POSTMODERN AMERICAN POETRY

A NORTON ANTHOLOGY

Second Edition

POSTMODERN AMERICAN POETRY

A NORTON ANTHOLOGY

Second Edition

EDITED BY

PAUL HOOVER

San Francisco State University

W. W. NORTON & COMPANY

New York • London

For information about special discounts for bulk purchases, please contact
W. W. Norton Special Sales at specialsales@wwnorton.com or 800-233-4830

Manufacturing by RR Donnelley, Harrisonburg
Book design by Chris Welch
Production manager: Louise Mattarelliano

Library of Congress Cataloging-in-Publication Data

Postmodern American poetry : a Norton anthology / edited
by Paul Hoover, San Francisco State University. — Second edition.
        pages cm
Includes bibliographical references and index.
ISBN 978-0-393-34186-7 (pbk.)
1. American poetry—20th century. 2. American poetry—21st century.
3. Postmodernism (Literature)—United States.
PS615.P669 2013
811'.540801—dc23
                        2012039473

W. W. Norton & Company, Inc.
500 Fifth Avenue, New York, N.Y. 10110
www.wwnorton.com

W. W. Norton & Company Ltd.
Castle House, 75/76 Wells Street, London W1T 3QT

1 2 3 4 5 6 7 8 9 0

Contents

POETICS

Preface

The first edition of *Postmodern American Poetry* had a powerful and surprising impact on contemporary American poetry. In canonizing new practices such as language poetry and honoring the avant-garde in general, it issued a challenge to many poets working in the "workshop" mode of expression of the 1990s. Seeing that other paths were open, they began to migrate across the boundaries, creating a cleft between their early and recent works. At the same time, poets of the avant-garde began to be hired as professors in MFA creative writing programs, where they were confronted by the professional demands of academic life. As happens with every generation, the new wins the day and the broader writing culture is altered by its theories and practices. Like the other arts, poetry experiences aesthetic turns as historical events and generational temperament impact the poetics of our time. Just as Beat poetry was a neo-Romantic turn away from the formalist rule of the New Criticism of the 1940s, new practices since the early 1990s have reflected a turn from poetry as an expression of the metaphysical and transcendent toward proceduralism and nontraditional forms. In 1994 the newest poetics was that of language poetry. Today the new is represented by conceptual poetry, Newlipo, cyberpoetry including Flarf, and the postlanguage lyric.

In 2009 W. W. Norton published the anthology *American Hybrid*, edited by Cole Swensen and David St. John, which argued against the avant-garde cycle of the new and proposed an end to the oppositional, vanguard-versus-mainstream theory of poetry. It's an interesting concept, rather like Francis Fukuyama's 1989 essay, "The End of History," which posits a "post-political" world condition. I would argue to the contrary. There will be no settled and permanent condition of poetry. New practices will continue to appear under the pressure of historical, technological, and generational changes. Who imagined that Alfred Jarry's theory of 'Pataphysics would influence the digital age, that poetry would be produced via online search engines, and that a transcription of an issue of the *New York Times* would be valued as "unoriginal writing"? Just as Jackson Pollock dispensed with the brush, conceptual poets Kenneth Goldsmith and Craig Dworkin have dispensed with the author. We had thought that language poetry had gone as far as possible. Now we see the vulnerability of its glorification of author as stylist.

With a few exceptions, all of the poets anthologized in this volume are from or based in the United States. The work of two Canadian authors appears because they have lived for a significant period of time in the United States or been intimately involved in the development of a new practice influential in this country. Poets in this volume are organized chronologically by date of birth, and poems are dated according to their first appearance in a book by that author, in the right margin directly following the poem. Dates in the left margin or in proximity to the title indicate the date of composition.

This anthology began when, in 1991, I spoke to Barry Wade of W. W. Norton about the need for an anthology of poetry of the "other tradition," as none had been published since Donald Allen's *The New American Poetry: 1945–1960.* He was receptive to the idea and asked for a proposal, which led to the publication of the first edition of *Postmodern American Poetry: A Norton Anthology* in 1994. Under the supervision of Norton editor Julia Reidhead, the book was a great success in its first trade season and became the classroom standard for teachers and students interested in new developments in poetry. For help with this second edition, I express my gratitude to Carly Fraser Doria, associate editor, for her wisdom and superb organizational skills in guiding this edition, as well as Hannah Blaisdell, assistant editor, whose help in the preparation of the manuscript was invaluable. I would also like to thank Julia Reidhead, now editorial director for the college division, for helping to make this second edition possible. Thanks also to the scholars Marjorie Perloff, Charles Altieri, and Sianne Ngai for their evaluations of the table of contents. My heartfelt thanks go to María Baranda for her advice and support throughout the development of this project. I am grateful as always to Maxine Chernoff; my children Koren, Philip, and Julian; and my grandson Dorian Michael Hoover.

Introduction

What Is Postmodern Poetry?

The poet Charles Olson used the word "postmodern" as early as an October 20, 1951, letter to Robert Creeley from Black Mountain, North Carolina. Doubting the value of historical relics when compared with the process of living, Olson states: "And had we not, ourselves (I mean postmodern man), better just leave such things behind us—and not so much trash of discourse, & gods?"[1] As used in this anthology, "postmodern" covers the historical period following World War II, and refers to avant-garde poetry by American poets from 1950 to the present. Broadly speaking, the term suggests an experimental approach to composition, as well as a worldview that sets itself apart from mainstream culture and the sentimentality and self-expressiveness of its life in writing. Arising from within the economic context of postwar consumer society marked by the overwhelming influence of large corporations, the philosophical context of existentialism, and the technological context of ever-more-powerful mass communications, the period contains several markers: 1975, the end of the Vietnam War; 1989, the dissolution of the Soviet Union; and September 11, 2001, whose tragic events are coincident with the expansion of global capitalism. Over the decades covered in this anthology, the term "postmodern" has received acceptance in all areas of culture and the arts; it has even come to be considered a reigning style, one that continues in the twenty-first century.

Despite such enormous changes and turbulent events, culturally the situation is much the same as 1991, when critic Frederic Jameson wrote, "It is safest to grasp the concept of the postmodern as an attempt to think about the present historically in an age that has forgotten how to think historically in the first

1. *Charles Olson and Robert Creeley: The Complete Correspondence*, Vol. 8, Santa Rosa, 1987, p. 79.

place."[2] The postmodern view reacts not to history as much as to cultural and aesthetic production, preferring the image to the object, the copy to the original, the maximal to the minimal, surface to depth. Its style has been described as "quotationist," "citationist," and "double-coded."[3] Messy rather than neat, plural rather than singular, mannered and oblique rather than straightforward, it prefers the complications of the everyday and the found to the simplicities of the heroic. Its tongue is seriously in its cheek. It is all styles rather than one.

Jameson has argued that postmodernism represents a break with nineteenth-century romanticism and early twentieth-century modernism. In his words, postmodernism is characterized by "aesthetic populism," "the deconstruction of expression," "the waning of affect," "the end of the bourgeois ego," and "the imitation of dead styles" through the use of pastiche.[4] In Jameson's opinion, postmodernism is the perfect expression of late capitalist culture as dominated by multinational corporations. If Jameson is correct, "deconstruction of expression" is symptomatic of the loss of individuality in a consumer society and, under the 2002 Homeland Security Act, stronger limits on privacy and individual rights. As history finds its "end" in liberal democracy and consumerism, it loses its sense of struggle and discovery. This results in the affectless or "blank" style of some of today's conceptual poets, as well as language poetry's preference for Gertrude Stein's "continuous present." Similarly, Jameson's "aesthetic populism" would reflect the triumph of mass-media communication over the written word. In this new edition, there are several "authorless" texts. Kenneth Goldsmith's "Seven American Deaths and Disasters" contains not one word of his own expression; it consists of transcripts of police tapes and mass communications reports. The text is mediated and edited but, strictly speaking, it is not authored. Such an approach presents a challenge to authorship's treasured concept of originality.

Others argue that postmodernism is an extension of romanticism and modernism, both of which still thrive. Thus what Jameson calls pastiche, a patchwork of styles, is simply a further development of modernist collage—today's cultural pluralism can be identified in Eliot's *The Waste Land,* Pound's *The Cantos,* and Picasso's Cubist appropriation of the ceremonial masks of Benin; the self-reflexiveness of postmodern art can be found in Joyce's *Finnegans Wake* and as far back as *Tristram Shandy;* performance poetry is simply the most recent of many attempts, including those of Wordsworth and William Carlos Williams, to renew poetry through the vernacular. The poetry of John Ashbery is quintessentially postmodern, yet it is influenced by the modernist

2. *Postmodernism, or, The Cultural Logic of Late Capitalism,* Durham, NC, 1991, p. ix.   3. Matei Calinescu, *Five Faces of Modernity: Modernism, Avant-Garde, Decadence, Kitsch, Postmodernism,* Durham, NC, 1987, p. 285.   4. *New Left Review,* No. 146, July/August 1984, pp. 53–92.

romantic Wallace Stevens and the modernist Augustan W. H. Auden. John Cage's use of the "prepared piano" and his emphasis on indeterminacy in language represent high postmodernism, yet they can also be situated, along with the Aeolian harp, a stringed instrument on which the wind played, in the history of romanticism. The contemporary emphasis on machine poetics, constructivism, proceduralism, the death of subjectivity, and found material can be traced to Dada and aesthetic materialism of the early Soviet period. To further confuse the picture, some poetic practices that appear to work against expression, like the Dada cut-up poem and Google sculpting, resemble ancient divinatory practices. For example, the West African practice of Ifa divination depends on the casting of sixteen cowrie shells. How the shells fall directs the *babalawo*, or priest, to recite one of 256 poems of the Ifa canon, which then serves as the supplicant's cure. The cyberpoet takes samples from the great online stream of digital consciousness; the resulting poem will bear the evidence of our cultural and psychic condition. Acts of chance in divination and art are often highly methodical. John Cage *prepared* his piano for dissonance by hampering certain strings.

In the first edition of this anthology, we chose "postmodern" for the title over "experimental," "avant-garde," and "millennial" because it is the most encompassing term for the variety of new practices since World War II, ranging from the oral poetics of Beat and performance poetries to the more "writerly" work of the New York School and language poetry. Now it is called upon to encompass the further developments of the postlanguage lyric, conceptual poetry, cyberpoetics, and proceduralism. These new poetics tend to work in opposition to the motives of mid-twentieth-century romanticism, which served as the dominant model from 1950 to 1990. While language poetry has been the major influence and theoretical model since 1990, newer directions are divided between the postlanguage lyric, which seeks the expressive, and conceptual, cybernetic, and procedural poetics, which work against writing as expression. Once feared for desiring to run lyric poetry out of the canon, language poetry has provided Barbara Guest, Ann Lauterbach, Rosmarie Waldrop, and Andrew Joron, among many other solitary singers, with fresh resources. Nevertheless, the poetics standoff remains the division between the ghost (the human figure, myth, and song) and the machine (structure, method, and wit). Both styles are postmodern. One might even speak of early and late postmodernisms. The early consists of Beat, projectivist, New York School, deep image, and aleatory poetics (Cage and Mac Low), while late postmodernism represents a digital and media-conscious shift to cybernetic and machine poetics.

The concept of the postmodern has come under criticism, but no other term has arisen that seems adequate to describe the cultural condition since World War II. The scholar John Frow casts it into past tense in "What Was Postmodernism?," but in the end points out the difficulty of dispensing with the word "postmodern" and, by implication, what it represents: "The very persistence of the word, however irritating this may be, seems to indicate that something is at stake, something that cannot be brushed aside as a theoretical fashion."[5] More importantly, the philosophical foundations of the postmodern are existential rather than metaphysical and derive from the philosophers of crisis, identified by one commentator as Nietzsche, Heidegger, Foucault, and Derrida.[6] Gregory Bruce Smith writes, "Nietzsche meant that it would no longer be possible for man to believe in anything that transcends the immanent, temporal world, that the bases of the values that had previously shielded humanity were destroyed once and for all. . . . Eternity was driven out completely, and therewith Being, to be replaced by the unrelenting reign of Becoming."[7] Eternity is reduced to Ethernity, the cybernetic universe that can be shared by all, much of which is mundane and profane. It is not that postmodernism lacks foundations, as some have suggested, but rather that the foundations have shifted from the transcendent to the everyday; from surrealism's search for the absolute to the emphasis in Dada on found materials, performance art, and conceptualism; from the necessary and natural to the arbitrary, contingent, and manmade. Instead of playing in the fields of the Lord, the poet plays with the material substance of the language. Heidegger wrote of his approach to philosophy, "I have left an earlier standpoint, not in order to exchange it for another one, but because even the former standpoint was merely a way-station along a way. The lasting element in thinking is the way. And ways of thinking hold within them that mysterious quality that we can walk them forward and backward, and that indeed only the way back will lead us forward."[8] Being on the way (*unterwegs*) is a principle factor of postmodern, process-driven writing, from Olson, Ginsberg, and Ashbery to the language poets. Instead of succumbing to history, postmodernism remains stubbornly underway by appropriating and refashioning established practices. The way forward is the way back to Jarry, Tzara, Duchamp, and Stein.

According to critic Peter Bürger, avant-garde art opposes the bourgeois model of consciousness by attempting to close the gap between art and life. However, "an art no longer distinct from the praxis of life but wholly absorbed in it will lose the capacity to criticize it."[9] Vanguardism thus collaborates with nineteenth-century aestheticism in the diminishment of art's social function even as it attempts to advance it. The risk is that the avant-garde will become

---

5. *Time & Commodity Culture: Essays in Cultural Theory and Postmodernity*, Oxford, 1997, p. 23.   6. Allan Megill, *Prophets of Extremity: Nietzsche, Heidegger, Foucault, Derrida*, Berkeley, CA, 1987.   7. *Nietzsche, Heidegger and the Transition to Postmodernity*, Chicago, 1996, p. 71.   8. "Dialogue on Language between a Japanese and an Inquirer," trans. Peter D. Hertz, *On the Way to Language*, San Francisco, p. 12.   9. *Theory of the Avant-Garde* (1974), trans. Michael Shaw, Minneapolis, 1984, p. 50.

an institution with its own self-protective rituals, powerless to trace or affect the curve of history. When the first edition of this anthology appeared, the newest development was language poetry, a Marxist-feminist poetics that, despite its opposition to the romantic and insistence on the word as such, shared in many of the cultural assumptions of the Beats, such as resistance to commodity culture. The more recent schools of thought may seem comparatively post-historical in approach. They may even appear to revel in aspects of American culture and mass media that Charles Olson called "pejorocracy." In fact, following the situationists, many of today's conceptual and cyberpoets turn violence and mass-media manipulation back on itself by holding the mirror of its own language up to it.

This anthology hopes to assert that avant-garde poetry endures in its resistance to dominant and received modes of poetry; it is the avant-garde that renews poetry as a whole through new, but initially shocking, artistic strategies. The "normal" way of writing in any period was first the practice of the innovators of previous generations. In the introduction to the first edition of this book, we suggested, "By this reasoning, recent postmodern aesthetics like performance poetry and language poetry will influence mainstream practice in the coming decades." This has proved to be an understatement. The leading language poets hold endowed chairs at leading universities, and their practice has become so historicized that, since the turn of the millennium, critics have referred to a "postlanguage" generation. With the rise of creative writing graduate programs and the increasing professionalization of what academics call "the discipline," even the outsiders and vanguardists find teaching positions available. Born in 1969, the conceptual poet Craig Dworkin is professor of English at the University of Utah, where he edits a conceptual poetry website, *eclipse*. The covers of his books are proudly displayed on the English department website. The majority of the books are academic studies on conceptual poetry, about which he is a brilliant commentator. There is nothing in this very successful profile to slander Craig Dworkin; quite to the contrary. The point is that, on many fronts, the old oppositions of town and gown, bohemian and academic, have broken down. Apparently nobody in the English department demands that Craig Dworkin alter his poetics to serve the greater aesthetic or moral good, or commence upon a sonnet sequence. In the history of such relations, this is a relatively new development. One of the leading practitioners of the cyberpoetry mode called Flarf, K. Silem Mohammad, did indeed write a sonnet sequence, which he calls sonnagrams, based on anagrams of the lines of Shakespeare's lines. Because such a procedure requires the use of an online anagram generator, the resulting translations can be trifling or profane. It's up to the poet as editor to make the best of the procedure to which she or he has committed. As the new movements of their day, Dada, surrealism, modernism, and the Beats were considered silly and/or transgressive. This is true also of today's new movements. It is only with time and close consideration that the necessity of these works emerges, beyond what at first seems their ludic arbitrariness. The issue today is not the survival of avant-garde, but rather the astonishing speed with which it triumphs.

Postmodernism is not a single style with its departure in Pound's *Cantos* and its arrival in language poetry; it is, rather, an ongoing resistance to and comment upon dominant practices. William Carlos Williams railed against the sonnet, Ezra Pound against pentameter; today's conceptual poets Kenneth Goldsmith and Craig Dworkin question creativity itself. With each new development, we recognize that the language game of poetry is continually in play. No matter how sharp the break with a former tradition, new methods and means of attending to the poem result in a "having said." Someone who stands before us as priest has cast the cowrie shells once more.

In the 1960s, in opposition to the impersonal, Augustan poetry encouraged by the New Criticism, the postmodern revolt was primarily in the direction of a personal, oral, and "organic" poetry that saw each voice as unique. Frank O'Hara's injunction, "You just go on your nerve,"[10] called for an improvisatory poetics of the everyday that was essentially neoromantic. Yet, in its intense casualness, his poetry also argued against the romantic concept of self; in its disregard for the metaphysical, it broke with the "transcendental signified." By the late 1970s, a new generation of postmodernists had begun to challenge the speech and breath-based poetics of Olson and Ginsberg. Nevertheless, most innovators since 1945 have valued writing-as-process over writing-as-product. They have elevated the pluralistic, which Charles Olson called "the real biz of reality," over the singular, which Olson called "the whole ugly birth of the 'either-or.'"[11] Postmodernism decenters authority and encourages a "panoptic" or many-sided point of view. It prefers "empty words" to the "transcendental signified," the actual to the metaphysical. In general, it follows a constructivist rather than an expressionist theory of composition. Its "I" is often another. Method vies with intuition in driving poetic composition. With the death of God and the unfortunate but inevitable distancing of nature, appropriation becomes a reigning device. Our books become our civilization and our nature; at the same time, the words are just words. Having no conclusion to come to, narrative doubles back on itself with overlapping and sometimes contradictory versions. For example, Italo Calvino's novel *If on a winter's night a traveler* (1979) consists of the first ten chapters of ten novels, none of which is developed or concluded. To begin again and again is to create the "continuous present" that Gertrude Stein called for as the "now and then now" of writing. What

10. "Personism: A Manifesto," in *The Collected Poems of Frank O'Hara,*" New York, 1972, p. 498.
11. Letter to Robert Creeley, October 20, 1951, in *Charles Olson and Robert Creeley: The Complete Correspondence,* Vol. 8, p. 73.

a text means has more to do with how it was written than what it expresses. As Robert Creeley wrote, "Meaning is not importantly *referential*."[12] Quoting Charles Olson, Creeley continues, *"That which exists through itself is what is called the meaning."*[13] Like Williams's plums, "so sweet / and so cold," the thing is valued for itself, not for its symbolism. In general, postmodern poetry opposes the centrist values of unity, significance, linearity, expressiveness, and any heroic portrayal of the bourgeois self and its concerns. The poetry in this volume employs a wide variety of strategies, from the declaratory writings of the Beats to the more theoretical work of the language poets. The empty sign, like the use of transgressive material by the Beats and Flarf, is but one means of resistance to any settled definition of poetry. However, for many poets in this anthology, of both the pre- and postlanguage lyric, signs are far from empty and require no grieving. The empty sign, like Hölderlin's weather vane clattering in cold weather, may actually be the one that's too full.

The Battle of the Anthologies

In analyzing American poetry after 1945, it is traditional to point to the so-called battle of the anthologies that occurred with the publication of *New Poets of England and America* (1962), edited by Donald Hall and Robert Pack, and *The New American Poetry: 1945–1960* (1960), edited by Donald Allen. The former put forth a literature that was more traditional, formal, and refined. Its contributors were schooled in the assumptions of the New Criticism, which held that poems are sonorous, well-made objects to be judged independently of the author's experiences; they speak to and from their place in the ongoing tradition of sonorous, well-made objects. Cleanth Brooks's *The Well-Wrought Urn* (1947), universally assigned in poetry literature classes, placed emphasis on the poem's craftsmanship, uses of paradox, thematic and formal weights and balances, and self-consistency. To use Robert Lowell's terminology, borrowed from Claude Levi-Strauss, the poetry of the Hall/Pack anthology was more "cooked" than "uncooked." Trusting in tradition, its contributors were not eager to reject the influence of British letters in favor of a home-grown idiom. Yeats was preferred to Williams, the mythical to the personal, the rational to the irrational, the historical to the living moment, and decorum and restraint to spontaneity. However, the early confessional poems of Sylvia Plath and Anne Sexton were included, perhaps an indication that New Criticism's demand for objectivity and critical distance was already under question. Rob-

---

12. Introduction to *Selected Writings of Charles Olson*, New York, 1966, p. 9.   13. The same.

ert Pack's introduction to his selection of American poets under forty (Hall selected the British poets) shows his distaste for spontaneous poetry:

> The idea of a raw, unaffected, or spontaneous poetry misleads the reader as to what is expected of him. It encourages laziness and passivity. He too can be spontaneous, just sit back and respond. A good poem, rather, is one that deepens upon familiarity. . . . It is not enough to let a poem echo through your being, to play mystical chords upon your soul. The poem must be understood and felt in its details; it asks for attention before transport.[14]

Pack sides here with the formalism of the New Criticism, which required consistency of structure and poetic detail. Positioning himself against the romanticism of Beat poetry, he stresses "attention" (the close-reading style of New Criticism) and "familiarity" (tradition). He implies that the only worthwhile poems are those that lend themselves to study. The overall defensiveness of the remark suggests that the new poetry had already begun to make its mark.

In 1955, five years before the publication of the Donald Allen anthology, the San Francisco Renaissance burst on the scene with a single momentous reading at Six Gallery, 3119 Fillmore Street. Jack Kerouac described the event in *The Dharma Bums*:

> Anyway I followed the whole gang of howling poets to the reading that night, which was, among other important things, the night of the birth of the San Francisco Renaissance. Everyone was there. It was a mad night. And I was the one who got things jumping by going around collecting dimes and quarters from the rather stiff audience standing around the gallery and coming back with three huge gallon jugs of California burgundy and getting them all piffed so that by eleven o'clock when Alvah Goldbrook [Allen Ginsberg] was reading his, wailing his poem "Wail" drunk with arms outspread everybody was yelling "Go! Go! Go!" (like a jam session) . . . .[15]

In fact, as poet and critic Michael Davidson points out, there had been earlier activity in San Francisco. As early as 1944, Robert Duncan had begun to set the stage for a publicly gay role in literature by publishing his essay "The Homosexual in Society." In 1949, Jack Spicer wrote, "We must become singers, become entertainers," a prophecy of the Beat movement's return of poetry to its bardic roots.[16] Since the 1920s, Kenneth Rexroth had been a

---

14. *New Poets of England and America*, Cleveland, 1962, p. 178.   15. New York, 1958, p. 13
16. "The Poet and Poetry—a Symposium," *One Night Stand and Other Poems*, San Francisco, 1980, p. 92.

significant avant-garde figure in the Bay area, organizing "at homes" for writers and artists and reading poetry to jazz long before the Beat poets made the activity popular. The Six Gallery reading galvanized media interest in a variety of alternative poetries. It also introduced the concept of poetry as public performance.

If Robert Pack's model poet "deepens upon familiarity," Donald Allen's deepens upon strangeness, preferring the irrational and improvised to the decorous and well made. In the tradition of Walt Whitman and William Carlos Williams, the poets in Allen's anthology also emphasized the American idiom and place. Although predominantly male, many of these poets were Jewish, Irish, Italian, black, and gay—that is, from "new" ethnic and social groups. They lived primarily in New York City and San Francisco, where they were influenced by other arts, especially jazz and painting. None of them taught at a university; the distinction between bohemia and academia was clear in 1960. The radicalism that inspired many poets of the 1960s has found expression in critical approaches such as feminism and multiculturalism that are central to the study of liberal arts.

The most public of the new poetries was the Beat movement led by Allen Ginsberg, Gregory Corso, Gary Snyder, Lawrence Ferlinghetti, and the fiction writers Jack Kerouac and William Burroughs. The word "beat," suggesting exhaustion, beatitude, and the jazz improvisation that inspired many of its writers, was first used by Jack Kerouac, who also provided the titles for Ginsberg's *Howl* and Paul Carroll's notable literary magazine *Big Table*. Kerouac's novel *On the Road* (1957), written on a continuous roll of teletype paper, provided the Beat model of composition, which Kerouac also dubbed "spontaneous bop prosody." "Not 'selectivity' of expression," Kerouac insisted, "but following free deviation (association) of mind into limitless blow-on-subject seas of thoughts."[17] In Ginsberg's *Howl*, this verbal improvisation and jazz sense of measure can be heard in lines such as "ashcan rantings and kind king light of mind." According to Ginsberg, Kerouac believed that "the gesture he made in language was his mortal gesture, and therefore unchangeable."[18] It could no more be revised than the act of walking across a room. Spontaneous composition is not, however, without discipline. "What this kind of writing proposes," Ginsberg once said, "is an absolute, almost Zen-like, complete absorption, *attention* to your own consciousness . . . so that the attention does not waver while writing, and doesn't feed back on itself and become self-conscious."[19] With its roots in the poetry of Blake, Whitman, and William Carlos Williams, Beat writing is public, direct, performative, ecstatic, oral, and incantatory. It is both irreverent and spiritually aware. Ginsberg's

17. "Essentials of Spontaneous Prose," *The Moderns*, ed. LeRoi Jones, New York, 1963, p. 343.
18. *Allen Verbatim*, ed. Gordon Ball, New York, 1974, p. 145.   19. The same, p. 147

line, "angelheaded hipsters burning for the ancient heavenly connection to the starry dynamo in the machinery of night," searches for meaning high and low. Ginsberg experimented with drugs, was expelled from Columbia University for writing an obscenity on the window of his dorm room, and spent time in the psychiatric ward of Rockland State Hospital. At a time that demanded form, decorum, refinement, and impersonality, his poetry was vivid, profane, loud, and personal. The "secret hero" of *Howl* is Neal Cassady, also immortalized as Dean Moriarty of *On the Road,* who lived the exuberant and ultimately self-destructive life the bohemian tradition so much admires. In 1968, Cassady died in Mexico at age forty-one from a lethal mixture of alcohol and sleeping pills; Kerouac died the following year. The Beat influence has been sustained by each new generation's attraction to its mythologies of youth and visionary ambition. Beat poetry remains the ideal of art made with all the immediacy of life. It is Blake's figure of the powerful youth, Orc, rising up in verbal flames, as opposed to the exhausted Urizen (your reason), crawling on his hands and knees.

Central figures of the New York School, which emerged parallel to the Beat movement, are John Ashbery, Frank O'Hara, Kenneth Koch, James Schuyler, and Barbara Guest. Ashbery, O'Hara, and Koch attended Harvard; all the men but Koch were gay; and all five figures lived in Manhattan. Strongly influenced by the French avant-garde, especially the novels of the eccentric amateur Raymond Roussel, they founded the magazines *Locus Solus* and *Art and Literature* and set upon the most self-consciously nonprogrammatic poetics of the period. However, something of a general stance can be found in O'Hara's essay "Personism: A Manifesto," written as a parody of Charles Olson's "Projective Verse." O'Hara states that one day in 1959, while writing a poem for a specific person, he realized that he could "use the telephone instead of writing the poem, and so Personism was born."[20] Personist poetry speaks with immediacy and directness of everyday experience, in everyday language. O'Hara's statement, "You just go on your nerve," is reminiscent of the spontaneity and antiformalism of the Beats; his insistence that Personism "does not have to do with personality or intimacy"[21] suggests that the self for O'Hara was objectified, a being among other beings. Much of the work of James Schuyler has the intimacy and easeful charm of Personism; it is also among the most lyrical of the group. But the Personist mode is not characteristic of all New York School poetry and is only part of O'Hara's production. Although formally radical in *The Tennis Court Oath* (1962), John Ashbery also loves traditional but minor forms like the sestina, pantoum, and haibun. Likewise, Kenneth Koch wrote his comic epics *Ko* and *The Duplications* in ottava rima, the stanza of Byron's *Don Juan.* Like Byron, Koch and the rest of the New York School poets admire

20. O'Hara, p. 499.   21. The same.

wit, daring, urbanity, and offhanded elegance. As courtly eccentrics, they set a tone that is distinct from the more earnest bohemianism of the Beats. The New York School has a fondness for parody (Koch's "Variations on a Theme of William Carlos Williams") and pop culture (Ashbery's Popeye sestina, "Farm Implements and Rutabagas in a Landscape"). It also works within the avant-garde tradition of the "poet among the painters." As a curator for the Museum of Modern Art and organizer of major exhibits, Frank O'Hara was the Apollinaire of New York painting in the late fifties and early sixties. John Ashbery was editor of *ARTnews,* and James Schuyler and Barbara Guest were frequent contributors to art journals such as *Art in America.*

It is important to note the leading role of John Ashbery in American poetry since the publication of *Self-Portrait in a Convex Mirror* (1975). Perhaps because his poetry expresses the period's most important theme, indeterminacy, Ashbery has become a major poet in an age suspicious of the term. Indeterminacy means the conditionality of truth, as well as a compositional tendency away from finality and closure; the text is in a state of unrest or undecidability. Characterized by sudden shifts in tone and a wide range of reference, making frequent use of the self-canceling statement, Ashbery's poetry has the capacity, to quote Frank O'Hara, for "marrying the whole world."[22] Through circuitousness and obliqueness, Ashbery alludes to things in the process of avoiding them; in saying nothing, he says everything. In the words of David Lehman, "Ashbery's poetry points toward a new mimesis, with consciousness itself as the model."[23] Mimesis refers to representation in art—for example, the ability of a painter to make an apple look like an apple. Ashbery paints a picture of the mind at work rather than the objects of its attention. He has remarked, "Most reckless things are beautiful, just as religions are beautiful because of the strong possibility that they are founded on nothing."[24]

While O'Hara and Schuyler can be grouped as Personist and intimist—the New York School quotidian—much of the poetry of John Ashbery and Barbara Guest falls into the category of the "abstract lyric." Guest is especially adept at this philosophical mode, as can be seen in the majestic "Wild Gardens Overlooked by Night Lights." The abstract lyric can also be located in the work of Ann Lauterbach, Marjorie Welish, and, to some degree, Michael Palmer. Because her thinking tends to be about perception itself, the work of the language poet Lyn Hejinian sometimes seems related to the abstract lyric mode. Abstract lyric rarely seeks to solve a philosophical issue; rather, it follows the path of indeterminacy. But we are usually provided with symbolic figures in the discourse. In Ann Lauterbach's "Platonic Subject," for instance:

22. "Poem Read at Joan Mitchell's," *The Collected Poems of Frank O'Hara,* New York, 1972, p. 266.
23. "The Shield of a Greeting," in *Beyond Amazement: New Essays on John Ashbery,* ed. David Lehman, Ithaca, 1980, p. 118.   24. "The Invisible Avant-Garde," in *Avant-Garde Art,* eds. Thomas B. Hess and John Ashbery, London, 1968, p. 184.

But here is a twig in the form of a wishbone.
Aroused, I take it, and leave its outline
scarred in snow which the sun will later heal:
form of the real melts back into the ideal
and I have a twig.[25]

In the late sixties a second generation of New York School poets, including Ted Berrigan, Ron Padgett, Alice Notley, Anne Waldman, and Bernadette Mayer, came into their strength. Through readings at St. Mark's Church on the Lower East Side and through journals such as *The World, Telephone,* and *C,* they brought a more bohemian tone to the New York School "dailiness" and wit. As the presiding figure of the scene, Ted Berrigan influenced a large number of younger poets, including the youngest poet in this volume, Ben Lerner, whose "Doppler Elegies" share with Berrigan's *The Sonnets* (1964) a shifting, cut-up, combinatory sense of the line. A classic of the period, *The Sonnets* applied the cut-up method of Dada poet Tristan Tzara to the sonnet form. Because the same phrases and lines would intermittently reappear, Berrigan seemed also to be taking the lines out of a hat.[26] With Ron Padgett and Joe Brainard, he wrote the notable volume *Bean Spasms* (1967). Other significant books produced by this generation were Padgett's *Great Balls of Fire* (1969) and Alice Notley's *How Spring Comes* (1981). Anne Waldman, with her extraordinary skills as a poet, performer, and organizer, provided much of the energy that made the Poetry Project at St. Mark's Church and later Naropa University in Boulder, Colorado, powerful literary centers.

Projectivist or Black Mountain poetry evolved under the leadership of Charles Olson at Black Mountain College in North Carolina. The leading alternative college of its time, Black Mountain was home to an extraordinary number of major figures, including painters Josef Albers and Robert Rauschenberg, composers John Cage and Stefan Wolpe, dancer and choreographer Merce Cunningham, and futurist thinker Buckminster Fuller, creator of the geodesic dome. The poets Robert Creeley, Ed Dorn, Denise Levertov, and Robert Duncan were in residence. Black Mountain poetics, which is more programmatic than that of the Beats or New York School, depends primarily on the essays and teachings of Charles Olson, especially "Projective Verse" (1950), where he calls for an "open" poetry in which "FIELD COM-

---

25. *Before Recollection*, Princeton, NJ, 1987, p. 28.   26. In "To Make a Dadaist Poem," Tristan Tzara wrote: "Take a newspaper. / Take some scissors. / Choose from this paper an article of the length you want to make your poem. / Cut out the article. / Next carefully cut out each of the words that make up the article and put them all in a bag. / Shake gently. / Next take out each cutting one after the other. Copy conscientiously in the order in which they left the bag. The poem will resemble you. / And there you are—an infinitely original author of charming sensibility, even though unappreciated by the vulgar herd." *Seven Dada Manifestos and Lampisteries*, translated by Barbara Wright, Kalamazoo, MI, 1981/1992, p. 39.

POSITION" replaces the "closed form" of the past. Field composition means that the poet "puts himself in the open," improvising line by line, syllable by syllable, rather than using an "inherited line" such as iambic pentameter.[27] Olson quotes the young Robert Creeley as saying that "Form is never more than an extension of content."[28] Form and content are therefore inextricably linked. Quoting his mentor Edward Dahlberg, Olson writes, "One perception must immediately and directly lead to a further perception."[29] To this he adds the injunction that "always one perception must must must MOVE, INSTANTER, ON ANOTHER."[30] This compositional pressure includes close attention to the syllable, which is "king."

Let me put it baldly. The two halves are:

> the HEAD, by way of the EAR, to the SYLLABLE
> the HEART, by way of the BREATH, to the LINE[31]

Attention to the line as a unit of breath is a major principle of Black Mountain composition, though, as a technique, it was flexible rather than prescribed. Each breath is a unit or measure of utterance; this is reflected in the length of the line, and, with Creeley's work especially, how the line is broken. Recordings of Olson and Creeley, whose speech patterns are quite different, reveal the importance of the line and breath to their spoken words. A similar emphasis is found in Ginsberg's statements that each strophe of *Howl* is ideally a unit of "Hebraic-Melvillean bardic breath."[32] The relation of speech and breath to the poem is organic and thereby urgent and necessary. Speech and breath are sanctified and relate to proprioception, the body's knowledge of itself.

Another important aspect of Olson's essay is his concept of ego: "getting rid of the lyrical interference of the individual as ego . . . that peculiar presumption by which western man has interposed himself between what he is as a creature of nature . . . and those other creations of nature which we may, with no derogation, call objects."[33] Olson's goal was to avoid the self-congratulatory mode, with its inevitable drift toward pathos. This is not to say that Projectivist poetry is necessarily impersonal. Olson's "The Librarian," among other poems, deals with his own life; the same is true of work by Robert Creeley, Denise Levertov, and Robert Duncan. The monumental figure of Olson as a man (he was six feet eight inches in height) is reflected in the figure of Maximus in *The Maximus Poems* (1960).

Influenced by Zen Buddhism and Dada, the poetry of John Cage and Jackson Mac Low reflects an interest in the use of aleatory, or chance, procedures;

---

27. *Charles Olson: Selected Writings*, New York, 1966, p. 16.   28. The same.   29. The same, p. 17.   30. The same.   31. The same, p. 19.   32. "Notes for Howl and Other Poems," in *The Poetics of the New American Poetry*, eds. Donald M. Allen and Warren Tallman, New York, 1973, p. 318.   33. "Projective Verse," p. 24.

Mac Low was also among the first to practice digital poetics. Cage's *Themes & Variations* (1982) depends on a "library of mesostics in one hundred and ten different subjects and fifteen different names to make a chance-determined renga-like mix."[34] Cage used *I Ching* operations to focus his project, as well as to link a notebook of ideas with the names of friends. The purpose was "to find a way of writing which though coming from ideas is not about them; or is not about ideas but produces them."[35] By employing mesostics, a form of acrostic in which emphasized letters spell out words vertically at the center of horizontal lines of poetry, Cage attempts to free the language from syntax. This "demilitarizes" it. "Nonsense and silence, so familiar to lovers, are produced. We actually begin to live together," he writes in the foreword to *M: Writings '67–'72*."[36] In his preface to *The Pronouns*, Jackson Mac Low explains that the series of poems involved a "set of 3-by-4-inch filing cards on which there are groups of words and of action phrases around which dancers build spontaneous improvisations."[37] Due to a "correspondence of format to syntax, each verse line, *including its indented continuation,* if any, is to be read as one breath unit."[38] Thus the series of poems not only stands as script for the dance, but also provides its own instructions for oral performance.

Aleatory poetry was not widely practiced initially by the generations of avant-gardists to follow Cage and Mac Low. Yet its emphasis on the indeterminate and accidental, its reliance on rigid structures and methods to achieve randomization, its use of appropriation and found materials, and its willingness to lend itself equally to performance and the poetics of language poetry, make it the essence of postmodernism. Cage's work also bridges the earlier European avant-garde, especially Dada, and more recent American developments such as conceptual art, Flarf, cyberpoetry, and the procedural aspects of Newlipo.

In the first postwar generation, only a few women, such as Denise Levertov, Diane Di Prima, and Barbara Guest, rose to prominence within the avant-garde. However, the 1970s saw the arrival of a number of significant women poets, from Anne Waldman, Bernadette Mayer, and Alice Notley among the New York School to Susan Howe, Mei-mei Berssenbrugge, Rosmarie Waldrop, Rae Armantrout, Lyn Hejinian, Leslie Scalapino, and Carla Harryman, among others, associated with language poetry and related innovation. Implicit in the language poets' break with traditional modes such as narrative, with its emphasis on linearity and closure, is a challenge to the male-dominant hierarchy. In her essay, "The Rejection of Closure," Lyn Hejinian quotes Elaine Marks regarding the desire of French feminist writers to "use language as a passageway, and the only one, to the unconscious, to that which had been repressed and which

34. John Cage, *Introduction to Themes & Variations*, Barrytown, NY, 1982, p. 8.   35. The same, p. 6.   36. Middletown, CT, 1973, p. 2.   37. Barrytown, NY, 1979, p. viii.   38. The same, p. ix.

would, if allowed to rise, disrupt the symbolic order, which Jacques Lacan has dubbed 'the Law of the Father.'"[39] At the same time, Hejinian sees the limit of complete openness: "The (unimaginable) complete text, the text that contains everything, would be in fact a closed text. It would be insufferable."[40] Wanda Coleman's "Brute Strength" refers to sexual conflict directly, using narrative elements to intensify the drama of the poem. Because it is more forceful rhetorically, the poem may seem more political than the work of women language poets. Yet the comparatively oblique work of Leslie Scalapino frequently alludes to the intrusive power of the male gaze and sexualized public space.

By 1990, two relatively marginal influences of the seventies, language poetry and performance poetry, had become increasingly significant as postmodern modes. The first emphasized textuality, therefore a degree of intellectual difficulty. Strongly based in theory, it required an initiated reader. In its complexity and literariness, language poetry was reminiscent of the high modernism of T. S. Eliot and Ezra Pound. Yet language poetry was Marxist and feminist in theory and disdained Pound and Eliot for their politically conservative themes. Performance poetry, especially as it evolved into poetry "slams," had its chief appeal with the popular audience of noninitiates. Its commitment was not to the "poem as poem," but rather in using the words as script for spoken word performance. In its verbal intensity, it recalled the Beat coffeehouse readings of the 1950s. Among the poets here represented, Anne Waldman, Wanda Coleman, Christian Bök, and Edwin Torres have the largest commitment to performance.

Language poetry found its disparate precursors in Gertrude Stein's *Tender Buttons* (1914); the writings of Russian Futurist Velimir Khlebnikov, a creator of *zaum*, or "transrational language"; Louis Zukofsky's *"A"* (1959/1978) and the Objectivist movement in general; John Ashbery's most radical book, *The Tennis Court Oath* (1962); the early work of Clark Coolidge such as *Space* (1970); and the methodical procedures of Jackson Mac Low. Some aspects of Black Mountain poetics, especially Olson's statement against the individual ego, were also of interest to language poets, though they disassociated themselves from what Charles Bernstein called the "phallocentric syntax" of Olson's poetry.[41] Seeing a poem as an intellectual and sonic construction rather than a necessary expression of the human soul, language poetry raises technique to a position of privilege. Language poets see lyricism in poetry not as a means of expressing emotion but rather in its original context as the musical use of words. Rather than employ language as a transparent window onto experience, the language poet prizes the material nature of words. Because it

39. *Writing/Talks*, ed. Bob Perelman, Carbondale, IL, 1985, p. 282.   40. The same, p. 285.   41. "Undone Business," in *Content's Dream: Essays, 1975–1984*, Los Angeles, 1986, p. 329.

is fragmentary and discontinuous, language poetry may at first appear to be automatic writing; however, it is often heavily reworked to achieve the proper relation of materials. This approach is consistent with William Carlos Williams's definition of a poem as a "small (or large) machine made of words. When I say there's nothing sentimental about a poem I mean there can be no part, as in any other machine, that is redundant."[42]

However, the principle of sheer volume often found in language poetry tends to frustrate the economy of phrase, and its suggestion of organic form, inherent in Williams's model. Ron Silliman's *Tjanting* (1981) consists of 213 pages of prose poetry, the last paragraph of which starts on page 128. It begins, "What makes this the last paragraph?" The sprawl of such work is designed perhaps to communicate the democratic principle of inclusiveness. Its form is located in what Silliman calls "The New Sentence," sentences being "the minimum complete utterance" according to linguist Simeon Potter.[43] Favoring the prose poem for its formal freedom and exhaustiveness, Silliman builds up a mosaic structure by means of seemingly unrelated sentences and sentence fragments. This progression of non sequiturs frustrates the reader's expectation for linear development at the same time it opens a more complete world of reference. The emphasis in language poetry is placed on production rather than packaging (beginning, middle, and end) and ease of consumption. Gertrude Stein gave the credit for this egalitarian theory of composition to her favorite painter: "Cézanne conceived of the idea that in composition one thing is as important as another thing. Each part is as important as the whole."[44]

The author cedes his or her false authority as individual ego; broadly distributing wealth in the form of words, the author acquires a more trustworthy authority. Because the words are so freely given, they may seem scattered and disorganized. It is therefore necessary for the reader to participate actively in the creation of meaning. Charles Bernstein states in his essay "Writing and Method":

> The text calls upon the reader to be actively involved in the process of constituting its meaning. . . . The text formally involves the process of response/interpretation and in so doing makes the reader aware of herself or himself as a producer as well as consumer of meaning.[45]

A poem is not "about" something, a paraphrasable narrative, symbolic nexus, or theme; rather, it is the actuality of words. In the case of *Tjanting*, formal

---

42. Author's introduction to *The Wedge* (1944), in *The Collected Poems of William Carlos Williams*, Vol. 2, New York, 1988, p. 54.   43. *Modern Linguistics*, New York, 1964, p. 104.   44. "A Transatlantic Interview 1946," in *A Primer for the Understanding of Gertrude Stein*, ed. Robert B. Haas, Santa Barbara, 1976, p. 15.   45. *Content's Dream: Essays 1975–1984*, Los Angeles, 1986, p. 233.

interest is added through the use of the Fibonacci number sequence in determining the number of each paragraph's sentence count, as well as Silliman's astute musical sense of words.

Language poetry's resistance to closure, which infuses meaning throughout the poem rather than knotting it into lyrical and dramatic epiphanies, may prove to be one of its most lasting effects. It has also revealed the limits of a "natural" or "organic" concept of poetry. In language poetry, as in Marshall McLuhan's theory of television, the medium is the message. Words are not transparent vessels for containing and conveying higher truth; they are instead the material of which it is shaped. Gertrude Stein said that she was interested in two aspects of composition:

> . . . the idea of portraiture and the idea of the recreation of the word. I took individual words and thought about them until I got their weight and volume complete and put them next to another word, and at this same time I found out very soon that there is no such thing as putting them together without sense. It is impossible to put them together without sense.[46]

In much the same way an artist might view paint and stone, Stein conceived of words as the plastic material of her compositions in language. Each word has its own "weight and volume." It exists from an artistic viewpoint for its own "recreation." Such a view disinvests the language of metaphysics and returns it to the physical realm of daily use. Like Stein, language poets shatter the assumption that poetry is necessary and deep; it is, instead, arbitrary and contingent. Language poetry, too, rejects the idea of poetry as an oral form; it is written. To use Roland Barthes's terminology, it is more "writerly" than "readerly." Indeed, language poetry could be seen as fulfilling Barthes's prophecy of a "neutral" mode of writing:

> . . . writing thus passed through all the stages of progressive solidification; it was first the object of a gaze, (Châteaubriand) then of creative action, finally of murder, (Mallarmé) and has reached in our time a last metamorphosis, absence: in those neutral modes of writing, called here "the zero degree" of writing; we can easily discern a negative momentum . . . as if literature, having tended for a hundred years now to transmute its surface into a form with no antecedents, could no longer find purity anywhere but in the absence of all signs . . .[47]

46. "A Transatlantic Interview 1946," p. 18.   47. *Writing Degree Zero*, trans. Annette Lavers
and Colin Smith, New York, 1967, p. 5.

Early workers in what is now called language poetry—Jackson Mac Low, Clark Coolidge, and Michael Palmer—remain as important precursors. However, much of the critical theory and organizational energy have been the work of Charles Bernstein, whose numerous books of essays including *A Poetics* (1992) and *My Way* (1999) most effectively express the group's thinking. Among other important points, Bernstein rejects reading as an "absorption" into the text, wherein the reader is captured by mimesis. Like many other postmodern theorists, he also opposes the heroic stance, which "translates into a will to dominate language rather than let it be heard."[48] Early in the movement's development, theoretical energies were divided, like Rap, into East Coast (Charles Bernstein and Bruce Andrews) and West Coast (Lyn Hejinian, Ron Silliman, Bob Perelman) schools and resulted in its own battle of anthologies: Douglas Messerli's *"Language" Poetries* (1987) and Ron Silliman's *In the American Tree* (1986). Also of note was *Code of Signals: Recent Writings in Poetics,* edited by Michael Palmer (1983); Barrett Watten's *Total Syntax* (1985); Lyn Hejinian's *The Language of Inquiry* (2000); Steve McCaffery's *North of Intention* (2000); and Joan Retallack's *The Poethical Wager* (2003). Particularly significant to the early development of language poetry was *Writing/Talks* (1985), edited by Bob Perelman, a collection of talks given at the San Francisco gallery New Langton Arts in the late seventies and early eighties.

As language poetry began to sweep the field of poetics and became acceptable in English departments at leading universities, an important question was raised, that of the lyric poem. Any thought of a "language lyric" seemed impossible. Too many statements had been made against the bourgeois ego and transcendental signifier. However, there remained the option of depicting personal experience through the intermittency of the "new sentence." Each section of Lyn Hejinian's prose poem sequence *My Life* (1987) contained thirty-eight sentences, one for each year of her age. The scenes are brief but cumulative and also imply a fondness for one's own history. The same could be said of Ron Silliman's works in *Tjanting* (1981) and *Paradise* (1985). The sentences and fragments are brief and well modulated but resist narrative development. Nevertheless, it is recognizably Ron Silliman gazing at the thumb he sliced while carving roast beef. In short, though language poetry may bring the personal to bear, it rarely lends it the lyrical note of Keats's "silence and slow time." We find that lyrical note in the poetry of James Schuyler, Denise Levertov, and others of the first postmodern generation. But the survival of the lyric into the postlanguage period was largely due to the "abstract lyric" practiced by John Ashbery and Barbara Guest. Philosophical and often playful, this meditative mode is influenced by Wallace Stevens and, perhaps to some degree, in Ashbery and Laura Riding. But it was with Barbara Guest's

48. Undone Business," p. 329.

Fair Realism (1989) that the innovative lyric began its negotiation with language poetry. This engagement of language and lyric, often expressed through the fragment and Mallarmé's silence of the white page, would have a profound influence on the practice of young poets in the late nineties and into the new millennium.[49] The call back to Mallarmé, like conceptual poetry's dependence on Marcel Duchamp and the found object, is part of the avant-garde paradox. We often take a step back in art history to take a step forward.

Leading poets of the postlanguage lyric include Peter Gizzi, Elizabeth Willis, Cole Swensen, Mark McMorris, Rae Armantrout, Fanny Howe, and Elizabeth Robinson, among others of diverse practice. Postlanguage lyric cannot be said to constitute a school but rather the natural inclination of poetry toward sweetness and depth of expression; moreover, subjectivity, while often tempered with irony, is granted a role. Peter Gizzi's "A Panic That Can Still Come Upon Me" begins, "If today and today I am calling aloud / / If I break into pieces of glitter on asphalt / bits of sun, the din." The poem announces itself as a cry or plea, which is always done at emotional risk. Usually identified as a language poet, Rae Armantrout seems increasingly a poet of personal expression, as her recent works such as *Versed* (2009) are touched with self-elegy. The poetry of Fanny Howe sometimes deals directly with religious faith. Neither Armantrout nor Howe has substantially altered her style, but what they write has found a wider audience.

Postlanguage poetry also involves the emergence of three distinct schools of poetry: Newlipo, conceptual poetry, and cyberpoetry, which includes the popular practice of Flarf. Influenced by Dada, Situationism, and Oulipo, they find common ground in their love for cyberspace, the appropriation and manipulation of found texts, a delight in poetry machines, methods, and procedures, and the ironic use, as well as *détournement*, of mass media.

Newlipo adopts the practices of the French group Oulipo, or *Ouvroir de Littérature Potentielle* (Workshop for Potential Literature). Founded on November 24, 1960, by Raymond Queneau and François Le Lionnais, Oulipo consisted primarily of mathematicians and scientists who met for dinner and the discussion of new or "potential" forms of writing. Among such forms is the lipogram, which excludes one or more letters of the alphabet from the work being produced. Oulipo stalwart Georges Perec wrote a novel, *La disparition* (1969) that famously contained no letter "e." The leading poet of Newlipo is Christian Bök, whose best-selling poetry book *Eunoia* (2001) consists primar-

---

49. Mallarmé wrote in "Crisis in Poetry" (1895): "There will be none of the sublime incoherence found in the page-settings of the romantics, none of the artificial unity that used to be based on the square measurements of the book. Everything will be hesitation, disposition of parts, their alternations and relationships—all this contributing to the rhythmic totality, which will be the very silence of the poem, in its blank spaces, as that silence is translated by each structural element in its own way." In *Mallarmé: Selected Prose Poems Essays & Letters*, translated by Bradford Cook, Baltimore, 1956, p. 41.

ily of five prose poem sequences that, each in turn, uses only the vowels, "a," "e," "i," "o," and "u." His poem "Vowels," on the other hand, excludes all letters of the alphabet but those in the poem's title. Harryette Mullen made a sensation with her volume *Muse & Drudge* (1995), which employs the practice of homophonic translation to comment upon the cultural history and place of African Americans in U.S. society. In the work's opening stanza, "Sapphire's lyre styles / plucked eyebrows / bow lips and legs / whose lives are lonely too," Sapphire, the radio and television wife of Kingfish on the 1950s *Amos 'n' Andy Show*, is doubled with the Greek lyric poet Sappho. In *Sleeping with the Dictionary* (2002), Mullen adopts other Oulipo forms, such as N+7, which requires replacing all nouns of a preexisting work with the seventh noun to follow in whatever dictionary you possess.

Like Newlipo, twenty-first-century conceptual poetry draws upon an earlier international experimental movement. Beginning in 1956, the Brazilian *Noigrandes* group consisting of Haroldo de Campos, Augusto de Campos, and Décio Pignatari stirred international interest in their "poesia concreta" (concrete poetry), which they defined as "[the] tension of thing-words in space-time."[50] Creating verbal objects, they sought the materiality of the word as word, rather than as a vehicle for the transcendent. Such materializing of the word brought poetry closer to conceptual art and has influenced conceptual poetry in the United States. The American poet Aram Saroyan was creating conceptual poetry when he wrote the one-word work "lighght" in the 1960s[51] Ron Padgett's *Great Balls of Fire* (1969) is rich in conceptual poetry; for instance, his sonnet, "Nothing in That Drawer" repeats the title fourteen times. Of the postwar avant-garde, the New York School, with which Padgett is associated, has been most attracted to Oulipo practices.

A rich new phase of conceptualism arrived with Kenneth Goldsmith, Craig Dworkin, Robert Fitterman, and Vanessa Place. Goldsmith's *Day* (2003) consists of his word-by-word transcription of an entire issue of *The New York Times* from Friday, September 1, 2000. None of the words are his own. In appropriating the words of others, he sets forth two major principles of his practice, "hyperrealism" and "uncreative writing." The creativity of his work has nothing to do with the virtuosity and originality of his phrasing; in fact, there is none. The work's creative value begins and ends with its concept. We may also admire the writer's labor as the craftsman (that is, typist) of the work. Just as few read all of Joyce's *Finnegans Wake*, most people will not want to read the exhaustive result. A sample of the work suffices to authenticate its existence. Imagine the difference in the work's impact if the day selected

---

50. "From (Command) Line to (Iconic) Constellation.," UbuWeb, Kenneth Goldsmith. http://www.ubu.com/papers/goldsmith_command.html.   51. *Complete Minimal Poems,* Brooklyn, 2007, p. 31.

had been September 11, 2001. Would the result be too inherently dramatic to qualify as "unoriginal writing"?

Today's conceptual poet goes farther than Charles Olson's proscription of "the lyrical interference of the individual as ego." In conceptual works there may be no lyric, no author, no expression, and no act of original writing, unless the cutting and pasting of others' words is to be considered writing. Conceptual poetry defines itself as, "Unoriginality, illegibility, appropriation, plagiarism, fraud, theft, and falsification as its precepts; information management, word processing, databasing, and extreme process as its methodologies; and boredom, valuelessness, and nutritionlessness as its ethos."[52] Nevertheless conceptual works can be beautifully conceived and structured. Vanessa Place's *Dies: A Sentence* (2005) is a novel in verse consisting on a single sentence. Craig Dworkin's *Parse* (2008), consists entirely of parsing of the grammatical structures of Edwin A. Abbott's *How to Parse: An Attempt to Apply the Principles of Scholarship to English Grammar*, published in 1874. A major influence on such overwriting was Robert Rauschenberg's *Erased de Kooning* (1953), in which, with Willem de Kooning's permission, the little-known younger artist, age twenty-three, erased a drawing by one of the masters of abstract expressionism. The erased work of course was no longer de Kooning's but Rauschenberg's. Sherrie Levine's photographing of Walker Evans's iconic photos of the Great Depression is also an important influence.

Jason Christie offers the term "plundergraphia" to refer to the literary uses of found material: "I believe it is necessary at the outset," he writes, "to demonstrate how plundergraphia is distinct from plagiarism and reference, and shares little more than intention with found poetry. Plagiarism requires a person to desire to conceal a source for his or her benefit. . . . Found poetry appropriates previously conceived material into new arrangements but is still dependent upon the final product as a product. Plundergraphia is a more general praxis that situates words in a new context where they are changed by their transformation."[53] Christie identifies Ronald Johnson's treatment of Milton's *Paradise Lost* as having a plundergraphic attitude toward an original source: Johnson's "transformations of the original distort it beyond legibility into an entirely new creative expression."[54] Johnson creates out of Milton, who was no romantic, a prophetic tone reminiscent of William Blake. His means were both intuitive and procedural, and the result is clearly literature. In Kenneth Goldsmith's works, which are plundered from nonliterary sources, the original is not only recognizable but left virtually intact. Because readers are accustomed to the point of view of the imaginary—not what is, but what is

---

52. "Conceptual Poetics," Kenneth Goldsmith, Sibila online journal, http://www.sibila.com.br/index.php/sibila-english/410-conceptual-poetics/.   53. "Sampling the Culture: 4 Notes toward a Poetics of Plundergraphia and on Kenneth Goldsmith's *Day*," UbuWeb Open Letter, http://www.ubu.com/papers/kg_ol_christie.html.   54. The same.

possible—they may have difficulty in identifying Goldsmith's works with literature. They are, quite simply, the actual.

Not coincidentally, boredom is a positive aspect of many conceptual and cyberpoetry works. A year of New York City weather reports (Kenneth Goldsmith's *The Weather*, 2005) will be boring to most readers after a few pages; nevertheless, the concept remains amusing. Like the Andy Warhol movie, *Sleep* (1963), in which poet John Giorno is filmed sleeping for five hours and twenty minutes, such works use real rather than fictive time. As cyberpoet Tan Lin writes, "Change, like boredom, is the byproduct of time passing. One might add that Warhol's paintings like his novel *a: A Novel* (1968) and his films, are the byproduct of time repeating itself, and thus that thing known as desire. Warhol is the most Platonic of modern artists. He creates an endless series of simulacra of Eternal Forms. . . . Beauty can never be had; it can only be flirted with."[55] Kenneth Goldsmith quotes John Cage as saying: "If something is boring after two minutes, try it for four. If still boring, then eight. Then sixteen. Then thirty-two. Eventually one discovers that it is not boring at all."[56] From the perspective of real time, it's possible to view literatures of fictive time, such as the symbolist poem or romance novel, as absurdly willed into being.

As Walter Benjamin noted with regard to the work of art: "The presence of the original is prerequisite to the concept of authenticity. . . . The whole sphere of authenticity is outside technical—and, of course, not only technical—reproducibility."[57] With the rise of mechanical reproduction, such as moveable type, the lithograph, and the photograph, the aura of the original began to fade, ultimately leading, in our era, to a fondness for copies and mechanical means of production. The simulacrum, or copy, began to take on its own aura. Such is the state of affairs, when, long after McLuhan, the museum gallery most trafficked is the one with a video playing. With the loss of originality as a value, nature, the art of painting, heroism, originality, and the lyric poem begin to lose their savor, replaced by a Heraclitean stream of Internet words and images. Emerson wrote "under every deep a lower deep opens." In the new media streams, there are no depths but rather an insistent rushing of the shallows.

Referring to Borges's fable in which "the cartographers of the Empire draw up a map so detailed that it ends up covering the territory exactly," Baudrillard notes: "Today abstraction is no longer that of the map, the double, the mirror or the concept. Simulation is no longer that of a territory, a referential being, or a substance. It is the generation by models of a real without origin or reality: a hyperreal. The territory no longer precedes the map, nor does it survive it.

55. "Warhol's Aura and the Language of Writing," *Cabinet* 4, Fall 2001, http://cabinetmagazine .org/issues/4/linh.php.   56. Kenneth Goldsmith, *Uncreative Writing: Managing Language in the Digital Age*, New York, 2011, p. 134.   57. "The Work of Art in the Age of Mechanical Reproduction," *Illuminations: Essays and Reflections*, New York, 1955/1968, p. 220.

It is nevertheless the map that precedes the territory—precession of simulacra—that engenders the territory."[58] Ultimately, "it is all of metaphysics that is lost. No more mirror or being and appearances, of the real and its concept."[59] Ultimately, the real "is no longer anything but operational. In fact, it is no longer really the real, because no imaginary envelops it anymore. It is a hyperreal, produced from a radiating synthesis of combinatory models in a hyperspace without atmosphere."[60]

Cyberpoetry is defined by Brian Kim Stefans, a leading practitioner, as (1) "writing that takes advantage of the possibilities afforded by digital technologies—such as the internet, or graphics programs such as Illustrator or Photoshop, or animation/audio/interactive programs such as Flash—in their creation and presentation" or (2) "those forms of writing that are informed by new ways of thinking brought about by the way digital technology has impacted our world, i.e. forms of writing that are organized according to principles of the database, or that work primarily as texts distributed over the internet."[61] This includes recombinant poetics that can be done *without* the computer, such as William S. Burroughs's "cut-up" fictions, concrete poetry, and various Oulipo practices that address the language as replaceable physical matter rather than "necessary expression." Compositional tools expand to include poetry machines such as anagram and Gematria generators, as well as word randomizers like Cut'n'Mix that are created by algorithm. One of the first of these, Travesty (1984), was a simple DOS program codesigned by the scholar Hugh Kenner. Travesty allows for the input of a preestablished text, which can be randomized by letter count on a range from 1 to 9. One of Jackson Mac Low's favorite cyber tools was Diastext4, which analyzes and remixes the letters that appear in a source phrase. Cyberpoetry has also developed its own theoretical and critical vocabulary, with terms like "hacktivist," "wordtoys," "text/image complex," "generative text," and "database aesthetics."[62]

The primary technique of cyberpoetry is sampling; that is, the cutting and pasting of texts and/or images located on the Web onto a page where you have determined to construct a poem. Sampling begins with the use of an online search engine, into which a search phrase is entered. In many respects, cyber technique resembles collage. The field from which to sample is enormous, and it makes available material that ordinarily would fall outside poetry's range of reference. With each copy and paste comes the cultural stain of the Web. This explains the tone of Flarf, a cyberpoetry noted for the outrageousness of its content.

Brian Kim Stefans writes of his fellow cyberpoet: "Tan Lin seems to have gotten there before most of us. His first book, *Lotion Bullwhip Giraffe* (1996), glided along on riffs and rhythms that seemed as if Gerard Manley Hopkins's "dapple-

58. *Simulacra and Simulation,* Ann Arbor, 1994 (1981), p. 1.   59. The same, p. 2.   60. The same.   61. "What Is Electronic Writing?" in *Kluge: A Meditation, and Other Works,* New York, 2007, p. 121.   62. The same, pp. 122–23.

dawn-drawn Falcon" had gotten stuck in John Yau's English-as-a-Stammered-Language machine."[63] He then quotes from Lin's poem, "Talc Bull Dogface":

> Lu Hsun chews geisha cup. Geisha spits
> cup. Clouds form on back like worms
> in planetarium. How is tap-dancing
> nightingale distinguish
> from cleaning rag?[64]

Referring to the "scattershot" aspect of the writing and the "Chinaman in the clinamen," Stefans admires the "vast text dump" organized by "some hidden, reptilian algorithm" that bounds along until it glows "with a radium-like intensity."[65] The poem was probably created by an algorithmic text randomizer. However, Tan Lin's simulation of Hopkins's authorship may ultimately have felt too authored. He soon changed to the contrasting mode of "ambient literature":

> For me, the ambience is a mode of absorption. . . . I came out of this language poetry movement premised on difficulty, non-lyric, things that have not to do with memorization or the expression of a self or a voice. Ambience was, for me, a way of dealing in a sort of avant-garde or experimental context with some of these ideas, and to diffuse them, simply because I thought the aesthetic autonomy that was promulgated from within seemed, in some ways, slightly outmoded, in that, really, so much that we experience today has to do with ease of absorption, labeling[66] things.[67]

This ambience includes samplings from other poets such as Laura Riding, T. S. Eliot, and Emily Dickinson, which appear "slightly rewritten." As Tan Lin says, "I don't want there to be a shock of montage you would get in a T. S. Eliot 'Waste Land' poem; I wanted it to be effortless and float and soak over you."[68] To create a more accessible style (his friends had failed to understand his first book), Tan Lin turned to the established mode of the personal essay, the addition of fictive elements, such as an imaginary spinster aunt who lives sadly in Seattle, and uses of the everyday. In his essay, "Artifice of Absorption," Charles Bernstein had opposed a poetics of absorption and ease, call-

---

63. "Streaming Poetry," *Boston Review*, October/November 2004 archives, http://bostonreview .net/BR29.5/stefans.php.   64. The same.   65. The same.   66. *A Poetics*, Cambridge, MA, 1992, p. 29.   67. "Ambiently Breaking Reading Conventions: Colin Marshall Talks to Experimental Poet Tan Lin," *3 Quarks Daily*, July 5, 2010, http://www.3quarksdaily. com/3quarksdaily/2010/07/ambiently-breaking-reading-conventions-colin-marshall-talks-to-experimental-poet-tan-lin-html.   68. The same.

ing instead for the impermeability of artifice, distraction, and difficulty, and attention scattering. However, Tan Lin's ambient literature uses the devices of artifice and distraction to absorptive, easeful, and accessible ends. Likewise, his flirtation with boredom appears to be for his own, and the reader's, amusement.

Much digital poetry appears in online periodicals, and many literary magazines can be found only in digital format. However, collections of digital poetry still appear primarily as printed books. In his print collections, Tan Lin imports the visual look of the Web, such as an advertisement for Blimpie's, as a reminder of the work's origins. The results can be alternately fragmentary and jittery (sampling mode) or steady and banal (ambient mode). Tan Lin writes: "What are the forms of non-reading and what are the non-forms a reading might take? Poetry = wallpaper. . . . It would be nice to create works of literature that didn't have to be read but could be looked at, like placemats. The most exasperating thing at a poetry reading is always the sound of a poet reading."[69]

The cyberpoetry practice of Flarf was founded by Gary Sullivan in December, 2000, when, upset by his grandfather being scammed by a poetry contest, he set out to write the worst poem possible. That poem, "Mm-hmm," began with the lines:

> Mm-hmm
> Yeah, mm-hmm, it's true
> Big birds make
> Big doo! I got fire inside
> My "huppa"-chimp™5
> Gonna be agreesive, greasy aw yeah god

When Sullivan sent the poem to his friends online, they decided to write their own purposely bad poems. According to a Flarf historian, "They plugged random phrases into Google and emailed the 'poetic' results to their colleagues. That group, in turn, Googled the new lines of poetry, and massaged the results into verse—a poetic pyramid scheme. . . . The poems were so bad, they were good. A terrible beauty was born.[70] Sullivan also named the movement. "I found the word 'flarf' online on a police blotter where some stoner had described marijuana as flarfy," Sullivan said.[71]

Unlike most schools of poetry, Flarf has never issued an official statement of poetics. In this and other respects, it resembles Dada. However, Sullivan sees a more important connection to Camp: "Flarf is similar to Camp in that it

---

69. *Seven Controlled Vocabularies and Obituary 2004. The Joy of Cooking,* Middletown, CT, 2007, p. 16.   70. Rick Snyder, "The New Pandemonium: A Brief Overview of Flarf," *Jacket* 31, October 2006, http://jacketmagazine.com/31/snyder-flarf.html.   71. The same.

sets aside any pre-existing sense of 'good' and 'bad' in favor of another value, or set of values. It does not, however, as some believe, favor 'bad' over 'good.' It simply does not make the distinction."[72] Sullivan claims that the difference between the two resides primarily in their emphasis on form and content: "There is, in much Flarf, a superabundance of content. Often to an embarrassing or discomfiting degree."[73] Like Kitsch, Camp is an art style of the early 1960s that calls for an art so bad it becomes fashionable, as in the television series *Batman*. Vladimir Nabokov's novel *Lolita* has aspects of Camp, such as Humbert Humbert's adoration of Lolita's toenails.

By May of 2001, Sullivan had created the online Flarflist, which included Nada Gordon, Drew Gardner, Kasey Mohammad, Katie Degentesh, Mitch Highfill, Jordan Davis, Carol Mirakove, and, somewhat later, Maria Damon and Erik Belgum. The poets Michael Magee, Rodney Koeneke, and Rod Smith were also involved. Flarf traffic was initially heavy online, but after a few months enthusiasm began to wane. Sullivan recalls: "By September 2001, the list became relatively silent. Not too long after 9/11, people began posting again, though now all of the flarfs—many of which were parodies of AP News items—in some way or form addressed the aftermath of 9/11 including media portrayal of the same."[74] With works like Drew Gardner's "Chicks Dig War," Flarf can take moral action through the situationist *détournement* of the disagreeable aspects of culture.[75] But on the whole, the motive of Flarf is the pure amusement of the online carnival. Like the Pac-Man video game of yore, it represents the popular culture's appetite for its own products. Such a tone can be found in K. Silem Mohammad's essay "Excessivism," a parody of Frank O'Hara's "Personism: A Manifesto":

> Everything is in the European blinko (whatever that means), but at the risk of sounding like the Powerline Boys on a corndog-and-Super-Squishee bender, I will write to you because I just heard that the Police are reuniting for the Grammies. Now come on, I don't believe in God, so I don't have a problem. I hate Southwest Airlines, I always have. I may be spoiled, but I like airlines that offer advance seat assignments and first class cabins for upgrades. I don't even like whales. Please, feel free to observe the irony of my current situation: I love to sleep.[76]

72. Tom Beckett, "Interview with Gary Sullivan," e-x-c-h-a-n-g-e-v-a-l-u-e-s, May 14, 2006, http://willtoexchange.blogspot.com/2006/05/interview-with-gary-sullivan.html.   73. The same. 74. "The Flarf Files," Flarf website, http://epc.buffalo.edu/authors/bernstein/syllabi/readings/flarf.html.   75. Founded by the Letterist International and extensively developed by the Situationist International, *détournement*, or "derailing," involves the spoofing of a dominant system such as commodity capitalism by turning its expressions against itself. The works of artist Barbara Kruger are a prime example.   76. *Action Yes Online Quarterly* 1.5 (Spring, 2007), http://www.actionyes.org/issue5/excess/mohammad/mohammad1.html.

Flarf enjoys the controversial but strategically advantageous position of presenting what seems to be a new low in poetry. But its daring has opened new fields of reference and recuperated a populist, content-centered writing that had been missing during the comparatively theoretical reign of language poetry. As a postlanguage poetry, Flarf stands at the opposite pole from the postlanguage lyric, which, despite its uses of irony and oblique phrasing, maintains the gravitas of the human subject. In the Mohammad quote above, it's hard to decide what or whom he is spoofing. Is it Frank O'Hara, poetry as expression, or a culture that values the Powerline Boys, the Police, and Southwest Airlines? Is our silliness and profanity a form of sleep? Or is Mohammad attempting to awaken us to the real situation? Conceptual poetry and Flarf have the means to *détourn* society, but are they too entrenched in official art culture and infantilized by popular culture? Or are poets like Ann Lauterbach, Claudia Keelan, and Bob Perelman already saying, between the lines of their lyric poems or more directly with Perelman's irony, what will restore us to sense and right action?

An interesting and sometimes dispiriting debate on the current state of poetry occurred in 2009 between conceptual poet Kenneth Goldsmith and *Skanky Possum* editor Dale Smith.[77] Goldsmith wrote:

> Any notion of history has been leveled by the internet. Now, it's all fodder for the remix and recreation of works of art: free-floating toolboxes and strategies unmoored from context of historicity. . . . All types of proposed linear historical trajectories have been scrambled and discredited by the tidal wave of digitality, which has crept up on us and so completely saturated our culture that we, although deeply immersed in it, have no idea what hit us. In the face of the digital, postmodernism is the quaint last gasp of modernism.

To which Smith, who supports a "slow poetry" based on the expressive intuitions of individual authors, responded:

> We're surrounded by the past in the form of digitized archives. I understand that. But Benjamin's notion of history is rooted in a sense of the catastrophic failures of history in the twentieth century, too. Paradise is a dream—a true liberating force (an impossibility?)—that is rooted in a meaningful search for images. We are surrounded by artifacts, ending fodder for remixing, as you say. But how do we proceed with this

---

77. "The Tortoise and the Hare: Dale Smith and Kenneth Goldsmith Parse Slow and Fast Poetries," Monday, July 6, 2009–Saturday, July 25, 2009, *Jacket* 38, Late 2009, http://jacketmagazine.com/38/iv-smith-goldsmith.shtml.

material in respect to the catastrophe? Are we really free to ignore the contexts and situations produced by these images?

While Goldsmith celebrates the digital flood, Smith goes on to remind us that "the human psyche remains at best a kind of Paleolithic thing," as Gary Snyder, the Pound-Olson tradition, and others have long understood. For all the triumphal claims of conceptualism, no one is drowned but Icarus and the ship of history sails calmly on. History determined that Rae Armantrout, an experimental lyric poet and close observer of human experience, won the Pulitzer Prize for 2010. In the weights and measures of value, the lyric mode continues its negotiation with the most primal of technologies, the human mind and voice. It does its writing both by hand and on the computer, with craft and sometimes wisdom, and in varying degrees of silence and sound. It is difficult for the Internet to conceive of silence. As the poet Cole Swensen writes, "There does exist a territory of impression not accessible by language. The exploration of such a territory seems to me the particular domain of the arts."[78] When a cybernetic poet casts a Google search phrase onto the Internet, he or she invites the furies of wisdom and foolishness to attend the poem, as Ginsberg did in the writing of *Howl*. The challenge to authorship is always made by an author, who recognizes the mysteries of the actual and allows them, for a time and within a given artistic frame and intention, to speak. There are, finally, no empty words. Despite claims made for the digital revolution, the computer remains a research, editing, and compositional tool for the great majority of poets in this volume. The limit of the person is the limit of the machine.

As we noted in the previous edition, the avant-garde, which fractures tradition, has its own traditions and long history, which critic Marjorie Perloff views as beginning with Rimbaud in the second half of the nineteenth century: "It is Rimbaud who strikes the first note of that 'undecidability' we find in Gertrude Stein, in Pound, and in Williams . . . an undecidability that has become marked in the poetry of the last decades."[79] This inheritance includes Futurism, Dada, surrealism, modernism, and the varieties of postmodernism we are now experiencing. Despite the exhaustion we may feel at the political and economic levels, with each generation poetry does renew itself. The approaches taken by the poets in this anthology are broad and various, but certain patterns and schools of thought emerge. We should not imagine that a single style rules the period, such as language poetry, conceptual poetry, or the postlanguage lyric. It is all of the above. Perloff's term "undecidability" does not mean that the poets or the era have no determination. It is poetry

---

78. Poet's statement, *Writing from the New Coast: Technique*, o•blēk 12, Spring/Fall, 1993, ed. Peter Gizzi and Juliana Spahr, p. 91.   79. *The Poetics of Indeterminacy*, Evanston, 1983, p. 4.

itself that thrives on a certain uncertainty. That principle was first stated by Keats in a letter to his brothers of December 22, 1817:

> It struck me what quality went to form a Man of Achievement, especially in Literature, and which Shakespeare possessed so enormously—I mean *Negative Capability,* that is, when a man is capable of being in uncertainties, mysteries, doubts, without any irritable reaching after fact and reason. Coleridge, for instance, would let go by a fine isolated verisimilitude caught from the Penetralium of mystery, from being incapable of remaining content with half-knowledge.[80]

Strange to quote Keats on this subject, but his insight holds for the poetry of our time, just as Heisenberg's uncertainty principle speaks to the measurements of science, that what we know of quantum events is changed by our perception of them. Our poetics assert a position, but a truth or beauty held too tightly slips away to other arms. Cole Swensen is correct, and Kenneth Goldsmith is correct. Will Alexander is correct when he writes: "Poetry commences by the force of biographical intensity, by the force of its interior brews, by the sum of its subconscious oscillations."[81] And Gertrude Stein, who was ahead of her time, was correct when she wrote, "No one is ahead of his time."[82] As Friedrich Hölderlin, who was mad half of his life, knew too well: "The god / is near and difficult to grasp."[83] That god, charm, or source of interest is what compels you to read a novel in verse consisting of one sentence, or Yeats's "Lapis Lazuli," or Caroline Knox's "Freudian Shoes." The poem was unsolvable and a little ugly, but lovely. It has so teased your interest that a couple of days later you want to read it again.

80. *The Complete Poetical Works and Letters of John Keats,* Cambridge Edition, Boston, 1899, p. 277.   81. "Poetry: Alchemical Anguish and Fire," Gizzi and Spahr, pp. 15–16. 82. Quoted in "Stacy Doris: Poet's Statement," Gizzi and Spahr, p. 133.   83. "Patmos," *Selected Poems of Friedrich Hölderlin,* trans. Maxine Chernoff & Paul Hoover, Richmond, CA, 2008, p. 283.

POSTMODERN AMERICAN POETRY

Second Edition

Charles Olson ─────────
1910–1970

In the winter of 1944–1945, in his midthirties, Charles Olson rejected a promising political career in the Roosevelt administration and turned to writing prose and poetry. His study of Herman Melville, *Call Me Ishmael*, appeared in 1947, followed shortly by his first book of poetry, *Y & X*, in 1948. The same year, Olson began a series of lectures at Black Mountain College, an experimental institution in North Carolina, where his success led to his replacing his mentor Edward Dahlberg as a visiting lecturer. Olson wrote his best early poetry at Black Mountain, including "In Cold Hell, in Thicket" and "The Kingfishers," as well as his manifesto "Projective Verse," published in *Poetry New York* in 1950. From 1951 until its closing in 1956, Olson served as rector of Black Mountain College, inviting poets such as Robert Creeley, Denise Levertov, and Robert Duncan to teach. By 1960, the year in which he published *The Distances*, Olson was recognized as a major figure of American poetry.

If Allen Ginsberg was the popular and spiritual leader of the postwar experimental poetry, Charles Olson was its leading thinker and strategist. Like Ginsberg, he reconnected poetry with the body, emphasizing what he called the "proprioceptive," or inward, character of human speech. For Olson, each line of poetry was both idiosyncratic and "necessary" as a result of each speaker's particular breath.

The first sentence of *Call Me Ishmael* is "I take SPACE to be the central fact to man born in America, from Folsom Cave to now." The poetics of place is basic to Olson's thinking. In *The Maximus Poems*, his epic poem, that place is his hometown of Gloucester, Massachusetts. Also important to Olson's poetics is what the philosopher Alfred North Whitehead called "presentational immediacy." Art and life fail, Olson stressed in his essay "Human Universe," when the passive replaces the active, for it is not in "spectatorism" that culture is earned but rather in work. The descriptive and the metaphysical fail because they "crowd out participation" in the same way "monopolies of business and government . . . protect themselves from the advancement in position of able men."[1] Summarizing perception rather than presenting it, the symbolic also falls short. "Art does not seek to describe but to enact," Olson writes.[2] Emphasizing poetry as process, the postmodern poet replaces what Olson called the "Classical-representational" with the *"primitive-abstract."*[3] Thus Olson predicts the shamanistic poetries of Allen Ginsberg and Gary Snyder, among others, as well as the current trend toward cultural pluralism.

1. *Selected Writings*, New York, 1966, p. 58.   2. The same, p. 61.   3. "Letter to Elaine Feinstein" (May 1959), in *Selected Writings*, p. 28.

In Cold Hell, in Thicket

In cold hell, in thicket, how
abstract (as high mind, as not lust, as love is) how
strong (as strut or wing, as polytope, as things are
constellated) how
strung, how cold
can a man stay (can men) confronted
thus?

All things are made bitter, words even
are made to taste like paper, wars get tossed up
like lead soldiers used to be
(in a child's attic) lined up
to be knocked down, as I am,
by firings from a spit-hardened fort, fronted
as we are, here, from where we must go

God, that man, as his acts must, as there is always
a thing he can do, he can raise himself, he raises
on a reed he raises his

Or, if it is me, what
he has to say

1

What has he to say?
In hell it is not easy
to know the traceries, the markings
(the canals, the pits, the mountings by which space
declares herself, arched, as she is, the sister,
awkward stars drawn for teats to pleasure him, the brother
who lies in stasis under her, at ease as any monarch or
a happy man

How shall he who is not happy, who has been so made unclear,
who is no longer privileged to be at ease, who,
                                        in this brush, stands
reluctant, imageless, unpleasured, caught in a sort of hell, how
shall he convert this underbrush, how turn this unbidden place

how trace and arch again
the necessary goddess?

2

The branches made against the sky are not of use, are
already done, like snow-flakes, do not, cannot service
him who has to raise (Who puts this on, this damning

of his flesh?)
he can, but how far, how sufficiently far can he raise

the thickets of
this wilderness?

How can he change, his question is
these black and silvered knivings, these
awkwardnesses?

How can he make these blood-points into panels,

into sides
for a king's, for his own
for a wagon, for a sleigh, for the beak of,

the running sides of
a vessel fit for
moving?

How can he make out, he asks,
of this low eye-view,
size?

And archings traced and picked enough to hold
to stay, as she does, as he, the brother, when,
here where the mud is, he is frozen, not daring
where the grass grows, to move his feet from fear
he'll trespass on his own dissolving bones, here
where there is altogether too much remembrance?

3

The question, the fear he raises up himself against
(against the same each act is proffered, under the eyes
each fix, the town of the earth over, is managed) is: Who
am I?

Who am I but by a fix, and another,
a particle, and the congery of particles carefully picked
                                        one by another,

          as in this thicket, each
          smallest branch, plant, fern, root
          —roots lie, on the surface, as nerves are laid open—
          must now (the bitterness of the taste of her) be
          isolated, observed, picked over, measured, raised
          as though a word, an accuracy were a pincer!
                                        this

               is the abstract, this
               is the cold doing, this
               is the almost impossible

     So shall you blame those
     who give it up, those who say
     it isn't worth the struggle?

                    (Prayer
     Or a death as going over to—shot by yr own forces—to
     a greener place?

                    Neither

     any longer
     usable)

               By fixes only (not even any more by shamans)
               can the traceries
               be brought out

                           II

ya, selva oscura, but hell now
is not exterior, is not to be got out of, is
the coat of your own self, the beasts
emblazoned on you   And who
can turn this total thing, invert
and let the ragged sleeves be seen
by any bitch or common character?   Who
can endure it where it is, where the beasts are met,

where yourself is, your beloved is, where she
who is separate from you, is not separate, is not
goddess, is, as your core is,
the making of one hell

>   where she moves off, where she is
>   no longer arch

(this is why he of whom we speak does not move, why
he stands so awkward where he is, why
his feet are held, like some ragged crane's
off the nearest next ground, even from
the beauty of the rotting fern his eye
knows, as he looks down, as,
in utmost pain if cold can be so called,
he looks around his battlefield, this
rotted place where men did die, where boys
and immigrants have fallen, where nature
(the years that she's took over)
does not matter, where

>   that men killed, do kill, that woman kills
>   is part, too, of his question

2

That it is simple, what the difference is—
That a man, men, are now their own wood
and thus their own hell and paradise
that they are, in hell or in happiness, merely
something to be wrought, to be shaped, to be carved, for use, for
others

does not in the least lessen his, this unhappy man's
obscurities, his
confrontations

He shall step, he
will shape, he
is already also
moving off

into the soil, on to his own bones

he will cross

(there is always a field,
for the strong there is always
an alternative)

But a field
is not a choice, is
as dangerous as a prayer, as a death, as any
misleading, lady

He will cross

And is bound to enter (as she is)
a later wilderness.
Yet
what he does here, what he raises up
(he must, the stakes are such

this at least
is a certainty, this
is a law, is not one of the questions, this
is what was talked of as
—what was it called, demand?)

He will do what he now does, as she will, do
carefully, do
without wavering,
without
as even the branches,
even in this dark place, the twigs
how

even the brow
of what was once to him a beautiful face

as even the snow-flakes waver in the light's eye

as even forever wavers (gutters

in the wind of loss)

even as he will forever waver

precise as hell is, precise
as any words, or wagon,
can be made

1953

I, Maximus of Gloucester, to You

Off-shore, by islands hidden in the blood
jewels & miracles, I, Maximus
a metal hot from boiling water, tell you
what is a lance, who obeys the figures of
the present dance

1

the thing you're after
may lie around the bend
of the nest (second, time slain, the bird! the bird!

And there! (strong) thrust, the mast! flight

                (of the bird
                o kylix, o
                Antony of Padua
                sweep low, o bless
the roofs, the old ones, the gentle steep ones
on whose ridge-poles the gulls sit, from which they depart,

                And the flake-racks

of my city!

2

love is form, and cannot be without
important substance (the weight
say, 58 carats each one of us, perforce
our goldsmith's scale

           feather to feather added
           (and what is mineral, what
           is curling hair, the string
           you carry in your nervous beak, these
           make bulk, these, in the end, are
           the sum
           (o my lady of good voyage
           in whose arm, whose left arm rests
no boy but a carefully carved wood, a painted face, a schooner!
a delicate mast, as bow-sprit for

           forwarding

3

the underpart is, though stemmed, uncertain
is, as sex is, as moneys are, facts!
facts, to be dealt with, as the sea is, the demand
that they be played by, that they only can be, that they must
be played by, said he, coldly, the
ear!

By ear, he sd.
But that which matters, that which insists, that which will last,
that! o my people, where shall you find it, how, where, where shall you listen
when all is become billboards, when, all, even silence, is spray-gunned?

when even our bird, my roofs,
cannot be heard

when even you, when sound itself is neoned in?

when, on the hill, over the water
where she who used to sing,
when the water glowed,

black, gold, the tide
outward, at evening

when bells came like boats
over the oil-slicks, milkweed
hulls

And a man slumped,
attentionless,
against pink shingles

o sea city)

4

one loves only form,
and form only comes
into existence when
the thing is born

born of yourself, born
of hay and cotton struts,
of street-pickings, wharves, weeds
you carry in, my bird

of a bone of a fish
of a straw, or will
of a color, of a bell
of yourself, torn

5

love is not easy
but how shall you know,
New England, now
that pejorocracy is here, how
that street-cars, o Oregon, twitter
in the afternoon, offend
a black-gold loin?

how shall you strike,
o swordsman, the blue-red back

when, last night, your aim
was mu-sick, mu-sick, mu-sick
And not the cribbage game?

(o Gloucester-man,
weave
your birds and fingers
new, your roof-tops,
clean shit upon racks
sunned on
American
braid
with others like you, such
extricable surface
as faun and oral,
satyr lesbos vase

o kill kill kill kill kill
those
who advertise you
out)

6

in! in! the bow-sprit, bird, the beak
in, the bend is, in, goes in, the form
that which you make, what holds, which is
the law of object, strut after strut, what you are, what you must be, what
the force can throw up, can, right now hereinafter erect,
the mast, the mast, the tender
mast!

The nest, I say, to you, I Maximus, say
under the hand, as I see it, over the waters
from this place where I am, where I hear,
can still hear

from where I carry you a feather
as though, sharp, I picked up,
in the afternoon delivered you
a jewel,
it flashing more than a wing,

than any old romantic thing,
than memory, than place,
than anything other than that which you carry

than that which is,
call it a nest, around the head of, call it
the next second

than that which you
can do!

1953

Letter 3

Tansy buttons, tansy
for my city
Tansy for their noses

Tansy for them,
tansy for Gloucester to take the smell
of all owners,
the smell

Tansy
for all of us

Let those who use words cheap, who use us cheap
take themselves out of the way
Let them not talk of what is good for the city

Let them free the way for me, for the men of the Fort
who are not hired, who buy the white houses

Let them cease putting out words in the public print
so that any of us have to leave, so that my Portuguese leave,
leave the Lady they gave us, sell their schooners
with the greyhounds aft, the long Diesels
they put their money in, leave Gloucester
in the present shame of,
the wondership stolen by,
ownership

Tansy from Cressy's
I rolled in as a boy
and didn't know it was
tansy

1

Did you know, she sd, growing up there,
how rare it was? And it turned out later she meant exactly the long field
drops down from Ravenswood where the land abrupts,
this side of Fresh Water Cove, and throws out
that wonder of my childhood, the descending green does run
so,
by the beach

       where they held the muster Labor Day, and the engine teams
       threw such arcs of water

               runs with summer with

tansy

2

I was not born there, came, as so many of the people came,
from elsewhere. That is, my father did. And not from the Provinces,
not from Newfoundland. But we came early enough. When he came,
there were three hundred sail could fill the harbor,
if they were all in, as for the Races, say
Or as now the Italians are in, for San Pietro,
and the way it is from Town Landing, all band-concert,
and fireworks

So I answered her: Yes,
I knew (I had that to compare to it,
was Worcester)

As the people of the earth are now, Gloucester
is heterogeneous, and so can know polis
not as localism, not that mu-sick (the trick
of corporations, newspapers, slick magazines, movie houses,
the ships, even the wharves, absentee-owned

they whine to my people, these entertainers, sellers

they play upon their bigotries (upon their fears

these   they have the nerve
to speak of that lovely hour
the Waiting Station, 5 o'clock, the Magnolia bus, Al Levy
on duty (the difference
from 1 o'clock, all the women getting off
the Annisquam-Lanesville,
and the letter carriers

5:40, and only the lollers
in front of the shoe-shine parlor

these, right in the people's faces (and not at all as the gulls do it,
who do it straight, do it all over the "Times" blowing
the day after, or the "Summer Sun" catching on pilings, floating
off the Landing, the slime
the low tide reveals, the smell
then

3

The word does intimidate. The pay-check does.
But to use either, as cheap men

o tansy city, root city
let them not make you
as the nation is

I speak to any of you, not to you all, to no group, not to you as citizens
as my Tyrian might have. Polis now
is a few, is a coherence not even yet new (the island of this city
is a mainland now of who? who can say who are
citizens?

Only a man or a girl who hear a word
and that word meant to mean not a single thing the least more than
what it does mean (not at all to sell any one anything, to keep them anywhere,
not even
in this rare place

1953

Maximus, to himself

I have had to learn the simplest things
last. Which made for difficulties.
Even at sea I was slow, to get the hand out, or to cross
a wet deck.
        The sea was not, finally, my trade.
But even my trade, at it, I stood estranged
from that which was most familiar. Was delayed,
and not content with the man's argument
that such postponement
is now the nature of
obedience,

        that we are all late
        in a slow time,
        that we grow up many
        And the single
        is not easily
        known

It could be, though the sharpness (the *achiote*)
I note in others,
makes more sense
than my own distances. The agilities

        they show daily
        who do the world's
        businesses
        And who do nature's
        as I have no sense
        I have done either

I have made dialogues,
have discussed ancient texts,
have thrown what light I could, offered
what pleasures
doceat allows

        But the known?
This, I have had to be given,
a life, love, and from one man
the world.

Tokens,
But sitting here
I look out as a wind
and water man, testing
And missing
some proof

I know the quarters
of the weather, where it comes from,
where it goes. But the stem of me,
this I took from their welcome,
or their rejection, of me

And my arrogance
was neither diminished
nor increased,
by the communication

2

It is undone business
I speak of, this morning,
with the sea
stretching out
from my feet

1956

John Cage
1912–1992

Born in Los Angeles, John Cage was the son of an inventor who developed an explanation of the cosmos called "Electrostatic Field Theory."[1] This history predicts Cage's own innovations in music, a field he chose after early ambitions as a writer and painter. In 1933 he became the student of Arnold Schoenberg, who later called Cage not a composer but "an inventor—of genius."[2] Committed to experiment, especially the Dadaist example of Marcel Duchamp, Cage went on to pioneer a new conception of music based on the use of chance and other nonintentional methods. In this, he was aided by his study of Zen Buddhism and a pacifist social philosophy based in the writings of Thoreau. As William Carlos Williams had done in poetry, Cage expanded the definition of music to include all categories of sound, such as random everyday noises. As he writes in "The Future of Music": "*Klangfarbenmelodie* has not taken the place of *bel canto*. It has extended our realization of what can happen."[3]

In the 1960s, following his own example in music, as well as the work of Clark Coolidge and Jackson Mac Low, Cage turned his attention to poetry, using both nonintentional and intentional methods. He soon discovered the use of mesostics, a form of acrostics, as an aid to composition. He also began using the texts of honored predecessors, such as James Joyce and Ezra Pound, as the basis for his chance procedures. Such methods as the casting of the *I Ching* to determine relationships within the text are intended to bring about the politically desirable goal of "demilitarizing" the language. Cage's "indeterminacy," his challenge to the status of author as ego, and his use of appropriation and found materials have become defining characteristics of postmodern art in general. Likewise, his links to Dada, use of prepared piano, and cybernetic tools of composition have proved attractive to today's conceptual and cyber poets.

His work in language includes *A Year from Monday* (1967), *M: Writings '67–'72, Empty Words: Writings '73–'78,* and *X: Writings '79–'82.*

A frequent collaborator with choreographer Merce Cunningham, Cage lived in New York City.

1. John Cage, "Autobiography," in *Conversing with John Cage,* ed. Richard Kostelanetz, New York, 1988, p. 1.   2. The same, p. 6.   3. *Empty Words: Writings '73–'78,* Middletown, CT, 1979, p. 178.

25 Mesostics Re and Not Re Mark Tobey

it was iMpossible
  to do Anything:
  the dooR
  was locKed.

i won The first game.
   he wOn the second.
    in Boston,
     nExt
      Year, he'll be teaching philosophy.

         the house is a Mess:
              pAintings
           wheRever
         you looK.

     she told Me
      his wAy
     of Reading
assumes that the booK he's reading is true.

      why doesn'T
         he stOp painting?
        someBody
       will havE
       to spend Years cataloguing, etc.

         The girl checking in the baggage
      reduced Our overweight to zero
        By counting it
   on a first-class passEnger's ticket: the heaviest handbag
had been hidden unnecessarilY

       forTunately, we were with hanna,
      antOinette,
   and hanna's two Boys.
       thE girl at the counter
gave one of the boYs a carry-on luggage tag as a souvenir.

            My
           strAtegy:
       act as though you'Re home;
         don't asK any questions.

instead of Music:
thunder, trAffic,
      biRds, and high-speed military planes/producing sonic booms;
now and then a chicK en (pontpoint).

      each Thing he saw
    he asked us tO look at.
        By
          thE time we reached the japanese restaurant
    our eYes were open.

    the rooM
        dAvid has in the attic
      is veRy
  good for his worK.

  how much do The paintings
       cOst?
    they were Bought
on the installmEnt plan:
there was no moneY.

he played dominoes and drank calvados unTil
               fOur in the morning.
    carpenters came aBout
        sEven
          thirtY to finish their work in his bedroom.

    you can find ouT
      what kind Of art is up to the minute
        By visiting
      thE head office
of a successful advertising companY.

    i'M helpless:
    i cAn't do a thing
  without Ritty in paris
and mimi in new yorK (artservices).

"is There
anything yOu want
Brought
from thE
citY?" no, nothing. less mass media, perhaps.

waiting for the bus, i happened to look at the paveMent
i wAs standing on;
noticed no diffeRence between
looKing at art or away from it.

the chinese children accepted the freedoMs
i gAve them
afteR
my bacK was turned.

pauline served lunch on The
flOor
But
objEcted
to the waY galka was using her knife and fork.

norTh
Of paris, june '72:
colly Bia platyphylla,
plutEus cervinus, pholiota
mutabilis and several *hYpholomas.*

The
dOors and windows are open.
"why Bring it back?
i'd forgottEn where it was.
You could have kept it."

he told Me
of A movie they'd seen,
a natuRe film.
he thought we would liKe it too.

<pre>
                The paintings
        i had decided tO
                    Buy
            wEre superfluous; nevertheless,
        after several Years, i owned them.

                    sold Them
                            tO write music. now there's a third.
                i must get the first two Back.
                    whEre
                    are theY?

                        all it is is a Melody
                            of mAny
                            coloRs:
                                Klangfarbenmelodie.
                                                1973
</pre>

To write the following text I followed the rule given me by Louis Mink, which I also followed in *Writing for the Third (and Fourth) Time through Finnegans Wake*, that is, I did not permit the appearance of either letter between two of the name. As in *Writing for the Fourth Time through Finnegans Wake*, I kept an index of the syllables used to present a given letter of the name and I did not permit repetition of these syllables.

Writing through the Cantos

<pre>
        and thEn with bronZe lance heads beaRing yet Arms 3–4
                    sheeP slain Of plUto stroNg praiseD
            thE narrow glaZes the uptuRned nipple As 11
                    sPeak tO rUy oN his gooDs
        arE swath blaZe mutteRing empty Armour 14–15
    Ply Over ply eddying flUid beNeath the of the goDs
                    torchEs gauZe tuRn of the stAirs 16
        Peach-trees at the fOrd jacqUes betweeN ceDars
            as gygEs on topaZ and thRee on the bArb of 17
    Praise Or sextUs had seeN her in lyDia walks with
                    womEn in maZe of aiR wAs 18
</pre>

Put upOn lUst of womaN roaD from spain

sEa-jauZionda motheR of yeArs 22

Picus de dOn elinUs doN Dictum 23

concubuissE y cavals armatZ meRe succession And 24

Peu mOisi plUs bas le jardiN olD

mEn's fritZ enduRes Action 25

striPed beer-bOttles bUt *is* iN floateD

scarlEt gianoZio one fRom Also 28

due disPatch ragOna pleasUre either as participaNt wD.

sEnd with sforZa the duchess to Rimini wArs 31

Pleasure mOstly di cUi fraNcesco southwarD

hE abbaZia of sant apollinaiRe clAsse 36

serPentine whOse dUcats to be paid back to the cardiNal 200 Ducats

corn-salvE for franco sforZa's at least keep the Row out of tuscAny 43

s. Pietri hOminis reddens Ut magis persoNa ex ore proDiit 44

quaE thought old Zuliano is wRite thAt 50

Peasant fOr his *sUb de malatestis* goNe him to Do in

mo'ammEds singing to Zeus down heRe fAtty 51

Praestantibusque bOth geniUs both owN all of it Down on

papEr bust-up of braZilian secuRities s.A. securities 55

they oPerated and there was a whOre qUit the driNk saveD up 56

his pay monEy and ooZe scRupulously cleAn 61

Penis whO disliked langUage skiN profiteers Drinking

bEhind dung-flow cut in loZenges the gaiteRs of slum-flesh bAck- 64

comPlaining attentiOn nUlla fideNtia earth a Dung hatching 65

inchoatE graZing the swill hammeRing the souse into hArdness 66

long sleeP babylOn i heard in the circUit seemed whirliNg heaD 68

hEld gaZe noRth his eyes blAzing

Peire cardinal in his mirrOr blUe lakes of crimeN choppeD

icE gaZing at theiR plAin 69

nymPhs and nOw a swashbUckler didN't blooDy 70

finE of a bitch franZ baRbiche Aldington on 71

trench dug through corPses lOt minUtes sergeaNt rebukeD him

for lEvity trotZsk is a bRest-litovsk Aint yuh herd he 74

sPeech mOve 'em jUst as oNe saiD 75

'Em to Zenos metevsky bieRs to sell cAnnon 80–81

Peace nOt while yew rUssia a New keyboarD

likE siZe ov a pRince An' we sez wud yew like

his Panties fer the cOmpany y hUrbara zeNos's Door

with hEr champZ don't the felleRs At home 84

uP-Other Upside dowN up to the beD-room 85

stubby fEllow cocky as khristnoZe eveRy dAmn thing for the
hemP via rOtterdm das thUst Nicht Days 86
gonE glaZe gReen feAthers 91
of the Pavement brOken disrUpted wilderNess of glazeD 92
junglE Zoe loud oveR the bAnners
fingers Petal'd frOm pUrple olibaNum's wrappeD floating
bluE citiZens as you desiRe quellA 96
Pace Oh mUrdered floriNs paiD 97
ovEr doZen yeaRs conveyAnce
be Practicable cOme natUre moNtecello golD 98
wishEd who wuZ pRice cAn't 101
Plane an' hOw mr. bUkos the ecoNomist woulD 102
savE lattittZo the giRl sAys it'z 106
shiP dOwn chUcked blaNche forDs 107
of ocEan priZes we have agReed he hAs won 110
Pay nOstri qUickly doN't seeD combs
two grEat and faictZ notRe puissAnce 113
Priest sent a bOy and the statUes Niccolo tolD him 114
sEnt priZe a collaR with jewels cAme 123
Prize gOnzaga marqUis ferrara maiNly to see sarDis
of athEns in calm Zone if the men aRe in his fAce 129
Part sOme last crUmbs of civilizatioN Damn
thEy lisZt heR pArents 135
on his Prevalent knee sOnnet a nUmber learNery jackeD up 136
a littlE aZ ole man comley wd. say hRwwkke tth sAid
Plan is tOld inclUded raNks expelleD 137
jE suis xtZbk49ht *paRts of this* to mAdison 154
in euroPe general washingtOn harangUed johN aDams 155
through a wholE for civiliZing the impRovement which begAn 158
to comPute enclOse farms and crUsoe Now by harD
povErty craZy geoRge cAtherine 159
Picked the cOnstant a gUisa agaiN faileD
all rEcords tZin vei le Role hAve 163
Page they adOpted wd. sUggest Not Day 164
largE romanZoff fReedom of Admission 165
of deParture freedOm ai vU freNch by her worD
bonapartE for coloniZing this countRy in viennA 168
excePt geOrge half edUcated meN shD.
concErns mr fidascZ oR nAme we 172
resPect in black clOthes centUry-old soNvabitch gooD is
patiEnt to mobiliZe wiRe deAth for 173

Pancreas are nObles in fact he was qUite potemkiN marrieD
a rEaltor a biZ-nis i-de-a the peRfect peAutiful chewisch 174
schoP he gOt dhere and venn hiss brUdder diet tdeN Dh
vifE but topaZe undeRstood which explAins 179
Pallete et sOld the high jUdges to passioNs as have remarkeD 180–181
havE authoriZed its pResident to use funds mArked 183
President wrOte fUll fraNk talk remembereD
in sorrEnto paralyZed publicly answeRed questions thAn 186
duol che soPra falseggiandO del sUd vaticaN expresseD 187
politE curiosity as to how any citiZen shall have Right to pAy 209
sPecie wOrkers sUch losses wheNso it be to their shoulD 210
usEd *luZ* wheRe messAge 229
is kePt stOne chUrch stoNe threaD 230
nonE waZ bRown one cAse 231
couPle One pUblished Never publisheD 232
oragE about tamuZ the Red flAme going 236
seed   two sPan twO bUll begiN thy seaborD 237
fiElds by kolschitZky Received sAcks of 240
Pit hOld pUt vaN blameD 241
amErican civil war on Zeitgeist Ruin After d. 249
Preceded crOwd cried leagUe miNto yelleD
Evviva Zwischen die volkeRn in eddying Air in 251
Printed sOrt fU dyNasty Dynasty 254–255
Eighth dynasty chaZims and usuRies the high fAns 257–258
simPles gathered gOes the mUst No wooD burnt
gatEs in an haZe of colouRs wAter boiled in the wells 259–269
Prince whOm wd/ fUlfill l'argeNt circule that cash be lorD to 270
sEas of china horiZon and the 3Rd cAbinet 286–287
keePin' 'Osses rUled by hochaNgs helD up
statE of bonZes empRess hAnged herself 291
sPark lights a milliOn strings calcUlated at sterliNg haD by 292
taozErs tho' *bonZesses* of iRon tAng 294
Princes in snOw trUe proviNce of greeD 295
contEnt with Zibbeline soldieRs mAy
Paid 'em tchOngking mUmbo dishoNour wars boreDom of 296
rackEt 1069 ghingiZ tchinkis heaRing of heAring 300
'em Pass as cOin was stUff goverNor 3⅓rD 301
triEd oZin wodin tRees no tAxes 302–303
Prussia and mengkO yU tchiN D. 1225
nEws lord lipan booZing king of fouR towns opened gAtes 316–317
to Pinyang destrOying kU chiNg ageD

thronE and on ghaZel tanks didn't woRk fAithful 318
echo desPerate treasOns bhUd lamas Night Drawn
Each by Zealously many dangeRs mAde 328
to Pray and hOang eleUtes mohamedaNs caveD 329
gavE put magaZines theRe grAft 335
Pund at mOderate revenUe which Next approveD
un fontEgo in boston gaZette wRote shooting stArted 344
Putts Off taking a strUggle theN moveD
somE magaZine politique hollandais diRected gen. wAshington 346
to dePuties at der zwOl with dUmas agaiNst creDit
with bankErs with furZe scaRce oAk or other tree 374
minced Pie and frOntenac wine tUesday cleaN coD 375
clEar that Zeeland we signed etc/ commeRce heAven 376
remPlis d'un hOmme she mUle axletree brokeN to Dry 377
curE appriZed was the dangeR peAce is 379
Passed befOre i hear dUke maNchester backeD
frEnch wd/ back Ζεῦ ἀΡχηγ'ε estetA 421–1
mi sPieghi ch'iO gUerra e faNgo Dialogava 2–3
cEntro impaZiente uRgente e voce di mArinetti 4
in Piazza lembO al sUo ritorNello D'un toro
chE immondiZia nominaR è pArecchio 5
Più gemistO giÙ di pietro Negator' D'usura 6
vEngon' a bisanZio ne pietRo che Augusto 8
Placidia fui suOnava mUover è Nuova   baDa
a mE Zuan cRisti mosAic till our 425
when and Plus when gOld measUred doNe fielD 426
prEparation taishan quatorZe juillet and ambeR deAd the end 434
suPerb and brOwn in leviticUs or first throwN thru the clouD
yEt byZantium had heaRd Ass 439
stoP are strOnger thUs rrromaNce yes yes bastarDs
slaughtEr with banZai song of gassiR glAss-eye wemyss 442
unPinned gOvernment which lasted rather less pecUliar thaN reD 443
firE von tirpitZ bewaRe of chArm
sPiritus belOved a Ut veNto ligure is Difficult 444
psEudo-ritZ-caRlton bArbiche 447
Past baskets and hOrse cars mass'chUsetts cologNe catheDral
paolo uccEllo in danZig if they have not destRoyed is meAsured by 455
tout dit que Pas a small rain stOrm eqUalled momeNts surpasseD 456
quE pas barZun had old andRe conceAl the sound 472
of its foot-stePs knOw that he had them as daUdet is goNcourt sD/
martin wE Zecchin' bRingest to focus zAgreus 475

sycoPhancy One's sqUare daNce too luciD 476–477
squarEs from byZance and befoRe then mAnitou 489
sound in the forest of Pard crOtale scrUb-oak viNe yarDs 490
clicking of crotalEs tsZe's biRds sAy 491–495
hoPing mOre billyUm the seNate treaD 496
that voltagE yurr sZum kind ov a ex-gReyhound lArge 503
centre Piece with nOvels dUmped baNg as i cD/ 504
makE out banking joZefff may have followed mR owe initiAlly 506
mr P. his bull-dOg me stUrge m's bull-dog taberNam Dish
robErt Zupp buffoRd my footbAth 514
sliP and tOwer rUst loNg shaDows 515
as mEn miss tomcZyk at 18 wobuRn buildings tAncred 524
Phrase's sake and had lOve thrU impeNetrable troubleD
throbbing hEart roman Zoo sheeR snow on the mArble snow-white 538
into sPagna t'aO chi'ien heard mUsic lawNs hiDing a woman
whEn sZu' noR by vAin 546
simPlex animus bigOb men cUt Nap iii trees prop up clouDs 547–549
praEcognita schwartZ '43 pRussien de ménAge with four teeth out 566
Paaasque je suis trOp angUstiis me millet wiNe set for wilD 567
gamE *chuntZe* but diRty the dAi 580–581
toPaze a thrOne having it sqUsh in his excelleNt Dum
sacro nEmori von humboldt agassiZ maR wAy 598
desPair i think randOlph crUmp to Name was pleaseD 599
yEars tZu two otheRs cAlhoun
Pitching quOits than sUavity deportmeNt was resolveD on 600
slavEs and taZewell buRen fAther of 602
Price sOldiers delUged the old hawk damN saDist 603
yEs nasZhong bRonze of sAn zeno buy columns now by the 614
stone-looP shOt till pUdg'd still griN like quiDity 615
rhEa's schnitZ waR ein schuhmAcher und 621
corPse & then cannOn ϑΥγάτηρ apolloNius fumbleD 622–623
amplE cadiZ pillaRs with the spAde 638–639
εΠι έλϑΟν and jUlia έλληνίξοΝτας the Dawn
onE Λιзζιγฦфฦ lock up & cook-fiRes cAuldron 661
Plaster an askÓs αῩξει τῶN has covereD 662
thEir koloboZed ouR coinAge 663–664
Pearls cOpper tissUs de liN hoarD 665
for a risE von schlitZ denmaRk quArter 672
of sPain Olde tUrkish wisselbaNk Daily
papErs von schultZ and albuqueRque chArles second c.5 674
not ruled by soPhia σΟφία dUped by the crowN but steeD

askEd douglas about kadZu aceRo not boAt　683–684

Pulchram Oar-blades ϑΙνα ϑαλάσσης leUcothoe rose babyloN of

caDmus　685

linE him analyZe the tRick fAke　712

Packed the he dOes habsbUrg somethiNg you may reaD　713

posing as moslEm not a trial but kolschoZ Rome baBylon no sense of 732

Public destrOyed de vaUx 32 millioN exhumeD with　733–734

mmE douZe ambRoise bluejAys　741

his Peers but unicOrns yseUlt is dead palmerstoN's worse oviD　742

much worsE to summariZe was in contRol byzAnce　743–744

sPartan mOnd qUatorze kiNg lost fer some gawD

fool rEason bjjayZus de poictieRs mAverick　749–750

rePeating this mOsaic bUst acceNsio shepherD to flock

tEn light blaZed behind ciRce with leopArd's by mount's edge　754

over broom-Plant yaO whUder ich maei lidhaN flowers are blesseD　755

aquilEia auZel said that biRd meAning　780

Planes liOns jUmps scorpioNs give light waDsworth in　781–782

town housE in

1982

Robert Duncan
1919–1988

Although he declared himself a derivative poet who borrowed from sources as diverse as Dante, Pound, Blake, H.D., Stein, Cocteau, Yeats, Riding, García Lorca, Arp, and St. John of the Cross, Robert Duncan's work is a highly original blend of experimental and traditional influences. Attracted to the mystical, he was also one of the more erudite poets associated with Black Mountain poetics. "Soul is the body's dream of its continuity in eternity—a wraith of mind," he wrote in "Pages from a Notebook," a statement of poetics.[1] Yet later in the same essay, Duncan moves beyond romantic unity: "I don't seek a synthesis, but a melee."[2]

Like many poets of the Pound tradition, Duncan is critical of the work and influence of T. S. Eliot. "Eliot is deficient on a formal level; that's why he talks about form."[3] His own struggle to find a new form he credits to an extensive correspondence with Denise Levertov, who urged him toward a new poetics rather than the traditional influences that attracted him in the early 1950s. But Duncan claimed an important difference with Olson's concept of "field composition"; that is, open rather than closed form: "If we have a field, how can we throw out closed forms. They are only forms within a field."[4]

Born in Oakland, California, Duncan encountered the work of Ezra Pound as a student at the University of California in Berkeley. In 1947, the year of his first meeting with Charles Olson, he published his first book, *Heavenly City, Earthly City*. The first book of his major period, *The Opening of the Field*, was published in 1960, followed by *Roots and Branches* (1964). According to the poet Michael Palmer, following the publication of *Bending the Bow* (1968), Duncan chose not to publish a new collection for fifteen years:

> This decision would free him to listen to the demands of his (supremely demanding) poetics and would liberate the architecture of his work from all compromised considerations. He would allow the grand design ("grand collage") to emerge in its own time from the agonistic dance of Eros and Thanatos, chaos and form, darkness and light, permission and obligation. It was not until 1984 that *Ground Work I: Before the War* appeared, to be followed in February 1988, the month of his death, by *Ground Work II: In the Dark*.[5]

His work also includes *Fictive Certainties* (1983), a volume of essays; *Selected Poems* (1993); *Selected Prose* (1995); and *The H.D. Book* (2011), begun in 1959 as an homage to the poet who had so influenced him.

1. *The New American Poetry: 1945–1960*, ed. Donald Allen, New York, 1960, p. 401.   2. The same, p. 406.   3. Robert Duncan, *Allen Verbatim,* ed. Gordon Ball, New York, 1974, p. 108. 4. "Interview: Robert Duncan," in *Towards a New American Poetics,* ed. Ekbert Faas, Los Angeles, p. 61.   5. "On Robert Duncan's *Ground Work,*" *Active Boundaries: Selected Essays and Talks,* New York, 2008, p. 18.

Often I Am Permitted to Return to a Meadow

as if it were a scene made-up by the mind,
that is not mine, but is a made place,

that is mine, it is so near to the heart,
an eternal pasture folded in all thought
so that there is a hall therein

that is a made place, created by light
wherefrom the shadows that are forms fall.

Wherefrom fall all architectures I am
I say are likenesses of the First Beloved
whose flowers are flames lit to the Lady.

She it is Queen Under The Hill
whose hosts are a disturbance of words within words
that is a field folded.

It is only a dream of the grass blowing
east against the source of the sun
in an hour before the sun's going down

whose secret we see in a children's game
of ring a round of roses told.

Often I am permitted to return to a meadow
as if it were a given property of the mind
that certain bounds hold against chaos,

that is a place of first permission,
everlasting omen of what is.

1960

Poetry, a Natural Thing

Neither our vices nor our virtues
further the poem. "They came up
and died
just like they do every year
on the rocks."

The poem
feeds upon thought, feeling, impulse,
    to breed   itself,
a spiritual urgency at the dark ladders leaping.

This beauty is an inner persistence
        toward the source
striving against (within) down-rushet of the river,
        a call we heard and answer
in the lateness of the world
        primordial bellowings
from which the youngest world might spring,

salmon not in the well where the
        hazelnut falls
but at the falls battling, inarticulate,
        blindly making it.

This is one picture apt for the mind.

A second: a moose painted by Stubbs,
where last year's extravagant antlers
        lie on the ground.
The forlorn moosey-faced poem wears
        new antler-buds,
        the same,

"a little heavy, a little contrived",

his only beauty to be
        all moose.

                                        1960

Bending the Bow

We've our business to attend Day's dutie
bend back the bow in dreams as we may
til the end rimes in the taut string
with the sending. Reveries are rivers and flow
where the cold light gleams reflecting the window upon the
    surface of the table,

the presst-glass creamer, the pewter sugar bowl, the litter
    of coffee cups and saucers,
carnations painted growing upon whose surfaces. The whole
composition of surfaces leads into the other
                current disturbing
what I would take hold of. I'd been

in the course of a letter—I am still
in the course of a letter—to a friend,
who comes close in to my thought so that
the day is hers. My hand writing here
there shakes in the currents of . . . of air?
of an inner anticipation of . . . ?   reaching to touch
ghostly exhilarations in the thought of her.

            At the extremity of this
                design
"there is a connexion working in both directions, as in
            the bow and the lyre"—
only in that swift fulfillment of the wish
                that sleep
            can illustrate my hand
                sweeps the string.

You stand behind the where-I-am.
The deep tones and shadows I will call a woman.
The quick high notes . . . You are a girl there too,
    having something of sister and of wife,
                inconsolate,
        and I would play Orpheus for you again,

                recall the arrow or song
                to the trembling daylight
                from which it sprang.

                                                1968

The Torso   Passages 18

        Most beautiful!   the red-flowering eucalyptus,
            the madrone, the yew

        Is he . . .

So thou wouldst smile, and take me in thine arms
The sight of London to my exiled eyes
Is as Elysium to a new-come soul

If he be Truth
I would dwell in the illusion of him

His hands unlocking from chambers of my male body

such an idea in man's image

rising tides that sweep me towards him

. . . *homosexual?*

and at the treasure of his mouth

pour forth my soul

his soul   commingling

I thought a Being more than vast, His body leading
into Paradise,   his eyes
quickening a fire in me,   a trembling

hieroglyph: At the root of the neck

the clavicle, for the neck is the stem of the great artery
upward into his head that is beautiful

At the rise of the pectoral muscles

the nipples, for the breasts are like sleeping fountains
of feeling in man, waiting above the beat of his heart,
shielding the rise and fall of his breath, to be
awakend

At the axis of his mid hriff

the navel, for in the pit of his stomach the chord from
which first he was fed has its temple

At the root of the groin

the pubic hair, for the torso is the stem in which the man
flowers forth and leads to the stamen of flesh in which
his seed rises

a wave of need and desire over   taking me

cried out my name

(This was long ago.   It was another life)

and said,

What do you want of me?

I do not know, I said. I have fallen in love.   He
has brought me into heights and depths my heart
would fear   without him.   His look

pierces my side . fire eyes .

I have been waiting for you, he said:
I know what you desire

you do not yet know   but through me .

And I am with you everywhere.   In your falling

I have fallen from a high place.   I have raised myself

from darkness in your   rising

wherever you are

my hand in your hand   seeking   the locks, the keys

I am there.   Gathering me, you gather

your Self .

For my Other is not a woman but a man

the King upon whose bosom let me lie.

1968

Songs of an Other

If there were another . . .

if there were an other
person I am   he would
be heavy as the shadow

in a dying tree.   The light
thickens into water
welling up to liven

whose eyes?   who   hides his mother
behind him mirrord in his
bride's gaze   when the flame

darkens the music as he plays?
for I am here the Master of a Sonata
meant for the early evening

when in late Spring
the day begins to linger on
and we do not listen to the news

but let the wars and crises go
revering strife in a sound of our own,
a momentary leading of a tone

toward a conflicting possibility and then
fury so slowd down it lapses
into the sweetening melancholy of

a minor key, hovering toward refrain
it yet refrains from,   I come into
the being of this other me,

exquisitely alone,   everything   about the voice
has its own solitude the speech
addresses and, still accompanied,

kindled thruout by you,   every thought
of bride and groom comes to,
           my other

cannot keep his strangeness separate
there is such a presence of "home"
in every room I come to.

1984

Close

At the brim, at the lip

the water   the word   trembles   fills

to flooding   every thing

(Olson's "elements in trance")   advancing

this river   deeper than Jordan   flows

everywhere   the spirit bird/fish   comes down into the medium

comes up into the medium   lighter than Jordan

the Grail-Heart holds   this Mystery

does not fill in time   but through out time   fills

—dove-sound,   sparrow-song, whippoorwill-cry—

—salmon-swirl,   trout stream,   gold carp in the shadow pool—

Wish   the daimon of this field   force
             force before the gods came.

All the rest is archetype: Plato's in the Mind
    or Jung's in psyche,   yes,   glorious

            imaginal   But this clime

is Fancy's   that something beyond the given
      come into it—   that
      this rare   threatend— I too want to

prove it out—
              imaginary Love
I do not "really" feel   I live by.

So it is not the Holy Ghost,
I do not have the Ghost of a Chance in it,

      still, at the brim, at the lip

What else trembling   but this pretend
    pretentious   pre-text   Child's play of answering

    where   what was not calld for

this too   this playing-house   hold

—You think I have some defense for it,   in it?
    do not know the critical impossibility?

I make my realm this realm in the
        patently irreal—   History
    will disprove my existence.

The Book will not hold this poetry   yet
    all the vain song I've sung comes into it

        spirit-bird cuckoo's   Song of Songs

one tear of vexation as if it were beautiful

       falls into the elixir

     one tear of infatuation follows
       as if it were love

Let something we must all wonder about   ensue
    one tear I cannot account for   fall

this: the flooding into the flooding

this: the gleam of the bowl in its not holding—

Feb. 19, 1982   1987

Lawrence Ferlinghetti

b. 1919

Lawrence Ferlinghetti's early life was characterized by change. His father, an Italian immigrant, died six months before Ferlinghetti's birth, and his mother was committed to an asylum in his infancy. After a brief residency in a New York orphanage, Emily Monsanto, a relative of his mother, adopted Ferlinghetti and took him to live with her in France, where French became his first language. Around 1924, Monsanto took a position as a governess with the wealthy Bisland family in Bronxville, New York. Ferlinghetti spent the remainder of his childhood with the Bislands, even after Monsanto disappeared. Educated at the University of North Carolina, Columbia University, and the Sorbonne, Ferlinghetti settled in San Francisco in 1952, where he founded the country's first all-paperback bookstore, City Lights Books, as well as the City Lights publishing imprint, which brought to light such notable works as Ginsberg's *Howl*. Early in his development as a poet, he regularly attended discussions at the home of Kenneth Rexroth, a leading figure among San Francisco's literary outsiders. Thus his bohemianism predates the arrival of Ginsberg and Kerouac in the mid-1950s.

Ferlinghetti's own poetry collection, *A Coney Island of the Mind*, has sold over a million copies since it was first published in 1958. Other books of poetry include *Pictures of the Gone World* (1955), *The Secret Meaning of Things* (1969), *Open Eye, Open Heart* (1973), *Landscapes of Living and Dying* (1979), *Endless Life: Selected Poems* (1981), and *Over All the Obscene Boundaries* (1984). Among Ferlinghetti's other works are two novels, *Her* (1960) and *Love in the Days of Rage* (1988), and translations of the poetry of Jacques Prevert and Pier Paolo Pasolini, poets who share Ferlinghetti's own lightness, openness, lyricism, and political commitment as anarchist poet-statesmen.

Ferlinghetti's stylistic achievement, according to Allen Ginsberg, is his adaptation of "French loose verse—that you get out of Prevert and Cendrars and a few other poets—to the American style."[1] Ferlinghetti has indicated that some of the poems in *A Coney Island of the Mind*, including the enormously popular "I Am Waiting," were "conceived specifically for jazz accompaniment and as such should be considered as spontaneously written 'oral messages' rather than as poems written for the printed page."[2]

In 1998, he was named as the first San Francisco Poet Laureate, and in 2003 he was awarded the Robert Frost Memorial Medal and elected to the American Academy of Arts and Letters. His recent books of poetry include *These Are My Rivers: New & Selected Poems* (1993), *A Far Rockaway of the Heart* (1998), *San Francisco Poems* (2001), and *Poetry as Insurgent Art* (2007).

1. Barry Silesky, *Ferlinghetti: The Artist in His Time*, New York, 1990, p. 265.   2. *A Coney Island of the Mind*, New York, 1958, p. 48.

[In Goya's greatest scenes we seem to see]

In Goya's greatest scenes we seem to see
                                    the people of the world
                exactly at the moment when
                    they first attained the title of
                                        'suffering humanity'
                They writhe upon the page
                            in a veritable rage
                                        of adversity
                Heaped up
                        groaning with babies and bayonets
                                        under cement skies
                    in an abstract landscape of blasted trees
                    bent statues bats wings and beaks
                            slippery gibbets
                cadavers and carnivorous cocks
                and all the final hollering monsters
                    of the
                            'imagination of disaster'
                    they are so bloody real
                                it is as if they really still existed

And they do

                Only the landscape is changed

They still are ranged along the roads
            plagued by legionnaires
                        false windmills and demented roosters

    They are the same people
                        only further from home
                on freeways fifty lanes wide
                        on a concrete continent
                        spaced with bland billboards
                illustrating imbecile illusions of happiness

The scene shows fewer tumbrels
                but more maimed citizens
                            in painted cars
        and they have strange license plates
    and engines
                that devour America

                                        1958

[In Golden Gate Park that day]

In Golden Gate Park that day
                    a man and his wife were coming along
        thru the enormous meadow
                    which was the meadow of the world
He was wearing green suspenders
                    and carrying an old beat-up flute
                                    in one hand
        while his wife had a bunch of grapes
                    which she kept handing out
                                    individually
            to various squirrels
                            as if each
            were a little joke

And then the two of them came on
                        thru the enormous meadow
    which was the meadow of the world
                        and then
        at a very still spot where the trees dreamed
        and seemed to have been waiting thru all time
                                for them
        they sat down together on the grass
                        without looking at each other
            and ate oranges
                    without looking at each other
                            and put the peels
        in a basket which they seemed
                        to have brought for that purpose
        without looking at each other

And then
        he took his shirt and undershirt off
        but kept his hat on
                    sideways
                            and without saying anything
            fell asleep under it
                        And his wife just sat there looking
    at the birds which flew about
        calling to each other
                    in the stilly air

as if they were questioning existence
                    or trying to recall something forgotten

But then finally
            she too lay down flat
                    and just lay there looking up
                                at nothing
            yet fingering the old flute
                        which nobody played
            and finally looking over
                    at him
        without any particular expression
                            except a certain awful look
            of terrible depression

                                            1958

[Constantly risking absurdity]

        Constantly risking absurdity
                            and death
            whenever he performs
                        above the heads
                                of his audience
        the poet like an acrobat
                    climbs on rime
                        to a high wire of his own making
        and balancing on eyebeams
                        above a sea of faces
            paces his way
                    to the other side of day
        performing entrechats
                        and sleight-of-foot tricks
        and other high theatrics
                        and all without mistaking
                any thing
                    for what it may not be

            For he's the super realist
                        who must perforce perceive
                taut truth
                        before the taking of each stance or step

in his supposed advance
                        toward that still higher perch
where Beauty stands and waits
                        with gravity
                                to start her death-defying leap
And he
        a little charleychaplin man
                        who may or may not catch
                her fair eternal form
                        spreadeagled in the empty air
        of existence

                                                        1958

A Dark Portrait

She always said '*tu*' in such a way

as if she wanted to sleep with you

or had just had

            a most passionate

                        orgasm

And she *tutoyéd* everyone

But she

            was really like Nora in *Nightwood*

        long-gaited and restless as a mare

and coursed the cafés

                through revolving doors and nights

        looking for the lover

                who would never satisfy her

And when she grew old

                slept among horses

                                                        1984

Barbara Guest
1920–2006

Born in Wilmington, North Carolina, and raised in California, Barbara Guest received her B.A. from the University of California Berkeley before moving to New York City. There she became involved in the art scene and gained recognition as a member of the first generation of the New York School of poetry.

Guest's early poetry collections include *The Location of Things* (1960), *The Blue Stairs* (1968), *Moscow Mansions* (1973), *The Countess from Minneapolis* (1976), and *The Türler Losses* (1979). She then published *Herself Defined: The Poet H.D. and Her World* (1986), a critical biography of the great Imagist poet. But it was the collection *Fair Realism* (1989), winner of the Lawrence Lipton Prize for Literature, which established her as an increasingly important experimental figure. Guest is not a poet of social statement; neither is she confessional; her work focuses instead on the possibilities of language. Critic Anthony Manousos writes, "Given this preoccupation with verbal elements as objects that can be arranged to dazzle, astonish, and move, . . . it is not surprising that many of her poems are ultimately concerned with the process of composition."[1]

With *Fair Realism*, Guest's poetry moved toward the obliquity and abstraction of language poetry, yet it retains the color and momentum of action painting. Like other poets of the New York School, Guest was a frequent contributor to art journals; from 1951 to 1954, she served as an associate editor of *ARTnews*. A clue to Guest's poetics might be found in her novel, *Seeking Air* (1978):

> Yet one should not forsake the melodic line. It rests here like a cloud, there like the blue. Because it can be overheard it should be listened to. If not regularly, then intermittently, but a certain constancy should be maintained. And that will chalk up the memory account. Something like a postcard remaining of a visit to Spain. But sufficient. Like geometry, perhaps. One recalls only the isosceles passage. Yet geometric figures cling to a life, fortunately without one having to take any particular notice.[2]

Her later works include *Musicality* (1988), *Defensive Rapture* (1992), *Rocks on a Platter* (1999), *Miniatures and Other Poems* (2002), *The Red Gaze* (2005), and *The Collected Poems* (2008). She also wrote a book of essays on her practice of poetry, *Forces of Imagination: Writing on Writing* (2003).

In 1999, Guest was awarded the Robert Frost Medal for Lifetime Achievement. A longtime resident of Southampton, New York, she lived in Berkeley, California, from 1994 until her death.

1. *Dictionary of Literary Biography*, vol. 5, ed. Donald J. Greiner, Detroit, 1980, p. 298.
2. Santa Barbara, 1978, p. 75.

Red Lilies

Someone has remembered to dry the dishes;
they have taken the accident out of the stove.
Afterward lilies for supper; there
the lines in front of the window
are rubbed on the table of stone

The paper flies up
then down as the wind
repeats, repeats its birdsong.

Those arms under the pillow
the burrowing arms they cleave
at night as the tug kneads water
calling themselves branches

The tree is you
the blanket is what warms it
snow erupts from thistle
to toe; the snow pours out of you.

A cold hand on the dishes
placing a saucer inside
her who undressed for supper
gliding that hair to the snow

The pilot light
went out on the stove

The paper folded like a napkin
other wings flew into the stone.

1973

River Road Studio

Separations begin with placement
that black organizes the ochre
         both earth colors,

Quietly the blanket assumes its shapes
as the grey day loops along leaving
an edge (turned like leaves into something else),

Absolutes simmer as primary colors
and everyone gropes toward black
where it is believed the strength lingers.

I make a sketch from your window
the rain so prominent earlier
now hesitates and retreats,

We find bicycles natural
under this sky composed of notes,

Then ribbons, they make noises
rushing up and down the depots
at the blur exchanging
its web for a highway.

Quartets the quartets
are really bricks and we are
careful to replace them
until they are truly quartets.

1976

Prairie Houses

Unreasonable lenses refract the
sensitive rabbit holes, mole dwellings and snake
climes where twist burrow and sneeze
a native species

into houses

corresponding to hemispheric requests
of flatness

euphemistically, sentimentally
termed prairie.

On the earth exerting a willful pressure

something like a stethoscope against the breast

only permanent.

Selective engineering architectural submissiveness
and rendering of necessity in regard to height,
eschewment of climate exposure, elemental
      understandings,
constructive adjustments to vale and storm

historical reconstruction of early earthworks

and admiration

for later even oriental modelling

for a glimpse of baronial burdening
we see it in the rafters and the staircase heaviness
a surprise yet acting as ballast surely

the heavens strike hard on prairies.

Regard its hard-mouthed houses with their
robust nipples the gossamer hair.

                                           1976

Wild Gardens Overlooked by Night Lights

Wild gardens overlooked by night lights. Parking
lot trucks overlooked by night lights. Buildings
with their escapes overlooked by lights

They urge me to seek here on the heights
amid the electrical lighting that self who exists,
who witnesses light and fears its expunging.

I take from my wall the landscape with its water
of blue color, its gentle expression of rose,
pink, the sunset reaches outward in strokes as the west wind
rises, the sun sinks and color flees into the delicate
skies it inherited,
I place there a scene from "The Tale of the Genji."

An episode where Genji recognizes his son.
Each turns his face away from so much emotion,
so that the picture is one of profiles floating
elsewhere from their permanence,
a line of green displaces these relatives,
black also intervenes at correct distances,
the shapes of the hair are black.

Black describes the feeling,
black is recognized as remorse, sadness,
black is a headdress while lines slant swiftly,
the space is slanted vertically with its graduating
need for movement,

Thus the grip of realism has found
a picture chosen to cover the space
occupied by another picture
establishing a flexibility so we are not immobile
like a car that spends its night
outside a window, but mobile like a spirit.

I float over this dwelling, and when I choose
enter it. I have an ethnological interest
in this building, because I inhabit it
and upon me has been bestowed the decision of changing
an abstract picture of light into a ghost-like story
of a prince whose principality I now share,
into whose confidence I have wandered.

Screens were selected to prevent this intrusion
of exacting light and add a chiaroscuro,
so that Genji may turn his face from his son,
from recognition which here is painful,
and he allows himself to be positioned on a screen,
this prince as noble as ever,
songs from the haunted distance
presenting themselves in silks.

The light of fiction and light of surface
sink into vision whose illumination
exacts its shades,

The Genji when they arose
strolled outside reality
their screen dismantled,
upon that modern wondering space
flash lights from the wild gardens.

1989

An Emphasis Falls on Reality

Cloud fields change into furniture
furniture metamorphizes into fields
an emphasis falls on reality.

"It snowed toward morning," a barcarole
the words stretched severely

silhouettes they arrived in trenchant cut
the face of lilies. . . .

I was envious of fair realism.

I desired sunrise to revise itself
as apparition, majestic in evocativeness,
two fountains traced nearby on a lawn. . . .

you recall treatments
of 'being' and 'nothingness'
illuminations apt
to appear from variable directions—
they are orderly as motors
floating on the waterway,

so silence is pictorial
when silence is real.

The wall is more real than shadow
or that letter composed of calligraphy
each vowel replaces a wall

a costume taken from space
donated by walls . . .

These metaphors may be apprehended after
they have brought their dogs and cats
born on roads near willows,

willows are not real trees
they entangle us in looseness,
the natural world spins in green.

A column chosen from distance
mounts into the sky while the font
is classical,

they will destroy the disturbed font
as it enters modernity and is rare. . . .

The necessary idealizing of your reality
is part of the search, the journey
where two figures embrace

This house was drawn for them
it looks like a real house
perhaps they will move in today
into ephemeral dusk and
move out of that into night
selective night with trees,

The darkened copies of all trees.

1989

Valorous Vine

Lifts a spare shadow
            encircling vine,
does not tarnish   bauble
    from overseas   and out of silver mine,
drop in clamor and volume.

        Along the footpath
    returned to mourning a lost stem,

gauzy the stem-like saving, or ruled
over stone to develop muscular difficulty.

In the wind
and overhead, held back lightning. Did
not surrender or refuse visibility and pliancy obtained.

Or confuse VIOLETRY with stone
or dissipate the land   land unshackled,
budding in another country
while dark here.

ii

It can be seen she encouraged the separation of flower from the page, that
she wished an absence to be encouraged. She drew from herself a technique
that offered life to the flower, but demanded the flower remain absent. The
flower, as a subject, is not permitted to shadow the page. Its perfume is
strong and that perfume may overwhelm the sensibility that strengthens the
page and desires to initiate the absence of the flower. It may be that absence
is the plot of the poem. A scent remains of the poem. It is the flower's appari-
tion that desires to remain on the page, even to haunt the room in which the
poem was created.

1999

Freed Color

The branches are placed in a wet cloth,
clover reaches out.

They cannot locate a blue vine.
Purple fills the agenda. Red is on the plant,
the setting of a hibiscus tree.
They are warned not to linger in the purple shade.

Are these bitter colors? Are they accompanied
by rhyme to cheer them when they cross
into that land where color is rare?

They hasten to make use of freed color
who bends to no one,
who dwells in a tent like rhythm
continuously rolled.

To stop the riot of color, to hasten the quiet paucity of rhythm,
to sleep when it is time.

And doors open into a narrow surprise.
The jingle of crystal follows you everywhere,
even into the whistling corridor.

2005

Jackson Mac Low
1922–2004

Since 1954, when he first composed verbal texts by "nonintentional" procedures, Jackson Mac Low has been a pioneer of such methods in poetry.[1] In this, he has taken inspiration from several sources—John Cage's music composed by chance operation, Zen Buddhism, the *I Ching* ("Book of Changes"), and the Jewish mystic Abraham Abulafia.[2] Mac Low's nonintentional methods—for example, his experiments in "reading through" a text acrostically with the aid of computer programs—aim to avoid the intrusions of the author as ego and to foreground language as such.

Mac Low's works were often performed in collaboration with dancers and musicians. *The Pronouns* (1964) was written both as poems and instructions for a dance. Created from an earlier work, *Nuclei for Simone Forti* (1961), it consists of "groups of words & of action phrases around which dancers build spontaneous improvisations."[3] Other works include *Stanzas for Iris Lezak* (1972); *Asymmetries 1–260* (1980); *"Is That Wool Hat My Hat?"* (1982); *Bloomsday* (1984); *French Sonnets* (1984); *Representative Works: 1938–1985* (1986); *Twenties: 100 Poems* (1991); *Pieces o' Six: 33 Poems in Prose* (1992); *Barnesbook* (1996), based on works of Djuna Barnes; *20 Forties* (1999); and *Struggle Through* (2001), based on a poem by Andrew Levy.

Mac Low's "59th Light Poem: for La Monte Young and Marian Zazeela—6 November 1982" is, in part, an acrostic on the dedicatees' names.[4] The words of "Antic Quatrains" were drawn systematically from a 3,000-line computer printout of word groups; these groups were in turn derived by a randomizing program from a 5,000-word list of partial anagrams of the poem's dedicatee, Annie Brigitte Gilles Tardos.

Mac Low's methodical approach to composition is attractive to the language poets, with whom he came to be associated, and opened the way for today's generation of cybernetic poets. He also experimented with more deliberate "intentional" forms of composition in works such as "Trope Market" and the poems in the "Twenties" series, which, despite the appearance of being produced through chance operations, were written "intuitively, spontaneously, and directly."[5]

In 1999, he was awarded both the Dorothea Tanning Award and the Wallace Stevens Award of the Academy of American Poets.

Born in Chicago, Mac Low lived in New York City.

---

1. "Jackson Mac Low, Interviewed by Kevin Bezner," *New American Writing*, no. 11 (1993), p. 110.   2. The same, p. 109.   3. Jackson Mac Low, "Preface to the 1979 Revised Edition of *The Pronouns*, Barrytown, NY, 1979, p. viii.   4. Jackson Mac Low, Preface to *Bloomsday*, Barrytown, NY, 1984, p. ix.   5. *New American Writing*, p. 116.

FROM *The Pronouns*

1st Dance—Making Things New—
6 February 1964

He makes himself comfortable
& matches parcels.

Then he makes glass boil
while having political material get in
& coming by.

Soon after, he's giving gold cushions or seeming to do so,
taking opinions,
shocking,
pointing to a fact that seems to be an error & showing it to be
      other than it seems,
& presently paining by going or having waves.

Then after doing some waiting,
he disgusts someone
& names things.

A little while later he gets out with things
& finally either rewards someone for something or goes up under
      something.

6th Dance—Doing Things with Pencils—
17–18 February 1964

I do something consciously,
going about & coming across art.

After that I boil some delicate things
while doing something under the conditions of competition
& going under someone or something
& taking opinions,
& then, when making or giving something small, I monkey with
      something that's not white.

Later I quietly chalk a strange tall bottle.

Then, being a band or acting like a bee
& being a brother to someone,
I discuss something brown.

Either I will myself dead or I come to see something narrow.

I give gold cushions or I seem to do so,
but I get by.

I keep to the news.

I put society at odds with a family,
letting a new sound be again,
& I send a warm thing by spoon over a slow one.

Again I discuss something brown.

& once again I'm willing myself dead or I'm coming to see
        something narrow.

Once more I quietly chalk a strange tall bottle.

Finally I'm saying something between thick things.

Trope Market

In the network, in the ruin,
flashing classics gravitate,
snared, encumbered voicelessly.

Teak enticements seek, leaping
fan-shaped arras corners
snore among in backward dispatch.

Panels glow, groan, territorialize
fetishistically in nacreous
instantaneity spookily shod.

4 July 1983
New York

1984

59th Light Poem: for La Monte Young and Marian Zazeela—6 November 1982

Late light allows us to begin.
Altair's light on an altar guides us onward.

Many lights are seen where mountains cluster.
Orange lights are spangled over hillsides.
Neutral light glows above their ridges.
Tiny lights of many kinds begin to be discernible.
Evanescent lights arise and die.

Yellow light momently overspreads.
Ochre light succeeds it.
Umber light in a while is all that is left.
Nearly nonexistent light increases rapidly.
Green light envelops everything.

Magenta light glows over the farther peaks.
Alabaster lights suddenly shoot upward.
Red lights cross the sky diagonally.
Incandescent-lamp light glows in the foreground.
Acetylene-lamp light splits the ambience.
No light at all supervenes.

Zodiacal light replaces light's absence.
Algae-green light maculates the glow.
Zincz light flares amid the highest oaks.
Escaping light illumes Lithuanian paths.
Earthlight grows near the Baltic.
Lithuanian light lessens environing earthlight.
All the light there *can* be won't be enough.

6 November 1982   1984
(rev. 21 February 1984)
New York

Antic Quatrains

derived from the computer print-out phase of
"A Vocabulary for Annie Brigitte Gilles Tardos"

Along a tarn a delator entangled a dragline,
Boasting o' tonnages, doggies, ants, and stones
As long as Lind balled Gandas near a gas log
As it late lit rigatoni and a tag line.

In Dis libidinal radians o' tigons
Deter no generals, no ordinaries,
No Adlerians tarring arteries' DNA,
Triliteral arsenal o' nitid groins.

Begone, senile Tiresias, raser o' tanneries!
Gastonia's grants-in-aid, sestertia to Liebig,
Are raising glissading sergeants' titillation
In lairs o' daisies, glarier and estranging.

Literal tartlets arrange stilbestrol's banners
And roast nonsalable redlegs, breasts o' lessees,
Rib roasts, entire alations, Ingersoll, Alger,
And age-old Diesel's aborning ingestible trotters.

Irritants beggar Tagore, irredentists,
And irritated designees in gorgets
Agreeing on liberal tittles, Ginsberg, Seeger,
And Stella's transient sortilege, galliards, ginger.

Do gerardias register tanglier antibioses
Or sillier Latrobe allegorise eared seals?
Do literati's binges iodate sand tables?
Internists banter teetotalers in bordels.

Tilden's Iliad tabled alliteration
And a gainless Sartrian ass aired abattoirs
As tonsils' orneriness assigned Ortega
To distillations antedating Sade.

Erelong GI's' ideas girdle Borstals

And toadies retrain Orientals as Borgia desserts:
Elated at iodine on starting gates,
Do sonnetising Britons lead orbed otters?

Ill borage's large attendants in bodegas,
Labiating gristlier translations,
Belie agreeable garnerings. No? 'Tain't so?
Go greet Titania in an insensate snit!

Granados labeled a gateleg table stable
As droll goaltenders tensed at tenebrist rites
And an elegant internee sensed godlier litanies
In gangrened slattern lotteries in Laredo.

A belligerent gent tainted a nationalist
And an ill-starred seer slogged near Odin's targe
As Rosetta retested gastral allegories,
Riled at a brainless trio's rosaries.

Aretino's gist is bearable
And Lister's treatises are greatening:
Siberian gentianella's deteriorating
And loneliness endangers libraries.

March 1980   1984
New York

Twenties 26

Undergone swamp ticket   relative
whist   natural sweep   innate   bicker
flight notion reach out tinsel reckoning
bit   straddle iniquitous ramble stung

Famous furniture instant paschal
passionate Runnymede licorice
feature departure   frequency gnash
lance   sweat lodge rampart crow

Neck   Bedlam philosophaster rain drape
lack fragile limitation   bitartrate

fence lengthen tinge impinge classed
Fenster planetary knocked market

Glass killjoy vanity infanta part song
king cleanse vast chromium watch it
neat intense yellow cholera
ornithology insistence pantry

Torque normal fax center globe host
yammer ratchet zinc memory
yield texture tenure Penelope
reed liter risible stashed incomprehension

11 February 1990
Kennedy Airport, New York
en route to San Diego

1991

Twenties 27

Last carpenter feelie pocket guru
nest shelf clumsy rennet cliffhanger
linked frontline pence innocence leafmold
rank panel cracker follow-up

Nail dream camel *Lieder* fleetest
teen needle gash guest tensor
panatella cage apprentice embracement
negative gleam apparatus crop gut

Femur enamel dust leftover tendency
cleat dissection narcissist clip gap
deal dilate lumber later glum prompt hoax
flouted fortune orchid conation

Zeal for a Vegan penoplain parch
considered ducks' muckery twine embolden
peaking Gloucester Tamil lever wrist
fledge intent took crust

Desk   leper ledger regional ornament
Kansas enact   cancel
clasp   grippe   ontological
toe claustrophobia garish Parkinson's twilight trim bark

11 February 1990   1991
Kennedy Airport, New York
en route to San Diego

NOTE: Caesural spaces in Mac Low's "Twenties" series indicate the length of silences: three letter spaces equal one unaccented syllable; six letter spaces equal one accented syllable or "beat"; nine letter spaces equal one accented and one unaccented syllable or one and a half "beats"; twelve letter spaces equal two "beats."

Philip Whalen
1923–2002

Born in Portland, Oregon, Philip Whalen attended Reed College in the late 1940s, where Gary Snyder was also a student. In the early 1950s, he moved to San Francisco, where he met Allen Ginsberg and Jack Kerouac. Whalen participated with Ginsberg, Snyder, Kenneth Rexroth, Michael McClure, and Philip Lamantia in the much-noted Six Gallery reading on October 13, 1955, and was included in a special "San Francisco Scene" issue of *Evergreen Review*; he was thus identified as one of the Beat poets.

Whalen's poetry embraces the world with Whitmanesque openness and gentleness. Yet the wit of Whalen's writing reminds critic and poet Michael Davidson of the eighteenth-century satirists Alexander Pope and John Dryden.[1] Davidson further observes that Whalen's "emphasis on the situational frame resembles the 'personism' of New York poets like Frank O'Hara and Ted Berrigan, whose poetry insists on the temporary and contingent in art."[2] Poetry, Whalen has said," is the graph of the mind's movement."[3] Whalen wrote his poems in a notebook, often accompanying them with drawings and doodles. In *Scenes of Life at the Capital*, he states his belief that copying poems from the notebook to the typewriter suppresses the material.[4] His style of writing was therefore notational and improvisatory. In his public readings, he would often read directly from the notebook, flipping from page to page as his own curiosity demanded. Whalen's notational style would influence Ted Berrigan in writing the long poems "Tambourine Life" and "Bean Spasms."

Whalen's books of poetry include *Like I Say* (1960), *On Bear's Head* (1969), *Severance Pay* (1970), *Scenes of Life at the Capital* (1971), *The Kindness of Strangers* (1976), and *Enough Said: Poems 1974–1979* (1980). *Overtime: Selected Poems*, ed. Michael Rothenberg, was published in 1999, followed by *The Collected Poems of Philip Whalen* in 2007. Whalen also published the novels *You Didn't Even Try* (1967), *Imaginary Speeches for a Brazen Head* (1972), and *The Diamond Noodle* (1980). *Off the Wall: Interviews with Philip Whalen* was published in 1978. Ordained as an *unsui,* or Buddhist monk, he lived at the San Francisco Zen Center from 1972 until his death. Gary Snyder writes of Whalen's monastery years: "His quirks became his pointers, and his frailties his teaching method. Philip was always the purest, the highest, the most dry, and oddly cosmic of the Dharma-poets—we are all greatly karmically lucky to have known him."[5]

1. *The San Francisco Renaissance: Poets and Community at Mid-Century,* Cambridge, England, 1989, p. 113.   2. The same, p. 117.   3. *On Bear's Head,* New York, 1969, p. 93.   4. Leslie Scalapino, Introduction to *Overtime: Selected Poems,* New York, 1999, p. xvii.   5. "Highest and Driest," Foreword to *The Collected Poems of Philip Whalen,* 2007, p. xxix.

Sourdough Mountain Lookout

Tsung Ping (375–443): "Now I am old and infirm. I fear I shall no more be able to roam among the beautiful mountains. Clarifying my mind, I meditate on the mountain trails and wander about only in dreams."
—in The Spirit of the Brush, tr. by Shio Sakanishi, p. 34.

for Kenneth Rexroth

I always say I won't go back to the mountains
I am too old and fat there are bugs mean mules
And pancakes every morning of the world

Mr. Edward Wyman (63)
Steams along the trail ahead of us all
Moaning, "My poor old feet ache, my back
Is tired and I've got a stiff prick"
Uprooting alder shoots in the rain

Then I'm alone in a glass house on a ridge
Encircled by chiming mountains
With one sun roaring through the house all day
& the others crashing through the glass all night
Conscious even while sleeping

    Morning fog in the southern gorge
    Gleaming foam restoring the old sea-level
    The lakes in two lights green soap and indigo
    The high cirque-lake black half-open eye

Ptarmigan hunt for bugs in the snow
Bear peers through the wall at noon
Deer crowd up to see the lamp
A mouse nearly drowns in the honey
I see my bootprints mingle with deer-foot
Bear-paw mule-shoe in the dusty path to the privy

Much later I write down:
    "raging. Viking sunrise
      The gorgeous death of summer in the east"
(Influence of a Byronic landscape—
Bent pages exhibiting depravity of style.)

Outside the lookout I lay nude on the granite
Mountain hot September sun but inside my head
Calm dark night with all the other stars

HERACLITUS: "The waking have one common world
But the sleeping turn aside
Each into a world of his own."

I keep telling myself what I really like
Are music, books, certain land and sea-scapes
The way light falls across them, diffusion of
Light through agate, light itself . . . I suppose
I'm still afraid of the dark

  "Remember smart-guy there's something
  Bigger something smarter than you."
  Ireland's fear of unknown holies drives
  My father's voice (a country neither he
  Nor his great-grandfather ever saw)

  A sparkly tomb a plated grave
  A holy thumb beneath a wave

Everything else they hauled across Atlantic
Scattered and lost in the buffalo plains
Among these trees and mountains

From Duns Scotus to this page
A thousand years

  (". . . a dog walking on his hind legs—
  not that he does it well but that he
  does it at all.")

Virtually a blank except for the hypothesis
That there is more to a man
Than the contents of his jock-strap

EMPEDOCLES: "At one time all the limbs
Which are the body's portion are brought together
By Love in blooming life's high season; at another

Severed by cruel Strife, they wander each alone
By the breakers of life's sea."

Fire and pressure from the sun bear down
Bear down centipede shadow of palm-frond
A limestone lithograph—oysters and clams of stone
Half a black rock bomb displaying brilliant crystals
Fire and pressure Love and Strife bear down
Brontosaurus, look away

My sweat runs down the rock

HERACLITUS: "The transformations of fire
are, first of all, sea; and half of the sea
is earth, half whirlwind. . . .
It scatters and it gathers; it advances
and retires."

I move out of a sweaty pool
                (The sea!)
And sit up higher on the rock

Is anything burning?

The sun itself! Dying
Pooping out, exhausted
Having produced brontosaurus, Heraclitus
This rock, me,
To no purpose
I tell you anyway (as a kind of loving) . . .
Flies & other insects come from miles around
To listen
I also address the rock, the heather,
The alpine fir

BUDDHA: "All the constituents of being are
Transitory: Work out your salvation with diligence."

(And everything, as one eminent disciple of that master
Pointed out, has been tediously complex ever since.)

There was a bird
Lived in an egg

And by ingenious chemistry
Wrought molecules of albumen
To beak and eye
Gizzard and craw
Feather and claw

My grandmother said:
"Look at them poor bed-
raggled pigeons!"

And the sign in McAlister Street:

"IF YOU CAN'T COME IN
SMILE AS YOU GO BY
L♡VE
THE BUTCHER

I destroy myself, the universe (an egg)
And time—to get an answer:
There are a smiler, a sleeper and a dancer

We repeat our conversation in the glittering dark
Floating beside the sleeper.
The child remarks, "You knew it all the time."
I: "I keep forgetting that the smiler is
Sleeping; the sleeper, dancing."

From Sauk Lookout two years before
Some of the view was down the Skagit
To Puget Sound: From above the lower ranges,
Deep in forest—lighthouses on clear nights.

This year's rock is a spur from the main range
Cuts the valley in two and is broken
By the river; Ross Dam repairs the break,
Makes trolley buses run
Through the streets of dim Seattle far away.

I'm surrounded by mountains here
A circle of 108 beads, originally seeds
    of *ficus religiosa*
        Bo-Tree
A circle, continuous, one odd bead

Larger than the rest and bearing
A tassel (hair-tuft) (the man who sat
      under the tree)
In the center of the circle,
A void, an empty figure containing
All that's multiplied;
Each bead a repetition, a world
Of ignorance and sleep.

Today is the day the goose gets cooked
Day of liberation for the crumbling flower
Knobcone pinecone in the flames
Brandy in the sun
Which, as I said, will disappear
Anyway it'll be invisible soon
Exchanging places with stars now in my head
To be growing rice in China through the night.
Magnetic storms across the solar plains
Make Aurora Borealis shimmy bright
Beyond the mountains to the north.

Closing the lookout in the morning
Thick ice on the shutters
Coyote almost whistling on a nearby ridge
The mountain is THERE (between two lakes)
I brought back a piece of its rock
Heavy dark-honey color
With a seam of crystal, some of the quartz
Stained by its matrix
Practically indestructible
A shift from opacity to brilliance
(The Zenbos say, "Lightning-flash & flint-spark")
Like the mountains where it was made

What we see of the world is the mind's
Invention and the mind
Though stained by it, becoming
Rivers, sun, mule-dung, flies—
Can shift instantly
A dirty bird in a square time

Gone
Gone

REALLY gone
Into the cool
O MAMA!

Like they say, "Four times up,
Three times down." I'm still on the mountain.

Sourdough Mountain 15:viii:55
Berkeley 27–28:viii:56

The Chariot

for Jess Collins

I stand at the front of the chariot
The horses run insane, there are no reins
The curtains behind me don't flutter or flap

I don't look worried. Is the chariot headed
      for the edge of a cliff?

Behind the curtains a party's going on
      laughing and talking and singing

I prefer to stand here, my arms folded
      Ben Hur
Or one hand leaning lightly on the guard rail

Watch the horses galloping

Mother and father behind the curtains
      they argue, naturally
      "Who's driving, anyway?"

Wind whistles through my spiky crown
Some hero, some king!

30:iii:62

Denise Levertov ─────────────
1923–1997

Daughter of Paul Levertoff, a Russian Jew who became an Anglican priest, and Beatrice Spooner-Jones of Wales, Denise Levertov was born and raised in Ilford, Essex, England. Her first book of poetry, *The Double Image,* was published in England in 1946. Shortly thereafter, she married American writer Mitchell Goodman and moved with him to New York City. In 1949 she began a friendship with Robert Creeley that led to her publication in *Origin,* Cid Corman's magazine that grew out of the Black Mountain influence, as well as in Creeley's own *Black Mountain Review.* Her first American book, *Here and Now,* was not published until 1957, but was soon followed by numerous collections, including *Overland to the Islands* (1958), *With Eyes at the Back of Our Heads* (1959), *The Jacob's Ladder* (1961), *O Taste and See: New Poems* (1964), *The Sorrow Dance* (1967), *The Freeing of the Dust* (1975), *Candles in Babylon* (1982), *Oblique Prayers* (1984), *Selected Poems* (1986), *A Door in the Hive* (1989), *Evening Train* (1992), and *This Great Unknowing* (2000). Her many awards include the Shelley Memorial Award, the Robert Frost Medal, the Lenore Marshall Prize, the Lannan Award, and a Guggenheim Fellowship. For a time the poetry editor of *The Nation,* she was in fervent opposition to the Vietnam War.

Following William Carlos Williams, Levertov rejects the iambic pentameter line for a more "organic" form. "For me," she writes, "back of the idea of organic form is the concept that there is a form in all things (and in our experience) which the poet can discover and reveal."[1] A poet is therefore *"brought to speech"* by "perceptions of sufficient interest."[2] The ultimate goal is "the splendor of the authentic," the creation of which involves the writer "in a process rewarding in itself."[3]

In later years, Levertov's intense lyricism, reminiscent of Rilke, joined with themes of visionary Christianity. This conjunction is especially evident in *Breathing the Water* (1987) and *The Door in the Hive* (1989). Mysticism has a long tradition in Levertov's family: her mother was descended from a Welsh mystic, Angel Jones of Mold; ancestors on her mother's side include Russian rabbi Schneour Zaimon, who was reputed to understand the language of birds. Levertov's metaphysics, which emphasize beauty and wholeness, set her apart from the post-existentialist poetics of the language poets.

Her works of prose included *The Poet in the World* (1973), *Light Up the Cave* (1981), *New & Selected Essays* (1992), *Tesserae: Memories & Suppositions* (1995), and two volumes of correspondence, with William Carlos Williams and Robert Duncan.

1. "Some Notes on Organic Form," in *The Poet in the World,* New York, p. 7.   2. The same, p. 8.   3. The same, p. 13.

Overland to the Islands

Let's go—much as that dog goes,
intently haphazard. The
Mexican light on a day that
'smells like autumn in Connecticut'
makes iris ripples on his
black gleaming fur—and that too
is as one would desire—a radiance
consorting with the dance.
               Under his feet
rocks and mud, his imagination, sniffing,
engaged in its perceptions—dancing
edgeways, there's nothing
the dog disdains on his way,
nevertheless he
keeps moving, changing
pace and approach but
not direction—'every step an arrival.'

                                             1958

Illustrious Ancestors

The Rav
of Northern White Russia declined,
in his youth, to learn the
language of birds, because
the extraneous did not interest him; nevertheless
when he grew old it was found
he understood them anyway, having
listened well, and as it is said, 'prayed
               with the bench and the floor.' He used
what was at hand—as did
Angel Jones of Mold, whose meditations
were sewn into coats and britches.
               Well, I would like to make,
thinking some line still taut between me and them,
poems direct as what the birds said,
hard as a floor, sound as a bench,
mysterious as the silence when the tailor
would pause with his needle in the air.

                                             1958

The Ache of Marriage

The ache of marriage:

thigh and tongue, beloved,
are heavy with it,
it throbs in the teeth

We look for communion
and are turned away, beloved,
each and each

It is leviathan and we
in its belly
looking for joy, some joy
not to be known outside it

two by two in the ark of
the ache of it.

1964

The Wings

Something hangs in back of me,
I can't see it, can't move it.

I know it's black,
a hump on my back.

It's heavy. You
can't see it.

What's in it? Don't tell me
you don't know. It's

what you told me about—
black

inimical power, cold
whirling out of it and

around me and
sweeping you flat.

But what if,
like a camel, it's

pure energy I store,
and carry humped and heavy?

Not black, not
that terror, stupidity

of cold rage; or black
only for being pent there?

What if released in air
it became a white

source of light, a fountain
of light? Could all that weight

be the power of flight?
Look inward: see me

with embryo wings, one
feathered in soot, the other

blazing ciliations of ember, pale
flare-pinions. Well—

could I go
on one wing,

the white one?

1966

Stepping Westward

What is green in me
darkens, muscadine.

If woman is inconstant,
good, I am faithful to

ebb and flow, I fall
in season and now

is a time of ripening.
If her part

is to be true,
a north star,

good, I hold steady
in the black sky

and vanish by day,
yet burn there

in blue or above
quilts of cloud.

There is no savor
more sweet, more salt

than to be glad to be
what, woman,

and who, myself,
I am, a shadow

that grows longer as the sun
moves, drawn out

on a thread of wonder.
If I bear burdens

they begin to be remembered
as gifts, goods, a basket

of bread that hurts
my shoulders but closes me

in fragrance. I can
eat as I go.

1966

Williams: An Essay

His theme
over and over:

the twang of plucked
catgut
from which struggles
music,

the tufted swampgrass
quicksilvering
dank meadows,

a baby's resolute fury—metaphysic
of appetite and tension.

Not
the bald image, but always—
undulant, elusive, beyond reach
of any dull
staring eye—lodged

among the words, beneath
the skin of image: nerves,

muscles, rivers
of urgent blood, a mind

secret, disciplined, generous and
unfathomable.
                    Over

and over,
his theme
                hid itself and
smilingly reappeared.

                        He loved
persistence—but it must
be linked to invention: landing

backwards, 'facing
into the wind's teeth,'

>   to please him.

He loved
the lotus cup, fragrant
upon the swaying water, loved

the wily mud
pressing swart riches into its roots,

and the long stem of connection.

>   1982

Where Is the Angel?

Where is the angel for me to wrestle?
No driving snow in the glass bubble,
but mild September.

Outside, the stark shadows
menace, and fling their huge arms about
unheard. I breathe

a tepid air, the blur
of asters, of brown fern and gold-dust
seems to murmur,

and that's what I hear, only that.
Such clear walls of curved glass:
I see the violent gesticulations

and feel—no, not nothing. But in this
gentle haze, nothing commensurate.
It is pleasant in here. History

mouths, volume turned off. A band of iron,
like they put round a split tree,
circles my heart. In here

it is pleasant, but when I open
my mouth to speak, I too
am soundless. Where is the angel

to wrestle with me and wound
not my thigh but my throat,
so curses and blessings flow storming out

and the glass shatters, and the iron sunders?

1989

James Schuyler ─────────────────
1923–1991

Known for the direct, conversational style of his work, as well as its charm and musicality, James Schuyler has come to be regarded as one of the most accomplished and insightful of the New York School poets. As David Lehman writes in his review of *Selected Poems*, Schuyler has "an accurate ear for the cadences of speech and the rhythms of consciousness, and a gift for being lyrical without resorting to false poeticism." Although he lived much of his life in Manhattan, including a long residence at the Chelsea Hotel, Schuyler is paradoxically one of the finest nature poets in contemporary American poetry. His powerful long poem, "The Morning of the Poem" (1980), reveals an accomplished miniaturist whose eye is always on the actual.

Reviewing Schuyler's *Collected Poems* (1993), the poet Peter Gizzi wrote: "Modesty, fortunately, is not one of Mr. Schuyler's virtues and the world he artfully presents, as we are keenly aware in every line, is neither his nor ours, even when the recognition of the real in his observations is so stunning we can only acquiesce. Objects are never as real in life as they appear in Schuyler's poems."[1]

Schuyler's considerable charm and descriptive skills are apparent in his letter to Frank O'Hara of October 8, 1954:

> The most intoxicating thing has happened to the weather here. At the beginning of the week, the sun went into hiding for a couple of days, and when it came back, its light had turned as gold as a grape. It's marvelous to have gotten to know Venice well, and then have it turn in a day into something so much more beautiful—all the hard whites have turned to cream and roses, and the dry stucco colors have gotten as rich as autumn leaves. How I wish you were here—they say it happens again in the spring, and I know it will next October—ought we to begin to plan?[2]

Born in Chicago, James Schuyler attended Bethany College in West Virginia. After serving in the navy in World War II, he moved to New York City, where he became an associate editor of *ARTnews* and took a curatorial position at the Museum of Modern Art. His poetry is collected in the volumes *Freely Espousing* (1969); *The Crystal Lithium* (1972); *Hymn to Life* (1974); *The Morning of the Poem* (1980), winner of the Pulitzer Prize; *A Few Days* (1985); and *Selected Poems* (1988). He is also the author of three novels, including a collaboration with John Ashbery, *A Nest of Ninnies* (1975).

For most of his career Schuyler did not give public readings, but when he finally did in the late 1980s the literary Lower East Side turned out in force.

1. *Lingo*, August, 1993.   2. "Letters from Italy, Winter 1954–55—from James Schuyler to Frank O'Hara," *The Letters of James Schuyler to Frank O'Hara*, ed. William Corbett, New York, 2006, p. 18.

A Man in Blue

Under the French horns of a November afternoon
a man in blue is raking leaves
with a wide wooden rake (whose teeth are pegs
or rather, dowels). Next door
boys play soccer: "You got to start
over!" sort of. A round attic window
in a radiant gray house waits like a kettledrum.
"You got to start . . ." The Brahmsian day
lapses from waltz to march. The grass,
rough-cropped as Bruno Walter's hair,
is stretched, strewn and humped beneath a sycamore
wide and high as an idea of heaven
in which Brahms turns his face like a bearded thumb
and says, "There is something I must tell you!"
to Bruno Walter. "In the first movement
of my Second, think of it as a family
planning where to go next summer
in terms of other summers. A material ecstasy,
subdued, recollective." Bruno Walter
in a funny jacket with a turned-up collar
says, "Let me sing it for you."
He waves his hands and through the vocalese-shaped spaces
of naked elms he draws a copper beech
ignited with a few late leaves. He bluely glazes
a rhododendron "a sea of leaves" against gold grass.
There is a snapping from the brightwork
of parked and rolling cars.
There almost has to be a heaven! so there could be
a place for Bruno Walter
who never needed the cry of a baton.
Immortality—
in a small, dusty, rather gritty, somewhat scratchy
Magnavox from which a forte
drops like a used Brillo pad?
Frayed. But it's hard to think of the sky as a thick glass floor
with thick-soled Viennese boots tromping about on it.
It's a whole lot harder thinking of Brahms
in something soft, white and flowing.
"Life," he cries (here, in the last movement),
"is something more than beer and skittles!"
"And the something more

is a whole lot better than beer and skittles,"
says Bruno Walter,
darkly, under the sod. I don't suppose it seems so dark
to a root. Who are these men in evening coats?
What are these thumps?
Where is Brahms?
And Bruno Walter?
Ensconced in resonant plump easy chairs
covered with scuffed brown leather
in a pungent autumn that blends leaf smoke
(sycamore, tobacco, other),
their nobility wound in a finale
like this calico cat
asleep, curled up in a breadbasket,
on a sideboard where the sun falls.

1969

The Crystal Lithium

The smell of snow, stinging in nostrils as the wind lifts it from a beach
Eye-shuttering, mixed with sand, or when snow lies under the street
    lamps and on all
And the air is emptied to an uplifting gassiness
That turns lungs to winter waterwings, buoying, and the bright
    white night
Freezes in sight a lapse of waves, balsamic, salty, unexpected:
Hours after swimming, sitting thinking biting at a hangnail
And the taste of the—to your eyes—invisible crystals irradiates the world
"The sea is salt"
"And so am I"
"Don't bite your nails"

                and the metal flavor of a nail—are these brads?—
Taken with a slight spitting motion from between teeth and
    whanged into place
(Boards and sawdust) and the nail set is ridged with cold
Permanently as marble, always degrees cooler than the rooms of air
    it lies in
Felt as you lay your cheek upon the counter on which sits a blue-
    banded cup
A counter of condensed wintry exhalations glittering infinitesimally
A promise, late on a broiling day in late September, of the cold kiss
Of marble sheets to one who goes barefoot quickly in the snow and early

Only so far as the ashcan—bang, dump—and back and slams the door:
Too cold to get up though at the edges of the blinds the sky
Shows blue as flames that break on a red sea in which black coals float:
Pebbles in a pocket embed the seam with grains of sand
Which, as they will, have found their way into a pattern between
　　　foot and bedfoot
"A place for everything and everything in its place" how wasteful,
　　　how wrong
It seems when snow in fat, hand-stuffed flakes falls slow and steady
　　　in the sea
"Now you see it, now you don't" the waves growl as they grind
　　　ashore and roll out
At your feet (in boots) a Christmas tree naked of needles
Still wound with swags of tarnishing tinsel, faintly alarming as the
　　　thought
Of damp electricity or sluggish lightning and for your health-
　　　desiring pains
The wind awards: Chapped Lips: on which to rub Time's latest
　　　acquisition
Tinned, dowel-shaped and inappropriately flavored sheep wool fat
A greasy sense-eclipsing fog "I can't see
Without my glasses" "You certainly can't see with them all steamed up
Like that. Pull over, park and wipe them off." The thunder of a
　　　summer's day
Rolls down the shimmering blacktop and mowed grass juice
　　　thickens the air
Like "Stir until it coats the spoon, remove from heat, let cool and chill"
Like this, graying up for more snow, maybe, in which a small flock
Of—sparrows?—small, anyway, dust kitty-colored birds fly up
On a dotted diagonal and there, ah, is the answer:
Starlings, bullies of birdland, lousing up
The pecking order, respecters of no rights (what bird is) unloved (oh?)
Not so likeable as some: that's temperate enough and the temperature
Drops to rise to snowability of a softness even in its scent of roses
Made of untinted butter frosting: Happy Name Day, Blue Jay, staggering
On slow-up wings into the shrunk into itself from cold forsythia snarl
And above these thoughts there waves another tangle but one
　　　parched with heat
And not with cold although the heat is on because of cold settled all
About as though, swimming under water, in clearly fishy water, you
Inhaled and found one could and live and also found you altogether
Did not like it, January, laid out on a bed of ice, disgorging

February, shaped like a flounder, and March with her steel bead
    pocketbook,
And April, goofy and under-dressed and with a loud laugh, and May
Who will of course be voted Miss Best Liked (she expects it),
And June, with a toothpaste smile, fresh from her flea bath, and
    gross July,
Flexing itself, and steamy August, with thighs and eyes to match,
    and September
Diving into blue October, dour November, and deadly dull
    December which now
And then with a surprised blank look produces from its hand the
    ace of trumps
Or sets within the ice white hairline of a new moon the gibbous rest:
Global, blue, Columbian, a blue dull definite and thin as the first day
Of February when, in the steamed and freezing capital cash built
Without a plan to be its own best monument its skyline set in stacks
Like poker chips (signed, "Autodidact"), at the crux of a view there
    crosses
A flatcar-trailer piled with five of the cheaper sort of yachts,
    tarpaulined,
Plus one youth in purple pants, a maid in her uniform and an "It's
    not real
Anything" Cossack hat and coat, a bus one-quarter full of strangers and
The other familiar fixings of lengthening short days: "He's outgrown them
Before you can turn around" and see behind you the landscape of the past
Where beached boats bask and terraced cliffs are hung with oranges
Among dark star-gleaming leaves, and, descending the dizzying
    rough stairs
Littered with goat-turd beads—such packaging—you—he—she—
One—someone—stops to break off a bit of myrtle and recite all the lines
Of Goethe that come back, and those in French, *"Connais-tu . . . ?"* the air
Fills with chalk dust from banged erasers, behind the February dunes
Ice boats speed and among the reeds there winds a little frozen stream
Where kids in kapok ice-skate and play at Secret City as the sun
Sets before dinner, the snow on fields turns pink and under the
    hatched ice
The water slides darkly and over it a never before seen liquefaction
    of the sun
In a chemical yellow greener than sulphur a flash of petroleum by-
    product
Unbelievable, unwanted and as lovely as though someone you knew
    all your life

Said the one inconceivable thing and then went on washing dishes:
    the sky
Flows with impersonal passion and loosening jet trails (eyes tearing
    from the cold)
And on the beach, between foam frozen in a thick scalloped edging
    so like
Weird cheek-mottling pillowcase embroidery, on the water-darkened
    sand the waves
Keep free of frost, a gull strangles on a length of nylon fishline and
    the dog
Trots proudly off, tail held high, to bury a future dinner among cut
    grass on a dune:
The ice boats furl their sails and all pile into cars and go off to the
    super market
Its inviting foods and cleansers sold under tunes with sealed-in
    memory-flavor
"Hot House Rhubarb" "White Rock Girl" "Citrus Futures" "Cheap
    Bitter Beans" and
In its parking lot vast as the kiss to which is made the most
    complete surrender
In a setting of leaves, backs of stores, a house on a rise admired for being
Somewhat older than some others (prettier, too?) a man in a white
    apron embraces a car
Briefly in the cold with his eyes as one might hug oneself for
    warmth for love
—What a paint job, smooth as an eggplant; what a meaty chest,
    smooth as an eggplant
—Is it too much to ask your car to understand you? the converse
    isn't and the sky
Maps out new roads so that, driving at right angles to the wind,
    clouds in ranks
Contrive in diminishing perspective a part of a picture postcard of a
    painting
Over oak scrub where a filling station has: gas, a locked toilet (to
    keep dirt in)
A busted soda pop machine, no maps and "I couldn't tell you *thet*" so
The sky empties itself to a color, there, where yesterday's puddle
Offers its hospitality to people-trash and nature-trash in tans and
    silvers
And black grit like that in corners of a room in this or that cheap dump
Where the ceiling light burns night and day and we stare at or into each

Other's eyes in hope the other reads there what he reads: snow, wind
Lifted; black water, slashed with white; and that which is, which is beyond
Happiness or love or mixed with them or more than they or less,
    unchanging change,
"Look," the ocean said (it was tumbled, like our sheets), "look in my eyes"
1972

Letter to a Friend: Who Is Nancy Daum?

All things are real
no one a symbol:
curtains (shantung
    silk)
potted palm, a
bust: flat, with pipe—
  M. Pierre Martory
a cut-out by Alex
       Katz:
Dreaming eyes
    and pipe
Contiguous to
en terre cuite
      Marie
Antoinette
her brown and seeming
living curls
and gaze seen as
Reverie: *My Lady*
of My Edgeworth
("Prince Albert in
the can?" "Better
let him out, I . . .")
pipe dream. Some
vitamins; more
Flying Buzzard
    ware:

a silver chain—my
silver chain
from Denmark from
you by way
of London—
(I put it on: cold
and I love
its weight:
        argento
                pessante)
a *sang de boeuf*
                spittoon
or Beauty bowl,
a compact
with a Red Sea
        scene
holding little
pills (Valium
for travel strain),
this French
        lamp
whose stem of
    glass
Lights softly
                        up
entwined with
autumn trees
(around the base
        are reeds)
its glass shade
        slightly oiled
as is the dawn
above a swamp
lagoon or fen where
        hunters lurk and
        down marc or cognac
or home-made rotgut
    of their choice,
I—have lost
        my place:
No, here it is:

Traherne,
Poems, Centuries
and Three
Thanksgivings,
a book beneath
the notebook
in which I write.
Put off the light—
the French lamp
(signed, somewhere)
And put it on:
the current
flows.
My heart
beats. Nerves,
muscles,
the bright invisible
red blood—*sang*
d'homme
helps (is
that the word?)
propel
this ball-point
pen:
black ink is
not black
blood.
Two other books:
The Gay
Insider
—good—*Run*
Little Leather
Boy awaits
assessment
on my Peter Meter.
A trove of glass
within a
cabinet
near my
knees
I wish I were on

my knees
embracing
   yours
      my cheek
against the suiting of
          whatever
suit—about now—
or soon, or late—
("I'm not prompt"
   you said, rueful
         factual
"I" I said, "climb
walls")
O Day!
   literal
and unsymbolic
         day:
silken: gray: sunny:
   in salt and pepper
tweed soot storm:
guide, guard,
     be freely
        pierced
by the steel and
gold-eyed
needle passes—stitches
—of my love, my
       lover,
          our
      love,
his lover—I
     am he—
  (is not
at any tick
each and every life
at hazard: *faites
vos jeux,
   messieurs*)
...Where am I?
  en route to
    a literal

Vermont. It's
    time
      to
—oh, do this
   do that—.
I'll call.
Perhaps we'll
 lunch? We
already
said goodbye a
long farewell
for a few weeks'
   parting!
My ocean liner,
 I am your
tug. "Life
is a bed
   of roses:
rugosas,
nor is it always
   summer."
Goodbye. Hello.
    Kiss
Hug. I
 gotta
run. Pierre
Martory,
his semblance,
smokes a St.
   Simonian
pipe and thinks
Mme de Sévigné
-type thoughts.
He was, when
   posing,
perhaps, projecting
A Letter to a Friend.
   (signed)—
all my
—you know—
  ton

                              Dopey.
                    PS The lamp is
                       signed, Daum,
                          Nancy.
                    Hence I surmise
                       she made
                    or, at least,
                                  designed it.
                    Who *is* Nancy Daum?

                                                    1972

Korean Mums

beside me in this garden
are huge and daisy-like
(why not? are not
oxeye daisies a chrysanthemum?),
shrubby and thick-stalked,
the leaves pointing up
the stems from which
the flowers burst in
sunbursts. I love
this garden in all its moods,
even under its winter coat
of salt hay, or now,
in October, more than
half gone over: here
a rose, there a clump
of aconite. This morning
one of the dogs killed
a barn owl. Bob saw
it happen, tried to
intervene. The airedale
snapped its neck and left
it lying. Now the bird
lies buried by an apple
tree. Last evening
from the table we saw
the owl, huge in the dusk,
circling the field

on owl-silent wings.
The first one ever seen
here: now it's gone,
a dream you just remember.

The dogs are barking. In
the studio music plays
and Bob and Darragh paint.
I sit scribbling in a little
notebook at a garden table,
too hot in a heavy shirt
in the mid-October sun
into which the Korean mums
all face. There is a
dull book with me,
an apple core, cigarettes,
an ashtray. Behind me
the rue I gave Bob
flourishes. Light on leaves,
so much to see, and
all I really see is that
owl, its bulk troubling
the twilight. I'll
soon forget it: what
is there I have not forgot?
Or one day will forget:
this garden, the breeze
in stillness, even
the words, Korean mums.

1980

Kenneth Koch
1925-2002

A central figure in the New York School of poets, Kenneth Koch was born in Cincinnati and educated at Harvard and Columbia. His poetry is strongly influenced by the French avant-garde tradition, especially Guillaume Apollinaire, the poet and art critic who named cubism and surrealism; Max Jacob's prose poems, from which Koch claims to have learned "the possibility of being funny and lyrical at the same time"; the melancholy lyricism of Pierre Reverdy; and the surrealists Paul Eluard and Rene Char. Koch also greatly admired the work of Spanish poet Federico García Lorca.[1] Some of Koch's earliest poetry, published in *When the Sun Tries to Go On* (1953/1969), was written in a rigorously nonnarrative style. His turn toward the simpler, more narrative style of his later work he credits to three influences: falling in love and getting married; the counsel of his friend Frank O'Hara, who praised modesty and directness in art; and seeing a production of *Peter Pan,* the simplicity and even "dumbness" of which he admired.[2]

In such lighthearted polemics as "Fresh Air" and "The Art of Poetry," Koch speaks for a poetry of spontaneity and joy and against what he calls an "exigent" poetry characterized by caution and revision. His fondness for humor, parody, and popular culture is ironically part of his seriousness as a poet. Koch's comic epics in ottava rima, "The Duplications" and "Ko, or A Season on Earth," and his meditative and elegiac "Seasons on Earth" reveal his mastery of traditional form.

Koch's poetry collections include *Thank You and Other Poems* (1962), *The Pleasures of Peace and Other Poems* (1969), *The Art of Love* (1975), *The Burning Mystery of Anna in 1951* (1979), *Days and Nights* (1982), *On the Edge* (1986), *One Train* (1994), *On the Great Atlantic Rainway: Selected Poems 1950–1988* (1994),and *New Addresses* (2000). He also wrote an experimental novel, *The Red Robins* (1975); a volume of short plays, *One Thousand Avant-Garde Plays* (1988); and influential books on teaching the writing of poetry, most notably *Wishes, Lies, and Dreams* (1970). With John Ashbery, Harry Mathews, James Schuyler, and Frank O'Hara, he edited the short-lived but noteworthy magazine of the 1950s, *Locus Solus*. He was awarded the Bollingen Prize for Poetry in 1994.

A much-loved and influential professor of comparative literature at Columbia University, Kenneth Koch lived in New York City and Southampton, Long Island.

1. David Shapiro, "A Conversation with Kenneth Koch," *Field* 7 (Fall 1972), p. 61.   2. The same, p. 57.

To You

I love you as a sheriff searches for a walnut
That will solve a murder case unsolved for years
Because the murderer left it in the snow beside a window
Through which he saw her head, connecting with
Her shoulders by a neck, and laid a red
Roof in her heart. For this we live a thousand years;
For this we love, and we live because we love, we are not
Inside a bottle, thank goodness! I love you as a
Kid searches for a goat; I am crazier than shirttails
In the wind, when you're near, a wind that blows from
The big blue sea, so shiny so deep and so unlike us;
I think I am bicycling across an Africa of green and white fields
Always, to be near you, even in my heart
When I'm awake, which swims, and also I believe that you
Are trustworthy as the sidewalk which leads me to
The place where I again think of you, a new
Harmony of thoughts! I love you as the sunlight leads the prow
Of a ship which sails
From Hartford to Miami, and I love you
Best at dawn, when even before I am awake the sun
Receives me in the questions which you always pose.

1962

Variations on a Theme by William Carlos Williams

1

I chopped down the house that you had been saving to live in next
  summer.
I am sorry, but it was morning, and I had nothing to do
and its wooden beams were so inviting.

2

We laughed at the hollyhocks together
and then I sprayed them with lye.
Forgive me. I simply do not know what I am doing.

3

I gave away the money that you had been saving to live on for the next
  ten years.
The man who asked for it was shabby
and the firm March wind on the porch was so juicy and cold.

4

Last evening we went dancing and I broke your leg.
Forgive me. I was clumsy, and
I wanted you here in the wards, where I am the doctor!

1962

Alive for an Instant

I have a bird in my head and a pig in my stomach
And a flower in my genitals and a tiger in my genitals
And a lion in my genitals and I am after you but I have a song in my
  heart
And my song is a dove
I have a man in my hands I have a woman in my shoes
I have a landmark decision in my reason
I have a death rattle in my nose I have summer in my brain water
I have dreams in my toes
This is the matter with me and the hammer of my mother and father
Who created me with everything
But I lack calm I lack rose
Though I do not lack extreme delicacy of rose petal
Who is it that I wish to astonish?
In the birdcall I found a reminder of you
But it was thin and brittle and gone in an instant
Has nature set out to be a great entertainer?
Obviously not A great reproducer? A great Nothing?
Well I will leave that up to you
I have a knocking woodpecker in my heart and I think I have three
  souls
One for love one for poetry and one for acting out my insane self
Not insane but boring but perpendicular but untrue but true
The three rarely sing together take my hand it's active
The active ingredient in it is a touch

I am Lord Byron I am Percy Shelley I am Ariosto
I eat the bacon I went down the slide I have a thunderstorm in my
    inside I will never hate you
But how can this maelstrom be appealing? do you like menageries? my god
Most people want a man! So here I am
I have a pheasant in my reminders I have a goshawk in my clouds
Whatever is it which has led all these animals to you?
A resurrection? or maybe an insurrection? an inspiration?
I have a baby in my landscape and I have a wild rat in my secrets from you.

1975

Aesthetics of a Small Theatre

Don't bring a horse
Into a small theatre
But, if you must,
Put it on stage.

Aesthetics of Creating Something

This doesn't happen:
It happens to you.

Aesthetics of Lorca

Federico García Lorca stands alone
Luna, typewriter, plantain tree, and dust
The moon is watching him. It is watching over him.

Aesthetics of Feeling Fine

Feel fine
Then go away.

Aesthetics of Being a Mouse

Look at the floor.
Look up.
Look at the wall.

Aesthetics of Poetry and Prose

Chekhov told Bunin
Not to begin writing
Until he felt cold as ice.
Keats wrote to Shelley
"I am a fever of myself!"

Aesthetics of Comedy Asleep

Don't wake the clown
Or he may knock you down.

Aesthetics of Silence

Silence is not everything.
It is half of everything
Like a house.

Aesthetics of the Aesthetician

What is the aesthetician
But a mule hitched to the times?

1994

Jack Spicer

1925–1965

Jack Spicer was born in Los Angeles and spent his brief but significant poetic career in San Francisco. While dying of alcoholism, his last words were, "My vocabulary did this to me." Spicer believed in poetry as a form of magic, most potent when spoken aloud. In 1957, he organized a "Poetry as Magic" workshop at the Berkeley Public Library. Spicer was also an enthusiastic participant, and sometimes host, of Blabbermouth Night at The Place, a San Francisco literary bar. Blabbermouth Night, a bardic competition in which poets uttered unrehearsed "babble" into the microphone, underscored Spicer's belief in an oral poetics, as stated in "The Poet and Poetry—A Symposium" (1949):

> The truth is that pure poetry bores everybody. It is a bore even to the poet. The only real contribution of the New Critics is that they have demonstrated this so well. They have taken poetry (already removed from its main source of human interest—the human voice) and have completed the job of denuding it of any remaining connection with person, place, and time. . . .
>
> Live poetry is a kind of singing. It differs from prose, as song does, in its complexity of stress and intonation. Poetry demands a human voice to sing it and demands an audience to hear it. Without these it is naked, pure, and incomplete—a bore.[1]

Yet Spicer's poems in the volume *Language* (1964), with their emphasis on linguistics, anticipate the later development of language poetry, which rejects an exclusively oral poetics.

The poet's most significant contribution came with his work on the serial poem, which has greatly influenced contemporary practice. In a series of talks he gave in Vancouver in June, 1965, Spicer offered a definition of seriality:

> A serial poem, in the first place, has the book as its unit—as an individual poem (a dictated poem, say, as we were talking about on Sunday night) has the poem as its unit, the actual poem that you write at the actual time, the single poem. And there is a dictation of form as well as a dictation of the individual form of an individual poem.
>
> And you have to go into the serial poem not knowing what the hell you're doing. You have to be tricked into it. It has to be some path that you've never seen on a map.[2]

Individual poems were to become obsolete in Spicer's practice, mere "one night stands"; after discovering the serial poem, he wrote only books. *The Holy Grail* (1962) consisted of seven books of seven poems each. Although the poems must remain in the chronological order of their composition, they are necessarily incomplete in themselves. Spicer credited his friend and fellow serialist, Robin Blaser (*The Holy Forest*), with comparing each work to a dark room: "A light is turned on for a minute. Then it's turned off again and you go into a different room where a light is turned on and turned off."[3] What Spicer called the poem's dictation comes from the "Outside," from the "Lowghost," a pun on the Greek word *logos,* meaning word. Spicer credits Robert Duncan with having written serial poetry in "The Structure of Rime" series that threads through *The Opening of the Field* (1960). Spicer's serial poem doesn't strive for the open-ended purity and breathlessness of Mallarmé, but rather instances of the real. "I'd say that I wasted quite a great deal of time trying to write perfect little poems." Spicer declared. "If you want to be dignified, there's no reason to be a poet. I mean it's the most undignified thing in the world, other than the person who hands out towels in the Turkish bath."[4]

Much attention has been paid to Spicer's work in recent years. This includes *The Collected Books of Jack Spicer,* edited by Robin Blaser (1989); *The House That Jack Built: The Collected Lectures of Jack Spicer* (1998); and *My Vocabulary Did This to Me: The Collected Poetry of Jack Spicer* (2008), edited by Peter Gizzi and Kevin Killian.

1. *One Night Stand and Other Poems,* San Francisco, 1980, p. 91.   2. "Vancouver Lecture 2: The Serial Poem and the Holy Grail," *The House that Jack Built: The Collected Lectures of Jack Spicer,* ed. Peter Gizzi, Middletown, CT, 1998, p. 52.   3. The same, p. 55.   4. The same, p. 75.

Song for Bird and Myself

I am dissatisfied with my poetry.
I am dissatisfied with my sex life.
I am dissatisfied with the angels I believe in.
     Neo-classical like Bird,
     Distrusting the reality
     Of every note.
     Half-real
     We blow the sentence pure and real
     Like chewing angels.

"Listen, Bird, why do we have to sit here dying
In a half-furnished room?
The rest of the combo
Is safe in houses
Blowing bird-brained Dixieland,
How warm and free they are. What right

Music."
"Man,
We
Can't stay away from the sounds.
We're *crazy,* Jack
We gotta stay here 'til
They come and get us."

Neo-classical like Bird.
Once two birds got into the Rare Book Room.
Miss Swift said,
"Don't
Call a custodian
Put crumbs on the outside of the window
Let them
Come outside."
Neo-classical
The soft line strains
Not to be neo-classical.
But Miss Swift went to lunch. They
Called a custodian.
Four came.
Armed like Myrmidons, they
Killed the birds.
Miss Munsterberg
Who was the first
American translator of Rilke
Said
"Suppose one of them
Had been the Holy Ghost."
Miss Swift,
Who was back from lunch,
Said
"Which."
But the poem isn't over.
It keeps going
Long after everybody
Has settled down comfortably into laughter.
The bastards
On the other side of the paper
Keep laughing.
LISTEN
STOP LAUGHING

THE POEM ISN'T OVER. Butterflies.
I knew there would be butterflies
For butterflies represent the lost soul
Represent the way the wind wanders
Represent the bodies
We only clasp in the middle of a poem.
See, the stars have faded.
There are only butterflies.
Listen to
The terrible sound of their wings moving.
Listen,
The poem isn't over.

Have you ever wrestled with a bird,
You idiotic reader?
Jacob wrestled with an angel.
(I remind you of the image)
Or a butterfly
Have you ever wrestled with a single butterfly?
Sex is no longer important.
Colors take the form of wings. Words
Have got to be said.
A butterfly,
A bird,
Planted at the heart of being afraid of dying.
Blow,
Bird,
Blow,
Be,
Neo-classical.
Let the wings say
What the wings mean
Terrible and pure.

The horse
In Cocteau
Is as neo-classical an idea as one can manage.
Writes all our poetry for us
Is Gertrude Stein
Is God
Is the needle for which
God help us
There is no substitute

Or the Ace of Swords
When you are telling a fortune
Who tells death.
Or the Jack of Hearts
Whose gypsy fortune we clasp
In the middle of a poem.

"And are we angels, Bird?"
"That's what we're trying to tell 'em, Jack
There aren't any angels except when
You and me blow 'em."

So Bird and I sing
Outside your window
So Bird and I die
Outside your window.
This is the wonderful world of Dixieland
Deny
The bloody motherfucking Holy Ghost.
This is the end of the poem.
You can start laughing, you bastards. This is
The end of the poem.

1955–1956

FROM The Holy Grail

The Book of Gawain

1.

Tony
To be casual and have the wish to heal
Gawain, I think,
Had that when he saw the sick king squirming around like a
    half-cooked eel on a platter asking a riddle maybe only
    ghostmen could answer
His riddled body. Heal it how?
Gawain no ghostman, guest who could not gather
Anything
There was an easy grail.
Later shot a green knight

In a dead forest
That was an easy answer
No king
No riddle.

2.

In some kind of castle some kind of knight played chess with an
      invisible chessplayer
A maiden, naturally.
You can hear the sound of wood on the board and some kind of
      knight breathing
It was another spoiled quest. George
Said to me that the only thing he thought was important in
      chess was killing the other king. I had accused him of lack of
      imagination.
I talked of fun and imagination but I wondered about the nature
      of poetry since there was some kind of knight and an
      invisible chessplayer and they had been playing chess in the
      Grail Castle.

3.

The grail is the opposite of poetry
Fills us up instead of using us as a cup the dead drink from.
The grail the cup Christ bled into and the cup of plenty in Irish
      mythology
The poem. Opposite. Us. Unfullfilled.
These worlds make the friendliness of human to human seem
      close as cup to lip.
Savage in their pride the beasts pound around the forest
      perilous.

4.

Everyone is impressed with courage and when he fought him
      he won
Who won?
I'm not sure but one was wearing red armor and one black armor
I'm not sure about the colors but they were looking for a cup
      or a poem
Everyone in each of the worlds is impressed with courage and
      I'm not sure if either of them were human or that what they

were looking for could be described as a cup or a poem or
    why either of them fought
They made a loud noise in the forest and the ravens gathered in
    trees and you were almost sure they were ravens.

5.

On the sea
(There is never an ocean in all Grail legend)
There is a boat.
There is always one lone person on it sailing
Widdershins.
His name is Kate or Bob or Mike or Dora and his sex is almost
    as obscure as his history.
Yet he will be met by a ship of singing women who will embalm
    him with nard and spice and all of the hallows
As the ocean
In the far distance.

6.

They are still looking for it
Poetry and magic see the world from opposite ends
One cock-forward and the other ass-forward
All over Britain (but what a relief it would be to give all this up
    and find surcease in somebodyelse's soul and body)
Thus said Merlin
Unwillingly
Who saw through time.

7.

Perverse
Turned against the light
The grail they said
Is achieved by steady compromise.
An unending
The prize is there at the bottom of the rainbow—follow the
    invisible markings processwise
I, Gawain, who am no longer human but a legend followed the
    markings
Did
More or less what they asked

My name is now a symbol for shame
I, Gawain, who once was a knight of the Grail in a dark forest.

The Book of Percival

1.

Fool-
Killer lurks between the branches of every tree
Bird-language.
Fooled by nature, I
Accepted the quest gracefully
Played the fool. Fool-
Killer in the branches waiting.
Left home. Fool-Killer left home too. Followed me.
Fool-
Killer thinks that just before the moment I will find the grail
     he will catch me. Poor
Little boy in the forest
Dancing.

2.

Even the forest felt deserted when he left it. What nonsense!
The enormous trees. The lakes with carp in them. The wolves
     and badgers. They
Should feel deserted for a punk kid who has left them?
Even the forest felt deserted. There were no leaves dropping or
     sounds anybody could hear.
The wind met resistance but no noise, the sky
Could not be heard through the water.
Percival
Fool, like badger, pinetree, broken water,
Gone.

3.

"Ship of fools," the wise man said to me.
"I used to work in Chicago in a department store," I said to the
     wise man never knowing that there would be a ship

Whose tiny sails, grail bearing
Would have to support me
All the loves of my life
Each impossible choice I had been making. Wave
Upon wave.
"Fool," I could hear them shouting for we were becalmed in
        some impossible harbor
The grail and me
And in impossible armor
The spooks that bent the ship
Forwards and backwards.

4.

If someone doesn't fight me I'll have to wear this armor
All of my life. I look like the Tin Woodsman in the Oz Books.
Rusted beyond recognition.
I am, sir, a knight. Puzzled
By the way things go toward me and in back of me. And finally
        into my mouth and head and red blood
O, damn these things that try to maim me
This armor
Fooled
Alive in its
Self.

5.

The hermit said dance and I danced
I was always meeting hermits on the road
Who said what I was to do and I did it or got angry and didn't
Knowing always what was not expected of me.
She electrocuted herself with her own bathwater
I pulled the plug
And there was darkness (the Hermit said)
Deeper than any hallow.

6.

It was not searching the grail or finding it that prompted me
It was playing the fool (Fool-killer along at my back
Playing the fool.)

I knew that the cup or the dish or the knights I fought didn't
     have anything to do with it
Fool-killer and I were fishing in the same ocean
"And at the end of whose line?" I asked him once when I met
     him in my shadow.
"You ask the wrong questions" and at that my shadow jumped
     up and beat itself against a rock, "or rather the wrong
     questions to the wrong person"
At the end of whose line
I now lie
Hanging.

7.

No visible means of support
The Grail hung there like june-berries in October or something
     I had felt and forgotten.
This was a palace and an ocean I was in
A ship that cast its water on the tide
A grail, a real grail. Snark-hungry.
The Grail hung there with the seagulls circling round it and the
     pain of my existence soothed
"Fool," they sang in voices more like angels watching
"Fool."

1962

Frank O'Hara
1926–1966

Raised in Grafton, Massachusetts, and educated at Harvard, where he met John Ashbery and Kenneth Koch, O'Hara published only two full-length books in his lifetime: *Meditations in an Emergency* (1957) and the influential *Lunch Poems* (1964). These collections, as well as the essay "Personism: A Manifesto," have by and large established the public image of the New York School of poetry. Characterized by wit, charm, and everydayness, his work extended William Carlos Williams's emphasis on the American vernacular into urban popular culture of the 1950s and 1960s.

The poet John Ashbery writes of O'Hara that "the poetry that meant the most to him when he began writing was either French—Rimbaud, Mallarmé, the surrealists: poets who speak the language of every day into the reader's dream—or Russian—Pasternak and especially Mayakovsky, from whom he picked up what James Schuyler has called the 'intimate yell.'"[1]

Another of O'Hara's important predecessors was the French poet Guillaume Apollinaire. Gathering random snatches of overheard conversation on his Paris walks, Apollinaire composed what he called "Poèmes conversations." Using a similar conversational style and spirit of chance encounter, O'Hara's poem beginning "Lana Turner has collapsed!" was written on the Staten Island ferry on the way to a poetry reading, where he read it along with his prepared manuscript. In his famous manifesto, written in part as a spoof of Charles Olson's "Projective Verse," O'Hara claimed that Personism was born when he realized that, instead of writing a poem for a friend, he could just as well use the telephone.

In a statement for the anthology *The New American Poetry*, O'Hara wrote: "I don't think of fame or posterity (as Keats so grandly and genuinely did), nor do I care about clarifying experiences for anyone or bettering (other than accidentally) anyone's state or social relation, nor am I for any particular development in the American language simply because I find it necessary. What is happening to me, allowing for lies and exaggerations which I try to avoid, goes into my poems."[2] Immediacy, honesty, and fearlessness are among the attractive qualities of his style: "You're sort of galloping into the midst of a subject. . . . You're not afraid to think about anything and you're not afraid of being stupid and you're not afraid of being sentimental. You just sort of gallop right in and deal with it."[3]

His numerous manuscripts, which were casually stuck into drawers or handed off to friends, were published posthumously in *The Collected Poems of Frank O'Hara* (1972). Other O'Hara volumes are *Poems Retrieved* (1977), containing poems discovered by editor Donald Allen after the publication of *Collected Poems*; *Selected Plays* (1978); and a collection of essays and interviews, *Standing Still and Walking in New York* (1983).

1. Introduction to *The Collected Poems of Frank O'Hara*, New York, 1972, p. vii.   2. *The Collected Poems of Frank O'Hara*, p. 500.   3. Edward Lucie-Smith, "An Interview with Frank O'Hara," taped in October 1965, in *Standing Still and Walking in New York*, San Francisco, 1983, p. 25.

Poem

The eager note on my door said "Call me,
call when you get in!" so I quickly threw
a few tangerines into my overnight bag,
straightened my eyelids and shoulders, and

headed straight for the door. It was autumn
by the time I got around the corner, oh all
unwilling to be either pertinent or bemused, but
the leaves were brighter than grass on the sidewalk!

Funny, I thought, that the lights are on this late
and the hall door open; still up at this hour, a
champion jai-alai player like himself? Oh fie!
for shame! What a host, so zealous! And he was

there in the hall, flat on a sheet of blood that
ran down the stairs. I did appreciate it. There are few
hosts who so thoroughly prepare to greet a guest
only casually invited, and that several months ago.

1957

Meditations in an Emergency

Am I to become profligate as if I were a blonde? Or religious as if I were French?

Each time my heart is broken it makes me feel more adventurous (and how the same names keep recurring on that interminable list!), but one of these days there'll be nothing left with which to venture forth.

Why should I share you? Why don't you get rid of someone else for a change?

I am the least difficult of men. All I want is boundless love.

Even trees understand me! Good heavens, I lie under them, too, don't I? I'm just like a pile of leaves.

However, I have never clogged myself with the praises of pastoral life, nor with nostalgia for an innocent past of perverted acts in pastures. No. One need never leave the confines of New York to get all the greenery one wishes—I can't even enjoy a blade of grass unless I know there's a subway handy, or a record store or some other sign that people do not totally *regret* life. It is more important to affirm the least sincere; the clouds get enough attention as it is and even they continue to pass. Do they know what they're missing? Uh huh.

My eyes are vague blue, like the sky, and change all the time; they are indiscriminate but fleeting, entirely specific and disloyal, so that no one trusts me. I am always looking away. Or again at something after it has given me up. It makes me restless and that makes me unhappy, but I cannot keep them still. If only I had grey, green, black, brown, yellow eyes; I would stay at home and do something. It's not that I'm curious. On the contrary, I am bored but it's my duty to be attentive, I am needed by things as the sky must be above the earth. And lately, so great has *their* anxiety become, I can spare myself little sleep.

Now there is only one man I love to kiss when he is unshaven. Heterosexuality! you are inexorably approaching. (How discourage her?)

St. Serapion, I wrap myself in the robes of your whiteness which is like midnight in Dostoevsky. How am I to become a legend, my dear? I've tried love, but that hides you in the bosom of another and I am always springing forth from it like the lotus—the ecstasy of always bursting forth! (but one must not be distracted by it!) or like a hyacinth, "to keep the filth of life away," yes, there, even in the heart, where the filth is pumped in and slanders and pollutes and determines. I will my will, though I may become famous for a mysterious vacancy in that department, that greenhouse.

Destroy yourself, if you don't know!

It is easy to be beautiful; it is difficult to appear so. I admire you, beloved, for the trap you've set. It's like a final chapter no one reads because the plot is over.

"Fanny Brown is run away—scampered off with a Cornet of Horse; I do love that little Minx, & hope She may be happy, tho' She has vexed me by this Exploit a little too.—Poor silly Cecchina! or F: B: as we used to call her.—I wish She had a good Whipping and 10,000 pounds." Mrs. Thrale.

I've got to get out of here. I choose a piece of shawl and my dirtiest suntans. I'll be back, I'll re-emerge, defeated, from the valley; you don't want me to go where you go, so I go where you don't want me to. It's only afternoon, there's a lot ahead. There won't be any mail downstairs. Turning, I spit in the lock and the knob turns.

1957

Ode to Joy

We shall have everything we want and there'll be no more dying
    on the pretty plains or in the supper clubs
for our symbol we'll acknowledge vulgar materialistic laughter
    over an insatiable sexual appetite
and the streets will be filled with racing forms
and the photographs of murderers and narcissists and movie stars
    will swell from the walls and books alive in steaming rooms
    to press against our burning flesh not once but interminably
as water flows down hill into the full-lipped basin
and the adder dives for the ultimate ostrich egg
and the feather cushion preens beneath a reclining monolith
    that's sweating with post-exertion visibility and sweetness
    near the grave of love

                      No more dying

We shall see the grave of love as a lovely sight and temporary
    near the elm that spells the lovers' names in roots
and there'll be no more music but the ears in lips and no more wit
    but tongues in ears and no more drums but ears to thighs
as evening signals nudities unknown to ancestors' imaginations
and the imagination itself will stagger like a tired paramour of ivory
    under the sculptural necessities of lust that never falters
like a six-mile runner from Sweden or Liberia covered with gold
as lava flows up and over the far-down somnolent city's abdication
and the hermit always wanting to be lone is lone at last
and the weight of external heat crushes the heat-hating Puritan
    whose self-defeating vice becomes a proper sepulchre at last
    that love may live

Buildings will go up into the dizzy air as love itself goes in
    and up the reeling life that it has chosen for once or all

while in the sky a feeling of intemperate fondness will excite the bird
    to swoop and veer like flies crawling across absorbed limbs
that weep a pearly perspiration on the sheets of brief attention
and the hairs dry out that summon anxious declaration of the organs
    as they rise like buildings to the needs of temporary neighbors
pouring hunger through the heart to feed desire in intravenous ways
like the ways of gods with humans in the innocent combination of light
and flesh or as the legends ride their heroes through the dark to found
great cities where all life is possible to maintain as long as time
    which wants us to remain for cocktails in a bar and after dinner
    lets us live with it

No more dying

1960

The Day Lady Died

It is 12 : 20 in New York a Friday
three days after Bastille day, yes
it is 1959 and I go get a shoeshine
because I will get off the 4 : 19 in Easthampton
at 7 : 15 and then go straight to dinner
and I don't know the people who will feed me

I walk up the muggy street beginning to sun
and have a hamburger and a malted and buy
an ugly NEW WORLD WRITING to see what the poets
in Ghana are doing these days
                I go on to the bank
and Miss Stillwagon (first name Linda I once heard)
doesn't even look up my balance for once in her life
and in the GOLDEN GRIFFIN I get a little Verlaine
for Patsy with drawings by Bonnard although I do
think of Hesiod, trans. Richmond Lattimore or
Brendan Behan's new play or *Le Balcon* or *Les Nègres*
of Genet, but I don't, I stick with Verlaine
after practically going to sleep with quandariness

and for Mike I just stroll into the PARK LANE
Liquor Store and ask for a bottle of Strega and
then I go back where I came from to 6th Avenue
and the tobacconist in the Ziegfeld Theatre and

casually ask for a carton of Gauloises and a carton
of Picayunes, and a NEW YORK POST with her face on it

and I am sweating a lot by now and thinking of
leaning on the john door in the 5 SPOT
while she whispered a song along the keyboard
to Mal Waldron and everyone and I stopped breathing

1959   1964

Personal Poem

Now when I walk around at lunchtime
I have only two charms in my pocket
an old Roman coin Mike Kanemitsu gave me
and a bolt-head that broke off a packing case
when I was in Madrid the others never
brought me too much luck though they did
help keep me in New York against coercion
but now I'm happy for a time and interested

I walk through the luminous humidity
passing the House of Seagram with its wet
and its loungers and the construction to
the left that closed the sidewalk if
I ever get to be a construction worker
I'd like to have a silver hat please
and get to Moriarty's where I wait for
LeRoi and hear who wants to be a mover and
shaker the last five years my batting average
is .016 that's that, and LeRoi comes in
and tells me Miles Davis was clubbed 12
times last night outside BIRDLAND by a cop
a lady asks us for a nickel for a terrible
disease but we don't give her one we
don't like terrible diseases, then
we go eat some fish and some ale it's
cool but crowded we don't like Lionel Trilling
we decide, we like Don Allen we don't like
Henry James so much we like Herman Melville

we don't want to be in the poets' walk in
San Francisco even we just want to be rich
and walk on girders in our silver hats
I wonder if one person out of the 8,000,000 is
thinking of me as I shake hands with LeRoi
and buy a strap for my wristwatch and go
back to work happy at the thought possibly so

1959

1964

A Step away from Them

It's my lunch hour, so I go
for a walk among the hum-colored
cabs. First, down the sidewalk
where laborers feed their dirty
glistening torsos sandwiches
and Coca-Cola, with yellow helmets
on. They protect them from falling
bricks, I guess. Then onto the
avenue where skirts are flipping
above heels and blow up over
grates. The sun is hot, but the
cabs stir up the air. I look
at bargains in wristwatches. There
are cats playing in sawdust.
                                    On
to Times Square, where the sign
blows smoke over my head, and higher
the waterfall pours lightly. A
Negro stands in a doorway with a
toothpick, languorously agitating.
A blonde chorus girl clicks: he
smiles and rubs his chin. Everything
suddenly honks: it is 12:40 of
a Thursday.
                        Neon in daylight is a
great pleasure, as Edwin Denby would
write, as are light bulbs in daylight.
I stop for a cheeseburger at JULIET'S

CORNER. Giulietta Masina, wife of
Federico Fellini, *è bell' attrice.*
And chocolate malted. A lady in
foxes on such a day puts her poodle
in a cab.
            There are several Puerto
Ricans on the avenue today, which
makes it beautiful and warm. First
Bunny died, then John Latouche,
then Jackson Pollock. But is the
earth as full as life was full, of them?
And one has eaten and one walks,
past the magazines with nudes
and the posters for BULLFIGHT and
the Manhattan Storage Warehouse,
which they'll soon tear down. I
used to think they had the Armory
Show there.
            A glass of papaya juice
and back to work. My heart is in my
pocket, it is Poems by Pierre Reverdy.

1956   1964

Ave Maria

Mothers of America
                    let your kids go to the movies!
get them out of the house so they won't know what you're up to
it's true that fresh air is good for the body
                                        but what about the soul
that grows in darkness, embossed by silvery images
and when you grow old as grow old you must
                                        they won't hate you
they won't criticize you they won't know
                    they'll be in some glamorous country
they first saw on a Saturday afternoon or playing hookey

they may even be grateful to you
                            for their first sexual experience

which only cost you a quarter
                              and didn't upset the peaceful home
they will know where candy bars come from
                                   and gratuitous bags of popcorn
as gratuitous as leaving the movie before it's over
with a pleasant stranger whose apartment is in the
                                        Heaven on Earth Bldg
near the Williamsburg Bridge
                            oh mothers you will have made the little tykes
so happy because if nobody does pick them up in the movies
they won't know the difference
                              and if somebody does it'll be sheer gravy
and they'll have been truly entertained either way
instead of hanging around the yard
                                   or up in their room
                                              hating you
prematurely since you won't have done anything horribly
                                                 mean yet
except keeping them from the darker joys
                                    it's unforgivable the latter
so don't blame me if you won't take this advice
                              and the family breaks up
and your children grow old and blind in front of a TV set
                                                 seeing
movies you wouldn't let them see when they were young

1960   1964

Steps

How funny you are today New York
like Ginger Rogers in *Swingtime*
and St. Bridget's steeple leaning a little to the left

here I have just jumped out of a bed full of V-days
(I got tired of D-days) and blue you there still
accepts me foolish and free
all I want is a room up there
and you in it
and even the traffic halt so thick is a way

for people to rub up against each other
and when their surgical appliances lock
they stay together
for the rest of the day (what a day)
I go by to check a slide and I say
that painting's not so blue

where's Lana Turner
she's out eating
and Garbo's backstage at the Met
everyone's taking their coat off
so they can show a rib-cage to the rib-watchers
and the park's full of dancers and their tights and shoes
in little bags
who are often mistaken for worker-outers at the West Side Y
why not
the Pittsburgh Pirates shout because they won
and in a sense we're all winning
we're alive

the apartment was vacated by a gay couple
who moved to the country for fun
they moved a day too soon
even the stabbings are helping the population explosion
though in the wrong country
and all those liars have left the U N
the Seagram Building's no longer rivalled in interest
not that we need liquor (we just like it)

and the little box is out on the sidewalk
next to the delicatessen
so the old man can sit on it and drink beer
and get knocked off it by his wife later in the day
while the sun is still shining

oh god it's wonderful
to get out of bed
and drink too much coffee
and smoke too many cigarettes
and love you so much

1961   1964

Poem

Lana Turner has collapsed!
I was trotting along and suddenly
it started raining and snowing
and you said it was hailing
but hailing hits you on the head
hard so it was really snowing and
raining and I was in such a hurry
to meet you but the traffic
was acting exactly like the sky
and suddenly I see a headline
LANA TURNER HAS COLLAPSED!
there is no snow in Hollywood
there is no rain in California
I have been to lots of parties
and acted perfectly disgraceful
but I never actually collapsed
oh Lana Turner we love you get up

1962

1964

Why I Am Not a Painter

I am not a painter, I am a poet.
Why? I think I would rather be
a painter, but I am not. Well,

for instance, Mike Goldberg
is starting a painting. I drop in.
"Sit down and have a drink" he
says. I drink; we drink. I look
up. "You have SARDINES in it."
"Yes, it needed something there."
"Oh." I go and the days go by
and I drop in again. The painting
is going on, and I go, and the days
go by. I drop in. The painting is
finished. "Where's SARDINES?"
All that's left is just
letters, "It was too much," Mike says.

But me? One day I am thinking of
a color: orange. I write a line
about orange. Pretty soon it is a
whole page of words, not lines.
Then another page. There should be
so much more, not of orange, of
words, of how terrible orange is
and life. Days go by. It is even in
prose, I am a real poet. My poem
is finished and I haven't mentioned
orange yet. It's twelve poems, I call
it ORANGES. And one day in a gallery
I see Mike's painting, called SARDINES.

1971

Allen Ginsberg
1926–1997

Born in Newark, New Jersey, Allen Ginsberg attended Columbia University, where he met Jack Kerouac. With novelist William Burroughs, author of *Naked Lunch,* Ginsberg and Kerouac became major figures of the Beat generation. In place of the reigning style of the early postwar period, which called for decorum, formalism, and intellectual complexity, Ginsberg proposed a return to the immediacy, egalitarianism, and visionary ambitions of Blake and Whitman. However, it was not until he followed William Carlos Williams's urging that he write in the contemporary American idiom that Ginsberg found his own distinctive voice.

Ginsberg was also guided by Jack Kerouac's stance that writing as a spontaneous expression would only be weakened by revision. According to Ginsberg, Kerouac's "spontaneous bop prosody" required "an absolute, almost Zen-like complete absorption, *attention* to your own consciousness, to the act of writing."[1] Ginsberg also quotes William Blake in this respect: "First thought is best in Art, second in other matters."[2] The spontaneous approach to composition is reflected in Ginsberg's poems *Howl* and *Kaddish,* long established as classics of the period.

Of his use of personal materials, Ginsberg said, "There is a tradition of prose in America, including Thomas Wolfe and going through Kerouac, which is personal, in which the prose sentence is completely personal, comes from the writer's own person—his person defined as his body, his breathing rhythm, and his actual talk."[3] Walt Whitman had called for "Large conscious American Persons." Ginsberg responded by writing himself large on the American landscape while retaining an appealing modesty. The young boy in "To Aunt Rose" who stands "on the thin pedestal / of my legs in the bathroom—Museum of Newark" provides the characteristic Ginsberg persona, simultaneously revealing and vulnerable.

In 1974, at the urging of his spiritual leader, Chögyam Trungpa, Ginsberg and Anne Waldman founded the Jack Kerouac School of Disembodied Poetics at the Naropa Institute in Boulder, Colorado.

His early books, *Howl and Other Poems* (1956), *Kaddish and Other Poems* (1961), *Reality Sandwiches* (1963), and *Planet News* (1971) are among his most influential. He won the National Book Award for *The Fall of America* (1974) and was inducted into the Academy of American Poets and the National Institute of Arts and Letters in 1979. But his achievement ran far beyond the accomplishments of a literary career. His poetry was not only of its time; it helped to change the times.

1. *Allen Verbatim: Lectures on Poetry, Politics, Consciousness,* ed. Gordon Hill, New York, 1974, p. 147.   2. "Mind Writing Slogans," *Sulfur* 32 (Spring, 1993), p. 125.   3. *Allen Verbatim,* p. 153.

FROM *Howl*

For Carl Solomon

I

I saw the best minds of my generation destroyed by madness, starving
    hysterical naked,

dragging themselves through the negro streets at dawn looking for an angry
    fix,

angelheaded hipsters burning for the ancient heavenly connection to the
    starry dynamo in the machinery of night,

who poverty and tatters and hollow-eyed and high sat up smoking in the
    supernatural darkness of cold-water flats floating across the tops of
    cities contemplating jazz,

who bared their brains to Heaven under the El and saw Mohammedan angels
    staggering on tenement roofs illuminated,

who passed through universities with radiant cool eyes hallucinating Arkansas
    and Blake-light tragedy among the scholars of war,

who were expelled from the academies for crazy & publishing obscene odes
    on the windows of the skull,

who cowered in unshaven rooms in underwear, burning their money in
    wastebaskets and listening to the Terror through the wall,

who got busted in their pubic beards returning through Laredo with a belt of
    marijuana for New York,

who ate fire in paint hotels or drank turpentine in Paradise Alley, death, or
    purgatoried their torsos night after night

with dreams, with drugs, with waking nightmares, alcohol and cock and
    endless balls,

incomparable blind streets of shuddering cloud and lightning in the mind
    leaping toward poles of Canada & Paterson, illuminating all the
    motionless world of Time between,

Peyote solidities of halls, backyard green tree cemetery dawns, wine
    drunkenness over the roof tops, storefront boroughs of teahead
    joyride neon blinking traffic light, sun and moon and tree vibrations
    in the roaring winter dusks of Brooklyn, ashcan rantings and kind
    king light of mind,

who chained themselves to subways for the endless ride from Battery to holy
    Bronx on benzedrine until the noise of wheels and children brought
    them down shuddering mouth-wracked and battered bleak of brain all
    drained of brilliance in the drear light of Zoo,

who sank all night in submarine light of Bickford's floated out and sat through

the stale beer afternoon in desolate Fugazzi's, listening to the crack of
doom on the hydrogen jukebox,

who talked continuously seventy hours from park to pad to bar to Bellevue to
museum to the Brooklyn Bridge,

a lost battalion of platonic conversationalists jumping down the stoops off fire
escapes off windowsills off Empire State out of the moon,

yacketayakking screaming vomiting whispering facts and memories and
anecdotes and eyeball kicks and shocks of hospitals and jails and wars,

whole intellects disgorged in total recall for seven days and nights with brilliant
eyes, meat for the Synagogue cast on the pavement,

who vanished into nowhere Zen New Jersey leaving a trail of ambiguous
picture postcards of Atlantic City Hall,

suffering Eastern sweats and Tangerian bone-grindings and migraines of
China under junk-withdrawal in Newark's bleak furnished room,

who wandered around and around at midnight in the railroad yard wondering
where to go, and went, leaving no broken hearts,

who lit cigarettes in boxcars boxcars boxcars racketing through snow toward
lonesome farms in grandfather night,

who studied Plotinus Poe St. John of the Cross telepathy and bop kabbalah
because the cosmos instinctively vibrated at their feet in Kansas,

who loned it through the streets of Idaho seeking visionary indian angels who
were visionary indian angels,

who thought they were only mad when Baltimore gleamed in supernatural
ecstasy,

who jumped in limousines with the Chinaman of Oklahoma on the impulse of
winter midnight streetlight smalltown rain,

who lounged hungry and lonesome through Houston seeking jazz or sex or
soup, and followed the brilliant Spaniard to converse about America
and Eternity, a hopeless task, and so took ship to Africa,

who disappeared into the volcanoes of Mexico leaving behind nothing but
the shadow of dungarees and the lava and ash of poetry scattered in
fireplace Chicago,

who reappeared on the West Coast investigating the FBI in beards and
shorts with big pacifist eyes sexy in their dark skin passing out
incomprehensible leaflets,

who burned cigarette holes in their arms protesting the narcotic tobacco haze
of Capitalism,

who distributed Supercommunist pamphlets in Union Square weeping and
undressing while the sirens of Los Alamos wailed them down, and
wailed down Wall, and the Staten Island ferry also wailed,

who broke down crying in white gymnasiums naked and trembling before the
machinery of other skeletons,

who bit detectives in the neck and shrieked with delight in policecars for committing no crime but their own wild cooking pederasty and intoxication,

who howled on their knees in the subway and were dragged off the roof waving genitals and manuscripts,

who let themselves be fucked in the ass by saintly motorcyclists, and screamed with joy,

who blew and were blown by those human seraphim, the sailors, caresses of Atlantic and Caribbean love,

who balled in the morning in the evenings in rosegardens and the grass of public parks and cemeteries scattering their semen freely to whomever come who may,

who hiccuped endlessly trying to giggle but wound up with a sob behind a partition in a Turkish Bath when the blond & naked angel came to pierce them with a sword,

who lost their loveboys to the three old shrews of fate the one eyed shrew of the heterosexual dollar the one eyed shrew that winks out of the womb and the one eyed shrew that does nothing but sit on her ass and snip the intellectual golden threads of the craftsman's loom,

who copulated ecstatic and insatiate with a bottle of beer a sweetheart a package of cigarettes a candle and fell off the bed, and continued along the floor and down the hall and ended fainting on the wall with a vision of ultimate cunt and come eluding the last gyzym of consciousness,

who sweetened the snatches of a million girls trembling in the sunset, and were red eyed in the morning but prepared to sweeten the snatch of the sunrise, flashing buttocks under barns and naked in the lake,

who went out whoring through Colorado in myriad stolen night-cars, N.C., secret hero of these poems, cocksman and Adonis of Denver—joy to the memory of his innumerable lays of girls in empty lots & diner backyards, moviehouses' rickety rows, on mountaintops in caves or with gaunt waitresses in familiar roadside lonely petticoat upliftings & especially secret gas-station solipsisms of johns, & hometown alleys too,

who faded out in vast sordid movies, were shifted in dreams, woke on a sudden Manhattan, and picked themselves up out of basements hungover with heartless Tokay and horrors of Third Avenue iron dreams & stumbled to unemployment offices,

who walked all night with their shoes full of blood on the snowbank docks waiting for a door in the East River to open to a room full of steam-heat and opium,

who created great suicidal dramas on the apartment cliff-banks of the Hudson

under the wartime blue floodlight of the moon & their heads shall be
crowned with laurel in oblivion,

who ate the lamb stew of the imagination or digested the crab at the muddy
bottom of the rivers of Bowery,

who wept at the romance of the streets with their pushcarts full of onions and
bad music,

who sat in boxes breathing in the darkness under the bridge, and rose up to
build harpsichords in their lofts,

who coughed on the sixth floor of Harlem crowned with flame under the
tubercular sky surrounded by orange crates of theology,

who scribbled all night rocking and rolling over lofty incantations which in the
yellow morning were stanzas of gibberish,

who cooked rotten animals lung heart feet tail borsht & tortillas dreaming of
the pure vegetable kingdom,

who plunged themselves under meat trucks looking for an egg,

who threw their watches off the roof to cast their ballot for Eternity outside of
Time, & alarm clocks fell on their heads every day for the next decade,

who cut their wrists three times successively unsuccessfully, gave up and were
forced to open antique stores where they thought they were growing
old and cried,

who were burned alive in their innocent flannel suits on Madison Avenue amid
blasts of leaden verse & the tanked-up clatter of the iron regiments of
fashion & the nitroglycerine shrieks of the fairies of advertising & the
mustard gas of sinister intelligent editors, or were run down by the
drunken taxicabs of Absolute Reality,

who jumped off the Brooklyn Bridge this actually happened and walked away
unknown and forgotten into the ghostly daze of Chinatown soup
alleyways & firetrucks, not even one free beer,

who sang out of their windows in despair, fell out of the subway window,
jumped in the filthy Passaic, leaped on negroes, cried all over the
street, danced on broken wineglasses barefoot smashed phonograph
records of nostalgic European 1930s German jazz finished the whiskey
and threw up groaning into the bloody toilet, moans in their ears and
the blast of colossal steamwhistles,

who barreled down the highways of the past journeying to each other's hotrod-
Golgotha jail-solitude watch or Birmingham jazz incarnation,

who drove crosscountry seventytwo hours to find out if I had a vision or you
had a vision or he had a vision to find out Eternity,

who journeyed to Denver, who died in Denver, who came back to Denver
& waited in vain, who watched over Denver & brooded & loned in
Denver and finally went away to find out the Time, & now Denver is
lonesome for her heroes,

who fell on their knees in hopeless cathedrals praying for each other's salvation
and light and breasts, until the soul illuminated its hair for a second,

who crashed through their minds in jail waiting for impossible criminals with
golden heads and the charm of reality in their hearts who sang sweet
blues to Alcatraz,

who retired to Mexico to cultivate a habit, or Rocky Mount to tender Buddha
or Tangiers to boys or Southern Pacific to the black locomotive or
Harvard to Narcissus to Woodlawn to the daisychain or grave,

who demanded sanity trials accusing the radio of hypnotism & were left with
their insanity & their hands & a hung jury,

who threw potato salad at CCNY lecturers on Dadaism and subsequently
presented themselves on the granite steps of the madhouse with shaven
heads and harlequin speech of suicide, demanding instantaneous
lobotomy,

and who were given instead the concrete void of insulin Metrazol electricity
hydrotherapy psychotherapy pingpong & amnesia,

who in humorless protest overturned only one symbolic pingpong table,
resting briefly in catatonia,

returning years later truly bald except for a wig of blood, and tears and fingers,
to the visible madman doom of the wards of the madtowns of the
East,

Pilgrim State's Rockland's and Greystone's foetid halls, bickering with the
echoes of the soul, rocking and rolling in the midnight solitude-bench
dolmen-realms of love, dream of life a nightmare, bodies turned to
stone as heavy as the moon,

with mother finally °°°°°°, and the last fantastic book flung out of the tenement
window, and the last door closed at 4 A.M. and the last telephone
slammed at the wall in reply and the last furnished room emptied
down to the last piece of mental furniture, a yellow paper rose twisted
on a wire hanger in the closet, and even that imaginary, nothing but a
hopeful little bit of hallucination—

ah, Carl, while you are not safe I am not safe, and now you're really in the total
animal soup of time—

and who therefore ran through the icy streets obsessed with a sudden flash of
the alchemy of the use of the ellipsis catalog a variable measure and
the vibrating plane,

who dreamt and made incarnate gaps in Time & Space through images
juxtaposed, and trapped the archangel of the soul between 2 visual
images and joined the elemental verbs and set the noun and dash of
consciousness together jumping with sensation of Pater Omnipotens
Aeterne Deus

to recreate the syntax and measure of poor human prose and stand before
you speechless and intelligent and shaking with shame, rejected yet

confessing out the soul to conform to the rhythm of thought in his
    naked and endless head,

the madman bum and angel beat in Time, unknown, yet putting down here
    what might be left to say in time come after death,

and rose reincarnate in the ghostly clothes of jazz in the goldhorn shadow of
    the band and blew the suffering of America's naked mind for love into
    an eli eli lamma lamma sabacthani saxophone cry that shivered the
    cities down to the last radio

with the absolute heart of the poem of life butchered out of their own bodies
    good to eat a thousand years.

1956

A Supermarket in California

What thoughts I have of you tonight, Walt Whitman, for I walked
down the sidestreets under the trees with a headache self-conscious looking
at the full moon.

In my hungry fatigue, and shopping for images, I went into the neon
fruit supermarket, dreaming of your enumerations!

What peaches and what penumbras! Whole families shopping at night!
Aisles full of husbands! Wives in the avocados, babies in the tomatoes!—and
you, García Lorca, what were you doing down by the watermelons?

I saw you, Walt Whitman, childless, lonely old grubber, poking among
the meats in the refrigerator and eyeing the grocery boys.

I heard you asking questions of each: Who killed the pork chops?
What price bananas? Are you my Angel?

I wandered in and out of the brilliant stacks of cans following you, and
followed in my imagination by the store detective.

We strode down the open corridors together in our solitary fancy tasting
artichokes, possessing every frozen delicacy, and never passing the cashier.

Where are we going, Walt Whitman? The doors close in an hour.
Which way does your beard point tonight?

(I touch your book and dream of our odyssey in the supermarket and
feel absurd.)

Will we walk all night through solitary streets? The trees add shade to
shade, lights out in the houses, we'll both be lonely.

Will we stroll dreaming of the lost America of love past blue automobiles
in driveways, home to our silent cottage?

Ah, dear father, graybeard, lonely old courage-teacher, what America did you have when Charon quit poling his ferry and you got out on a smoking bank and stood watching the boat disappear on the black waters of Lethe?

Berkeley, 1955   1956

To Aunt Rose

Aunt Rose—now—might I see you
with your thin face and buck tooth smile and pain
            of rheumatism—and a long black heavy shoe
                for your bony left leg
limping down the long hall in Newark on the running carpet
            past the black grand piano
                in the day room
                    where the parties were
        and I sang Spanish loyalist songs
            in a high squeaky voice
                (hysterical) the committee listening
            while you limped around the room
                collected the money—
Aunt Honey, Uncle Sam, a stranger with a cloth arm
        in his pocket
            and huge young bald head
                of Abraham Lincoln Brigade

—your long sad face
        your tears of sexual frustration
            (what smothered sobs and bony hips
                under the pillows of Osborne Terrace)
—the time I stood on the toilet seat naked
        and you powdered my thighs with calamine
            against the poison ivy—my tender
                and shamed first black curled hairs
    what were you thinking in secret heart then
                knowing me a man already—
    and I an ignorant girl of family silence on the thin pedestal
            of my legs in the bathroom—Museum of Newark.

Aunt Rose
Hitler is dead, Hitler is in Eternity; Hitler is with
        Tamburlane and Emily Brontë

Though I see you walking still, a ghost on Osborne Terrace
    down the long dark hall to the front door
  limping a little with a pinched smile
    in what must have been a silken
        flower dress
  welcoming my father, the Poet, on his visit to Newark
    —see you arriving in the living room
      dancing on your crippled leg
    and clapping hands his book
      had been accepted by Liveright

Hitler is dead and Liveright's gone out of business
The Attic of the Past and *Everlasting Minute* are out of print
    Uncle Harry sold his last silk stocking
    Claire quit interpretive dancing school
      Buba sits a wrinkled monument in Old
        Ladies Home blinking at new babies

last time I saw you was the hospital
    pale skull protruding under ashen skin
      blue veined unconscious girl
        in an oxygen tent
    the war in Spain has ended long ago
      Aunt Rose
Paris, June 1958

                                        1961

First Party at Ken Kesey's with Hell's Angels

Cool black night thru the redwoods
cars parked outside in shade
behind the gate, stars dim above
the ravine, a fire burning by the side
porch and a few tired souls hunched over
in black leather jackets. In the huge
wooden house, a yellow chandelier
at 3 A.M. the blast of loudspeakers
hi-fi Rolling Stones Ray Charles Beatles
Jumping Joe Jackson and twenty youths
dancing to the vibration thru the floor,
a little weed in the bathroom, girls in scarlet
tights, one muscular smooth skinned man
sweating dancing for hours, beer cans

bent littering the yard, a hanged man
sculpture dangling from a high creek branch,
children sleeping softly in their bedroom bunks.
And 4 police cars parked outside the painted
gate, red lights revolving in the leaves.

December 1965   1971

On Neal's Ashes

Delicate eyes that blinked blue Rockies all ash
nipples, Ribs I touched w/my thumb are ash
mouth my tongue touched once or twice all ash
bony cheeks soft on my belly are cinder, ash
earlobes & eyelids, youthful cock tip, curly pubis
breast warmth, man palm, high school thigh,
baseball bicept arm, asshole anneal'd to silken skin
                all ashes, all ashes again.

August 1968   1971

Robert Creeley ─────────────────────
1926–2005

Born in Arlington, Massachusetts, Robert Creeley attended Harvard but dropped out before getting his degree. After living in the south of France in Aix-en-Provence and Majorca, Spain, where he founded the Divers Press, he joined the faculty of Black Mountain College in 1954 at the invitation of Charles Olson. There he founded the *Black Mountain Review*. While Creeley left the college itself in 1955, his influence on Black Mountain poetics has been significant. Associated with the State University of New York at Buffalo since 1966, he was named poet laureate of the state of New York in 1992. In 1991, he joined colleagues Susan Howe, Charles Bernstein, Raymond Federman, Robert Bertholf, and Dennis Tedlock in founding the Poetics Program at Buffalo. There was, however, a sense that Creeley remained independent of the diminishments of academic life.

Creeley's work, which has been described as "Minimus" to Charles Olson's "Maximus," is lyrical and romantic in the tradition of the troubadours even at the same time as it is experimental in syntax. William Carlos Williams, whose poetry was the primary influence on Creeley's work, wrote that Creeley has "the subtlest feeling for the measure that I encounter anywhere except in the verses of Ezra Pound."[1] In Creeley's view the poem does not point toward anything outside itself but is a self-sufficient and sinuous gesture. In his essay "To Define," he rejects poetry as a "*descriptive* act, I mean any act which leaves the attention outside the poem."[2]

His poetry explores the immediate sensation but in language that is often oblique and evocative rather than direct and descriptive; the hesitation offered by his short lines and his use of enjambment suggest both the graceful stumbles of everyday speech and the lyrical cadence of song. In the tradition of the objectivists, Creeley scraps nineteenth-century "symbolism," as the poet Louis Zukofsky wrote, for the actual; it is Creeley's "*thoughtfulness* that makes the shape—the metaphysics of loneliness."[3]

When Creeley died at age seventy-eight from the complications of pneumonia, the innovative poetry community felt a great loss, as of a father figure. He had been in many ways the most reliable link to the modernist past, and his generosity to young poets was legendary. Although he was awarded the Bollingen Prize and elected to the Academy of Arts and Letters, he was never awarded a major publication prize such as the National Book Award and Pulitzer Prize. His poetry collection *For Love* (1962) stands with Ginsberg's *Howl* and O'Hara's *Lunch Poems* as one of the defining volumes of the postwar period.

1. Letter to Creeley, January 18, 1960, quoted in *Robert Creeley's Life and Work: A Sense of Increment,* ed. John Wilson, Ann Arbor, 1987, p. 30.   2. *A Quick Graph: Collected Notes and Essays,* ed. Donald Allen, San Francisco, p. 23.   3. Letter to Creeley, October 11, 1955, in *Robert Creeley's Life and Work,* p. 32.

After Lorca

for M. Marti

The church is a business, and the rich
are the business men.
When they pull on the bells, the
poor come piling in and when a poor man dies, he has a wooden
cross, and they rush through the ceremony.

But when a rich man dies, they
drag out the Sacrament
and a golden Cross, and go *doucement, doucement*
to the cemetery.

And the poor love it
and think it's crazy.

1962

A Form of Women

I have come far enough
from where I was not before
to have seen the things
looking in at me through the open door

and have walked tonight
by myself
to see the moonlight
and see it as trees

and shapes more fearful
because I feared
what I did not know
but have wanted to know.

My face is my own, I thought.
But you have seen it
turn into a thousand years.
I watched you cry.

I could not touch you.
I wanted very much to

touch you
but could not.

If it is dark
when this is given to you,
have care for its content
when the moon shines.

My face is my own.
My hands are my own.
My mouth is my own
but I am not.

Moon, moon,
when you leave me alone
all the darkness is
an utter blackness,

a pit of fear,
a stench,
hands unreasonable
never to touch.

But I love you.
Do you love me.
What to say
when you see me.

1962

The Rain

All night the sound had
come back again,
and again falls
this quiet, persistent rain.

What am I to myself
that must be remembered,
insisted upon
so often? Is it

that never the ease,
even the hardness,

of rain falling
will have for me

something other than this,
something not so insistent—
am I to be locked in this
final uneasiness.

Love, if you love me,
lie next to me.
Be for me, like rain,
the getting out

of the tiredness, the fatuousness, the semi-
lust of intentional indifference.
Be wet
with a decent happiness.

1962

For Love

for Bobbie

Yesterday I wanted to
speak of it, that sense above
the others to me
important because all

that I know derives
from what it teaches me.
Today, what is it that
is finally so helpless,

different, despairs of its own
statement, wants to
turn away, endlessly
to turn away.

If the moon did not . . .
no, if you did not
I wouldn't either, but
what would I not

do, what prevention, what
thing so quickly stopped.
That is love yesterday
or tomorrow, not

now. Can I eat
what you give me. I
have not earned it. Must
I think of everything

as earned. Now love also
becomes a reward so
remote from me I have
only made it with my mind.

Here is tedium,
despair, a painful
sense of isolation and
whimsical if pompous

self-regard. But that image
is only of the mind's
vague structure, vague to me
because it is my own.

Love, what do I think
to say. I cannot say it.
What have you become to ask,
what have I made you into,

companion, good company,
crossed legs with skirt, or
soft body under
the bones of the bed.

Nothing says anything
but that which it wishes
would come true, fears
what else might happen in

some other place, some
other time not this one.

A voice in my place, an
echo of that only in yours.

Let me stumble into
not the confession but
the obsession I begin with
now. For you

also (also)
some time beyond place, or
place beyond time, no
mind left to

say anything at all,
that face gone, now.
Into the company of love
it all returns.

1962

The Language

Locate *I*
love you some-
where in

teeth and
eyes, bite
it but

take care not
to hurt, you
want so

much so
little. Words
say everything.

I
love you
again,

then what
is emptiness
for. To

fill, fill.
I heard words
and words full

of holes
aching. Speech
is a mouth.

1967

The Window

Position is where you
put it, where it is,
did you, for example, that

large tank there, silvered,
with the white church along-
side, lift

all that, to what
purpose? How
heavy the slow

world is with
everything put
in place. Some

man walks by, a
car beside him on
the dropped

road, a leaf of
yellow color is
going to

fall. It
all drops into
place. My

face is heavy
with the sight. I can
feel my eye breaking.

1967

The World

I wanted so ably
to reassure you, I wanted
the man you took to be me,

to comfort you, and got
up, and went to the window,
pushed back, as you asked me to,

the curtain, to see
the outline of the trees
in the night outside.

The light, love,
the light we felt then,
greyly, was it, that

came in, on us, not
merely my hands or yours,
or a wetness so comfortable,

but in the dark then
as you slept, the grey
figure came so close

and leaned over,
between us, as you
slept, restless, and

my own face had to
see it, and be seen by it,
the man it was, your

grey lost tired bewildered
brother, unused, untaken—
hated by love, and dead,

but not dead, for an
instant, saw me, myself
the intruder, as he was not.

I tried to say, it is
all right, she is
happy, you are no longer

needed. I said,
he is dead, and he
went as you shifted

and woke, at first afraid,
then knew by my own knowing
what had happened—

and the light then
of the sun coming
for another morning
in the world.

1967

Self-Portrait

He wants to be
a brutal old man,
an aggressive old man,
as dull, as brutal
as the emptiness around him,

He doesn't want compromise,
nor to be ever nice
to anyone. Just mean,
and final in his brutal,
his total, rejection of it all.

He tried the sweet,
the gentle, the "oh,
let's hold hands together"
and it was awful,
dull, brutally inconsequential.

Now he'll stand on
his own dwindling legs.

His arms, his skin,
shrink daily. And
he loves, but hates equally.

1983

Bresson's Movies

A movie of Robert
Bresson's showed a yacht,
at evening on the Seine,
all its lights on, watched

by two young, seemingly
poor people, on a bridge adjacent,
the classic boy and girl
of the story, any one

one cares to tell. So
years pass, of course, but
I identified with the young,
embittered Frenchman,

knew his almost complacent
anguish and the distance
he felt from his girl.
Yet another film

of Bresson's has the
aging Lancelot with his
awkward armor standing
in a woods, of small trees,

dazed, bleeding, both he
and his horse are,
trying to get back to
the castle, itself of

no great size. It
moved me, that
life was after all
like that. You are

in love. You stand
in the woods, with
a horse, bleeding.
The story is true.

1983

When I think

When I think of where I've come from
or even try to measure as any kind of
distance those places, all the various
people, and all the ways in which I re-
member them, so that even the skin I
touched or was myself fact of, inside,
could see through like a hole in the wall
or listen to, it must have been, to what
was going on in there, even if I was still
too dumb to know anything—When I think
of the miles and miles of roads, of meals,
of telephone wires even, or even of water
poured out in endless streams down streaks
of black sky or the dirt roads washed clean,
or myriad, salty tears and suddenly it's spring
again, or it was—Even when I think again of
all those I treated so poorly, names, places,
their waiting uselessly for me in the rain and
I never came, was never really there at all,
was moving so confusedly, so fast, so driven
like a car along some empty highway passing,
passing other cars—When I try to think of
things, of what's happened, of what a life is
and was, my life, when I wonder what it meant,
the sad days passing, the continuing, echoing deaths,
all the painful, belligerent news, and the dog still
waiting to be fed, the closeness of you sleeping, voices,
presences, of children, of our own grown children,
the shining, bright sun, the smell of the air just now,
each physical moment, passing, *passing*, it's what
it always is or ever was, just then, just there.

2006

Paul Blackburn
1926–1971

Born in St. Albans, Vermont, Paul Blackburn was raised by his grandmother until age fourteen, when he moved to New York City to live with his mother, the poet Frances Frost. As a student at the University of Wisconsin, he began corresponding with Ezra Pound, who was then institutionalized at St. Elizabeth's Hospital in Washington, D.C. In 1951 Pound encouraged him to make the acquaintance of Robert Creeley, who introduced him to Charles Olson and other poets.

Though often associated with Black Mountain poetics, Blackburn actively resisted categorization, taking inspiration from the troubadour poets of twelfth-century Provence, whom he translated into English, with the help of a 1967 Guggenheim Fellowship; García Lorca's *Obras Completas* and European experimental poetry in general; and the emerging Beat scene in New York City in the early sixties. Blackburn founded several reading series on the Lower East Side out of which grew the Poetry Project at St. Mark's Church.

In a 1954 statement, Blackburn wrote:

> Personally, I affirm two things:
>   the possibility of warmth & contact
>   in the human relationship :
> as juxtaposed against the materialistic pig of a technological world,
> where relationships are only 'useful' i.e., exploited, either
> psychologically or materially.
>
>   2⁰, the possibility of s o n g
> within that world: which is like saying 'yes' to sunlight.[1]

The scholar M. L. Rosenthal wrote of a Blackburn poem, "The Watchers": "The ear at work here is remarkably attuned to both sophistical and ordinary speech. Of all the successors to Pound and Williams, Blackburn comes closest to their ability to mix the colloquial and formal, and to their instinct for melodic patterning and for volatile improvisational immediacy."[2]

His books include *Brooklyn-Manhattan Transit* (1960), *The Nets* (1961), *The Cities* (1967), *In. On. Or About the Premises* (1968), and the posthumous volumes *Early Selected Y Mas* (1972), *Halfway Down the Coast* (1975), *The Journals* (1977), and *The Parallel Voyages* (1987). All of these are represented in *The Collected Poems of Paul Blackburn* (1985).

1. *The Parallel Voyages*, 1987, quoted in *Jacket* 12, http://jacketmagazne.com/12/blac-stat .html.   2. "Foreword," *The Selected Poems of Paul Blackburn*, New York, 1989, p. viii.

Brooklyn Narcissus

Straight rye whiskey, 100 proof
you need a better friend?
Yes.   Myself.

The lights
the lights
the lonely   lovely   fucking   lights
and the bridge on a rainy Tuesday night
Blue/green double-stars   the line
that is the drive and on the dark alive
gleaming river
Xmas trees of tugs scream and struggle

        Midnite

Drops on the train window wobble . stream
              My trouble
                    is
  it is her fate to never learn to make
                    anything grow
                be born or stay
Harbor beginnings and that other gleam . The train
is full of long/way/home and holding lovers whose
        flesh I would exchange for mine
        The rain, R.F.,

        sweeps the river as the bridges sweep
        Nemesis is thumping down the line
        But I have premises to keep
        & local stops before I sleep
        & local stops before I sleep
                            The cree-
                            ping train
                            joggles
                            rocks across
                            I hear
          the waves below lap against the piles, a pier
                        from which ships go
                                to Mexico
a sign which reads

PACE O MIO DIO

    oil

        "The flowers died when you went away"

Manhattan Bridge
a bridge between
we state, one life and the next, we state
is better so
is no
    backwater, flows
           between us is
our span our bridge our
naked eyes
open here
see
bridging whatever impossibility . . . PACE!

PACE O MIO DIO

    oil

        "The flowers died . . ."
        Of course they did

Not that I was a green thing in the house

        I was once.
        No matter.

The clatter of cars over the span, the track
      the spur
the rusty dead/pan ends of space
    of grease

We enter the tunnel.

The dirty window gives me back my face

1958   1960

El Camino Verde

The green road lies this way.
I take the road of sand.

One way the sun burns hottest, no relief, the other
sun (the same) is filtered thru
        leaves that cast obscene
        beautiful patterns
        on roads and walls . And

        the wind blows all day.
Hot . sirocco, a chain
of hot wind rattles across
high over the mountains
rushes down from the peaks to the sea
laving men's bodies in the fields between
        Days when
the serpent of wind plucks and twists the harp of the sun.
        In the green road, pale
        gray-green of olives, olive-wood twisted
        under the burning wind, the wet
        heat of an armpit, but in the mouth

this other road. And the dry heat of the mouth is the pitiful
        possibility
of finding a flower in the dust.   Sanity . See
        there, the white
        wing of a gull over blindness of water,
the black black wing of a hawk over stretches of forest .
        Wish
to hold the mind clear in the dark honey of evening light, think
of a spring
in an orchard
in flower
in soft sun amid ruins, down there
a small palm offers its leaves to the wind .
        On the mountain, olive,
        o, live wood,
its flawless curve hangs from the slope.

Hot . sirocco . covers everything
and everyone, all day, it blows all day as if
this were choice, as if
the earth were anything else but
what it is, a hell. But
blind, bland, blend the flesh.
Mix the naked foot with the sand that caresses it, mix
with the rock that tears it,   enter
                          the hot world.

Cave of the winds .
What cave?   the
                          reaches of Africa
                          where an actual
                              measure
                                  exists.

1955   1961

Park Poem

From the first shock of leaves their alliance
with love, how is it?

Pages we write and tear
Someone in a swagger coat sits and waits on a hill

It is not spring, may-
be it is never spring

    maybe it is the hurt end of summer
    the first tender autumn air
    fall's first cool rain over the park
    and these people walking thru it

The girl thinking:
                      life is these pronouns
the man : to ask / to respond / to accept
                      bird-life . reindeer-death
                      Life is all verbs, vowels and verbs
They both get wet

If it is love, it is to make
love, or let be
'To create the situation / is love
and to avoid it, this is also
Love'
as any care of awareness, any
other awareness might might

have been
but is now

hot flesh
socking it into hot flesh
until reindeer-life   /   bird-death

You are running, see?
you are running down slope across this field
I am running too
to catch you round

This rain is yours
it falls on us
we fall on one another

Belong to the moon
we do not see

It is wet and cool
bruises our skin
might have been
care and avoidance
but we run . run

to prepare
love later

1961

1967

John Ashbery ━━━━━━━━━━━━━━━━━━━━━━━━━
b. 1927

With the publication in 1975 of *Self-Portrait in a Convex Mirror,* which won both the National Book Award and the Pulitzer Prize, John Ashbery was recognized as the leading poet of his generation. This critical acceptance was somewhat unexpected, given the experimental nature of his work, most radically expressed in *The Tennis Court Oath* (1962). Ashbery's work draws from a poetics of "indeterminacy," which favors the process of writing over the drawing of conclusions; while his work is lyrical and meditative, it resists closure and narrative. Not surprisingly, his chosen form is the long poem.

One of his primary devices, periphrasis (roundabout speech or circumlocution), is consistent with the unusual length of some of his work. As he announces in an early long poem, "The Skaters" (1966), he intends to push poetry past the "dismal two-note theme / Of some sodden 'dump' or lament" into a fuller kind of reference. Critic and poet David Lehman writes that the subject of "The Skaters" is "the unbegun journey to the unattainable place," a phrase appropriate to Ashbery's work in general.[1] Ashbery's long poem *Self-Portrait in a Convex Mirror,* based on Parmigianino's painting of the same title, displays the self-reflexiveness of his poetry. But Ashbery avoids narcissism by multiplying and confusing the perspective; it is the movement of consciousness rather than the narrow concerns of self that is finally depicted.

Like other poets of the New York School, Ashbery admires French avant-garde writing, in particular the novels of Raymond Roussel, author of *Locus Solus* and *Impressions of Africa.* In *How I Wrote Certain of My Books,* Roussel declared that his novels were derived from elaborate sets of puns—the conjunction, for example, of *pillard* (plunderer) and *billard* (billiard table).[2] Ashbery shares Roussel's delight in artifice; as an eccentric formalist, his love of unusual poetic forms such as the sestina, pantoum, and villanelle single-handedly made these minor forms attractive to some younger New York School poets. Ashbery also expresses a great fondness for *Hebdomeros,* the dreamlike novel by the painter Giorgio de Chirico. His literary forebears in the English language include Laura Riding Jackson, the modernist poet who abandoned her highly original poetry of abstraction for the study of linguistics; Wallace Stevens, whom Ashbery succeeds as a major poet of romantic epistemology; and W. H. Auden, who selected Ashbery's first book, *Some Trees* (1956), for publication in the Yale Series of Younger Poets and whose love of formalism Ashbery shares.

Perhaps because of his commitment to eccentric letters, Ashbery's work is often considered difficult. However, in its inconclusiveness and linguistic play, Ashbery's poetry captures the philosophical spirit of the age, as otherwise reflected in the thought of Ludwig Wittgenstein and Jacques Derrida.

Among his many other books are *Rivers and Mountains* (1966), *The Double Dream of Spring* (1970); the widely admired prose meditation, *Three Poems* (1972); *Houseboat Days* (1977); *Shadow Train* (1981); *A Wave* (1984); *April Galleons* (1987), *Wakefulness* (1998); the book-length poem, *Girls on the Run* (1999), inspired by the work of Henry Darger; *Where Shall I Wander* (2005); *A Worldly Country* (2007); and *Planisphere* (2009). Ashbery was formerly editor of *ARTnews* and gave the distinguished Charles Eliot Norton series of lectures at Harvard in 1989–1990. His *Selected Prose* was published in 2005.

He is currently professor of literature at Bard College. Among his numerous honors, Ashbery was awarded the National Book Foundation's 2011 Medal for Distinguished Contribution to American Letters.

1. "The Shield of a Greeting," in *Beyond Amazement: New Essays on John Ashbery*, ed. David Lehman, Ithaca, 1980, p. 123.   2. Trans. Trevor Winkfield, New York, 1975, p. 3.

The Picture of Little J. A. in a Prospect of Flowers

He was spoilt from childhood
by the future, which he mastered
rather early and apparently
without great difficulty.
—Boris Pasternak

I

Darkness falls like a wet sponge
And Dick gives Genevieve a swift punch
In the pajamas. "Aroint thee, witch."

Her tongue from previous ecstasy
Releases thoughts like little hats.

"He clap'd me first during the eclipse.
Afterwards I noted his manner
Much altered. But he sending
At that time certain handsome jewels
I durst not seem to take offence."

In a far recess of summer
Monks are playing soccer.

II

So far is goodness a mere memory
Or naming of recent scenes of badness
That even these lives, children,
You may pass through to be blessed,
So fair does each invent his virtue.

And coming from a white world, music
Will sparkle at the lips of many who are
Beloved. Then these, as dirty handmaidens
To some transparent witch, will dream
Of a white hero's subtle wooing,
And time shall force a gift on each.

That beggar to whom you gave no cent
Striped the night with his strange descant.

III

Yet I cannot escape the picture
Of my small self in that bank of flowers:
My head among the blazing phlox
Seemed a pale and gigantic fungus.
I had a hard stare, accepting

Everything, taking nothing,
As though the rolled-up future might stink
As loud as stood the sick moment
The shutter clicked. Though I was wrong,
Still, as the loveliest feelings

Must soon find words, and these, yes,
Displace them, so I am not wrong
In calling this comic version of myself
The true one. For as change is horror,
Virtue is really stubbornness

And only in the light of lost words
Can we imagine our rewards.

1956

"How Much Longer Will I Be Able to Inhabit the Divine Sepulcher . . ."

How much longer will I be able to inhabit the divine sepulcher
Of life, my great love? Do dolphins plunge bottomward
To find the light? Or is it rock
That is searched? Unrelentingly? Huh. And if some day

Men with orange shovels come to break open the rock
Which encases me, what about the light that comes in then?
What about the smell of the light?
What about the moss?

In pilgrim times he wounded me
Since then I only lie
My bed of light is a furnace choking me
With hell (and sometimes I hear salt water dripping).

I mean it—because I'm one of the few
To have held my breath under the house. I'll trade
One red sucker for two blue ones. I'm
Named Tom. The

Light bounces off mossy rocks down to me
In this glen (the neat villa! which
When he'd had he would not had he of
And jests under the smarting of privet

Which on hot spring nights perfumes the empty rooms
With the smell of sperm flushed down toilets
On hot summer afternoons within sight of the sea.
If you knew why then professor) reads

To his friends: Drink to me only with
And the reader is carried away
By a great shadow under the sea.
Behind the steering wheel

The boy took out his own forehead.
His girlfriend's head was a green bag
Of narcissus stems. "OK you win
But meet me anyway at Cohen's Drug Store

In 22 minutes." What a marvel is ancient man!
Under the tulip roots he has figured out a way to be a religious animal
And would be a mathematician. But where in unsuitable heaven
Can he get the heat that will make him grow?

For he needs something or will forever remain a dwarf,
Though a perfect one, and possessing a normal-sized brain
But he has got to be released by giants from things.
And as the plant grows older it realizes it will never be a tree,

Will probably always be haunted by a bee
And cultivates stupid impressions
So as not to become part of the dirt. The dirt
Is mounting like a sea. And we say goodbye

Shaking hands in front of the crashing of the waves
That give our words lonesomeness, and make these flabby hands seem
    ours—
Hands that are always writing things
On mirrors for people to see later—

Do you want them to water
Plant, tear listlessly among the exchangeable ivy—
Carrying food to mouth, touching genitals—
But no doubt you have understood

It all now and I am a fool. It remains
For me to get better, and to understand you so
Like a chair-sized man. Boots
Were heard on the floor above. In the garden the sunlight was still purple

But what buzzed in it had changed slightly
But not forever . . . but casting its shadow
On sticks, and looking around for an opening in the air, was quite as if it
    had never refused to exist differently. Guys
In the yard handled the belt he had made

Stars
Painted the garage roof crimson and black
He is not a man
Who can read these signs . . . his bones were stays . . .

And even refused to live
In a world and refunded the hiss

Of all that exists terribly near us
Like you, my love, and light.

For what is obedience but the air around us
To the house? For which the federal men came
In a minute after the sidewalk
Had taken you home? ("Latin . . . blossom . . .")

After which you led me to water
And bade me drink, which I did, owing to your kindness.
You would not let me out for two days and three nights,
Bringing me books bound in wild thyme and scented wild grasses

As if reading had any interest for me, you . . .
Now you are laughing.
Darkness interrupts my story.
Turn on the light.

Meanwhile what am I going to do?
I am growing up again, in school, the crisis will be very soon.
And you twist the darkness in your fingers, you
Who are slightly older . . .

Who are you, anyway?
And it is the color of sand,
The darkness, as it sifts through your hand
Because what does anything mean,

The ivy and the sand? That boat
Pulled up on the shore? Am I wonder,
Strategically, and in the light
Of the long sepulcher that hid death and hides me?

1962

FROM *The Skaters*

I

These decibels
Are a kind of flagellation, an entity of sound
Into which being enters, and is apart.

Their colors on a warm February day
Make for masses of inertia, and hips
Prod out of the violet-seeming into a new kind
Of demand that stumps the absolute because not new
In the sense of the next one in an infinite series
But, as it were, pre-existing or pre-seeming in
Such a way as to contrast funnily with the unexpectedness
And somehow push us all into perdition.

Here a scarf flies, there an excited call is heard.

The answer is that it is novelty
That guides these swift blades o'er the ice
Projects into a finer expression (but at the expense
Of energy) the profile I cannot remember.
Colors slip away from and chide us. The human mind
Cannot retain anything except perhaps the dismal two-note theme
Of some sodden "dump" or lament.

But the water surface ripples, the whole light changes.

We children are ashamed of our bodies
But we laugh and, demanded, talk of sex again
And all is well. The waves of morning harshness
Float away like coal-gas into the sky.
But how much survives? How much of any one of us survives?
The articles we'd collect—stamps of the colonies
With greasy cancellation marks, mauve, magenta and chocolate,
Or funny-looking dogs we'd see in the street, or bright remarks.
One collects bullets. An Indianapolis, Indiana man collects
    slingshots of all epochs, and so on.

Subtracted from our collections, though, these go on a little
    while, collecting aimlessly. We still support them.
But so little energy they have! And up the swollen sands
Staggers the darkness fiend, with the storm fiend close behind him!

True, melodious tolling does go on in that awful pandemonium,
Certain resonances are not utterly displeasing to the
    terrified eardrum.
Some paroxysms are dinning of tambourine, others suggest piano
    room or organ loft
For the most dissonant night charms us, even after death. This, after all,

may be happiness: tuba notes awash on the great flood, ruptures
  of xylophone, violins, limpets, grace-notes, the musical instrument
  called serpent, viola da gambas, aeolian harps, clavicles, pinball
  machines, electric drills, que sais-je encore!
The performance has rapidly reached your ear; silent and tearstained, in
  the post-mortem shock, you stand listening, awash
With memories of hair in particular, part of the welling that is you,
The gurgling of harp, cymbal, glockenspiel, triangle, temple block,
  English horn and metronome! And still no presentiment, no
  feeling of pain before or after.
The passage sustains, does not give. And you have come far indeed.

Yet to go from "not interesting" to "old and uninteresting,"
To be surrounded by friends, though late in life,
To hear the wings of the spirit, though far. . . .
Why do I hurriedly undrown myself to cut you down?
"I am yesterday," and my fault is eternal.
I do not expect constant attendance, knowing myself
  insufficient for your present demands
And I have a dim intuition that I am that other "I" with which
  we began.
My cheeks as blank walls to your tears and eagerness
Fondling that other, as though you had let him get away forever.

The evidence of the visual henceforth replaced
By the great shadow of trees falling over life.

A child's devotion
To this normal, shapeless entity . . .

Forgotten as the words fly briskly across, each time
Bringing down meaning as snow from a low sky, or rabbits
  flushed from a wood.
How strange that the narrow perspective lines
Always seem to meet, although parallel, and that an insane
  ghost could do this,
Could make the house seem so much farther in the distance, as
It seemed to the horse, dragging the sledge of a perspective line.
Dim banners in the distance, to die. . . . And nothing put to
  rights. The pigs in their cages

And so much snow, but it is to be littered with waste and ashes
So that cathedrals may grow. Out of this spring builds a tolerable

Affair of brushwood, the sea is felt behind oak wands,
      noiselessly pouring.
Spring with its promise of winter, and the black ivy once again
On the porch, its yellow perspective bands in place
And the horse nears them and weeps.

So much has passed through my mind this morning
That I can give you but a dim account of it:
It is already after lunch, the men are returning to their
      positions around the cement mixer
And I try to sort out what has happened to me. The bundle
      of Gerard's letters,
And that awful bit of news buried on the back page of
      yesterday's paper.
Then the news of you this morning, in the snow.
      Sometimes the interval
Of bad news is so brisk that . . . And the human brain, with its
      tray of images
Seems a sorcerer's magic lantern, projecting black and orange
      cellophane shadows
On the distance of my hand . . . The very reaction's puny,
And when we seek to move around, wondering what our position
      is now, what the arm of that chair.

A great wind lifted these cardboard panels
Horizontal in the air. At once the perspective with the horse
Disappeared in a *bigarrure* of squiggly lines. The image with
      the crocodile in it became no longer apparent.

Thus a great wind cleanses, as a new ruler
Edits new laws, sweeping the very breath of the streets
Into posterior trash. The films have changed—
The great titles on the scalloped awning have turned dry and
      blight-colored.
No wind that does not penetrate a man's house, into the very
      bowels of the furnace,
Scratching in dust a name on the mirror—say, and what
      about letters,
The dried grasses, fruits of the winter—gosh! Everything
      is trash!
The wind points to the advantages of decay
At the same time as removing them far from the sight of men.

The regent of the winds, Aeolus, is a symbol for all
    earthly potentates
Since holding this sickening, festering process by which
    we are cleansed
Of afterthought.
                A girl slowly descended the line of steps.

The wind and treason are partners, turning secrets over to
    the military police.

Lengthening arches. The intensity of minor acts.
    As skaters elaborate their distances,
Taking a separate line to its end. Returning to the mass,
    they join each other
Blotted in an incredible mess of dark colors, and again
    reappearing to take the theme
Some little distance, like fishing boats developing from the
    land different parabolas,
Taking the exquisite theme far, into farness, to Land's End,
    to the ends of the earth!

But the livery of the year, the changing air
Bring each to fulfillment. Leaving phrases unfinished,
Gestures half-sketched against woodsmoke. The abundant sap
Oozes in girls' throats, the sticky words, half-uttered,
    unwished for,
A blanket disbelief, quickly supplanted by idle questions
    that fade in turn.
Slowly the mood turns to look at itself as some urchin
Forgotten by the roadside. New schemes are got up, new taxes,
Earthworks. And the hour becomes light again.
Girls wake up in it.

It is best to remain indoors. Because there is error
In so much precision. As flames are fanned, wishful
    thinking arises
Bearing its own prophets, its pointed ignoring.
    And just as a desire
Settles down at the end of a long spring day, over heather
    and watered shoot and dried rush field,
So error is plaited into desires not yet born.

Therefore the post must be resumed (is being falsified
To be forever involved, tragically, with one's own image?).
The studio light suddenly invaded the long
        casement—values were what
She knows now. But the floor is being slowly pulled apart
Like straw under those limpid feet.
And Helga, in the minuscule apartment in Jersey City
Is reacting violet to the same kind of dress, is drawing death
Again in blossoms against the reactionary fire . . . pulsing
And knowing nothing to superb lambent distances that intercalate
This city. Is the death of the cube repeated. Or in the
        musical album.

It is time now for a general understanding of
The meaning of all this. The meaning of Helga, importance
        of the setting, etc.
A description of the blues. Labels on bottles
And all kinds of discarded objects that ought to be described.
But can one ever be sure of which ones?
Isn't this a death-trap, wanting to put too much in
So the floor sags, as under the weight of a piano,
        or a piano-legged girl
And the whole house of cards comes dinning down around
        one's ears!

But this is an important aspect of the question
Which I am not ready to discuss, am not at all ready to,
This leaving-out business. On it hinges the very importance
        of what's novel
Or autocratic, or dense or silly. It is as well to call attention
To it by exaggeration, perhaps. But calling attention
Isn't the same thing as explaining, and as I said I am not ready
To line phrases with the costly stuff of explanation, and shall not,
Will not do so for the moment. Except to say that the carnivorous
Way of these lines is to devour their own nature, leaving
Nothing but a bitter impression of absence, which as we know
        involves presence, but still.
Nevertheless these are fundamental absences, struggling to
        get up and be off themselves.

This, thus is a portion of the subject of this poem
Which is in the form of falling snow:

That is, the individual flakes are not essential to the
      importance of the whole's becoming so much of a truism
That their importance is again called in question, to be
      denied further out, and again and again like this.
Hence, neither the importance of the individual flake,
Nor the importance of the whole impression of the storm,
      if it has any, is what it is,
But the rhythm of the series of repeated jumps, from
      abstract into positive and back to a slightly less
      diluted abstract.

Mild effects are the result.

I cannot think any more of going out into all that, will stay here
With my quiet *schmerzen.* Besides the storm is almost over
Having frozen the face of the bust into a strange style with the lips
And the teeth the most distinct part of the whole business.

It is this madness to explain. . . .

What is the matter with plain old-fashioned cause-and-effect?
Leaving one alone with romantic impressions of the trees, the sky?
Who, actually, is going to be fooled one instant by these
      phony explanations,
Think them important? So back we go to the old,
      imprecise feelings, the
Common knowledge, the importance of duly suffering and
      the occasional glimpses
Of some balmy felicity. The world of Schubert's lieder.
      I am fascinated
Though by the urge to get out of it all, by going
Further in and correcting the whole mismanaged mess.
      But am afraid I'll
Be of no help to you. Good-bye.

As balloons are to the poet, so to the ground
Its varied assortment of trees. The more assorted they are, the
Vaster his experience. Sometimes
You catch sight of them on a level with the top story of a house,
Strung up there for publicity purposes. Or like those bubbles
Children make with a kind of ring, not a pipe, and probably
      using some detergent

Rather than plain everyday soap and water. Where was I?
        The balloons
Drift thoughtfully over the land, not exactly commenting on it;
These are the range of the poet's experience. He can hide in trees
Like a hamadryad, but wisely prefers not to, letting the balloons
Idle him out of existence, as a car idles. Traveling faster
And more furiously across unknown horizons, belted into the night
Wishing more and more to be unlike someone, getting the
        whole thing
(So he believes) out of his system. Inventing systems.
We are a part of some system, thinks he, just as the sun is part of
The solar system. Trees brake his approach. And he seems
        to be wearing but
Half a coat, viewed from one side. A "half-man" look
        inspiring the disgust of honest folk
Returning from chores, the milk frozen, the pump heaped high
        with a chapeau of snow,
The "No Skating" sign as well. But it is here that he is best,
Face to face with the unsmiling alternatives of his nerve-wracking
        existence.
Placed squarely in front of his dilemma, on all fours before the
        lamentable spectacle of the unknown.
Yet knowing where men *are* coming from. It is this, to hold the
        candle up to the album.

                                                    1966

Farm Implements and Rutabagas in a Landscape

The first of the undecoded messages read: "Popeye sits in thunder,
Unthought of. From that shoebox of an apartment,
From livid curtain's hue, a tangram emerges: a country."
Meanwhile the Sea Hag was relaxing on a green couch: "How pleasant
To spend one's vacation *en la casa de Popeye*," she scratched
Her cleft chin's solitary hair. She remembered spinach

And was going to ask Wimpy if he had bought any spinach.
"M'love," he intercepted, "the plains are decked out in thunder
Today, and it shall be as you wish." He scratched

The part of his head under his hat. The apartment
Seemed to grow smaller. "But what if no pleasant
Inspiration plunge us now to the stars? *For this is my country.*"

Suddenly they remembered how it was cheaper in the country.
Wimpy was thoughtfully cutting open a number 2 can of spinach
When the door opened and Swee'pea crept in. "How pleasant!"
But Swee'pea looked morose. A note was pinned to his bib. "Thunder
And tears are unavailing," it read. "Henceforth shall Popeye's
    apartment
Be but remembered space, toxic or salubrious, whole or scratched."

Olive came hurtling through the window; its geraniums scratched
Her long thigh. "I have news!" she gasped. "Popeye, forced as you
    know to flee the country
One musty gusty evening, by the schemes of his wizened, duplicate
    father, jealous of the apartment
And all that it contains, myself and spinach
In particular, heaves bolts of loving thunder
At his own astonished becoming, rupturing the pleasant

Arpeggio of our years. No more shall pleasant
Rays of the sun refresh your sense of growing old, nor the scratched
Tree-trunks and mossy foliage, only immaculate darkness and
    thunder."
She grabbed Swee'pea. "I'm taking the brat to the country."
"But you can't do that—he hasn't even finished his spinach."
Urged the Sea Hag, looking fearfully around at the apartment.

But Olive was already out of earshot. Now the apartment
Succumbed to a strange new hush. "Actually it's quite pleasant
Here," thought the Sea Hag. "If this is all we need fear from spinach
Then I don't mind so much. Perhaps we could invite Alice the Goon
    over"—she scratched
One dug pensively—"but Wimpy is such a country
Bumpkin, always burping like that." Minute at first, the thunder

Soon filled the apartment. It was domestic thunder,
The color of spinach. Popeye chuckled and scratched
His balls: it sure was pleasant to spend a day in the country.

1970

▪

The One Thing That Can Save America

Is anything central?
Orchards flung out on the land,
Urban forests, rustic plantations, knee-high hills?
Are place names central?
Elm Grove, Adcock Corner, Story Book Farm?
As they concur with a rush at eye level
Beating themselves into eyes which have had enough
Thank you, no more thank you.
And they come on like scenery mingled with darkness
The damp plains, overgrown suburbs,
Places of known civic pride, of civil obscurity.

These are connected to my version of America
But the juice is elsewhere.
This morning as I walked out of your room
After breakfast crosshatched with
Backward and forward glances, backward into light,
Forward into unfamiliar light,
Was it our doing, and was it
The material, the lumber of life, or of lives
We were measuring, counting?
A mood soon to be forgotten
In crossed girders of light, cool downtown shadow
In this morning that has seized us again?

I know that I braid too much my own
Snapped-off perceptions of things as they come to me.
They are private and always will be.
Where then are the private turns of event
Destined to boom later like golden chimes
Released over a city from a highest tower?
The quirky things that happen to me, and I tell you,
And you instantly know what I mean?
What remote orchard reached by winding roads
Hides them? Where are these roots?

It is the lumps and trials
That tell us whether we shall be known
And whether our fate can be exemplary, like a star.
All the rest is waiting

For a letter that never arrives,
Day after day, the exasperation
Until finally you have ripped it open not knowing what it is,
The two envelope halves lying on a plate.
The message was wise, and seemingly
Dictated a long time ago.
Its truth is timeless, but its time has still
Not arrived, telling of danger, and the mostly limited
Steps that can be taken against danger
Now and in the future, in cool yards,
In quiet small houses in the country,
Our country, in fenced areas, in cool shady streets.

1975

The Other Tradition

They all came, some wore sentiments
Emblazoned on T-shirts, proclaiming the lateness
Of the hour, and indeed the sun slanted its rays
Through branches of Norfolk Island pine as though
Politely clearing its throat, and all ideas settled
In a fuzz of dust under trees when it's drizzling:
The endless games of Scrabble, the boosters,
The celebrated omelette au Cantal, and through it
The roar of time plunging unchecked through the sluices
Of the days, dragging every sexual moment of it
Past the lenses: the end of something.
Only then did you glance up from your book,
Unable to comprehend what had been taking place, or
Say what you had been reading. More chairs
Were brought, and lamps were lit, but it tells
Nothing of how all this proceeded to materialize
Before you and the people waiting outside and in the next
Street, repeating its name over and over, until silence
Moved halfway up the darkened trunks,
And the meeting was called to order.

                                    I still remember
How they found you, after a dream, in your thimble hat,
Studious as a butterfly in a parking lot.
The road home was nicer then. Dispersing, each of the

Troubadours had something to say about how charity
Had run its race and won, leaving you the ex-president
Of the event, and how, though many of those present
Had wished something to come of it, if only a distant
Wisp of smoke, yet none was so deceived as to hanker
After that cool non-being of just a few minutes before,
Now that the idea of a forest had clamped itself
Over the minutiae of the scene. You found this
Charming, but turned your face fully toward night,
Speaking into it like a megaphone, not hearing
Or caring, although these still live and are generous
And all ways contained, allowed to come and go
Indefinitely in and out of the stockade
They have so much trouble remembering, when your
    forgetting
Rescues them at last, as a star absorbs the night.

1977

Paradoxes and Oxymorons

This poem is concerned with language on a very plain level.
Look at it talking to you. You look out a window
Or pretend to fidget. You have it but you don't have it.
You miss it, it misses you. You miss each other.

The poem is sad because it wants to be yours, and cannot.
What's a plain level? It is that and other things,
Bringing a system of them into play. Play?
Well, actually, yes, but I consider play to be

A deeper outside thing, a dreamed role-pattern,
As in the division of grace these long August days
Without proof. Open-ended. And before you know
It gets lost in the steam and chatter of typewriters.

It has been played once more. I think you exist only
To tease me into doing it, on your level, and then you aren't there
Or have adopted a different attitude. And the poem
Has set me softly down beside you. The poem is you.

1981

Life Is a Dream

A talent for self-realization
will get you only as far as the vacant lot
next to the lumber yard, where they have rollcall.
My name begins with an A,
so is one of the first to be read off.
I am wondering where to stand—could that group of three
or four others be the beginning of the line?

Before I have the chance to find out, a rodent-like
man pushes at my shoulders. "It's *that* way," he hisses.
"Didn't they teach you *anything* at school? That a photograph
of *anything* can be real, or maybe not? The corner of the stove,
a cloud of midges at dusk-time."

I know I'll have a chance to learn more
later on. Waiting is what's called for, meanwhile.
It's true that life can be anything, but certain things
definitely aren't it. This gloved hand,
for instance, that glides
so securely into mine, as though it intends to stay.

2000

Involuntary Description

That his landscape could have been the one you meant,
that it meant much to you, I never doubted,
even at the time. How many signifiers have you?
Good, I have two. I took my worries on the road
for a while. When we got back little cherubs were nesting
in the arbor, below the apple tree. We were incredulous,
and whistled. The road came back to get them
just as darkness was beginning.
The comic and the bathetic were our interior.
They kept integers at bay, and, when it was over,
toasted a little cheese to prove it never happened—
It had been reflected in a needle by the road's side.
The lovely sandlot was purple or gray.

Sometimes I think it's all one big affectation.
The forty jars, each holding its thief, draw closer
to me, trying to eavesdrop. But the only sound is water
dripping in the last millennium. I try and say it too;
you are glad it's over, except for a ton of sleep
and the half dreams that people it—people you knew,
but they weren't those people, only figures on a beach.

2006

Feverfew

It all happened long ago—
a murky, milky precipitate
of certain years then drawing to a close,
like a storm sewer upheaval. Road rage had burst its flanks;
all was uncertain on the Via Negativa
except the certainty of return, return
to the approximate.

Night and morning a horn sounded,
summoning the faithful to prayer, the unfaithful to pleasure.
In that unseemly alley I first exhaled
a jest to your comic, crumb-crusted lips:
What if we are all ignorant of all that has happened to us,
the song starting up at midnight,
the dream later, of lamb's lettuce and moss
near where Acheron used to flow?

But it's only me, now, I came because you cried and I had to.
Plaited bark muffles the knocker, but the doorbell
penetrates deep into the brain of one who lived here.
O brackish clouds and dangerous,
the moon is unambiguous.

2007

Opposition to a Memorial

"Come back, in a few days."
—William Empson

Not that it was needed that much, this much
was clear. A little cleverness would do
as well, a lei woven of servility
and something like affection. He would crawl through

the long days, dreaming of something else,
just to be near and not caught out.
A famished throng followed, always keeping
the same distance. What is it like to mend

and be shattered, weep and not know what you're
laughing about? The mother's tone was severe.
She spoke, but very little. It was time to go away
into the pageant night had promised:

There were prisms and lanterns at the outer edge
and toward the center a vacancy one knew.
This is what it means then,
to be in a dream and suck sleep from a jar

as though only the polished exterior mattered.
Inside all was crabbed notes and lines,
the reason of the doing. The reader frowns
and shuts the book. Another time, perhaps,

there will be effusions, random exclamations.
Today it's clear the rent has come due again.
And though you're offered a ride back, it's not so much
a favor as an occasion to brood.

What were the rights and the right ways?
Did we invest our strength in the kind grains
of conversation that blew across our page, and out?
Is this the time to tackle a major oeuvre,

or are we banished to shallows of content,
when one hears a companion curse and pick up the load

again, coming out into temporary sunshine and the past has waxed
benign, one more time? Is this launch definitive?

2007

Litanies

1.

Objects, too, are important.
Some of the time they are.
They can furrow their brow,
even offer forgiveness, of a sort.

You ask me what I'm doing here.
Do you expect me to actually read this?
If so, I've got a surprise for you—
I'm going to read it to everybody.

2.

Spring is the most important of the seasons.
It's here even when it's not here.
All the other seasons are an excuse for it.
Spring, idle spring,
you poor excuse for summer—
Did they tell you where they mislaid you,
on which arterial road piercing the city,
fast and faster like breath?

3.

It is important to be laid out
in a man-made shape. Others will try
to offer you something—on no account
accept it. Reflected in the window
of a pharmacy you know the distance you've come.

Let others taste you.
Sleep happily;
the wind is over there.
Come in. We were expecting you.

2007

The Ecstasy

We wandered in and out of the lobby
of a large house in history.
There was little to see at first,
then our eyes growing accustomed to the darkness
we could make out figures on a bridge
who waved to us, seeming to want us to come nearer.

We decided not to do that.
You thought the place was scary.
I found it relaxing, invigorating even.
There was a smell of that kind of musk
that is less than a warning, more than a confirmation.
The furniture was all of a piece,
alas; the air moved nearer.
It was my breathing as I had often feigned it.

Going down the slope the next day
there was nothing in the brilliant, awful annals
that let us see
just to the margin, and no further.
I want out now.
I have traveled in this country
longer than anyone should, or has.
It's natural to want a little sweetness
along with one's hunger, to put nothing aside
for the blistery winter when friendships come unknotted
like tie-dyed scarves, and the weathervane's a mate,
only you can't see it pointing backwards.

We left early for the reception,
though swooning and sherbets no longer seemed viable,
and there was a hidden tax in all this.
Yet we stayed, longer and longer. The dancing came to an end,
then started up again, one had no say in the matter.
In the morning it was warm, period. I went out on some pretext
and stayed for twenty years.
When I returned you asked if I had forgotten anything,
and I answered no, only the milk. Which was the truth.

2007

Larry Eigner
1927–1996

Larry Eigner was born in Swampscott, Massachusetts, north of Boston. Since childhood he was confined to a wheelchair by cerebral palsy. "For Larry Eigner," Samuel Charters wrote, "the circumstances of his life have given a form and shape to his poetry . . . his life has been spent in a glassed-in front porch of a frame house on a side street in a small Massachusetts town. Through the windows—and through the windows of his bedroom—he follows the world of seasons, the sky, the trees."[1] He was very close to his mother, Bessie, who arranged for his homeschooling, which resulted in degrees from Swampscott High School and the University of Chicago.

Eigner's poetry, which deals with everyday events such as the passing of people and cars on the street, begins with what he calls an "imitation of attention."[2] In the short essay, "Statement on Words," he writes that "abundant moments in various places persist . . . a poem can be assay(s) of things come upon, can be a stretch of thinking."[3] Eigner's method is one of understatement and happenstance, working outward from the small and partial. The egoless discontinuity of his poetry is admired by the language poets; his attention to local detail and integrity of poetic line provides a link to both the Williams tradition and Black Mountain poetry. His poetics however were based in practice rather than theory.

The poet Charles Bernstein describes Eigner's work as "a democracy of particulars, as against the craving for highlights, for the heightened, that is as much a literacy aesthetic as a consumer imperative. For Eigner, this didn't mean a flattening of affect; on the contrary it meant a luminosity of every detail: the perceptual vividness that his work so uncannily concatenates. This acknowledgment of the daily, a series of remarks on the otherwise unremarkable, a sort of poetic alchemy that is not dissimilar to one strain of Jewish mysticism (a strain in which the mysticism dissolves into an active apprehension of the real)."[5] In the poem "p o e t r y," written on November 26, 1974, Eigner defined the art in four lines: "assessments / immediacies / one calculus / in the world."[6]

The first of Eigner's numerous books, *From the Sustaining Air* (1953), was published in Mallorca by Robert Creeley's Divers Press. His other books include *Things Stirring Together or Far Away* (1974), *The World and Its Streets, Places* (1977), *Waters/Places/a Time* (1983), *Windows/ Walls/Yard/Ways* (1994), and a collection of short prose, *Country/Harbor/ Quiet/Act/Around* (1978). *The Collected Poems of Larry Eigner* was published in 2010.

After the death of his father, Eigner moved to Berkeley, California, where he lived on a trust fund established by his brother, Richard. Until his death of pneumonia at age sixty-eight, he was given assistance in his living arrangement by Bay Area poets and friends.

1. Biographical note in Larry Eigner, *The World and Its Streets, Places,* Santa Barbara, 1977, p. 182.   2. "Method from Happenstance," in *areas lights heights: Writings 1954–1989,* p. 6.   3. *areas lights heights,* p. 3.   4. Unpublished letter to Ina Forster, February 11, 1987, http://wings.buffalo.edu/epc/ezines/passages/passages5/forster.html.   5. February 5, 1996, post to the SUNY/Buffalo Poetics site, http://wings.buffalo.edu/epc/documents/obits/eigner .html.   6. *Windows/Walls/Yard/Ways,* Santa Rosa, 1994, p. 53.

[trees green   the quiet sun]

trees green   the quiet sun

    shed metal truck in the next street
    passing the white house you listen
               onwards

      you heard

        the dog

          through   per
             formed circles

     the roads near the beach

      rectangular

        rough lines of the woods

        tall growth   echoing

        local water

                      1977

W h o l e s

For a while a year is a long time
as things increase in their number
  and walls break
familiarity comes

familiarity of life, which sinks
to a level of sorts,   space

(empty except for
the rabbits-hat of things

Before crumbling, the walls streak
with some tangent of minutes

and life takes on a size

                                                        1977

[a temporary language]

a temporary language

as temporary things

and poetry the

math. . of

everyday

life

what time

Of the day is it

lad what

have you

to do with

or gotten

done

                                                        1977

[the sun solid]

the sun solid
                  ground   it soaks

    what bird took

            wing

            a minute ago

        now there are others

                some white stuff

            they eat and build

            farther

                        there an ample world

                    in which

                            their sounds are quiet

                                                1983

[Out of the wind   and leaves]

    Out of the wind   and leaves

                first rustle

            the rain straight

                    down

                the wall within

                    the wall of sound

                                        1983

June 19–September 9 90

the window opening
　no, opened already
　　　nothing but the wind

　　the window opening

　no,　already opened

　　　nothing but the wind up

　　　　　　　　　　　1994

Kenward Elmslie
b. 1929

Born in Colorado Springs, Colorado, and educated at Harvard, Kenward Elmslie's first experiences as a writer were as a lyricist and librettist. Elmslie has written librettos for three operas, three of which, *The Seagull* (1976), *Washington Square* (1976), and *Three Sisters* (1986) were composed by Pulitzer Prize nominee Thomas Pasatieri. His other librettos are *The Sweet Bye and Bye* (1956), *Miss Julie* (1965; music by Ned Rorem), and *Lizzie Borden* (1965). He also wrote the book and lyrics for the Broadway show *The Grass Harp* (1971), with music by Claibe Richardson, based on the Truman Capote novel. He wrote the lyrics for "Love Wise," a "top forty" song recorded by Nat King Cole in the 1950s.

Elmslie credits his turn to poetry to hearing Kenneth Koch read his "The History of Jazz" at the Five Spot in 1965, accompanied by Larry Rivers on saxophone. "My guffaw meter went bong," Elmslie says in an interview. "Kenneth transported the zest, the dippy angstlessness of musical comedy into poetry."[1] Elmslie's books of poetry include *Motor Disturbance* (1971), *Circus Nerves* (1971), *Tropicalism* (1975), *Moving Right Along* (1980), *Champ Dust* (1994), and *Routine Disruptions: Selected Poems and Lyrics* (1998). Among the first generation of New York School poets, his work is unique for its carnivalesque diction and theatrical character.

In the early 1980s, he turned his attention to creating performance works in collaboration with visual artists Ken Tisa (*Bimbo Dirt*), Donna Dennis (*26 Bars*), and Joe Brainard (*Sung Sex*), as well as the musician Steven Taylor.

Motor Disturbance won the Frank O'Hara Award for Poetry in 1971, the first year that prize was awarded.

A grandson of publisher Joseph Pulitzer, Kenward Elmslie lives in Vermont and Manhattan's West Village.

1. W. C. Bamberger, "An Interview with Kenward Elmslie," *New American Writing* 8/9 (Fall 1991), pp. 181–82.

Shirley Temple Surrounded by Lions

In a world where kapok on a sidewalk looks like an "accident"
—innards—would that freckles could enlarge, well, meaningfully
   into kind of friendly brown kingdoms, all isolate,
with a hero's route, feral glens,
   and a fountain where heroines cool their mouths.

Scenario: an albino industrialiste, invited to the beach at noon
(and to such old exiles, oceans hardly teem with ambiguities)
   by a lifeguard after her formulæ, though in love—
"Prop-men, the gardenias, the mimosa need anti-droopage stuffing."
Interestingly slow, the bush and rush filming.

Hiatus, everyone. After the idea of California sort of took root,
we found ourselves in this cookie forest; she closed the newspaper,
groped past cabañas, blanched and ungainly.

The grips watched Marv and Herm movies of birds tweeting,
fluttering around and in and out an old boat fridge, on a reef,
when eek, the door, or was it "eef"? "Shirl" said the starling, end of.

  The janitors are watching movies of men and women ruminating.
         Then a cartoon of two clocks licking.
         Chime. Licking. Chime. *Then* a?
After that, photos of incinerators in use moved families more
         than the candy grass toy that retches. Dogs.
         For the dressers, *Mutations,*
about various feelers. For the extras, movies of revenge that last.

This spree has to last. "Accept my pink eyes, continual swathing,"
Shirley rehearsed. "Encase me in sand, then let's get kissy."
         Do children have integrity, i.e. eyes?
         Newsreels, ponder this.
How slow the filming is for a grayish day with its bonnet
         bumping along the pioneer footpath,
         pulled by—here, yowly hound.

                                            1971

Feathered Dancers

Inside the lunchroom the travelling nuns wove
sleeping babies on doilies of lace.
A lovely recluse jabbered of bird lore and love:
      "Sunlight tints my face

      and warms the eggs outside
      perched on filthy columns of guilt.

In the matted shadows where I hide,
buzzards moult and weeds wilt."

Which reminds me of Mozambique
in that movie where blacks massacre Arabs.
The airport runway (the plane never lands, skims off) is bleak—
scarred syphilitic landscape—crater-sized scabs—

painted over with Pepsi ads—
as in my lunar Sahara dream—giant net comes out of sky,
encloses my open touring car. Joe slumps against Dad's
emergency wheel turner. Everyone's mouth-roof dry.

One interpretation. Mother hated blood!
When the duck Dad shot dripped on her leatherette lap-robe,
dark spots not unlike Georgia up-country mud,
her thumb and forefinger tightened (karma?) on my ear-lobe.

Another interpretation. Motor of my heart stalled!
I've heard truckers stick ping-pong balls up their butt
and jounce along having coast-to-coast orgasms, so-called.
Fermés, tousled jardins du Far West, I was taught—tight shut.

So you can't blame them. Take heed, turnpikes.
Wedgies float back from reefs made of jeeps: more offshore debris.
Wadded chewy depressants and elatants gum up footpaths. Remember Ike's
"Doctor-the-pump-and-away-we-jump" Aloha Speech to the Teamsters?
      "The—"

he began and the platform collapsed, tipping him onto a traffic island.
An aroused citizenry fanned out through the factories that day
to expose the Big Cheese behind the sortie. Tanned,
I set sail for the coast, down the Erie and away,

and ate a big cheese in a café by the docks,
and pictured every room I'd ever slept in:
toilets and phone-calls and oceans. Big rocks
were being loaded, just the color of my skin,

and I've been travelling ever since,
so let's go find an open glade,

like the ones in sporting prints,
(betrayed, delayed, afraid)

where we'll lie among the air-plants
in a perfect amphitheatre in a soft pink afterglow.
How those handsome birds can prance,
ah . . . unattainable tableau.

Let's scratch the ground clean,
remove all stones and trash,
I mean open dance-halls in the forest, I mean
where the earth's packed smooth and hard. Crash!

It's the Tale of the Creation. The whip cracks.
Albatrosses settle on swaying weeds.
Outside the lunchroom, tufts and air-sacs
swell to the size of fruits bursting with seeds.

1971

Japanese City

Centennial of Melville's birth this morning.
Whale balloons drift up released by priests. Whale floats parade
followed by boats of boys in sou'westers jiggled by runners
followed by aldermen in a ritual skiff propelled by "surf"—girls.
In my hotel room with its cellophane partitions (underwatery)
I phone down for ice-water, glass, tumbler, and the cubes.

Cattle for the Xmas Market fill the streets.
Black snouts—a rubby day indeed. Bump the buildings, herds.
A Mexican seamstress brings back my underthings shyly
six, seven times a day. One sweats so, lying about.
She mentions marvelous pistachio green caverns
where one canoes through cool midgy Buddha beards

where drafts of polar air sound like cicadas, where—
About the partitions. The other travellers seem—
There were beautiful hairs in the wash-basin this A.M.—
thick, and they smelled of limes

(good, that jibes with mine—ugh!—)
but mine, how perverse! Form a hoop, you there. Mine,

mine smell like old apples in a drawer. Jim the Salesman
and his cohorts are massaging my feet—a real treadmill example.
They're in lawn décor, ether machines, and nocturnal learning clasps.
And Jim? Plays cards in his shorts, moves black fish around.
Black houses, the capitol. Hotel chunks. Sky chunks. The squeeze:
green odd numbers—white air, amputations and eagles, respite.

Red even numbers—body sections, the ocean sac, the great beach.
Green even numbers—oval jewels, quicksand, the haven behind the falls.
Jim's stammer is contagious, zen smut about hatcheries in the suburbs,
how the women in the canneries came down with the "gills,"
hence bathtub love-makings, couplings in the sewers. The ice-water comes.

The room-clerk's pate shines up through the transparent floor.
Soon the sin couples will start arriving, and the one-way mirror teams
and the government professionals with their portable amulets—
shiny vinyl instruments that probe and stretch.
Much visiting back and forth. Pink blobs. Revels and surveys.
Many olive eyes'll close in a sleep of exhaustion. More ice-water!

The celebrants in metal regalia jangle and tinkle
moving past the red-roofed villas of the Generals,
past the cubicles of the nakeds and into the harbor,
past the glum stone busts of the Generals, sitting in the water.
Out they go, (Jim etc.) into the sweet emptied city, leaving behind
the red odd numbers untouched: pleasure beaches, monsoons and sun.

1971

Ed Dorn
1929–1999

Born in Villa Grove, Illinois, Ed Dorn studied at the University of Illinois and Black Mountain College in North Carolina. "I think I'm rightly associated with the Black Mountain 'school,'" he said, "not because of the way I write, but because I was there."[1]

Dorn's four-volume epic poem *Slinger* (1968) has been described by the critic Marjorie Perloff as "one of the most ambitious and interesting long poems of our time, a truly original cowboy-and-indian saga, rendered in the most ingenious mix of scientific jargon, Structuralist terminology, junkie slang, Elizabethan sonneteering, Western dialect, and tough talk."[2]

His books include *The Newly Fallen* (1961), *From Gloucester Out* (1964), *Geography* (1965), *The North Atlantic Turbine* (1967), *Recollections of Gran Apacheria* (1974), and *Hello, La Jolla* (1978), as well as volumes of collected and selected works. From the beginning, Dorn's poetry was both sardonic and lyrical; his later work, included in *Abhorrences* (1990), is more caustic in its political expression.

Finding in Dorn's poetry the wit, song, and pronunciamento of the Augustan satirists, the critic Donald Wesling has written that his pervasive tone "is that of a Jonathan Swift trapped in Democracy."[3] Dorn claimed not to share "the current aversion directed at the words 'ironic' and 'sarcastic.' In fact, I value those modes because they save us from the pervasively jerky habits of straightforwardness."[4] For all his uses of irony, however, Dorn's poems like "Geranium" and "The Rick of Green Wood" are among the most convincingly lyrical of the period. As is evident in "On the Debt My Mother Owed to Sears Roebuck," he was also unique in his ability to depict the difficult circumstances of working people.

One of Dorn's titles, "The Cosmology of Finding Your Place," provides a good description of his project—that is, finding one's place in the cultural and political landscape. The American West gave Dorn the setting of that quest.

1. David Ossman, "*The Sullen Art* Interview," in *Edward Dorn: Interviews*, Bolinas, 1980, p. 1.   2. *The New Republic*, April 24, 1976.   3. *Internal Resistances: The Poetry of Edward Dorn*, ed. Donald Wesling, Berkeley, 1985, p. 15.   4. Stephen Fredman, "Road Testing the Language," in *Edward Dorn: Interviews*, p. 98.

The Rick of Green Wood

In the woodyard were green and dry
woods fanning out, behind
                                        a valley below
a pleasure for the eye to go.

Woodpile by the buzzsaw. I heard
the woodsman down in the thicket. I don't
want a rick of green wood, I told him
I want cherry or alder or something strong
and thin, or thick if dry, but I don't
want the green wood, my wife would die

Her back is slender
and the wood I get must not
bend her too much through the day.
Aye, the wood is some green
and some dry, the cherry thin of bark
cut in July.

My name is Burlingame
said the woodcutter.
My name is Dorn, I said.
I buzz on Friday if the weather cools
said Burlingame, enough of names.

    Out of the thicket my daughter was walking
singing—
          backtracking the horse hoof
      gone in earlier this morning, the woodcutter's horse
      pulling the alder, the fir, the hemlock
      above the valley
            in the november
air, in the world, that was getting colder
as we stood there in the woodyard talking
pleasantly, of the green wood and the dry.

                                    1956

Geranium

I know that peace is soon coming, and love of common object,
and of woman and all the natural things I groom, in my mind, of
faint rememberable patterns, the great geography of my lunacy.

I go on my way frowning at novelty, wishing I were closer to home
than I am. And this is the last bus stop before Burlington,

that pea-center, which is my home, but not the home of my mind.
That asylum I carry in my insane squint, where beyond
the window a curious woman in the station door
has a red bandana on her head, and tinkling things hand themselves
to the wind that gathers about her skirts. In the rich manner of her kind
she waits for the bus to stop. Lo, a handsome woman.

Now, my sense decays, she is the flat regularity, the brick
of the station wall, is the red Geranium of my last Washington stop.
Is my object no shoes brought from India
can make exotic, nor hardly be made antic would she astride
a motorcycle (forsake materials and we shall survive together)
nor be purchased by the lust of schedule.

No,

on her feet therefore, are the silences of nothing. And leather
leggings adorn her limbs, on her arms are the garlands of ferns
come from a raining raining forest and dripping lapidary's dust.
She is a common thief of fauna and locale (in her eyes
are the small sticks of slender land-bridges) a porter
standing near would carry her bundle, which is scarlet too,

as a geranium and cherishable common that I worship and that I sing
ploddingly, and out of tune as she, were she less the lapwing
as she my pale sojourner, is.

                                                                        1961

From Gloucester Out

It has all
come back today.
That memory for me is nothing
there ever was,
                    That man

so long,
when stretched out
and so bold
                    on his ground
and so much
lonely anywhere.

But never to forget
                    that moment

when we came out of the tavern
and wandered through the carnival.
They were playing
the washington post march
but I mistook it for manhattan beach
for all around were the colored lights
of delirium
                    to the left the boats
of Italians
and ahead of us, past the shoulders
of St. Peter the magician of those fishermen

the bay
stood, and immediately in it the silent
inclined pole where tomorrow the young men
of this colony
so dangerous on the street
will fall harmlessly
into the water.

They are not the solid
but are the solidly built
citizens, and they are about us
as we walk across
                    the square
with their black provocative
women
slender, like whips of
sex in the sousa filled night.

Where edged
by that man in the music
of a transplanted time and
enough of drunkenness
to make you senseless of all
but virtue
                    (there is never
no, there is never a small complaint)
(that all things shit poverty,
and Life, one wars on with

many embraces) oh it was a time that was perfect
but for my own hesitating
to know all I had not known.
Pure existence, even in the crowds
I love
will never be possible for me

even with the men I love
                              This is
the guilt
that kills me
                    My adulterated presence

but please believe with all men
I love to be

    •

That memory
of how he lay out
on the floor in his great length
and when morning came,
late,
we lingered
in the vastest of all cities
in this hemisphere
                              and all other movement
stopped, nowhere
else was there a stirring known to us
yet that morning I stood
by the window up 3 levels
and watched a game
of stick ball, thinking of going away,
and wondering what would befall that man
when he returned to his territory.
The street as you could guess
was thick with their running
and cars,
themselves, paid that activity
such respect I thought a ritual
in the truest sense,
where all time and all motion
part around the space of men
in that act

as does a river flow past
the large rock.

•

And he slept.
in the next room, waiting
in an outward slumber
                    for the time

we climbed into the car, accepting all things
from love, the currency of which is
parting, and glancing.

Then went
out of that city to jersey
where instantly we could not find our way
and the maze of the outlands west
starts that quick
where you may touch
your finger to liberty
and look so short a space
to the columnar bust
of New York
and know those people exist
as a speck in your own lonely heart
who will shortly depart,
taking a conveyance for the
radial stretches
past girls on corners
past drugstores, tired hesitant
creatures who I also love
in all their alienation were it not so
past all equipment of country side
to temporary homes
where the wash of sea and other
populations come
once more to whisper only one thing
for all people: a late and far-away
night yearning for
and when he gets there
I want him to stay away
from the taverns of familiarity
I want him to walk by the seashore alone

in all height
which is nothing more than
a mountain. Or the hailing of a mast
with big bright eyes.

So rushing,
        all the senses
come to him
as a swarm of golden bees
and their sting is the power
he uses as parts of
the oldest brain. He hears
the delicate thrush
of the water attacking
He hears the cries, falling gulls
and watches silently the gesture of grey
bygone people. He hears their cries
and messages, he never

ignores any sound.
As they come to him he places them
puts clothes upon them
and gives them their place
in their new explanation, there is never
a lost time, nor any inhabitant
of that time to go split by prisms or unplaced
and unattended,
            that you may believe

is the breath he gives
the great already occurred and nightly beginning world.
So with the populace of his mind
you think his nights? are not
lonely. My God. Of his
loves, you know nothing and of his
false beginning
you can know nothing,
            but this thing to be marked

again
    only

he who worships the gods with his strictness
can be of their company
the cat and the animals, the bird he took
from the radiator
of my car saying it had died
a natural death, rarely seen in a bird.

To play, as areal particulars can out of the span
of Man, and of all, this man
does not
        he, does, he
   walks
        by the sea
in my memory

and sees all things and to him
are presented at night
the whispers of the most flung shores
from Gloucester out

1964

On the Debt My Mother Owed to Sears Roebuck

Summer was dry, dry the garden
our beating hearts, on that farm, dry
with the rows of corn the grasshoppers
came happily to strip, in hordes, the first
thing I knew about locust was they came
dry under the foot like the breaking of
a mechanical bare heart which collapses
from an unkind and incessant word whispered
in the house of the major farmer
and the catalogue company,
from no fault of anyone
my father coming home tired
and grinning down the road, turning in
is the tank full? thinking of the horse
and my lazy arms thinking of the water
so far below the well platform.

On the debt my mother owed to sears roebuck
we brooded, she in the house, a little heavy
from too much corn meal, she
a little melancholy from the dust of the fields
in her eye, the only title she ever had to lands—
and many ways winged their way to her through the mail
saying so much per month
so many months, this is yours, take it
take it, take it, take it
and in the corncrib, like her lives in that house
the mouse nibbled away at the cob's yellow grain
until six o'clock when her sorrows grew less
and my father came home

On the debt my mother owed to sears roebuck?
I have nothing to say, it gave me clothes to
wear to school,
and my mother brooded
in the rooms of the house, the kitchen, waiting
for the men she knew, her husband, her son
from work, from school, from the air of locusts
and dust masking the hedges of the fields she knew
in her eye as a vague land where she lived,
boundaries, whose tractors chugged pulling harrows
pulling discs, pulling great yields from the earth
pulse for the armies in two hemispheres, 1943
and she was part of that *stay at home army* to keep
things going, owing that debt.

                                                    1964

Gregory Corso _____
1930–2001

Gregory Nunzio Corso was born on Manhattan's Bleecker Street to Italian immigrant parents. His mother died when he was a child, and his father moved back to Italy, leaving him in the care of an orphanage and four foster homes. When Corso was twelve, his father remarried and took custody of him; however, he ran away and wound up in the Tombs, a New York prison, for stealing a radio in a boys' home. At age thirteen, he spent time in the children's ward at New York's Bellevue Hospital, where he was given a series of mental tests. Paradoxically, it was while serving a prison sentence for theft at age seventeen that Corso was introduced to literature through books—such as *The Brothers Karamazov* and *The Red and the Black*—given to him by an elderly inmate who wished to further Corso's education.[1] Corso began writing poems in prison.

Although Corso had only a sixth-grade education, he left prison in 1950 "well read and in love with Chatterton, Marlowe, and Shelley."[2] In the same year, he met Allen Ginsberg, who further guided his education as a poet. In 1954, he went to Cambridge, Massachusetts, at the invitation of Harvard and Radcliffe students who later gathered the money for publishing his first book, *The Vestal Lady on Brattle* (1955).[3]

Corso's travels with Ginsberg to San Francisco and Mexico inspired the poems in *Gasoline* (1958). Later collections include *The Happy Birthday of Death* (1960), *Long Live Man* (1962), *Elegiac Feelings American* (1970), *Herald of the Autochthonic Spirit* (1981), and *Mindfield: New and Selected Poems* (1989). His poem "Marriage," with its exuberant voice, bohemian counsel, and surrealist figures such as "penguin dust," captures much of the appeal of the Beat aesthetic. Allen Ginsberg called Corso a "divine Poet Maudit, rascal poet Villonesque and Rimbaudian."[4]

While making the film *Corso: The Last Beat*, Corso expressed his desire off-camera to be buried near Shelley and Keats in the Protestant Cemetery in Rome. Although the cemetery had been closed to newcomers for years, following Corso's death a special dispensation was made. His ashes lie at the feet of Shelley, the poet he most admired.[5]

---

1. Gregory Corso, *The New American Poetry*, New York, 1960, p. 429.   2. The same, p. 430.   3. The same.   4. "On Corso's Virtues," in Gregory Corso's *Mindfield: New and Selected Poems*, New York, 1989, p. xv.   5. Eliot Katz, July 2006, "Some Recollections of Gregory," at the website Gregory Corso Biography, http://gregorycorsobiography.blogspot.com.

Italian Extravaganza

Mrs. Lombardi's month-old son is dead.
I saw it in Rizzo's funeral parlor,
A small purplish wrinkled head.

They've just finished having high mass for it;
They're coming out now
. . . wow, such a small coffin!
And ten black cadillacs to haul it in.

1958

The Mad Yak

I am watching them churn the last milk
    they'll ever get from me.
They are waiting for me to die;
They want to make buttons out of my bones.
Where are my sisters and brothers?
That tall monk there, loading my uncle,
    he has a new cap.
And that idiot student of his—
    I never saw that muffler before.
Poor uncle, he lets them load him.
How sad he is, how tired!
I wonder what they'll do with his bones?
And that beautiful tail!
How many shoelaces will they make of that!

1958

Last Night I Drove a Car

Last night I drove a car
    not knowing how to drive
    not owning a car
I drove and knocked down
    people I loved
    . . . went 120 through one town.

I stopped at Hedgeville
    and slept in the back seat
       . . . excited about my new life.

1958

Dream of a Baseball Star

I dreamed Ted Williams
leaning at night
against the Eiffel Tower, weeping.

He was in uniform
and his bat lay at his feet
—knotted and twiggy.

'Randall Jarrell says you're a poet!' I cried.
'So do I! I say you're a poet!'

He picked up his bat with blown hands;
stood there astraddle as he would in the batter's box,
and laughed! flinging his schoolboy wrath
toward some invisible pitcher's mound
—waiting the pitch all the way from heaven.

It came; hundreds came! all afire!
He swung and swung and swung and connected not one
sinker curve hook or right-down-the-middle.
A hundred strikes!
The umpire dressed in strange attire
thundered his judgement: YOU'RE OUT!
And the phantom crowd's horrific boo
dispersed the gargoyles from Notre Dame.

And I screamed in my dream:
God! throw thy merciful pitch!
Herald the crack of bats!
Hooray the sharp liner to left!
Yea the double, the triple!
Hosannah the home run!

1960

I Held a Shelley Manuscript

written in Houghton Library, Harvard

My hands did numb to beauty
as they reached into Death and tightened!

O sovereign was my touch
upon the tan-ink's fragile page!

Quickly, my eyes moved quickly,
sought for smell for dust for lace
      for dry hair!

I would have taken the page
breathing in the crime!
For no evidence have I wrung from dreams—
yet what triumph is there in private credence?

Often, in some steep ancestral book,
when I find myself entangled with leopard-apples
      and torched-mushrooms,
my cypressean skein outreaches the recorded age
and I, as though tipping a pitcher of milk,
pour secrecy upon the dying page.

                          1960

Marriage

Should I get married? Should I be good?
Astound the girl next door with my velvet suit and faustus hood?
Don't take her to movies but to cemeteries
tell all about werewolf bathtubs and forked clarinets
then desire her and kiss her and all the preliminaries
and she going just so far and I understanding why
not getting angry saying You must feel! It's beautiful to feel!
Instead take her in my arms lean against an old crooked tombstone
and woo her the entire night the constellations in the sky—

When she introduces me to her parents
back straightened, hair finally combed, strangled by a tie,

should I sit knees together on their 3rd degree sofa
and not ask Where's the bathroom?
How else to feel other than I am,
often thinking Flash Gordon soap—
O how terrible it must be for a young man
seated before a family and the family thinking
We never saw him before! He wants our Mary Lou!
After tea and homemade cookies they ask What do you do for a

living?

Should I tell them: Would they like me then?
Say All right get married, we're losing a daughter
but we're gaining a son—
And should I then ask Where's the bathroom?

O God, and the wedding! All her family and her friends
and only a handful of mine all scroungy and bearded
just wait to get at the drinks and food—
And the priest! he looking at me as if I masturbated
asking me Do you take this woman for your lawful wedded wife?
And I trembling what to say say Pie Glue!
I kiss the bride all those corny men slapping me on the back
She's all yours, boy! Ha-ha-ha!
And in their eyes you could see some obscene honeymoon going

on—

Then all that absurd rice and clanky cans and shoes
Niagara Falls! Hordes of us! Husbands! Wives! Flowers!

Chocolates!

All streaming into cozy hotels
All going to do the same thing tonight
The indifferent clerk he knowing what was going to happen
The lobby zombies they knowing what
The whistling elevator man he knowing
The winking bellboy knowing
Everybody knowing! I'd be almost inclined not to do anything!
Stay up all night! Stare that hotel clerk in the eye!
Screaming: I deny honeymoon! I deny honeymoon!
running rampant into those almost climactic suites
yelling Radio belly! Cat shovel!

O I'd live in Niagara forever! in a dark cave beneath the Falls
I'd sit there the Mad Honeymooner
devising ways to break marriages, a scourge of bigamy
a saint of divorce—

But I should get married I should be good
How nice it'd be to come home to her
and sit by the fireplace and she in the kitchen
aproned young and lovely wanting my baby
and so happy about me she burns the roast beef
and comes crying to me and I get up from my big papa chair
saying Christmas teeth! Radiant brains! Apple deaf!
God what a husband I'd make! Yes, I should get married!
So much to do! like sneaking into Mr Jones' house late at night
and cover his golf clubs with 1920 Norwegian books
Like hanging a picture of Rimbaud on the lawnmower
like pasting Tannu Tuva postage stamps all over the picket fence
like when Mrs Kindhead comes to collect for the Community Chest
grab her and tell her There are unfavorable omens in the sky!
And when the mayor comes to get my vote tell him
When are you going to stop people killing whales!
And when the milkman comes leave him a note in the bottle
Penguin dust, bring me penguin dust, I want penguin dust—

Yet if I should get married and it's Connecticut and snow
and she gives birth to a child and I am sleepless, worn,
up for nights, head bowed against a quiet window, the past behind
                                                                                    me,

finding myself in the most common of situations a trembling man
knowledged with responsibility not twig-smear nor Roman coin
                                                                                    soup—

O what would that be like!
Surely I'd give it for a nipple a rubber Tacitus
For a rattle a bag of broken Bach records
Tack Della Francesca all over its crib
Sew the Greek alphabet on its bib.
And build for its playpen a roofless Parthenon

No, I doubt I'd be that kind of father
not rural not snow no quiet window

but hot smelly tight New York City
seven flights up, roaches and rats in the walls
a fat Reichian wife screeching over potatoes Get a job!
And five nose running brats in love with Batman
And the neighbors all toothless and dry haired
like those hag masses of the 18th century
all wanting to come in and watch TV
The landlord wants his rent
Grocery store Blue Cross Gas & Electric Knights of Columbus
Impossible to lie back and dream Telephone snow, ghost parking—
No! I should not get married I should never get married!
But—imagine If I were married to a beautiful sophisticated woman
tall and pale wearing an elegant black dress and long black gloves
holding a cigarette holder in one hand and a highball in the other
and we lived high up in a penthouse with a huge window
from which we could see all of New York and even farther on
                                                   clearer days
No, can't imagine myself married to that pleasant prison dream—

O but what about love? I forget love
not that I am incapable of love
it's just that I see love as odd as wearing shoes—
I never wanted to marry a girl who was like my mother
And Ingrid Bergman was always impossible
And there's maybe a girl now but she's already married
And I don't like men and—
but there's got to be somebody!
Because what if I'm 60 years old and not married,
all alone in a furnished room with pee stains on my underwear
and everybody else is married! All the universe married but me!

Ah, yet well I know that were a woman possible as I am possible
then marriage would be possible—
Like SHE in her lonely alien gaud waiting her Egyptian lover
so I wait—bereft of 2,000 years and the bath of life.

                                                   1960

Gary Snyder
b. 1930

Born in San Francisco and educated at Reed College in Oregon, Gary Snyder was attracted as a young poet to the poetry of Carl Sandburg, D.H. Lawrence, Walt Whitman, and William Carlos Williams, poets who share his own romantic and democratic views; he also admired the more conservative T. S. Eliot as an "elegant ritualist of key Occidental myth-symbols."[1] Snyder was equally influenced by Chinese poetry of the Tang dynasty, translations of Native American song and myth, especially those from the Haida and Kwakiutl traditions, and Japanese poetry and culture. A Zen Buddhist, he associates his daily practice of zazen, or meditation, with the disciplined freedom of poetry, both of which require the individual to "go into *original mind*."[2] A poet does not express his or her self, but rather *"all* of our selves."[3] "Breath," Snyder writes, "is the outer world coming into one's body. With pulse—the two always harmonizing—the source of our inward sense of rhythm."[4]

A leading poet of the San Francisco Renaissance, Snyder is identified with the Beat poets; unlike many of the Beats, however, he rarely deals in urban subjects. "My political position," he has said, "is to be a spokesman for wild nature."[5] Committed to the politics of ecology, he prefers the elemental creative force that predates human civilization to the empty sophistications of Eurocentric culture. In poetry, Snyder seeks continuity with the "paleolithic" through the figure of the "shaman-dancer-poet" who sees beyond the illusions of class structure and modern technology. Snyder's shaman is the source of an expressly *spoken* poetry, for it is through speech, or "mother tongue," that poetry achieves its "gleaming daggers and glittering nets of language."[6] For Snyder, then, the poetry of nonliterate cultures has more to offer than formal literature, a view that has proved prophetic of the rise of performance and related oral poetries.

His books include *Riprap and Cold Mountain Poems* (1959), *The Back Country* (1968), *Earth House Hold* (1969), the Pulitzer Prize–winning *Turtle Island* (1974), *Myths and Texts* (1978), *The Real Work: Interviews & Talks, 1964–1979* (1980), *Axe Handles* (1983), *Left Out in the Rain: New Poems 1947–1985* (1986), *The Practice of the Wild* (1990), *No Nature: New and Selected Poems* (1992), *Mountains and Rivers Without End* (1996), *Danger on Peaks* (2005), and *A Place in Space: Ethics, Aesthetics, and Watersheds* (2008).

Snyder's dharma name is "Chofu" ("Listen to the Wind").

1. "The Real Work," in *The Real Work: Interviews & Talks, 1964–1979*, New York, 1980, p. 57.   2. The same, p. 65.   3. The same.   4. "Poetry and the Primitive: Notes on Poetry as an Ecological Survival Technique," in *Earth House Hold*, New York, 1969, p. 123.   5. "Knots in the Grain," in *The Real Work*, p. 49.   6. "Poetry and the Primitive," p. 118.

Hay for the Horses

He had driven half the night
From far down San Joaquin
Through Mariposa, up the
Dangerous mountain roads,
And pulled in at eight a.m.
With his big truckload of hay
      behind the barn.
With winch and ropes and hooks
We stacked the bales up clean
To splintery redwood rafters
High in the dark, flecks of alfalfa
Whirling through shingle-cracks of light,
Itch of haydust in the
      sweaty shirt and shoes.
At lunchtime under Black oak
Out in the hot corral,
—The old mare nosing lunchpails,
Grasshoppers crackling in the weeds—
"I'm sixty-eight" he said,
"I first bucked hay when I was seventeen.
I thought, that day I started,
I sure would hate to do this all my life.
And dammit, that's just what
I've gone and done."

            1959

Riprap

Lay down these words
Before your mind like rocks.
      placed solid, by hands
In choice of place, set
Before the body of the mind
      in space and time:
Solidity of bark, leaf, or wall
      riprap of things:
Cobble of milky way,
      straying planets,

These poems, people,
           lost ponies with
Dragging saddles—
           and rocky sure-foot trails.
The worlds like an endless
           four-dimensional
Game of *Go*.
           ants and pebbles
In the thin loam, each rock a word
           a creek-washed stone
Granite: ingrained
           with torment of fire and weight
Crystal and sediment linked hot
           all change, in thoughts,
As well as things.

                                        1959

The Bath

Washing Kai in the sauna,
The kerosene lantern set on a box
           outside the ground-level window,
Lights up the edge of the iron stove and the
           washtub down on the slab
Steaming air and crackle of waterdrops
           brushed by on the pile of rocks on top
He stands in warm water
Soap all over the smooth of his thigh and stomach
           "Gary don't soap my hair!"
           —his eye-sting fear—
           the soapy hand feeling
           through and around the globes and curves of his body
           up in the crotch,
And washing-tickling out the scrotum, little anus,
           his penis curving up and getting hard
           as I pull back skin and try to wash it
Laughing and jumping, flinging arms around,
           I squat all naked too,
                              is this our body?

Sweating and panting in the stove-steam hot-stone
           cedar-planking wooden bucket water-splashing

kerosene lantern-flicker wind-in-the-pines-out
    sierra forest ridges night—
Masa comes in, letting fresh cool air
    sweep down from the door
    a deep sweet breath
And she tips him over gripping neatly, one knee down
    her hair falling hiding one whole side of
    shoulder, breast, and belly,
Washes deftly Kai's head-hair
    as he gets mad and yells—
The body of my lady, the winding valley spine,
    the space between the thighs I reach through,
    cup her curving vulva arch and hold it from behind,
    a soapy tickle   a hand of grail
The gates of Awe
That open back a turning double-mirror world of
    wombs in wombs, in rings,
    that start in music,
                  is this our body?

The hidden place of seed
The veins net flow across the ribs, that gathers
    milk and peaks up in a nipple—fits
    our mouth—
The sucking milk from this our body sends through
    jolts of light; the son, the father,
    sharing mother's joy
That brings a softness to the flower of the awesome
    open curling lotus gate I cup and kiss
As Kai laughs at his mother's breast he now is weaned
    from, we
    wash each other,
                  this our body

Kai's little scrotum up close to his groin,
    the seed still tucked away, that moved from us to him
In flows that lifted with the same joys forces
    as his nursing Masa later,
    playing with her breast,
Or me within her,
Or him emerging,
                this is our body:

Clean, and rinsed, and sweating more, we stretch
    out on the redwood benches hearts all beating
Quiet to the simmer of the stove,
    the scent of cedar
And then turn over,
    murmuring gossip of the grasses,
    talking firewood,
Wondering how Gen's napping, how to bring him in
    soon wash him too—
These boys who love their mother
    who loves men, who passes on
    her sons to other women;

The cloud across the sky. The windy pines.
    the trickle gurgle in the swampy meadow

    this is our body.

Fire inside and boiling water on the stove
We sigh and slide ourselves down from the benches
    wrap the babies, step outside,

black night & all the stars.

Pour cold water on the back and thighs
Go in the house—stand steaming by the center fire
Kai scampers on the sheepskin
Gen standing hanging on and shouting,

"Bao! bao! bao! bao! bao!"

This is our body. Drawn up crosslegged by the flames
    drinking icy water
    hugging babies, kissing bellies,

Laughing on the Great Earth

Come out from the bath.

                                1974

Avocado

The Dharma is like an Avocado!
Some parts so ripe you can't believe it,
But it's good.
And other places hard and green
Without much flavor,
Pleasing those who like their eggs well-cooked.

And the skin is thin,
The great big round seed
In the middle,
Is your own Original Nature—
Pure and smooth,
Almost nobody ever splits it open
Or ever tries to see
If it will grow.

Hard and slippery,
It looks like
You should plant it—but then
It shoots out thru the
         fingers—
gets away.

1974

As for Poets

As for poets
The Earth Poets
Who write small poems,
Need help from no man.

The Air Poets
Play out the swiftest gales
And sometimes loll in the eddies.
Poem after poem,
Curling back on the same thrust.

At fifty below
Fuel oil won't flow
And propane stays in the tank.

Fire Poets
Burn at absolute zero
Fossil love pumped back up.

The first
Water Poet
Stayed down six years.
He was covered with seaweed.
The life in his poem
Left millions of tiny
Different tracks
Criss-crossing through the mud.

With the Sun and Moon
In his belly,
The Space Poet
Sleeps.
No end to the sky—
But his poems,
Like wild geese,
Fly off the edge.

A Mind Poet
Stays in the house.
The house is empty
And it has no walls.
The poem
Is seen from all sides,
Everywhere,
At once.

1974

Axe Handles

One afternoon the last week in April
Showing Kai how to throw a hatchet
One-half turn and it sticks in a stump.
He recalls the hatchet-head
Without a handle, in the shop
And go gets it, and wants it for his own.

A broken-off axe handle behind the door
Is long enough for a hatchet,
We cut it to length and take it
With the hatchet head
And working hatchet, to the wood block.
There I begin to shape the old handle
With the hatchet, and the phrase
First learned from Ezra Pound
Rings in my ears!
"When making an axe handle
       the pattern is not far off."
And I say this to Kai
"Look: We'll shape the handle
By checking the handle
Of the axe we cut with—"
And he sees. And I hear it again:
It's in Lu Ji's *Wên Fu,* fourth century
A.D. "Essay on Literature"—in the
Preface: "In making the handle
Of an axe
By cutting wood with an axe
The model is indeed near at hand."
My teacher Shih-hsiang Chen
Translated that and taught it years ago
And I see: Pound was an axe,
Chen was an axe, I am an axe
And my son a handle, soon
To be shaping again, model
And tool, craft of culture,
How we go on.

1983

Right in the Trail

Here it is, near the house,
A big pile, fat scats,
Studded with those deep red
Smooth-skinned manzanita berries,
Such a pile! Such droppings,
Awesome. And I saw how

The young girl in the story,
Had good cause to comment
On the bearscats she found while
Picking blueberries with her friends.
She laughed at them
Or maybe with them, jumped over them
(Bad luck!), and is reported
To have said "wide anus!"
To amuse or annoy the Big Brown Ones
Who are listening, of course.

They say the ladies
Have always gone berrying
And they all join together
To go out for the herring spawn,
Or to clean green salmon.
And that big set of lessons
On what bears really want,
Was brought back by the girl
Who made those comments:
She was taken on a year-long excursion
Back up in the mountains,
Through the tangled deadfalls,
Down into the den.
She had some pretty children by a
Young and handsome Bear.

Now I'm on the dirt
Looking at these scats
And I want to cry not knowing why
At the honor and the humor
Of coming on this sign
That is not found in books
Or transmitted in letters,
And is for women just as much as men,
A shining message for all species,
A glimpse at the Trace
of the Great One's passing,
With a peek into her whole wild system—
And what was going on last week,
(Mostly still manzanita)—

Dear Bear: do stay around. Be good.
And though I know
It won't help to say this,

Chew your food.

Kitkitdizze X.88

1992

No Shadow

My friend Deane took me into the Yuba Goldfields. That's at the
lower Yuba River outflow where it enters the Sacramento valley
flatlands, a mile-wide stretch between grass and blue oak meadows.
It goes on for ten miles. Here's where the mining tailings got dropped
off by the wandering riverbed of the 1870s—forty miles downstream
from where the giant hoses washed them off Sierra slopes.

We were walking on blue lupine-covered rounded hundred-foot
gravel hills til we stood over the springtime rush of water. Watched
a female osprey hunting along the main river channel. Her flight
shot up, down, all sides, suddenly fell feet first into the river and
emerged with a fish. Maybe fooling the fish by zigzagging, so—
no hawk shadow. Carole said later, that's like trying to do zazen
without your self entering into it.

Standing on a gravel hill by the lower Yuba
can see down west a giant airforce cargo plane from Beale
hang-gliding down to land
strangely slow over the tumbled dredged-out goldfields
—practice run
shadow of a cargo jet—soon gone

no-shadow of an osprey

still here

2004

Keith Waldrop _____

b. 1932

Keith Waldrop was born in Emporia, Kansas, and studied at Aix-Marseille University and the University of Michigan. He is currently the Brooke Russell Astor Professor of Humanities at Brown University, and codirector of Burning Deck Press, a leading publisher of experimental poetry.

Waldrop's many books include *A Windmill Near Calvary* (1968), *The Garden of Effort* (1975), *The Space of Half an Hour* (1983), *A Shipwreck in Haven* (1989), *The Opposite of Letting the Mind Wander: Selected Poems and a Few Songs* (1990), *Analogies of Escape* (1997), *Well Well Reality* (with Rosmarie Waldrop, 1998), *Haunt* (2000), *The Real Subject: Queries and Conjectures of Jacob Delafon, with Sample Poems* (2005), *Several Gravities* (2009), and *Transcendental Studies: A Trilogy*, which won The National Book Award for Poetry in 2009. He has also translated the work of contemporary French poets Claude Royet-Journoud, Anne-Marie Albiach, and Edmond Jabès, as well as new translations of Baudelaire's *The Flowers of Evil* (2006) and *Paris Spleen* (2009).

Drawing on the technique of collage, Waldrop uses other texts to create his own; for example, he describes his work *The Antichrist and Other Foundlings* (1970) as the text of Bram Stoker's *Dracula* "with most of the words removed."[1] Waldrop deliberately plays on the compositional value of inattention—"a frame of mind that lets in strays"—to create poems with multiple points of focus.[2] Viewing his poems as "constructions," Waldrop is fascinated by *"background"*; that is, "those aspects of the scene we can't really scrutinize, cannot (by definition) attend to."[3] *Transcendental Studies: A Trilogy* was produced by the same method.

Asked about the relation of collage to translation, Waldrop noted, "Collage is not a form of translation, or vice versa, but they're related. Translation and collage are both movements from one surface to another. In translation, one takes a poem, subtracts all its words—and refills it with other words, words of a different language. . . . Collage is the opposite movement. It takes words . . . and removes them from their context and therefore from the form which they were part of. . . . A translation has an original it is working from and to. That's why translating a poem is so much harder than simply writing a poem; one has all the same difficulties, *plus* the necessity of respecting the original. A collage doesn't have an original."[4]

Keith Waldrop lives in Providence, Rhode Island.

1. "Notes for a Preface," in *The Opposite of Letting the Mind Wander*, Providence, 1990, n.p.   2. The same.   3. The same.   4. Peter Gizzi, "On Collage: An Interview with Keith Waldrop," Siglio Press website, http://www.sigliopress.com/library/waldrop/kw_petergizzi.htm.

A Shipwreck in Haven (I)

1

Balancing. Austere. Life-
less. I have tried to keep
context from claiming you.

Without doors. And there are
windows. How far, how
far into the desert have we come?

Rude instruments, product
of my garden. Might also be
different, what I am thinking of.

So you see: it is
not symmetrical, dark
red out of the snow.

2

Enemies for therapy, the
rind of the lime-tree
in elaborate garlands.

Strew the table. Let the hall
be garlanded and lit, the will
to break away. Welcome your couches.

Witness these details. Your judgement, my
inclination. Hear. Touch. Taste.
Translate. Fixed: the river.

Disquieting thought, I am not
ultimate, full moon, memory.
Prepare for rout.

3

Here, even in the
sand. Among the rocks, I have
heard, remnant of a cloud.

Unfleshed, short, thin, pointed.
Independent of you, a
revelation. A great city.

Flatly unknown, you do not
know of yourself, do not know
yourself, not stuck full of nails.

Under such illumination, darkness
becomes terror. Under this high
wall, dark ground.

4

High marble wall, broken mid-
way. Dark unphenomenality, like
the hand of a clock. Sun-baked.

No *direct* communication likely. Marble
terrace. Suffusing with soft-
tinted glow. Images first.

The gods and you come later, a wealth
of approaches. Within the portico:
marble. Bundled like qualities.

Not—the world—one of
several, as if it could be
different. Nothing. Nothing different.

5

I mean translated, though some
charms are pre-determined. Shall I
not delve and deliver?

If I could think it. Our
wings are broken. As easily might
plunge. In a violent sweat.

The desert. And might be
the same: lemurs
swim down gutters.

And might be threshold, never
hesitate, ship on the high sea.
The desert in the house.

6

Intrinsic, your un-
thinkability. Casts over all created
things annihilating shadow.

An opening for possible
storms, as a deity enters
the world, a stranger.

The bed we are not in: can-
not surprise it. What passes
in the street? Pure picture.

In the world these
limits, almost occult—only signals
corporeal. To think of something.

7

I was hardly dead, when you
called. Now are you convinced?
Infinitely soft strum.

As if night. As if im-
perceptibly. Slowly you fall. Break
somewhat the blackness of the day.

Might also be any
direction, every start
takes us to other time.

Forth across the sands. From
sky or from the liver,
divined. Endless beginning.

8

Need not end. Indeed, *nothing*. Step
out. Grist for wits. Shadow of your
shell. Stand there.

No other ground. No
other. And the world concerns you every-
where, but do not identify with it.

Let light onto us. Flowers through the
gate, flowers skimming
the wall. A carpet of petal.

Treasures below the earth. Neither in
this world nor another, guarding.
Nothing but fade and flourish.

9

Now there is a door and whoever
very beautiful and very
very strange. Near you a table.

Laughing. Singing. Calling to one
another, the crack of whips. Cloud to
cloud in ricochet.

Music of hooves and wheels. The heavenly
Jerusalem from shards of Babylon
destroyed. Now a door.

Where thinking ends, house and temple
echo, possible objects of
admiration. Will you go?

10

Oh yes and wheels on the pavement,
angels of incidence, rebounding from
waves, but precisely. Reflective angels.

Like the hand of a clock which, minute
by minute, crosses its appointed
spaces. Oh! You are passing!

Things are ready. All
things, because something
must be settled. Slung.

Answering laughter. Mixture of
diamond and diamond
and blood, a rope of flowers.

1989

Plurality of Worlds

And each inhabited. And each
inhabitant resolves. And I, I with
my various processes. I stumble, I
revolve.

As one
sees, in the desert, water
welling, always distant, forever
unapproachable.

A view of the chase
from the battlements. To see something—any-
thing—I always step back. And then:
where am I?

Distant. Unapproachable. My
name. Jericho. Absurdly—I mean, out of
tune. And forgetfulness? deceit?
error?

For us to grow
old, the moon must rise. From invisible
fire, flames leap into view. A dream
of bodily heaven.

Hot colors, subtle
nuances. Motives recast in site
after site. Figures absorbed by
a plethora of drapery.

I must remove all this:
evening chill, an impression of transparency, your
presence—remove it all, without
letting anything go.

I was born in December
and things seem always to come at me like
January. The fifty-third bird in the
tree this morning.

Joy, laughter,
lamentation—it's like a map. Minuet.
Waltz. Ninety percent too
dark to see.

Let me think now. Roads.
Tombs. Temples. I could list my
Friends . . . What will I
forget next?

Light, analyzed by
dusk, and then? The specters
still there. A painterly softening. Almost
heraldic poses.

Long narrow
slits of light, dark bars against bright
ground, or straight-line borders peculiarly
oriented.

Looking one way, everything
is lost. The other direction: nothing to

lose. In a crystal I glimpse, maybe, my
waking state.

My soul's
fictitious body . . . Think. My
health: the world's long
lingering illness.

Pain, hot-cold, mere
contact. Crude sensory modalities. These
remain after destruction of the sensory
cortex. Pain.

Shock waves. Feathery
feet of barnacles. It does not
reach us, the sun's bottomless
profundo.

Things age and, when old
enough, no longer able to resist,
become animate. Unable to stay
free of life.

What remains of
ancient rites? Grammar. I
would never give up anything I have, in
return for mere certainty.

1995

Competing Depth

As the wave reaches the church, it
separates right and left and the edifice
is embraced. Confabulation fills the gap.

Still, the sound-shadow is only partial. Errors
in recognizing the surroundings are
paralleled by misjudgments of time and trouble.

The pulse advances, squeezes the particles to-
gether. Meaningless patterns distorted,
so as to make them look familiar.

When a long sea roller meets an isolated
rock in its passage, it rises against the rock,
clasps it all around. Past events, pushed.

1995

Michael McClure
b. 1932

Born in Marysville, Kansas, Michael McClure grew up in Seattle and Wichita and attended the University of Arizona at Tucson before moving to San Francisco. He gave his first reading as a participant in the 1955 Six Gallery event that launched the San Francisco Renaissance, and he remains one of the leading poets of the Beat generation.

The graphic design of many of his poems, suggestive of mushroom clouds and flowers, serves a purpose for McClure. "The deliberate depersonalizations of grammar, and alterations of accepted written syntax, are for me like the splashings of paint in modern canvases. I continue to see the poem as an extension of myself, as a gesture, and as an organism seeking life."[1] McClure sees both politics and poetry as rooted in biology, and the history of humans as animals driven and animated by biological forces: "It is thrilling to be in this waste and destruction and re-creation. That is one of the sensualities of American culture. Our primate emotions sing to us in the midst of it."[2]

His books include *Hymn to Saint Geryon* (1959), *Meat Science Essays* (1963), *September Blackberries* (1974), *Jaguar Skies* (1975), *Fragments of Perseus* (1983), *Simple Eyes & Other Poems* (1992), *Rain Mirror* (1999), *Plum Stones: Cartoons of No Heaven* (2002), *Mysteriosos and Other Poems* (2010) and *Of Indigo and Saffron: New and Selected Poems* (2011). McClure regularly performs his poetry with the accompaniment of Ray Manzarek, keyboardist for the rock group The Doors. His plays include *Josephine: The Mouse Singer* (1980) and *The Beard* (1965), a "poem-play of a confrontation between Billy the Kid and Jean Harlow," which was suppressed by the San Francisco and Los Angeles police for obscenity but won two Obie Theatre Awards in New York for 1967–1968. He also wrote the song "Mercedes Benz" popularized by singer Janis Joplin.

1. "Author's Note," in *Selected Poems*, New York, 1986, pp. vii, 90.   2. *Selected Poems*, p. 90.

Gray Fox at Solstice

Waves crash and fluff jewel sand
in blackness. Ten feet from his den
the gray fox shits on the cliff edge
enjoying the beat of starlight
on his brow, and ocean
on his eardrums. The yearling
deer watches—trembling.

The fox's garden trails
down the precipice:
ice plant, wild strawberries,
succulents.
Squid eggs
in jelly bags (with moving
embryos) wash up on
the strand.
It is the night of the solstice.
The fox coughs,
"Hahh!"
Kicks his feet—
stretches.
Beautiful claw toes
in purple brodiaea lilies.
He dance-runs through
the Indian paintbrush.
Galaxies in spirals.
Galaxies in balls.
Near stars and white mist swirling.

1974

Mexico Seen from the Moving Car

THERE ARE HILLS LIKE SHARKFINS
and clods of mud.
The mind drifts through
in the shape of a museum,
in the guise of a museum,
dreaming dead friends:
Jim, Tom, Emmet, Bill.
—Like billboards their huge faces droop
and stretch on the walls,
on the walls of the cliffs out there,
where trees with white trunks
make plumes on rock ridges.

My mind is fingers holding a pen.

Trees with white trunks
make plumes on rock ridges.

Rivers of sand are memories.
Memories make movies
      on the dust of the desert.
Hawks with pale bellies
      perch on the cactus,
their bodies are portholes
      to other dimensions.

This might go on forever.

I am a snake and a tiptoe feather
at opposite ends of the scales
as they balance themselves
against each other.
This might go on forever.

1993

The Butterfly

YELLOW AND BLACK,
   black and yellow . . . in a smooth flicker
the butterfly raises and lowers
her wings,
      in a smooth flicker,
   as she steps
   in an awkward walk
   like a dancer.
   She sips the taste of the mountain
   from the red-black mud,
   from the red-black mud
   near the river.

The gray-silver clouds are ocelot spots
and a stone peak stares from a notch in green cliffs.

   She sips the taste of the mountain
   from the red-black mud
   and
   a cowbell rings
      in the shadow of clouds.

the Sierra Madre
1993

The Cheetah

See the face
of a beautiful
 and highly
  intelligent
   child
    in
     the
     profile
of the cheetah.
   SHE
   IS
   BEYOND
   ALL
   GOOD
    and
EVIL
and more like us
than we can ever
imagine.

The black stripes
at the tip of her tail
twitch
and she closes her eyes
as my mother used to do,
with pleasure.

Her three large kittens
nod and grin in the sun.

What is human
is so much more obvious
in beings with tails.

Samburu, Kenya
1993

Thoreau's Eyes

two poems for Kazuaki Tanahashi

one

REVEL IN THE CONTRADICTIONS OF LOVE AND PAIN
AND DEEP THOUGHT.
Thoreau's eyes are there to thank you a lot
for the courage to bear the curse
and laugh at the actions you make in your stealth.
In Thoreau's worn eyes is a glory of health.
We are part sweatly stallion and part opalescent elf—
AND
IT
IS
ALL
O.K.
as a long-gone childhood pouring forth the odor of hay

2002

Amiri Baraka (LeRoi Jones)
b. 1934

Born in Newark, New Jersey, where he currently resides, LeRoi Jones attended Howard University and served in the United States Air Force before settling in Greenwich Village in 1957. In 1958 he married Hettie Cohen, with whom he edited the avant-garde literary magazine *Yugen,* publishing the work of Frank O'Hara, William Burroughs, and Charles Olson, among others. An organizer of great energy, Jones also founded Totem Press, served as poetry editor of Corinth Press, and coedited the important literary magazine *The Floating Bear* with poet Diane di Prima.

His early poetry, included in *Preface to a Twenty Volume Suicide Note* (1961) and *The Dead Lecturer* (1964), is associated with Beat and Black Mountain poetics. With the production of his plays *The Slave* (1964) and *Dutchman* (1964), the second of which received the Obie Theatre Award, he rose to national prominence. But with the death of Malcolm X in 1965, Jones left the predominantly white literary world of Greenwich Village for Harlem, where he founded the Black Arts Repertory Theatre and began an intense involvement in Black Nationalism. Returning to live in Newark, he became founding director of Spirit House theatre, and married Sylvia Robinson (Bibi Amina Baraka).

In 1968 he took the Bantu-Muslim name Imamu Amiri Baraka, which means "spiritual leader," "prince," and "blessed one"; he also became the main theorist of the Black Arts movement, which sought to replace white models of consciousness with African American language and values. For Baraka, the ideal black artist was jazz saxophonist John Coltrane: "Trane is a mature swan whose wing span was a whole new world. But he also showed us how to murder the popular song. To do away with weak Western forms."[1]

In 1974, dropping "Imamu" from his name, he rejected Black Nationalism as racist and turned to Third World Marxism, which emphasizes social class over race. "Poetry for the Advanced" (1979) strongly represents this period in Baraka's development. "American culture is multinational," he said in a 1984 radio interview. "It's not just white. It's not European (it's definitely not European—it's got some European origins like it's got some African origins) . . . American culture is multinational."[2]

Baraka's 1963 essay "Expressive Language," in which he challenges the dominance of standard English and upholds the originality and beauty of black dialect, is prophetic of the multicultural movement. He is the author of an important study, *Blues People: Negro Music in White America* (1963) and the novel *The System of Dante's Hell* (1965).

Baraka's poetics are deeply linked to his love of music. Like the musi-

cians he most admires, John Coltrane and James Brown, he desires to speak
directly to people rather by academic means and the delay of book publica-
tion: "Most of the poetry that's written by the academy is not intended to
be read at all. It's usually meant so people can get tenure and then it goes
to a library. But I think that for those of us who are interested in people
hearing it and listening to it, it always has got to be close to music, 'cause
that's where it began . . . close to music, close to dance. . . . The first poetry
that I knew was the poetry of the blues. That's the first poetry that had any
meaning to me."[3]

According to poet Nathaniel Mackey, "Baraka refers to John Coltrane,
Sonny Rollins, and others as 'this new generation's private assassins,' and the
association of the music with acts of subversion, sabotage, and revolution or,
at the very least, contempt carries over into his poetry, his fiction, and his
plays."[4]

In 2002, Baraka's poem "Somebody Blew Up America," was accused of
anti-Semitism for the following lines: "Who knew the World Trade Center was
gonna get bombed? / Who told 4,000 Israeli workers at the Twin Towers / To
stay home that day / Why did Sharon stay away?" After a failed attempt by Gov-
ernor McGreevy to remove him from his post as Poet Laureate of New Jersey,
state lawmakers voted in July 2003 to eliminate the position of poet laureate
altogether.[5]

Recipient of grants from the Rockefeller Foundation, the Guggenheim
Foundation, and the National Endowment for the Arts, he coauthored the
autobiography of Quincy Jones and was a supporting actor in the Warren
Beatty film *Bulworth.*

1. *Black Music,* New York, 1968, p. 174.   2. *The LeRoi Jones/Amiri Baraka Reader,* ed.
William J. Harris (New York, 1991), p. 250.   3. Graham Hodges, "Amiri Baraka, Sterling
Plumpp, and Curtis Lyle: An Interview," 1982. *Another Chicago Magazine* 12 (1985), pp. 186–94.
Conversations with Amiri Baraka, ed. Charlie Reilly (University Press of Mississippi, 1994), pp.
222–23.   4. "The Changing Same: Black Music in the Poetry of Amiri Baraka." *Discrepant
Engagement: Dissonance, Cross-Culturality, and Experimental Writing* (Cambridge University
Press, 1993), 28.   5. Library of Congress, U.S. State Poets Laureate, New Jersey, www.loc
.gov/rr/main/poets/newjersey.html.

Duncan Spoke of a Process

And what I have learned
of it, to repeat, repeated
as a day will repeat

its color, the tired sounds
run off its bones. In me, a balance.

Before that, what came easiest. From
wide poles, across the greenest earth,
eyes locked on, where they could live, and
whatever came from there, where the hand
could be offered, like Gideon's young troops
on their knees at the water.

                    I test myself,
with memory. A live bloody skeleton. Hung as softly
as summer. Sways like words' melody, as ugly as any
lips, or fingers stroking lakes, or flesh like a
white frightened scream.

What comes, closest, is
closest. Moving, there
is a wreck of spirit,
               a heap of broken feeling. What

was only love
or in those cold rooms,
opinion. Still, it made
color. And filled me
as no one will. As, even
I cannot fill
myself.

        I see what I love most and will not
leave what futile lies
I have. I am where there
is nothing, save myself. And go out to
what is most beautiful. What some noncombatant Greek
or soft Italian prince
would sing, "Noble Friends."
                Noble Selves. And which one

  is truly
  to rule here? And
  what country is this?

                                    1964

Political Poem

(for Basil)

Luxury, then, is a way of
being ignorant, comfortably
An approach to the open market
of least information. Where theories
can thrive, under heavy tarpaulins
without being cracked by ideas.

(I have not seen the earth for years
and think now possibly "dirt" is
negative, positive, but clearly
social. I cannot plant a seed, cannot
recognize the root with clearer dent
than indifference. Though I eat
and shit as a natural man. (Getting up
from the desk to secure a turkey sandwich
and answer the phone: the poem undone
undone by my station, by my station,
and the bad words of Newark.) Raised up
to the breech, we seek to fill for this
crumbling century. The darkness of love,
in whose sweating memory all error is forced.
Undone by the logic of any specific death. (Old gentlemen
who still follow fires, tho are quieter
and less punctual. It is a polite truth
we are left with. Who are you? What are you
saying? Something to be dealt with, as easily.
The noxious game of reason, saying, "No, No,
you cannot feel," like my dead lecturer
lamenting thru gipsies his fast suicide.

1964

The New World

The sun is folding, cars stall and rise
beyond the window. The workmen leave
the street to the bums and painters' wives

pushing their babies home. Those who realize
how fitful and indecent consciousness is
stare solemnly out on the emptying street.
The mourners and soft singers. The liars,
and seekers after ridiculous righteousness. All
my doubles, and friends, whose mistakes cannot
be duplicated by machines, and this is all of our
arrogance. Being broke or broken, dribbling
at the eyes. Wasted lyricists, and men
who have seen their dreams come true, only seconds
after they knew those dreams to be horrible conceits
and plastic fantasies of gesture and extension,
shoulders, hair and tongues distributing misinformation
about the nature of understanding. No one is that simple
or priggish, to be alone out of spite and grown strong
in its practice, mystics in two-pants suits. Our style,
and discipline, controlling the method of knowledge.
Beatniks, like Bohemians, go calmly out of style. And boys
are dying in Mexico, who did not get the word.
The lateness of their fabrication: mark their holes
with filthy needles. The lust of the world. This will not
be news. The simple damning lust,

> float flat magic in low changing
> evenings. Shiver your hands
> in dance. Empty all of me for
> knowing, and will the danger
> of identification,

> Let me sit and go blind in my dreaming
> and be that dream in purpose and device.

> A fantasy of defeat, a strong strong man
> older, but no wiser than the defect of love.

1969

Leadbelly Gives an Autograph

Pat your foot
and turn
    the corner. Nat Turner, dying wood

of the church. Our lot
is vacant. Bring the twisted myth
of speech. The boards brown and falling
away. The metal banisters cheap
and rattly. Clean new Sundays. We thought
it possible to enter
the way of the strongest.

But it is rite that the world's ills
erupt as our own. Right that we take
our own specific look into the shapely
blood of the heart.
                          Looking thru trees
the wicker statues blowing softly against
the dusk.
Looking thru dusk
thru dark-
ness. A clearing of stars
and half-soft mud.

The possibilities of music. First
that it does exist. And that we do,
in that scripture of rhythms. The earth,
I mean the soil, as melody. The fit you need,
the throes. To pick it up and cut
away what does not singularly express.

Need.
Motive.
The delay of language.

A strength to be handled by giants.
The possibilities of statement. I am saying, now,
what my father could not remember
to say. What my grandfather
was killed
for believing.
                    Pay me off, savages.
                    Build me an equitable human assertion.

One that looks like a jungle, or one that looks like the cities
of the West.   But I provide the stock. The beasts

and myths.
　　　　　The City's Rise!
　　　　　　　　　(And what is history, then? An old deaf lady
　　　　　　　　　burned to death
　　　　　　　　　in South Carolina.

　　　　　　　　　　　　　　　　　　　　1969

Ka 'Ba

A closed window looks down
on a dirty courtyard, and black people
call across or scream across or walk across
defying physics in the stream of their will

Our world is full of sound
Our world is more lovely than anyone's
tho we suffer, and kill each other
and sometimes fail to walk the air

We are beautiful people
with african imaginations
full of masks and dances and swelling chants
with african eyes, and noses, and arms,
though we sprawl in gray chains in a place
full of winters, when what we want is sun.

We have been captured,
brothers. And we labor
to make our getaway, into
the ancient image, into a new

correspondence with ourselves
and our black family. We need magic
now we need the spells, to raise up
return, destroy, and create. What will be

the sacred words?

　　　　　　　　　　　　　　　　　　　　1969

Leroy

I wanted to know my mother when she sat
looking sad across the campus in the late 20's
into the future of the soul, there were black angels
straining above her head, carrying life from our ancestors,
and knowledge, and the strong nigger feeling. She sat
(in that photo in the yearbook I showed Vashti) getting into
new blues, from the old ones, the trips and passions
showered on her by her own. Hypnotizing me, from so far
ago, from that vantage of knowledge passed on to her passed on
to me and all the other black people of our time.
When I die, the consciousness I carry I will to
black people. May they pick me apart and take the
useful parts, the sweet meat of my feelings. And leave
the bitter bullshit rotten white parts
alone.

1969

The Rare Birds

for Ted Berrigan

brook no obscurity, merely plunging deeper
for light. Hear them, watch the blurred windows tail
the woman alone turning and listening to another time
when music brushed against her ankles and held a low light
near the table's edge. These birds, like Yard and
Bean, or Langston grinning at you. Can't remember the shadow
pulled tight around the door, music about to enter. We hum
to anticipate, more history, every day. These birds, angular
like sculpture. Brancusian, and yet more tangible like Jake's
colored colorful colorado colormore colorcolor, ahhh, it's about
these birds and their grimaces. Jake's colors, and lines. You
remember the eyes of that guy Pablo, and his perfect trace of
life's austere overflowings.

Williams writes to us
of the smallness of this American century, that it splinters into worlds it
cannot live in. And having given birth to the mystery
splits unfolds like gold shattered in daylight's beautiful hurricane.
(praying Sambos blown apart) out of which a rainbow of anything you need.
I heard these guys. These lovely ladies, on the road to Timbuctoo
waiting for Tu Fu to register on the Richter scale. It was called
Impressions, and it was a message, from like a very rare bird.

1987

J. said, "Our whole universe is generated by a rhythm"

Is Dualism, the shadow inserted
for the northern trip. as the northern
trip. minstrels of the farther land,
the sun, in one place, ourselves, somewhere
else. The Universe
is the rhythm
there is no on looker, no outside
no other than the real, the universe
is rhythm, and whatever is only is as
swinging. All that is is funky, the bubbles
in the monsters brain, are hitting it too,
but the circles look like
swastikas, the square is thus
explained, but the nazis had dances, and even some of the
victims would tell you that.

There is no such thing as "our
universe", only degrees of the swinging, what
does not swing is nothing, and nothing swings
when it wants to. The desire alone is funky
and it is this heat Louis Armstrong scatted in.

What is not funky is psychological, metaphysical
is the religion of squares, pretending no one
is anywhere.

Everything gets hot, it is hot now, nothing cold exists
and cold, is the theoretical line the pretended boundary
where your eye and your hand disappear into desire.

Dualism is a quiet camp near the outer edge of the forest.
there the inmates worship money and violence. they are
learning right now to sing, let us join them for a moment
and listen. Do not laugh, whatever you do.

1996

Ted Berrigan
1934–1983

A leading figure of the New York School's second generation, Ted Berrigan was born in Providence, Rhode Island. After three years in the U.S. Army, he finished his college degree and earned a master's degree at the University of Tulsa. It was in Oklahoma that he met poets Ron Padgett and Dick Gallup and artist and poet Joe Brainard, who arrived with Berrigan in New York City as a "Tulsa group." In 1963 he founded *C Magazine,* with Ed Sanders's *Fuck You: A Magazine of the Arts* and Ron Padgett's *White Dove Review,* one of the more significant little magazines of the period.

During the late sixties and throughout the seventies, Berrigan was a charismatic leader in the bohemian poetry scene of the Lower East Side, especially in relation to the Poetry Project at St. Mark's Church. His first major publication, *The Sonnets* (1967), remains among his finest work. Using cut-ups from a variety of sources, including his own writing, he renewed interest in the sonnet form. Berrigan's sonnets may also be seen as a key development linking Dada and proceduralist practices of today. The everydayness of Berrigan's work, which he openly appropriates from Frank O'Hara's "I do this I do that" poems, balances and counters his natural tendency toward elegy. Besides O'Hara, Berrigan's literary influences include Paul Blackburn and Philip Whalen, whose volume *On Bear's Head* he greatly admired.

His many books of poetry include *Many Happy Returns* (1969), *In the Early Morning Rain* (1970), *Train Ride* (1971), *Red Wagon* (1976), and *Nothing for You* (1977), all of which are represented in *So Going Around Cities: New & Selected Poems 1958–1979* (1980). A posthumous volume, *A Certain Slant of Sunlight,* consisting of poems designed to fit on a series of postcards, appeared in 1988; his *Collected Poems* in 2005. With Ron Padgett, Berrigan wrote *Bean Spasms* (1967), a book containing poems by both authors, as well as works written in full collaboration. The fact that none of the poems in *Bean Spasms* was assigned authorship was consistent with the sixties' challenge both to individual ownership and to a hierarchical concept of authorship.

Berrigan died on July 4, 1983, following years of health problems compounded by amphetamine use. In 1991, *Nice to See You: Homage to Ted Berrigan* was published, a volume of essays, poems, and reminiscences by his many friends recounting Berrigan's widespread influence on poets of his generation.

FROM *The Sonnets*

II

Dear Margie, hello. It is 5:15 a.m.
dear Berrigan. He died
Back to books. I read
It's 8:30 p.m. in New York and I've been running around all day
old come-all-ye's streel into the streets. Yes, it is now,
How Much Longer Shall I Be Able To Inhabit The Divine
and the day is bright gray turning green
feminine marvelous and tough
watching the sun come up over the Navy Yard
to write scotch-tape body in a notebook
had 17 and 1/2 milligrams
Dear Margie, hello. It is 5:15 a.m.
fucked til 7 now she's late to work and I'm
18 so why are my hands shaking I should know better

XV

In Joe Brainard's collage its white arrow
He is not in it, the hungry dead doctor.
Of Marilyn Monroe, her white teeth white-
I am truly horribly upset because Marilyn
and ate King Korn popcorn," he wrote in his
of glass in Joe Brainard's collage
Doctor, but they say "I LOVE YOU"
and the sonnet is not dead.
takes the eyes away from the gray words,
Diary. The black heart beside the fifteen pieces
Monroe died, so I went to a matinee B-movie
washed by Joe's throbbing hands. "Today
What is in it is sixteen ripped pictures
does not point to William Carlos Williams.

XXXVI

after Frank O'Hara

It's 8:54 a.m. in Brooklyn it's the 28th of July and
it's probably 8:54 in Manhattan but I'm
in Brooklyn I'm eating English muffins and drinking

pepsi and I'm thinking of how Brooklyn is New
York city too how odd I usually think of it as
something all its own like Bellows Falls like Little
Chute like Uijongbu
                           I never thought on the Williams-
burg bridge I'd come so much to Brooklyn
just to see lawyers and cops who don't even carry
guns taking my wife away and bringing her back
                                                    No
and I never thought Dick would be back at Gude's
beard shaved off long hair cut and Carol reading
his books when we were playing cribbage and
watching the sun come up over the Navy Yard
across the river
                     I think I was thinking when I was
ahead I'd be somewhere like Perry street erudite
dazzling slim and badly loved
contemplating my new book of poems
to be printed in simple type on old brown paper
feminine marvelous and tough

LXXXVIII

A FINAL SONNET

for Chris

How strange to be gone in a minute!   A man
Signs a shovel and so he digs   Everything
Turns into writing a name for a day
                                    Someone
is having a birthday and someone is getting
married and someone is telling a joke   my dream
a white tree   I dream of the code of the west
But this rough magic I here abjure   and
When I have required some heavenly music   which even
     now
I do   to work mine end upon *their* senses
That this aery charm is for   I'll break
My staff   bury it certain fathoms in the earth
And deeper than did ever plummet sound
I'll drown my book.
It is 5:15 a.m.   Dear Chris, hello.

                                                    1967

Words for Love

for Sandy

Winter crisp and the brittleness of snow
as like make me tired as not. I go my
myriad ways blundering, bombastic, dragged
by a self that can never be still, pushed
by my surging blood, my reasoning mind.

I am in love with poetry. Every way I turn
this, my weakness, smites me. A glass
of chocolate milk, head of lettuce, dark-
ness of clouds at one o'clock obsess me.
I weep for all of these or laugh.

By day I sleep, an obscurantist, lost
in dreams of lists, compiled by my self
for reassurance. Jackson Pollock   René
Rilke   Benedict Arnold   I watch
my psyche, smile, dream wet dreams, and sigh.

At night, awake, high on poems, or pills
or simple awe that loveliness exists, my lists
flow differently. Of words bright red
and black, and blue.   Bosky.   Oubliette.   Dis-
severed. And O, alas

Time disturbs me. Always minute detail
fills me up. It is 12:10 in New York. In Houston
it is 2 p.m. It is time to steal books. It's
time to go mad. It is the day of the apocalypse
the year of parrot fever! What am I saying?

Only this. My poems do contain
wilde beestes. I write for my Lady
of the Lake. My god is immense, and lonely
but uncowed. I trust my sanity, and I am proud. If
I sometimes grow weary, and seem still, nevertheless

my heart still loves, will break.

1969

Bean Spasms

to George Schneeman

New York's lovely weather
                    hurts my forehead

                    in praise of thee
                                        the? white dead
                                        whose eyes know:
                what are they
        of the tiny cloud my brain:
The City's tough red buttons:
                                        O Mars, red, angry planet, candy

                                    bar, with sky on top,
                "why, it's young Leander hurrying to his death"
            what? what time is it in New York   in these here alps
            City of lovely tender hate
                                and beauty making beautiful
                                            old rhymes?

        I ran away from you
    when you needed something strong
                then I leand against the toilet bowl (ack)
            Malcolm X
                    I love my brain
            it all mine now is
            saved not knowing
                    that &
                    that (happily)
                    being that:

        "wee kill our selves to propagate our kinde"
                                        John Donne
        yes, that's true
                        the hair on yr nuts & my
                                big blood-filled cock are a part in that
                        too

PART 2

Mister Robert Dylan doesn't feel well today
That's bad
This picture doesn't show that
It's not bad, too

it's very ritzy in fact

here I stand I can't stand
to be thing
I don't use   atop
                                        the empire state
                                        building
                                        & so sauntered out that door
That reminds me of the time
I wrote that long piece about a gangster name of "Jr."
O Harry James! had eyes to wander but lacked tongue to praise
                                        so later peed under his art

          paused only to lay a sneeze

                                        on Jack Dempsey
                                        asleep with his favorite Horse

               That reminds me of I buzz
                    on & off Miró pop
                         in & out a Castro convertible
          minute by minute   GENEROSITY!

          Yes now that the seasons totter in their walk
               I do a lot of wondering about Life   in praise of ladies dead of
& Time plaza(s), Bryant Park by the Public   eye of brow
Library, Smith Bros. black boxes, Times
                    Square
               Pirogi Houses
                         with long skinny rivers thru them
               they lead the weary away
                    off! hey!
                    I'm no sailor
                    off a ship
                              at sea   I'M HERE
                         & "The living is easy"

It's "HIGH TIME"
              & I'm in shapes
              of shadow, they
              certainly can warm, can't they?

     Have you ever seen one?   NO!
                   of those long skinny Rivers
                        So well hung, in New York City
              NO!   in fact
                             I'm the Wonderer
& as yr train goes by   forgive me, René!   "just oncet"
I woke up in Heaven
                   He woke, and wondered more; how many angels
         on this train huh?   snore

                        for there she lay
                   on sheets that mock lust   done that 7 times
                                                 been caught
                        and brought back
                   to a peach nobody.

                   To Continue:
                   Ron Padgett & Ted Berrigan
                        hates yr brain
                             my dears
                             amidst the many other little buzzes
                   & like, Today, as Ron Padgett might say
                             is
                   "A tub of vodka"
                                  "in the morning"

         she might reply
and that keeps it up
         past icy poles
                        where angels beg fr doom then zip
                             ping in-and-out, joining the army
                   wondering about Life
                   by the Public Library of
                             Life
                                  No Greater Thrill!
                   (I wonder)

Now that the earth is changing I wonder what time it's getting to be
        sitting on this New York Times Square
    that actually very ritzy, Lauren   it's made of yellow wood or
           I don't know something   maybe
          This man was my   it's been fluffed up
         friend
              He had a sense for the
                 vast   doesn't he?
        Awake my Angel! give thyself
           to the lovely hours   Don't cheat
      The victory is not always to the sweet.
        I mean that.

Now this picture is pretty good here
Though it once got demerits from the lunatic Arthur Cravan
He wasn't feeling good that day
Maybe because he had nothing on
                paint-wise I mean

PART 3

       I wrote that
        about what is
     this empty room   without a heart
       now in three parts
       a white flower
       came home wet & drunk   2 Pepsis
      and smashed my fist thru her window
               in the nude
  As the hand zips you see
      Old Masters, you can see
     well hung in New York   they grow fast here
      Conflicting, yet purposeful
        yet with outcry vain!

PART 4

      Praising, that's it!
you string a sonnet around yr fat gut
   and falling on your knees
             you invent the shoe
            for a horse. It brings you luck

while sleeping
"You have it seems a workshop nature"
Have you   "Good Lord!"
                                            Some folks is wood
seen them?   Ron Padgett wd say
                          amidst the many other little buzzes
                    past the neon on & off
                       night & day   STEAK SANDWICH
                 Have you ever tried one Anne?   SURE!
        "I wonder what time 'its'?"
              as I sit on this new Doctor
NO   I only look at buildings they're in
as you and he, I mean he & you & I buzz past
                          in yellow ties   I call that gold
                 THE HOTEL BUCKINGHAM
        (facade) is black, and taller than last time
is looming over lunch   naked   high time   poem   & I, equal in
                                            perfection & desire
        is looming   two eyes   over coffee-cup (white) nature
                    and man: both hell on poetry.
                 Art is art and life is
                       "A monograph on Infidelity"
            Oh. Forgive me stench of sandwich
            O pneumonia in American Poetry

      Do we have time?   well look at Burroughs
            7 times been caught and brought back to Mars
                       & eaten
"Art is art & Life
is home," Fairfield Porter said that
                          turning himself in
                             Tonight arrives again in red
some go on   even in Colorado   on the run
                       the forests shake
            meaning:
                    coffee   the cheerfulness of this poor
                                     fellow is terrible, hidden in
                                     the fringes of the eyelids
                 blue mysteries' (I'M THE SKY)
      The sky is bleeding now
                 onto 57th Street
                 of the 20th Century &

HORN & HARDART'S

Right Here. That's PART 5

I'm not some sailor off a ship at sea
I'm the wanderer   (age 4)
                         & now everyone is dead
                    sinking bewildered of hand, of foot, of lip
   nude, thinking
laughter burnished brighter than hate

                                                   Goodbye.
                   André Breton said that
                                        what a shit!
Now he's gone!
                   up bubbles all his amorous breath
                   & Monograph on Infidelity entitled
                                             The Living Dream
I never again played
                         I dreamt that December 27th, 1965
                    all in the blazon of sweet beauty's breast

        I mean   "a rose"   Do you understand that?
                         Do you?
The rock&roll songs of this earth
commingling absolute joy AND
incontrovertible joy of intelligence
                                   certainly can warm
                              can't they?   YES!
                         and they do.
                   Keeping eternal whisperings around

                                        (Mr. Macadams writes in
                                        the nude: no that's not
                                        me that: then zips in &
(we want to take the underground   out the boring taxis, re-
    revolution to Harvard!)   fusing to join the army
                                        asleep "on the springs"
          and yet this girl has   of red GENEROSITY)
                so much grace
                   I wonder!
             Were all their praises simply prophecies
        of this
                   the time!   NO GREATER THRILL
                         my friends

But I quickly forget them, those other times, for what are they
but parts in the silver lining of the tiny cloud my brain
drifting up into smoke the city's tough blue top:

I think a picture always
leads you gently to someone else
Don't you? like when you ask to leave the room
& go to the moon.

1966   1969

A Certain Slant of Sunlight

In Africa the wine is cheap, and it is
on St. Mark's Place too, beneath a white moon.
I'll go there tomorrow, dark bulk hooded
against what is hurled down at me in my no hat
which is weather: the tall pretty girl in the print dress
under the fur collar of her cloth coat will be standing
by the wire fence where the wild flowers grow not too tall
her eyes will be deep brown and her hair styled 1941 American
            will be too; but
I'll be shattered by then
But now I'm not and can also picture white clouds
impossibly high in blue sky over small boy heartbroken
to be dressed in black knickers, black coat, white shirt,
            buster-brown collar, flowing black bow-tie
her hand lightly fallen on his shoulder, faded sunlight falling
across the picture, mother & son, 33 & 7, First Communion Day, 1941—
I'll go out for a drink with one of my demons tonight
they are dry in Colorado 1980 spring snow.

1988

My Autobiography

For love of Megan I danced all night,
fell down, and broke my leg in two places.
I didn't want to go to the doctor.
Felt like a goddam fool, that's why.
But Megan got on the phone, called

my mother.   Told her, Dick's broken
his leg, & he won't go to the doctor !
Put him on the phone, said my mother.
Dickie, she said, you get yourself
up to the doctor right this minute !
Awwww, Ma, I said.   All right, Ma.
Now I've got a cast on my leg from
hip to toe, and I lie in bed all day
and think.   God, how I love that girl !

1988

In Your Fucking Utopias

Let the heart of the young
    exile the heart of the old :   Let the heart of the old
Stand exiled from the heart of the young :   Let
    other people die :   Let Death be inaugurated.
Let there be Plenty Money.   & Let the
Darktown Strutters pay their way in
To The Gandy-Dancers Ball.   But Woe unto you, O
    Ye Lawyers, because I'll be there, and
        I'll be there.

1988

Diane di Prima
b. 1934

Born in Brooklyn and educated at Swarthmore College, Diane di Prima began corresponding with poets Ezra Pound and Kenneth Patchen at age nineteen. Her first book of poems, *This Kind of Bird Flies Backwards*, was published in 1958, followed by a book of prose, *Dinners and Nightmares*, in 1960. In 1961, while living on Manhattan's Lower East Side, she began editing the literary magazine *The Floating Bear* with LeRoi Jones. The same year, the editors were arrested by the FBI for alleged obscenity, but the case was thrown out by the grand jury. Her second poetry collection, *The New Handbook of Heaven*, appeared in 1963.

In 1968 she moved to San Francisco, where she studied with Zen master Shenryu Suzuki Roshi. Her most popular early collection, *Revolutionary Letters*, was published in 1971. The same year, she began writing the long poem *Loba*, parts 1–8 of which were published in 1978. The poem began with a dream di Prima had in Wyoming of being followed by a wolf:

> . . . at some point, I turned around and looked this creature in the eye, and I recognized, in my dream . . . this huge white wolf, beautiful white head, recognized this as a goddess that I'd known in Europe a long long time ago. Never having read about any European wolf-goddesses, I just recognized this as deity. And we stood and looked at each other for a long moment.[1]

Like Jerome Rothenberg, di Prima is interested in alternative European spiritual traditions such as "Paganism, Gnosticism, alchemy"; she is also devoted to the "Way-seeking Mind" of Buddhism.[2] Associated with the Beat movement, di Prima writes poetry of "magical evocation," to borrow from one of her titles, that has a Keatsian lyricism and roundness of phrasing.

Cofounder of the New York Poets Theatre, di Prima taught at the Jack Kerouac School of Disembodied Poetics, Naropa Institute, from 1974 to 1997. A collection of selected poems, *Pieces of a Song*, was published in 1990. In 2001, she published the memoir *Recollections of My Life as a Woman: The New York Years*. In 2009, Di Prima was named Poet Laureate of San Francisco.

1. Diane di Prima, "The Birth of Loba," in *Symposium of the Whole: A Range of Discourse Toward an Ethnopoetics*, ed. Jerome Rothenberg, Berkeley, 1983, p. 442.　　2. The same, p. 444.

The Practice of Magical Evocation

The female is fertile, and discipline
(contra naturam) only
confuses her
—Gary Snyder

i am a woman and my poems
are woman's: easy to say
this   the female is ductile
and
        (stroke after stroke)
built for masochistic
calm.   The deadened nerve
is part of it:
awakened sex, dead retina
fish eyes;   at hair's root
minimal feeling

and pelvic architecture functional
assailed inside & out
(bring forth)   the cunt gets wide
and relatively sloppy
bring forth men children only
                           female
                           is
                           ductile

woman, a veil thru which the fingering Will
twice torn
twice torn
              inside & out
the flow
what rhythm add to stillness
what applause?

1975

On Sitting Down to Write, I Decide Instead to Go
to Fred Herko's Concert

As water, silk
the quiver of fish

or the long cry of goose
  or some such bird
  I never heard
your orange tie
a sock in the eye
  as Duncan
  might forcibly note
are you sitting under the irregular drums
of Brooklyn Joe Jones
(in a loft which I know to be dirty
& probably cold)
or have you scurried already
   hurried already
uptown
on a Third Avenue Bus
toward smelly movies & crabs I'll never get
and you all perfumed too
as if they'd notice

O the dark caves of obligation
into which I must creep
  (alack)
like downstairs & into a coat
  O all that wind
Even Lord & Taylor don't quite keep out
that wind
and that petulant vacuum
I am aware of it
sucking me into Bond Street
into that loft
  dank
  rank
I draw a blank
at the very thought

   Hello
I came here
  after all

         1975

For H.D.

1

trophies of pain I've gathered.   whose sorrow
do I shore up, in trifles?   the weavings,
paintings, jewels, plants, I bought

with my heart's hope.   rocks from the road
to Hell, broken pieces of statuary, ropes,
bricks, from the city of Dis.

encrusted.   they surround me: nest
the horror of each act from which I saved
a dried, dismembered hand.   poisoned

amulets, empty vials still fuming.   their tears
saved lovingly as my own.   to have
"lived passionately"   this secret

hoarding of passion.   Truth turned against itself.

2

Heart's truth, spat out of sleep, was only hate.
I caught it, on my pillows.   Tried
to turn it to diamonds.   Sometimes succeeded

so far as quartz in the hand.   Like ice it melted.
Heat of my will   burns down the walls around me
time after time.   Yet there remain

encrustations of old loves.   Filthy barnacles
sucking my marrow.   My illness:
that I am not blind,   yet cannot transmute

In body cauldron I carried
hate or indifference, anger,   clothed it
in child flesh,   & in the light

it seemed I had worked magic. But the stone
sticks in their throats. Night screams & morning tears
phantoms of fathers,   dead skin hung on

old bones.   Like jewels in the hair.

3

"I am a woman of pleasure"   & give back
salt for salt. Untrammeled by hope or knowledge
I have left these

in the grindstones of other thresholds.   Now only bedrock
basalt to crack your breath.   Beloved.   To suck for drink.
I am not fair.   But you are more than fair.

You are too kind.   Still water   in which,
like a crystal, the phantoms dance.
Each carrying death like a spear,   for we die

of each other's hate, or indifference.   Draw blood
to draw out poison.   But it has seat
in heart of our heart, the hollow of the marrow

of our bones.   Salt for salt   & the desert
is infinite   it drinks
more juice than we carry.

4

O, I'd yet beg bread, or water,   wd lie
in the dry wash & pray the flood wd come
That my eyes unstick,   that I see stars

as I drown.   For 25 years, bruised, wounded,
I've hid in rocks.   Fed by hyenas, vultures, the despised
that chew carrion   & share the meal

which, sharing,   you lose caste;   forget
human laws.   My blood
tastes in my mouth like sand.

5

humiliated   time & again   by song
laughter from cracked lips.
power of incantation stirring to life

what shd sleep, like stone.   yet the turquoise
sparkles.   "happy to see you"   stars
beat against my skin.   what is mine:

cold prickles,   moving out
from spine.   pulsing skull
pushing to light.   burning bushes

that lie.   snow mountains where gods
leave laws, like stones.   Anubis in Utah.
and tears.   and tears.   and tears.

to bless my desert   and give back
song for salt.

1975

Backyard

where angels turned into honeysuckle & poured nectar into my mouth
where I french-kissed the roses in the rain
where demons tossed me a knife to kill my father in the stark
    simplicity of the sky
where I never cried
where all the roofs were black
where no one opened the venetian blinds
O Brooklyn! Brooklyn!
where fences crumbled under the weight of rambling roses
and naked plaster women bent eternally white over birdbaths
the icicles on the chains of the swings tore my fingers
& the creaking tomato plants tore my heart as they wrapped their
    roots around fish heads rotting beneath them
& the phonograph too creaked Caruso come down from the skies;
    Tito Gobbi in gondola; Gigli ridiculous in soldier uniform;
    Lanza frenetic
& the needle tore at the records & my fingers
tore poems into little pieces & watched the sky

where clouds torn into pieces & livid w/neon or rain
scudded away from Red Hook, away from Gowanus Canal, away
from Brooklyn Navy Yard where everybody worked, to fall to pieces
    over Clinton Street
and the plaster saints in the yard never looked at the naked women
    in the birdbaths
and the folks coming home from work in pizza parlor or furniture
    store, slamming wrought iron gates to come
    upon brownstone houses,
never looked at either: they saw that the lawns were dry
were eternally parched beneath red gloomy sunsets we viewed from
    a thousand brownstone stoops
leaning together by thousands on the same
wrought-iron bannister, watching the sun impaled
on black St. Stephen's steeple

                                                1975

The Loba Addresses the Goddess / or The Poet as Priestess Addresses the Loba-Goddess

Is it not in yr service that I wear myself out
running ragged among these hills, driving children
to forgotten movies? In yr service
broom & pen. The monstrous feasts
we serve the others on the outer porch
(within the house there is only rice & salt)
And we wear exhaustion like a painted robe
I & my sisters
                wresting the goods from the niggardly
           dying fathers
healing each other w / water & bitter herbs
that when we stand naked in the circle of lamps
(beside the small water, in the inner grove)
we show
no blemish, but also no superfluous beauty.
It has burned off in watches of the night.
O Nut, O mantle of stars, we catch at you
    lean   mournful
    ragged   triumphant
     shaggy as grass
our skins ache of emergence / dark o' the moon

                                                  1978

Clayton Eshleman
b. 1935

Born and raised in Indianapolis, where his father was an efficiency expert in a slaughterhouse, Clayton Eshleman attended Indiana University. It was as editor of the English department's literary magazine, *Folio,* that he became acquainted with Paul Blackburn, Jerome Rothenberg, and Robert Kelly, poets with whom he has been associated.

Following graduation, Eshleman discovered the poetry of Pablo Neruda and César Vallejo and began to teach himself Spanish in order to know their work better. While living in Mexico in the summers of 1958 and 1959, he began his distinguished career as translator of poetry by translating some of Neruda's *Residencias* to English. His translation, with José Rubia Barcia, of *César Vallejo: The Complete Posthumous Poetry* won the 1979 National Book Award. His translation of Vallejo's *The Complete Poetry* was published in 2007. He has also edited two of the most important literary magazines of the postmodern period, *Caterpillar* (1967–1973) and *Sulfur* (1981–2000).

Eshleman's poetry has affinities with the writings of Blake, Vallejo, Artaud, and Césaire, as well as the psychological theories of Wilhelm Reich and Carl Jung. He also claims a connection with the music of Bud Powell and paintings of Chaim Soutine. Since the mid-1970s, he has incorporated what he calls "Paleolithic Imagination and the Construction of the Underworld" into his poetry. His vision of the underworld was shaped significantly by his visits to the Dordogne region of France in 1974 and 1978, where he studied the prehistoric cave paintings in the Lascaux, Combarelles, and Trois Frères caves. A book by the archetypal psychologist James Hillman, *The Dream and the Underworld,* established for Eshleman that Paleolithic art was less concerned with the empirical reality of "daytime activity" than with the ancient and ongoing worlds of dream, archetype, and myth.[1] Embodying a virtual "history of the image," the signs and animals of the cave walls "become a language upon which all subsequent mythology has been built."

According to the critic Eliot Weinberger, Eshleman is "the primary American practitioner of what Mikhail Bahktin calls 'grotesque realism.' It is an immersion in the body; not the body of the individual, the 'bourgeois ego,' but the body of all."[2]

Among Eshleman's numerous books are *Indiana* (1969), *Coils* (1973), *Hades in Manganese* (1981), *Hotel Cro-Magnon* (1989), *Under World Arrest* (1994), *An Alchemist with One Eye on Fire* (2006), *Grindstone of Rapport: A Clayton Eshleman Reader* (2008), and *Anticline* (2010). His prose volumes include *Antiphonal Swing: Selected Prose 1962–1987* (1989), *Companion Spider* (essays) in 2002, and *Juniper Fuse: Upper Paleolithic Imagination & the Construction of the Underworld* (2003).

Among other institutions, Eshleman taught at the California Institute of

Technology, where he served as Dreyfuss Poet-in-Residence, and at Eastern
Michigan University. He lives in Ypsilanti.

1. Preface to *Hades in Manganese*, Santa Barbara, 1981, p. 10.　　2. Introduction to Eshleman's
The Name Encanyoned River: Selected Poems 1960–1985, Santa Barbara, 1986, p. 14.

The Lich Gate

Waiting, I rest in the waiting gate.
Does it want to pass my death on,
or to let my dying pass into the poem?
Here I watch the windshield redden
the red of my mother's red Penney coat,
the eve of Wallace Berman's 50th birthday drunk
truck driver smashed Toyota,
a roaring red hole, a rose in whirlpool
placed on the ledge of a bell-less shrine.
My cement sits propped against the post. To live
is to block the way and
to move over at the same time, to hang
from the bell-less hook, a tapeworm in the packed
organ air, the air resonant with fifes, with mourners
filing by the bier
resting in my hands, my memory coffer
in which an acquaintance is found.
Memory is acquaintance. Memory is not a friend.
The closer I come to what happened,
the less I know it, the more I love
what I see beyond the portable
frame in which I stand—I, clapper, never free,
will bang, if the bell rope is pulled.
Pull me, Gladys and Wallace say to my bell, and you
will pass through, the you of I, your
pendulum motion, what weights
you, the hornet-nest shaped
gourd of your death, your scrotal
lavender, your red glass crackling
with fire-embedded mirror. In vermillion and black
the clergyman arrives. At last
something can be done about this
weighted box. It is the dead who come forth to
pull it on. I do nothing here.
When I think I do, it is the you-hordes

leaning over my sleep with needle-shaped
fingers without pause they pat
my still silhouette which shyly moves.
The lich gate looks like it might collapse.
Without a frame in which to wait,
my ghoul would spread. Bier in lich,
Hades' shape, his sonnet prism reflecting
the nearby churchyard, the outer hominid limit,
a field of rippling meat. I have come here
to bleed this gate, to make my language fray
into the invisibility teeming against
The Mayan Ballcourt of the Dead, where
I see myself struggling intently,
flux of impact, the hard
rubber ball bouncing against the stone hoop.

                                                              1979

Iraqi Morgue

Blackened semi-smile
   eyelidlifted turned

rust fur   Can't get a
fix on

mangled slab of splintered bone,
stringy red muscles.

Armpit trying to raise
mouth milk,
                    eyes
staring at something great.

Eyes like headlights still on
in twisted steel.

0070 64 F 04 is sad,
he's looking up to the right
cheeks bulging.

Some are camouflaged, it seems,
with death labels &

plastic label bags
    —ears show,
    a tooth rip.

Black skin rubble
no eyes   upper teeth
        in death lisp.

Faceless, no, burned to
    a congealed
insectile smear.

Shattered lit
skull rubble through which
one eye blasts.

Maroon head skin
tucked up about its bag shoulder
as if asleep.

What am I looking at?
At horror looking through
an 1899 update:
after the lynch picnic,
the knuckles of Sam Hose displayed
in the window of an Atlanta grocery.

340 04 v 04
nearly all blood.

    Very old man gray
turned head cupped
in death sheet blossom.

                                                        2006

In Memory of George Butterick

Fortress of summer. Heat a connecting rod.
Black leaf mouth of the redbud chewing everywhichway.

Thoughts of George back in the hospital
so overwhelmed the light in those leaf jaws

I called Colette:
George was home,
                              difficult to speak, but he did,
courageous even, asking about Paul Blackburn.
"Where did his start?" Or more specifically: "Did it start
    in the esophagus?   I thought so . . ."

              Poetry, a nativity
                      poised
          on an excrement-flecked blade—

Paradise, you are wadding,
to plug one big gap?
                      Dogtown to be
so total a place in Charles Olson's desire
that concepts of hell, or any mountain-climbed heaven
become inadequate to the congruence of earth's facets.

But then there is the Celan-
hole, the no-one God, void of the ovens.

Dear George, I am moved by how many lives lived
are ivy.

By how life breaks through wall after wall only to provide
more stone.

How each is less than he is,
and more.

Self-knotted Nile of the anticline in which
we curl.

[9 July 1987–2008]   2010

Combarelles

The horse showing through
the cave wall showing through the horse. Goal
                              of engraving:
to arrive
        As reciprocity.

★

A limestone lightning rod for the new mind's animal-
flashing borderless rinks, in-bordered
                              with a line
                        scraped between me
and the thee of cosmic indivisibility.

★

The fine sand of creature life poured through the mind's riven mesh.

★

In the jigsaw puzzle of creation, the desire to not
just fit, but to allow, through
                        sudden aperture,
the hiss of the shuddering other.

2010

Eternity at Domme

Between the junipers flows the Dordogne.
My home is near, as close as gone—
identity in the archaic region of the soul.
Between the junipers flows the Dordogne.

Sunlit crags with chestnuts, lindens overgrown.
What chambers, what cavalcades engraved—
I'll never reach the pillowed rock Laussel arranged.
Between the junipers flows the Dordogne.

Can arrival at yearning's core
be said to decorticate home? Is home my immured
animality, the phantom lurking in my stain?

I'm ancient as never before this afternoon,
charged with karstic urge, fully born.
Between the junipers flows the Dordogne.

[9 June 2007]   2010

Ronald Johnson
1935–1998

Born in Ashland, Kansas, Ronald Johnson graduated from Columbia University and lived for a time in New York, where he met the poet and publisher Jonathan Williams and was introduced to poets of the Black Mountain influence. Although associated primarily with the Black Mountain poets, Johnson began to experiment with concrete poetry and proceduralism in the late 1960s. His long poem *RADI OS*, for instance, is a systematic erasure of Milton's *Paradise Lost*. In the 1970s, he served as Writer in Residence at the University of Kentucky, and he held the Roethke Chair for Poetry at the University of Washington. Eventually he moved to San Francisco, where he lived for twenty-five years.

Johnson's volumes of poetry include *A Line of Poetry, A Row of Trees* (1964), which he dedicated to Charles Olson; *The Book of the Green Man* (1967), inspired by his walking trip of England; *Valley of the Many-Colored Grasses* (1969); *Eyes and Objects* (1976); and *ARK,* his visionary epic begun in the early 1970s and published in its entirety in 1995. *ARK* consisted of three sections of thirty-three poems: *The Foundations* (made up of Beams), *The Spires,* and *The Ramparts* (whose cantos are called Arches). In the words of scholar Eric Murphy Selinger:

> Over these, as a metaphorical dome, rests ARK 100, a rewriting of *Paradise Lost* by excision. There is a temporal sequence to the poems as well, since *The Foundations* begin at sunrise and end at noon, *The Spires* go to sundown, and *The Ramparts* overlook a midnight of the Soul even as they show the *ARK* transformed into a metaphorical starship ("all arrowed a rainbow midair, / ad astra per aspera / countdown for Lift Off").[1]

In an interview, Johnson comments on the architecture of his epic: "I think that at the heart of *ARK* is my father's lumber yard. . . . It was a huge building with these slots for different kinds and lengths of wood. And it was kind of a maze of wood—a wooden maze. And there were secret rooms and belfries—with bats, there was one with bats. . . . Oh, it was a secret playground which had many stalls."[2] He also reveals the process by which *RADI OS* was created: "*RADI OS* happened before *ARK.* It was when I was teaching at the University of Washington. I went to a party at a student's one night and they played a Lukas Foss record called 'Baroque Variations.' His Handel piece, his strategy was to take Handel and erase things so that it had a modern, modish feel, but it was definitely Handel. . . . [T]he next day I went to the bookstore and bought a Milton *Paradise Lost.* And I started crossing out. I got about halfway through it crossing out anything because I thought it would be funny. But I decided you don't tamper with Milton to be funny. You have to be serious."[3]

Johnson's last book of poetry, *The Shrubberies,* was published in 2001. He died at his father's home in Topeka, Kansas.

1. Biography of Ronald Johnson, *The Dictionary of Literary Biography,* reprinted at http://www .trifectapress.com/Johnson/interview1.html.   2. Peter O'Leary, "Ronald Johnson Interview, November 19, 1995," http://www.trifectapress.com/johnson/interview1.html.   3. The same.

FROM *Ark: The Foundations*

Beam 6, The Musics

Let flick his tail, the darkling Lion, down to the primal
  huddle fiddling DNA.

Let the Elephant ruffle the elements in The Great Looped
  Nebula with his uplift trunk.

Let the Binary, orange, emerald, and blue, in the foot of
  Andromeda run awhisker with Mouse.

Let the Dickcissel, in Cock's-foot, Foxtail, & Tottering,
  ring one molecular ornamentation on tau Ceti.

Let the Switch Snake lilt bluegrass back and forth between
  pellucid cells.

Let Porcupine rattle quill, in a Casseopia of Hollyhock.

Let the whinny of Pigeons' wings trigger similar strains
  from elm to Triangulum.

Let a score for matter's staccato to cornstalk be touted to
  stars clustering The Archer's wrist.

Let the stripes of Zebra be in time with the imaginary
  House of Mozart, on Jupiter.

1980

Beam 8

Line eye us.
Web stir us.

—as the eye leaves outside of itself the object it sees—
the mind weaves it
of itself
incessant shuttle to external's
shelf
point . circle . point
(a double cone in counterpoint)
within, without
AS I PASS THROUGH A WINDOW REFLECTED BEHIND ME
in a glass
held in my hand, behold:

wind Os wind Os

wind Os wind Os

wind Os wind Os

wind Os wind Os

—ripple-intersecting circles
Open, Close—

in equipoise through the nuclei's 'quadrupole
moments'

mag-nets-nets-nets

&c.

1980

Beam 33

pyre, eyrie
From here, barred owls ladder winter sun's
resounding arroyos'
"earths of different colours, as blue, a kind of crimson,

grass-green, shining black, chalkwhite, and ochre"
against

Montagnes de Pierres Brillants,
now Rockies.
Or there, a stand of scarlet sumac (with bobolink
sphericling the hereabouts
lit with a fine straw-colored light like the spirits of trees
—some Appalachia for backdrop)

drinks in all green wide summer
to a berry.
Off the porch, I see twelve miles into the sunflower patch.
High noon stands still as a just picked apple.
prairie, prairie
These are The Foundations.

1980

FROM *RADI OS*

O   tree
into the World,
                                    Man

————————————————————————————— the chosen ———————————————————————

Rose out of Chaos:

                                                    song,

                                                        outspread,
                                    on the vast

Illumine,

I

   Say first—

                              what time

                                   aspiring

                        equal

Raise

        headlong

To bottomless

                      fire

    times the space that measures

                                thought

Both

                               eyes,

At once,

                on all sides round,

                                    fed
With
        place Eternal

In utter darkness,

        from the centre

                    whirlwind

        "If

        Myriads

        Joined
        In Equal

                    thunder:
The force of

                        outward lustre,   mind,

                            raised

        Innumerable

                        on the plains of
        And
        All is
        And
        And

And
That

Who, from the terror of this

empyreal

Irreconcilable
of joy

answered

Too well I see

: for the mind

swallowed up

entire,

in the heart   to work in fire,

words the Arch

being

!

the gates of

lightning

through the vast and boundless

rest,

With head uplift above the wave, and eyes

1977

Gustaf Sobin
1935–2005

Born in Boston and educated at Brown University, Gustaf Sobin first visited Provence in 1962 to see the French poet René Char, whose work he greatly admired. The following year, carrying only a bag and a briefcase, he moved to the village of Gordes, in the Vaucluse region of Provence, where he bought a stone cottage for $800. He lived there for the rest of his life.

According to the critic Paul Christensen, Sobin's well-crafted poems can be compared to his *borie* (a hive-shaped rock shelter common to Vaucluse) in that they comprise "a structure of mortarless emjambments."[1] Yet Sobin also strongly holds to an organic theory of composition. "Language is the husk of experience," he told Christensen in conversation, "as when the milk is bound by the juice of the fig." The first line or phrase of a poem, which Sobin calls its nexus," contains "the entire poem in its yet-unraveled trajectory: i.e., not only its 'message,' but both the direction of its thrust and the rate of its movement, its meter." Because poems have a decided momentum, "poetry is as kinetic as cinema, its movement . . . irresponsible as breath."[2] Besides René Char, Sobin claims the American poets Robert Duncan and George Oppen as his most important predecessors—Duncan for his orphic sense of "language as the generator, the mother, the source of all being," and Oppen for the "focused intensity" of the work.[3]

Sobin's work includes the New Directions volumes, *Wind Chrysalid's Rattle* (1980), *The Earth as Air* (1984), *Voyaging Portraits* (1988), and *Breaths' Burials* (1995). Following the death of publisher James Laughlin, his books were published by Talisman House; they include *By the Bias of Sound: Selected Poems, 1974–1994* (1995), *Toward the Blanched Alphabets* (1998), *In the Name of the Neither* (2002), *The Places as Preludes* (2005), and *Collected Poems* (2010). His novels include *Venus Blue* (1992), The *Fly Truffler* (2000), and *In Pursuit of a Vanishing Star* (2002). He published three books of essays, most notably *Luminous Debris: Reflecting on Vestige in Provence and Languedoc* (2000).

1. "A Noble Wave," review of Voyaging Portraits, in *Temblor* 7, 1988, p. 24.   2. "A Few Stray Comments on the Cultivation of the Lyric," in *Talisman* 10, 1993, p. 41.   3. Edward Foster, "An Interview with Gustaf Sobin," *Talisman* 10, 1993, p. 35.

What the Music Wants

In Memory of George Oppen

what the music
wants is
pod and tentacle (the thing
wiggling,
wild

as washed
hair, spread).   is our-
selves, in-

serted.   within
our
own rhythms: wrapt, voluted,
that miracle
of
measure-

ascendant.   *to*
stand, that there's some-
where to

stand.   marble
over

moorings, the
scaffolds, now, as if
vanished, and the steps, the
floors: spoken
forth.   *to*
stand, stand there, with-
in
sound alone,
that

miracle!

                 is what the
waters comb, and the

bells,
beating,
count (faint, now, over the

waves, in a
garland
of
bells). *is*

somewhere, and
wrapt

in the bulb
of its
voices, are buoyant, among.

1988

Eleven Rock Poems

for Emmanuel Muheim

sent myself the   length
    of my own metaphors (boxwood, then cistus, the
swallows going white in the   high winds).   a
    body wrapt a-

bout the mirror of its   breath, slept
        nights in the shallow, black waves of the   rocks.

---

    where ice lacquered the
red arrows rose, a wrist hoisted
        its ankles   after.   lapped muscles, the
    limbs-chromatic, would
reach, touch, be drawn through the   roots of
                            that reaching.

---

    up, out of the last, lime-
stone cirque, on footpaths a   half-
        foot wide, looked down.   saw my-

self, as if
dissolving—washed blue, the back
                              still bent—as I climbed.

———————————

the eyes rising through those random
stations, their
                    wedged breath- holds (as if
'something' drew, pulled, as if
                              a 'somewhere,' finally, were).

———————————

as much dust as   snow, the
trail's driven into
              those deep, mineral creases (had carried
          shadows, the bundled sticks of their tinder.   over
the soft, billowing shrouds, had beaten

          breath, pulled light from the thin meats of
                              each murmur).

———————————

all space, as it muscles in   sound (im-
mensity driven, com-
                    pressed into such quick passages . . .).

———————————

chord the   body hauls a-
cross the washed minerals, sporadic blacks
              of the stout ilex, saw the   fixed intervals
moving (and 'the
                    harmonies' as they shattered, strayed, re-

                    grouped).

———————————

high, now, over the river, where
millgirls, once, set the long- wicked snails
              flaming downstream, the

          path vanishes, breaks
into boxwood, cade.   (shall weigh shadows; where the   thin

winds shiver, read
    their mineral palm).

––––––––––––

 for that itinerant breath- pilgrim, may
the rock be hollow, *be*
   grotto; within it, may the
 ashes of those last opaque vocables a-
      light.

––––––––––––

 loss, each time, descending, as the
rhythms catch
  on the quick loops of re-
entry, and out, over the shoulders, the
    rocks sprout, rise, un-
      fold.

––––––––––––

 had plumbed space, sideways. blown,
through its god-
  less body, these showers of thin, hissing
 splinters. (that the

emptiness be edged, wedged, that pierced, it
    spread open).

        1988

Genesis

 from the very outset, a
 needle, a
 no-thread,
 run inextricable
 through the living mass. flared, then

 guttered, that
 ore, that either, that *isn't* that

 is. wasn't this
 what you'd flex to, sink

through: gaze so much lighter than all
the

oleander it ever
lingered
in?

1998

Under the Bright Orchards

for M.W.

. . . ink's for the
phosphorous white eyelets, for sprinkling the
pages with
blown
phonemes. a counterworld, you'd

called it: an erratic calligraphy
of
hatched shadows (*was what
had brought us, carried us, in dark drafts, a-
cross the
vaporous landscapes of the
rigorously*

pre-
scribed). a squiggle, then, for the
first hornet, pale
tracery

for the rush, clustering, of
bud. does it curl, will it catch? wrap us, this
very instant, in the
folds of our

own dictation? here, here's
a
dash, and there, the scooped hull of some sudden
imperative. drags, now,
in deep loops, our

hearts under, holds us in the
spell of
its running numbers. rocks, walls, the laddered
light: what the knuckles,
a-

lone, substantiate. passage, a passage, at
last, through the blanched
im-

measurable. yes, here, in a shiver of
blossoms, gloss of
winds, draws us —in
the
hollow coil of our own dark scribbles—past.

1998

Rosmarie Waldrop

b. 1935

Rosmarie Waldrop was born in Germany and lives in Providence, Rhode Island, where she codirects Burning Deck Press, a leading publisher of innovative poetry. Editor of *Serie d'écriture,* a journal of recent French poetry in translation, she is also a brilliant translator from French and German.

Waldrop's books include *The Aggressive Ways of the Casual Stranger* (1972), *The Road Is Everywhere or Stop This Body* (1978), *Streets Enough to Welcome Snow* (1986), *A Key into the Language of America* (1994), *Another Language: Selected Poems* (1997), *Split Infinites* (1998), *Love, Like Pronouns* (2003), *Blindsight* (2004), *Splitting Image* (2006), *Curves to the Apple* (2006), and *Driven to Abstraction* (2010). While she works very effectively in verse ("I love the way verse refuses to fill up all of the available space of the page so that each line acknowledges what is *not*"[1]), her chosen form is the prose poem, most effectively displayed perhaps, in her trilogy: *The Reproduction of Profiles* (1987), *Lawn of the Excluded Middle* (1993), and *Reluctant Gravities* (1999). Her attraction to the sentence as the organizing feature of her writing suggests an association with language poetry—for example, Ron Silliman's concept of the "new sentence":

> I must cultivate the cuts, discontinuities, ruptures, cracks, fissures, holes, hitches, snags, leaps, shifts of reference, and emptiness *inside* the semantic dimension. *Inside* the sentence. Explode its snakelike beauty of movement.[2]

However, her influences are primarily European and precede the arrival of language poetry. She cites living in Paris from 1970 to 1971, where she met the French poets Claude Royet-Journoud and Anne-Marie Albiach and began to translate the work of Edmond Jabès, as the turning point in her career as a poet. Referring to the varied language of Jabès's work, she says, "In my own work, too, I don't have one single mode. I write in a particular mode, and when at a certain point it runs dry, I try to do something different."[3] Waldrop is opposed to "the prophetic stance—the poet as vates, as priest, seer." Believing that God is absent from considerations of meaning, she holds that the "one transcendence available to us, that we can enter into, is language. It *is* like a sea. I often think of it as a space."[4]

Waldrop has been widely honored for her work, including the Harold Morton Landon translation award in 1994 for *The Book of Margins* by Edmond Jabès, a 2003 grant from the Foundation for Contemporary Arts, and the 2008 PEN Award for Poetry in Translation for Ulf Stolterfoht's *Lingos I–IX*. For her service to French literature, she was named a *Chevalier des Arts et des Lettres* by the French government and in 2006 was elected to the American Academy of Arts and Sciences.

Her prose works include two novels and a book of criticism, *Lavish Absence: Recalling and Rereading Edmond Jabès* (2002) and *Dissonance (if you are interested)*, 2005.

1. "Why Do I Write Prose Poems When My True Love Is Verse," *Dissonance (if you are interested)*, Tuscaloosa, 2005, p. 260.   2. The same, p. 262.   3. Edward Foster, "An Interview with Rosmarie Waldrop," *Talisman* 6, Spring 1991, p. 29.   4. The same, p. 31.

FROM Pre & Con or Positions and Junctions

For Craig Watson

1

The sun's light and
is compounded
and lovers and
emphatically

and cast long and shadows
of and a look
and on the
and face of a girl

waiting for and
the night and with imperfect
repose and secret
and craving

and bodies operate
and upon one and
another and blue
may differ
and in depth

2

Of bodies
of various
sizes of
vibrations

of blue excite
of never except
in his early
in childhood has he touched

of the space of
between of
to allow
of for impact

now of that color
has slowed
its pitch
or of skin

of but light
no deep foundation
nor of leans into
the blue

3

When vibrations
when impinge on when ends
of the nerve

pure when reason
the aqueous pores of
when capillamenta

but children are never
when mentioned
only the blue when

fills the when night
when incomprehension
enters itself

as when a fleet
when of ships in
when classical times

never leaves
never when sight of
when land

For Bernadette Mayer

4

The biggest
vibrations with
strongest red

plum
blossoms
yellow peach

with a confusion
with all with white with
with brain

the right
conjunction with
loss a whole world

great mansions
in with ruins along
with the bay held

up by
their reflection in
with water

5

And possibly color is
divided
into the octave

gradations of
into love into
impalpable

in spite of into careful
attention into
leaves blown

into autumn blown
into tension into
between

growing into and
into ungrowing
desire into and into

1998

CONVERSATION 1
On the Horizontal

My mother, she says, always spread, irresistibly, across the entire room, flooding me with familiarity to breed content. I feared my spongy nature and, hoping for other forms of absorption, opened the window onto more water, eyes level with its surface. And lower, till the words "I am here" lost their point with the vanishing air. Just as it's only in use that a proposition grinds its lens.

Deciphering, he says, is not a horizontal motion. Though the way a sentence is meant can be expressed by an expansion that becomes part of it. As a smile may wide-open a door. Holding the tools in my mouth I struggle uphill, my body so perfectly suspended between my father's push and gravity's pull that no progress is made. As if consciousness had to stay embedded in carbon. Or copy. Between camp and bomb. But if you try to sound feelings with words, the stone drops into reaches beyond fathoms.

I *am* here, she says, I've learned that life consists in fitting my body to the earth's slow rotation. So that the way I lean on the parapet betrays dried blood and invisible burns. My shadow lies in the same direction as all the others, and I can't jump over it. My mother's waves ran high. She rode them down on me as on a valley, hoping to flush out the minerals. But I hid my bones under sentences expanding like the flesh in my years.

Language, he says, spells those who love it, sliding sidelong from word to whole cloth. The way fingers extend the body into adventure, print, lakes, and Deadman's-hand. Wherever the pen pushes, in the teeth of fear and malediction, even to your signature absorbing you into sign. A discomfort with the feel of home before it grows into inflamed tissue and real illness. With symptoms of grammar, punctuation, subtraction of soul. And only death to get you out.

1999

CONVERSATION 2
On the Vertical

We must decipher our lives, he says, forward and backward, down through cracks in the crystal to excrement, entrails, formation of cells. And up. The way the lark at the end of night trills vertically out of the grass—and even that I know too vaguely, so many blades and barely sharper for the passing of blindness—up into anemic heights, the stand-still of time. Could we call this God? or meaning?

The suck of symbol, rather, she quotes. Or an inflection of the voice? Let the song go on. And time. My shadow locks my presence to the ground. It's real enough and outside myself, though regularly consumed at high noon. So maybe I should grant the shoot-out: light may flood me too, completely. But it won't come walking in boots and spurs, or flowing robes, and take my hand or give me the finger with the assurance of a more rational being. And my body slopes toward yours no matter how level the ground.

If we can't call it God, he says, it still perches on the mind, minting strangeness. How could we recognize what we've never seen? A whale in through the window, frame scattered as far as non-standard candles. The sky faints along the giant outline, thar she blows under your skin, tense, a parable right through the body that remains so painfully flesh.

So pleasurably flesh, she says, and dwells among us, flesh offered to flesh, thick as thieves, beginning to see. Even the lark's soar breaks and is content to drop back into yesterday's gravity. Which wins out over dispersion, even doubt, and our thoughts turn dense like matter. The way the sky turns deep honey at noon. The way my sensations seem to belong to a me that has always already sided with the world.

1999

CONVERSATION 3
On Vertigo

That's why thought, he says, means fear. Sicklied o'er with the pale cast. And the feel of a woman. No boundary or edge. No foothold. Blast outspins gravity, breath to temples, gut to throat, propositions break into gasps. Then marriage. The projectile returns to the point of firing. Shaken, I try to take shelter in ratios of dots on a screen.

A narrow bed, she says. Easier to internalize combustion under a hood while rain falls in sheets, glazing a red wheelbarrow for the hell of it. I don't bait fabled beasts to rise to the surface of intonation. But I once watched a rooster mate, and he felt hard inside me, a clenched fist, an alien rock inside me, because there was no thinking to dissolve him. So to slide down, so unutterably, so indifferent.

I don't understand, he says, how manifest destiny blows west with the grass, how the word "soul" floats through the language the way pollen pervades tissue. Worry pivots in the gut, a screeching brake, so scant the difference between mistake and mental disturbance. Is language our cockadoodledoo? Is thinking a search for curves? Do I need arrowheads or dreadlocks to reach my rawest thoughts? A keyboard at their edge?

The longer I watched, she says, the more distinctly did I feel the snap of that shot flat inside me. So simple the economy of nature: space appears along with matter. So to slide down and stand there. Such self-gravity. So narrow the gap between mistake and morning sickness.

1999

Object Relations

How differently our words drift across danger or rush toward a lover. Meaning married to always different coordinates. I married a foreigner, in one sense. In another, no word fits with another.

Your smile breaks from any point of your body. I need a more complicated picture. This falls among crow's-feet and bears no fruit. What did it try? Replace your body?

My doubts stand in a circle around us. Like visitors around the well under the house. They advise to board it up. Dampness unhinges. And decay of fish.

It would mean all night. Hands scraped on rough surmise. Remembering I too am a monster.

The objective character of statements has shifted to relations. Boiling water and the length of a column of mercury? Or that you mean me when you say "you?"

When I say "we were standing close" am I saying: we were not touching? To replace a laugh. Which could be described as: wish, yellowish, fish.

What if there is no well? What if language is not communication? If facts refuse coordinates? Detachment vanishes, as if thinned.

Meaning you consists in thinking of your body. There are no fish in my mouth.

2003

We Will Always Ask, What Happened?

Imagine a witch in the form of a naked girl. Now say her name. Is it foreign? Was the idea of the witch complete before you named the girl? Did you go down a passage that does not exist toward a well of dark water?

Your mind makes small rudimentary motions. Because the joke is against it? Because it does not know which way to turn and keeps reviewing the field of possible action? Aches? Actresses?

I hear you sighing. Intention is neither an emotion nor yet lip-synch of longing. It is not a state of consciousness. It does not have genuine duration. I say, are you alright?

Can you have an intention intermittently? abandon it like a soldier paralyzed the moment before battle? and resume it?

Could I order you to understand this sentence? just as I could tell you to run forward? Into the fire?

Would the understanding cast a shadow on the wall even though a premonition is not a bullet hole?

One symptom is that space is forced into a mirror. As if the event stood in readiness behind the silver. You move your hand, and it goes the other way. Then the earth opens up and you slide down your darkest desires.

Witches were killed by fire, by water, by hanging in air, burying in earth, by asphyxiation, penetration, striking, piercing, crushing in a thousand and one ways.

What was that name you gave her?

2003

Kathleen Fraser
b. 1937

Kathleen Fraser grew up in Oklahoma, Colorado, and California. After moving to New York for a career in journalism, she began studying poetry with Stanley Kunitz and Kenneth Koch. She was soon publishing poems in *The Nation, Poetry,* and *The New Yorker.* In 1964, she received the YMHA Poetry Center's Discovery Award and the New School's Frank O'Hara Poetry Prize, later followed by a National Endowment for the Arts Fellowship in poetry and a Guggenheim Fellowship. At the same time, she was coming to be associated with Black Mountain and New York School poets. In 1972, she returned to California to direct the Poetry Center at San Francisco State University, where she founded the American Poetry Archives and became a professor of Creative Writing.

She was cofounder, with Beverly Dahlen and Frances Jaffer, of *HOW(ever),* an influential journal devoted to the writing of experimentalist women such as Gertrude Stein, H.D., Lorine Niedecker, Mina Loy, and Barbara Guest. The journal also sought to include the writings of women in a theoretical discourse that had been primarily male. Her own critical writings are collected in *Translating the Unspeakable: Poetry and the Innovative Necessity* (2000).

Her poetry volumes include *Change of Address* (1966); *Magritte Series* (1977), a sequence of poems based on the paintings of the Surrealist painter; *New Shoes* (1978); *Each Next* (1980); *Something (even voices) in the foreground, a lake* (1984), *Notes Preceding Trust* (1987); *When New Time Folds Up* (1993); *WING* (1995); *Il cuore : the heart—New & Selected Poems 1970–1995* (1997); and *Discrete Categories Forced into Coupling* (2004). Over the course of these volumes, she has moved from an image-based poetics to one that is more linguistic in orientation. While this reflects her growing interest in language poetry, her identity as a poet remains independent of that movement.

In an essay on the poetic line, she writes: "The line, for a poet, locates the gesture of longing brought into language. It is the visual enactment of perspective and difference. . . . The poetic line is a primary defining place, the site of watchfulness where we discover *how* we hear ourselves take in the outside world and tell it back to ourselves."[1]

In 1993, she left her position at San Francisco State University to devote herself exclusively to her writing. She now divides her time between San Francisco and Rome.

1. "Line. One the Line. Lining Up. Lined with. Between the Lines. Bottom Line." In *The Line in Postmodern Poetry,* eds. Robert Frank and Henry Sayre, Champaign-Urbana (1988).

re : searches
(fragments, after Anakreon,
for Emily Dickinson)

inside
(jittery
burned language)
the black container

•

white bowl, strawberries
perfumy from sun
two spoons   two women
deferred pleasure

•

pious   impious
reason could not take
precedence

•

latent content
extant context

•

"eee wah yeh
my little owlet"
not connected up
your lit-up exit

•

just picked—
this red tumbling mound
in the bowl
this fact and its arrangement
this idea and who
determines it

•

this strawberry is
what separates her tongue
from just repetition

•

the fact of her
will last only
as long as she continues
releasing the shutter, she thinks

•

her toes are not
the edible boys'
toes Bernini carved,
more articulate
and pink in that gray
marble

•

his apprentice finished off
the wingy stone
splashing feathers from each
angel's shoulder but
Bernini, himself,
did the toes, ten-
der gamberoni,
prawnha, edible and
buttery under
the pink flame

•

this is what you looked like at ten,
held for an instant,
absorbed by the deep ruffle
and the black patent
shine of
your shoes

•

lying with one knee up
or sitting straight (yearning)
as if that yellow towel
could save you (some music about to hear you)

•

beside the spread, narrow surface, the
yellow terra
firma, the blue wave

longing to be her own
future sedative,
no blemish,
blond

•

wounded sideways,
wound up as if
     disqualified

•

externally, E-
ternal city,
sitting   hereafter,
laughter

•

her separate person-
ality, her
father's neutrality
ity

•

equalibrium
(cut her name
out of every
scribble)
hymn   himnal now, equal-
lateral

•

pronounced with
partially closed
lips

•

pink pearl eraser
erasing her face her
eee face ment
her face meant

•

he cut out
of her, her name
of each thing
she sang
each letter she
hung, on line
(divine)

•

this above
all to be who,
be nature's two,
and though heart
be pound-
ing at door,
cloud   cuckoo

•

radial activ-
ity, who cow now,
who moo

•

not random, these
crystalline structures, these
non-reversible orders, this
camera forming tendencies, this
edge of greater length, this
lyric forever error, this
something embarrassingly clear, this
language we come up against

1987

your back to me inside the black suit

Your back to me inside the black suit, inside your back and shoulders fitted into
sleeves marked with chalk at the insets. After this discovery, appearing to be exactly
identical in intensity to every other part of the backdrop, a person leaning against
it as if you,

assigned one full day in which necessity plays its part. Necessary to have a private pink human in the cosmic field: brown window shades delivering glimpses, propelling through to you. (Delete the anxiety of someone's chewing on a word before opening its

pronoun.) What did you mean by the series of inked life stages littering the lower half of a uniformly lined paged? Delivering my cool waters rowing through your own personal throat? No need to obscure when a cough can be heard in almost any room—

your precedent for going away. Away is nothing ready for use that has not been preparing itself.

2004

notebook 5: "in spite of gradual deficits"

Through deep parabolas of air you swim up to her.
The room says *I'm a little bit out of this world* but

you are inside her when you paint
and you like the pink embankments of her shoulders

A certain muscular ditch is flawless between two points
You can find both sides of her later

She gives you her colors when you scrape her down and layer her
again with rose madder bleached by repetitions of white in the width of big

embankments, as if you thought of her
as a road to somewhere called "dedication to light"

•

Everything sifts through the painter's torso which is central
in spite of gradual deficits and paired helical filaments,

"like a plasterer laying thin coats of sparkling paste" incised
with charcoal   Turning, staring at nothing, the hand holds

the hard paint tube oozing fresh pigment, stretched & trimmed
Yet her swollen red passages in crystalline absence and array

Drawing from early numbed chatter, trailing bright ridges
of silence   Or the lost year he tried to open her, smearing apart

Again and again pour of turpentine, plaques and tangles
roughly proportional to loss

2004

Susan Howe

b. 1937

Born in Ireland, Susan Howe emigrated with her family to the United States as a child. Her mother, Mary Manning, wrote plays and acted for Dublin's Abbey Theatre, and her father, Mark DeWolfe Howe, was a professor at Harvard Law School. One of the most prolific and widely admired poets of our time, she was an actress and assistant stage designer at Dublin's Gate Theatre, a painter, radio producer, and literary critic before beginning her tenure at the State University of Buffalo, 1989–2006. There she cofounded the Poetics Program. Her sister is the noted poet Fanny Howe.

Susan Howe's greatest influences are Charles Olson, especially in his attraction to the history and culture of New England, and Emily Dickinson, about whom Howe wrote the notable book of criticism *My Emily Dickinson* (1985). Howe also considers the early Puritan writers, especially Cotton Mather, to be important influences on her writing.

She has twice received the Before Columbus Foundation American Book Award, in 1980 for *Secret History of the Dividing Line* (1979) and in 1987 for *My Emily Dickinson.* Among her other books are *Pythagorean Silence* (1982), *Defenestration of Prague* (1983), *Articulation of Sound Forms in Time* (1987), *The Europe of Trusts: Selected Poems* (1990), *The Nonconformist's Memorial* (1993), *Frame Structures: Early Poems 1974–1979* (1996), *The Midnight* (2003), and *That This* (2010), an elegy upon the death of her husband Peter Hare. Each of her books focuses on a unique area of historical interest, such as the life and work of linguist Charles S. Pierce (*Pierce-Arrow,* 1998) and the Labadists, a Utopian Quietest sect of Cecil County Maryland, 1684–1722 (*Souls of the Labadie Tract,* 2007).

Of *Singularities* (1990), the critic Marjorie Perloff has written, "Susan Howe is unique in her ability to make history her own, to transform the archive and chronicle into an elusive, elliptical, and yet deeply personal drama in which the New England of the Indian wars, the New England of Thoreau enter the consciousness of the woman artist working into the American fin de siècle." Howe credits her interest in history to growing up during World War II: "The deaths of millions of people in Europe and Asia . . . prevented me from ever being able to believe history is only a series of justifications, or that tragedy and savagery can be theorized away."[1] She believes that "poetry brings similitude and representations to configurations waiting from forever to be spoken. . . . I write to break out into perfect primeval Consent. I wish I could tenderly lift from the dark side of history, voices that are anonymous, slighted—inarticulate."[2]

Recipient of the distinguished Bollingen Prize for 2011, Howe lives in Guilford, Connecticut.

1. Edward Foster, "An Interview with Susan Howe," *Talisman,* No. 4, 1990, p. 22.   2. *The Europe of Trusts,* 1990, Los Angeles, p. 14.

FROM Taking the Forest

Girl with forest shoulder
Girl stuttering out mask or trick

aria out of hearing

Sound through cult annunciation
sound through initiation Occult

Enunciate barbarous jargon
fluent language of fanaticism

Green tree of severance
Green tree girdled against splitting

Transmutation of murdered Totem

Foresters move before error
forgotten forgiven escaping conclusion

Oak and old hovel grow gossamer

■

Shoal kinsmen trespass Golden
Smoke splendor trespass

Symmetry carried from country
frail counterfeit well met

Lost among equivocations
Emancipator at empyrean center

Anarchy into named theory
Entangled obedience

muffled discourse from distance
mummy thread undertow slough

Eve of origin Embla the eve
soft origin vat and covert

Green hour avert grey future
Summer summon out-of-bound shelter

▪

Hook intelligence quick dactyl

Bats glance through a wood
bond between mad and made

anonymous communities bond and free

Perception crumbles under character
Present past of immanent future

Recollection moves across meaning
Men shut their doors against setting

Flocks roost before dark
Coveys nestle and settle

Meditation of a world's vast Memory

Predominance pitched across history
Collision or collusion with history

▪

Summary of fleeting summary
Pseudonym cast across empty

Peak proud heart

Majestic caparisoned cloud cumuli
East sweeps hewn flank

Scion on a ledge of Constitution
Wedged sequences of system

Causeway of faint famed city
Human ferocity

dim mirror Naught formula

archaic hallucinatory laughter

Kneel to intellect in our work
Chaos cast cold intellect back

▪

Hemmed trammels of illusion
rooted to shatter random

Firstborn of Front-sea
milestone by name farewell

Milestones bewitched millstones
Sleep passage from Europe

Otherworld light into fable

Negative face of blank force

Winds naked as March
bend and blend to each other

Fledgling humming on pathless

Old Double and old beginning Vain
Covergesture

▪

Latin ends and French begins

Golden page third voyage
Caravels bending to windward

Crows fly low and straggling
Civilizations stray into custom

Struts structure luminous region
Purpose or want of purpose

Part of each kingdom of Possession

Only conceived can be seen
Original inventors off Stray

Alone in deserts of Parchment
Theoreticians of the Modern

—emending annotating inventing
World as rigorously related System

Pagan worlds moving toward destruction

▪

Visible surface of Discourse

Runes or allusion to runes
Tasks and turning flock

Evening red enough for chivalry

Algorithms bravadoes jetsam
All Wisdom's plethora pattern

paper anacoluthon and naked chalk

Luggage of the prairie
Wagons pegged to earth

Tyrannical avatars of consciousness
emblazoned in tent-stitch

Five senses of syntax

Dear Unconscious scatter syntax
Sythe mower surrender hereafter

Dear Cold cast violet coronal

World weary flesh by Flesh bygone
Bridegroom

▪

Last line of blue hills

Lost fact dim outline

Little figure of mother

Moss pasture and wild trefoil
meadow-hay and timothy

She is and the way She was

Outline was a point chosen
Outskirts of ordinary

Weather in history and heaven

Skiff feather glide house

Face seen in a landscape once

▪

To kin I call in the Iron-Woods
Turn I to dark Fells last alway

Theirs was an archheathen theme
Soon seen stumbled in lag Clock

Still we call bitterly bitterly
Stern norse terse ethical pathos

Archaic presentiment of rupture
Voicing desire no more from here

Far flung North Atlantic littorals

Lif sails off longing for life
Baldr soars on Alfather's path

Rubble couple on pedestal
Rubble couple Rhythm and Pedestal

Room of dim portraits here there
Wade waist deep maidsworn men

Crumbled masonry windswept hickory

1987

FROM Bedhangings

To the Compiler of Memories

Frequent exposure to night air
An inattention to the necessity
of changing damp clothes

Sweet affliction sweet affliction
Singing as I wade to heaven

■

Soon swerved from what
people of his charge took him
to be

Not only alone but on foot
with his luggage on his back
On the first of January 1801

Something over against is
what surprised the sadder
and wiser

■

Sandemanian sentiments of
course he never preached as
the denomination admits no
correlative save Christ and his
apostles for the rote of ethic
Embracing the sentiments of
the Sandemanians he was dis-

missed and his apostle until
the church became extinct a
study of odd relic aforesaid

■

I am going to confine myself
beneath disguises a catalogue
of categories relative to coeval
apostle represented as a plain
if practical preacher I come to
you with neither crook nor shoe
nor scrip a Presbyterian cloak
though admittedly eyelet holes
As if two weathercocks refer
to another class of settlement

■

You disconcert a maxim
of Pragmatism scorning
small doses of induction
Pragmaticism so far as it
goes if A is true C is true
What is it that is absolute
This is not shown at all
Proceeding to the wood
along with some coeval
you hope to fell a first tree

■

You are he who felled by
tree deducts the maxims
of Pragmaticism scorning
by a point propitious ab-
duction hedged by paper
you appear to me walking
across the text to call an
unconverted soul King James
lyricism another C minor
Coeval decades hereafter

■

Ten thousandth truth
Ten thousandth impulse
Do not mince matter
as if tumbling were apt
parable preached in
hedge-sparrow gospel
For the lily welcomes
Owl! art thou mad?
Why dost thou twit me
with foreknowledge

■

To this the Nihtegale
gave answer that twig
of thine thou shouldst
sing another tune Owl
Still in Ovid cloth of
scarlet the Owl and her
"Old Side" blue thread
Listen! Let me speak!
the Wren replied I do
not want lawlessness

■

Everyone knows in a rough way
the impious history of sensation
Earlier times resemble ice to the
fourth parish or enthusiast class
Sheets and pillows are initiated
Permanent thought permanent
Before inviolate love knots are
edged with paper in the manner
of braided binding valences before
a long night's sleep with closure

■

Subject to experience Mr. Sprout
was sent as a vagrant person
from constable to constable
Sandemanian views have not
spread though they have not
become extinct as rapidly as
might be expected in Andrew
Fuller's *Works* whether this
is true or not is a question of
experience in itself sensation

▪

Evening for the Owl
spoke wisely and well
willing to suffer them
and come flying night
from the Carolingian
mid owl falcon fable
In their company saw
all things clearly wel
Unfele I could not do

▪

Nihtegale to the taunt
Owl a preost be piping
Overgo al spoke iseon
sede warme inome nv
stille one bare worde
Go he started mid ivi
Grene al never ne nede
Song long ago al so
sumere chorless awey

▪

Milk they drink and also whey they
know not otherwise bitter accent
I do not remember any crying out
falling down or fainting to signify

revelation preached from Isaiah 60
I have not known visions trances
Who are they that fly as a cloud as
doves to their windows have pity
From terrible and deep conviction
Brandish unreconciled yet arrows

▪

Pensive itinerants and exhorters
gathering manna in the morning
Thirty pages then the rest mostly
children enact ruin enthusiastical
impressions in my mind though
not to my knowledge it seems he
still believed he was conversing
with an invisible spirit however
the sharp weather his wet jacket
Finding himself alive went home

2003

Caroline Knox
b. 1938

Born and raised in Boston, Caroline Knox graduated from the Putney School and Radcliffe College and received a Ph.D. in English, with an emphasis in creative writing, from the University of Wisconsin Milwaukee. She taught at the University of Connecticut at Avery Point (Groton) and lives in Westport, Massachusetts. Knox is known for the high spirit, intelligence, and wit of her poetry evidenced in the beginning of her poem, "Freudian Shoes":

> Freudian shoes, the puddings or orthopedic flight
> marginally confining doves of feet which might actually be a
>   female Everyman's[1]

Fond of antiquity and oddity, hers is an intensely social poetry. It bears no theory, no particular poetics or grudge against tradition save for the curiosities of life as it is lived: "They're Quaker guns, a creative ruse, the kind you couldn't and wouldn't / fire: they're flotsam, jetsam, or any old trees, ship's logs."[2] She is a very keen observer of people and things in their places, particularly the New England culture she lives in. One reviewer comments: "Knox's obsessive attention to historical detail, as in a poem that is in essence a list of presumably extinct and rather Baroque-sounding varieties of cider apples, suggests the categorizing mind of the librarian or auction house antiquarian. . . . To inhabit this historical no-man's-land is also to enter into the American idiom in the very process of its creation . . . the unnerving quality of this work results from subtly rendering English as if it has been translated from English."[3]

Knox's work has appeared in *The American Scholar, Boston Review, New American Writing, The New Republic, The Paris Review, Ploughshares, Tri-Quarterly, The Times Literary Supplement,* and other leading literary journals. Her poems in *Poetry* won the publication's Bess Hokin Prize. She has also received awards from the National Endowment for the Arts and the Ingram Merrill Foundation.

1. *To Newfoundland*, Athens, GA, 1989, p. 19.　　2. *Quaker Guns*, Seattle, 2008, p. 10.　　3. Sarah Eggers, "'A Map of Itself': Language and Representation in Caroline Knox's *Nine Worthies*," the the poetry blog, February 2, 2011, www.thethepoetry.com, p. 1.

Freudian Shoes

> Freudian shoes, the puddings of orthopedic flight
> marginally confining doves of feet which might actually be a
>   female Everyman's,

but with this sublime caveat: vermilion please not to say alizarin
crimson flame-stitch and water-silk uppers
with the atavism of barefoot people—everyone is promiscuous
    upstairs,
Oh feet, poise in repose, mit luftpost, glands and serifs for the legs.

Jungian days—a pair of shoes *sur le tapis*
manfully complete the narrative with no legs attached!
What could they be doing what could they be doing
Will they shave themselves on this personal day?

But we live in an age where these shoes are yours.
Flying in the face of whatever (mutable) sumptuary laws are
    going down,
please (gratitude relieving stress) accept them the both of them
for free in rosy tissue paper I beseech in size 7-1/2 medium left
    and right, one for each foot.

                                           1989

Movement Along the Frieze

Who are these people who have got their grammar and their
    diction levels
the way they want them. Who are their sweethearts
and who is their friend that they call up in McKeesport
and say something to. A plain tale. Please like their work.
Please like what men and women and children present the
line-breaks of. How did they get their act together
in the matter of sentence fragments, which are sacraments,
and of all those Nortony things, in their English-teacher costumes
or barn clothes and out partying in Bayonne, New Jersey,
    writing stuff down all the time.
Please anyway read what they brought out of the despair
of the boringness of expected word order and what got printed
    with margins
on four sides of it, in what somebody else, a graphics person,
figured out for a typeface; oh please like all these
and the cover of paper which is supposed to decompose
so that they will have something to write their elegiac and mutability
poems about, some of them even MID-party arguing in oral
    comma splice

that written comma splice is a form of parallel structure
and so not only justified but welcome! and others loudly disagreeing
totally. (And one of the noisiest avers that incremental repetition
is a form of parallel structure!) Some write syntax down goofy
and then go back and put profundity in
—which is fine—in an air of peace and freedom
as some of them have fasted or will fast or otherwise
sacrifice. A trace of movement along the frieze.
"For a symbolic hand," says this one or the other,
"lies on the pulse of protean co-Americans,
the very hand on the light table, the gong's mallet,
an instrument like my word: confusion of stillness
and motion, the *horror vacui,* and the ancient
nobility of fictive farce!" Perhaps, please,
among blot and stipple and among these nattering damned
didactic SAT and vocabulary words, which are boring
or stunning (in exigency of plot as metaphor) sometimes
to read, the poems are honored by your time and attention.

                                                              1989

Sleepers Wake

    Karen made a poem
    walking to rehearsal
    about children making angels
    seeing angels in the chimney flames
    Karen is the tall one
    with braids down her back
    She's old enough to be
    like a lady and have the braids
    on her head like a princess

    This is the song called *Glory in the*
    Highest, it has to be loud
    It's just about all one note
    and we have to hold our mouths right
    for this one especially, *Glory*
    I'm sorry for the altos
    They have to sing O on A
    for bars and bars
    Karen is the solo, she is a snob

The breathing
is theatrical as all getout
There are almost no crescendos
We're so loud now
we couldn't make one anyway
Not one of us knows anything about it
but we have to sing in German
and over again in English
translated by Henry S. Drinker:

Wake awake for night is FLAAAAAAAAAH-
ying. The watchman on the height
is CRAAAAAAH-
ying. It's Cantata No. 140
Wachet auf by J. S. Bach with an extended
(is it ever) chorale in the middle

Going home in the snow is boring
It's so dry and dark and cold
I am a fabulous robot
We boot the snow and squeak it and shower the others
Karen will tell, she can mind her own beeswax
and just like the dark in summer, spring and fall
Mom and Dad will do their boring joke

SHADRACH MESHACH AND TOBEDWEGO

1994

Famous Bigshots

Famous bigshots of the world unite
in black tie and nutria stormcoats,
omnicompetent, handsome dreamboats
totally snazzy and slightly snobby
exclusive hotshots with prodigious bankrolls
for clandestine bombshells, gaslight escorts,
splendidly outfitted armfuls of cashmere
adjudged diaphanous. Old blister,

old beano: auspicious dearies
and snooded consorts, fiscal eggheads
and erstwhile tightwads eleemosynary
to the scrumptious amanuensis.
With brass putter, vermeil niblick,
bronze mashie and deco Ronson,
footed salver with deckled message,
hammered flask and acajou stick;
with great hat! grand leghorn—these foxy moderns—crafty
    sophisticates,
putative expatriates—they leave their unread half-calf first
edition of *Trilby* by George du Maurier
on the faux-malachite plinth, and they scarpa.
This is a true account of famous bigshots.
Not one word has been distorted or omitted.

                                              1994

Quaker Guns

Your handsome workmanlike fourmaster,
out on a reach, no sight of land,
mirrors the adventure tales for children and grownups—oh, isn't the brightwork
bright; oh, the cannon royal, the twenty-four pounders.
It's safe to assume that you have eighty-six guns.

But these aren't worth the powder
it takes to blow them to hell.
Shipmasters long ago thought up this protection.

They're Quaker guns, a creative ruse, the kind you couldn't and wouldn't
fire: they're flotsam, jetsam, or any old trees, ships' logs.
They're broken masts. They're the Friends of the Friends.
These logs are laid in the loading trays—
you have twelve cannon at most, but they look like an armada.
So privateers mistake the logs for guns, and scarper,
afraid of driftwood posing as ordnance.
No pirate would go anywhere near you.

                                              2008

Dreyken

Dreyken fabe, wer ingete dreyken
(dor droy rittavittastee orn canar).
Preb. Refen ingete inget. Preb.

Santona nofa Xeroc;
ter quittz mivin movip.
Morm faria greel Florida
faria greel pandeck.

Bathrobes

We took our bathrobes and stuck them in the washer.
(Ritta put hers in the blue laundry machine.)
I said, "Refen ingete inget."

Nocturnes are hard to Xerox;
birds follow the glare of water.
We prepare tax returns for people in Florida,
people in Florida whom we have never met.

(Translated by the author and Caroline Knox)

2008

Bill Berkson
b. 1939

Associated with the New York School, Bill Berkson attended Brown, Columbia, and The New School for Social Research, where he won the Dylan Thomas Memorial Poetry Award and studied with Kenneth Koch. The association with Koch led to his discovery of French poetry, especially that of Pierre Reverdy and the surrealist prose poet Henri Michaux, and his growing involvement with the work of Ashbery, O'Hara, and Koch himself. After working for *ARTnews* and teaching at The New School and Yale, he moved to San Francisco in 1970. In 1984, he began teaching art history and literature at San Francisco Art Institute, where he also served as interim dean in 1990 and Director of Literature and Science from 1993 to 1998.

Berkson edited the poetry anthology *Best & Company* (1969); *Homage to Frank O'Hara* (1978); a collection of essays and other writings about O'Hara; and the poetry journal *Big Sky*. His poetry collections include *Enigma Variations* (1975); with drawings by Philip Guston; *Blue Is the Hero: Poems 1960–1975* (1976); *Lush Life* (1984); *Serenade: Poetry and Prose 1975–1989* (2000); *Fugue State* (2001); *Our Friends Will Pass Among You Silently* (2007); *Goods and Services* (2008); and *Portrait and Dream: New and Selected Poems 1959–2008* (2009). Notable among his works of collaboration are *Hymns of St. Bridget & Other Writings* (with Frank O'Hara, 1975/2001), *Enigma Variations* (with Philip Guston, 1975), and *Gloria* (with Alex Katz, 2008). His works of art commentary are *Ronald Bladen: Early and Late* (1990), *The Sweet Singer of Modernism & Other Writings 1985–2003* (2004), and *Sudden Address: Selected Lectures 1981–2006* (2007).

Married to art curator Constance Lewallen, he lives in San Francisco's Eureka Valley.

Merit

Sorry for the suffering, world,
reaper of sutures, in point of other surface
beneath the silly sheets

What conditions lack is truth
in the absence of conditions
same blank din, soon to be released

Oh boy, oh boy,
the color of your knowing this,
when you do

Tromping through the snow
to see the pictures, cleanly made
by this year's nut

2001–2008   2009

Goods and Services

Are you a 15th-century Italian monk of present-day ill repute?
No, I am not Savonarola.

Whenever anyone steals something it is Prometheus
But theft is ascribed to Hermes.

Word went out that the missing husband had been found
Behind the house, washing his pants.

So Lady Light lets drop another of her interminable fireballs
And you are no longer suspicious, only all the more turned around.

My class notes are illegible.
False Spring casts its ballot of blue. Code name: "Clemency."

2001–2008   2009

In Costume

The endangered energy guys are coming on a Monday
And the steamed-up picture window (time being what it is, its prolonged
Disconnect elaborately personified) wavers blue-ishly spotlit,
Affecting a slight concussion to face the styptic deer.

In the parlance of permanence many bulbs need replacing.
I heard the woods speaking but they went about it the wrong way around,
Panting like mutts in the leafy strata.
Unlikely lunch: Dark toast soaked in soup du jour.

Agnes Moorehead, Goddess of Nimbly Erected Spite, tell us,
What is it that will make life palatable when so it is?
And lunch absorbs from light executive privilege
At the high end of the cerebral cortex afloat on my fiery palatial plank.

She flies! The saucer can't *not* act.
The clock is whole, its animations invariably tingling,
Recruited to receive pronouncement of the final
Anagram hastily received dark nights long before graduation.

2001–2008   2009

After the Medusa

I have to spring lightly to make or thwart a meaning
bare thump at the Safeway's automated door
birds in their vanishing act above or near the U.S. Mint

My mistake, I holler
but poetry comes first
democratizing confluence
despite terror greed

No big deal, larger than life or death
I hear fifes in the outward calm
granite humps and chins
sweet sizeable orpiment
seldom repetitive, un-saying the echo.

2001–2008   2009

Song for Connie

The sun met the moon at the corner
noon in thin air

Commotion you later
choose to notice

Love shapes the heart
      that once was pieces

You take in hand
      the heart in mind

Your fate's consistent
      alongside mine

Unless a mess
      your best guess

That is right, thanks, the intimate
      fact that you elect it

At corners, dressed or naked, with lips taste
      full body, time thick or thin, fixated

Love, take heart
      as heart takes shape

And recognition
      ceases to be obscure

One line down the center
      another flying outward enters

2001–2008   2009

Clark Coolidge
b. 1939

Clark Coolidge traces his development as a poet to reading Jack Kerouac's novel *On the Road* as a college student: "Everything that happened to me, the minutest details of sunlight on a shoe, began to seem vastly important, had to be scribbled down, with *extensions*. . . . I had thought the writer must first have it all in his head and only *then* put it into words, but no. I began to see how it was really excitingly done: You wrote from what you didn't know toward whatever could be picked up in the act."[1]

Coolidge composed his early poetry, collected in *Space* (1970), with the use of a dictionary in an attempt to break with normal syntax and broaden what he felt was the limited vocabulary of poetry. His arrangement of seemingly unrelated words without the aid of sentences can create a puzzle of disjunction for the uninitiated reader. Yet, once the reader suspends any demand for narrative or linear organization, the words are free to come into relation, like the abstract yet liquid shapes in a Tanguy painting, or like the geologic formations that have fascinated Coolidge since childhood. Coolidge perceives poetic composition as an "arrangement" of discrete materials (words), just as quartz and calcite are an arrangement of molecules.[2]

Arrangement and movement are the tensions at play in Coolidge's imagery, a subject on which he likes to quote painter Philip Guston:

> It cannot be a settled, fixed image. It must of necessity be an image which is unsettled, which has not only not made up its mind where to be but must feel as if it's been in many places all over this canvas, and indeed there's no place for it to settle—except momentarily.[3]

"I don't want to use the word *form*," Coolidge said in a lecture, "I want to use the word *forms*. The word is plural always, plural. You never have just one."[4] Influenced by the rhythm and movement of jazz, Coolidge's style of public reading is characterized by a driving tempo.

His poetics focus on "obduration" and the refusal of cultural assimilation: "The history of 20th century art is so much one of assimilation, that art itself is finally becoming inseparable from the main mechanisms of society: business, education, government, the church. Therefore the artist must reject art to keep clear. The artist must also make his or her way through a confusing proliferation of forms. Coolidge sees the artist's current condition in Beckett's statement of 1961: "To find a form that accommodates the mess, that is the task of the artist now."[5]

Coolidge's many books include *The Maintains* (1974), *Polaroid* (1975),

Mine: The One That Enters the Stories (1982), *The Crystal Text* (1986), *Solution Passage* (1986), *At Egypt* (1988), *The Book of During* (1991), *The Rova Improvisations* (1994), *Far Out West* (2001), *The Act of Providence* (2010), and *This Time We Are Both* (2010). He is the editor of *Philip Guston: Collected Writings, Lectures, and Conversations* (2010).

Raised in Providence, Rhode Island, where his father was a professor of music at Brown University, Coolidge has lived in New York City, San Francisco, Rome, and New Lebanon, New York. He currently resides in Petaluma, California.

1. "A First Reading of *On the Road* and Later," *Talisman* 3, Spring, 1989, p. 100.   2. "Arrangement," in *Talking Poetics from Naropa Institute*, Boulder, 1978, pp. 144 and 147.   3. The same, p. 151.   4. The same, p. 147.   5. From *Notebooks (1976–1982)*, in *Code of Signals: Recent Writings in Poetics*, New York, 1983/2005, p. 173.

Brill

```
        emotional the
    fox at an am            land kept chess           dim after him
        two things               shrink very barren
                            parts of the 6                wind but
    act no like                    canvas can
        A he up                                          very least
            or may in that            lonely like part
    merely Davis 1956   body very     red soapy
                    complexity it           means fees
            it to out                  can't ready doing
        scratched up once         in the seemed the in
                    life crab                    but by so
        cigs or visits      last d                    his the
    like darkness      past is root              "Woolp-klo"
            wings nohow        planet three speed
            fast like not
                        column stood still
    sin        sun        wig                coin in what in
                            dry  one                        tat
        fun          six      not          hell      pall
                                new
            tic        way      was            yes        two
                                    not            bud
        bar      sip      has      day              you
```

```
          get           here
pip   now   guy   air   wen   hod   no
```

1970

Styro

```
    quite is high
    quatic
              deliverance rates   dial   3
  in ex
          trees palling steins   ing
  snail of it, acrid, the dumps
                      the "sill row"
      to knees smoke
                sir fins


  drub in minnow the elicit of haunt (bite)
  crust, stub, crayon, chives
                      Galatea dumbing hard
      cawl o'wrist it?
                nubs
                   (Nile)
  an green    and ever attack
                        styrene mistachio dubloon
  rack sun correct ratchet
                Dumbo in      size


   sign or hone win
     gold when aft
       whom      whine
  it, state
```

1970

On Induction of the Hand

Perhaps I've got to write better longer thinking of it as
grown up out of the same singular lost. The pattern is in, or is it
under, the hands? Better be in or it's gone from the brain
choking on airless. The outside leaves stain the sands of my

sleep even through glass and alerted in this very chair as I
thought I snoozed by the strings of this world. What world?,
evening of syntax brought full over the mounds of these what
lives but hopes. There is a wrench that a certain staring at
while balancing humours we call words in state pours wings
of edgy fondness bound useless in calm of lucidity down the
chute of the sentence. So-called duty roster activity when
typing at the seeming to be nodded at by trees. They yearn?
Saying that I am out there, with a loop I hope carries me
swaying back to here by means of them there. A tree could even
be a monad to this use, though never is it held in my heat to
be even. I let myself off myself never, no dope again trembling
my attic wires loose from their packets. Containments of such
that I never think them sendable. A poet used the word
"lozenge," he didn't write it. Some other and more careless
scribe wanted me to write one of those but the hell with what
    lies off
him. I remain stormy in my paradise. I pull up my pants when
the itch takes me, drops hitting page. Writing *is* a prayer for
always it starts at the portal lockless to me at last leads
to the mystery of everything that has always been written.
The state of that, trembles and then fades back in leaving
the hole where it's gone. But I pout instead of kneel. I
would rather confess, but there's no mouth to pour toward at
the poem. Perhaps it's just that the words have all been said
but not by me, and the process *is* a trial. What those leaves
are awaiting, every day my burden's finality in hand. Beneath
it are the faces I've yet to replace in a rock as stern and fluid as
Piero's Christless blue. But all the while I eye you, demon,
your bird hoards are clustering here. Sent for calm and
brought crazy still.

1978–1981   1986

Noon Point

I think I wrote a poem today but I don't know well.
Though well do I seize the trees shake but am not given pause.
The lights are every one of them out, we see it all so well.
Nothing is taken care of, everything lies.
Everyone rise.

1978–1981   1986

FROM This Time We Are Both

I.

Dark hands pass
dark with no silence
lights in the smoke
hands that start, that light
pass the particles, link penetrations
to an amphitheater smell, that each corner well
treat the carriers, they small, they dark in the wind
the mind rose, the cable hands, a drench
of light smalls, close, a building of hair entire
how it dips in the time to see, we hear
they go forwards past
the inclination
darkening corners to form

The never rest dark forms a sample
a shattered sugar
blades in the dark near time
tastes more than dark but lines
then not to rest

Dark fur past
taste high window
elbow in move, placed than dark
height then links, pin strikes
wrist across, of pain takes a sample
septic smell of nerve say
but high, dare I light?

There is number, and it is a vanished vast here
broken cable of light sugar to pin on blue
flash particulars waiting, high down, tapped across
I live dark in particular waiting, city high and
over is the choice on this corner tonight

Time is in labels peeling, keep up the time-green neons
and spell a spark but past links air things swept
strike title the ways strong of pack smoke
gap to all this razor its windows
left of trap so I am one, my own but of two

over dicey caliper sweep, out of the well walls
one word dips to drop at a glance or
what if you lived over that streetlight change?
a certain soup, quick lead snap, snuff up
is the story of that corner
a lick snap spark to cross its rails
so dark the hands to cross with

Are you the one who moved, or me that came?
over these wells lived walls, a razor for windows
no neons for windows, in face the frames and blare wreck
today to dismal the fall repeats, unparticular labels titling out
peel from my spares, like nerve never rest never touch
now, what if soup in the streetlight change
straight to lick that rail then cross the palm
with steel as the sapphire fired its points
this seriously put together with tears, what is torn
remind, some signs replaced

But the neighborhood where the people, smoke
where the pole wires, a fist of needles and says
we extend farther than you do and will get you
no doubt of those poles wires in a fist
and I have the urge to shake you
flats of sun fill blind vitamins simply
share the urge to seize stars violet like soup from
that rail, pretend flat out those vistas are alarming
trolley pack, and spring, flash bait, wait and we wave
broken gum, a flat rock of sugar

A brown dawn wins with wireless opticals, rooves from which
the nerves retreat, and the standing so early is not to
release this corner
a shoulder full of hands, stop me if you've heard
but are these lights the same night? of turpentine wind
gnarls, full sail, grant dark its plain airs
the petrified bags, the polished TV
all in here above is not near
we are out, all night plummet, held around the same
a corner where these people show, regain a spot to urge
store down late to notice to stay, dark has its corners

where the same picks are made, tucks, grain spill
of the nightly spice truck, whatever will stay
denizen alert
belts all to their steel urge my plan

And gone off strung horn of coffees this horizon
motion?
at the darkness hurdles the people sleep on showing
off all dreams
to come from a time the coal in cones

2010

Ed Roberson
b. 1939

Ed Roberson was born in Pittsburgh, Pennsylvania, and studied painting as an undergraduate at the University of Pittsburgh, where he was drawn to the mixed-media collages of Romare Bearden. He also has a graduate degree in creative writing from Goddard College. At age twenty-three, he won the Grand Prize in the *Atlantic Monthly* poetry contest and published his first book, *When Thy King Is a Boy,* as early as 1970, but his emergence as an important figure came with the Iowa Poetry Prize in 1995 and a Lila Wallace Reader's Digest Award in 1998. According to critic Brent Hayes Edwards, like Amiri Baraka's "changing same" and Nathaniel Mackey's "discrepant engagement," Roberson's title phrase "On the Calligraphy of Black Chant" reminds us that there was a "full range of black postmodernism, in which a vernacular poetics does not simply imply the faithful transcription of some inviolate primary orality."[1] Instead, Roberson's poems "manipulate the spacing and enjambment of repeated lines to suggest a plurality of voices: the visual differentiation from repetition to repetition suggests a shift in inflection and even perspective."[2]

Committed to the poetic sequence and seriality, Roberson cites his desire to achieve universality of expression:

> You take a word and it means layers and layers of things that resonate through all human experience. . . . You put your arms around half the world with certain poems. Nobody treated Black poetry like that, particularly during the Black Arts movement. So I wanted to write poems that have layer upon layer, circles upon circles of universality. . . . And I began to play with that: not putting them together as finished poems, but noting how they string each other up. . . ."[3]

Roberson's books of poetry include *Lucid Interval as Integral Music* (1985), *Voices Cast Out to Talk Us In* (1995), *Just In: Word of Navigational Challenges: New and Selected Work* (1998), *Atmosphere Conditions* (2000), *City Eclogue* (2006), *The New Wing of the Labyrinth* (2009), and *To See the Earth before the End of the World* (2010). He has received the Shelley Memorial Award and the Stephen Henderson Award for outstanding achievement in poetry.

Joseph Donahue sees divination as a feature of Roberson's practice:

> The poem will divinize reading itself. . . . And the white space will accrue to itself immense metaphoric power. In fact we can intuit here how the gap in the line means more than a pause. It theologizes print. In Roberson, the gnostic call is echoed in the very lineation. The breaks wake us. They, on occasion, whack us. Sometimes in the recursive drift of the eye, they take on a choral aura.[4]

Another commentator writes that, instead of casting out voice, the postmodern strategy of the language poets, Roberson is postmodern "through his refusal of a singular, unified lyric voice, and his deployment, in its stead, of multiple voices."[5] Critic Andrew Welsh refers to Roberson's poetry as "a lattice of voices."[6]

Ed Roberson has taught at Rutgers University, Columbia College Chicago, the University of Chicago, and Northwestern University. He lives in Chicago.

1. "Black Serial Poetics: An Introduction to Ed Roberson," *Callaloo* 33.3, 2010, p. 623.   2. The same.   3. Spoken comment at Black Serial Poetics: A Conversation and a Reading," Poets House, New York, 12 November 2004, in Brent Hayes Edwards, the same, p. 627.   4. "Metaphysical Shivers: Reading Ed Roberson," *Callaloo* 33.3, 2010, p. 701.   5. Robert Zamsky, "The Umbilicate Ear: Audition in Ed Roberson's Lucid Interval as Integral Music," *Callaloo* 33.3, 2010, p. 684.   6. Introduction to *Voices Cast Out to Talk Us In, Iowa City,* 1995, p. xii.

Sit In What City We're In

1

Someone may want
to know one day how many steps we took
          to cross one of our streets,
to know there were hundreds
in one city   streets in one direction
          and as many
as could fit between the land's contours
crossing those,
          our hive grid as plumb
as circles flanked into the insect
hexagonals,
          our stone our steel.

Others may want more
to know what steps aside the southern streets required
          to flow at last free to clear,
to know how those kept out
set foot inside, sat down, and how
          the mirrors around the lunch counter
reflected the face
to face—the cross-mirrored depth reached
          infinitely back into either—

the one pouring the bowl over the head of
the one sitting in
                        at that counter

                        this regression this seen stepped
back into nothing both ways
From which all those versions of the once felt sovereign
                self   locked together in the mirror's
march from deep caves of long alike   march back
into the necessary   together
                        living   we are
reflected in the face to face we are
a nation facing ourselves our back turned
                        on ourselves   how
that reflection sat in demonstration
of   each face
                        mirror reflecting into mirror generates

a street cobbled of the heads of
our one
                        long likeness
the infinite regressions.
The oceans, themselves one,   catch their image
                        hosed by riot cops down the gutter into
The sphere surface
river
                        looked into   reflects
                        one face.

                        2

A here and not-here division of things,
where the future is in the same
                        place as the past, is
maybe one of the African
masquerades of time   like these facing mirrors
                        in which time is making faces
at you from the elemental
moment,   the faced and yet to be
                        faced
in one frame   where from, where to are faces of here.

Where a few in the crowd at that lunch counter
                    face their actions.

Where what dark is revealed
in the face to face   is a back to back.
                    The words of that god
against us. In the glass, the face
observed, changes the looking at that face, cancels both
                        their gaze to transparence, opens
around it a window containing right here
around us;   and in that window these
                    same
—in the lapped frame of this one moment—
are the other one's
                    world we see into in ours:

You can't smash the mirror   there but it break here.
And in it you see   that you can't see
                    your own back,
your angel of the unfamiliar, of that not like
your face . . . See. and
                        relax that hand raised against
your impossible
hand   that reaches to give the pat, to okay   touch you
                    at the unfamiliar, those stubs of your
back.

                    3

From mirror to window   glass   to thin air
between   and finally, us with no you nor I
                    but being
—with all our world—   inside the other;
but there only in   our each part yet having
                    no displacement of the other,
just as each wishes   the self not lost, shared
being in common in each other   being
                    as different as
night and day still   of one spin.
The sphere surface
                    of this river.

To know ourselves as a god would know us
would make us gods
                    of ourselves   we are so
fused in communication we happen at once,
as if as one   gazing
                    ball pivot of critical gardens,
cocked Creations.   Here, in the glass of the city,
a godlike simply knowing doesn't determine
                    what built
raft of citizen draughts where the street runs
up the walk to the door   ocean teased apart
                    to its each drop
                    of rain.
Someone is riding a bus, too tired
for everything   except what is right;
                    a god has his back against the wall
of a church in Birmingham;
the marchers take to the streets.
                    Someone may want to know
what city we're in
that curves glowing over the edge
                    into an earth.

2006

Urban Nature

Neither New Hampshire nor Midwestern farm,
nor the summer home in some Hamptons garden
thing, not that Nature,   not a satori
-al leisure come to terms peel by peel, not that core
whiff of beauty as the spirit. Just a street
pocket park, clean of any smells, simple quiet—
simple quiet not the same as no birds sing,
definitely not the dead of no birds sing:

The bus stop posture in the interval
of nothing coming, a not quite here running
sound underground, sidewalk's grate vibrationless
in open voice, sweet berries ripen in the street
hawk's kiosks. The orange is being flown in
this very moment picked of its origin.

2006

Open / Back Up (breadth of field)

To state for the case of poetry
the most recent open field I've crossed
would have to be the block long park lost
in the midst of the security

of local campus mounted police.
Black people get stopped regularly
to show they have university
I.D. by the ones in cars; the auspice

of the animal mounted doesn't fly.
Really, neither do the comic cops. Nature
life and limb gone through divestiture
of place from point
                              reads to the lie
of open
          breasts of field   Elysian,
nor the narrow badge number of the gun.

                                                                2006

Monk's Bird Book

Mourning doves are not owls after a while
away from the city   not because the country
appears of a softer feather   less predatory

          you're thinking a sound more naturally friendly
          less edgy and dangerous than the subway
but because the

city city to city within itself so sharply
details for you   actually walks you through
a training in the amplitudes of form

          after a while that sharpness wipes the smile
the natural had you putting on everything.
Really owls   are so soft   their deadly

accuracy of flight depending on it
they are all but silent   a recognizable law
nobody says shit you learn   the city

has taught you to pick up on   which wings
bring the disk of their sun for around
your neck each day

and which take you out;
and that your green act of good is natural
in that it too depends on the weather.

2006

A Sampler

Depending   on how the center attends
most closely what is around, she hears

or sees him approach, then feels his weight
take up the loose plank bench left beside her

where she sits, placing her in the balance.
She has levels of smell, some she'll drop

into   below that attention, ape sense
with only the language of chemistries,

others are what he wears gives her   his taste
on sweat's index of   his activities.

All this communication, nothing said.
Nothing is voiced.   The moon embroiders

with its almost texture   the sky, the seen
wears its satiny light over what is there

to say.
But the question, What is there to say? is
never answered, and as you see, Nothing

is not that answer. There is something;
something can be said. There isn't anything

that is not the answer; everything is.
It's just that word is not all the saying.

She is listening for safety to arrive
from him   as his shadow saying those lines to

simply the benign direction of light.
She is feeling her survival take note

on a tissue level, the positive
of fear: he's okay. She remembers once

a silence of commuter stop in a dream,
her hands' attention in that sky on her lap.

2006

Psalm

My hands were Molotov cocktails
and I was pounding on the streets
as on a table   buildings jumped
and lives fell over and shattered,
the blood wine and glass all over the ground
of any social fabric spread
between people   certain dishes
of issue   dropped abruptly and concluded.

Surprised my effect
wakes the reverse of what I dreamed
now   I hate cause.   I hate gravity
I want the hands of anything that holds
off me.   If nothing held true
the way I see   then nothing holds.
I want whatever does or is
if not my way   done away.

God is allowed
to kill for the table
the more dead the more is understood that
to be fed   the ham of your enemy's thigh
the blackened ribs
of your own   is to hate the calves of this meal

as your fullest table.
and to be not filled I hate God   I eat my lips
His laurel kiss.

2006

The Counsel of Birds

An alarm waiting a battery
shoved down its throat for some time now   chirps
from its plastic nest attached to the ceiling,
a hybrid re-birthing   anti-fire strain of phoenix.

Nigeria has a bird whose call sounds
like the busy signal of the telephone
and a snake who hangs it up.   Ecuador has
the Galapagos   who hid the messages.

The risen night sweat up   a pacing fog
of nightmare   dries away to waking.
A beeping sun pecks through the dark,
the orange number in its beak   breaking

due into the vapor molecules of its
missed,   its overage of too late
come morning   thin air   augury's loon
singing its insides out out of sight: a dew.

The dawn meadow of coattail-pull pulls me told
to naked. The nothing new of nothing
permanent all I have on. The crow's scare of skin.
Its cocked and trigger of wing, code figure of birds

exploding to flight   free, screams attention blind,
instruction deaf and dumb   before word is these
are gun fire.   And without enough answers answering
the alarm is our alarms are not working.

2006

Fanny Howe

b. 1940

Fanny Howe grew up in Cambridge, Massachusetts, and attended Stanford University for three years before dropping out to get married at age twenty. She never received her B.A. degree. She lived in the Bay Area and Riverside, California, but the marriage was brief and she returned to live in New York City and Boston. While working as a reader for Avon Books, she wrote five unpublished novels, but had been writing poetry since she was young. For a time she worked for CORE on housing violations in Boston. After marrying again and having three children in four years, she began teaching and publishing her poetry and fiction. From 1969 until 1987 her concerns were with "liberation theology, poetry, continental philosophy, fiction and the lives of children that made my days interesting."[1] A single mother, she moved to San Diego to teach at the University of California San Diego/La Jolla, and traveled frequently to England and Ireland, where her mother, Mary Manning, had lived before moving to Massachusetts. "Since 2000," she writes, "I have lived in the New England area, but have taken teaching jobs wherever I could find them, because I retired too soon."[2]

Fanny Howe has had an extraordinary career as a poet, including the Lenore Marshall Poetry Prize (2001), the Griffin Poetry Prize (2005), and The Ruth Lilly Poetry Prize (2009). However, her works of fiction dominated the early years of her production. By the mid-1980s, she turned primarily to poetry, with such volumes as *Robeson Street* (1985), *The Vineyard* (1988), *The Quietist* (1992), *O'Clock* (1995), *One Crossed Out* (1997), *Selected Poems* (2000), *Gone* (2003), *On the Ground* (2004), *The Lyrics* (2007), and *Come and See* (2011). She has also produced two notable essay collections, *The Wedding Dress* (2003) and *The Winter Sun: Notes on a Vocation* (2009).

Howe is unusual in the postmodern age of irony and doubt as one who credits the spiritual agency of poetry, not as a rigid system of belief or credo, but rather through uncertainty, as she wrote in 2003:

> There is a Muslim prayer that says, "Lord, increase my bewilderment," and this prayer belongs both to me and to the stranger Whoever who goes under the name of "I" in my poems—and under the multiple names in my fiction—where error, errancy, and bewilderment are the main forces that signal a story.
>
> A signal does not necessarily mean that you want to be located or described. It can mean that you want to be known as Unlocatable and Hidden. This contradiction can drive the "I" in the lyrical poem into a series of techniques that are the reverse of the usual narrative movements around courage, discipline, conquest, and fame.[3]

Bewilderment is therefore a positive force for Howe: "The whirling that is central to bewilderment is the natural way for the lyric poet. A dissolving of particularities into one solid braid of sound is her inspiration."[4]

Fanny Howe currently lives in Cambridge, Massachusetts.

1. Unpublished biographical statement, 2011.   2. The same.   3. "Bewilderment," in *The Wedding Dress*, Berkeley, 2003, p. 6.   4. The same, p. 18.

FROM Veteran

I don't believe in ashes; some of the others do.
I don't believe in better or best; some of the others do.
I don't believe in a thousand flowers or the first robin
of the year or statues made of dust. Some of the others do

I don't believe in seeking sheet music
by Boston Common on a snowy day, don't believe
in the lighting of malls seasonably
When I'm sleeping I don't believe in time
as we own it, though some of the others might

Sad lace on green. Veterans stamping the leafy snow
I don't believe in holidays
long-lasting and artificial. Some of the others do
I don't believe in starlings of crenelated wings
I don't believe in berries, red & orange, hanging on
threadlike twigs. Some of the others do

I don't believe in the light on the river
moving with it or the green bulbs hanging on the elms
Outdoors, indoors, I don't believe in a gridlock of ripples
or the deep walls people live inside

Some of the others believe in food & drink & perfume
I don't. And I don't believe in shut-in time
for those who committed a crime
of passion. Like a sweetheart
of the iceberg or wings lost at sea

the wind is what I believe in,
the One that moves around each form

1988

FROM *The Quietist*

■

Mad God, mad thought
Take me for a walk
Stalk me. Made God,
Wake me with your words.
Believe in what I said

Just shadows
Shadows on sheets
Grass, seed . . .

Push my anguish down—
Coffee, smokes & creams—
Tongue-dainties
To scare compulsion away
Compulsion to die

■

Two waters—squared
by an alley—

Three acorns—
One wet chair

Several yellow
chestnuts—

A man's erect
nipples

It was enemy class
travel

with the devil
who's red for a reason

Pleasure bloodies his underskin
Thin skin

▪

My bedclothes were stuffed with ashes
The spreads were incarnadine

Our match had burned at both ends
Since temptation concludes where the middle is nothing

Can a desire be a mistake?
The theme can be wrong, but not the music

And I lay there dying
For my asylum

Was myself

1992

FROM *O'clock*

▪

Go on out but come back in
you told me to live by, so I went
with my little dog trotting

at my side out of the garden
into woods colored rotten.

I did this several times, out and in,
it was of course a meditation.

The out surrounds me now
a whole invisible O to live in:

tender tantrums, sky gone suddenly gray—
still soften light but no one brings

papers here to sign. The top of the water
shudders under the brush of wind.

Past? Present? Future? No such things.

▪

Hive-sized creams are on the chestnut tree
alive for—and with—bees—boughs
of copper beech gives birds a ride

for their whistles—clouds
course overhead—the gorse
is buttery sweet—it's May

—the day the right hand gives to the left.

While the lamb pecks at the tit
of its mother—it seems
the rest of the field has gone to sleep.

Now milk drips down its brand new lips
and bubbles of grass wet the ewe's.

She stops chewing and turns her face
to gaze at the feast at her waist.

▪

I feel like the end
of a long day
near Druid stones
and ghosts and hedgerows

thick as storms
where mist takes form
in a water garden.
It seems I am back

in Glan and want
to stay close
to childish things
like milk and sugar

in my tea, a mother
who calls darling
—to clouds darkening
the daily hills.

322 ■ FANNY HOWE

Sometimes it seems
my sight's turned in
on a place dark green
and undefiled

and I am as old
as the young
will ever be.
No, I mean wild!

■

Wild garlic flowers
whiten the forest—children love their brothers—

people are hope-filled—and skuthers
of wind wear down the quarries.

And worries wear down the man aging
to something as light as a trout

but more lonely from breathing.

■

He was a cold-hearted Saxon
whose sex was as busy as a farm
and left the room warm
with the scent of hounds.

Believe me, he could have had it with anyone—
man or woman—but he wanted to be good.

These are the dangerous ones.

1995

FROM Forty Days

18.

Because my secret wedding
Was enduring and the rest

Was not—I think disclosure
Is dangerous.

What is heavier than lead?
The need for bread.

What is crueler than a boss?
The need for praise.
What is shorter than a step?
An indrawn breath.

My secret wedding was to whom?
A promise not a human.

2007

23.

Hey, afraid
The disenfranchised
Made the first machines of labor?
So to build prisons
Around themselves?

What if the man said "walking stick"
Instead of "get to work"?
What if he said "You are your own
Trap and lock"?

Afraid the rape bed
Was comfy?
No pleasure, no me?

Stop at the little beehive
Behind that tree.

2007

Lyn Hejinian
b. 1941

One of the leading language poets, Lyn Hejinian was editor and publisher of Tuumba Press and coeditor, with Barrett Watten, of *Poetics Journal*. She currently codirects the Atelos Publishing Project. Her prodigious output of poetry books includes *A Thought Is the Bride of What Thinking* (1976), *Writing Is an Aid to Memory* (1978), *The Guard* (1984), *My Life* (1987), *Oxata: A Short Russian Novel* (1991), *The Cell* (1992), *The Cold of Poetry* (1994), *Happily* (2000), *Slowly* and *The Beginner* (2002), *The Fatalist* (2003), *Saga / Circus* (2008), and *The Book of a Thousand Eyes* (2012). She has also written an influential work of criticism, *The Language of Inquiry* (2000).

Like Leslie Scalapino and Carla Harryman, she is attracted to the complexities of narrative. In *My Life*, Hejinian gradually creates a portrait of her own childhood through a mosaic of discontinuous sentences and glimpses, wherein the "title" of one section of the book-length sequence finds its way into the text of another. "Repetition, and the rewriting that repetition becomes, make a perpetual beginning," she writes in her essay "The Rejection of Closure."[1] Such writing of "this and again this" is reminiscent of Gertrude Stein's "continuous present."

Her book *Oxota* consists of 270 "sonnets" inspired by Pushkin's *Evgeny Onegin*, through which she creates a portrait of post-Soviet Russia. Hejinian is the translator of the contemporary Russian poet Arkadii Dragamoschenko, whom she first met in Moscow in 1983. Her attraction to Russian literature was first established, however, through the writings of Velimir Khlebnikov, Viktor Shklovsky, Roman Jakobson, and others who share Hejinian's interest in the "constructedness" of a literary text.

In an assessment of the poetic line, Hejinian writes, "The integrity of the individual line, and the absorbing discontinuities that often appear between lines—the jumpiness that erupts in various sections of the work (whether the result or the source of disjunctive semantics)—are so natural to my 'real life' experience that they seem inevitable—and 'true.'"[2] In the prose-poem sequence *My Life*, however, that disjunctiveness finds its expression in the associational gaps between sentences and sentence fragments.

Hejinian lives in Berkeley, California.

1. *Writing/Talks*, ed. Bob Perelman, Carbondale, 1985, p. 273.   2. "Line," in *The Line in Postmodern Poetry*, eds. Robert Frank and Henry Sayre, Urbana, 1988, p. 191.

FROM *Writing Is an Aid to Memory*

I.

apple is shot nod
            ness seen know it around saying
                think for a hundred years
      but and perhaps utter errors direct the point to a meadow
              rank fissure up on the pit
arts are several branches of life
           little more science is brought where great
          need is required
            out becomes a bridge of that name
         in the painting is a great improvement
bit ink up on the human race
and return if the foot goes back
          in the trunks of trees behoove a living thing
               wedge war common saw
        hard by that length of time the great demand is
             very dear
ashes in water
              that might be a slip of architecture
              think was reduced to an improper size
     blocks to interest who can visit
              variations on ideas are now full
        problems
     from a point of increasing
at only as to four or we who nine
a little grace familiar with simple limbs and the sudden
       reverse

                          1978

FROM *My Life*

A pause, a rose,
something on paper

A moment yellow, just as four years later when my father returned home from the war, the moment of greeting him, as he stood at the bottom of the stairs, younger, thinner than when he had left, was purple—though moments are no longer so colored. Somewhere, in the background, rooms share a pattern of small roses. Pretty is as pretty does. In certain families, the meaning of necessity is at one with the sentiment of pre-necessity. The better things were gathered in a pen. The windows were narrowed by white gauze curtains which were never loosened. Here I refer to irrelevance, that rigidity which never intrudes. Hence, repetitions, free from all ambition. The shadow of the redwood trees, she said, was oppressive. The plush must be worn away. On her walks she stepped into people's gardens to pinch off cuttings from their geraniums and succulents. An occasional sunset is reflected on the windows. A little puddle is overcast. If only you could touch, or, even, catch those gray great creatures. I was afraid of my uncle with the wart on his nose, or of his jokes at our expense which were beyond me, and I was shy of my aunt's deafness who was his sister-in-law and who had years earlier fallen into the habit of nodding, agreeably. Wool station. See lightning, wait for thunder. Quite mistakenly, as it happened. Long time lines trail behind every idea, object, person, pet, vehicle, and event. The afternoon happens, crowded and therefore endless. Thicker, she agreed. It was a tic, she had the habit, and now she bobbed like my toy plastic bird on the edge of its glass, dipping into and recoiling from the water. But a word is a bottomless pit. It became magically pregnant and one day split open, giving birth to a stone egg, about as big as a football. In May when the lizards emerge from the stones, the stones turn gray, from green. When daylight moves, we delight in distance. The waves rolled over our stomachs, like spring rain over an orchard slope. Rubber bumpers on rubber cars. The resistance on sleeping to being asleep. In every country is a word which attempts the sound of cats, to match an inisolable portrait in the clouds to a din in the air. But the constant noise is not an omen of music to come. "Everything is a question of sleep," says Cocteau, but he forgets the shark, which does not. Anxiety is vigilant. Perhaps initially, even before one can talk, restlessness is already conventional, establishing the incoherent border which will later separate events from experience. Find a drawer that's not filled up. That we sleep plunges our work into the dark. The ball was lost in a bank of myrtle. I was in a room with the particulars of which a later nostalgia might be formed, an indulged childhood. They are sitting in wicker chairs, the legs of which have sunk unevenly into the ground, so that each is sitting slightly tilted and their postures make adjustment for that. The cows warm their own barn. I look at them fast and it gives the illusion that they're moving. An "oral history" on paper. *That* morning this morning. I say it about the psyche because it is not optional. The overtones are a denser shadow in the room characterized by its habitual readiness, a form of charged waiting, a perpetual attendance, of which I was thinking when I began the paragraph, "So much of childhood is spent in a manner of waiting."

As for we who "love
to be astonished"

You spill the sugar when you lift the spoon. My father had filled an old apothecary jar with what he called "sea glass," bits of old bottles rounded and textured by the sea, so abundant on beaches. There is no solitude. It buries itself in veracity. It is as if one splashed in the water lost by one's tears. My mother had climbed into the garbage can in order to stamp down the accumulated trash, but the can was knocked off balance, and when she fell she broke her arm. She could only give a little shrug. The family had little money but plenty of food. At the circus only the elephants were greater than anything I could have imagined. The egg of Columbus, landscape and grammar. She wanted one where the playground was dirt, with grass, shaded by a tree, from which would hang a rubber tire as a swing, and when she found it she sent me. These creatures are compound and nothing they do should surprise us. I don't mind, or I won't mind, where the verb "to care" might multiply. The pilot of the little airplane had forgotten to notify the airport of his approach, so that when the lights of the plane in the night were first spotted, the air raid sirens went off, and the entire city on that coast went dark. He was taking a drink of water and the light was growing dim. My mother stood at the window watching the only lights that were visible, circling over the darkened city in search of the hidden airport. Unhappily, time seems more normative than place. Whether breathing or holding the breath, it was the same thing, driving through the tunnel from one sun to the next under a hot brown hill. She sunned the baby for sixty seconds, leaving him naked except for a blue cotton sunbonnet. At night, to close off the windows from view of the street, my grandmother pulled down the window shades, never loosening the curtains, a gauze starched too stiff to hang properly down. I sat on the windowsill singing sunny lunny teena, ding-dang-dong. Out there is an aging magician who needs a tray of ice in order to turn his bristling breath into steam. He broke the radio silence. Why would anyone find astrology interesting when it is possible to learn about astronomy. What one passes in the Plymouth. It is the wind slamming the doors. All that is nearly incommunicable to my friends. Velocity and throat verisimilitude. Were we seeing a pattern or merely an appearance of small white sailboats on the bay, floating at such a distance from the hill that they appeared to be making no progress. And for once to a country that did not speak another language. To follow the progress of ideas, or that particular line of reasoning, so full of surprises and unexpected correlations, was somehow to take a vacation. Still, you had to wonder where they had gone, since you could speak of reappearance. A blue room is always dark. Everything on the boardwalk was shooting toward the sky. It was not specific to any year, but very early. A German goldsmith covered a bit of metal with cloth in the 14th century and gave mankind its first button. It was hard to know this as politics, because it plays like the work of one person, but nothing is isolated in history—certain humans are situations. Are your fingers in the margin. Their random procedures make monuments to fate. There is something still surprising when the green emerges. The blue fox has ducked its head. The front rhyme of harmless with harmony. Where is my honey running. You cannot linger "on the lamb." You cannot determine the nature of progress until you assemble all of the relatives.

Like plump birds along the shore Summers were spent in a fog that rains. They were mirages, no different from those that camelback riders approach in the factual accounts of voyages in which I persistently imagined myself, and those mirages on the highway were for me both impalpable souvenirs and unstable evidence of my own adventures, now slightly less vicarious than before. The person too has flared ears, like an infant's reddened with batting. I had claimed the radio nights for my own. There were more storytellers than there were stories, so that everyone in the family had a version of history and it was impossible to get close to the original, or to know "what really happened." The pair of ancient, stunted apricot trees yielded ancient, stunted apricots. What was the meaning hung from that depend. The sweet aftertaste of artichokes. The lobes of autobiography. Even a minor misadventure, a bumped fender or a newsstand without newspapers, can "ruin the entire day," but a child cries and laughs without rift. The sky droops straight down. I lapse, hypnotized by the flux and reflux of the waves. They had ruined the Danish pastry by frosting it with whipped butter. It was simply a tunnel, a very short one. Now I remember worrying about lockjaw. The cattle were beginning to move across the field pulled by the sun, which proved them to be milk cows. There is so little public beauty. I found myself dependent on a pause, a rose, something on paper. It is a way of saying, I want you, too, to have this experience, so that we are more alike, so that we are closer, bound together, sharing a point of view—so that we are "coming from the same place." It is possible to be homesick in one's own neighborhood. Afraid of the bears. A string of eucalyptus pods was hung by the window to discourage flies. So much of "the way things were" was the same from one day to the next, or from one occasion (Christmas, for example, or July 4th) to the next, that I can speak now of how we "always" had dinner, all of us sitting at our usual places in front of the placemats of woven straw, eating the salad first, with cottage cheese, which my father always referred to as "cottage fromage" that being one of many little jokes with which he expressed his happiness at home. Twice he broke his baby toe, stubbing it at night. As for we who "love to be astonished," my heartbeats shook the bed. In any case, I wanted to be both the farmer and his horse when I was a child, and I tossed my head and stamped with one foot as if I were pawing the ground before a long gallop. Across the school playground, an outing, a field trip, passes in ragged order over the lines which mark the hopscotch patch. It made for a sort of family mythology. The heroes kept clean, chasing dusty rustlers, tonguing the air. They spent the afternoon building a dam across the gutter. There was too much carpeting in the house, but the windows upstairs were left open except on the very coldest or wettest of days. It was there that she met the astonishing figure of herself when young. Are we likely to find ourselves later pondering such suchness amid all the bourgeois memorabilia. Wherever I might find them, however unsuitable, I made them useful by a simple shift. The obvious analogy is with music. Did you mean gutter or guitar. Like cabbage or collage. The book was a sort of protection because it had a better plot. If any can be spared from the garden. They hoped it would rain before somebody parked beside that section of the curb. The fuchsia is a plant much like a person, happy in the out-of-doors in the same sun and breeze that is most comfortable to a person sitting nearby. We had to wash the windows in order to see them. Supper was a different meal from dinner. Small fork-stemmed boats propelled by wooden spoons wound in rubber bands cruised the trough. Losing its balance on the low horizon lay the vanishing vernal day.

1987

FROM *Slowly*

I wake to the waking shadow of the world the waking have in common for one long visit slowly

I walk rather than speed up the ordinary unfolding

One has to wait for the lateness of the day with recalcitrance circulating to stop in the midst of traffic in a blindspot that flows around one smoothly to regard the dark building without apology

Movement prolongs the finitudes a person moving achieves which lacks finality imperceptibly

Out the dark door over black leaves putting into motion what painters have known for years I see that the night is in the mind before it ever gets to day

Colors creating forms are left for the imagination to turn from birds in flight to photographs of same or nearly same

The middle of my face aches as if with cold a physicist can detect as an acceleration I'm slowing

Or there might be scores a physician scorning dreams
should nonetheless excise as extended omens
Omens always have a psychological twist indomitable will
exercises
What one clearly sees comes up momentarily in implausibly
submerged assertions as generosity
Slowly things partly because of damage are represented as
ghosts grown too quickly
Repetitive exposure to anything provokes sensations

I'm always moving around incessantly which is dubious
animation seemingly not chosen
The old city skyscraper rises today with pathos that propels
the change from one sensation to another daily bound a short way
I recognize it as a skyscraper by going mentally around the
information given
It inclines its crown
Its walls come from a dune
Its shadow briefly falls like light upon the patterns of
motion of the mottled pigeons that flutter in the gutter and like a
photograph captures the feeling of transience
Light the eye adds to the evidence falls on a scene as the
scene outside its shadow
Lettered passersby pass by what history has for us
The vanquished sit at the center of their world
intransigently outskirting
My eye caught the light, a rock approximately the size of a
head, and something was said regarding fate surreptitiously
Each fate is phrased
Fate in sequences
My hand mentally grabs the glass just before it hits the floor
suddenly
Fate is a term for the present, a name for time regained
Clichés develop in the dark and they are known in a flash
as hallucinations
In the one called "wouldn't you know it!" a dachshund
comes out from under the bed
It is the usual dachshund, the decisively irascible fat one
If I had it to do all over again I'd call it "Beethoven" and
after awhile "Lately"

But the hallucination known as "to do it all over again"
takes the kind of time we are immediately fated not to have

Someone I have known for a long time like the green we
ascribe without seeming effort to the surface of leaves lives not far
away
Landmarks auspiciously intervene
Lamplight and strange diction and the duration that's
required for something very ordinary to occur (the rice to cook, the
rain to fall, the dust to dull the stripes of the zebra immobilized in
a museum diorama as if to highlight our knowledge of zebras) are of
course of interest of necessity
The hardest knowledge to acquire to continue is that of
unfleeting characteristic incidents
Strange tales can be quickly heard
The kissing of a snowball, the connection glimpsed
between the legs of a pedestrian to lions in a dream of this, the kiss
to think that connection in a hurry
Is *that* love?
There is a species of moth whose individuals are differently
colored but which together at nightfall form a horde that hangs from
a branch, the palest as anchor and the others by degrees until the
whole looks like a flower and produces the observation that vivid
botanical lives invite briefly ebullient imitations
If what is is all there is, then it is impossible for what is to
be imperfect—that's one way to think of things
The encyclopedic is slowed by a totality ("reality")

The inability to remember except perhaps some vague
and distant storeroom causes doubt whose reach is independent
of everything that might happen after breakfast tomorrow but the
present
The bird we saw yesterday in the tree constantly sings
outwardly
Fate can never in a new way nor as before overcome its
dependence on the present once and for all
When inertia sets in, things that are in motion stay in
motion, things that are stationary stay put
For the onlooker tossing in her bed given too much
information the magic square judiciously disappears
The information whispered by the wristwatch counts not

for but to nothing it continues
    Its brief halts for repentance erroneously considered an
instant of knowledge are always on the question
    Contrition is itself a form of query

    Strange kinds of dreams sometimes result from the
confusion caused by their remnants
    Outwardly calm, sincerely yours, gradually fading, etc
    Then there's ambivalence and strong suspicion loosely
connected
    An idea takes shape taking shapes such and such
    The inability to see as if through an insect's eye seeing
numerous different images is not a true detriment
    We shift position and fiddle with our subjectivity
    The several states of the self separate unequally distributed
    I climb my way to the backgammon board and comb my
hair
    I "wait," "cease," "race," now to be languid incessantly
    I shake a head of lettuce and lie back to hear my brother
play the cello
    To keep my balance I remain obedient to the laws of
physics governing my times thoroughly
    Ideas have no autonomy
    We don't see someone off who is just going around the
house suspiciously

2002

FROM *The Beginner*

This is a good place to begin.
From something.
Something beginning in an event that beginning overrides.
Doubt instruction light safety fathom blind.
In the doorway is the beginning thus and thus no denial.
A little beat of time, a little happiness quite distinct from
misery as yet.
The sun shines.
The sun is perceived as a bear, then a boat, then an
instruction: see.
The sun is a lily, then a whirlpool turning a crowd.

The shadows lengthen, the sun-drenched line of arriving strangers are all admitted, seen in the day and not the same at night, host and guest alike.

Two things then, both occurring as the beginner arrives: acceptance and the reconstruction of the world which that acceptance implies.

In the first twenty-four hours nearly blind and with hands swelling, the gaze fierce, face scowling, the beginner faces scowling.

The beginner is a figure of contradiction, conditions what has begun.

Someone could say clouds suddenly, correctly, there's a change in the low-lying blue, the space for it having diminished, its limits are almost certainly black.

Yes, black is right, it's for certainty, yellow for cattle, brown for the violin, pink is fortuitous except in flowers especially the rose, rose is for the rose, gray for clocks and the time they keep, orange for lips or for cups, also sponges, ochre for shadows at noon and sleep, silver for fish and memory, fissures and their accompanying sentiment, gold for blue and iconography and geographical distance, red is for the forest and for the alphabet, blue is for intelligence, purple for the old neighbors smelling of wool, green is for sweat, and out of white comes what we can say.

The face is made from paste and paper, this is what's known as clay, the skull is formed of clay supported by feeling twigs into which feeling flows.

Some degree of risk is involved, but no one pities the beginner.

How can they until he or she has begun (to be pitiable or enviable, happy or sad (one can't experience happiness without catching a glimpse of life (February 1) since that's what happiness is: the awareness of the sensation of having seen something of life), rich or poor (money is both signifier and signified, and poverty is like the notorious gap between them (February 5)), well or ill (inevitably in the course of time one will be both, though for some wellness is the norm and illness the marked condition (for these people illness is an injury) while for others it's the other way around (illness befalling the ill is an insult)), etc.).

And then it's too late for pity.

If in the 19th century, as Gertrude Stein said, people saw parts and tried to assemble them into wholes, while in the 20th century people envisioned wholes and then sought parts appropriate to them, will the 21st century carry out a dissemination of wholes into all parts and thus finish what the 19th century began (February 7)?

Even when nothing happens there is always waiting submerged in the task of beginning and task it is in thoughts to begin afresh.

The beginner makes a beginning, and if optimism is in the air (or pessimism, that mordant state of mind that says things can't possibly improve), the beginner proclaims it a good place to begin.

That is beginning.

Something and other things in a sequence simultaneously.

Ants on a white sill buried.

A harbinger in the light.

A child composed nudely.

A side of a tree cut into squares at a shout from a man under an umbrella.

A furtive marked moth fluttering into a beam of light.

A woman at a door falling.

The beginner is diverted.

Follow me.

—

Beginning will be an experience, unfolding more it runs its course, we will follow, doing and undergoing.

We have no particular end or plan.

We could head out, in, off, over, north, we are doing so.

Which?

The answer must be deferred just as I write this, a child comes into the room with a book always a little differently, he says, I don't like gloom, so much the better, I say.

Something is happening.

To the book?

Yes, to me.

The child is holding a spider on his palm, perhaps he'll be very strong, minds will fly to meet his, I'd say thinking, hello, what can I teach the flesh about his body, the snow, cake, time, without question nothing is more amazing than the millions of years.

The spider jumps off his hand, whoops, no calculation, the transition is sudden and remains elusive, there is a spider and then it takes power with a "tightening of the heart strings," it takes itself off.

A beginner (a tragic as well as a comic beginner) must have a sense of timing, though perhaps not of time, which can come only later, as lateness, animals too, cats, zebra, frogs, etc., they must know whether the time is wrong or right, that is timing, whether the given moment will be a passage into or out of disturbance.

Whether we lie in a field or sit in a small room, we know we are living in an expanding universe (March 19), there is mathematical uncertainty and certainty about it, F = freedom, there's an echo, mockery, perhaps.

I've begun without stopping maybe lurching and poorly fitting.

There's no heroism involved, heroics come to a stop.

The snapping of whistles, rumpling of twigs, spinning of bricks into bridges goes on in confusion trivialities cross.

You think of confusion as rapid?

As it proceeds at a turtle's pace by halves?

Coming or going?

One can't tell.

The turtle halves in motion, etc., as et cetera in celebration—we don't know wholes (heroes (March 21)).

I can believably anticipate breezes in weather, memory, precision, noises of birds or perhaps cellos or both alternating, some by day some by night with its stars, cravings, evaluations, distractions, goals, and fumblings where there are no goals, since beginning is undertaken but not always with the goal of beginning nor with any goal at all.

I would never want to suggest that one begins by oneself and not in conjunction with one's own life and with all the rest of life besides, with its conflicting tendencies.

That would be a mistake, not an impossibility, mistakes do happen.

Still one may begin unawares or one may be well on one's way but feel it perpetually to be a beginner's way, one might insist on that, an old hand at beginning and getting to an edge for the love of it.

Hesiod says love is a loosener of limbs.

But it is fate that has given the spider freedom and it runs for cover, it doesn't exhaust its possibilities

2002

Joan Retallack
b. 1941

The poet and literary scholar Joan Retallack received her B.A. from the University of Illinois and her M.A. from Georgetown University. Widely admired for her critical study *The Poethical Wager* (2004) and books on Gertrude Stein and John Cage, she is John D. and Catherine T. MacArthur Professor of Humanities at Bard College.

Retallack's works of poetry include *Circumstantial Evidence* (1985), *Errata Suite* (1993), *Icarus FFFFFalling* (1994), *Afterrimages* (1995), *How to Do Things with Words* (1998), *Mongrelisme: A Difficult Manual for Desperate Times* (1998), *Steinzas en mediation* (2002), *Memnoir* (2004), and *Procedural Elegies* (2010).

Although associated with the language poets, Retallack is primarily influenced by John Cage, whose work and ideas showed that a different concept of space-time was possible for writing. Instead of the need for "certain privileged beginnings leading to a very specific and precious kind of development," the artist "could simply exist at whatever intersection in space-time" she found herself in and bring that into the work.[1] As a result of that realization, Retallack's poetics turned away from fictive time, which in its measured presentation of person, place, and event privileges authorial voice over the complexities of the real: "I really began to see that kind of work as having to do with a vanishing point perspective, that everything was moving toward the last punctum where the conflict—the conflict that had been artificially imported in the first place—would be resolved."[2] Her works therefore model difficulty rather than ease of expression.

Retallack posits a "poethical" poetry that makes a wager on the new. Like all wagers, the poethical "bet" comes with the necessary risk of breaking identity with your own established style, which may also be the popular mode of the day. Retallack writes, "Your poethical work begins when you no longer wish to shape materials (words, visual elements, sounds) into legitimate progeny of your own poetics. When you are released from filling in the delimiting forms. This swerve, of course, comes about only as the result of a wrenching crisis."[3] Retallack continues, "For the work to become poethical it seems it must risk a period of invisibility, unintelligibility. This is what happened with Stein, Joyce, Beckett, Wittgenstein, Cage."[4] She further argues that the language "must fly from the poet, like Zeno's arrow, in an imperiled, imperiling trajectory subject to cultural weather, chance, vagaries of all kinds beyond the poet's intentionality."[5]

1. Joan Retallack Interviewed by Redell Olsen, London, Sunday May 16, 1999, *how2* 1.6 (2001), http://www.asu.edu/pipercwcenter/how2journal/archieve/online_archive/v1_6_2001/current/radings/encounters/olsen.html.   2. The same.   3. "The Poethical Wager," *The Poethical Wager,* Berkeley, 2003, p. 38.   4. The same, p. 40.   5. The same.

Curiosity and the Claim to Happiness

Studies have shown that the brain
prefers unpredictable pleasures.

PRESENT TENSE

it's said that it happens even in nature e.g. during the
childhood the mother might have (had) a taste for film
noir and take(n) the child along

my machine is hooked up to my machin things inaccessible
to the precise methods of e.g. a Brazilian bookmobile
being hijacked in a dark underground garage fiction is
precisely what they now call non-fiction too get a bit too
personal i.e. Eurydice my dark darling don't worry I can
bear your not looking at me she cri(ed) out i.e. hoping it
(was) true

(now) (here) together in the mix of the modern metropolis
Rio Vienna Paris Tokyo Moscow Hong Kong Lagos New
York Bombay London Mumbai he and she both feel close
to the idealized neuron in the book

▪

some of the diffuse sensations of early childhood may still
surprise us as we consider their names e.g. joy frustration
shame anxiety love rage fear anger wonder curiosity
disgust surprise longing humor pride self-respect fear but
not terror fear but not horror

the mother however might not like surprises e.g. wanting
to know for how many generations a Negro in the
bloodlines can produce a *throwback* the word is memory
the child recalls this use of memory does not know what
to say for a very long time: The soul is inwardness, as
soon as and insofar as it is no longer outwardness; it is
memoria, insofar as it does not lose itself in *curiositas*.

▪

otherwise one could ask at any moment e.g. in what story
does an uninvited goddess walk in and roll a golden ball
down the hall or why not enjoy the story of lovers in the
same vein from different centuries but in the same story
from different worlds but in the same story I write down
my dreams this is probably not one of them i.e. for a very
long time the child want(ed) more than she could say to
not want more than she could say i.e. impossible according
to any simple formula for mirroring formulas

■

if e.g. but for the accidental clause the swerve of curiosity
on the monkey bars the flash-bulb memory the wall of fire
outside the window and or something as vague as living in
time i.e. for a time near what seem to be near things swept
into the stream of self-translation in the coincidental flow
of events near disregarded syllables suddenly audible vol up
sudden outburst of song sudden Ha it's too funny how
funny it is to feel sometimes and not others how to
remotely sense a sweet violence in the brevity i.e. the spilt
second glance

      without yards of shimmering adjectives
      description: is description possible can a sunrise
      be described by yards of shimmering adjectives

■

While the curate was saying this, the lass in boy's clothing
stood as if spell-bound, looking first at one and then at
another, without moving her lips or saying a word, like a
rustic villager who is suddenly shown some curious thing
that he has never seen before . . . she gave a deep sigh and
broke her silence at last. . . . Doing her best to restrain her
tears, she began the story of her life, in a calm, clear voice.

■

without the carefully constructed container
story: is story possible: can a life even a portion
of a life be contained in a story: would songs
be better to repair the brain

when if it's curiosity that draws attention to curiosity even
the other animals like us even in nature if for only the
space of time e.g. at the watering hole e.g. during those
times when it's too wide or too narrow for ambiguity the
range of genres might now include humor and but or
horror even (then) there

this voltage through the body is brought on by the senses
senses strictly speaking in logic nothing is accidental the
world divides us into seekers after facts seekers after gold
dig up much earth and find little

▪

or less than a port royal stain it's super being natural not
wishing to symbolize the wish to return to feel as much at
home in e.g. a fortunate sentence as in i.e. an unfortunate
century

some may see at this point which is not an Archimedean
point the necessity to invent a game in which all vowels
are serially replaced with x mxgxcxlly txrnxng prxmxtxrx
txrrxr xntx pxlxtxblx pxst-pxst xrxny xtc.

▪

or that it is not an idle game after all to forgive that they
or we in the slit second of a single pulse to reveal the tear
the tears in all the pages in all their ambiguity paging
through x number of photo albums knowing and not
knowing all that is is not there with only a few clues to
go by e.g. fake cheetah fur fake cowboy hat small dog
straining at leash small notebook or any other kind of book
that can be open and closed at the same time

▪

i.e. all this and more with the ontological thickness of a
scratch and win sheet

look see the red blue yellow green space at the watering
hole hear the animals slurp see the animals roll in the mud
witness the archeological trace of some thing less visible
than a zoological park the mother the father stiff in Sunday
best the insistent curiosity of the child the timing the
timing is all that is off

it is that that is the problem with the timing that it is
always off while it can not be off at all

PRESENT TENSE: CHOICE

e.g. so to not choose the wrong thing to choose nothing
nothing and all given the diversity of forms that even a
soap film or any other minimal surface can at this time at
or on this point that is not e.g. an Archimedean point

or to consider the mother i.e. Archimedea on point to
point out to all how to punch out the holes according to
the instructions that could have (been) the point to
begin with

■

or e.g. any point that can be made into a world view i.e. a
wild idea the wild idea one has just (had) as a hummingbird
flies by just as one thinks that's a fine deluxe model
bumble bee engine with mechanical wings beating the sky
into a wild idea a hot majestic interlude containing
improbable beauty profanity violence graphic photos of
murder victims all this and more before the clouds part
and the sun turns into a coffee mug or a doughnut

■

and but though over the years mathematicians have been
able to prove that every noninteresting closed curve is

spanned by at least one smooth minimal surface or surface
reflecting the twisting of the sun into someone's bird's eye
view or the limits of any horizon always being a point of
view just like the one unflooding here

and then the first question on the examination turns out
to be i.e. drymouth #2 pencil poised: What license does
the program of curiosity as the motor of progress of the
sciences give itself and or us? not to say them

and then the child may or may not find that to find one's
position on the graph using xy coordinates one must
reconfigure the geometry of attention in order to comb
the snakes from her hair

PRESENT TENSE: STILL

they would go often to the movies hot majestic interludes
containing profanity violence & graphic photos of murder
victims in black and white interlard(ed) with bitter irony
of if

in this the context of the extreme sport of everyday life it
is necessary to put this in the context of e.g. the extreme
sport of everyday life

or the most extreme object of medical curiosity that one
could hope to hit upon here i.e. the e.g. clarification of the
connections between the way the body moves and feels the
way the mind thinks and feels if one dares to seek these
bonds in the brain of a living animal

▪

or to zoom in on the scene in the darkened room on the
screen the shadow of the murderous aunt is moving across
the screen along the far wall of the screen one can tell it is
the murderous aunt from the feather in the hat and the
dagger in the hand of the silhouette of the shadow on the
wall

or the scene in the neighborhood playground the boy
falling back the boy falling back and back after being (shot)
about to take another bite of his Mars Bar or any other
chocolate treat with a paper or plastic wrapper in the
country where many fear(ed) God & AIDS & Elephants &
Castles & Car Windows & pop goes the weasel on the way
home from school

■

is it too trivial to ask is this a scale too trivial to ask about
to ask if it is more tragic or more poignant that the child
had hoped to finish i.e. e.g. the candy bar before he (was)
(shot) can the tragic be poignant and vice versa and verso
and recto and the pant cuff gets caught in the spokes and
e.g. the anonymous rider falls off the bike and the optics of
the horizon is questioned on the spot by the Mennonite
Italian who feels his father watch(ed) too many Sinatra
movies and puts too much ham in his omelets

catastrophe theorists say that if we backtrack along the
previous path there will be no catastrophe this time i.e.
not this time

2004

Ron Padgett

b. 1942

Born in Tulsa, Oklahoma, Ron Padgett received his B.A. degree from Columbia University, where he studied with Kenneth Koch, who was a major influence on his writing. Padgett's love for French poetry led him to study in Paris in 1965–1966 as a Fulbright Scholar. Subsequently, he translated French poetry and fiction, notably that of Blaise Cendrars and Guillaume Apollinaire.

From his influential first major collection, *Great Balls of Fire* (1969), to *How Long* (2011), Padgett has displayed a playful attitude that is consistent with Dada. His chapbook *In Advance of the Broken Arm* (1964) takes its title from Marcel Duchamp's found object, an ordinary snow shovel propped against a wall. Like Duchamp, Padgett is a conceptual artist who likes to challenge the status of the art object in the context of the contingent and everyday. His poem "Nothing in That Drawer" is a sonnet parody consisting of fourteen identical lines; the prose poem "Falling in Love in Spain or Mexico" is structured as a short play in which the main character's lines are borrowed from a Spanish-language phrase book. As seen in the poem "Wonderful Things," Padgett's poetry often carries a multitude of moods, from the elegiac to the offhanded, which is characteristic of New York School practice.

Padgett's enthusiasm for collaboration, influenced by the French surrealist poets' practice of the *cadavre exquis* (exquisite corpse) in which two or more poets take turns writing the lines of a poem, led to his working with poet Ted Berrigan on the classic work *Bean Spasms* (1967) and with painter Jim Dine on *The Adventures of Mr. and Mrs, Jim and Ron* (1970).

His other books and collaborations include *Crazy Compositions* (1974); *Toujours l'amour* (1976); *Tulsa Kid* (1979); *Triangles in the Afternoon* (1979); *How to Be a Woodpecker,* with Trevor Winkfield (1983); *Light as Air,* with Alex Katz, (1987); *The Big Something* (1990); *New and Selected Poems* (1995); *You Never Know* (2001); *How to Be Perfect* (2007); and *How Long* (2011).

A former director of the Poetry Project at St. Mark's Church in the Bowery, Padgett lives on the Lower East Side of Manhattan and in Calais, Vermont.

Wonderful Things

Anne, who are dead   and whom I loved in a rather asinine fashion
            I think of you often
        buveur de l'opium chaste et doux

                            Yes I think of you
        with very little in mind

as if I had become a helpless moron

Watching zany chirping birds

That inhabit the air

And often ride our radio waves

So I've been sleeping lately with no clothes on
The floor   which is very early   considering the floor
Is made of birds and they are flying and I am
Upsidedown and ain't it great to be great!!

Seriously I have this mental (smuh!) illness

which causes me to do things

on and away

Straight for the edge
Of a manicured fingernail
Where it is deep and dark   and green   and silent

Where I may go at will
And sit down and tap
My forehead against the sunset

Where he takes off the uniform
And we see he is God

God get out of here

And he runs off chirping and chuckling into his hand

And that is a wonderful thing
. . . a tuba that is a meadowful of bluebells

is a wonderful thing

and that's what I want to do

Tell you wonderful things

1969

Nothing in That Drawer

Nothing in that drawer.
Nothing in that drawer.
Nothing in that drawer.
Nothing in that drawer.
Nothing in that drawer.
Nothing in that drawer.
Nothing in that drawer.
Nothing in that drawer.
Nothing in that drawer.
Nothing in that drawer.
Nothing in that drawer.
Nothing in that drawer.
Nothing in that drawer.
Nothing in that drawer.

1969

Falling in Love in Spain or Mexico

A handsome young man and a veiled woman enter. They stroll slowly across the stage, stopping from time to time, so that their entrance coincides with the first spoken word and their exit the last.

JOSÉ: I am happy to meet you. My name is José Gomez Carrillo. What is your name? This is my wife. I like your daughter very much. I think your sister is beautiful. Are you familiar with the U.S.? Have you been to New York? Your city is very interesting. I think so. I don't think so. Here is a picture of my wife. Your daughter is very beautiful. She sings very well. You dance very well. Do you speak English? Do you like

American movies? Do you read books in English? Do you like to swim? To drive a car? To play tennis? Golf? Dance? Do you like American music? May I invite you to dance? I like to play tennis. Will you drive? Do you live here? What is your address? Your phone number? I am here for four days. Two weeks. One month only. Would you like a cigarette? A glass of wine? Anything? Help yourself. To your health! With best regards. Many happy returns! Congratulations! With best wishes! Merry Christmas! My sincere sympathy. Good luck! When can I see you again? I think you are beautiful. I like you very much. Do you like me? May I see you tomorrow? May I see you this evening? Here is a present for you. I love you. Will you marry me?

GIRL: *(She lifts and throws back her veil, revealing her face, which is extremely and extraordinarily beautiful.)* Yes!

THE END

1969

Who and Each

I got up early Sunday morning
because it occurred to me that the word
which
might have come from a combination of *who* and *each*
and reached for the *OED*
which for me
(I think of it not
as the *Oxford English Dictionary*
but as the *O Erat Demonstrandum)*
has the last word:
"Hwelc, huelc, hwaelc, huaelc, huoelc, hwaelc, wheche, weche,
whech, qwech, queche, qheche, qwel, quelk, hwilc, wilc, hwilch,
wilch, whilc, whillc, whilk, whylke, whilke, whilk, wilke,
whylk, whilk, quilc, quilke, qwilk, quylk, quhylk, quilk, quhilk,
hwic, wic, hwich, wyche, wich, hwych, wiche, whiche, whyche,
wych, whych, which quiche, quyche, quich, quych, qwiche,
qwych, qwych, quhich, hwylc, hwulch, hulch, wulc, whulc,
wulch, whulche": Teutonic belching.
    But in little tiny type: "For the compounds *gewilc,
aeghwilc,* see *Each.*"
Now, if you want to talk *belching. . . .*

It was raining outside
with the blue-gray hiss of tires
against the wet street
I would soon walk my dog in,
the street I drove an airplane up
earlier this morning in a dream
in which the Latin word *quisque* appeared to me,
as if it meant *each which*
in the sea of *eisdem, quicumque,* and *uterque.*
Thus I spend my days,
waiting for my friends to die.

1990

Irish Song by an English Man

O there's a listening in the air
There's a hovering nearby
I know because I'm there
And it is I

O there's a mountain in the stream
All to ribbons torn
Almost a dream
The moment you are born

O my mother came to me
Without a reason why
I wanted to be free
Of her and die

I loved her like a harp
Whose strings have gone away
To ripple in the dark
No songs anyway

Except O the one I hear
And no one hears but I
A listening in the air
A hovering nearby

2011

I'll Get Back to You

What was I thinking about
a few minutes ago when
another thought
swept me away?
Can't I have (pepper)
several thoughts at the same time
(carnival midway) or go back and forth
between (hyphen) them?
I guess so!
But since people (ooga) don't
like that kind of thinking (factory)
we don't do it (doghouse) much.
I never wanted to live (tree)
in a doghouse.
Now to get back (folding
map) to that earlier thought.
(President is guarding it.)
(No sense in asking *him* for it.)
It had something to do
with numbers (flying up
all over the place) and how
(smoke) sequence has properties
that (gleaming faucets) induce
certain thoughts and feelings,
such as reassurance.
I guess that's a good argument
for linearity. Don't you prefer
linearity in the long run?
(Low clouds over the winter field.)

2011

Ann Lauterbach
b. 1942

In Ann Lauterbach's view, "poetry is the aversion to the assertion of power. Poetry is that which resists dominance."[1] Like the poet John Ashbery, Lauterbach employs an oblique yet sumptuous style that often concerns itself with themes of poetic imagination. In her poem "Mimetic," which takes its theme from Wallace Stevens's "The Idea of Order at Key West," Gene Tierney, the 1940s movie actress, "walks along the cliffs, reflective," a figure of the poet as maker. Neither Tierney nor the poem "mirrors" the world; their veracity lies in *being* the world. In Lauterbach's view, the self in poetry is "construed across the entire surface of the poem." The poem can be seen as "an act of self-construction, the voice its threshold."[2]

Like Stevens, Ashbery, and Guest, whose work is concerned with issues of representation, Lauterbach is essentially a philosophical poet. In "Platonic Subject," for instance, a wishbone-shaped twig exists at many levels: the ideal twig, the real twig, the image of the twig in snow, and the twig as poetic image. "Poetry resists false linkages," Lauterbach writes. Both "conventional narrative strategies" and "the mimesis of visual description" are therefore inadequate to the demands of contemporary experience."[3] In an essay on Emerson she writes:

> At the heart of Emersonian thought, for me, is an almost constant desire to reconcile what he called "polarities" into manifestations of flow, circuits and cycles, relation and concordance. . . . Within this typology of reconciliation comes an immense intellectual permission to explore the moody and mercurial shapes of life, to be digressive and uncertain. He writes, "There are no fixtures in nature. The universe is fluid and volatile. Permanence is but a word of degrees."[4]

The same patterns of flow and resistance are characteristic of Lauterbach's poetry, which seeks the moment rather than the conclusion. On the other hand, the poet Tim Peterson sees a break toward "a more edgy heteroglossia" at the time of *Clamor* when Lauterbach's sister died. Characterized by what he calls "rootless elegiac," these new poems "voice displeasure with both the present and the past, but always stated with a kind of backward nod."[5]

Born and raised in New York City, Lauterbach has taught at Columbia, Princeton, and Brooklyn College. Since 1997, she has served as the David and Ruth Schwab Professor of Languages and Literature, Milton Avery Graduate School of the Arts, Bard College. She has published eight volumes of poetry, including

Before Recollection (1987), *Clamor* (1991), *If in Time: Selected Poems, 1975–2000* (2001), *Hum* (2005), and *Or to Begin Again* (2009). Her essays are collected in *The Night Sky: Writings on the Poetics of Experience* (2005). She has received a MacArthur Fellowship and a Guggenheim Fellowship.

Ann Lauterbach lives in Germantown, New York.

1. "Links without Links: The Voice of the Turtle," *The American Poetry Review*, Jan./Feb. 1992, p. 37.   2. The same.   3. The same.   4. "On Emerson," *The Night Sky: Writings on the Poetics of Experience*, New York, 2005, p. 237.   5. "Rootless Elegiac: An Interview with Ann Lauterbach," Mappemunde, April 17, 2004, http://mappemunde.typepad.com/mappemunde/2004/04/rootless_elegia.html.

Platonic Subject

Momentum and wash of the undefined,
as if clarity fell through the sieve of perception,
announced as absence of image.
But here is a twig in the form of a wishbone.
Aroused, I take it, and leave its outline
scarred in snow which the sun will later heal:
form of the real melts back into the ideal
and I have a twig.

1987

Clamor

1.

It was a trance: thieves, clowns, and the blind girl
Passed symmetrically under the wide structure
As a floor passes under a rug,
Was this enough to go on, this scrap?
Had I entered, or was I pacing the same limits:
The room brought forward to another landscape,
Its odd birds, its train, its street lamp
Stationed like an unmoving moon. At night, the cries
Assembled into the ordinary speech of lovers before love
As the train pulled up the space, passing and passing.

Were these categories to be kept—thief, clown, blind girl—
Or were they too narrowly forensic, too easily found,
The whining insatiable drift insufficiently modeled.
They were an invitation to appear, appease, applaud,
In short to respond, be magical.
In the old days, we howled.
In the old days we chanted our lists until they
Were deciphered, lifted the leaves, touched the broken clay,
Counted the steps quickly, saying this is the one with the key,
This is the one for whom I will awaken.

2.

Affection is merciless: the wind, the excluder.
So much ruptured attention, so much pillaged from the stalk.
Even the nerves stray from precision, announcing
Their stunned subject. Merciless: a field of snow
Flying like jargon, sweeping the issue away
In a halo of cold, its purpose
Lifted from the flat climate, from its nub or throb.
Lifted on impossible wings we are generous, we dare.
But affection is merciless: the dead in their thin garb
Walking the ruined streets, inventing us in stride and envy.
It is said they will make their way
Back to us, as what rises saves itself, falls.
What is the speed of this doctrine, what dividends,
What annual yield?
When will he give it back,
When will I laugh in the untidy yard
And when will her eyes, staring at me
Because she sees only her departure from me,
See me left here. Further adventure is further delay.
I used to count the days. I do not want to count the days.

1991

New Brooms

Of representation (*frame*)
from one to another (*use*)
between the articulation (*space*)

of language *(tree)*
of clarity by means of *(intent)*
of humans *(speech)*
on the contrary *(response)*
with itself, in its own density *(earth)*
for it is not *(image)*
from the first to the second *(wave)*
seizes upon *(law)*
within the other *(us)*
without those of *(tradition)*
point by point *(nature)*
of or to *(the same)*

and so on into a possible good
the waxed carnation's cribbed flounce
shade distinctly wound among new brooms
panache of the ever-tan September

          And so what is said   is at an angle

architectural

      over the floor from which the soliloquy drafts
          upwards, as if restitution
             could be a chant surrounding disaster.

Bruise on the arm lingers in absentia.
Buzz saw in the alley.

Speech, oracle of intention, dissolves
into the sea's remission
as up through an imperfect net comes another exaltation.

2.

Some here twitch along a heading, out
out, and came thou back along the periphery,
shroud tracked, foregathered,
tune integrating chorale
tautly drawn into rainspit, down
through the breaking mirror's reminiscent shield, *bethou*
said the maiden, *bethou* said the monk.

Not yet, said the bird, elongating distance,
high among pines and pale rock.
But had we spoken of the quarry?
Or were we in a room, video-taped, among dry towels
and the humid inquisition of the crowd?
We were in the crowd, *"you and I" "he and she"* and so
transpired over its edge into
bodily harm: an eye for a hand, some mantra of war.
The stipulating crew began to assert its origins
and what pale and what golden
shimmied into paradox, whittling the streets with monograms,
the walls with cool but generative dust.
The pictures came back from their instants.
A genetic stroke of luck is not to have this receptor.
Yet another instruction, one we still cannot read.

to Thomas Dumm

2000

Instruction

To maximize the dim effects of dream
declaw the cat. Also,
name the mother in the dream, that one, spilling
on the first violinist in the quartet who sways in a crimson
gown. Or that one, sad on her cot
with only one eye, blinking at the wreath
hung on the wall where the fire was.
That is not a dream. Get rid of it.
To maximize the dim effects of dream
read Nabokov and listen to
rain. The woman with the long dark hair in the corner
was that the mother? The rich Christians in the west
speak in tongues. What do they say?
Are they speaking to God risen like a sun
over mountains? The mother was not there, so that also
is not the dream. Nabokov spoke in tongues, the hilarity of
his rue and rage teased from his mother's as from the milk
of human kindness. Drink the apparition.

2005

Constellation in Chalk

These ready-mixed colors are available only in
case of emergency, dial
power
with one arm showing
green, then orange flashing, then green.
An airplane? Plane of content—sleep's sound
harvests twenty stamps, each with
floral arrangement, and poison
merit, ultra in the night,
the drawing on the left
a creature in want of wings.

The Third New International
harbors a bug roving, its minor journey
neither in nor out, where the pointing is.
Sandpiper below Essex, Park,
their finish three stories above a hollow noise.

                              Door hauling.

                                        I would like

five red apples, please,
but omit the five and the apples.

This was an episode in description.

Morning's adapter came without
messages from the near—far near, only
mobile structures, flanged and muddy,
mind spooled at the knot, counting without measuring,
a topography of cost scratched into the floor.
Rug slide. Box shapes, and moist smoke
leaning on the environment
like an Idealist colony speaking in tongues,
climbing the hill in period costume,
bothers, sisters, before we hear what was said.

Record of records, the paradoxical mouth.

On that side of the river
a ghetto bus replaced the high orchestral cloud,

rose to ragweed, field with visual noise,
the elders' parade
dragged toward the crows' damaged carillon.

There was a splinter, or leak, in the habitat of selves,
more names than things on the
stage. Only the recording had remembered
and it was shard. *I paint what I paint
said Rivera.* In a dusty window, a sad-eyed doll
caused one to point as at a final moon, an
instrument long surpassed: thought-ghost reads the *fi*
the *fa,* child invents, sighs, scribbles
outside the faint stance of the ready-mades.

How much is that? One or two themes
slink away, scented in derision and
the decision not to play.
Tendresse mystery genre whose fast horses
and arcadian themes
question the robed dawn. *Hehe hehe*
as careful as a ladder leaning on air, nonsense chapters
drawn onto the figural ground.
She swallows the poison, waits and counts. Psyche's
pool of omission reflects the flying horse as the villain leaves
his semen card in her body of reams (operatic ring of gold).
She draws the Empress from the
deck, its familiar headdress of snakes, one for each
known dead. Nobody's diary, somebody's curse.
From his niche in the anthology the Hero speaks,
eyeing her bloody or painted toes, her livid mouth.
Strip the prayer from the kiss web,
it is merely sham. Salvation has undone
her eternal soul into little itinerant drops,
each younger than dew.
The moon's strap slips off the shoulder of night.
Night of Nights it is called; all must follow.

In memory of Barbara Guest

2009

Michael Palmer
b. 1943

Although published in anthologies of language poetry, Michael Palmer's work goes outside the bounds of language poetry and cannot be strictly limited to the movement. In his critical writings, Palmer recognizes the inevitability of narrative in much writing: "Ultimately there is a *definition* that occurs as Gregory Bateson argues 'by relation,' in fact a story, defining that form as a 'knot or complex of that species of connectedness we call relevance.'"[1] But story, as well as autobiography, always involves a degree of concealment: "What is taken as a sign of openness—conventional narrative order—may stand for concealment, and what are understood generally as signs of withholding or evasion—ellipsis, periphrasis, etc.—may from another point of view stand for disclosure."[2] Palmer's poetry is of the second kind, using devices of concealment such as the third person ("He loved the French poets / fell through the partly open door"). Yet even when openly autobiographical ("As Robert's call on Tuesday asking whether I knew that Zukofsky had died . . ."), there is a hermetic tone and refusal of certainty in Palmer's work centered in "Whether I know whatever I know."

In contrast with the language poets, he holds steadfastly to the lyric poem, which he calls "analytic lyric," while recognizing the excesses of subjectivity among the confessional poets. In opposing the "mawkish posturing and exhausted rhetoric" of the Robert Lowell poem "Middle Age," he stands with the Objectivists Zukofsky and Oppen, in their call for sincerity, directness, and objectification.[3] In his view, models of the analytic lyric can be found in Edmond Jabès's mystical poetry of exile, Paul Celan's packed inwardness, the Madrid school of Lorca, Hernandez, and Aleixandre, and the Peruvian poet César Vallejo. In all cases, the lyric contains "a critique of the discourse of power" as a means of poetry's renewal.[4]

Born in New York City and educated at Harvard in history and comparative literature, Palmer has lived in San Francisco since 1969. His books of poetry include *Plan of the City of O* (1971), *Blake's Newton* (1972), *The Circular Gates* (1974), *Without Music* (1977), *Notes for Echo Lake* (1981), *First Figure* (1984), *Sun* (1988), *At Passages* (1995), *The Lion Bridge: Selected Poetry 1972–1995* (1998), *The Promises of Glass* (2000), *Company of Moths* (2005), and *Thread* (2011). He has translated the work of Emmanuel Hocquard, Vicente Huidobro, and Alexei Parshchikov, among others, and coedited the anthology *Nothing the Sun Could Not Explain: 20 Contemporary Brazilian Poets* (1997). Editor of *Code of Signals: Recent Writings in Poetics* (1983), his works of prose include *Active Boundaries: Selected Essays and Talks* (2008). He is also well known for his collaborations with the dancer Margaret Jenkins and the painters Irving Petlin and Sandro Chia. Appointed as a chancellor of the Academy of American Poets in 1999, he was awarded the academy's Wallace Stevens Prize for poetry in 2005. He has also received the Shelley Memorial Award from the Poetry Society of America.

1. "Autobiography, Memory, and Mechanisms of Concealment," in *Writing/Talks*, ed. Bob Perelman, Carbondale, 1985, p. 210.   2. The same, p. 227.   3. "On Objectivism," in *Active Boundaries: Selected Essays and Talks*, New York, 2008, p. 229.   4. "Counter-Poetics and Current Practice," the same, pp. 256–57.

Notes for Echo Lake   3

Words that come in smoke and go.

Some things he kept, some he kept and lost. He loved the French poets fell through the partly open door.

And I as it is, I as the one but less than one in it. I was the blue against red and a voice that emptied, and I is that one with broken back.
While April is ours and dark, as something always stands for
what is: dying elm, headless man, winter—

salamander, chrysalis,

fire—
    grammar and silence.

Or grammar against silence. Years later they found themselves talking in a crowd. Her white cat had been killed in the woods behind her house. It had been a good possibly even a terrible winter. Ice had coated the limbs of the hawthorn and lilac, lovely but dangerous. Travel plans had been made then of necessity abandoned. At different times entire weeks had seemed to disappear. She wondered what initially they had agreed not to discuss.

Some things he kept while some he kept apart.

As Robert's call on Tuesday asking whether I knew that Zukofsky had died a couple of days before. The call came as I was reading a copy of Larry Rivers' talk at Frank O'Hara's funeral (July, 1966), "He was a quarter larger than usual. Every few inches there was some sewing composed of dark blue thread. Some stitching was straight and three or four inches long, others were longer and semi-circular . . ."

As Robert's call on Tuesday a quarter larger than usual asking whether I knew whether I knew. Blue thread every few inches, straight and semi-circular, and sand and wet snow. Blue snow a couple of days before. Whether I know whatever I know.

The letters of the words of our legs and arms. What he had seen or thought he'd seen within the eye, voices overheard rising and falling. And if each conversation has no end, then composition is a placing beside or with and is endless, broken threads of cloud driven from the west by afternoon wind.

The letters of the words of our legs and arms. In the garden he dreamt he saw four bearded men and listened to them discussing metaphor. They are standing at the points of the compass. They are standing at the points of the compass and saying nothing. They are sitting in the shade of a flowering tree. She is holding the child's body out toward the camera. She is standing before the mirror and asking. She is offering and asking. He-she is asking me a question I can't quite hear. Evenings they would walk along the shore of the lake.

Letters of the world. Bright orange poppy next to white rose next to blue spike of larkspur and so on. Artichoke crowding garlic and sage. Hyssop, marjoram, orange mint, winter and summer savory, oregano, trailing rosemary, fuchsia, Dutch iris, day lily, lamb's tongue, lamb's ears, blackberry, feverfew, lemon verbena, sorrel, costmary, never reads it as it is, "poet living tomb of his / games."

Eyes eyeing what self never there, as things in metaphor cross, are thrown across, a path he calls the path of names. In the film *La Jetée* she is thrown against time and is marking time.

> sun burns thru the roars
> dear eyes, *all eyes*, pageant
> bay inlet, garden casuarina, spittle-spawn
> (not laurel) nameless we name
> it, and sorrows dissolve—human

In silence he would mark time listening for whispered words. I began this in spring, head ready to burst, flowers, reddening sky, moon with a lobster, New York, Boston, return, thin coating of ice, moon while dogs bark, moon dogs bark at, now it's late fall.

And now he told me it's time to talk.

Words would come in smoke and go, inventing the letters of the voyage, would walk through melting snow to the corner store for cigarettes, oranges and a newspaper, returning by a different route past red brick townhouses built at the end of the Civil War. Or was the question in the letters themselves, in how by chance the words were spelled.

In the poem he learns to turn and turn, and prose seems always a sentence long.

1981

The Project of Linear Inquiry

[Let *a* be taken as . . .]
a liquid line beneath the skin
and *b* where the blue tiles meet
body and the body's bridge
a seeming road here, endless

rain pearling light
chamber after chamber
of dust-weighted air
the project of seeing things
so to speak, or things seen

namely a hand, namely
the logic of the hand
holding a bell or clouded lens
the vase perched impossibly near the edge
obscuring the metal tines.

She said "perhaps" then it echoed.
I stood there torn
felt hat in hand
wondering what I had done
to cause this dizziness

"you must learn to live with."
It reveals no identifiable source
(not anyway the same as a forest floor).
A vagrant march time, car
passes silently, arm rests at his side

holding a bell or ground lens
where *c* stands for inessential night—
how that body would
move vs how it actually does—
too abstract &/or not abstract enough

but a closed curve in either case
she might repeat
indicating the shallow eaves
nothing but coats and scarves below the window
his-her face canted to the left

nothing imagined or imaginable
dark and nothing actually begun
so that the color becomes exactly as it was
in the minuscule word for it
scribbled beside an arrow

on the far wall
perfectly how else continuous with memory.
There are pomegranates on the table
though they have been placed there
salt, pepper, books and schedules

all sharing the same error
and measure of inattention.
What she says rolls forward.
I shouted toward motion, other gestured,
child laughs, sky,

traffic, photograph. I
gave real pain, expelled
breath, decided. Both arms in thought,
mirror otherwise, abandoned
structures mostly, the glass

door with its inscription lay open
before us, nothing to fear.

1981

Voice and Address

You are the owner of one complete thought

Its sons and daughters
march toward the capital

There are growing apprehensions to the south

It is ringed about
by enclaves of those who have escaped

You would like to live somewhere else

away from the exaggerated music
in a new, exaggerated shirt

a place where colored stones have no value

This hill is temporary
but convenient for lunch

Does she mean that the afternoon should pass

in such a manner
not exactly rapidly

and with a studied inattention

He has lost his new car
of which you were, once,

a willing prisoner

a blister in your palm
identical with the sky's bowl

reflected in the empty sentence

whose glare we have completely shed
ignoring its freshness

The message has been sent

across the lesser fractures in the glass
where the listeners are expendable

The heart is thus flexible

now straight now slightly bent
and yesterday was the day for watching it

from the shadow of its curious house

Your photo has appeared
an island of calm

in a sea of priapic doubt

You are the keeper of one secret thought
the rose and its thorn no longer stand for

You would like to live somewhere

but this is not permitted
You may not even think of it

lest the thinking appear as words

and the words as things
arriving in competing waves

from the ruins of that place

1984

I Do Not

Je ne sais pas l'anglais.
—Georges Hugnet

I do not know English.

I do not know English, and therefore I can have nothing to say about this
latest war, flowering through a nightscope in the evening sky.

I do not know English and therefore, when hungry, can do no more than point repeatedly to my mouth.

Yet such a gesture might be taken to mean any number of things.

I do not know English and therefore cannot seek the requisite permissions, as outlined in the recent protocol.

Such as: May I utter a term of endearment; may I now proceed to put my arm or arms around you and apply gentle pressure; may I now kiss you directly on the lips; now on the left tendon of the neck; now on the nipple of each breast? And so on.

Would not in any case be able to decipher her response.

I do not know English. Therefore I have no way of communicating that I prefer this painting of nothing to that one of something.

No way to speak of my past or hopes for the future, of my glasses mysteriously shattered in Rotterdam, the statue of Eros and Psyche in the Summer Garden, the sudden, shrill cries in the streets of São Paulo, a watch abruptly stopping in Paris.

No way to tell the joke about the rabbi and the parrot, the bartender and the duck, the Pope and the porte-cochère.

You will understand why you have received no letters from me and why yours have gone unread.

Those, that is, where you write so precisely of the confluence of the visible universe with the invisible, and of the lens of dark matter.

No way to differentiate the hall of mirrors from the meadow of mullein, the beetlebung from the pinkletink, the kettlehole from the ventifact.

Nor can I utter the words science, séance, silence, language and languish.

Nor can I tell of the aboreal shadows elongated and shifting along the wall as the sun's angle approaches maximum hibernal declination.

Cannot tell of the almond-eyed face that peered from the well, the ship of stone whose sail was a tongue.

And I cannot report that this rose has twenty-four petals, one slightly cancred.

Cannot tell how I dismantled it myself at this desk.

Cannot ask the name of this rose.

I cannot repeat the words of the Recording Angel or those of the Angle of
    Erasure.

Can speak neither of things abounding nor of things disappearing.

Still the games continue. A muscular man waves a stick at a ball. A woman in
    white, arms outstretched, carves a true circle in space. A village turns to
    dust in the chalk hills.

Because I do not know English I have been variously called Mr. Twisted, The
    One Undone, The Nonrespondent, The Truly Lost Boy, and Laughed-
    At-By-Horses.

The war is declared ended, almost before it has begun.

They have named it The Ultimate Combat between Nearness and Distance.

I do not know English.

2000

Autobiography 2 (hellogoodby)

The Book of Company which
I put down and can't pick up

The Trans-Siberian disappearing,
the Blue Train and the Shadow Train

Her body with ridges like my skull
Two children are running through the Lion Cemetery

Five travelers are crossing the Lion Bridge
A philosopher in a doorway insists

that there are no images
He whispers instead: Possible Worlds

The Mind-Body Problem
The Tale of the Color Harpsichord

Skeleton of the World's Oldest Horse
The ring of O dwindles

sizzling around the hole until gone
False spring is laughing at the snow

and just beyond each window
immense pines weighted with snow

A philosopher spreadeagled in the snow
holds out his Third Meditation

like a necrotic star. He whispers:
archery is everywhere in decline,

photography the first perversion of our time
Reach to the milky bottom of this pond

to know the feel of bone,
a knuckle from your grandfather's thumb,

the maternal clavicle, the familiar
arch of a brother's brow

He was your twin, no doubt,
forger of the unicursal maze

My dearest Tania, When I get a good position in the courtyard
I study their faces through the haze

Dear Tania, Don't be annoyed,
please, at these digressions

They are soldering the generals
back onto their pedestals

for A.C.

2000

Of

Of this photograph no one has taken

Eyes both a veil and sexual organ
The play as they always say

of light against shadow
first light then shadow then the shadow-play

Is it in color or black and white?

Yes it is in color or black and white

There are leaves drifting down,
a tiny skiff prepared to embark

across the waters of a painter's studio
toward a tower of clouds beyond the glass

The scatter of things

the room choking on pages
and the torn remnants of pages

No one to answer the telephone's ring
(Dearest Reader are there still phones still rings?)

They are afloat the two of them
in a sea of something

or perhaps they are drowning
or waiting for the wind to gather them up

into a palinode, a canticle, a stanza

If she has a question
will it go unasked?

(Are there still questions and questions unasked
Dearest Reader from the future-past?)

Berries brilliant orange on the hawthorn
this Wednesday late November

Blurred wing at the edge of the frame

Eyes unfocussed lost in her
thoughts as they always say

Eyes at once fixed and in motion

gilded aleph emerging from her mouth
mouth emerging from her mouth

So, it's claimed, an age begins

This photograph no one has seen
offers itself in evidence

2005

The Phantom of Liberty

The summer snows, a bit of a surprise,
and the new turn our love-making has taken—

The Imam's Delight, The Secret Glyph, The Trial Balloon.
Why do such discoveries take so long?

We began, I remember, with the ordinary—
sips of juice, strips of bacon of a morning,

eggs over easy. So the decades passed
and pasture reverted to woodland

and the ghosts we thought long gone
returned, bearing fresh robes it's true,

and the sheep in the fields wandered up to the fence
and greeted them, come anew.

Snow coating the stone walls, the eaves, the little boat.
Snow on the wintergreen and the scarlet oak.

And the Emperors, Green Foresters, China Marks,
tracing and retracing their arcs

in the late, slant light.
And the ghosts with names and the ghosts with none.

2005

Leslie Scalapino
1944–2010

Leslie Scalapino's project was remarkably consistent from the beginning of her career. Through overlapping narratives that often retell actual events with different beginning and end points, she examined the nature of external events in relation to the narrator's perception of them. Scalapino wrote of *that they were at the beach—aeolotropic series:* "I intended this work to be the repetition of historically real events the writing of which punches a hole in reality. (As if to void them, but actively). Also, to know what an event is."[1]

In the opinion of the poet and critic Benjamin Hollander, Scalapino's work deals in "the mutability of identity across time and place, and on how contiguously enacted histories inform, defer, break down, and inhabit an individual in the present."[2] Scalapino typically makes her narrator a psychological actor in the experiences he or she reports: "I am trying to use the writing to be an examination of the mind in the process of whatever it's creating."[3] Scalapino's formal influences, according to the critic Tyrus Miller, include "the ellipses of objectivist poetry, the grammaticalism of Gertrude Stein, and the typographical quirkiness of Emily Dickinson."[4]

Though sometimes grouped with the language poets and a frequent collaborator with the language poet Lyn Hejinian, she maintained her own poetics. Although her work was considerably different from that of Beat poets Philip Whalen and Michael McClure, she published, edited, and wrote introductions to their works.

Fanny Howe wrote of her work: "A solitary, an original. What other way could there be for someone with a mind so electric, independent and restless except out into the space-time continuum? Because she is thoroughly modern, every moment of experience is interrupted and unstable, accompanied by introspection and sidelong glimpses at the social. The poet here is a horrified witness, a perpetual child, a sexually alert female who keeps looking back to believe what she has seen."[5]

Scalapino's books of poetry include *Considering how exaggerated music is* (1982), *that they were at the beach—aeolotropic series* (1985), *way* (1988), the trilogy *The Return of Painting, The Pearl, and Orion* (1991), and *Crowd and not evening or light* (1992), *Sight* (with Lyn Hejinian, 1999), *New Time* (1999), *Day Ocean State of Star's Night: Poems & Writings, 1989 & 1999–2006*, and *It's go in horizontal: Selected Poems 1974–2006* (2008). She also wrote the fictions *The Return of Painting* (1990), *Defoe* (1995), *The Front Matter, Dead Souls* (1996), and *Orchid Jetsam* (2001), as well as the cross-genre works *How Phenomena Appear to Unfold* (1991) and *Zither & Autobiography* (2003). Her plays included *Goya's L.A.* (with music by Larry Ochs, 1994) and *The Weatherman Turns Himself In* (1999).

Scalapino was born in Santa Barbara, California. She attended Reed College and received an M.A. in English from the University of California at Berkeley. Founder and editor of O Books, a publisher of experimental poetry, she lived in Oakland.

1. "Note on My Writing," in *How Phenomena Appear to Unfold,* Elmwood, CT, 1989, p. 21.   2. Review of *that they were at the beach—aeolotropic series, Conjunctions* 9, 1986, p. 272.   3. Edward Foster, "An Interview with Leslie Scalapino," *Talisman* 8, Spring 1992, p. 32.   4. *Sulfur* 26, Spring 1990, p. 222.   5. Jacket comment, *It's go in horizontal: Selected Poems 1974–2006,* Middletown, CT, 2008.

FROM *Zither*

Note: 'his' — such as, 'his'-quiet or 'his'-fan — is 'the fact,' is or means 'there is someone else' (aware 'there is someone other').

Separate to the side — continuous — one's

and   a — it's not
refugees — are in   — in —
    — the middle — with   one — outside shape
[famine] — first   — hasn't that space
                                                       ahead in one — [is]

    to walk
in
an unstable and ungoverned country
            array [of] —
armed factions   — to one side
are still — fighting   *outside*
                                  [one's breathing]

                                          shape, *as shape,* is on the side
                                          [as it — at all]

                                          one's
                                  breathing has to
                                          realign — *to* — it
                                  can't — [yet]

        the
        few trickling — back in

— said [they're]
— dying
of thirst dysentery in panicked

flight

                       their — refugees
               — space — outside — one's
               breathing
               then
               being inside — the *'outside'*

        anticipated first, not known before

               being heard *when* it hasn't been
          heard
          first — one

    yet — they [factions]
want starving
      waiting to feed
ends — them [refugees]

               breathing — is
             — in — outside — one's
               — outside shape
         has
         forgotten
         ...

    The soft dark sides of the horse lying being kicked in the long grass with
their coming through the sea of grass from all sides
    to hold too much

    The soft dark rolling sides-cage of curled horse lying — mounds in grass
They're (their) kicking in at the sides

        train on parch cracks
        is freighter — at night

    A man, the interior nature of muscular dove — cage — one stretches out
on the throat-breast raking it, the base of it while his dove moves — remaining
soaked
    one

        not changing

by
the middle — being
in

one — or side is
one is that

He applies his brilliant gentle mind to the fact in the grass. The kicking
people in long grass yet being a tyrant one is respected *per se,* for that.
    This is not the movement in the grass.
    Nor is their movement zither — we had a zither, as children; there is freighter
they are themselves *in fact*
    Hemmed in by the long spears, the other in the middle — spears through
grass, the people holding them on the other ends on all sides — the other is
hemmed pricking as spear-punctures that are on her sides.
    One first — the other does — runs in before (before them being there) —
One is running out — something occurs *then,* when one is running

    not anticipating, as in happiness — running out — before is happy, something
occurring does not change that then. experiencing being happy is in the present,
that it *will* be. (*Is* in the future then, at the same time.)

. . .

    Lear is the viewer. One might even loosen this faculty (sensual as exterior /
interior at once) of apprehension further from one's stream. (*Zither* is the rewriting
of *King Lear* as Kurasawa's *Ran* — which doesn't have this in it)

A little white owl springs up gliding toward one

the girl with eyebrows curved like bows follows it into the plumed grass
the moon or sun resting on the plumed grass, both then

walk on plumed grass

horse

    down crowds coming in from the long plumes eyebrows arch following
phosphorescent owl gliding in

    in fireflies crowds sides running on its sides

    crowds running on its sides wallows on black grass

    crowds wallow eyebrows on moon-edged horse-blackness

    crowds wallow grass horse gliding moon

    eyebrows arching through grass wallow moon

eyebrows wallow crowd on the horse

the man at the café outside in the light appears to be wearing magpie's glistening black feathers gliding blackness
crowd comes in plumed grass to little white owl

head in blackness and running legs in plumed grass

seated roils in sun and moon both then on half-plumed wall-grass
crowd in sun and moon both then wallows on wall-plumes and seated to the side the half

horse
alone walking beside man who's seated at café in glistening black wall to plumed grass in crowd

. . .

— as freedom in rickshaws
early freedom

ocean ball — in future span sky [is in] — too at all one's —
Two — starting out in rickshaws — no supervision then in the city

early freedom — leading to blossomed spring
separation — as one — leading to bud

— as no authority existing at all is only — so it's not itself even —
children insulted in school racially — too there — early freedom

nothing is based
on anything

One exists now on only past (present) as 'nothing' (as that being in fact, events — since placing the past at present *is* dissolved)
Humiliating children regarding their race until they stamped and screamed.
then they did also, the adults got out of the way. the realignment by present-adult didn't work. we're not. past.
to change. the past. 'at' present. *no need.*
She dotes on everything that has balls — to sustain them, fanning their ego, so there cannot be love, that is despair — if one doesn't have balls though one is not sustained

by anything

Look get this straight, I dote on everything that has balls. [This is said by the Mayfly, who later in the comic book scenario is wearing the swastika.]
Everyone begins writing in in letters, Look, she dotes on everything that has balls, meaning favorably of that.

[Mayfly seated at café table still holds swathed balls and with her glistening sails pinned wide black fans outside: Fact in occurrence (past) — is in one's physical frame — too, dawn.]

Then the ballooned fans turn red in the black sun.

The load is so great one'll have to be carried off to the loony bin and *will* here sustain one —

here we're

pretending

I think we should get to utter level of infant [an inner track of despair] — has something to do with dying one isn't now that's it — but that really — as infantile [thin track, line], humps of the colostomy bags on brownshirts them gliding to one and one hits them swatting with newspaper to have them continue gliding

say how.

. . .

One cannot tell a separation between them with humps gliding and their pretending. One's pretending and theirs are so similar as simply pretending — how are we going to be an infant without being infant?

demystify life — so one can do it.

saw curled woman on motorcycle
another waiting for her — on span ahead

— separated from one's — thorax, there

(not) breathing at all — bursting — breathing there

thorax black in shining blue wide
thin — place — of *their* moving
then one's thorax loosened laughs in space

[One suddenly ceased to breathe seeing a curled woman flying on motorcycle bumble-bee-like on vast bridge span where another woman waited curled on motorcycle ahead at the end of the span. One was asphyxiating. *Then,* seeing them, one laughing and weeping at the same time could breathe. One's response was associated with the recent death of a relative, but the sight (of the motorcyclists) was not related in any way.]

boy on skateboard speeding downhill — the thorax opens — one's
one's — black thorax in pelting rain opens
[separately] *slow*

. . .

fans-forest. there

yet
'the'.
outer-fan — there is no outer fan — is
his

————

'reverse grace'
and fans-forest
blackening fan — is wind
one's — as outside walking
[his]

— to

notice
'reverse grace' — him — 'love'

early fan
outer walking

early

his
— walking on trees

— one — [and] — he — loves — [in the middle]
his
— walking on trees

'at'

red-rain's fan — early
— and — 'in' night

————

his
planks as dawn [heart's valve — rungs] — goes on
opened so people's leaving camps
at night
people's tendons being hacked in many — in
along —
in planks [his — dawn] leaps one him their — to side

     night
     base — there is no base

     breaks past rungs while in their middle —
dawn's
     his — people's — fleeing camps — one's
bursting — 'in' it — separate — is — on his
     his quiet's
[[his] 'heart's' — valve] burst 'on' — a — dawn time — one's

        ————

     his quiet's
people fleeing
rungs' planks

     his one's rungs
trees' red-rain's planks

          ...

forest existing
his

a center — hurls —

[just] — [and] one's his-quiet

        ————

     the airs thin falls
'in' one — to be — close [to it]
     planks — people not caring for one
only — dread — at being
no moving away — in airs early
[captured in life — 'as' dying]
     — as 'shape' of early — one's
— in 'his'-quiet's dawn also —
     no other activities — just one's

thin fans-rose forest existing only
       ...

outer
fan — there isn't any
     — in it

captured in life in utter early

freedom
      and dying / others one
at all

and no outer fan
his

[his — [and]
fans-dawn 'there' — now]
         …

— crowds surrounding before — to pull
the place down — they call in the army

    where
one walks on water — his quiet's-
    base — jump [one] in middle 'at'-dawn's
'there'
    'base's' middle 'yet' — [and]
— crowds surrounding —

    — on huge river — one's-dawn's
one jumps to or goes to [it]

    — not — [captured in life]
[is conflict 'one' — why?]
    — in early
— walking
    one has a pair [is]
at present — 'in' — 'at'
    night's — [it]

    ['it cannot be known']
falling — at night — in sky sleeping even — as one's
    present
base — space — 'it can be known' — is
    [transgressing social
ridiculed for 'it can be known' — 'in' [there being] 'no child'
    early child thinks

then, right away — that was
accurate — dawn's at sky
    present
base-falling as fan's present stripping away
    as transgressing 'even'

wide base-falling

                      . . .

    recent-past events — existing separate
sole

    as present ['in'] — 'is'
crowds crawling on black mounds
    singing — climbing —
one's walking on water 'there'
night — 'his'-base walks thin

    in 'his' present early-'one'

    red trees-fan early-forest

    no time is necessary that's now — is it

    ————

    his base walks
    one's — there's a space — in
between like throwing
    — dawn's-trees-fan — is — early-instant's

space — this instant in
    the same
one — one's base walks —
    his-thin
moon's-day early

    he will be outside
this instant's fall fans
    breath's alive at night 'his'
— 'at' night
separately early — where — one's base walks

    ————

are — their — rungs — there — breath's — ?
'in'

night — 'at' night
crawling lines on black mounds [coal] and
their climbing at night early — ?

his quiet's — no moving away — captured in life

———

   a switch

with flowers on it

   to take a switch

with flowers on it — night

additional-
   ly early

2003

Marjorie Welish

b. 1944

Marjorie Welish was born in New York City, where she now lives, and studied art history at Columbia University. An art critic since 1968, she has written articles for *Art in America, Art International*, and *ARTnews*, among other magazines, as well as the catalogues for a number of exhibitions. Her poetry collections include *Handwritten* (1979), *Two Poems* (1981), *The Windows Flew Open* (1991), *Casting Sequences* (1993), *The Annotated "Here" and Selected Poems* (2000), *Word Group* (2004), *Isle of the Signatories* (2008), and the mixed genre work *In the Futurity Lounge/Asylum for Indeterminacy* (2012). She has also published a volume of art criticism, *Signifying Art: Essays on Art after 1960* (1999).

As a painter, she is represented by Baumgartner Galley of New York City. A retrospective collection of papers given on her work as an artist was held at the University of Pennsylvania in 2001, resulting in the volume *Of the Diagram: The Work of Marjorie Welish.*

Meditative rather than narrative, her poetry has the rhetorical detachment and imagistic complexity of some of John Ashbery's work. Welish's poetry avoids conclusiveness and the grand gesture; instead it delights in ambiguity and abstraction and finds lyricism there. Of *The Windows Flew Open*, critic Adam Craig Hill writes, "The verbal address of these poems is highly rhetorical, though interspersed with restless imaging and competing versions of reality."[1]

Welish's fascination with those competing versions of reality is especially evident in poems such as "Within This Book, Called Marguerite": "I wonder if the mind will ever stop pursuing / rival minds or at least rival murmuring."

Welish is the Madelon Leventhal Rand Distinguished Lecturer in Literature at Brooklyn College.

1. "How the World Exists," *American Book Review*, December 1991, p. 22.

Respected, Feared, and Somehow Loved

> In the long run we must fix our compass,
> and implore our compass,
> and arraign our shadow play in heaven, among the pantheon
> where all the plea-bargaining takes place.
> Within the proscenium arch,

the gods negotiate ceaselessly,
and the words he chooses to express the baleful phrase
    dare to be obsessed
with their instrumentality. Please send for our complete catalogue.

As in the days of creation, the clouds gossip and argue,
    the gods waver.
The gods oversee such unstable criteria as fourthly, fifthly.
The rest are little timbral touches.
The gods waver. To reiterate a point, the gods oversee
the symposium on the life raft—a crazed father, a dead son;
                          an unwarranted curtailment of family.

Part of the foot, and thus part of the grace splinter in dismay,
and the small elite of vitrines where our body parts are stored
dies in a plane crash in Mongolia.
Why didn't someone do something to stop the sins of the climate,
                          and earlier,

why did not someone rewrite the sins of the vitrines, the windows
shipwrecked icily, the windows called away?

                                          1991

Within This Book, Called Marguerite

The sky is overcast and behind it an infinite regress
of vision is pulling nearer (and yet beneath)
in bashful ruts. I wonder if the mind will ever stop pursuing
rival minds or at least rival murmuring. It is a long sky
that convenes this endlessness.

                        Persons cunningly blent
to suggest a consensus—this is what is meant by serious
    entertainment
of opposing and hastening points of view, each of whose
sense of history is mutually exclusive.

                        Deck chairs
are making a return. I remember when stacking and ganging

chairs were innovative and David Rowland won an industrial award
for the campanile of steel chairs climbing to the sky.

As time separates us
from the evaporating architectonics to sweeten mythopoetic
substances, you start to count heroically,
hurled down upon a profile of an as yet
unrevealed know-how.

You are unaccompanied
like the great unaccompanied counting
for solo violin that has arisen from the other side
of the mind and hand, the dark, tangled side of the hand,
with its great length of stay.

1991

Twenty-three Modern Stories

Perpetually roughed up
by the dawdling, blushing drone of an airplane,

"the viola with a restrained, sometimes" restringing
made the plunge
upon these planks
because of all the shores that must be visited.

". . . and continuities, whose intersections"
spreading hot wax
on privation
and on the phrase "this text,"
united once again,
are inescapably drawn toward the open door.

The bells have ceased altogether.
"The air bit hard and cold"
spaced in such a way as to make a triad
of arrangements thus:
old and tired star, guitar and protean
interdisciplinary soprano.

1993

The World Map

Prospect in readiness, together with
the annexation of processes,

>> revealing—dissembles

landslides or pure lyric
by which to complete the fragmented prayer "as intended."

Dumping gravel

> on emancipated frontiers . . .

If H.B. really were
darkening a bildungsroman of irony, he would say of R.R.
he is second,

> that he is the second most interesting philosopher,

or that the tenderness of located
skimming stones

> across pain and dust

"helps us get what we antecedently decided."

A landslide

> idling in the mirror . . .

>> 2000

Possible Fires

Constitutive of stone put down
grown by melting silt; artifice meets sourdough there; there deduced from
fractured clay matrix—and culture: culture's modern loaf induced. Let a
leaf be cultural in this world; then, let a leaf's waxy index of antihistamine
eventually be an event it (the leaf) might not have issued. Issue anything
special. Anything medicinal, everything medicinal. Everything medicinal and
a breeze

pebbled with trial.
Over and under entities are a few pebbles, some trial and error.
The author has argued that error in Spain was commonplace.
Spain was a commonplace in Stein's alterity.

Stein featured Spain.
Down beneath the constructs, we tried "countenancing" a type;
here she tried automatism and "feature," in the sense of
     "structure, form or appearance esp. of a person":
a portrait void of appearance yet replete with animal gait.
A world with animals overlapped, with animals offset,
     offset in a sea change.

Everything medicinal and an afterthought—
but he had then to breathe
     giving cause
     creating occasion
intervening ambitiously in Spain's
reciprocating energies and commonplace.
Stein featured Spain
     as one featuring norms
     as one featuring a build
         a build of beginnings
         a build of subroutine
with animals
     boar?
     pig?
offset in a sea change.

2004

Norma Cole

b. 1945

Born in Toronto, Norma Cole received an M.A. in French from the University of Toronto in 1967, and moved to France in time to absorb the revolutionary atmosphere of the May 1968 strike. After returning to Toronto in the early 1970s, she migrated to San Francisco in 1977, where she has lived ever since. A member of the circle of poets around Robert Duncan in the 1980s, and associated with San Francisco's language poets, Cole also takes sustenance from her connection with the contemporary French poets Jacques Roubaud, Claude Royet-Journoud, and Emmanuel Hocquard. A prolific translator of French poetry, her translations include Danielle Collobert's *Notebooks, 1956–1978*, Anne Portugal's *Nude*, and *Crosscut Universe: Writing on Writing from France*. In the winter of 2004–2005, she created an art installation as part of the California Historical Society's Collective Memory installation series. She has received the Wallace Alexander Gerbode Award and a grant from the Foundation for Contemporary Arts.

Anne Waldman writes of Norma Cole's work: "An authentic daughter of Robert Duncan . . . there's an inscrutability of purpose & yearning toward the underside of meaning through picture, place, story, objects (an orange flight suit, a clamp, a biscuit), person, wit, and dream. I think about music reverberating in the interstices of Cole's spheres of sound. But the poem is a toy, as she says, with the structure of insomnia."[1]

Her many books of poetry include *Metamorphopsia* (1988), *My Bird Book* (1991), *Moira* (1995), *Contrafact* (1996), *MARS* (1997), *Spinoza in Her Youth* (2002), *Do the Monkey* (2006), *Natural Light* (2008), *Where Shadows Will: Selected Poems 1988–2008* (2009), and *Win These Posters and Other Unrelated Prizes Inside* (2012). Her prose work, *To Be at Music: Essays and Talks*, was published in 2010.

1. Jacket comment, *Where Shadows Will: Selected Poems 1988–2008*, San Francisco, 2009.

At the Port

The subject requires what fuels it, a change outside the scope of law repeated in the position of the sleeper. The shadow of the driven one falls upon the other, dated entropically. The consequence of seasons signs disorder.

"Or like her" exhaling crocuses. It takes the speed of speech and logic, a story every day or more than one. Laziest are the gods of the Greeks, refusing to write; and in the dark weather, always carry a stone to drop, to discover whether you are over land or water; and we still do not know how they looked in their Parthian scent of spikenard, cinnamon, crocus, cardamom, thyme, marjoram, wine, balm, honey, saffron, rosewood, lotus and gum of the styrax; and the fate or heart shaped leaf fills the alphabet; and you may not eat the fish that may have eaten of the phallus of the god. To say the name here is a choice.

One note per clear night, quoted as Selene's theme. There is a city and then a new city. There is no lack of construction. Down by the port, everything will be just as it is now, only a little more fictional.

1995

In Memory of My Future

Statement is already exaggeration, migration, inclusion, the film itself become the fuse. Confusion is general or at least mutual, no longer or not yet.

The thought of dust tightens the cords. A task is perceived
as a symbol of inevitability, caesura seeing it through for
what it is.

It doesn't lend itself to explanation, sealed in the world, letter become life at the limit of memory.

1996

Remaining in Light

for John Taggart

So quiet, the second theme appears first
called recapitulation

no reaction shot, its application
to all such sites of intention

Rembrandt, and your not losing your place
in the book, the light's violence

and your scrutiny, autopsy's relevance
a morning syntax "imagined" who reads intention

but if you had been reading Sappho
as you identify him with light

coming to the end of this something
as you come to identify him with light

they were trying to recall
we didn't expect to see alders here

after the red berries in clusters, edible, etc.
they could break this fall as long as the rope held

leather straps on his thighs resembled garters
bright violence says you are hardly this or that

the cold is bright, the woman
might be cold, she may relax

and speak in the dark
imperceptible finitude

experienced as endlessness
its property its illusion

1996

The Laws

of noise and time, laws of instead of. Whose traffic jam is whose? If you open
that window an alarm goes off. A minimum of energy is required to maintain
the folded state. You agree for once, the three-dimensional folded pattern
is not conclusion-driven. Your reaction to this redness is not indecent. What
we're all trying to do is clear a space or feel that idea. From the social angle,
the air is full of red-hot life-vests. The origins of the doctrine, it seems, are
very ancient. First moment I taste you it's the groping seeking agreement.

How's this, the illustrated version: the plane was going down into gray chop,
its belly about to scrape along the shoal of black lava rock, where it would

finally stop, teetering precariously, half in the water, your hands half around my waist? The smallest possible energy to dislodge your concern was the leak in the manifold. That you could live with an increase of temperature, in another time, full of salt, crossed with the other's formula.

The other music was enormous rotating blades. Cultural bodies piled on the back of straight-backed chairs began to melt or move. For example, the red jacket or redingote sporting flashy buttons. Auditions for the echo were taking place on the charred upper floor of the library. In both cases, the random coil of memory, the heat, the scent of ripe peaches on trees growing in a ditch that had been a moat protecting the fortress protecting the island.

In the window, a pile of boulders, mountains blocking the view of what? In any case, the haunting takes place in a forest, memory occurs in the present. Ideally, their bodies, the ocean, flat, white and full of facts.

2002

The Stationmaster

Pluto stands in the dark and
thinks

between the sky overhead directly
and dead anger

all bedrock, brutal and
puritanical

dance to the fire station of
faith

create deafness, come
taste

2009

Bernadette Mayer
b. 1945

Bernadette Mayer was born in Brooklyn and received her B.A. from The New School for Social Research. Her books of poetry include *Moving* (1964), *Memory* (1975), *Studying Hunger* (1975), *Midwinter Day* (1982), *Utopia* (1983), *Sonnets* (1989), *The Formal Field of Kissing* (1990), *A Bernadette Mayer Reader* (1992), *Two Haloed Mourners: Poems* (1998), *Scarlet Tanager* (2005), and *Poetry State Forest* (2008). She has also been editor of the magazines *0 to 9* (with Vito Acconci), *Unnatural Acts* (with Ed Friedman), and *United Artists* (with Lewis Warsh).

Mayer is associated with the New York School in her use of daily occasions and her attraction to traditional form, especially the sonnet. However, poems like "Gay full Story" ("Gay full story is authentic verve fabulous jay gull stork") suggest the work of Gertrude Stein and the language poets. In the essay "The Obfuscated Poem," Mayer writes, "The best obfuscation bewilders old meanings while reflecting or imitating or creating a structure of a beauty that we know."[1]

Mayer tends to organize her books around a concept, sometimes interdisciplinary in nature. By her own description, "*Memory* is a journal of the month of July 1971 based on notes and writings, and a series of 1,116 slides (36 pictures shot every day)."[2] Her prose poem "The Desires of Mothers to Please Others in Letters" is a "series of letters never sent, written to unidentified friends, acquaintances, political figures, and poets over a nine-month period and ending with the birth of a baby."[3]

Her poem "Midwinter Day" (119 pages in length when published) was written in a single day, December 22, 1978, at 100 Main Street, Lenox, Massachusetts. This extraordinary production gave a new meaning to the New York School concept of "dailiness." In "Bernadette Mayer's List of Journal Ideas," a document widely distributed by samizdat in the 1980s, she shared strategies for writing that included "Write a soothing novel in twelve short paragraphs" and "Write on a piece of paper where something is already written."

Mayer lived for many years on the Lower East Side and conducted workshops at The New School for Social Research and the Poetry Project at St. Mark's Church. She currently resides in East Nassau, New York.

1. In *Code of Signals*, ed. Michael Palmer, Berkeley, 1983, p. 166.   2. A *Bernadette Mayer Reader*, New York, 1992, p. vi.   3. The same, p. viii.

FROM *Midwinter Day*

Stately you came to town in my opening dream
Lately you've been showing up a lot

                                                         I saw clearly

You were staying in the mirror with me
You walk in, the hills are green, I keep you warm
Placed in this cold country in a town of mountains
Replaced from that balmier city of yours near the sea
Now it's your turn to fall down from the love of my look
You stayed in the hotel called your daughter's arms
No wonder the mother's so forbidding, so hard to embrace
I only wait in the lobby, in the bar

                                 I write

People say, "What is it?"
I ask if I must tell all the rest
For never, since I was born
And for no man or woman I've ever met,
I'll swear to that,
Have there been such dreams as I had today,
The 22nd day of December,
Which, as I can now remember,
I'll tell you all about, if I can

                              Can I say what I saw

In sleep in dreams
And what dreams were before your returning arms
Took me like a memory to the room I always return to
When thought turns to memory's best love, I learn to
Deny desire from an acquired habit of vigilant fear
Till again to my nursed pleasure you and this love reappear
Like a story
Let me tell you what I saw, listen to me
You must be, you are the beginning of the day
When we are both asleep you waken me
I'm made of you, you must hear what I must say

                              First I thought I saw

People all around me
Wondering what it is I write, I saw up close
The faces of animals, I slid down a long grassy hill
Past everyone doing everything, I was going faster
There were no streets to cross, no dignity lost,
A long story without pausing

I was racing, no one approved of what I was learning,
I saw a woman's daughter, we met on the stairs
I saw everything that was ever hidden or happening
I saw that my daughters were older than me
But I wanted to see further

                                Nobody including you
Of all the people doing things, was approving
Of my sliding like this down the long tilting hill
Past the place to play and all the past

                                I saw the moon's
Last quarter in the southern sky at dawn

                                Then I saw
The shawls of the dream as if they were the sky
And the dream's dark vests and the dream's collar and cuffs
Of black leather on the dream's black leather jackets
I was alone in the dream's dressing room trying on
Different styles of tough gang-wear or raingear
In the dream my daughters Sophia and Marie
Are always with me

                         Then we climb
A mountain to the Metcalf's house, Nancy's fixing us
The eighteen intricate courses of a Japanese dinner
We sit at a counter curving around the kitchen
Like what they call a kidney-shaped pool
Eating hearts of heads of wet red and green lettuce
In the most high and palmy state of friendly love
Then Paul takes us all on a trip

                           A while ago
The Japanese lady who lives next door smiled
When Marie smelled the fragrance of her cultivated rose
Sometimes dream is so rampant, so wild
As to seem more luxuriant than day's repose
So without riot spreading everywhere
How can I be both here and there?

                            Then I found
A message in an over-sized book
On the way to Allen Ginsberg's nursery school
Where Ken Kesey was conducting a big picnic

                             Then I saw
All the buildings of New York drawn to look
Like the illustrations in a children's book

                               I dreamed

The road was so slippery from a truck's oil spill
We had to stop at a truckstop
Though our friends who were ahead of us might lose us
All the food in this place is served in a big dollhouse
And the salad's in a hatbox, they're catering to us
It's hilarious, suddenly we all crack up
        We say
You don't just eat from the desire to see a vine
Which today is called a chicken sandwich
You do seem to eat because you wear a hat and so
The hat's box is empty and must be filled with food
Do you see what I mean, it was a special restaurant
I was with Grace Murphy
      Then I dreamed
I was ordering pompoms
Not those ornamental tufts on hats and not chrysanthemums
But a kind of rapid-firing machine gun
Really I can't figure out what's good and what's bad
I know I want to awaken feeling
Some remembered perfection
For which I crave a homeopathic dose of evil
Like the hair of the dog in the proverb
To offset the unsteady state of memory
        What man or woman
Could this be involving, so fleet it is indulging
In not quite flying but dreaming, flaunting
The short-lived continuity of a sound like hummingbirds
What is a story
    Can I say that here
Or should I wait till later wherever the question
Of life's chronology of satisfying the favored senses
Might better gratify the falling course of the grave day
As I must come closer to inevitably waking up
Like a dying man is dying spoiling the favor
You might grant me to extend this liberal time
And remit my punishment due though I've confessed already
And been forgiven
Are you going to convince me
There's nothing more to dream up
Like sins not committed but related anyway
To cover innocence
Always listening to everything you see,
Watching the sounds of the day

Wouldn't it be possible

To eat everything
All the collected foods even you
And one's self like the dinosaurs just dying out
In some unaccountable hungry fall, cunningly saintlike

The night cometh

When no man can work
And David saw that Saul was come out to seek his work

I dream

I vault the fence, there's a cheerleader
Who needs to be kissed and caressed, it's like a blizzard,
Like my father I lost my color wheel when I died
I go vaulting over the consequent fence and with my ambition
I meet Gregory Peck

I always do

He looks like you

We go to the movies again, we go to two, we always do
And all the children are put,
Thrust, driven, goaded, impelled and flung,
Urged and pushed into bed

Then I can dream

We move again to the house where I was born
I'm wandering and forgetting, we are arranging
What rooms each of the children will finally sleep in

"Can Marie sleep in the hall bedroom
or is Andrew still alive?"

Andrew, who's like Bill
Or Bill's like him,

this state of things in dreams
could kill friendship if I told all
even to Uncle Andrew
who's also alot like Clark

Anyway I know we must share this copied house
With my grandfather, another Andrew, who is a little mean
Now everybody's here in this room and we are a party to death
I look at the old uncle who is still young Andrew or Bill
I am trying to remember where in time I am
I study his face but all I see is plain expression
Not the look of a man who's dead and knows it
Like something or someone nobody absolutely needs to know
I decide not to say anything about it
Already I've looked closer without moving to him,
A man without responses but that's beyond all this,

I say to myself in dream it's all the same
All the people in this room will surely die some time
Who cares which ones are already dead, I'm just here now
In my dream like I always am among the charms
Of sweet Andrew, charming Bill, I can't go on
                                          Is there an end

To such love and the duty of dreaming,
Things seen eyes closed not seeming to be dreams
Like the blackest edges once I saw outlining
Each leaf in spring one year or the jewels I saw
With Grace lying together before a thunderstorm
I could suggest to her then and she to me
What kind of thing would appear to us next
In the train of the vision moving from right to left
Under love's closed eyes
                          I hope you can see as much
When I try to suggest among lines of the evaporating word
What idea I've seen, what image each dream heard
There's no end to a narration of forms
From all the ways of looking eyes closed
                                    Now I see

What's ordinary like a sky
Or weather I can hear without ever looking
As blind people suddenly given sight
Sometimes will abhor it and shut their eyes again
To be more conversant with the actual view

                                                    1982

On Sleep

I have a book full of beds but I'm not scared
Now I wont write the poem about sleeplessness since
I cant sleep again even with Dash who sleeps so well
& I wont about dreaming that sleep is 1/3rd Egg St.
Or about dreaming I finally got some sleep, I wont write:
Sleep, I cant come tonight
Or, I cant get to first base with sleep, oh restlessness
Or, Oh elusive sleep where art thou gone thou fuck
Sleep is you oh hops tea youngly and safely hopping about
    so healthily
Sleep is an illusion in the beginning of sleep

Why do I want you to be a certain way, sleep
& why am I so afraid you'll never come back
Especially since this weekend was so fucking hot
Too hot to make love to sleep, too hot to feel air in lungs
You could only feel the air like cold's envelope
    surrounding the body like sleep
Sleep is the lion in the bed who scares me by coming close
But I know how to act, I never get killed
Sleep is the stealing of beds inside and outside
And the simple finding of them
Sleep is my favorite thing to do, Sophia said. what was yours?
Sleep is the train my father saw in the sea during the tornado
We're in the last car, it's a spacious sleeping & dining car
Sleep is alot like the $21.50 taxi ride I took to my dentist
    in my dreams
I steal the beds inside of sleep again & see the buildings
    & jewels that sometimes begin sleep
I cant sleep, I cant sleep with you
I do not know how to write commercially though some commercial writers
    who are quite successful also cannot sleep I'll bet sleep means something,
    look it up in Skeats Etymological Dictionary. Let me tell you what
    I'm worried about, my unbent block of wood under rails, my slipping
    sinking gliding dormant soul of myself, I am worried about these things
    (and then I will get back to the subject of rigid sleep with unbent pots
    of teas, potent mixtures that make you sleep perhaps if you are lucky):
    I am worried that the New College of California will never pay me
    the thousand dollars they owe me for my Walt Whitman lectures, that
    therefore I wont be able to go back to the dentist (or that they will pay me
    and I will be able to go to the dentist), that I wont have enough money
    to get through the summer, that I wont be able to proofread two books
    and edit two books by a week from Monday, that in order to do that I'll
    have to deny myself sleep or even the attempt to sleep, that Dash wont
    love me because it's hot in New York and my front tooth is crooked, that
    I might die even sooner than my parents did cause I spent most of my
    life troubling my heart about them, not to even speak of inheriting their
    physical falsities, that I am a complete idiot, that I am lacking in courage,
    that my fears and hatreds of dentists and school principals and doctors
    will ultimately do in, that I will become a bitter person that I am so
    unrealistic as to be surprised about what happens in nuclear power plants
    and NYC public schools, plus something I cant say here about love.
I dream I am in a museum with Dash. He leads me through a small space to
    an ice cave. At first I'm scared & have to listen to the voice of god saying,

"Lead with your backpack." Then the space opens up. We go to see the
paintings of somebody named Johnson through fancy panelled halls &
stairs.

Another thing I worry about is all my writing that is unfinished and how
there is so little time for it and how there might never be & how who
cares? like, what's so special about that?

I dream there is a broken plant in my bed. A (named with names I cant say
here) character is sitting at the foot of the bed laughing at me because
I cannot move properly and I have broken the plant myself. Then a lion
hand-puppet comes floating unattached through the room and I notice
it's pouring out.

I know how to attend to the moment of the text and all this writing about
oneself, this is not to the point. I worry about that. Maybe if you went to
Harvard it's o.k. Besides not going to Harvard I worry about the other
mistakes I've made in my life, I wont trouble you with a list.

It was easy enough for Gertrude Stein, she had some cash. I guess we have
to think of ourselves as being like Catulluses these days. We might live
longer than he did but we wont write much more cause we have to spend
so much time earning a living. & then we cant really expect to have our
works like his lost for a thousand years & then found again because there
might not be any more world by then, at least not here

I worry about why the masses sort of love disasters

I worry that my own heart and the hearts of others beat too fast all the time
these days, though sometimes on the street or in the subways you see
somebody skipping about lithely and you know then you are replaceable

I thought of a new capitalist method of falling asleep: you say to yourself: I
have the ownership of sleep, sleep is mine. This is called the proprietary
or entrepreneurial or landlord method. The first time I tried this I fell
asleep right away, almost magically, and woke again soon with a start, my
heart pounding, having dreamt that my blankets were made of darts

You can also think of sleep as being "with" the moon, that sometimes works.
Or you can try the 20th century t.v.-ish marriage method and say to
sleep: "Sleep, compromise." Or, a variation on that, cross-cultural:
"Sleep, my comrade, compromise."

Another method of falling asleep is the negative or Aristotelian mode. You
say to yourself: though the water in my apartment is always rusty and
roily, nevertheless I am still entitled as a human being to sleep. You dont
even need an apartment to sleep, much less one on the Lower East Side
of NYC where sleeping conditions are so bad

After all if they want us all to move to the suburbs or to the country where
it's much quieter and cooler, there's plenty of other nuclear power plants
there we could live near so we could still worry homeopathically, which

concept in medicine is based on the notion of the hair of the dog that bit you, as you know

When you wake up in the middle of the night and that or the number of warheads on each missile worries you, always write down your thoughts about sleep. In the morning you might find that they are dreamlike enough to reassure you that you got more sleep than you thought

This is a work in progress. I invite you to contribute to it. A railroad tie is called a sleeper, that's why we sometimes sleep like logs

A word of warning: vodka is not a cure for radiation or sleep-lessness. As far as I can tell it only wakes you up and its glow is not conducive to the most artless lambency necessary for a really famous night's sleep in a world where the reclining reviewing of the day's and night's positions is perhaps more welcomed. But this is a question of good luck too, and now good evening

2004

Alice Notley

b. 1945

Born in Bisbee, Arizona, Alice Notley grew up in Needles, California, in the Mojave Desert. She received her undergraduate degree from Barnard College in 1967 and her MFA in poetry and fiction from The Writer's Workshop at the University of Iowa in 1969. It was at Iowa that she met the poet Ted Berrigan, whom she married in 1972 and with whom she had two sons, Anselm and Edmund. After Berrigan died in 1983, she raised her children in New York's East Village by herself. In 1992, she moved to Paris with her second husband, poet Douglas Oliver (1937–2000) and has remained there ever since, "practicing no profession except for the writing, publication, and performing of her work and teaching an occasional workshop." She has published over thirty books of poetry, as well as the essay collection, *Coming After* (2005).

In her early career, Notley's work was reminiscent of Marianne Moore and William Carlos Williams in its precise but unexpected word choices and use of local detail. Its orchestral fullness set her apart from the ironic minimalism of some New York School poets. At one point, her sudden turns and verbal brightness seemed to be verging on a language poetry aesthetic; the style and emphasis of her work changed, however, following Berrigan's death. Thereafter, the darker concerns of her work seemed to border on the mystical. Peter Leary perceives a powerful Gnostic theme in her epic poem "The Descent of Alette," which is influenced by an ancient Sumerian myth of the descent of the goddess Inanna into the Underworld.[1]

Notley has been a finalist for the Pulitzer Prize and winner of the Los Angeles Times Book Prize for *Mysteries of Small Houses* (1998). She has also won the Shelley Memorial Award of the Poetry Society of America. Her book *Grave of Light: New and Selected Poems 1970–2005* (2008) won the Lenore Marshall Poetry Prize.

Notley has spoken of the necessity for the artist to be in a state of "disobedience." In a review of her poetry book *In the Pines* (2007), Joel Brouwer wrote: "In her new book's long title sequence, Notley finds that space of perpetual defiance and christens it 'the pines.' There, she imagines all conventions of causality and rationality have fallen away, creating an opening for the purely accidental quality of each lived instant, a quality the poet identifies as 'love.'

> I am losing my because. In the pines.
> In chance, in fortune, in luck, there is no because.
> Once I had, and now I don't.
> In love there is no because."[2]

Referring to the Australian aborigines in Bruce Chatwin's *The Songlines*, Notley writes, "One purpose of language is probably to sing where you go, to name the landscape so you can make it exist & thus get from place to place (to create it). Everything you see is a song or a story—you barely notice it if it isn't."[3] She insists that "poetry is not about words, or how one thinks, or making things. It is about essence—the secret inside the material."[4]

1. "American Poetry & Gnosticism," in *The World in Time and Space: Towards a History of Innovative American Poetry in Our Time,* Talisman 23–26, 2002, p. 440.   2. "A State of Disobedience," *The New York Times Book Review,* October 14, 2007.   3. "Notes on the Poetry of Everyday Life," in *From a Work in Progress,* New York, 1988.   4. Notley's introduction to *The Scarlet Cabinet: A Compendium of Books* by Alice Notley and Douglas Oliver (New York, 1992).

Poem

You hear that heroic big land music?
Land a one could call one.
He starred, had lives, looks down:
windmill still now they buy only
snow cows. Part of a dream, she
had a long waist he once but yet
never encircled, and now I'm
in charge of this, this donkey with
a charmed voice. Elly, I'm
being sad thinking of Daddy.
He marshalled his private lady,
did she wear a hat or the
other side? Get off my own land? We
were all born on it to die on
with no writin' on it. But who are
you to look back, well he's
humming "From this valley," who's gone.
Support and preserve me, father. Oh
Daddy, who can stand it?

1981

Jack Would Speak through the Imperfect Medium of Alice

So I'm an alcoholic Catholic mother-lover
yet there is no sweetish nectar no fuzzed-peach
thing no song sing but in the word
to which I'm starlessly unreachably faithful

you, pendant & you, politically righteous & you, alive
you think you can peel my sober word apart from my drunken word
my Buddhist word apart from my white sugar Thérèse word my
word to comrade from my word to my mother
but all my words are one word my lives one
my last to first wound round in finally fiberless crystalline skein

I began as a drunkard & ended as a child
I began as an ordinary cruel lover & ended as a boy who
read radiant newsprint
I began physically embarrassing—"bloated"—&
ended as a perfect black-haired lady
I began unnaturally subservient to my mother &
ended in the crib of her goldenness
I began in a fatal hemorrhage & ended in a
tiny love's body perfect smallest one

But I began in a word & I ended in a word &
I know that word better
Than any knows me or knows that word,
probably, but I only asked to know it—
That word is the word when I say me bloated
& when I say me manly it's
The word that word I write perfectly lovingly
one & one after the other one

But you—you can only take it when it's that one & not
some other one
Or you say "he lost it" as if I (I so nothinged) could ever
lose the word
But when there's only one word—when
you know them; the words—
The words are all only one word the perfect
word—
My body my alcohol my pain my death are only
the perfect word as I
Tell it to you, poor sweet categorizers
Listen
Every me I was & wrote
were only & all (gently)
That one perfect word

1981

A California Girlhood

The Brothers Grimm grew weaker and flickered, blue light
      in the well. Hans Christian Anderson
and his tiny gossamer bride went to bed beneath a walnut shell
      encrusted with every star, Copenhagen's
Sky, dreamed Louisa May Alcott, but when we awaken
      in New England my head will rest on
my cousin's shoulder, beneath *my* tree.
Anna Sewell, that the shining aren't suffered to continue to
      shine! though, old, he finds
his way home, Carolyn Keene's blue roadster
      cannot replace the young horse. There's nothing
left of her, Michael Shayne, but lipstick and
      fingerprints on a cognac bottle; Erle Stanley Gardner
knows the Chief will never pass cross-examination
      and on to ripeness, the breasts!
Where is orphan Canada, Anne of Green Gables?
      the smell of a white dress it rained on because
it was graduation. Frank G. Slaughter
      has given him hands that heal her after
she sleeps through rape by a snob. Frank Yerby
      pierces right through the membrane she cries
out triumphantly, one of the others, skim
      bunches of adjectives.
Margaret Mitchell moved to the eye which
      watered 3 times: that bright moon moves on. But
you can't strain hydrogen and oxygen out of tears
      or Raphael Sabatini out of life, Captain
Blood, the sword is worn
      against my tattered petticoat.
Charlotte Brontë is tense and comely as a first child.
Emily Brontë walks out to copulate with a
      storm. Indigo to emerald to
indigo, the Mississippi "beter den rum darlin'"; then
      Mark Twain gets hit on the hammer
and glowers a whole other lifetime. Anya
Seton sighed. "If only angels be angels and witchery
      the fine art it is
                    I still have to
bother about something besides décolletage."
Gwen Bristow pulled the arrow out of her arm

and thrust it into the Indian's chest.
When a guy goes molten John Dickson Carr
        orders the witch is non-existent, yawn
Sigrid Undset loses her life and yet loses nothing
        as a river in her bed flows beneath
the stained-glass leaves, thy breath is sustenance.
She wouldn't rollerskate through the Swedish palace,
        Annamarie Selinko. Lawrence Schoonover
respects the first man to use a fork in Spain,
        a Jew of Inquisition times,
she dances in little but castanets, Kathleen
        Windsor, it's a scheming pussy wind
that ripples and funs with the bleak sea. Knowledge
        of evil an inadequate knowledge, as
Herman Melville would say, read National
        Geographic, for your first glimpse of nipples,
free maps, Arctic, Hibiscus. Jane Austen
        sneaks a suspicion. You look like the
flash with the cash.
        John Steinbeck. My name
                        is Rose o'Sharon
the gorgeous coarse prayer, as the sentimental horrors
encroach and recede, repeatedly. Edgar Allan Poe
is on purple alert. Alexander Dumas, fils, announces
My favorite song is Rainy Night in Georgia.
Daphne DuMaurier wept tiny drops of Dom Perignon. Did
        Lady Brett Ashley copulate? did
Herman Wouk read between the lines?
T. H. White allowed one her manhood; Guinivere is
        Jenny, but I know I carry a lance.
William Faulkner incomprehensible, an
        obsidian cliff, does the ballerina wear cleats?
She puts her ear to the delicate shell of Ernest
        Hemingway; hears
Willa Cather orchestrate her death. Victoria Holt
        is still, chastely, darkly in love.

                                        1981

FROM *Beginning with a Stain*

Beginning with a stain, as the Universe did perhaps
I need to tell you about for myself this stain
A stain of old blood on a bedspread (white)
—how can I set a pace?—I'm
afraid to speak, not of being indiscreet, but of
touching myself too near, too near to
my heart bed—the bedspread
was white & thin
I slept on her bed with my lover
and thus was never
sure whose stain hers or mine? And when I washed it, or
rather, he did, it remained. And then

And then she died unexpectedly, as they say
became away forever
except in the air, and somewhere near
my heart bed—But
the bedspread
became of her ashes a mingled part.
The stain, my stain, or hers, but mine
My love stain is part of her ashes, & I rejoice in that, whether
she & her lover, or I & my lover
were the ones who originally lay there, staining the bed
Our stain has gone with her, you see,
This is the stain that

invents the world, holds it together in color of
color of, color. Color of love.

This is the love they spend in order to be.
And she was quite young & I am much older (her step-mother)
But our stain was the same one
There is no double. And she is endlessly
clear; & good. Surround my heart bed
with my others at night
speak with me of the stain, that is our love, that
invents the world, that is
our purest one. Help me to stain, I say, my words with all us

(I love you I know you are there)

the song of one breath.
Outside where cars & cycles
I'm not afraid to begin again, with & from you.

1992

April Not an Inventory but a Blizzard

I met Ted at two parties at the same house
at the first he insulted me because, he said later,
he was mad at girls that night; at the second we danced
an elaborate fox-trot with dipping—he had once taken one lesson
at an Arthur Murray's. First I went into an empty
room and waited for him to follow me. I liked the way
his poems looked on the page open but delicately arranged.

I like him because he's funny he talks more like
me than like books or words: he likes my knowledge and
accepts its sources. I know that there are Channel swimmers
and that they keep warm with grease because of
an Esther Williams movie. We differ as to what kind
of grease it is I suggest bacon he says it's bear
really in the movie it was dark brown like grease from a car
Who's ever greased a car? Not him I find he prefers to white out
all the speech balloons in a Tarzan comic
and print in new words for the characters. Do you want
to do some? he says—No—We go to a movie where Raquel Welch
and Jim Brown are Mexican revolutionaries I make him
laugh he says something about a turning point in the plot
Do you mean, I say, when she said We shood have keeled him long ago?
Finally a man knows that I'm being funny

He's eleven years older than me and takes pills
I take some a few months later and write
I think it's eighty-three poems I forget about Plath and James Wright
he warns me about pills in a slantwise way See this
nose? he says, It's the ruins of civilization
I notice some broken capillaries who cares

I wonder who I am now myself though I haven't
anticipated me entirely I have such an appetite

to write not to live I'm certainly living quite fully
We're good together he says because we can be like
little boy and little girl I give him much later a
girl's cheap Dutch brooch Delft blue and white
a girl and a boy holding hands and windmills
But now it's summer in Iowa City he leaves for
Europe gives me the key to his library stored
in a room at The Writers Workshop
I write mildly yet oh there's a phrase "the Gilbert curve"
how a street turns that sensation to make it permanent
a daily transition as the curve opens and is walked on
of the kinds of experience still in between the ones
talked about in literature and even in Ted's library
which finally makes poetry possible for me but I've
not read a voice like my own like my own voice will be

1998

I Must Have Called and So He Comes

"You're accusing me of something in these poems."
"No Ted, I'm not accusing you—can't catch your voice though."
"Through dead curtains," he says. Gives me the disgusted
Berrigan moue, casts match aside lighting cigarette
"So what are you doing?" he says. I say, "As the giant lasagne
on Star Trek—remember, Spock mindmelds with her
and screams, Pain." "So this is pain?" he says.
"I suppose it is. Was. But not from you," I say.
"We don't say pain we say fucked-up," he says, "Or
Kill the motherraper. Inside yourself . . ." (he fades)
"I can't catch your voice . . ." (I say)
". . . there's a place inside you," he says, "a poetry self, made by
         pain but not
violated—oh I don't say violated,
you're not getting my dialogue right, you can't remember
         my style."
"Would you say touched, instead?" I say.
"There's this place in us," he says, "the so-called pain can't
         get to
like a shelter behind those spices—coffee and sugar, spices,
matches, cockroach doodoo on the kitchen shelf.
But I was exhausted from being good without pills—

went off them on Diversey you'll remember—and you were
wearing me out. Well just a little. I took pills to
keep from thinking, myself. Do something else don't think
you're a poet write a poem for chrissakes, you're not
      your thoughts;
but I was afraid . . . you were mad at me deep down then."
"I don't think so," I say . . . "Men were a problem—I
      see that better
in the future, but you, sometimes you were 'men'
usually not." "Then were men men?" he says, "I mean—"
"No, I'll interrupt," I say, "Someone was being those times
why else was I unhappy." "Do you want to know," he says,
"if I loved you in 1970?" "No," I say, "I don't."
"Anything later than Chicago? But I've just got
a minute," he says. "No that's either your business
or something I already know," I say, "I really enjoyed the late 70's
      in New York, you know."
"You haven't wanted to talk to me since I died," he says.
"That's true," I say, "Too dangerous. But I want to say there's no
      blame here. I see your
goodness, plainly. I want to be
clear; I'm a detachment"—"As I am obviously," he says,
his voice getting fainter.

                                                    1998

Anne Waldman
b. 1945

Raised in Greenwich Village, Anne Waldman was first attracted to poetry at Friends Seminary High School in New York City. She later graduated from Bennington College, where she submitted a creative thesis and study on the work of Theodore Roethke. However, it was the 1965 Berkeley Poetry Conference, where she attended readings by Charles Olson, Robert Duncan, and Allen Ginsberg, that determined her direction as a poet. Associated with the bohemian poetics of the Lower East Side, she cofounded the literary magazine *Angel Hair* and became the director of the St. Mark's Poetry Project, a position she held from 1968 to 1978.

Following Allen Ginsberg's urging that she write long poems, Waldman produced *Fast Speaking Woman* (1975/1978), a book-length list poem with chantlike repetition. The poem's shamanistic qualities were borrowed from Maria Sabina, a Mazatec poet-priestess whose chanting was intended to heal the physical and spiritual woes of supplicants. The success of *Fast Speaking Woman* with audiences made Waldman a leading advocate of oral poetics and performance-related poetry.

"Makeup on Empty Space," which is also chantlike and psalmic, "takes off from the idea in Buddhist psychology that the feminine energy tends to manifest in the world, adorning empty space. What we see in the world, the phenomena, is created by feminine energy."[1]

Waldman is cofounder, with Allen Ginsberg, of the Jack Kerouac School of Disembodied Poetics at the Naropa Institute in Boulder, Colorado. Editor of *The World* magazine in the late sixties and early seventies, she has also edited a number of anthologies, including *Out of This World: An Anthology of the St. Mark's Poetry Project 1966–1991* (1991) and *Nice to See You: Homage to Ted Berrigan* (1991). Her many books include *Cabin (1981/1984), Makeup on Empty Space* (1984), *Skin, Meat, Bones* (1985), *Helping the Dreamer: New & Selected Poems 1966–1988* (1989), *Vow to Poetry* (2001), *In the Room of Never Grieve: New and Selected Poems 1985–2003* (2008), *Outrider: Essays, Poems, Interviews* (2006), and *The Iovis Trilogy: Colors in the Mechanism of Concealment* (2011). Waldman is often identified with Beat poetics, especially the writings of Allen Ginsberg and Diane di Prima. Yet, as witnessed by the pantoums and rondeaux in *First Baby Poems* (1983), she is also drawn to the more formal procedures of the New York School.

Waldman resides in Boulder, Colorado.

1. Lee Bartlett, Anne Waldman interview in *Talking Poetry: Conversations in the Workshop with Contemporary Poets,* Albuquerque, 1987, p. 272.

Makeup on Empty Space

I am putting makeup on empty space
all patinas convening on empty space
rouge blushing on empty space
I am putting makeup on empty space
pasting eyelashes on empty space
painting the eyebrows of empty space
piling creams on empty space
painting the phenomenal world
I am hanging ornaments on empty space
gold clips, lacquer combs, plastic hairpins on empty space
I am sticking wire pins into empty space
I pour words over empty space, enthrall the empty space
packing, stuffing, jamming empty space
spinning necklaces around empty space
Fancy this, imagine this: painting the phenomenal world
bangles on wrists
pendants hung on empty space
I am putting my memory into empty space
undressing you
hanging the wrinkled clothes on a nail
hanging the green coat on a nail
dancing in the evening it ended with dancing in the evening
I am still thinking about putting makeup on empty space
I want to scare you: the hanging night, the drifting night,
the moaning night, daughter of troubled sleep I want to scare you
I bind as far as cold day goes
I bind the power of 20 husky men
I bind the seductive colorful women, all of them
I bind the massive rock
I bind the hanging night, the drifting night, the
moaning night, daughter of troubled sleep
I am binding my debts, I magnetize the phone bill
bind the root of my sharp pointed tongue
I cup my hands in water, splash water on empty space
water drunk by empty space
Look what thoughts will do   Look what words will do
from nothing to the face
from nothing to the root of the tongue
from nothing to speaking of empty space

I bind the ash tree
I bind the yew
I bind the willow
I bind uranium
I bind the uneconomical unrenewable energy of uranium
dash uranium to empty space
I bind the color red I seduce the color red to empty space
I put the sunset in empty space
I take the blue of his eyes and make an offering to empty space
renewable blue
I take the green of everything coming to life, it grows &
climbs into empty space
I put the white of the snow at the foot of empty space
I clasp the yellow of the cat's eyes sitting in the
black space I clasp them to my heart, empty space
I want the brown of this floor to rise up into empty space
Take the floor apart to find the brown,
bind it up again under spell of empty space
I want to take this old wall apart I am rich in my mind thinking
of this, I am thinking of putting makeup on empty space
Everything crumbles around empty space
the thin dry weed crumbles, the milkweed is blown into empty space
I bind the stars reflected in your eye
from nothing to these typing fingers
from nothing to the legs of the elk
from nothing to the neck of the deer
from nothing to porcelain teeth
from nothing to the fine stand of pine in the forest
I kept it going when I put the water on
when I let the water run
sweeping together in empty space
There is a better way to say empty space
Turn yourself inside out and you might disappear
you have a new definition in empty space
What I like about impermanence is the clash
of my big body with empty space
I am putting the floor back together again
I am rebuilding the wall
I am slapping mortar on bricks
I am fastening the machine together with delicate wire
There is no eternal thread, maybe there is thread of pure gold

I am starting to sing inside about the empty space
there is some new detail every time
I am taping the picture I love so well on the wall:
moonless black night beyond country plaid curtains
everything illuminated out of empty space
I hang the black linen dress on my body
the hanging night, the drifting night, the moaning night
daughter of troubled sleep
This occurs to me
I hang up a mirror to catch stars, everything occurs to me out in the
night in my skull of empty space
I go outside in starry ice
I build up the house again in memory of empty space
This occurs to me about empty space
that it is nevered to be mentioned again
Fancy this
imagine this
painting the phenomenal world
there's talk of dressing the body with strange adornments
to remind you of a vow to empty space
there's talk of the discourse in your mind like a silkworm
I wish to venture into a not chiseled place
I pour sand on the ground
Objects and vehicles emerge from the fog
the canyon is dangerous tonight
suddenly there are warning lights
The patrol is helpful in the manner of guiding
there is talk of slowing down
there is talk of a feminine deity
I bind her with a briar
I bind with the tooth of a tiger
I bind with my quartz crystal
I magnetize the worlds
I cover myself with jewels
I drink amrita
there is some new detail
there is a spangle on her shoe
there is a stud on her boot
the tires are studded for the difficult climb
I put my hands to my face
I am putting makeup on empty space
I wanted to scare you with the night that scared me

the drifting night, the moaning night
Someone was always intruding to make you forget empty space
you put it all on
you paint your nails
you put on scarves
all the time adorning empty space
Whatever-your-name-is I tell you "empty space"
with your fictions with dancing come around to it
with your funny way of singing come around to it
with your smiling come to it
with your enormous retinue & accumulation come around to it
with your extras come round to it
with your good fortune, with your lazy fortune come round to it
when you look most like a bird, that is the time to come round to it
when you are cheating, come to it
when you are in your anguished head
when you are not sensible
when you are insisting on the
praise from many tongues
It begins with the root of the tongue
it begins with the root of the heart
there is a spinal cord of wind
singing & moaning in empty space

1984

FROM *The Asian Notebook*

Admonitions of the Boudoir

—after Meng Chiao (751–814 B.C.E.)

keep away from sharp words
don't go near a beautiful woman
barbed semantics such as "missile" "debt" "ownership"
"depression" "cleansed" "torrential flood"
    wound your *logopoeia*

woman's beauty up close—gold tooth
    wrinkled brow

quixotic smile
a wit to vie with?
upsets desire

cancel assignations of a perigee moon!

dangers of the highway are not about distance either
or speed limits whatever vehicle you drive

danger of passion is not in loving too often
one hour with you, scarred for life

———

In the Room of Never Grieve

register
& escape
the traps

a last judgment

cheetah under her skin

one window on the sunny side

still life with stylus
w/rancor
still life w/daggers
size of a postcard

no harm will come to the dolls
of which I am the queen

ghosts gather—
scald
seethe

———

One Inch of Love Is an Inch of Ashes
Allen Ginsberg came to me in a dream:

> *it's goofy here,*
> *all the conversations are in my head*
> *the gods & goddesses get busy*
> > *(commune) with the world, day in day out*
> *they're distracted*
> *I have no body! No notebooks*
> *I'm scribing my good looks & dangerous poetry*
> > *on heaven*
> *Heaven's so BIG too, & there're lots of rogues*
> > *around*
> *I'm just a Nobody*

> *You know what the Chinese poet said, Anne,*
> *"one inch of love is an inch of ashes."*

2003

Wanda Coleman

b. 1946

Born and raised in the Watts district of Los Angeles, Wanda Coleman is the author of *Mad Dog Black Lady* (1979), *Imagoes* (1983), *Heavy Daughter Blues* (1987), *African Sleeping Sickness: Stories and Poems* (1990), *Hand Dance* (1993), *Bathwater Wine* (1998), *Mercurochrome* (2001), a National Book Award finalist in 2001, and *Ostinato Vamps* (2003). She is known for her dramatic performances of her poetry, recordings of which include *Twin Sisters* (with Excene Cervenka, 1985), *Black Angeles* (with Michelle Clinton, 1988), and the solo releases *High Priestess of Word* (1990), *Black & Blue News* (1991), and *Berserk on Hollywood Blvd.* (1991). Coleman has also published several works of fiction, including *A War of Eyes and Other Stories* (1988) and *Jazz and Twelve O'Clock Tales* (2008), and the works of prose nonfiction *Native in a Strange Land* (1996) and *The Riot inside Me* (2005). Coleman is also an Emmy-winning former scriptwriter for the daytime television drama *Days of Our Lives.*

She credits her development as a poet to attending Charles Bukowski's poetry readings at The Bridge, a Hollywood counterculture gathering spot, in the late sixties. Because she couldn't afford to buy Bukowski's books, she would read them standing up in bookstores. In time, Bukowski's publisher, John Martin of Black Sparrow Press, would publish her first book, *Art in the Court of the Blue Fag* (1977), and serve as a literary guide.

Like Bukowski and Amiri Baraka, Coleman deals directly and often profanely with the burdens of poverty and race. In poems like "the ISM" and "Essay on Language," she offers a potent critique of social class, color, and sex, while spoofing the currently fashionable academic jargon. In a statement of poetics, Coleman writes, "Being from the southwest, Los Angeles, in particular, I am a minority within a minority—racially, sexually, regionally. Once being Black ceases to be the major limitation, being West Coast comes into play. My poetic image has been one which reflects the bleakness of the mad terrain in which I survive—the dog, the warrior, the warrior queen."[1]

1. "On the Poetics of Wanda Coleman," *Catalyst* magazine, Summer 1990, p. 37.

the ISM

tired i count the ways in which it determines my life
permeates everything. it's in the air
lives next door to me in stares of neighbors

meets me each day in the office. its music comes out the radio
drives beside me in my car. strolls along with me
down supermarket aisles
it's on television
and in the streets even when my walk is casual/undefined
it's overhead flashing lights
i find it in my mouth
when i would speak of other things

1983

Brute Strength

last night blonde spitfire Angie Dickinson beat steel-eyed
Lee Marvin's impervious chest until she dropped to gangland's
floor exhausted *point blank*

aunt ora used to threaten us kids with whippings
if half bad, she used her hand
if real bad, we got the hard wood paddle
if monstrous, there was the horsewhip that hung above the door
in the den. one day my brother and i were half bad
she gave me the glad hand and i cried
she laid it to him and he laughed. so she got the paddle
and he laughed even harder
in consternation she abandoned his punishment
he was more daring after that

and then there was my geechie lover
i once went at him with a 2 × 4 as hard as i could
i clubbed his chest. he smiled at me
i dropped the 2 × 4 and ran

my first husband wasn't much. i could take
his best punch

1987

Essay on Language

who stole the cookie from the
cookie jar?

this began somewhere

     suggest middle passage. consider the dutch ship
     consider adam and eve and pinchmenot

blacks think in circles she said. no they don't
i said it too readily, too much on the defense. of course
blacks think in circles. i think in circles
why did i feel it necessary to jump on the defensive.
     defensiveness
is sure sign of being gored by unpleasant truth

equation: black skin + new money = counterfeit

i keep going back over the same thoughts all the time (the
     maze
     poverty poverty poverty
syndrome oft times accompanies social stigmata)
     sex sex sex
desperately seeking absolute understanding (the way out)—
     black black black
the impossible (my love relationship wears me thin) i know

number one stole the cookie

but knowing doesn't
stop me from thinking about it—trying to be the
best i can spurred by blackness but they keep telling me the
best fashion in which to escape linguistic ghettoization
is to
ignore the actuality of blackness blah blah blah and it will
cease to
have factual power over my life. which doesn't
make sense to me—especially when the nature of mirrors
is to reflect

when a mirror does not reflect what it is? not necessarily a
     window,
merely glass? can it be something other than a glass? and once
it becomes glass can it ever be a mirror again?

          violent animal can't take it no more can't
          take it anymore from anyone tired of being
          one in a world of everybodies and someones
          violent animal you throw chalk against the
          blackboard rocks at reluctant lovers assault
          money-grubbing landladies with cold dishwater
          they're all against you in that paranoiac $$$
          prism keep trying to see yourself/reflection
          oooh black as swamp bottom mired in muck you
          violent animal struggle struggle struggle to
          get to solid ground get free get solidified/

          grounded

substitute writer for mirror, visionary for window, hack for
     glass

                       who me? couldn't be

(smashing is addictive and leads to greater acts of violence/
throwing things, i.e. the first sign of danger)

equation: colorlessness + glibness = success

i am occasionally capable of linear thought, stream of
     consciousness
and hallucinate after a three day fast (have eyes will see)

i'm much too much into my head. stressed. i can't feel
anything
below the neck

                 number two stole the cookie

he says he hates me
and i'm wondering what in

hell on earth did i do except
be who he says he loves to hate

equation: circle + spear = spiral

going down and in at the same time going outward and up

absolutely

this ends and begins here

1987

Ron Silliman

b. 1946

Ron Silliman is a prolific poet and critic, and a founding member of the San Francisco contingent of language poets. His long poem consisting of several previously published volumes, *The Alphabet,* was published in its entirety in 2008; each volume, such as *ABC* (1978), *Paradise* (1985), *Demo to Ink* (1992), *Toner* (1992), and *Xing* (2004) represents one or more of the letters of the alphabet. This abecedarian strategy may have been suggested by the long poem "A," of the Objectivist poet Louis Zukofsky. Yet this is only part of Silliman's production, which numbered eight volumes before 1983.

Silliman has a preference for eccentric forms of his own invention. The book-length prose poem *Tjanting* (1981), for example, is written according to the Fibonacci number sequence, with the result that the number of sentences in each paragraph equals the number of sentences in the previous two paragraphs.[1] Described by the critics Anne Mack and J. J. Rome, Silliman's book *Paradise* (1985) "is a sequence of paragraphs each of which was written in one sitting, with these paragraphs arranged in 'monthly' groupings, and with the whole comprising 'a year's diary.,'"[2] Similarly, Silliman's poem "The Chinese Notebook" takes as its model Wittgenstein's *Philosophical Investigations.* Its numbered sequence, extending to 223 items, includes:

5. Language is, first of all, a political question.

In writing what he calls the "new sentence," Silliman frustrates the convention of the poetic line, as well as its political implication of closure. The "new sentence," primarily seen in prose poems, does not narrate like most prose fiction, but rather accumulates a collection of comparatively distinct units which, taken as a whole, produce a disjunctive mosaic. According to Silliman, "Sentence length is the unit of measure" in such poems.[3] Critic George Hartley asserts that Gertrude Stein's *Tender Buttons* (1914) provides Silliman's model for the form.[4]

Silliman has commented, "I have, from the beginning, taken poetry to be the most intense relation possible between self and language (hence meaning-mind-world), but, coming from a basically traditional background, it has taken years to drop the pretenses of prevailing modes and admit it: form is passion, passion form. Given forms (whether the sonnet or the Pound-derived Projectivist mode) disinterest me since they are usually ways of shoving the language in a work aside."

Born in Pasco, Washington, and raised in Albany, California, Silliman attended San Francisco State University and the University of California at Berkeley. Editor of the anthology *In the American Tree* (1986) and author of an important book of criticism, *The New Sentence* (1987), he has received the Levinson Prize from the Poetry Foundation, two fellowships from the National Endowment for the Arts, and the Pew Fellowship in the Arts. His blog, which offers poetry news, links to reviews and events, and Silliman's own essays, has received over three million hits. Resident of Berkeley, California, for many years, he now lives in Chester County, Pennsylvania.

1. Ron Silliman: The Poetry Foundation, http://www.poetryfoundation.org/bio/ron-silliman, p. 3.　　2. *"The Alphabet,* Spelt from Silliman's Leaves (A Conversation on the 'American Long-poem')," *South Atlantic Quarterly,* Fall 1990, p. 775.　　3. "The New Sentence," in *The New Sentence,* New York, 1987, p. 91.　　4. "Sentences in Space," review of *The New Sentence, Temblor,* No. 7, 1988, p. 89.

FROM *The Chinese Notebook*

1.　Wayward, we weigh words. Nouns reward objects for meaning. The chair in the air is covered with hair. No part is in touch with the planet.

2.　Each time I pass the garage of a certain yellow house, I am greeted with barking. The first time this occurred, an instinctive fear seemed to run through me. I have never been attacked. Yet I firmly believe that if I opened the door to the garage I should confront a dog.

3.　Chesterfield, sofa, divan, couch—might these items refer to the same object? If so, are they separate conditions of a single word?

4.　My mother as a child would call a pot holder a "boppo," the term becoming appropriated by the whole family, handed down now by my cousins to their own children. Is it a word? If it extends, eventually, into general usage, at what moment will it become one?

5.　Language is, first of all, a political question.

6.　I wrote this sentence with a ballpoint pen. If I had used another, would it have been a different sentence?

7.　This is not philosophy, it's poetry. And if I say so, then it becomes painting, music or sculpture, judged as such. If there are variables to consider, they are at least partly economic—the question of distribution, etc. Also differing critical traditions. Could this be good poetry, yet bad music? But yet I do not believe I would, except in jest, posit this as dance or urban planning.

8. This is not speech. I wrote it.

9. Another story, similar to 2: until well into my twenties the smell of cigars repelled me. The strong scent inevitably brought to mind the image of warm, wet shit. That is not, in retrospect, an association I can rationally explain. Then I worked as a legislative advocate in the state capitol and was around cigar smoke constantly. Eventually the odor seemed to dissolve. I no longer noticed it. Then I began to notice it again, only now it was an odor I associated with suede or leather. This was how I came to smoke cigars.

10. What of a poetry that lacks surprise? That lacks form, theme, development? Whose language rejects interest? That examines itself without curiosity? Will it survive?

11. Rose and maroon we might call red.

12. Legalistic definitions. For example, in some jurisdictions a conviction is not present, in spite of a finding of guilt, without imposition of sentence. A suspension of sentence, with probation, would not therefore be a conviction. This has substantial impact on teachers' credentials, or the right to practice medicine or law.

13. That this form has a tradition other than the one I propose, Wittgenstein, etc., I choose not to dispute. But what is its impact on the tradition proposed?

14. Is Wittgenstein's contribution strictly formal?

15. Possibility of a poetry analogous to the paintings of Rosenquist—specific representational detail combined in non-objective, formalist systems.

16. If this were theory, not practice, would I know it?

17. Everything here tends away from an aesthetic decision, which, in itself, is one.

18. I chose a Chinese notebook, its thin pages not to be cut, its six red-line columns which I turned 90°, the way they are closed by curves at both top and bottom, to see how it would alter the writing. Is it flatter, more airy? The words, as I write them, are larger, cover more surface on this

two-dimensional picture plane. Shall I, therefore, tend toward shorter terms—impact of page on vocabulary?

19. Because I print this, I go slower. Imagine layers of air over the planet. One closer to the center of gravity moves faster, while the one above it tends to drag. The lower one is thought, the planet itself the object of the thought. But from space what is seen is what filters through the slower outer air of representation.

20. Perhaps poetry is an activity and not a form at all. Would this definition satisfy Duncan?

21. Poem in a notebook, manuscript, magazine, book, reprinted in an anthology. Scripts and contexts differ. How could it be the same poem?

22. The page intended to score speech. What an elaborate fiction that seems!

23. As a boy, riding with my grandparents about Oakland or in the country, I would recite such signs as we passed, directions, names of towns or diners, billboards. This seems to me now a basic form of verbal activity.

24. If the pen won't work, the words won't form. The meanings are not manifested.

25. How can I show that the intentions of this work and poetry are identical?

1975–1976   1986

FROM *Tjanting*

Not this.
What then?
I started over & over. Not this.
Last week I wrote "the muscles in my palm so sore from halving the rump roast I cld barely grip the pen." What then? This morning my lip is blisterd.
Of about to within which. Again & again I began. The gray light of day fills the yellow room in a way wch is somber. Not this. Hot grease had spilld on the stove top.
Nor that either. Last week I wrote "the muscle at thumb's root so taut from carving that beef I thought it wld cramp." Not so. What then? Wld I begin? This morning my lip is tender, disfigurd. I sat in an old chair out behind the anise. I cld have gone about this some other way.

Wld it be different with a different pen? Of about to within which what. Poppies grew out of the pile of old broken-up cement. I began again & again. These clouds are not apt to burn off. The yellow room has a sober hue. Each sentence accounts for its place. Not this. Old chairs in the back yard rotting from winter. Grease on the stove top sizzled & spat. It's the same, only different. Ammonia's odor hangs in the air. Not not this.

Analogies to quicksand. Nor that either. Burglar's book. Last week I wrote "I can barely grip this pen." White butterfly atop the gray concrete. Not so. Exactly. What then? What it means to "fiddle with" a guitar. I found I'd begun. One orange, one white, two gray. This morning my lip is swollen, in pain. Nothing's discrete. I straddled an old chair out behind the anise. A bit a part a like. I cld have done it some other way. Pilots & meteorologists disagree about the sky. The figure five figures in. The way new shoots stretch out. Each finger has a separate function. Like choosing the form of one's execution.

Forcing oneself to it. It wld've been new with a blue pen. Giving oneself to it. Of about to within which what without. Hands writing. Out of the rockpile grew poppies. Sip mineral water, smoke cigar. Again I began. One sees seams. These clouds breaking up in late afternoon, blue patches. I began again but it was not beginning. Somber hue of a gray day sky filld the yellow room. Ridges & bridges. Each sentence accounts for all the rest. I was I discovered on the road. Not this. Counting my fingers to get different answers. Four wooden chairs in the yard, rain-warpd, wind-blown. Cat on the bear rug naps. Grease sizzles & spits on the stove top. In paradise plane wrecks are distributed evenly throughout the desert. All the same, no difference, no blame. Moon's rise at noon. In the air hung odor of ammonia. I felt a disease. Not not not-this. Reddest red contains trace of blue. That to the this then. What words tear out. All elements fit into nine crystal structures. Waiting for the cheese to go blue. Thirty-two. Measure meters pause. Applause.

A plausibility. Analogy to "quick" sand. Mute pleonasm. Nor that either. Planarians, trematodes. Bookd burglar. What water was, wld be. Last week I cld barely write "I grip this pen." The names of dust. Blue butterfly atop the green concrete. Categories of silence. Not so. Articles pervert. Exactly. Ploughs the page, plunders. What then? Panda bear sits up. Fiddle with a guitar & mean it. Goin' to a dojo. Found start here. Metal urges war. One white, two gray, one orange, two longhair, two not. Mole's way. This morning the swelling's gone down. Paddle. No thingdis crete. Politry. Out behind the anise I straddled an old chair. O'Hare airport. About a bit in part a like. Three friends with stiff necks. I did it different. Call this long hand. Weathermen & pilots compete for the sky. Four got. Five figures figure five. Make it naked. The way new stretches shoot out. Shadow is light's writing. Each finger functions. The fine hairs of a nostril. Executing one's choice. What then? Forms crab forth. Pen's tip snaps. Beetles about the bush. Wood bee. Braille is the world in six dots. A man, his wife, their daughter, her sons. Times of the sign. The very idea. This cancels this. Wreak havoc, write home. We were well within. As is.

Wait, watchers. Forcing to it one self. Read in. It wld be blue with a new pen. Than what? Giving to one itself. The roads around the town we found. Of about under to within which what without. Elbows' flesh tells age. Hands writing. Blender on the end-table next to the fridge. Out of rock piled groupies. Hyphenate. Smoke cigar, sip water. Mineral. This was again beginning. Begging questions. Seams one sees. Monopoly, polopony. Blue patches breaking clouds up in the late afternoon. Non senses. It was not beginning I began again. In Spain the rain falls mainly on the brain. The gray sky came into the yellow room. Detestimony. Bridges affix ridges. On the road I discovered I was. I always wake. Not this. The bear's trappings. Counting my fingers between nine & eleven. Factory filld at sunrise. Three rain-warpd wood chairs in the back yard. Minds in the mines look out. Cat naps on the bear rug. Bathetic. On the stove top grease sizzles & spits. Lunch pales. In paradise plain rocks are distributed evenly throughout the desert. Electricity mediates the voice. All difference, no same, all blame. Lampshade throws the light. Noon's moonrise. Burn sienna. Feel the disease. Denotes detonation. Not not not-not-this. The sun began to set in the north. Reddest trace contains red blue. Metazoans, unite. Of that to the this of then. Break or lure. Out what words tear. One ginger oyster between chopsticks rose to the lips. All elemental crystal structures are nine. Helicopters hover down into the dust. The blue cheese waits. No one agrees to the days of the week. Thirty-two times two. We left the forest with many regrets. Meters pace measure. New moons began to rise. Applause drops the curtain. The elf in lederhosen returns to the stomach of the clock. Chiropractice. Furnace fumes. Crayola sticks. Each word invents words. One door demands another. Bowels lower onto bowls. Come hug. Sunset strip. Holograms have yet to resolve the problem of color. Thermal. This is where lines cross. Hyperspace, so calld. Mastodons trip in the tar pits. These gestures generate letters. Industrial accident orphan. Driving is much like tennis. Orgasmic, like the slam dunk. We saw it in slomo. Cells in head flicker & go out. Zoo caw of the sky.

Sarcadia. A plausibility. Gum bichromate. Quick analogy to sand. Not this. Moot pleonasm. Cat sits with all legs tuckd under. Nor that either. Table lamp hangs from the ceiling, mock chandelier. Trematodes, planarians. Featherd troops. Books burgled. Blood lava. What wld be was water. Bone flute. I cld barely write "last week I grippd this pen." Allusions illude. Dust names. Not easy. Green butterfly atop the blue concrete. Pyrotechnics demand night. Kinds of silence. Each is a chargd radical. Not so. Photon. Pervert articles. Extend. Exactly. Descend. Plunders & ploughs the page. Read reed as red. What then? With in Panda bear claps. The far side of the green door is brown. Fiddle with a mean guitar. "I don't like all those penises staring at me." Go into a dojo. Mojo dobro. Here found start. Dime store sun visor. Metal urges worn. Only snuggle refines us. Two long-hairs, two gray, one white, one not, one orange. Spring forward, fall back. Mole's way in. Build an onion. This morning the blister gave way to pus & half-formd flesh. Hoarfrost. Paddleball. Tether: No thindgis creep. Tiny plastic dinosaur: Politry teaches just what each is. Cameroon tobacco wrapper. Out behind anise I stood on an old chair. Southpaw slant to the line. O'Hare airport bar: Sounds the house makes. About a bit in part of a like. Shutters rattle, stairs "groan." Three stiff friends with necks. Your own voice at a distance. Done differently. Monoclinic. This long hand call. "Her skirt rustled like cow thieves." Sky divides jets & weather. Far sigh wren: Got for. Bumble. Figure five figures five. Dear Bruce, dear Charles. Make naked it. Negative. Out the way new stretches shoot. A thin black strap to keep his glasses from falling. Light's writing is shadow. Rainbow in the lawn hose's shower. Each finger's function. Beneath the willow, ferns & nasturtiums. Nostril fine hairs. Stan writes from Kyoto of deep peace in the calligraphic: Executed one choice. Pall bearers will not glance into one another's eyes. What then? A storm on Mount Sutro. Forms crab forth from tide pool's edge. Refusal of personal death is not uncommon amid cannery workers. Snaps pen tip. An ant on the writing alters letters. About the bush beetles. This municipal bus lurches forward. Be wood. Several small storms cld be seen across the valley. The world in six braille dots. Gray blur of detail indicates rain. A woman, her husband, their daughter, her sons. A pile of old clothes discarded in the weeds of a vacant lot. Time of the signs. Some are storms. The idea very. Borate bombers swoopd low over the rooftops. This cancels not this. The doe stood still just beyond the rim of the clearing. Writing home wrought havoc. In each town there's a bar calld the It Club. We were within the well. Many several. Is as is. Affective effects. Humidity of the restroom. Half-heard humor. Old rusted hammer head sits in the dust. Clothespins at angles on a nylon line. Our generation had school desks which still had inkwells, but gone were the bottles of ink. Green glass broken in the grass. Every dog on the block began to bark. Hark. Words work as wedges or as hedges to a bet. Debt drives the nation. These houses shall not survive another quake. A wooden fence that leans in all directions. Each siren marks the tragic. Dandelions & ivy. A desert by the sea is a sight to see. A missile rose quickly from the ocean's surface. A parabola spelld his mind. He set down, he said, his Harley at sixty. It is not easy to be a narcissist. Afterwords weigh as an anchor. Cement booties. Not everyone can cause the sun to come up. On the telly, all heads are equal. In Mexico, the federales eat you up. The production of fresh needs is the strangest of all. I swim below the surface. Room lit by moonlight. Words at either edge of the page differ from those in between. An old gray church enclosed in bright green scaffolding. Left lane must turn left. A dog in his arms like an infant. Each sentence bends toward the sun. Years later, I recognized her walk a block away.

1981

FROM *Paradise*

A SENTENCE in the evening. Today the boxscores are green. Tonight the boxcars are groaning in the railyard. The indexical items are not coreferential. Hollywood caenfidential. You made Cheerios number one.

Mock snow: white petals from the plum tree swirl in the wind. I was working on a different poem. The dark patches to the clouds' glare are all we have of depth to this sky. The shudder of laundry down in the basement. A small table in one corner of the kitchen. White petals from the plum tree twirl in the wind. I slip in a pair of diskettes. Don't miss the opportunity to earn Pediatrics Review and Education Program (PREP) credits on an hour-for-hour basis at the plenary sessions as well as Category I credit toward the American Medical Association's Physician Recognition Award. The stapler sits on the table. When in reverse, that car emits an idiot tune. I own not one photograph of my father. The most beautiful of all the carpenter's tools is the level. Becoming identified with an inaccurate but provocative name enabled the Language Poets to rapidly deepen market penetration and increase market share. I turn the muffins over. Dot matrix. The rectangularity of windows is sometimes a shock. Verse is not in crisis, Isis, but only the capacity of academics to comprehend phenomena they cannot predict. Juju use of slide guitar. One less wine glass. Westinghouse is the largest investor in Toshiba. I'm just singing to the muse.

I was working in a different poem. Descriptions of daily life decay. The idea of long words. A glare in the cloud rose which we thought to be the sun, calling it day. Still the clear memory of my grandmother's icebox. Or that the washing machine with the ringer atop it would spot oil on the linoleum floor. So writing a poem *is* different from kissing a baby's tush. A complex series of perpendiculars leading to the second floor. Short fat bird in the plum tree whistles.

The poem is thinking (white cat chews grass). You only had a bowl of cereal one hour ago. The bruise I don't remember getting. The entropy of later life mocks symmetry. By leasing out the technology and buying back its products for assemblage into full computer systems, IBM avoids any investment in manufacturing plants whatsoever, and is thus free to move its capital as labor market conditions shift. Rhymes with theft. As for we who live to be astonied, basil makes the pesto. Yet as *USA Today* makes clear, condensare is not itself sufficient for dichtung. The shape of the alphabet is itself a system: poem composed in symmetrical letters. Glass in the drying rack turned upside down. Selfgentrification. Orthodox Marxology requires antacid. Adorno escapes Frankfort, locating in Manhattan, whereupon is declared the New York School. Two prostitutes on a day off visit the zoo. An old wicker hamper is repainted green. The female cop tucks her hair beneath her cap. In a crowded department store I get nauseous and disoriented, buying wildly. Peter's criticism gets around. My one goal is a clear mind—right now! Geographic isolation enables the Huichol to resist acculturation into the increasingly Europeanized daily life of modern Mexico. The baby sucks at the full breast. The March sun. The snail clings to the kale leaf. The neighbor's cat bounds from porch to porch like a rabbit. Mountains of clouds from over the sea. First the plum tree blossoms, then come the leaves. Subtlety is not instinctive. At the instant of orgasm you roll your eyes.

The difference between eggs and chairs, fat happy baby, is how the cat sleeps: light drizzle. I lean forward and then the words focus. Beneath the leaf the trunk of the plant stood in the moist earth gathered in a pot atop a saucer on the desk. The point at which you simply start piling books for want of room. Mom sends photos of my brother's new son. The oven is our only heat. A small child runs to the bus in the rain.

Sometimes I come home from work so tired that I don't know whether to cry or throw up or lie on the floor, shaking.

The slope is called the fall line and you proceed up hill with your skis perpendicular to it. In the cabin, the cubicles are like small jail cells composed of wood. The cross country instructor has decided which girl for the weekend. I don't mean woman. Snowblind.

Big slow jet, low over the horizon. Her eyes on me wide and brown. There is no pain equal to the memory of pain. I'm impatient that each word takes so long to write. As when, in the newspaper, an article on how to ride a camel brings tears. All cotton pleated chino twills. My life is not your symbol. Historians eke rhyme from fact. Aka will, verb transitive. Remember the days when Bob smoked dope *all* the time? Well, Masanori Murakami has been released. You're a commie, too.

1985

(G)hosts final passage

To confuse sleep with dream
(to fuse blue with a deep
yellow, yielding green) is to
complete the riddle with action

giving satisfaction to none
but who reach up or out
in our direction as tho
you and I form a we for any

but the most fleeting
transactions (eyes over ink
not even at the same moment
and these letters for me

shadowed by my own hand always,
tall shaft of the black pen
held straight over the lined green page
of this notebook) You

who "philosophize disgrace"
(the judgment of history)
aware now suddenly
that you too have a body

before which this open text
(my heart, my home) must soon
reach an end if not
conclusion the way shadows

fill a room (an old Sufi
from the Floating Lotus
Opera Company appears
one night at the Tredyffrin

Library), mockingbird
in perfect imitation
of electronic handshake
as if to remind

suburbs are as islands
volatile social ecology,
a typology for cul de sacs
hidden in the trees.

1985–1999   2008

Rae Armantrout

b. 1947

Rae Armantrout was born in Vallejo, California, raised in San Diego, and educated at the University of California, Berkeley, and San Francisco State University. Author of the poetry collections *Extremities* (1978), *The Invention of Hunger* (1979), *Precedence* (1985), *Necromance* (1991), *Made to Seem* (1995), *Veil: New and Selected Poems* (2001), *Up to Speed* (2004), *Next Life* (2007), *Versed* (2009), and *Money Shot* (2011), she has been associated with language poetry despite being suspicious of the term, which "seems to imply division between language and experience, thought and feeling, inner and outer."[1] *Versed* won the Pulitzer Prize for Poetry and the National Book Critics Circle Award for 2010. The previous year she was a finalist for the National Book Award.

In her essay "Poetic Silence," Armantrout reflects on her desire to use silence, which, due to the "media barrage," exists only as an ideal or aesthetic effect. "Words no longer come from silence, but from other words. . . . And there is the impulse to call a halt, the impulse to silence."[2] In her view, the nonnarrative, declarative sentences of many language-oriented prose poems leave little room for the experience of silence. Her approach to composition associates things more in clusters than in (narrative) lines. These associations are "neither transparent and direct nor arbitrary, but somewhere in between. . . . Doubt and choice can coexist in the reader's mind. For me this better corresponds to the character of experience."[3]

In "Cheshire Poetics," she writes, "When I was a teenager I was given an anthology, and the poets I most loved there were William Carlos Williams and Emily Dickinson. So I was drawn to poems that seemed as if they were either going to vanish or explode—to extremes, in other words, radical poetries. . . . I think my poetry involves an equal counterweight to assertion and doubt. It's a Cheshire poetics, one that points two ways then vanishes in the blur of what is seen and what is seeing, what can be known and what it is to know. That double-bind."[4] What at first appears to be opaque and discontinuous in her work often turns out to be a complexly figured wisdom: "Come close. // The crowd is made of / little gods // and there is still / no heaven."[5]

Recipient of a Guggenheim Fellowship for 2008, Armantrout teaches at the University of California, San Diego.

1. "Why Don't Women Do Language-Oriented Writing?" in *In the American Tree*, ed. Ron Silliman, Orono, 1986, p. 546.   2. *Writing/Talks*, ed. Bob Perelman, Carbondale, 1985, p. 31.   3. "Chains," *Poetics Journal* 5, May 1985, p. 94.   4. *Collected Prose*, San Diego, 2007, p. 55.   5. *Next Life*, Middletown, CT, 2007, p. 12.

Close

1

As if a single scream
gave birth

to whole families
of traits

such as "flavor," "color,"
"spin"

and this tendency to cling.

2

Dry, white frazzle
in a blue vase—

beautiful—

a frozen swarm
of incommensurate wishes.

3

Slow, blue, stiff
are forms

of crowd behavior,

mass hysteria.

Come close.

The crowd is made of
little gods

and there is still
no heaven

2007

Empty

The present
must be kept empty
so that anything
can happen:

> The Queen of England visits
> Amanda's hot tub

> as a prophylaxis?

a discrepancy
between one's view of things
and what comes to pass.

★

It's ironic when something
has a meaning to someone

> "Gotta go
> Gotta go
> Gotta go
> right now"

other than that
intended by the speaker.

> sings the bladder-control model
> from the fidgety TV
> above the dying woman's bed.

★

It's ironic when a set
contains no elements.

Of a person, frivolous.
Of a body, shrunken.

2007

Yonder

1

Anything cancels
everything out.

If each point
is a singularity,

thrusting all else
aside for good,

"good" takes the form
of a throng
of empty chairs.

Or it's ants
swarming a bone.

2

I'm afraid
I don't love
my mother
who's dead

though I once—
what does "once" mean?—
did love her.

So who'll meet me over yonder?
I don't recognize the place names.

Or I do, but they come
from televised wars.

2007

Later

1

To be beautiful
and powerful enough
for someone
to want to break me

up

into syndicated ripples.

Later I'll try
to rise from these dead.

2

How much would this body
have had to be otherwise in order
not to be mine,

for this world
not to exist?

When would that difference
have had to begin?

3

The old lady invited me to her soirée. Maybe I was even
older than she was. I was mysterious, at any rate, a rarity,
until the room filled up. Then not. When she handed
out chocolates, she forgot me. I gesticulated as if it were
funny and she gave me two pink creams. Me! As if I
would have ever wanted these!

4

They drive me
out to sea.

Secretly, I am still
_____, the mysterious.

I speak in splashes.

Later
I have the lonely dream

2009

Prayers

1

We pray
and the resurrection happens.

Here are the young
again,

sniping and giggling,

tingly
as ringing phones.

2

All we ask
is that our thinking

sustain momentum,
identify targets.

The pressure
in my lower back
rising to be recognized
as pain.

The blue triangles
on the rug
repeating.

Coming up,
a discussion
on the uses
of torture.

The fear
that all *this*
will end.

The fear
that it won't.

2011

Autobiography: Urn Burial

1

I could say
"authenticity"

will have been about trying
to overtake the past,

inhabit it
long enough to look around,

say "Oh,"

but the past is tricky,

holds off.

So are we really moving?

Or is this something
like the way

form appears
to chase function?

2

I might hazard that my life's course
has been somewhat unusual.
When I say that, I hear both
an eager claim
and a sentence that attempts to distance itself
by adopting the style
of a 19th-century English gentleman.
The failed authority
of such sentences is soothing,
like watching Masterpiece Theatre.
When I recount my experiences,
whatever they may have been,
I'm aware of piping tunes
I've heard before.
Or jumbled snatches of familiar tunes.
The fancy cannot cheat
for very long, can it?
In the moment of experience,
one may drown
while another looks on.

2011

Mei-mei Berssenbrugge
b. 1947

Born in Beijing of Chinese and Dutch parents Mei-mei Berssenbrugge was raised in Massachusetts and educated at Reed College and Columbia University.

Berssenbrugge's poetry is based on an epic scale of perception that equates the movement of a cloud or a chunk of Arctic ice with the human actions and actors in the poems. This lends a democracy of attention to her oblique and often multiple perspectives, which involve the mental states of her fictive characters (alternately "I," "you," and "she"), her own shifting focus as an author, and the points of view of her readers ("This is where they have concentrated you").

Describing Berssenbrugge's work as "fluid and filmic," the poet Kathleen Fraser writes that "Berssenbrugge wants the structure of experience to emerge precisely as the meandering / wandering intelligence delivers it; for her meaning arrives through sensation, the surprised juxtaposition of moment upon moment."[1] In Fraser's view, Berssenbrugge's voice "sees disembodiment, a withdrawal of self-consciousness, a merging of perception and the elemental."[2] Linda Voris writes: "With her expansive, metastatic line, Berssenbrugge has developed a method to strain the boundaries established by perceptual operations and repeated in lyrical conventions. . . . Proceeding by means of a 'sensitive empiricism,' Berssenbrugge continually disrupts narrative and rhetorical representations that simplify experience."[3]

Berssenbrugge's books include *Fish Souls* (1971), *Summits Move with the Tide* (1974), *Random Possession* (1979), *The Heat Bird* (1983), *Hiddenness* (with artist Richard Tuttle, 1987), *Empathy* (1989), *Sphericity* (also with Richard Tuttle, 1993), *Endocrinology* (1997), *Four Year Old Girl* (1998), *Nest* (2003), *Concordance* (with Kiki Smith, 2006), and *I Love Artists: New and Selected Poems* (2006).

Cofounder of the journal *Tyuonyi*, Berssenbrugge sits on the contributing editorial board of the literary magazine *Conjunctions*. She lives in rural New Mexico, where as a young woman she worked as an associate of Georgia O'Keefe.

1. "Overheard," *Poetics Journal* 4, May 1984, p. 101.   2. The same, p. 102.   3. "A Sensitive Empiricism: Berssenbrugge's Phenomenological Investigations," *American Women Poets in the 21st Century: Where Lyric Meets Language*, ed. Claudia Rankine and Juliana Spahr, Middletown, CT, 2002, pp. 68–69.

Alakanak Break-Up

1

To find out the temperature, she tosses a cup of water into the air
because it will evaporate before it hits the ground.
She goes outside and tosses a cup of alcohol into the air
and then she keeps looking into the air.

When her attention is discontinuous, this no longer means that she
is inattentive. In the same way, they can measure the plain, now,
although the plain and the temperature are vacuums her heat sweeps
across, even before she has turned.

When she turns, the ice she had been standing on is changing into
foam and is about to drift away. It rumbles as it is changing.
She watches it recede until it is a slit of light entering the brain,
because the brain is protecting itself against the light.

Here is the event horizon. You can focus on a cone-shaped rock
in the bay. You can make it larger and closer than the ice
surrounding it, because you have the power to coax the target.
This breaks up your settlement in a stretch of infinity.

Then you tie some string to a stick and toss it in front of you
as you are watching the rock. Then you keep drawing it back.
Sometimes the stick disappears in front of you, and you have to
draw it back. At these times, the rock becomes yourself

wearing soft bedclothes and with burned eyes.
You balance three horizons. In the same way you press down
on her shoulders and gently push the person into the ground,
which is constantly changing in the current and on the tide.

This is where they have concentrated you. All that time
you had been noting the direction of snowdrifts and stalks bent
in the south wind. Nevertheless, a storm can distract your attention.
Your attention becomes the rasping noise of a stick drawn across
the edge of a bowl at a party. It draws attention tenuously
from your fingers, the way your body starts to hurry in the wind.

This is where they have concentrated you, in order to be afraid
or in order to recreate the line between your mind and your mind

on the other side of a blue crack in the ice, so you can sit
facing each other, like ice floes folded up and cut up
and piled up against each other, and so you know enough to stop
as soon as you lose your direction.

Then, if you are on the ocean, with poor visibility, with no wind
and you cannot be seen, please go around the outside of an ice
floe, because the ocean has dust particles, which will sparkle
and indicate the direction of the sun, she says.

When you look up, you see a heavy frost has formed on the window,
which had been damp for a while each morning, and then would dry
up and begin to crackle. You pass the window. The ice begins
to melt and drops of water travel down the window diagonally,
because of your speed.

You take the window and place it in your mouth, and meanwhile
fishline attached to your red bandanna jiggles in the dark,
because you are losing consciousness. It swarms around the rag
when you look up at it against the sky.

The dashes you had applied so carefully, in order to record rotation
in the sky have been washed away, leaving milky traces of themselves
and of their trails, so your poor map is now a circuit of spirals you
can only decode into chrysanthemums, on a sleeve moving past cirrus clouds.

You are a blur of speed concentrating on heading in one direction.
It is the bank above you standing still, because you are being
held back. Sometimes in your path you see darkness that looks
like smoke. When you come to the edge of it, you realize you are
already veering away from it. You have to concentrate on the
dotted line of your lane, which is foretold in threes by the light
and ticks like a meter from your looking at them.

Sitting up, you think someone has been splashing water on your clothes.
Picking up a dash, which has become a warm I-beam in your hand,
you arrange them on a board, oblivious to the sky, because
you can conceive of yourself now, moving on the board or behind
the board. A square of the board lights up and becomes the single
headlight of a car, indicating another person.

If the gravity of this moment outweighs your knowledge of where
you are, that is pathetic. That is what makes the space above the

ocean so attractive, but you still know enough to travel in a
straight line through a patch of fog, and continue to walk when
you emerge, with some fog clinging to you, up to your waist.

Each time you forge an off-shoot of the river, you are hoping it
is the river. It is a little mild time. You see a row
of gulls lined up on the ice, their chests puffed toward the sun
which is the color of apricots on the snow.

You pass a man lying on the snow, moving his head up and down
and singing. At first the monotony of his movement makes it hard
to concentrate on what he is saying. The snow around him has
frozen into patterns of wavy lines, so there are luminous blue
shadows all around you. This is obviously an instrument for his
location which her voice is occupying. It is grating across the
pointed places in the form of vapor trails.

It is so mild, you are beginning to confuse your destination with
your location. Your location is all the planes of the animal
reconstituting itself in front of you.

2

Anyone who is all right would not be coming in covered with fog.

It is a pattern when it is moving. When it is moving collisions
of things that happen produce a wavering but recognizable image
that merges into the ground when it is still. It is a black diamond
that condenses you mentally as it collapses. It is a black diamond
on the ground, and the diamond is moving. Then it disappears
when you look at it, yourself having no coincidence.

The ground is covered with ice.

Many holes in the ice are glowing with light.
You could say one light is a slanting plank that interrupts the ice. It
could be a bridge, except where new ice is closing it off into a small
enclosure like a holding pen or a bed. The human shines through from behind
and below seams and holes in the ice. The human hovers like a mood.
On a molecular level, the human remains, as a delicate glittering accent
on the dateline, like a light flashing upriver, which can only be seen
by the first person who looks on it, because her looking is equivalent
to clocking its velocity in a chute or a tunnel to her.

She considers these the unconscious lessons of a dominant force
that is being born, and as it becomes, its being is received structure.
First ice crystals, then heavier glass obscures the light,
so she walks back and forth talking to herself in a white soundless
sphere past the trash of the village.

She crosses pressure ridges which form a fringe between old ice
and open water. And the ice responds to her haphazard movement.
The snow is moving about the ice, some of it settling, some of it blowing.
She notices certain portions are ice, while others are covered with snow
which is easy to make tracks on. And she is careful not to step on the snow.

Twenty miles of frozen ridges buckle under snow,
but when she travels under the ice, the ice would be like fog.
Inside the fog is a jail fire. Flames lure a quantity
of what is going to happen to her into equivocalness
by softening her body with heat, as if the house she is in
suddenly rises, because people still want her.

She prefers to lie down like a river, when it is frozen in the valley
and lie still, but bright lines go back and forth
from her mouth, as she vomits salt water.
This is the breakthrough in plane. The plane itself is silent.
Above and behind the plain lies the frozen delta. Above and in
front of her, fog sinks into the horizon, with silence as a material,
so she is walking among formations of rock. Once again, she can make
a rock in a distant wash move closer to her, where it splays out
like contents its occurrence there. Once again, her solitariness
can flow into the present moment, although she seems to know what
is going to happen.

This is an image represented by a line of ice slabs facing a line
of rocks. One rock seems a little heavier and darker than the others,
but for now, they are two lines of tinkling unaccompanied voices.

The rest can be correspondingly inferred, as a line of rocks
leading toward a distant mountain, as into a distorting mirror,
which once again grows darker and denser, crossing over into mass
for a while, before returning to the little saxophone repetition
with which it began, like rubble under her feet.

Still, anything can still happen. She is still unable to distinguish
one wave from another. This is her nervous system attempting

to maintain its sweep across the plain.
Everything is still moving, and everything is still one texture,
altered from sheer space to the texture of a wall.

The route-through tightens around the nervous system like a musculature.
It floats like a black mountain against the night sky, although she will remember
a mountain glimmering with ore. Then it darkens for her return.
The river branches, and the sea has become blank as mirrors each
branch of the river flows into.

3

Sometimes I think my spirit is resting in the darkness of my stomach.
The snow becomes light at the end of the winter. The summer
is an interruption of intervals that disappear, like his little dance
before the main dances, a veridical drug.

A wafer of space beneath the ice starts to descend, like
the edge of her sleeve across a camera lens. Pretty soon
the ice will be all broken up. There is no space left. You look
down on a break-up of little clouds over the plain, as if the house
you are in suddenly rises, to relieve the nervous pressure of light.

Twenty miles of frozen ridges become a lace of moss
and puddles too flat to see and which are breathing. Here is
a snowdrift that has begun to melt. Here is an old woman
talking about a young person who is androgynous, across a distortion
of radio waves, trying to locate you. She is only moving
from her knees down.

The snow becomes light at the end of winter. How ice changes
on either side of the boat is not a tactic. The drum is a boat.
The mail route is a line of controlled electric light.
They will scatter their clothes anywhere in this light. You leave
your shirt near the snow machine. It is the initial color on the tundra.

1989

Texas

I used the table as a reference and just did things from there
in register, to play a form of feeling out to the end, which is
an air of truth living objects and persons you use take on,
when you set them together in a certain order, conferring privilege
on the individual, who will tend to dissolve if his visual presence
is maintained, into a sensation of meaning, going off by itself.
First the table is the table. In blue light
or in electric light, it has no pathos. Then light separates
from the human content, a violet-colored net or immaterial haze, echoing
the violet iceplant on the windowsill, where he is the trace of a desire.

Such emotions are interruptions in landscape and in logic
brought on by a longing for direct experience, as if her memory of experience
were the trace of herself. Especially now, when things have been flying apart in all
    directions,
she will consider the hotel lobby the inert state of a form. It is the location
of her appointment. And gray enamel elevator doors are the relational state,
the place behind them being a ground of water or the figure of water. Now,
she turns her camera on them to change her thinking about them into a thought
in Mexico, as the horizon when you are moving can oppose the horizon inside
the elevator via a blue Cadillac into a long tracking shot. You linger
over your hand at the table. The light becomes a gold wing on the table. She sees
it opening, with an environment inside that is plastic and infinite,
but is a style that has got the future wrong.

                                            1989

Concordance

1

Writing encounters one who does not write and I don't try for him, but face-
to-face draw you onto a line or flight like a break that may be extended, the
way milkweed filling space above the field is "like" reading.

Then, it's possible to undo misunderstanding from inside by tracing the
flight or thread of empty space running through things, even a relation that's
concordant.

Seeds disperse in summer air.

Sunrays cease to represent parallel passages in a book, i.e., not coming from what I see and feel.

Relation is in the middle, relay, flower description *to* flower becoming of my eye between light and heart.

Now, information has released imaginative function from authors.

I send an interrupted line over the top of space, past the middle cinematically, when you can no longer stand what you put up with before.

At night, part of her numbed to pain and part woke to what occurred.

Working backward in sleep, the last thing you numbed to is what wakes you.

What if that image were Eros as words?

I write to you and you feel me.

What would it be like if you contemplated my words and I felt you?

Animals, an owl, frog, open their eyes, and a mirror forms on the ground.

When insight comes in a dream, and events the next day illuminate it, this begins your *streaming* consciousness, synchronicity, asymptotic lines of the flights of concordances.

An owl opens its eyes in deep woods.

For the first time, I write and you don't know me.

Milkweed I touch floats.

2

One can experience another's energy as stress.

At first, I felt attacked by this attribution of the symptoms of my illnesses.

I was frightened thoughts and feelings could be externalized.

Then, I saw sunrise frequencies emanate from your body, like music.

An excited person in light absorbs wavelengths she herself gives off, as if light were the nutrient for feeling.

Color is the mirror where we see ourselves with living things, scarlet neck feathers, infant asleep across your heart, like to like.

Attention gives light: shine on a baby's calf; as he hears what I say, I become that.

Look at my body as light reflecting the thought and feeling, it's not safe to be here.

Remove anxiousness over persons you yearn for, stepping back to observe, like an animal in the fourth dimension.

Since animals don't judge, their evolving cosmic skills are a source of richness for us.

A bird lands on the rim of your tub; a wolf licks your baby's head.

When she cries and the part of you who cries wakes, do you hold her to suppress feeling?

Yearning can't be split and the animal lost, ahead of time.

3

My words unroll a plane of consistence they do not pre-exist—particles, fluxes the colors of spring.

Desire individuates through affects and powers I place on a page or plane of light vibrations, like a flowering field.

His autonomic response is to constrict breath against the feminine, magnetism of gems, consciousness emanating from stars symbiotic with individuation.

When I hear ants are telepathic, I see tiny words trying to communicate.

Then, they file across my clock, it's time to go.

Life manifests everywhere in the cosmos, but as we eliminate species here, we lose access to other realms.

So, discovering a new species is a great event.

Numinousness in the psyche emerges as from morphic fields, our wish for the animal tuning to its light or waveform, like the light of sex.

When you doubt this, you place a piece of "someone" on a pedestal to examine, a gap.

Breathe the shard back into yourself.

In your memory, scarlet feathers of a beloved macaw begin a glow arising from the exact color of connection.

Warmth, which was parallel, moves across the shard, smoothes and makes it porous, matter breath, light materializing ants and words.

2006

Nathaniel Mackey
b. 1947

Nathaniel Mackey's poems often draw on African rituals and folk wisdom and the rhythms and repetitions of jazz. In his essay "Sound and Sentiment, Sound and Symbol," Mackey writes, "Poetic language is language owning up to being an orphan, to its tenuous relationship with the things it ostensibly refers to. This is why in Kaluli myth [of Papua New Guinea] the origin of music is also the origin of poetic language."[1]

Legba, the Haitian *loa,* or god, is Mackey's figure of the poet-priest: "Legba walks with a limp because his legs are of unequal lengths, one of them anchored in the world of humans and the other in that of the gods. . . . The master of polyrhymicity and heterogeneity, he suffers not from deformity but multiformity, a 'defective' capacity in a homogenous order given over to uniform rule."[2] In Mackey's view, Legba's limp is comparable to the "stutter" of jazz musicians Sonny Rollins, Thelonious Monk, and others.[3] In poetry, the "limp" of an experimental prosody suggests the song of the social outcast or orphan. The figure Ghede in Mackey's "Ghede Poem" is a Haitian voudoun god of mortality and sexuality who taunt's worshipper's pretensions with the traditional jibe: "You love, I love, he / love, she love. What does / all this loving make?"

Mackey was born in Miami, and attended Princeton and Stanford universities. Editor of the literary magazine *Hambone,* he has published the full-length poetry collections *Septet for the End of Time* (1983), *Eroding Witness* (1985), *Outlantish* (1992), and *School of Udhra* (1993), *Song of the Andoumboulou: 18–20* (1994), *Whatsaid Serif* (1998), and *Splay Anthem* (2006), which was awarded the National Book Award. He has also published two works of criticism, *Discrepant Engagement: Dissonance, Cross-Culturality, and Experimental Writing* (1993) and *Paracritical Hinge: Essays, Talks, Notes, Interviews* (2004), and four volumes of an ongoing novel entitled *From a Broken Bottle Traces of Perfume Still Emanate: Bedouin Hornbook* (1986), *Djbot Baghostus's Run* (1993), *Atet, A.D.* (2001), and *Bass Cathedral* (2008). He is coeditor of the anthology *Moment's Notice: Jazz in Poetry and Prose* (1992).

Mackey taught at the University of California Santa Cruz for over thirty years, and currently serves as the Reynolds Price Professor of Creative Writing at Duke University.

1. *The Politics of Poetic Form,* ed. Charles Bernstein, New York, 1990, p. 90.   2. The same, p. 100.   3. The same, p. 109.

Andoumboulouous Brush

—"mu" fifteenth part—

He turned his head,
spoke to my clavicle,
  whispered more than
spoke. Sprung bone
              the
    obtuse flute he'd
  long wanted, blew
    across the end of it
                  sticking
up … Blew across its
  opening. Blew as if
cooling soup . . . Someone
behind him blowing
              bigger
    than him giggled,
  muse whose jutting
    lips he kissed as he
could . . . "Mouth that
    moved my mouth,"
                  he
  soughed, hummed it,
    made it buzz . . . Hummed,
  hoped glass would break,
walls fall. Sang thru
              the
    cracks a croaking
                  song
  to end all song,

  tongue's tip seeking
    the gap between her
teeth, mouth whose
  toothy pout made
                  "mu"
  tear
loose

              •

World release come
down to his and
her fracture, no bat-wing
bones in her nose
                    but
him aroused all the
same, walls of an
extinct retreat no
more than ember,
                    his
own flared, filling with
                    snow . . .
His hand on her waist,
her hand on his, all
in either's head,
whichever, fetterless
touch whose roots,
                    they'd
heard, lay elsewhere,
world they'd have been
on their way into, taken
                    so,
exhaust-colored snow
along the street outside
their window, room
                    they
lay remembering
                    in

                •

Clavicle spill spoke
volumes, book after
book after book.
Spoke with a
muzzle on its
                    mouth,
called it music,
partings more than
words could number,
made myth,

"mu's"
equivalent, lisp . . .
Imminent departure
made more poignant.
Possessed, said all
they could, stuck
pins
in their tongues,
not that they awoke
but that they were
awake . . .

Anxious aubade. Abject
sun . . . Awkward beauty
had it been theirs to
assess, attend to in
words, bled among
the
sunlit, leaving, blurred
sight,
stabbed eyes made it
more than they could
see . . . Awoke to a dream,
dreamt return, dead kin . . .
Anyone's guess whose
world
it was, anyone's but
his. Thought of his
grandmother, mother,
uncle, brother, aunt,
anyone's guess but
his
what world it was,
"Drifter's
Blues" on the box again,
them running in place,
rotting plums glued
their feet to the floor . . .
Bigger
than grandmother, mother,
uncle, brother, aunt,

dreamt andoumboulouous
advent, at whose
                        advance
his collarbone spoke . . .
Clavicle spill strewn in
all directions . . . No
more than a croon
                        for
condolence, no con-
dolence . . . *We lay on*
                        our
backs whispered itself
it seemed as he lay
without sleep, adrift
off Cantaloupe Island's
                        lotus
coast

                ●

Hardly begun, began
would-be waking, not
to be taken in by
dreams, left off
dreaming, better
                        to be
numb they thought.
As if it were comfort
called it all in their
        minds, all meaning
only. So quick
                bidding
farewell it seemed
they sought
inoculation, never
done saying goodbye
once begun, reach
                        though
they would notwith-
standing, finality's
hand an abstraction,

answerless, aloof,
hoarse-
ness the note they were
after, audible witness
all but out of ear's
reach . . .

After the end. Before
the beginning . . .
All at once they
both wondered
which . . . Talked
with
their teeth clenched,
hard
to say who said
less, ansonance
an uncut grit they
ingested, jawsplint
walling
their way. What had
been won some
crude inducement,
to
have been otherwise
available, remote . . .
Stripped indolence
a
dream he dreamt
he dreamt he woke
from reeling, head
a rotating hindrance,
hit,
slapped hand pulled
away pulled up
in-
to it

2006

Spectral Escort

—"mu" seventeenth part—

Not exactly a boat or
　　not only a boat . . .
Weathervane, boat,
　　flag rolled into
one, furled spur
　　　　　　　　it
　　fell to us to
unravel . . . What
　　we'd risen above
　　tiptoed up in
back of us. Lipped
　　hollow, big
　　　　　　　　blow-thru
gust we roughed
　　　　　　　　our
heads with, we
of the andoumboulouous
　　brush . . . Bank of
　　　　　　　　shade,
　　mouth of shadow,
fraught mouth. Deep
　　song's bucketmouth,
　　Rubichi's caught mouth
　　　　　　　　moaned,
dreaming's *ever after*
　　intransigent, ultimacy's
ruse made more obdurate,
　　　　　　　　"mu" . . .

　　Chewed charcoal, spat
out pictures . . . Black
　　lips, black teeth,
　　black tongue . . .
　　　　　　　　Music's
tease held at arm's
　　length, hardly had
　　any arm left. Better
　　we took rocks for bread

than be led to
believe we'd be so
       embraced . . .
As if such a place as
Lipped Hollow existed,
  what had been wind
  a way of knowing's
        blown
   imprint supporting
 us, music's at, else-
  where, reached. What
had blown suddenly under
             us,
 walked on, better *as if*
         not
had been heard
from, hushed

      •

Crawled out of thicket
we wrongly called
 andoumboulouous ambush . . .
A cooling breeze cut
 the tips of our
      tongues
off. Something hit our
 heads and our hit
 heads hummed, curlicue
  winds caressing the
       backs
of our necks . . .
     As if
  as if had nothing to
  do with it, depth and
deferred ipseity arrived at,
        buffed
  heads bothered by drum
 thumps, metal plates put
 where we'd been hit.
      Caught
 light lit our heads with

shimmer, rubbed rabab
strings. Headshine,
synaesthetized light . . .
Each of us an O, each
made of
welded chrome. Lipped
Hollow a place abstruse
flutes

took us back to. Undersea
bubble it seemed albeit
inland, miragelike,
buoyed,

burst

•

Wind rife with ghost-hum
blew between the sheets
on the bed we slept in.
Flutes blew thru gristle
where we touched . . .
Suppressed
billow, blown bank, burred
voice we owed blowing,
holes cut on hollow
wood . . .
I held back, slipped
off by myself, stole
away, haunted head
spouting obsequies,
crawled,
kept close to the ground.
Some said I was dead,
some
a dream of the dead gone too
far, dragged feet leaving
marks in the dirt those yet to
decide
said said it
all

2006

Steve McCaffery

b. 1947

Steve McCaffery was born in Sheffield, England, and lived in the United Kingdom for most of his youth, attending University of Hull. He moved to Toronto in 1968 to seek out the poet bpNichol, with whom he later founded the Toronto Research Group, in order to explore alternative poetry forms. In 1970, he began to collaborate with fellow poets Rafael Barreto-Rivera, Paul Dutton, and bpNichol, thus forming the important sound-poetry group The Four Horsemen. McCaffery's sound poetry, influenced by The Dada Performances of Hugo Ball, challenges the logic and syntax of poetry to create a purely emotional response. Yet much of his poetry also addresses the intellect.

McCaffery's many books of poetry include *Dr. Sadhu's Muffins* (1974), *Ow's Waif* (1975), *Intimate Distortions* (1979), *Knowledge Never Knew* (1983), *Panopticon* (1984), *Evoba* (1987), *The Black Debt* (1989), *The Cheat of Words* (1996), and *Verse and Worse: Selected and New Poems 1989–2009* (2010). His volumes *Theory of Sediment* (1991) and *Seven Pages Missing* (2000) were nominated for a Governor General's Award (one of Canada's most prestigious prizes). McCaffery has also published two volumes of theory and criticism, *North of Intention: Critical Writings 1973–1986* and *Prior to Meaning: The Protosemantic and Poetics* (2001). With Jed Rasula, he edited *Imagining Language* (2001) an anthology of poetic innovations, like those of Joyce, Stein, and Beckett, that were wildly out of line of the literary standard of their day. McCaffery was one of five collaborators in the now-legendary work *Legend*, the others being language poetry founders Charles Bernstein, Bruce Andrews, Ray DiPalma, and Ron Silliman.

Asked in an interview about the relationship of science to language, McCaffery responded that science offers "a readily transportable, or 'highjackable' body of concepts that poetry can plunder. In my own poetic thinking, I thought the shift from the notion of poetic form to poetic economy opens up wider possibilities to practice and interpretation. Later in *Prior to Meaning* I adopt the notion of the dissipative structure, specifically Georges Bataille's theory of general economy. . . . A dissipative structure is a structure that, as it gains complexity, is defined more by what it expends than what it takes in and is usefully applicable to thinking and describing not only poems and literature as a whole, but also the patterns of cities, hemispherical economies and globalization itself."[1] McCaffery's interests spread across the avant-garde range, from visual and sound poetries, to language poetry and conceptual poetry. His poem "Digital Poetics" takes the form of an automated phone response; it serves to travesty the commodification of culture, including that of poetry commerce. In "Apologia Pro Vita Sua," the Cartesian page seems to have knowledge of its own being: I speak therefore I am.

McCaffery is the David Gray Chair of Poetry and Letters at SUNY Buffalo.

1. Ryan Cox, "Trans-Avant-Garde: an Interview with Steve McCaffery," *Rain Taxi*, Winter 2007/2008.

Apologia Pro Vita Sua

1

i am a page if i am not a page
i will be a page when i will not be a page
i want to be a page as i do not want to be a page
i have become a page but i have not become a page

2

i am a page if i am not
i will be a page when i will not be
i want to be a page as i do not want to be
i have become a page but i have not become

3

i have not become a page if i have been
i do not want to be a page when i do not want to be
i will not be a page as i will be
i am not a page but i am

4

i have not become the page i have become
i do not want to be the page i want to be
i will not be the page that i will be
i am not the page i am

2010

Suggestion but No Insult

"No ideas but in things"
    is wrong Bill
        the challenge
          is how to
            negotiate the shift
              from
                quiddity to ideation
                by
          a border-crossing yet
              around subversions to
                      a fold in
                          measure space
                      caesura as transplant
                      and all time
      to keep philosophy your friendly
          insomniac
    grammar born of
the hands that
          question where
the wings should go

                              2010

The Dangers of Poetry
(for Italo Calvino)

Maybe you don't like this poem or perhaps you don't want to read it perhaps you should do something else like wash last night's dishes or watch TV if I were you I'd try reading a good book or even start to write one but perhaps you haven't stopped reading this poem just yet while you're wondering what else you could read or perhaps your interest in this poem has miraculously changed maybe you're enjoying it or finding it a challenge or perhaps you're simply thinking it would be a waste of precious time having read it so far to not read it to the end or perhaps there's nothing you can do because perhaps this is a class that you can't get out of or the start of a conference you've paid a lot of money to attend or perhaps it's a punishment prescribed in a minimum security prison you're now in for five or even ten years or perhaps reading this poem has induced paralysis and you can't move not even to blink your eyes or perhaps you believe it can't get worse but it does get worse and you think all these thoughts again and then compare this poem to the start of Italo Calvino's novel *If on a Winter's Night a Traveller* and that the two might be related perhaps you think that this poem was actually written by Calvino under the pseudonym of Steve McCaffery and then you think that this might be the poem Calvino didn't write but wished he had and by this time an entire week has passed and you're still at your desk at the office because you never went home and perhaps you couldn't have anyway because a friend called to tell you that your house burned down and all your pets and family burned to death because you were still reading this poem.

2010

The Poem as a Thing to See

Somebody here got married in vitro
but why is mass being held
for a million televisions tendered
as deluxe facsimile ready-mades?

Perhaps a microbe's forming a Gordian knot around
uncle's breakfast demands for a family rendition
of Krummacher's story of the worm in the apple.

Shadows above the scratches of a language?

Or do we have the virus as a new archangel?

Either way it's modernity from next door
with it heavy-metal flamenco out
of focus

        a flower and indisputably
a cryptomorphic entry into legend

(The fate of the book sealed in Flaubert's
  famous letter to Louise Colet
    but nothing
     happens
      when you

plan it

2010

Correlata for a Cryptogram

It looks like California outside
the mudslides of pure mascara
but it's been said before:
you can't give an inch a new nail.

Curious, however,
the return to the mystic writing pad
for just the briefest scribble
of top-right Celtomania.

Around these parts
simultaneity in claws is
the puma's best form of disappearance
just follow the arrow from the national diagonals
to reach the correlate for a cryptogram
around the throat of America

the way milk escapes the entire history
of its blackness.

2010

Digital Poetics

To read this poem in French press 1, in German press 2, in Spanish press 3, in English press 4. To read an index of all reviews, books and articles written about this poem press 5. For previous readers' opinions of this poem press 6. To read all variorum drafts in facsimile manuscript of this poem press 7. To read the final proof copy before publication press 8. To read the first printed version of this poem press 9. For a total line count press 10. For a total word count press 11. For a total character count press 12. For a list of all colleges and universities where this poem is taught press 13. For a list of anthologies in which this poem has appeared press 14. For a photograph and biography of the author press 15. To read all musical adaptations of this poem press 16. To read a dramatic version of this poem press 17. To read the libretto of and score to the operatic version of this poem press 18. For a list of bookstores where all books containing this poem are currently available press 19. For a list of stores where the CD version is available press 20. To read a different poem by this author press 21. To read a different poem by another author press 22. To read a shorter poem by this author press 23. To read a longer poem press 24. To read a better poem press 25. To read an on-line version of this poem press 26. To repeat this menu press 27. To read a commentary on these commands and a critical discussion of the social phenomenon of interpellation press 28. To read a commentary on these commands and their relation to Vico's cyclical theory of history press 29. To read a comparison of this touch-tone method to John Dee's Enochian tables press 30. For more information on John Dee's Enochian Tables press 31. To read factual information about John Dee press 32. To read information on Enoch press 33.

2010

Bob Perelman
b. 1947

Bob Perelman was born in Youngstown, Ohio, and attended the University of Michigan, where he received a B.A. in English and an M.A. in classics, and the University of Iowa Writer's Workshop. In 1975, he moved to San Francisco, where he edited the magazine *Hills* and was centrally involved in the growing language poetry scene. From 1977 to 1981, he founded and curated the important San Francisco Talk Series, located primarily at the Langton Street Gallery, and edited *Writing/Talks* (1985), a collection of talks and writings from the series. The "talks" consisted of a presentation by a poet, during which the audience responded with its own thoughts.

Of the language poets, Perelman is one of the more overtly political in his view of consumer society. His satirical approach to the politics of language is also evident in his talks and essays. Quoting the linguist Noam Chomsky, Perelman writes, "Question: How do you tell a language from a dialect? Answer: A language is a dialect that has an army and a navy."[1]

Perelman holds that, just as Virgil's *The Aeneid* justifies empire, much contemporary poetry exists for "a sort of Monday-morning Emperor," the bourgeois reader, who can feel "in the exquisitely disposed syllables, the pain of repression that comes with the territory of world dominion."[2] Perelman calls instead for a "defamiliarization' of poetry by removing it from the comforting aegis of the oral: "Unlike the oral poet, who is reinforcing what the community already knows, the didactic *writer* will always have something new, and, possibly, unacceptable to get across."[3]

Perelman's poetry books include *Braille* (1975), *7 Works* (1978), *Primer* (1981), *a.k.a.* (1984), *The First World* (1986), *Face Value* (1988), the ambitious long poem *Captive Audience* (1988), *Virtual Reality* (1993), *Ten to One: Selected Poems* (1999), *Playing Bodies* (with artist Francie Shaw, 2003), and *IFLIFE* (2006). He has also written the critical studies *The Trouble with Genius: Reading Pound, Joyce, Stein, and Zukofsky* (1994), and *The Marginalization of Poetry: Language Writing and Literary History* (1996).

He lives in Philadelphia and teaches at the University of Pennsylvania.

1. "Words Detached from the Old Song and Dance," in *Code of Signals: Recent Writings in Poetics*, ed. Michael Palmer, Berkeley, 1983, p. 224.   2. The same, p. 232.   3. The same, p. 233.

Chronic Meanings

The single fact is matter.
Five words can say only.
Black sky at night, reasonably.
I am, the irrational residue.

Blown up chain link fence.
Next morning stronger than ever.
Midnight the pain is almost.
The train seems practically expressive.

A story familiar as a.
Society has broken into bands.
The nineteenth century was sure.
Characters in the withering capital.

The heroic figure straddled the.
The clouds enveloped the tallest.
Tens of thousands of drops.
The monster struggled with Milton.

On our wedding night I.
The sorrow burned deeper than.
Grimly I pursued what violence.
A trap, a catch, a.

Fans stand up, yelling their.
Lights go off in houses.
A fictional look, not quite.
To be able to talk.

The coffee sounds intriguing but.
She put her cards on.
What had been comfortable subjectivity.
The lesson we can each.

Not enough time to thoroughly.
Structure announces structure and takes.
He caught his breath in.
The vista disclosed no immediate.

Alone with a pun in.
The clock face and the.
Rock of ages, a modern.
I think I had better.

Now this particular mall seemed.
The bag of groceries had.
Whether a biographical junkheap or.
In no sense do I.

These fields make me feel.
Mount Rushmore in a sonnet.
Some in the party tried.
So it's not as if.

That always happened until one.
She spread her arms and.
The sky if anything grew.
Which left a lot of.

No one could help it.
I ran farther than I.
That wasn't a good one.
Now put down your pencils.

They won't pull that over.
Standing up to the Empire.
Stop it, screaming in a.
The smell of pine needles.

Economics is not my strong.
Until one of us reads.
I took a breath, then.
The singular heroic vision, unilaterally.

Voices imitate the very words.
Bed was one place where.
A personal life, a toaster.
Memorized experience can't be completely.

The impossibility of the simplest.
So shut the fucking thing.

Now I've gone and put.
But that makes the world.

The point I am trying.
Like a cartoon worm on.
A physical mouth without speech.
If taken to an extreme.

The phone is for someone.
The next second it seemed.
But did that really mean.
Yet Los Angeles is full.

Naturally enough I turn to.
Some things are reversible, some.
You don't have that choice.
I'm going to Jo's for.

Now I've heard everything, he.
One time when I used.
The amount of dissatisfaction involved.
The weather isn't all it's.

You'd think people would have.
Or that they would invent.
At least if the emotional.
The presence of an illusion.

Symbiosis of home and prison.
Then, having become superfluous, time.
One has to give to.
Taste: the first and last.

I remember the look in.
It was the first time.
Some gorgeous swelling feeling that.
Success which owes its fortune.

Come what may it can't.
There are a number of.
But there is only one.
That's why I want to.

1993

Confession

Aliens have inhabited my aesthetics for
decades. Really since the early 70s.

Before that I pretty much wrote
as myself, though young. But something

has happened to my memory, my
judgment: apparently, my will has been

affected. That old stuff, the fork
in my head, first home run,

Dad falling out of the car—
I remember the words, but I

can't get back there anymore. I
think they must be screening my

sensations. I'm sure my categories have
been messed with. I look at

the anthologies in the big chains
and campus bookstores, even the small

press opium dens, all those stanzas
against that white space—they just

look like the models in the
catalogs. The models have arms and

legs and a head, the poems
mostly don't, but other than that

it's hard—for me anyway—to
tell them apart. There's the sexy

underwear poem, the sturdy workboot poem
you could wear to a party

in a pinch, the little blaspheming
dress poem. There's variety, you say:

the button-down oxford with offrhymed cuffs.
The epic toga, showing some ancient

ankle, the behold! the world is
changed and finally I'm normal flowing

robe and shorts, the full nude,
the scatter—Yes, I suppose there's

variety, but the looks, those come
on and read me for the

inner you I've locked onto with
my cultural capital sensing device looks!

No thanks, Jay Peterman! No thanks,
"Ordinary Evening in New Haven"! I'm

just waiting for my return ticket
to have any meaning, for those

saucer-shaped clouds to lower! The authorities
deny any visitations—hardly a surprise.

And I myself deny them—think
about it. What could motivate a

group of egg-headed, tentacled, slimier-than-thou aestheticians
with techniques far beyond ours to

visit earth, abduct naive poets, and
inculcate them with otherworldly forms that

are also, if you believe the
tabloids, salacious? And these abductions always

seem to take place in some
provincial setting: isn't that more than

slightly suspicious? Why don't they ever
reveal themselves hovering over some New

York publishing venue? It would be
nice to get some answers here—

we might learn something, about poetry
if nothing else, but I'm not

much help, since I'm an abductee,
at least in theory, though, like

I say, I don't remember much.
But this writing seems pretty normal:

complete sentences; semicolons; yada yada. I
seem to have lost my avant-garde

card in the laundry. They say
that's typical. Well, you'll just have

to use your judgment, earthlings! Judgment,
that's your job! Back to work!

As if you could leave! And
you thought gravity was a problem!

1999

Current Poetics

Going into Iraqi refugees was the last thing on most investors' minds
but suddenly that was where all the money had gone
First thing anybody knew the sun had really set, gone down for good

It has the unbearable presence of a bad dream
a monster telethon where the mute isn't working
except you can feel pain too

Bad preaching and worse theology
with porn the only commodity still behaving itself
a marriage everyone should have seen coming

While somewhere in the extreme back yard
the fastest most expensive machines are rattling the cage of the enemy nation state
    de jour
even as your own is being rattled

There's a noble symmetry in human endeavor. Two hands, two eyes,
    mobile mouth
All that's desirable desiring

But this other spectacle is not for viewing

the secret fraternity torture with all the details in denial
but apparently shot on site
That's the current poetics
You can't imitate it and it doesn't have a plot
It's where they bury people and where people are born
—very young, as Zukofsky says and he would have known

        dream narrative with the usual neocon displacements
how the head pronoun was forced
            to gather shrieks of enemy combatants in a golden cup

2006

The Remote

        Lord's willing only to obeyers
                    roped in a circle
                    parents watch the scantest detail
        humane hate
                    based on group gods

                Heaven understands the catalogue of the methods
                    Shock as burning good
                        with a hot Messenger
            irons dripping acid Its will the skin is where it alights
                    torture prayer of that private Iraq

                    And with the new
                        elected of course
                    cutting out tongues
                        for personal rape strength

2006

Bin Ramke

b. 1947

Bin Ramke was born in Port Neches, Texas, and studied literature at Louisiana State University. His father was an engineer and his mother spoke Cajun French. He later received his Ph.D. from Ohio University and took his first teaching position at Columbus College in Georgia.

Ramke's first book, *The Difference between Night and Day* (1978), won the Yale Younger Poets Award. His other works include *White Monkeys* (1981), *The Language Student* (1986), *The Erotic Light of Gardens* (1989), *Massacre of the Innocents* (1995), *Wake* (1999), *Air, Waters, Places* (2001), *Matter* (2004), *Tendril* (2007), and *Theory of Mind: New & Selected Poems* (2009).

In "The Ruined World," Ramke describes his approach to writing, even as he is constructing such a work: "A place of consequence, of sequence. I pick up scraps of paper and smooth them, pushing with both hands flat against my thigh. The papers are various. I carry a tool for poking in debris. I live this way."[1] Ramke's use of found materials and collage methods is far from mechanical; they thread through his work thematically. Whatever is snatched from a muddy puddle "makes a music anyway," be it a quote from John Cage, Emmanuel Kant, or Randolph's *Beekeeping for Profit*.

Due to the complexity and intellectual distance of some of his work, Ramke has been mistaken for a language poet. However, his work seeks thematic relation within disjunction. Of *Theory of Mind,* Marjorie Perloff writes, "A compelling leitmotif that runs through Bin Ramke's recent poems comes from Wittgenstein's *On Certainty*: 'Where there is no doubt there is no judgment.' Doubt, pressed to its limits and hence break-through, is at the heart of the gorgeously sounded metaphysical poems Ramke has been writing for thirty years—poems that recall Henry Vaughan in their lyric intensity, their profound understanding of scientific theorem and the natural world—wind, cloud, water, light—and especially their fidelity to the truth of the human heart."[2]

Responding to the question "What's American about American poetry?" Ramke responded: "All American poetry is religious poetry, at least theological poetry, in that it must deal with the absence (or presence?) of Ultimate Authority. . . . We are such sad bullies, we Americans, regretting our transformation of the world, how young and undisciplined we've made it."[3]

From 1984 to 2005, Bin Ramke edited the University of Georgia Press's Contemporary Poetry Series. Editor of the *Denver Quarterly,* he holds the University of Denver English department's Phipps Chair and teaches on occasion at the School of the Art Institute of Chicago.

1. *Wake*, Iowa City, 1999, p. 1.   2. Publisher's website: http://www.omnidawn.com/ramke2/index.htm.   3. Poetry Society of America website, 1999, http://www.poetrysociety.org/psa/poetry/crossroads/qa_american_poetry/bin_ramke/.

The Ruined World

(Its Glory)

It makes a music anyway
it is filled with beige plants and charcoal birds
it lingers
sunsets continue, chronic circling
rain will always fall
music breaks its heart
the barren seeds feed the birds
something moves
the light of a sun insinuates
puddles gather into lakes
sounds mingle into new chords
toothed edges of dry leaves cut
it cannot be stopped
it varies inversely with the square of the distance
its lakes reflect, on calm days
it makes its noises
its despised birds fly
it continues its turnings
the light is general and various
the noise of waves in the stormy nights
the sound of anything is a cleverness

but it remains a world. A place of consequence, of sequence. I pick
up scraps of paper and smooth them, pushing with both hands flat
against my thigh. The papers are various. I carry a tool for poking
in debris. I live this way.

The ruined world is mainly gray but the occasional flash, like the
epauletted blackbird you remember, is all the sweeter now for its
rarity. The air has its taste and its grit. The water is always brown.

The boatmen continue to love the world. The random riches, the fish.

Across the largest lakes the tinny bells still call for the faithful, beg
for forgiveness and a return to the fold. It is only the wind moving
among the ruins.
Nothing has changed.

Like many a voice of one delight,	"Stanzas Written
The winds, the birds, the ocean floods,	in Dejection, Near
The City's voice itself, is soft like Solitude's.	Naples" —Shelley

(Overheard)

Never trust the words. I do not
like the noise I make. It's all
I have, the noise I make, the trust. To make the words

a human failing. Noble silence is dead. Out of the depths
I cry unto thee o lord, lord hear my voice

fade softly into the hard discussion
who wouldn't like to know
this kind of consolation

word

. . . there is a group of words which etymologists are inclined to
treat as being all forms of the word which in O. Eng. is *sund,*
meaning "swimming." These words are (I) the swim-bladder of a
fish; (2) a narrow stretch of water between an inland sea and the
ocean, or between an island and the mainland, &c., cf. SOUND, THE,
below; (3) to test or measure the depth of anything, particularly the
depth of water in lakes or seas . . . in these senses has frequently been
referred to Lat. *Sub unda,* under the water; and Fr. *Sombre,* gloomy,
possibly from *sub umbra,* beneath the shade, is given as a parallel.
    —"Sound," *Encyclopaedia Britannica,* eleventh edition

not threatening
to hear while
casually under sun
it sounds like

rain and shimmering
small secret life
say some
story circling its way some
where the words wind
into tight knots stop then start

over
she heard a sound

as an infant she made faint noises, was called Good Girl
later she listened to her little records
on her boxy machine, which made her happy
a girl should be happy it is a world of sunlight
and the darkness behind the door is not her fault
the sunlight is made of those particles that penetrate the ether
shadows are an absence yes but make
the same sound as light
she plays in the sunlight she plays in the sunlight
". . . as we were walking along
introduced me without warning to his habit

of suddenly quietly singing" —John Cage
A man at a public telephone in an airport
turns to the window to appear to be observing the landscape

("Using the term 'note' for a sound produced by a periodic
disturbance, there is no doubt that a well trained ear can resolve
a note into pure tones of frequencies equal to those of the
fundamental and its harmonics" —Encyclopaedia Britannica)

he cries a sound or two escapes he wears a dark suit
he carries a briefcase as he turns I pretend I am reading
I watch him leave I never see him again

How did he become who he is why does he
suffer

Kant: How can I know? What ought I to do? What may I hope?

to break the heart

thee o lord, lord hear my voice

My talkative friend bought a bicycle in his old age;
an interesting angularity, knees and elbows,   (S. Beckett)
walking stick attached to the handlebars for when he stopped.

All about bicycles he told, and about
the suicide, how hard it must have been

in that last moment to keep his aim for the tree;   (G. Oppen)
the one about the policeman during the war, in
Holland, who hummed constantly, they heard him coming, and his
          enemy the artist of contraband,   (S. Lenz)
how you could see a cyclist trying to escape for miles across
          that flat land;
and how the sounds of warning would carry,
and the whistling of the policeman, and the storms.

Boys say to fathers many words they have forgotten.

My father, too, knew words for things, the chemical compositions,
formulas that applied to the normal family. There was a terrible
dark form in the bottom of our bathtub, a vague shape rising
through the vitreous surface where he spilled hydrochloric acid.
He knew secrets of the soul, I am sure he did. He must have been
a man of passions, he would have told me if he could.

My friends all say there is much to talk about.
There is a sound to make that means happiness,
and there is a noise to accompany tears.

When Elizabeth Bishop wrote that the beach hissed like fat, what
did she damage? Not the future, which also hisses like fat. She said
the little birds skittered along the edge of the foam, that the
particles of sand when wetted by the seawater reassemble into a
denser surface and a sound results, a continuous sigh of the beach
itself, not the ocean. Oh the ocean has been known to speak for
centuries, such a claim is commonplace. And sand is a famous
symbol, to do with time. There is nothing more to be said.

On every continent even this very night
there are children crying, telling you of their guilt.
And there are chickens climbing into their roosts
muttering to themselves, beginning to nod
even as their lovely hard feet fasten tightly,
a special tendon doing the work all night.
And all the creatures of the world sigh
into their little futures, and close their eyes
and breathe for nothing but their need, quiet.

(Among Trees)

Among the laurus nobilis

conspiring molecules
quiver in light

fir or feathered
a tangle of tangent
the glitters radiant

pine and parameters
quercus virginiana
festooned

tillandsia usneoides
epiphytic bromeliads
bay

growing in my mother's yard also
laurel
hemlock

the light this way
green as if
it were one

thing
green as gravity
growing

Imaginably twisting groundward
and rot and riddling a massiveness of organization
organic, roots: mirrored by limbs and twirling loose
in air movement and marauding photons glancing
as if it were possible. Nothing more, as if from the bible
the love of trees something vastly and evil. Engorged.

The way to prophecy is to keep secrets.

We could speak of birds, or of air. Ether.

A hint is powerful. The way to god is ambiguity. A path
to his house, his hovel, his shelter under the trees.

A family among the trees begins to die, the generation

having gathered, all uncles and aunts to the world, the pace
of their aging not hurried but they die and gather a smaller
group each time around the gathering graves. Soon under
a liveoak one alone will wipe his brow and turn away.

"How tender the green tip before the leaf grows."
                    —Robert Duncan

The enormous deciduous climb the gradual plain
the effect the geology of it all gone
there is a glitter beneath the wires the wind
plucks them a tone emerges the shatter
beneath and like longing turned crystalline
light light light

If the clouds be full of rain, they empty *themselves* upon the earth:
and if the tree fall toward the south, or toward the north, in the
place where the tree falleth, there it shall be. Eccles. II: 3.

A fill of forests and the story fills
us with regret and sweetness. We love
one another. The trees are ancient
and the story is long but no one tires
listening and great libraries flutter
from each limb and there is more to read
than ever can be told and more time
from the shade of the tree saunters
in front of the following sun
and still the story lingers.

                             (Preface)

A darkening delivers us
a children's game or simply
human shaped and sharp
a cowboy or some ethnic profile
toy soldier
formulas for anything and crowds
starlings change
shape forming and reforming against sunset

(into brightness in the dark
by the flame of his match he
felt the warmth of her hand on his
dissolve into the night the dark
he never saw such a face such
a woman smoke in the street walking)

there is your pattern of flourish
in this forest around the river
where Hansel wandered and Gretel
a flourish of blossom in the spring of fruit in the autumn
sadly slender humans descend their own nervous systems
eye to brain to spine
men do this and boys they look

(The amateur beekeeper should never work among his bees
without a veil, for stings about the face are particularly painful
and embarrassing.
                    —*Beekeeping for Profit,* Randolph)

they look at
mingling with air, wave, waving there
awe and careless
through crowds of flesh the boys
look and burning with will they sell
buy and belong
(..it is characteristic of more refined humanity to respect "the
mask" and not to indulge in psychology and curiosity in the wrong
place.
                    —"What is Noble?" Nietzsche)

Lovely and true they are
to the ways of flesh, flash and awe

and teeth and lips and eyelids and lashes
jumbled flesh earlobes the tiny maze they dangle from
and the bones beneath to shape
a thing to gaze upon

he kept his most accurate
mirror in his own room well protected a little frightening

it is a game or toy a life is. I was happy
and you were beautiful and we danced like the movies
someone did. Those were the days.

And here Aeneas saw the son of Priam,
Deiphobus, all of his body mangled,
his face torn savagely, his face and both   Aeneid 6, 651–655
his hands, his ears lopped off his ravaged temples,
his nostrils slashed by a disgraceful wound.

I would amazed listen
to the radio on the river the captains of ships conversing
the mates and enginemen the crackling
of two-way radio the rhythmic noise
and unamazed my uncle's sullen face hearing
his eyes closed his hand taking a shorthand
his understanding complete. I continued my games
hiding among the ship's stores and commerce
crates and gear to sell to passing mariners.
It seemed a game, this kind of life, of making a living
making believe, believing. This he could do
like child's play, his face behind his hand, hearing.

                                                      1999

Aaron Shurin
b. 1947

Poet and essayist Aaron Shurin was born in Manhattan and raised there, in eastern Texas, and Los Angeles. He studied at the University of California at Berkeley and received an M.A. in poetics from New College of California, where he studied with Robert Duncan.

He writes that his work "is framed by the innovative traditions in lyric poetry as they extend the central purpose of the Romantic Imagination: to attend to the world in its particularities, body and soul. Poetry remains for me an act of investigation, by which the imagination makes itself visible in a real world—and through which the inhabitants of the realer world become dimensional."

His volumes of poetry include *The Night Sun* (1976), *A's Dream* (1989), *Into Distances* (1993), *The Paradise of Forms: Selected Poems* (1999), *A Door* (2000), *Involuntary Lyrics* (2005), and *Citizen* (2011). He has also written a powerful book of personal essays, *King of Shadows* (2008), about coming out as a gay man in San Francisco in the late 1960s, his identification with Shakespeare's characters Oberon and Puck, and his indebtedness to the poets Denise Levertov, Robert Duncan, and Frank O'Hara.

After fifteen years of writing primarily prose poetry, Shurin returned to verse with his proceduralist masterwork, *Involuntary Lyrics,* in which the end words of Shakespeare's sonnets were retained and all else replaced with Shurin's own expression. Poet and blogger Ron Silliman wrote of the volume: "Shurin seems to have no limit as to what he can do with a form more closed—in the constructivist sense—than anything a so-called New Formalist might e'er imagine. The sweep is startling & if there is any limit to this relatively slim volume it is only that he has not included translations (or whatever you might call them) for every single Shakespearean sonnet."[1] The influence of Oulipo is evident in Shurin's formal practice of erasure and replacement. In such works, it is to the benefit of the lyric that it is forced into balance with a constructivist motivation and structure.

A professor and former associate director of the M.F.A. in Writing program at the University of San Francisco, Shurin has lived in San Francisco since 1974.

1. Silliman's Blog, Thursday, November 17, 2005, http://ronsilliman.blogspot.com/2005/11/very-first-page-is-so-strong-it-nearly.html.

FROM *Involuntary Lyrics*

VIII

I come to café, I sit, I bear
my part in the general cruise. One, sadly
won't look at me, another
won't look away; ridiculous assumption and snarled consumer joy
in abeyance, ordering
quotidian life according to compulsions or ordered *by,* focus shifting
        but always aligned. Well, gladly
I'd mother
that guy with a stubble but he wants a father. I won't annoy
his diligent linearity. Man I just yesterday had sex with in park
        — sing
muse — said "Yum" and somehow knew to pull my head on his
        shoulder, little bleating sounds.
One heart, one mind, one chance but right now one
second's second chance he just walked by this café walkman in ear
real time I could've run and, what, left the poem? Composition
        deems none
such interruption permissible; shit, the sheer complexity confounds.

XVIII

Those guys with Christmas tree untrimmed
and me to help, nobody else came, party day
fade
away unless I hang 'em. So here's my faux-pearl earring and necklace
        set, temperate
compared to some, countering your scary Guatemalan death-squad
        burnt angel. But owe
me no thanks this shimmying electric May-
pole brightens December shade.
X didn't call me for a date
though I foisted number on him after severe flirtations, what he
        might grow
in proportion to those giant feet shines
elsewhere, someone else'll see
it. Still I've no complaint, except employment chances dimmed

but that's perennial this annual, the
season's one for newing, I'm drinking, it's raining, I saw a plum
　　　blossom lone bluey pink on live branch for which tired
　　　December declines.

XXXVII

It's a country road forty years ago, a country store
where propped outside, banded tans and gold, are sugar cane several
　　　feet's delight
taller than especially me, despised
outsider New Yorker in temporary captive preadolescent Texas
　　　youth,
stymied circumspect narrowed to hold it in mouth, give
pleasure like dog with bone chewing and sucking to spite
poverty East Texas limitless, oh, nothing, stupid pleasure sufficed.
Stupid pleasure suffices? Shop spend decorate mad for eye view
　　　prowl sex get it or don't eat truth's
live
with stuffing it. Dad(dead)'s right here to watch. That fucker had wit
but no brain rage but no heart figure but no beauty the
knowing failure terror of him lies in wait fifty years and more
but I've dealt with him! I've dealt with him! though he with me
ghostly not finished, patiently hides to seek, smiling, sit and wait,
　　　wait and sit. . . .

LXVI

Disabled
by seeing them touch — his head in *his* hands — put me verge of
　　　cry-
ing, having given them authority
over my shallow solitude. His head was borne
on the water of *his* hands. Then you appeared, a skill
of time, raising jollity
from my meatiness, the simplicity
of mutual proximity. . . . Oh I've sworn

to and *not to* in terrible self-sufficiency ill
from perfection. . . . The meteor shower last night showered
      misplaced
"grains of rice" (I started to write "grains of night") streaking trails
      over Healdsburg gone
California ecliptic archer to hunter trumpeted
into layered distances alone
and found me watching breathless you too watching focused there
      apex in ample solitude *un*disgraced.

Trails my summer dawn wind in other flesh strung together on scar impressions
of young Panama night. . . .
William Burroughs

CII

if you would come for days
whoever you are or seeming
to be then I'd appear
to be enveloped in our aura of intimacy now
as if in middle of night
I might turn in teeming
sheets a bough
creaking to meet the wind everywhere
so I'd under especially red flannel delight
to find your sweaty hulk like just the other day & spring
or be sprung upon flattened then that tongue
lays
bare breastbone flayed & circling down conjunctive song
I make you make me sing

CXLI

Claudio, Steffano, Salo, Jésus, Christian, Holger, Dirk, alone
without you my somber eyes
can
note

the
empty, well, platonic form in front of 'em & then despise
the man
or men I dote
on, fictive, no, not you. For you I'd be
myself again if you would be yourselves, delighted
in your loveliness, really, imagination's form so fine in real-time, gain
of human countenance the gaze I found in you, on you, or you in
     me, prone
before each mirroring eyes sprayed out acknowledgment as beauty
     kindly given, sweet, pain
only of the threshold tested, crossed, hushed, tense, into, *invited*. . . .

CXLII

friends walk; bones begin to creak; wild iris and dandelion; bay leaf
     scented air; each rents
body for mere seasons; lunch on kalamata olives, smoked turkey,
     hummus; hate
to hear those
bones creak; old friends defer to time loving
walking measure; slanted redwood shade; golden poppies splatter
     hills; who'd have foreseen this kind of elegiac afternoon the
casual alternation of rain and sun a state
of how it grows
and falls proving
exactly one's situation small between material forces and what
     pushes back; "be
steady" the poem said; this is what your
eyes are permitted to see, this may hide
beneath resplendent ornaments;
cracked boulders in shallow stream glaze orange; red walking dust,
     browned mud; nothing noticed will be denied:
all mine

2005

Will Alexander

b. 1948

Will Alexander was born in Los Angeles and grew up in the South Central section of the city.

Alexander's poetry books include *Vertical Rainbow Climber* (1987), *Archane Lavender Morals* (1994), *The Stratospheric Canticles* (1995), *Asia & Haiti* (1995), *Above the Human Nerve Domain* (1998), *Towards the Primeval Lightning Field* (1998), *Exobiology as Goddess* (2005), *Sunrise in Armageddon* (2006), *The Sri Lankan Loxodrome* (2010), and *Compression & Purity* (2011). His first poems were published in *River Styx* in the early 1980s at the suggestion of Clayton Eshleman, who thereafter published Alexander's work regularly in his own journal *Sulfur*.

Influenced by Bob Kaufman, Federico García Lorca, Wilfredo Lam, and the Négritude writers Aimé Césaire and Leon Damas, Alexander has cleared his own path independent of official black and white modes of expression. "I knew I was completely different than what we call 'Black poetry.' In fact I wasn't even interested in that. Because they just give you a little area to live in. So here's your church, here's your poetry."[1] His major influence is Césaire, especially in relation to his unusually rich poetic diction.

In his introduction to *Towards a Primeval Lightning Field,* Andrew Joron writes, "The lightning-stroke is an inscription, a natural hieroglyph that conveys the message: Eternity has already happened. So that, in an important sense, Alexander's philosophy begins at the end. Or more precisely, *after* the end, *before* the beginning. Now—at this strange juncture between time and timelessness—comes to pass the Emergency of Emergence. In which everything presents itself at once, as an event that, containing all other events, cannot contain itself."[2] This sense of the uncontainable can be found in the maximalist pressure Alexander exerts on the sentence, as if everything on earth were happening *now*. This is not a narrative poetry, nor is it the parataxis of language poetry, as Harryette Mullen has noted.[3] Andrew Joron reasons that, because Alexander's language, like lightning itself, is a "free expenditure" (Bataille) that "must transgress the boundaries of all restricted economies of meaning. Hence Alexander's aggressively transgressive use of language: the neologisms, archaisms, and etymological dislocations."[4]

Will Alexander lives in Los Angeles.

1. Harryette Mullen, "Hauling up Gold from the Abyss: An Interview with Will Alexander," *Callaloo* 22.2 (1999), p. 397.   2. Andrew Joron, "On Alexandrian Philosophy," introduction to *Towards the Primeval Lightning Field,* Oakland, 1998, p. 10.   3. "'A Collective Force of Burning Ink': Will Alexander's Asia & Haiti," *Callaloo* 22.2, 1999, p. 422.   4. Joron, the same, p. 12.

A Nexus of Phantoms

In a lorikeet cave
motions exist of disintegrated swans
in a translocated lake
brimming with harvested poisons
sealed by corruptive post-mortems

such swans
staggered by microbial reasoning
their aggressive nests
anatomical with anomaly
with drifts of strenuous incarnadine leanings
with a thirst which hurtles conspiratorial invasives
alive
with coronal oceanics
open
like a clouded trail of rendings

analogous
with the "Auks" the pelicans the mergansers
perhaps
with "the petrels & the gannets"
under the power of darted mocking orations

the swans
looking back on solemn blood perusal
like a form of death breaking roses on a shore

it is the example of phonograms
of lost & compacted lenses
turning
within a charismatic "Fall Line"
or an "isoneph"
or what an avian would announce in Greenland
as a "Katabatic Wind"*

the swans
like a haze of magnetism

* "Rapid downward motion of air."

or implied gondola locations
where the scent of each lorikeet is consumed
& brought to dazzling eclipse refulgence

in another foci
in another depth
their form self-challenged
in a cloak of suns
their power de-revealed
with 7 moons burning
reduced to 2 intense incendiary magnets

& these incendiary magnets
like a nexus of phantoms
scattered across a geometric optometry

2009

Thought as Philosophical Torment

In the mirror of excessive drift
there exist those values
which exist within schisms
within error wracked spectrums
which glow by means of vapour
above anti-dimensional obstruction

the visage of metrics
tuned to a mesmeric lisp
to a rancid facial dice
thrown across ethers
across 3 or 4 sierras or voids

so that each sculpting
each prism
advances
the apparitional understanding
to a macro-positional scalding
which collapses
which takes on the centigrade of absence
bound to invisible comradery

which means velocity is obscured
& resurrected
beyond the scope of a-positional turquoise
beyond the scope which defines its way as jaundice
by a circular language as dragon
the face in the scope of the millipedes
no longer condoned to withdrawal
to persecution as flaw or advancement

for instance
the blank theogony of vowels
or the in-homophony of distance
like an open vibrational nerve
or the hissing of ruins in a buried nautical port

one thinks
of a sublimated mountain illness
contradicted
as in a reddish form of dysentery
& in each intrinsic nuance all the symmetries obscured
the maps one comes to know
are but boulders which are shattered by spoilage

therefore
the fragments hung in peninsulas
are suspended
& the visage in its demeanour
like a de-ingested shrine
subsumed in the body as a rudderless coherence

2009

FROM *The Sri Lankan Loxodrome*

*. . . transmitting Egyptian cultural values . . . in the
domain of writing and navigation*
—Cheikh Anta Diop

As to whether I exist
squared
to the 9 originations of the carnal spirit body
of its clarifying poison or its wheat
does not condemn me
or destroy my fate as Loxodrome

perhaps
I am a mix
of Yemenese or Omani configuration
possessing a murderous carpentry
or a salubrious or insalubrious flexity
at the code at which dissident germs must invigorate
bronchial delay
or answer its breathing by dialectical probation

it is as if each of my lives
is condoned with inflationary drift
with deltas
with models of themselves
involving perhaps
4 or 10 dimensions
more stunning than the ambit of an ibis
transcribing its folios in trance

I exist
not as a technical brutality
not as a monotheistic transcription
or as a terse incapable pilot splitting his axis on rocks
but the mind in its aurific degree
completely incapable of limits
incapable of forming zones of bondage
by which my tertiary compass responds to hosannas

I have burned in previous lives
as one single body
as foiled idyllic moneran
given over
to the permanent ache of isolation
to the permanent ecclesiastical gaze of a brackish melancholia
instinctively kept alive by prolonged engagement
with a succubus
her names
Pyrexia°
Karina°
Mamaloi°

& I have not been able to divide

°Pyrexia: Fever or febrile condition.
°Karina: Egyptian demonology, a familiar attached to each child at birth.
°Mamaloi: Priestess-Magician associated with voodooism in the West Indies.

to re-engender my thirst
according to a sovereign maritime picture
I have never been able to see my own breathing
or begin to awe myself within a narcotic iridescence

my blood ignites & disperses before the sun & after feeding
contained in itself by crepuscular magenta
by origins of Babylonian erubescence
by a diamond-streaked fuchsia
sometimes drizzling
sometimes a curious sleet in the iris

at these moments I've felt
like an epileptic maharajah
as a salt burned incarnation
as satrap
as bey
as pasha
nauseous
figmental
somehow plagued with corrosives

I am Loxodrome
whose commission is to de-poison sea snakes
to somehow bottle their arteries in clouds
all my actions being noctambulous & wary

my command
to capture them as beasts
whose colour is aurulent & xanthic

2009

Bruce Andrews

b. 1948

Born in Chicago, Bruce Andrews studied international relations at Johns Hopkins and political science at Harvard. A founding editor of $L = A = N = G = U = A = G = E$, the magazine of poetics that gave language poetry its name, he is one of the originators of the movement and a tireless experimenter and theorist.

His books include *Edge* (1973), *Getting Ready to Have Been Frightened* (1988), *Sonnets—memento mori* (1980), *Give Em Enough Rope* (1985), *Executive Summary* (1991), *I Don't Have Any Paper So Shut Up (Or, Social Romanticism)* (1992), *Tizzy Boost* (1993), *Lip Service* (2001), *Designated Heartbeat* (2006), *Factura* (2008), and *You Can't Have Everything . . . Where Would You Put It!* (2011). He has also published a collection of critical essays, *Paradise & Method: Poetics & Praxis* (1996).

A professor of political science at Fordham University since 1975, his is a politics of radical dissent. He believes that change can be accomplished through a systematic disruption of the language. "There is no 'direct treatment' of the thing possible, except of the 'things' of language," he writes in the essay "Poetry as Explanation, Poetry as Praxis." "Crystalline purity—or transparency—will not be found in words. That classical ideal is an illusion."[1] Instead, radical praxis calls for "an infinitizing, a wide-open exuberance, a perpetual motion machine, a transgression."[2]

Andrews lives in New York City, where he serves as music director for Sally Silvers & Dancers. In concert with the dancers, he improvises the presentation of text he has prepared on strips of paper. He refers to the text aspect of performance as "live editing," because it does not involve the creation of newly invented phrases but rather the variable treatment of established material. Likewise, he does "live mixing" of the sound materials on a digital mixing board. The performance therefore changes from night to night.[3]

1. *The Politics of Poetic Form*, ed. Charles Bernstein, New York, 1990, pp. 24–25.   2. The same, p. 25.   3. Email to Paul Hoover, March 21, 2012.

Earth 5

Only the 'preparations' are complete; the result
  is empty spurious leverage
                      are you waiting for the translation?
                      animals with voice amplifiers
  incensed so apt merely by relation.
    Don't dance

sweat belies

                              shookless
                  arcfretquietfiatvisor
eerie doldrums;
       is as aim — folly vent
the bee-sting is not precise factual detail.
        Monotonous affinity
                  generic delicacy
abnormal proxy ignited subjected
                fake gram seeded error
enterprised by its, hounded by it
                carnal shutters point not meant
powerless against things
                      verb fact amiss
slippage really believes I get killed through the ears:
will *the* please identify itself,
       telegraph askances close less likely
markprone syllabic con
release preview of affects
                  (and that this wasn't good news)
                      forfeit arc
             unhorse misbalancing ideal rebuff
fictitious swerve incline
askew;
       indirect sentience, she's got that poodle tongue,
that thumbnail pant — sticky areas
              duplicitous emergency —
cocktail imprint bank on wrong for now so slip
              spasm's defense jacks the box:
let the pumps dart the dialing, nube, the hurt
is on — hungry matches will eat dirty liquid.
       Proof alibi lance diatribe
              lie from the bottom of your heart
seldom from air lid air virtue's *victim*
           alto assumption's voice
                  wound never breaks —
you never return, I never leave —
delicately channeled small is better epidermal *push*.
       Shock, subtraction
detail trenches salt start circumstances of scrupulosity
text incarcerates — avenger from — atmospherelessly
                  aerial dupes over hum

what synth, sky
swoops wrong.
    Flouts this
annulling finicky, magnified & magnificent:
                give us home thrust
                          custody correct
hard-edged pastels semaphoring unconsciousness
homogeneous inverse to address
tint wire
physio-logically
askew on one's two legs.

Earth 6

DEAR refine the line Sir: nobody wants you here, if you
want facts, discourage me from repeating yourself — without the
sign! — old luggage mouth nature learned by heart trick
connotes tremble enamor tints appall muffle group cue strictest
soon quick ignorance can't vouch,
    I cross my fingers emptied light foolish pitch indecisive
swoon from constipation of purchase, otherwise you can nickel-
&-dime yourself down cognitively, a previous unknown level
of *granularity* in the pastiche & hence untraceable, amphitheater
                      devil with the rest quietist in captions.
    Vexed transmit denatured hint over show
foolscap horns on court tress balanced naught in apparition
vestiges do succumb absolute addresses
reach ourselves impractically cloistered
                        I don't know
              zher ner kawngprahng pah —
              poovay voo mer trahdweer serssee
              collage unnerved pleasant to be orated to
windmill to point stint with tips doctoring this fraud.
    Pensible, smoked out by
form in the shape of a rooster, uncertain distance
always avaricious koan cuties seldom
                   pleasure spell slower chilling
drone this momently adjacent chew-toy to end all chew-toys —
these lies are
particularly ugly ones innocence cancels,
    the latest line

fronting intuitions is not tonight — fickle
indecorums, surface grew decoys shellacked to a fault;
but I, connote me off, am too lavish peradventure
in this subject.
    Awardless trick start overdrawn
headdresses (or he addresses)
                helpless so to speak bifocal
                sorry to comet
fratricide of the unexpected pretty but not edible.
    Posthaste attentions are scarce
                stuttered ether lame in lobes —
I like indoors, brain lumped over into the netted septic tank
& that's why attention span went off.

Earth 9

WATCHWORD is
contrary's falsity intuition
                tilts lapped asleep, frontispiece
                        un-form sporadic
                servile body in formation recess box
                      obliging
                      eclipsing
              hum to fault standoffish
trespass, obstinate imaginations in a shop window;
    arrows understood? —
                indiscernible color nominal bender
                what stint
                hoop tilt glazes same swollen daubs
                sturdy as a vacuum —
torso cure, what are you dripping at?
    While time services
                        sulphurous cipher
while time surfaces —
why always rectangles? —
                curt premium
until the real thing comes along.
    Wet horse metric holy insulation
fusillades his light through evidential envy, formula patriarch
in whatsoever sleight masked crypto at odds

curiosity just a sexual pick-me-up.
    Excuse collision:
aspiring basks
on alert spun drone literally licking the paper-
self-reflecting error.
    Weak connote anti-intimate mathematical
                                    retreat attentless
                    dervished fabric; material harping
antitype sympathy marry clear heat retracts
                    parallelogram on fingertip.
    Ominous means intimate
nubile topology takes property's facial imprint, mirror's
infinity dwarfed into
                    optics for sale.
    Transparent diction blows, transition, chalk still abnormal
prong disarming saints' leakage threshed passé passive glass sure
vaccinates the vision,
    sordid spatialized vicar of virtuals
the lessons of quiet — Don't Call Me —
immediacy of the flesh weighs heavily how it gets from zero
to one.

                                                    2001

Somehow That's Just the Way It Is and I Just Don't Really Care

Not a sign of people — My brains are in my heart — Why is my
heart so frail? — To be circumspect — Life's machinery — And far
more alarming — It's permissible — To your size — The bad in every
man — Keener reception — Do you mean — Nature is hard to deny —
No one belongs to me — Why behave? — I behave — No ambition —
No desire — And that's why some are nervous — Unphotographable
 — In toto — I could have bound you too — Estrange me — And that-a
is that-a — Verbatim — It's only natural — Too much — I'm your slave,
dear — Conceal it — Is part of the scheme — Fools rush in — Taking
things apart now — To be — Now I believe — Matter over mind — Of
opposite sexes — And read every line — With the well-known
double-cross — You have what I lack myself — To go your own sweet
way — What's the use of trying not to fall — My possession — The
sun won't set on our possessions — Convention I break —

Horizontally speaking — It was all prearranged — You forget your
alphabet — Change your wishes to demands — That I'd be playing
solitaire — But should she refuse to succumb — *Hush, hush; quiet* —
By four hands — Troubles will keep — I can't win but here I am —
Together

2006

Devo Habit

Hucksters bundle up detachment hives grows uselessness comfy to politicize a
retina. The gauge of illusion as illusion: experience is life — that is, therapy fuels
longshot plantation. Only absence of telos self-satisfaction's superfluity chinks.
Bits outrage neo directness as brain condom. Insist = privilege = art control.
Hysteria lack just repression secrets relaxed futurity, dwelling arrogant claims
attachment's lack of words writing without worms. Anti-entropic ghost status,
nonbeguiling orgy to object status ideas ready for things, readier than things.
No ideas but in sexism; only coldness is frank. Idiotic team-up non-humans to
fear non-death complacency makes robot repair unnecessary. Limits severely
frigid grid tempo talent pre-exacting. Function needs a fiction: it belies hope
by not being resisted enough. To err is statemental. Suggestion just talk &
sincerity fabrication imitation. Vital signs terminate words, the lonely gone
past barriers to manage gnosis trouble form better than life permission ego
hang-up. Strength gives up hatchet job for the finite coaching the exact. A
suspicious religious suburb copy feeling up a goose-step careened anything life
belief more than system's studious rigidity to cause a harbor of belief system
effects. Handicappers as cause-and-effect landscape never really happens
to prefer more anthemic ads. Follow the animals as *they* roam for food too,
purely happens as drug doctrine little thoughts not a sense of humor to resume
normal intrusion procedure.

2006

FROM *Factura*

ca	ja	a	th	an	ne	sh	th	wa	pe
qu	ci	fo	in	ba	wh	vi	re	se	th
eu	co	st	cu	wo	a l	su	cr	ce	re
in	ma	vi	si	ba	am	ch	qu	an	is
th	th	cu	ni	se	fa	wo	ap	se	th
pr	st	th	st	th	th	ac	wh	wh	pa
wi	ha	wa	ti	bo	pr	wo	fe	th	tr
fa	sp	if	so	th	th	pl	fo	to	tw

2008

Stephen Ratcliffe ───────────────────
b. 1948

Stephen Ratcliffe was born in Boston, Massachusetts, and has lived in California since he was four years old. He was a Stegner Fellow at Stanford and received a Ph.D. from the University of California at Berkeley. Publisher of Avenue B Press, he is a professor and former director in the M.F.A. program at Mills College in Oakland, California.

Ratcliffe's production as a poet has been prodigious. This is largely due to the exhaustiveness of his procedure, which includes the constraint of writing every day at the same time. Focusing on what occurs in the actual within his view, his "day" works are meditative, observational, notational, and objective. *Portraits & Repetition* (2002), *REAL* (2007), and *CLOUD/RIDGE* (2011) are three such works. Each book in the trilogy is 474 pages written in 474 days.[1]

Each poem in *REAL* consists of seventeen lines and five sentences, and "each sentence has one comma which moves around in its position in the sentence, thus making a connection to the 5-couplet structure of *Portraits & Repetition*. . . . As for content, every poem in *REAL* tries to write down exactly what happens in the moment of 'real' (actual) perception; i.e., "Underside / of a moth's white wings fluttering against black / of window, man in a blue sweatshirt's reflection / looking out at it."[2] Poet Carol Watts comments: "These works are all in different ways founded on a dedicated inquiry into repetition and time, repetition understood as a Steinian 'insistence,' perhaps, which works to capture 'that present something.'"[3]

In addition to *Portraits & Repetition*, *REAL*, and *CLOUD/RIDGE*, Ratcliffe's many books include *New York Notes* (1983), *[where late the sweet] BIRDS SANG* (1989), *Selected Letters* (1992), *Mallarmé: poem in prose* (1998), *SOUND / (system)* (2002), and *Conversation* (2011). His prose works include *Reading the Unseen: (Offstage) Hamlet* (2009), *Listening to Reading* (2000), and *Campion: On Song* (1981).

Stephen Ratcliffe lives in Bolinas, California.

1. "Note on Included Work," *The Double Room: A Journal of Prose Poetry and Flash Fiction*, Fall/Winter 2003, http://webdelsol.com/Double_Room/issue_three/Stephen_Ratcliffe_1 .html.   2. The same.   3. "Only, document: Stephen Ratcliffe's *REAL*," *Jacket2*, October 20, 2011, https://jacket2org/article/only-document.

FROM *REAL*

10.31

Register of crow's persistent three-note "caw"

accompanied by higher pitch of an unknown bird

darting about in foliage beyond white window,

after which its apparent mate arrives. DJ

claiming Johnny Cash sings like redemptive-

seeking flagallent, bright stars in dark sky

after the new moon sets. The seven year old

girl imitating her one-eyed father picking up

lint from the carpet a piece at a time, twenty

year old cat yowling in blue cage in back seat

as the driver of the grey car changes stations.

Grey-white clouds piling up above the freeway,

the short-haired woman reaching from the tub

to turn off blues on radio. Woman in green

noting opacity of paint in relation to ink,

through whose translucence light reflects

diagonally back from the page.

11.1

Shadow of three green rose leaves between circle

of light on ceiling and the surface of the plane

it falls across, line of lip in relation to left

eye of the subject. Black and white photograph

of man in blue sweatshirt holding grey and white

striped cat on his lap, left hand of the woman

on right knee of girl who took it. DiMaggio

liking fight game and girls and especially

blonds, Monroe thinking him unlike usual

Hollywood guys she used to hang around with.

Woman with hair pulled back kneeling down beside

man sitting beside short-haired woman whose left

knee is crossed, an accumulation of blue adding

up to Platonic idea of it. Grey gull on red

buoy below line of horizon, blue and white

reflection of sky in water across which motion

of small swells approaches.

11.2

Interval of silence between cries of invisible
red-tailed hawk positioned in eucalyptus branch
behind the pine, small green tree frog stretched
between blue of sky in flat plane and the window
it leans against. Man on phone taking pictures
of grain elevators in Idaho, silver-haired man
thinking of the time he watched himself leave
his body to walk on the water 100 yards away.
Shoulder of the ridge sloping to the right below
pale blue streak in grey-white sky, lone pelican
disappearing into space beyond the viewer's left
shoulder. Man with shaved head walking with boy
up steep hillside under full moon light, leaving
him in front of a rock. Dark shape of the moth
with wings pulled back on the upper right side
of the frame, a second smaller one flickering
about in the outside dark.

11.3

Two small birds lifting from corner into blue
absence of clouds in otherwise motionless sky,
the larger brown one angling over the passion
vine-covered fence. Woman with hair just cut
asking long-haired son to pull his back, short-
haired woman in red V-neck sweater leaning over
to look at a book on the table. Left shoulder
in grey jacket feeling a non-Platonic current
arriving from right shoulder in black jacket
beside it, dream of another woman wondering
whether he wanted to kiss her when he felt
desire coming from her lips. Driver seeing
everything slow down at 241 mph, small black
stones on the track for example. A thin blue-
white line of cloud in blue-white sky parallel
to horizontal line of ridge below it, brighter
white line of jet passing ahead of its sound.

11.4

Corner of sunlight on the mauve rectangular

shape in the plane leaning against the wall

above the dresser, shadows of tobacco plant

leaves on white wall to the left. Silver-haired

man in blue shirt on scaffold beside shaved-head

man nailing shingles to the wall, the triangular

shape of dark blue plane whose flatness appears

to stand between green of cypress tree on left

and a brown slope on the right. Short-haired

woman moving the man the way he moves her, hot

water coming out of the faucet when she reaches

for the cold. Shoulders of man in black wetsuit

hunched over in the glare reflected from surface

of opaque green water, viewer flying vertically

over lighter green back of right-breaking wave.

Rose branches in wavering light, a light east

wind made visible in the motion of its effects.

11.5

Small green tree frog crouched in triangular

space under a grey rock from Everest leaning

against the window, black line above left eye

extending from mouth to back of head. Two red

and yellow apples on mound of grass under still

half-leaved tree, a pile of faded yellow petals

fallen on the table. Woman in the red nightie

under a trenchcoat whose pockets are stuffed

with porn, 120 foot obelisk whose base is 10

feet underground. The blond woman with hair

pulled back looking through binoculars at man

paddling out on right, walking back down beach

when he comes in. Sudden disturbance of dozens

of small brown birds lifting from brush on left,

the spider coming down from its web above green

trim toward the fly whose wings and rust-orange

eyes stop moving.

2007

Eileen Myles
b. 1949

Born and raised in Cambridge, Massachusetts, Eileen Myles attended the University of Massachusetts in Boston. In 1974, she moved to New York City, where she was involved in the Poetry Project at St. Mark's Church in the Bowery, and took poetry classes from Ted Berrigan, Alice Notley, and Paul Violi, among others. In 2002, she accepted a teaching position at the University of California San Diego, where she directed the Creative Writing program. Five years later, she took early retirement and returned to live in New York.

Myles's personal and lyrical poetry has an affinity with the work of James Schuyler; this is most evident in her diaristic style of composition, narrative ease, and use of short, enjambed lines. But her intensity can also be very keen. The poem "Immanence" is so mystically piercing it evokes Rilke or one of the Desert Fathers.

For Myles, the performance of a poem occurs more at the moment of its composition than during its enactment before an audience. Referring to the creation of one of her poems, "Hot Nights," she writes, "The process of the poem . . . is central to an impression I have that life is the rehearsal for the poem, or the final moment of spiritual revelation. I literally stepped out of my house that night, feeling a poem coming on . . . I went over to Yaffa [a restaurant] and wrote it looking out the window."[1] In Myles's view, "going out to get a poem" is like hunting: "I felt '. . . erotic, oddly / magnetic . . .' like photographic paper. As I walked I was recording the details, I was the details, I was the poem."[2]

Myles's poetry collections include *The Irony of the Leash* (1978), *A Fresh Young Voice from the Plains* (1981), *Sappho's Boat* (1982), *Not Me* (1991), *Maxfield Parrish* (1995), *School of Fish* (1997), *Skies* (2001), *Sorry, Tree* (2007), *Pencil Poems* (2011), and *Snowflake/different streets* (2012). Her book of poetry, *Tow*, with drawings by Larry C. Collins, appeared in 2005. She has also published the works of fiction *Bread and Water* (1986), *Chelsea Girls* (1994), *Cool for You* (2000), *Inferno (a poet's novel)* (2010), and a work of "travel writing in art," *The Importance of Being Iceland* (2009).

She has received a Warhol Foundation/Creative Capital Writers Grant (2007) and the Shelley Award of the Poetry Society of America (2010).

1. "How I Wrote Certain of My Poems," in *Not Me*, New York, 1991, p. 201.   2. The same, p. 202.

December 9th

I have the same
birthday as John
Milton. Did
you know that?
So I don't have to
write long poems about
heaven & hell—everything's
been lost in my lifetime
& I'm usually blind drunk
and not so serious
either. However . . .
when I am nearly dead
will you read to me
in bed? Will you pre-
tend to be my daughter
or my wife, Whoever,
will you crawl in
& die with Me?

1982   1991

The Sadness of Leaving

Everything's
    so far away—
my jacket's
    over there. I'm terrified
        to go & you
won't miss me
        I'm terrified by the
bright blues of
        the subway
    other days I'm
        so happy &
prepared to believe
        that everyone walking
down the street is
        someone I know.
The oldness of Macy's
        impresses me. The

wooden escalators
as you get
higher up to the furniture,
credit, lampshades—
You shopped here
as a kid. Oh,
you deserve me! In
a movie called
Close Up—once in
a while the wiggly
bars, notice
the wiggly blue
bars of
subway entrances,
the grainy beauty,
the smudge. I won't
kill myself today. It's
too beautiful. My heart
breaking down 23rd
St. To share this
with you, the
sweetness of the
frame. My body
in perfect shape
for nothing but
death. I want
to show you this.
On St. Mark's Place
a madman screams:
my footsteps, the
drumbeats of Armageddon.
Oh yes bring me
closer to you Lord.
I want to die
Close Up. A handful
of bouncing yellow
tulips for David.   I
admit I love tulips
because they
die so beautifully.
                              I

see salvation in

their hanging heads.
A beautiful exit. How do
        they get to
            feel so free? I am
        trapped by love—
            over french fries
        my eyes wander to
            The Hue Bar. A blue
        sign. Across the
    life. On my way to
        making a point,
            to making
                logic, to not
    falling in love to-
            night and
        let my pain remain
            unwrapped—to push
    the machine—Paul's
        staying in touch, but
    oh remember Jessica
        Lange, she looked so
                beautiful all
            doped up, on her
        way to meet King
            Kong. I sit
    on my little red
        couch in February
        how do they get
            to feel so free
    1,000,000 women
            not me moving through
    the street tonight
        of this filmy
            city & I
                crown myself
            again & again
            and there
            can't be
                two kings.

1987   1991

Bleeding Hearts

Know what
I'm jealous of?
Last night.
It held
us both
in its
big black
arms
& today
I hold
between
my legs
a shivering
pussy.
Bleeding &
shaking
wet with
memory
grief &
relief.
I don't know
why the universe
chose me
to be female
so much beauty
& pain,
so much
going on
inside
all this
change
everywhere
coins falling
all over
the bed
& death
is a dream.
Deep in
the night
with thousands

of lovers
the sucking
snapping
reeling
flesh
deep in
the cavity
of endless
night across
mounds
of bodies
I peer over
is it
love or
war. The hollow
creeping
cheek
where
I was
born.

1995

Immanence

All the doors in my home are open.
There's a pulse outside I want to hear

The phone's unplugged.
The pastiche of you on me would be unforgivable now.

If there's a god squirming around
she sees me & is me.
I wish the birds were souls, invisible.
I wish they were what I think they are; pure sound.

1995

Each Defeat

Please! Keep
reading me
Blake
because you're going to make
me the greatest
poet of
all time

Keep smoothing
the stones in the
driveway
let me fry an egg
on your ass
& I'll pick up
the mail.

I feel your
absence in
the morning
& imagine your
instant mouth
let me move
in with you—
Travelling
wrapping your limbs
on my back
I grow man woman
Child
I see wild wild wild

Keep letting the
day be massive
Unlicensed
Oh please have
my child
    I'm a little
    controlling
    Prose has some
    Magic. Morgan
had a

whore in
her lap. You
Big fisherman
I love my
Friends.

I want to lean
my everything
with you
make home for your hubris
I want to read the words you circld over and over again
A slow skunk walking across the road
Yellow, just kind
of pausing
picked up the warm
laundry. I just saw a coyote
tippy tippy tippy
I didn't tell you about the creature with hair
long hair, it was hit by cars on the highway
Again and again. It had long grey hair
It must've been a dog; it could've been
Ours. Everyone loses their friends.

I couldn't tell anyone about this sight.
Each defeat
Is sweet.

2007

The Frames

In San Diego

where only the power

boxes

are painted

like art

I think the world

is a fucking mother

less

hole; flowers

scrambling around the

strong black

box.

I bought this

cd in Ireland.

It's a little morose

a little pretty

now I

learn it's

a hit

I wish

I were a boy

in England

not Irish

I wish I

was an American

knife

shiny

not

a life

2007

C. D. Wright
b. 1949

C. D. Wright was born and raised in Mountain Home, Arkansas, in the Ozarks. She attended public and state schools including the University of Memphis and briefly attended law school before leaving to pursue an M.F.A. from the University of Arkansas. Her father was a judge and her mother a court reporter. "Of the choices revealed to me," she says, "crime and art were the only ones with any sex appeal."[1] Her background undoubtedly prepared her for the public life of the word, which came full circle when she wrote with Deborah Luster *One Big Self: An Investigation* (2003), a book-length work based on her artist's residency at a woman's prison.

In 1979, she took a position at the Poetry Center, San Francisco State University, where she came into contact with the developing language poetry scene. In 1983, she moved to Providence, Rhode Island, to teach at Brown University, where she is Israel J. Kapstein Professor of English.

Wright's poetry books include *String Light* (1991), *Just Whistle* (1993), *Tremble* (1996), *Deepstep Come Shining* (1998), *Steal Away: New and Selected Poems* (2002), *Rising, Falling, Hovering* (2008), *40 Watts* (2009), and *One With Others* (2010). She has also written a book of essays, *Cooling Time* (2005).

In an essay on poetics, Wright has written, "If you have any particular affinity for poetry associated with the South, it is with idiom. I credit hill people and African Americans for keeping the language distinct. Poetry should repulse assimilation; each poet's task is to fight her own language's assimilation. Miles Davis said, 'The symphony, man, they got seventy guys all playing one note.' He also said, 'those dark Arkansas roads, that is the sound I am after.' He had his own sound. He recommended we get ours."[2]

Wright declares: "Unlike, say, Oppen, I am not a purist. I am capable and comfortable with many vulgarities both in word and deed, especially in word. And I did not understand when I made this commitment that to choose being a poet meant I would be speaking what David Antin refers to as a 'sacred language . . . the object of a specialized cult.' Or if I did have such an inkling when I first undertook to write poetry, I didn't think anything was wrong with that at the time. Now I am sure poetry's status is as he defined it and I oppose this exclusive and near meaningless status, yet I persist."[3]

Wright has received a Guggenheim Fellowship, a MacArthur Fellowship, the Griffin Poetry Prize, and the National Book Critics Circle Award.

---

1. Introduction to her section, *American Hybrid*, New York, 2009, p. 481.   2. C. D. Wright, "Provisional Remarks on Being / A Poet / Of Arkansas," *Southern Review* 30:4 (Autumn 1994), 809–811, found at Modern American Poetry, http://www.english.illinois.edu/maps/poets/s_z/cdwright/ownwork.htm.   3. "69 Hidebound Opinions, Propositions, and Several Asides from

a Manila Folder Concerning the Stuff of Poetry," from *By Herself*, ed. Molly McQuade, Port Townsend, WA, 1999, found at Modern American Poetry, http://www.english.illinois.edu/maps/poets/s_z/cdwright/opinions.htm.

FROM *One Big Self*

Count your fingers

Count your toes

Count your nose holes

Count your blessings

Count your stars (lucky or not)

Count your loose change

Count the cars at the crossing

Count the miles to the state line

Count the ticks you pulled off the dog

Count your calluses

Count your shells

Count the points on the antlers

Count the newjack's keys

Count your cards; cut them again

＊

Count heads. Count the men's. Count the women's. There are five main counts in the cell or work area. 4:45 first morning count. Inmate must stand for the count. The count takes as long as it takes. Control Center knows how many should be in what area. No one moves from area A to area B without Control knowing. If i/m is stuck out for the count i/m receives a write-up. Three write-ups, and i/m goes to lockdown. Once

in lockdown, you will relinquish your things:
plastic soapdish, jar of vaseline, comb or hairpick, paperback
Upon return to your unit the inventory officer
will return your things:

soapdish, vaseline, comb, hairpick, paperback
Upon release you may have your possessions:
soapdish, vaseline, comb, pick, book
Whereupon your True Happiness can begin

In the Mansion of Happiness:

Whoever possesses CRUELTY

Must be sent back to JUSTICE

Whoever gets into IDLENESS

Must come to POVERTY

Whoever becomes a SABBATHBREAKER

Must be taken to the Pillory and there remain until he loses 2 turns

      I want to go home, Patricia whispered.

                  I won't say I like being in prison, but I have
learned a lot, and I like experiences. The terriblest part is being away
from your families. — Juanita
              I miss my screenporch.

I know every word to every song on *Purple Rain.* — Willie

      I'm never leaving here. — Grasshopper, in front of the woodshop,
posing beside a coffin he built

      This is a kicks' camp. Nothing positive come out of here except the
praying. Never been around this many women in my life. Never picked
up cursing before. — down for manslaughter, forty years

              I've got three. One's seven. One, four. One, one.
I'm twenty-three. The way I found out is, I was in an accident with my
brother. He was looking at some boys playing ball. We had a head-on.

      At the hospital, the doctor says, Miss, why didn't you tell us you

were pregnant. I'm pregnant? I wasn't afraid of my mama. I was afraid of
my daddy. I was supposed to be a virgin. He took it real good though.

The last time you was here I had a headful of bees.

See what I did was, I accidentally killed my brother.
                                        He spoke without inflection.

Asked how many brothers and sisters did he have —
On my mother's side, two brothers, well now, one brother, and
    two sisters.
On my father's side, fifteen sisters.

When I handed Franklin his prints, his face broke.
Damn, he said to no one, *I done got old.*

                        I kept a dog.

When you walk through Capricorn, keep your arms down and close to
    your body.

                    That's my *sign*.

No, she can't have no mattress. No, she can't have no spoon.
    See if she throwed her food yet.

                            No, she can't have no more.

    I am only about thirty-four minutes from home. That's hard.
— George, field line seated on a bag of peas on a flatbed

    My auntie works here, and two of my cousins. If I get in trouble,
get a write-up, my mama knows before supper. — George

    My name is Patricia, but my real name is Zabonia, she spoke softly.

Some have their baby and are brought back on the bus the next day
and act like it doesn't bother them a bit. Some cry all the way. And for
days. — guard

                        That's hard.
                        I don't go there.

My mama was fifteen when she had me. That's common
in the country.

Some can learn, and will be okay.
Some could stay in the class forever and not learn. S—— when she was a
little girl was struck in the head with a machete, and I don't think she'll learn
much more . . .

She is *so* sweet. You wouldn't believe she had did all the things they say
she did.

Don't ask.

My mug shot totally turned me against being photographed.

I miss the moon.
I miss silverware, with a knife,
and maybe even something to cut with it.

I miss a bathtub.
And a toilet. With a lid. And a handle.
And a door.

When Grasshopper came to Big Gola his wife was pregnant. He saw the
baby once. Next when he was twenty. Now he's inside. In Texas. Second
time. But he's short now. He'll get out soon.

That's hard.
I don't go there.

I miss driving.

We're both here because of love. — Zabonia of herself and her best
friend

I am highly hypnotizable.

I would wash that man's feet and drink the water.

2007

Charles Bernstein

b. 1950

Born and raised in New York City, Bernstein attended Harvard University, where he studied with the philosopher Stanley Cavell.

The leading theorist of language poetry, Bernstein was coeditor with Bruce Andrews of the journal $L = A = N = G = U = A = G = E$ as well as *The L = A = N = G = U = A = G = E Book* (1984), a collection of essays. Bernstein's own essays are collected in *Content's Dream: Essays 1975–1984* (1986/2001), *A Poetics* (1992), *My Way* (1999), and *Attack of the Difficult Poems: Essays and Inventions* (2011). His numerous poetry books include *Poetic Justice* (1979), *Controlling Interests* (1980), *Islets/Irritations* (1983/1992), *The Sophist* (1987), *Rough Trades* (1991), *Dark City* (1994), *Republics of Reality: 1975–1995* (2000), *With Strings* (2001), *Girly Man* (2006), and *All the Whiskey in Heaven: Selected Poems* (2010). He has also written the libretto *Shadowtime* (music by Brian Ferneyhough).

In "Artifice of Absorption," an essay in verse, Bernstein makes a distinction between the terms *absorption* ("rhapsodic, spellbinding, / mesmerizing, hypnotic, total, riveting, / enthralling") and *impermeability* ("artifice, boredom, / exaggeration, attention scattering, distraction, digression, interruptive, transgressive"[1]). Absorptive literature depends on realism, transparency, and continuity, while the antiabsorptive, which Bernstein prefers, is comparatively artificial, opaque, and discontinuous in character.

"In my poems," he writes, "I / frequently use opaque & nonabsorbable / elements, digressions & / interruptions, as part of a technological arsenal to create a more powerful ('souped up') absorption than possible with traditional, / & blander, absorptive techniques." Ultimately, the project of "impermeable" writings is "to wake / us from the hypnosis of absorption."[2] Rather than be held captive by the text, the reader is required "to be actively involved in the process of constituting its meaning."[3] Despite the difficulties presented by Bernstein's poetry, it frequently displays an antic sense of humor.

He is series editor, with Hank Lazer, of the Modern and Contemporary Poetics book series; director, with Al Filreis, of PennSound; and editor of *Close Listening: Poetry and the Performed Word* (1998). One of the founding members of the Poetics Program at the State University of New York, Buffalo, Bernstein currently serves as Donald T. Regan Chair in the Department of English at the University of Pennsylvania.

1. *A Poetics*, Cambridge, MA, 1992, p. 29.   2. The same, pp. 52–54.   3. Charles Bernstein, "Writing and Method," in *Content's Dream*, Los Angeles, 1986, p. 233.

The Klupzy Girl

Poetry is like a swoon, with this difference:
it brings you to your senses. Yet his
parables are not singular. The smoke from
the boat causes the men to joke. Not
gymnastic: pyrotechnic. The continuousness
of a smile—wry, perfume scented. No this
would go fruity with all these changes
around. Sense of variety: panic. Like
my eye takes over from the front
yard, three pace. Idle gaze—years
right down the window. Not clairvoyance,
predictions, deciphering—enacting. Analytically,
i.e., thoughtlessly. Begin to push and cue
together. Or I originate out of this
occurrence, stoop down, bend on. The
Protest-ant's voice within, calling for
this to be shepherded, for moment's
expression's enthroning. Able to be
alibied (contiguity of vacuity). Or
do you think you can communicate
telepathetically? Verena read the epistle
with much deliberateness. If we are
not to be phrasemongers, we must
sit down and take the steps that will
give these policies life. I fumbled clumsily
with the others—the evocations, explanations,
glossings of "reality" seemed like stretching
it to cover ground rather than make
or name or push something through.
"But the most beautiful
of all doubts is when the downtrodden
and despairing raise their heads and
stop believing in the strength of their oppressors."
To be slayed by such sighs: a noble figure
in a removed entranceway.
"This is just a little note
to say that it was nice working with
all of you. It has been a rewarding
experience in many ways. Although I
am looking forward to my new position with

great anticipation, I shall never forget
the days I spent here. It was like
a home-away-from-home, everyone was
just so warm and friendly. I shall ever
remember you in my prayers, and I
wish you the best for the future." Preoccupations
immediately launch: to set straight, to glean
from her glance. Terrifically bored
on the bus. Any really you want
go to mixed on me. Sumptuous slump.
As it becomes apparent. Just that I thought.
Contraction that to you perhaps an
idealization. Have I kept. But that
point is—such repair as roads no
joint, what?, these few years must
admit to not expecting, as if the
silent rudeness might separate us out. &
maybe anger would be better than explaining.
When in tents or families in comparative.
Which sums digest. Disclaimer
alights what with begin. That's
maybe the first pace, the particular. I mean
I feel I've got to and a few while
I can just look to see unrelenting
amount of canny criticism whatever
occasions overriding for comparison
spin for the sake of intrinsic in that
or that I've already made although
against reaction's consequent proceeding.
But it's to the point that you've
begun to broach like you could almost
fault me on as if you were going to
use could become primarily propulsion
to affinity have itself so. She
gets nutty. Oh she settles in, she
settles the curdles, unhooks the latches,
but I, preferring hatches . . .
When batters, benumbs, the lights
in a basket, portable. Potted & make
believe—your rudeness amounts to not
noticing, i.e., I'm on a different
scale of jags. To be in replacement

for a number of linings. Tubes of turmoil.
To stroll on the beach is to be in
the company of the wage-earner and
the unemployed on the public way, but
to command a view of it from a vantage
both recessed and elevated is to enter
the bourgeois space; here vantage and view
become consumable. I can't describe
how insulted I felt, it's a ruthlessness
not so much I didn't know you possessed
as that I didn't think you'd turn
on me. When you stop acting in good
faith any residue of the relationship
gets really unpleasant and the gratuitous
discounting severs what I can't necessarily
define the circumferences of. "There are a
number of calls in the June bill
which I have been unable to document. We
believe these calls were made by S———
O———who is no longer employed by
this project. We presume these calls
to be program related although she
did not keep a log of long distance
calls as requested in the memo
circulated March 11, 1980." It has
more to me than please to note acquits
defiant spawn. But your letter does
not scan its view nor serve our
own resolve. Little noticing sectored
demonstration, or flail with inheld
throng. Content to meet or not to meet
what inlays subsequent flustered
adjustment. "The Good *is*
for the fact that I will it, and apart
from willing it, it has no existence."
"There is no document of civilization
that is not at the same time a
document of barbarism." Blue suede pestilence.
Binds bins. History and civilization
represented as aura—piles
of debris founded on a law and mythology
whose bases are in violence, the release

from which a Messianic moment
in which history itself is vanquished.
That's why I'm perplexed
at your startlement, though obviously
it's startling to see contexts changed on you
to have that done to you and
delivered unbeknownst. The Ideal
swoops, and reascends. "With real
struggle, genuine tax relief
can be won." A manic
state of careless grace. Mylar juggernauts
zig-zag penuriously. Car smashed into;
camera stolen; hat lost; run out of
money, write for money, money doesn't come.
Long interruption as I talk to woman
most of the way back—a runner,
very pleasant. Get off in Boston and everything
seems to go crazy.

> All of gets where
> Round dog-eared head
> The clear to trying
> Forgets issues of trembles
> Address vestiges to remain
> These years after all
> Fog commends in discourse

1983

Dysraphism

Did a wind come just as you got up or were
you protecting me from it? I felt the abridgement
of imperatives, the wave of detours, the saber-
rattling of inversion. *All lit up and no
place to go.* Blinded by avenue and filled with
adjacency. Arch or arched at. So there becomes bottles,
hushed conductors, illustrated proclivities for puffed-
up benchmarks. Morose or comatose. "Life is what
you find, existence is what you repudiate." A good example
of this is 'Dad pins puck.' Sometimes something
sunders; in most cases, this is no more than a hall.
No where to go but pianissimo (protection of market

soaring). "Ma always fixes it just like I
like it." Or here valorize what seem to put off
in other. No excuse for that! You can't
watch ice sports with the lights on! Abnormal fluid retention,
inveterate inundation. Surely as wrongheaded as
but without its charm. No identification, only
restitution. But he has forced us to compel this offer;
it comes from policy not love. "Fill
the water glasses—ask each person
if they would like
more coffee, etc." *Content's
dream.* The
journey is
far, the
rewards inconsequential. Heraldically defamed.
Go—it's—gotten. Best
of the spoils: gargoyles. Or is a pretend wish
that hits the springs to sing with sanguine
bulk. "Clean everything from the table except
water, wine, and ashtrays; use separate plate to
remove salt & pepper." Ignorant
I confront, wondering at
I stand. We need
to mention that this is one
that applies to all eyes and that its application is only on the
most basic and rudimentary
level. Being
comfortable with and also
inviting and satisfying.
The pillar's tale: a windowbox onto society.
But heed not the pear that blows in your
brain. God's poison is the concept of
conceptlessness—anaerobic breath.
No less is culled no more vacated—temptation's
flight is always to
beacon's hill—the soul's
mineshaft.
Endless strummer. There is never annul-
ment, only abridgement. The Northern Lights is
the universe's paneled basement. Joy
when jogged. Delight in
forefright. Brushstrokes

on the canals of the . . . , moles on
sackcloth. "People like you don't need
money—you breed contempt." Some way such
toxic oases. This growth of earls, as on a failing
day, gurgling arboreally. Shoes that
shock. I'd
give to you my monkey, my serenade, my shopping bag;
but you require constancy, not weights. Who
taking the lump denies the pot, a beam of
buckram. Or they
with their, you
with your. Another
shot, another stop—dead
as floor board. Pardon my declension: short
parade. "Refill platter and pass to
everybody." A
sound is a sum—a sash
of seraphs. Bored loom.
Extension is never more than a form of content. "I
know how you feel, Joe. Nobody likes to admit
his girl is that smart." "I feel how you know,
Joe, like nobody to smart that girl is his admit."
A wavering kind of sort—down the tube, doused
in tub, a run of the stairs. You should shoot! But
by the time I'd sided. Magisterially calm and pompous.
Pump ass! A wash
of worry (the worldhood of
the whirl). Or: "Nice being here with anybody." Slips
find the most indefatigable invaginations, surreptitious
requiems.
Surfeit, sure fight.
Otherwise—flies,
detergent whines, flimflam psychosis. Let's:
partition the petulance, roast
the arrears, succor the sacred. "If you don't keep up
with culture, culture will keep up
with you." Sacral dosing, somewhat
hosting. Thread
threads the threads, like
thrush. Thrombolytic cassette. "While all of this is
going on, young Sir Francis Rose—a painter of dubious
gifts whom Gertrude Stein espoused for the last decade

of her life—appears as if out of nowhere with a
painting." If you mix with him you're mixing
with a metaphor. "It's
a realistic package, it's a
negotiable package, it's
not a final package." Glibness
of the overall, maybe: there is always something dripping
through.
We seem to be retreading the same tire
over and over, with no additional traction. Here
are some additional panes—optional. Very busy
by now reorganizing and actually, oddly, added
into fractionation ratio, as you might say. Or just
hitting against, back to everybody.
Reality is always greener
when you haven't seen her.
Anyway just to go on and be where you weren't or couldn't be
before—steps, windows, ramps. To let
all that other not so much dissolve as
blend into an horizon of distraction, distension
pursued as homing ground
(a place to bar the leaks). Say,
vaccination of cobalt emissaries pregnant with bivalent
exasperation, protruding with inert material. I
can't but sway, hopeful in my way. Perhaps
portend, tarry. The galoshes are, e.g.,
gone; but you are here. Transient cathexis, Doppler
angst. And then a light comes on
in everybody's head. "So I think
that somewhere we ought to make the point that it's really
a team approach." Riddled
with riot. What
knows not scansion admits
expansion: tea leaves
decoy
for the grosser fortune—the slush
of afternoon, the morning's replay. Prose,
pose—relentless
furrier.
Poem, chrome. "I
don't like the way you think":
a mind is a terrible thing to spend.
That is, in prose you start with the world

and find the words to match; in poetry you start
with the words and find the world in them. "Bring
soup in—very hot." "You
couldn't find your way
out of a blanched potato." Silence
can also be a tool
but it is seldom as effective as blindness.
His quarter, and heir to his heart, whom he purpled
with his fife, does bridle purpose to pursue
tides with unfolded scowls, and, pinched in this
array, fools compare with slack-weary ton.
Dominion demands distraction—the circus
ponies of the slaughter home. Braced
by harmony, bludgeoned by decoration
the dream surgeon hobbles three steps over, two
steps beside. "In those days you didn't have to
shout to come off as expressive." One by one
the clay feet are sanded, the sorrows remanded.
A fleet of ferries, forever merry.
Show folks know that what the fighting man wants
is to win the war and come home.

1987

Whose Language

Who's on first? The dust descends as
the skylight caves in. The door
closes on a dream of default and
denunciation (go get those piazzas),
hankering after frozen (prose) ambiance
(ambivalence). Doors to fall in bells
to dust, nuances to circumscribe.
Only the real is real: the little
girl who cries out "Baby! Baby!"
but forgets to look in the mirror
—of a . . . It doesn't really
matter whose, only the appointment
of a skewed and derelict parade.
My face turns to glass, at last.

1991

Virtual Reality

For Susan

Swear
   there is a sombrero
of illicit
    desquamation
(composition).

    I forgot to
get the
    potatoes but the lakehouse
(ladle)
   is spent
asunder. Gorgeous
   gullibility—
or,
   the origin
   of testiness
(testimony).

Laura
  does the laundry, Larry
lifts lacunas.

    Such that
details commission of
      misjudgment over 30-day
intervals.

         By
the sleeve is the
    cuff & cuff
link (lullaby, left offensive,
    houseboat).
Nor
    let your unconscious
get the better of you.
    Still, all ropes
lead somewhere, all falls
    cut to fade.

I.e.: 4 should always be followed
    by 6, 6 by 13.

  Or if
      individuality is a false
front, group solidarity is a
   false fort.

"ANY MORE FUSSING & YOU'LL
     GO RIGHT TO YOUR ROOM!"

She flutes that slurp
admiringlier.

     Any more blustering & I
  collapse as deciduous
        replenishment.

  So away the
swivels, corpusculate the
  dilatations.
    For I've
learned that relations
      are a small
twig in the blizzard
    of projections
 & expectations.
  The story
not capacity but care—
     not size but desire.

  & despair
makes dolts of any persons, shimmering
in the quiescence of
longing, skimming
    disappointment & mixing it
with
    breeze.

   The sting of
  recognition triggers
  the memory & try to

take that apart (put
that together).

Popeye
no longer sails, but Betty
Boop will always
sing sweetlier
sweetliest
than the crow who fly
against the blank
remorse of castles made
by dusk, dissolved in
day's baked light.

1994

A Defence of Poetry

For Brian McHale

My problem with deploying a term liek
nonelen
in these cases is acutually similar to
your
cirtique of the term ideopigical
unamlsing as a too-broad unanuajce
interprestive proacdeure.
You say too musch lie a steamroller when
we need dental (I;d say jeweller's)
tools.
(I thin youy misinterpret the natuer of
some of the poltical claims go; not
themaic
interpretatiomn of evey
evey detail in every peim
but an oeitnetation towatd a kind of
texutal practice
that you prefer to call "nknsense" but
for *poltical* purpses I prepfer to call
ideological!
, say Hupty Dumpty)

Taht is, nonesene see,msm to reduce a
vareity of fieefernt
prosdodic, thematic and discusrive
enactcemnts into a zeroo degree of
sense. What we have is a vareity of
valences. Nin-sene.sense is too binary
andoppostioin, too much oall or nithing
account with ninesense seeming by its
very meaing to equl no sense at all. We
have preshpas a blurrig of sense, whih
means not relying on convnetionally
methods of *conveying* sense but whih may
aloow for dar greater sense-smakinh than
specisigusforms of doinat disoucrse that
makes no sense at all by irute of thier
hyperconventionality (Bush's speeches,
calssically). Indeed you say that
nonsenese shed leds on its "antithesis"
sense making: but teally the antithsisi
of these poems you call nonselnse is not
sense-making itslef but perhps, in some
cases, the simulation of sense-making:
decitfullness, manifpulation, the
media-ization of language, etc.
I don't agree with Stewart that "the
more exptreme the discontinuities . . . the
more nonsisincial": I hear sense
beginning to made in this sinstances.
Te probelm though is the definaitonof
sense. What you mean by nomsense is
soething like a-rational, but ratio (and
this goes back to Blake not to meanion
the pre-Socaratics) DOES NOT EQUAL
sense! This realtioes to the sort of
oscillation udnertood as rhytmic or
prosidci, that I disusccio in Artiofice.
Crucialy, the duck/rabitt exmaple is one
of the ambiguity of *aspects* and clearly
not a bprobelm of noneselnse: tjere are
two competing, completely sensible,
readings, not even any blurring; the

issue is context-depednece)otr
apsrevcyt blindness as Witegenstein
Nonesesen is too static. Deosnt't
Prdunne even say int e eoem "sense occurs
"at the contre-coup:: in the process of
oscillatio itself.
b6y the waylines 9–10 are based on an
aphorism by Karl Kraus: *the closer we
look at a word the greater the distance
from which it stares back.*

1999

This Line

This line is stripped of emotion.
This line is no more than an
illustration of a European
theory. This line is bereft
of a subject. This line
has no reference apart
from its context in
this line. This line
is only about itself.
This line has no meaning:
its words are imaginary, its
sounds inaudible. This line
cares not for itself or for
anyone else—it is indifferent,
impersonal, cold, uninviting.
This line is elitist, requiring,
to understand it, years of study
in stultifying libraries, poring
over esoteric treatises on
impossible to pronounce topics.
This line refuses reality.

1999

Castor Oil

For Emma

I went looking for my soul
In the song of a minor bird
But I could not find it there
Only the shadow of my thinking

The slow sea slaps slow water
On the ever farther shore
And myself pulled under
In the uneven humming
Of the still wavering warps

Tuneless, I wander, sundered
In lent blends of remote display
Until the bottom bottoms
In song-drenched light, cradled fold

2006

Cecil S. Giscombe

b. 1950

Cecil Giscombe was born and raised in Dayton, Ohio. He received degrees from the State University of New York at Albany and Cornell, where he was editor of *Epoch*. He has taught at Cornell, Syracuse, Illinois State, and Penn State universities. He currently teaches at the University of California at Berkeley.

Giscombe's books of poetry include *Here* (1994), *Giscome Road* (1998), which won the Carl Sandburg Award for poetry, and *Prairie Style* (2008), as well as the chapbooks *Postcards* (1977), *At Large* (1989), and *Two Sections from Giscome Road* (1995). His comparatively spare production reflects the precision of his research, as well as the meditative depth at which he conducts it, often by traveling to a place close at hand, on bicycle.

Giscome Road is a unique and also characteristic project, a "powerful, understated meditation on place," based on Giscombe's travels to specific locales in northern British Columbia named for the nineteenth-century Jamaican miner John Robert Giscome, believed to be the poet's ancestor. Giscombe's work is therefore a poetry of place, in the tradition of William Carlos Williams's *Paterson*, Charles Olson's *Maximus*, and Ed Dorn's *Gunslinger*. It is also a poetry of race. The "Indianapolis, Indiana" section of *Prairie Style* is introduced by the following: "The Tribe of Ishmael, or Ishmaelites, was a tightly-knit nomadic community of African, Native American, and 'poor white' descent, estimated to number about 10,000. Fugitives from the South, they arrived in the central part of the Old Northwest at the beginning of the nineteenth century, preceding the other pioneers. After a century of fierce culture conflict with the majority society, the tribe was forcibly dispersed."[1]

In an interview, Giscombe commented, "I see that poetry, race, property, and geography are not one but form a very rag-tag and uncertain army, one with shifting ranks and alliances. What's interesting to me here is that it's possible or even necessary (at least for me) to read each one in the context of the others."[2]

Paula Koneazny writes, "Although true, it would be an oversimplification to say that Giscombe writes about place. It may be more accurate to say that he writes from places. His poetry is nomadic, both in inspiration and execution, always exploring what he aptly refers to as 'range.' At the same time, his is a settled nomadism. Even though always about location's ambiguity, what he refers to as 'the verb for location' in *Giscome Road*, his poems do not just pass through. They are attentive to their surrounds; they stay a while and get to know a place."[3]

Giscombe has also published the prose work *Into and Out of Dislocation* (2000).

1. Hugo Prosper Leaming, *The Ben Ishmael Tribe: Fugitive Nation of the Old Northwest*, in *Prairie Style,* Normal, IL, 2008, p. 87.   2. Mark Nowak, "Prairie Style: an Interview with C. S. Giscombe," Harriet the Blog, http://www.poetryfoundation.org/harriet/2008/08/prairie-style-an-interview-with-cs-giscombe.   3. Review of *Prairie Style, Rain Taxi* Online Edition, Summer, 2009, http://raintaxi.net/online/2009summer/giscombe.shtml.

All (Facts, Stories, Chance): 1–3

to Ken McClane

1.

I'm at no center, big & slack as I am

in my evil nature, in the whole blue funk,

in this for thee & myself—

but source, the argument goes, *gives* denotation,

even our having fanned out can't keep the nomenclature from overtaking us

(at which point/s it finds its own level, suggests the argument)—

the attitude is all locations

being temporary are

themselves "fugitive"—

that is all location is the way out (*north*

in the archetype)—

in the long view that that stays in

held back behind the face keeps *it* whole whatever happens—

the rivers flow outward (as it were) getting wide, an incalculable sum

to the spate of water (metaphoric depth & rush),

all locations are emphatic & come

to know one place
& the various landscape here

the variation of the edges here—

       the railroad sits up there on its bridges up through town, one

line crossing others (metaphoric height & rumble),

the headlight on the Niagara Rainbow might find us if we stood just
right,

before the tracks curved off toward the frontier at the Falls itself—

I dreamed I saw us on the coast

wading in the Atlantic off Senegal, off Gambia,

the coast of beautiful Gabon or Cameroon, I couldn't tell,

but there were white people on the cliffs above us

the pale voices clearly phrased in the wind

at our backs as usual & waking I saw it had been the dunes on Lake
Ontario I saw,

that we'd been at the end of Rte 414, at the end of upstate N.Y.,

that it was Canada across the water,

more ambiguous than we'd thought for an archetype

all invisible etc to be so big

2.

In another we walked through a small shopping center near here, the
far edge

of which was dominated in the dream by a K-Mart store, & out

through the store's dark back-rooms past
                the stacked boxes & the time clock, all
the service doors looked out
on the employees' parking lot & the dumpsters
                   but one, which opened
onto a path through tall grass & up

an embankment, across a gravel road
               & then down through the trees under a hillside—

            all the trouble

& misinformation about which door
was which had made us short w/ one another & so our faces closed up

getting all exact,

all unhidden & still the shapelessness of, even as we walked on,

the relation to *here,* our source between us at face level

    ✿ ✿ ✿

(In another the archetypal convict had escaped & it fell to thee & me,
old buddy,

to bring him in, we in our Ivy League suits, he

at large—
           When the captain sd "Where's the trail?" we sd "It swam on"

      —yet *we* were ambivalent, of many minds vis-à-vis serving

the state: culture was more than indefinite, it was an archipelago

of colonies, all names
had fled from memory & from the map both,

I saw typescript loose in the air all around our location when we spoke
in the dream,

the sentences disembodied but readable—

                    (You'd wanted to go start in Cuba
by talking to Guillen about vodun & santeria,
I'd wanted to head back to Dayton, Dayton being curiously the furthest
back

I was willing to extend, the view being the all-but-truly-Negro country
SW of the city proper,

the long view at the apparently stable edge,

the convergence of landscape

along the long roads in

from out of the landscape

—the view past the corporation markers framed by them, the
markers—

the ambivalence starting just out there (in memory)

    ❀ ❀ ❀

                  I'm at no center myself, we were at
in fact, in a *true* story, the edge of Ithaca, N.Y. where

the country comes *in* on hillsides & in triangles

and there 3 black boys were,

feeding a horse grass from the outside of the fence around him—

"Look," I sd as we went by in your Omni on our way

to East Hill Plaza, my long view connected &
detached both,

unrepeating but caught in looking & looking & looking,

in a tendency towards the sentimental,

in a fit

(in a funk),

in the way in & further in at the look itself

of some home or some one

of the metaphors,

the past's whole long self giving the name

to some thing at loggerheads w/ nothing—

   I'd have disclosed it willingly if I could've

        3.

A long song flows out of the future, noise

from no locations, sounding like nothing,

the chance voices edged out,

which were central to it,

not in theory but which waded

through the music as though the singers were looking *for* something

as though the singers were intent on missing nothing

of what they could see in the music

of what they could say in the music:

this was no "universal"—

lost in no old blue woods along the flood at morning,

lost along no railroad under some moon, looking somewhere off ahead:

this was not natcheral or unnatcheral either one.

I'm large, though, at

all edges

& pleased at the company on the trip to near home

on the way to near home

which is an unempathic landscape so

smooth to the eye, a repeating un-

deceptive surface bisected, fanning out,

more than the little intrigue memory is

the agreement sustained
& waiting both, someplace

(everyplace source was

(now music's at the lips,

at soul's opaque & unbroken surface that looked

so smooth from far off,

unimaginably intricate at the thick lip

1994

Far

Inland suffers its foxes: full-moon fox, far-flung fox — flung him yonder!
went the story — or some fox worn like a weasel round the neck. Foxes are a
simple fact, widespread and local and observable — *Vulpes fulva,* the common
predator, varying in actual color from red to black to rust to tawny brown, pale
only in the headlights.

It's that this far inland the appearance of a fox is more reference than
metaphor. Or the appearance is a demonstration. Sudden appearance, big like
an impulse; or the watcher gains a gradual awareness — in the field, taking

shape and, finally, familiar. The line of sight's fairly clear leaving imagination little to supply. It's a fact to remember, though, seeing the fox and where or, at night, hearing foxes (and where). The fox appearing, coming into view, as if to meet the speaker.

Push comes to shove. Mistah Fox arriving avec luggage, sans luggage.

2008

Day Song

Nothing to the sky but its blank endless chaos — old blue skies — , nothing to it when it meets the eye. To me half a belief's better by far or one broken into halves.

Trim paragraphs of uninflected speech hung over the prairie, sound's origin. Eros came up out of its den in the embankment — came out tawny, came out swarthy, came out more "dusky" than "sienna." The sky was a glass of water. White men say cock and black men say dick. One gets even in the midwest, one gets even in the midwest, one gets even in the midwest. Eros was a common barnyard pest, now coming to be seen in suburban settings as well, a song with lyrics, clarified and "refined" both. The day lengthened like they do but everything was over by nightfall. To me, it's foxes (most days).

2008

Prairie Style

The direction giving out — in the business past direction then and avoiding love's blunt teeth there. Done with houses and wanting to be seen as a boundary or as a line of plot re-appearing, done with all that too. Houses cleave and, to me, it all gets hammered out in overstatement — love's a terror, a revelation cleaving to contours. Love's a terror, in town and out of town too.

I was an unqualified marker, some days the ache of an implicit region. Nothing to the bear but bad hair. Having missed the trace the first time through I found coming a specificity hard to pronounce: river of unaccented speech, a single voice to mark it all off. Well this is namelessness up here, this is inward, and nothing but the curl will do.

Love's over there, to me, the old terror.

2008

John Yau
b. 1950

John Yau was born in Lynn, Massachusetts, a year after his parents emigrated from China. He was educated at Bard College and Brooklyn College, where he studied with John Ashbery.

His poetry books include *The Sleepless Night of Eugene Delacroix* (1980), *Broken Off by the Music* (1981), *Corpse and Mirror* (1983), *Radiant Silhouette: New & Selected Work 1974–1988* (1989), *Edificio Sayonara* (1992), *Forbidden Entries* (1996), *Borrowed Love Poems* (2002), *Paradiso Diaspora* (2006), and *Exhibits* (2010). He has written art criticism for *Art in America, Artforum, ARTnews,* and *Vogue,* among other magazines. His books on art include *In the Realm of Appearances: The Art of Andy Warhol* (1993), *The United States of Jasper Johns* (1996), *A Thing Among Things: The Art of Jasper Johns* (2009) and *The Passionate Spectator* (2006).

Despite the cool surfaces and uncommitted tone of his early work, which suggest Ashbery's influence, Yau's poetry is not associated with the New York School sensibility. In the mid-1970s, he composed poems using word-substitution games suggested by the work of French novelist Raymond Roussel.[1] By the late 1970s, he had turned to more narrative forms of poetry that also communicate a dreamlike sense of discontinuity. He also began to emphasize political ironies, which made his humor broader and more frontal.

Yau's use of narrative draws on film techniques. "I'm also influenced by movies," Yau claims, "that kind of *speed* of seeing, the seamless jumps, the echoes, and the way something dissolves something else." Although he often uses the materials of memory, Yau believes that "to write about one's life in terms of a subjective 'I' . . . is to fulfill the terms of the oppressor. I suppose I don't know who this 'I' would or could speak for. Myself, what for?"[2]

Yau lives in Brooklyn and has served as art editor of *The Brooklyn Rail* since 2004. He currently teaches art criticism at Mason Gross School of the Arts, Rutgers University. His numerous awards include the Lavan Award from the Academy of American Poets, the Jerome J. Shestack the Award from *American Poetry Review,* and a Guggenheim Fellowship.

1. Edward Foster, "An Interview with John Yau," *Talisman* 5, Fall 1990, p. 43.   2. The same, pp. 48, 49.

Unpromising Poem

I am writing to you from the bedroom of my ex-wife, where I have been stenciling diagrams on sheets and ceiling, intricate star charts of the paths modern soldier ants take to reach the lips waiting at the end of their long journey. There are no red messages in the balloons floating overhead, no tasty tidbits left from the first meeting. I have been told that the soft meat gets softer in the harsh helixes of the second sun.

I am writing to you from the bedroom of my ex-wife, the room in which flocks of birds have returned to the shelves of their one-syllable caves.

Dust settles on the eyelids of those who have yet to emerge from the shadows. Blue sparks etch the edges where the sky falls away, and black clouds fill the chalkboard with sleeping children.

I am writing to you from the bedroom my ex-wife keeps in her bedroom, the Library of Unusual Exceptions, Book of Gaudy Exemptions, Ledger of Lost Opportunities, wavelengths of archaeological soot drifting through the screen.

I am writing to you from the sleeping car temporarily disabled in the bedroom of my ex-wife. Dear Corraded Clouds, Dear Correspondence Principle, Dear Axle, Enzyme, and Ash, Dear Example of Excellence,
are you Frigg or Freya? Hoop Snake or Hoosegow?

O turtle in a kirtle, why must you chortle so?

Dear Hangman of Harbin, why did I wake in the bedroom of my ex-wife?

Dear ex-wife, I have learned to accept the small pleasures that come with being
    called
The Hangman of Harbin.

                                      2005

Screen Name

John Yau is calling, his name has come up on the screen of my cell phone. This makes me uneasy because I am John Yau, and I would like to believe that I am always answering to myself. I decide not to press the green button and see if the caller will leave a message. Since he has my name, and I his, maybe he knows what I was thinking when the phone started vibrating in my shirt pocket, pressed up hard against my nipple, my hands thrust in my pockets, and the air tingling. The shaking subsides, but no envelope indicating that I have received a message floats towards me. I fold up the phone and put it back in my breast pocket. It is

Wednesday, and the long-necked geese have started returning to the chimneys of my hometown.

After I realized that I must be the only one who thinks of a cell phone as a cell phone, and not as an efficient means of achieving a heightened spiritual state, I wondered how many friends would tell me the true purposes to which they put their cell phone, and if any found it to be an efficient instrument of physical satisfaction. I decided to call my friends and ask them if they have used or know of anyone who has used a cell phone as a vibrator.

Since the advent of the electric toothbrush, the idea that a common household object could be used to achieve sexual satisfaction of at least the second rank is not a completely foreign particle entering imagination's petrie dish. This hard oblong shape, some with extensions, could have been used in a variety of other ways, but I want to limit the scope of my research. There could be a new definition of phone sex that hasn't become part of our patois.

Might not the following scenario have already transpired countless times in places like Pompeii, Illinois, and Gutenberg, Kansas?? Sheila has gotten out of the shower and, after vigorously drying herself off with her new deep pile purple towel, placed her red cell phone in the appropriate position. After punching a series of buttons, she leans back in her Mies Van Der Rohe recliner, and waits for her favorite daytime romance to come on, a show that is broadcast from an island and therefore not subject to the same restrictions governing similar shows broadcast from places closer to her modest tract home. It is a little past nine in the morning, and Sheila is waiting for her boyfriend Tyson to call, as he does every morning whenever he is away on business.

Standing at a different latitude and longitude is Tyson, who has just jammed his cell phone deep into his pants' pocket. It is Thursday and he is waiting for Sheila to call him, as she does every Thursday that he is away. He is alone at the bus stop, trying to remember which bus will carry him to his destination. He is unsure if he should go north, towards the industrial park, its tasteful array of gleaming towers, or south towards the new amusement center, its computer managed drums of centrifugal force. The sun seems brighter than yesterday, when he was closer to the equator. His phone begins vibrating, slowly at first, and then faster and faster and faster. He is no longer sure what conditions prevail in the time zone that he has entered. Suppose it is Thursday only here, and it is not Sheila who is calling, but his brother who will ask him for a non-refundable loan, or someone from work, checking to see if he has his papers in order. He is glad that he got his and Sheila's phone customized. He was happy to have commissioned a friend of a friend whose specialty is ermine cell phone pouches. His phone keeps becoming agitated, as if its mission remains unaccomplished. Doesn't he have an appointment to meet someone? Isn't he supposed to meet a man by the name of John How or Chow? He is unsure of how to pronounce the man's surname, which sounds simple but a competitive co-worker or jealous underling might have set a trap. Even though it is past noon, he decides he must call Sheila, who has had more experience with the pitfalls one encounters when dealing with foreign names.

A cell phone in another time zone begins vibrating and vibrating. A hand moves it to another location.

2005

Ing Grish

You need to speak Singlish to express a Singaporean feeling.
—CATHERINE LIU

I never learned Singlish

I cannot speak Taglish, but I have registered
the tonal shifts of Dumglish, Bumglish, and Scumglish

I do not know Ing Grish, but I will study it down to its
black and broken bones

I do not know Ing Gwish, but I speak dung and dungaree,
satrap and claptrap

Today I speak barbecue and canoe

Today I speak running dog and yellow dog

I do not know Spin Gloss, but I hear humdrum and humdinger,
bugaboo and jigaboo

I do not know Ang Grish, but I can tell you that my last name
consists of three letters, and that technically all of them are vowels

I do not know Um Glish, but I do know how to eat with two sticks

Oh but I do know English because my father's mother was English
and because my father was born in New York in 1921
and was able to return to America in 1949
and become a citizen

I no speak Chinee, Chanel, or Cheyenne
I do know English because I am able to tell others
that I am not who they think I am

I do not know Chinese because my mother said that I refused to learn it
from the moment I was born, and that my refusal
was one of the greatest sorrows of her life,
the other being the birth of my brother

I do know Chinese because I understood what my mother's friend told her
one Sunday morning, shortly after she sat down for tea:
"I hope you don't that I parked my helicopter on your roof"

Because I do not know Chinese I have been told that means
I am not Chinese by a man who translates from the Spanish.
He said that he had studied Chinese and was therefore closer
to being Chinese than I could ever be. No one publicly disagreed with him,
Which, according to the rules of English, means he is right

I do know English and I know that knowing it means
that I don't always believe it

The fact that I disagree with the man who translates from the Spanish
is further proof that I am not Chinese because all the Chinese
living in America are hardworking and earnest
and would never disagree with someone who is right.
This proves I even know how to behave in English

I do not know English because I got divorced and therefore
I must have misunderstood the vows I made at City Hall

I do know English because the second time I made a marriage vow
I had to repeat it in Hebrew

I do know English because I know what "fortune cookie" means
when it is said of a Chinese woman

The authority on poetry announced that I discovered that I was Chinese
when it was to my advantage to do so

My father was afraid that if I did not speak English properly
I would be condemned to work as a waiter in a Chinese restaurant.
My mother, however, said that this was impossible because
I didn't speak Cantonese, because the only language
waiters in Chinese restaurants know how to speak was Cantonese

I do not know either Cantonese or English, Ang Glish or Ing Grish

Anguish is a language everyone can speak, but no one listens to it

I do know English because my father's mother was Ivy Hillier.
She was born and died in Liverpool, after living in America and China,
and claimed to be a descendant of the Huguenots

I do know English because I misheard my grandmother and thought
she said that I was a descendant of the Argonauts

I do know English because I remember what "Made in Japan" meant
when I was a child

I learn over and over again that I do not know Chinese.
Yesterday a man asked me how to write my last name in Chinese,
because he was sure that I had been mispronouncing it
and that if this was how my father pronounced it,
then the poor man had been wrong all his life

I do not know Chinese even though my parents conversed in it every day.
I do know English because I had to ask the nurses not to put my mother
in a straitjacket, and reassure them that I would be willing to stay with her
until the doctor came the next morning

I do know English because I left the room when the doctor told me
I had no business being there

I do not know Chinese because during the Vietnam War
I was called a gook instead of a chink and realized
that I had managed to change my spots without meaning to

I do not know English because when father said that he would
like to see me dead, I was never sure quite what he meant

I do not know Chinese because I never slept with a woman
whose vagina slanted like my mother's eyes

I do not know either English or Chinese and, because of that,
I did not put a gravestone at the head of my parents' graves
as I felt no language mirrored the ones they spoke.

2005

Maxine Chernoff

b. 1952

Born and raised in Chicago and chair of Creative Writing at San Francisco State University since 1996, Maxine Chernoff is author of thirteen books of poetry including, most recently, *World: Poems 1991–2001* (2001), *Evolution of the Bridge: New and Selected Prose Poems* (2003), *Among the Names* (2005), *The Turning* (2008), *A House in Summer* (2011), *To Be Read in the Dark* (2011), and *Without* (2012). Long associated with the prose poem, her work has also employed an ingenious variety of verse forms. Examples include the abecedarium *Japan* (1987), which adopts a strictly proceduralist approach as well as abstract, but beautifully lyric wordplay, and *Among the Names*, a researched but lyrical work based on the anthropological study of gifts and reciprocity. In *The Turning*, she employs a variety of strategies. The poem "What It Contains," for instance, was constructed by using the Google search phrase "the novel contains." The reader quickly realizes the novel of which the poem speaks is in fact a large number of quite different works. To haunting effect, the poem "Scenes from Ordinary Life" inserts the characters of Martin Heidegger and Hannah Arendt into the script for a bunraku drama, *The Love Suicides at Sonezaki*, circa 1725. "The Commons," on the other hand, is a serial plaint about the loss of common ground in contemporary life. We increasingly live in separate and gated communities, from which we anxiously look out.

The poet Aaron Shurin writes, "Chernoff coaxes moral and ethical perspectives up from their Americanized hiding places. The bracing result is a kind of vatic quotidian: a new form of Speaking the Real."[1]

Chernoff is also noted for her works of fiction, which include the books of short stories *Bop* (1986), *Signs of Devotion* (a *New York Times* Book of the Year, 1993), *Some of Her Friends That Year: New & Selected Stories* (2002), and the novels *Plain Grief* (1991), *American Heaven* (1996), and *A Boy in Winter* (1999). She is coeditor of the literary magazine *New American Writing*. With Paul Hoover, she edited and translated *Selected Poems of Friedrich Hölderlin* (2008), winner of the 2009 PEN-USA Translation Award. She has traveled widely to present her work, including China, Russia, Brazil, and the Czech Republic.

1. Jacket comment, *The Turning*, Berkeley, 2008.

What It Contains

Thomas contends that the novel contains scenes of violence and the detailed description of a sexual assault on a young boy.

Indeed, the novel contains one of the earliest discussions of how the conditions of slave life might be ameliorated.

In addition, the novel contains the revelations of a few hitherto well-guarded secrets.

Although the novel contains adult language and situations, it will appeal to all audiences.

The novel contains many scenes of characters being compelled to write "the truth."

The novel contains many descriptions of mouth-watering food that at the same time can be seen as homely and erotic.

In support of the pessimistic perspective, the novel contains many truly dark moments to offset the colorful ones.

As usual with Irving, the novel contains some brilliant moments of cultural observations.

But the novel contains the parallel and contrasting love of Konstantin Levin.

The novel contains a great deal of religious imagery.

The novel contains several bullfighting references, especially in the name of Tess' boat Quernica (the spot in the ring where the bull feels protected).

The novel contains a large amount of ethnographic material to make it seem "authentic," and there is more than a whiff of authorial exploitation here.

The novel contains a complementary story: the relationship of Glen and Miriam, who are attracted to each other but always tend to resist each other.

Those who know a bit about Church history and Scripture recognize that the novel contains much error and unsubstantiated theorizing.

An interesting feature from the linguistic perspective is that the novel contains a number of 'Newspeak' words (such as Miniluv, doublethink, plusgood, etc.).

The novel contains a large number of minor players: neighbors, coworkers, friends, relatives and other incidental participants.

The novel contains a wealth of ideas and scientific information that could spawn research that will lead to actual inter-species communication.

The novel contains many powerful vignettes, including two memorable and controversial sex scenes—a touching one between Janet and a teenage earth female.

All copies were confiscated because the novel contains descriptions of Mao Zedong's portrait being defaced.

The novel contains many different kinds of love: intellectual, spiritual, sexual, maternal. Which moves you most and why?

As the novel contains a double focus on morality and fantasy, it is also discussed as a dystopia, which is closely related to both satire and science.

It is also true that the main thread of the novel contains the love story of Chin Pao-yu and Lin Tai-yu.

Banned in Rochester, Michigan, the novel contains and makes reference to religious matters.

The second paragraph of the novel contains the same paragraph from a first-grade primer.

The novel contains several non-beautiful, even grotesque characters such as Bessie, Whitey, the pierced waitress, Judge, and Miss Ella.

Published in 1894, the novel contains brutally realistic depictions of war.

The novel contains excellent scientific details about the Everglades and their ecological diversity.

The novel contains twenty-five episodes, many of which have ludic titles.

The novel contains many descriptions of people looking at each other with anger, supplication, pity, and understanding.

The novel contains profanity and racial slurs.

The novel contains some clichés about manhood (the "real man" and his "inner red dog," for example).

What Bakhtin's concept of dialogism suggests is that we also need a book showing that every theory of the novel contains the Quixote within it.

The novel contains the first published reference to what would become The Dark Towers mythos, as King's uber-villain Randall Flagg is introduced.

2008

Scenes from Ordinary Life

(Supertitles: The Love Suicides at Sonezaki *(circa 1725) describes in realistic fashion a young merchant of soy sauce who commits suicide with the prostitute he loves. Chikamatsu sought in his domestic plays to depict on the stage the tragedies which occur in ordinary life rather than the mythical struggles of the gods.)*

Characters: Martin Heidegger and Hannah Arendt.

Time: 1925

Martin: Why is love rich beyond all possible human experience
and a sweet burden to those seized in its grasp?
Because we become what we love and yet remain ourselves.

Hannah: Do not forget me, and do not forget how much
and how deeply I know that our love has become
the blessing of my life.

(Dejection would be more vividly suggested if each in turn stood by a drooping willow when they spoke.)

Time: 1932

Hannah: I had read the fairy tale about Dwarf Nose, whose nose
gets so long nobody recognizes him anymore.
My mother pretended that had happened to me.
I still vividly recall the blind terror with which
I kept crying: but I am your child, I am your Hannah.—
That is what it was like today.

Martin: That I supposedly don't say hello to Jews
is such a malicious piece of gossip that in any case
I will have to take note of it for the future.

(She had gone to the entrance of the sake shop as if to strain for a glimpse of him. She strikes an attitude of anxious reflection, one hand thrust into the bosom of her kimono.)

Time: 1950

Martin: It is beautiful to be an "and."
But it is the secret of the goddess.
It happens before all communication.
It rings from the deep sound of
the "ou" in you.

Elfride thanks you for your wishes
and sends her best. Please give
your husband our best too.

(The operator holds him almost motionless for twenty minutes.)

Time: 1960

Hannah: You will see that the book does not contain
          a dedication. If things had ever worked out
          properly between us, and I mean *between,*
          that is neither you nor me—I would have asked you
          if I might have dedicated it to you.

(She sews cloth or plays a musical instrument.)

Time: 1969–1975

Martin in tableau: Letters letters letters visits.

Hannah in tableau: Visits visits letters etc.

(The characters must suggest the world of darkness but also the inner light that guides them.)

Time: 1975

Martin: It was a merciful death. Of course,
        in human terms, it came too soon.

(He plays the samisen, which Paul Claudel likened to the sound of a nerve being plucked.)

Appendix:

Poem to Martin from Hannah: We'll meet in that hour
                            White lilac in flower
                            My kisses your screen
                            All you'll need. (excerpt 1923 or '24)

Poem to Hannah from Martin: The stranger,
                            even to yourself,
                            she is:
                            mountain of joy
                            sea of sorrow,

> desert of desire,
> dawn of arrival. (excerpt 1950)

(Heard on a radio. Stage empty.)

Curtain

2008

The Commons

The house . . . is never seen, either by the eyes of the body or those of the mind. —HANNAH ARENDT

1.

Woods, meadows, streams
shared by community
in old German law:
so green will have a dwelling.

2.

The language was shared.
They had it in common.
Prepositions were their tonic.
Every morning they made love.

3.

Without a public realm,
freedom has no worldly reality.
Despots banish people to their homes,
where they speak in whispers.

4.

"I miss the village green
and all the simple people.
I miss the village green:
the church, the clock, the steeple."

5.

People flee a city
when buildings start to fall.
Only rats and pigeons—
we have them on surveillance.

6.

I had dreamed it so:
a threshold and a grave.
All the world's a slum
and we its shadow workers.

7.

Here to speak of ruin
in an age of plenty.
Fresh Kills filled with sofas.
Human flesh remains.

8.

Meanwhile in Manila
children play a game,
blindfolded in the dump,
reaching out their hands.

9.

When tsunamis come,
they also cleanse the world.
Everything flowing over,
tumbling into grace.

10.

So a fool said
on his way to church.
Let us praise the dead
with chilling nonchalance.

11.

I had thought I knew
how the world would end,
but all I really know
is how to stare and point.

12.

No one goes there now.
There is not a place—
our commons but a song
lost as it is sung.

2008

Carla Harryman

b. 1952

Born and raised in the towns of Orange and Costa Mesa, California, Carla Harryman was educated at the University of California at Santa Barbara and San Francisco State Unviersity.

Author of *Percentage* (1979), *The Middle* (1983), *Vice* (1987), *Animal Instincts: Prose, Plays, Essays* (1989), *In the Mode of* (1991), *The Words: After Carl Sandburg's Rootabaga Stories and Jean-Paul Sartre* (1994), *There Never Was a Rose Without a Thorn* (1995), *Baby* (2005), and *Adorno's Noise* (2008), Harryman likes to blend fictive and essayistic elements in her chosen form, the prose poem: "I prefer to distribute narrative rather than deny it," she writes. "Narrative exists, and arguments either for or against it are false."[1] She has edited a special issue of *The Journal of Narrative Theory* on the subject of Non/Narrative (2011). She also coedited *Lust for Life: On the Writings of Kathy Acker* (2006).

In Harryman's view, "narrative might be thought to be a character," the defects of which lie in the "'potential to observe his own practice of making falsehoods.' If this narrative is imitating anything, it's the intention to convince the audience to enjoy its imitation, whatever the lack of truth or reasonableness."[2] Harryman's narratives are intentionally marked by interruptions so that, as she writes in *The Middle*, "Causality is dimmed." Her work is self-reflexive and often humorously erotic: "Since I am often forced to write in the nude, I often fantasize wearing beautiful clothes," she writes. "In this way I never suffer from abuse, since my characterlessness is not perceived."[3]

The scholar Carla Billitteri writes: "Harryman's works are hybrid texts in Bakhtin's sense, not fusions of genres in which new forms are created and in which old forms are changed beyond recognizability, but heterogenous mixtures 'belonging simultaneously to two or more systems.'"[4] Billitteri notes that the word "delirium" has the root meaning "'to go out of the furrow,' an act of wandering, of digressing, or going astray"; in this sense the work of Carla Harryman is perfectly delirious in its "continuous, restless movement."[5]

A playwright and cofounder of the San Francisco Poets Theater, which produced experimental plays in San Francisco from 1978 to 1984, Harryman is associated with the language poets and lived for many years in the Bay Area. In 1995, she moved to Detroit. She currently teaches at Eastern Michigan University, as well as the Milton Avery School of the Arts at Bard College.

1. "Toy Boats," *Poetics Journal* 5, May 1985, p. 104.   2. The same.   3. San Francisco, 1983, p. 4.   4. "The Necessary Experience of Error," in *how2*, vol. 3, no. 3, p. 1, http://www.asu.edu./pipercwcenter/how2journal/vol_3_no_3/harryman/billetteri.html.   5. The same.

Noise for Adorno

Across sculpted surfaces glowworms manage excess with initials some call instincts and others choose to relish for their own sake. How many times has a gift become a crisis?

Beatles do not ask this question. They ask another question. Will the debris linger on the anchor? Much has been made of baleful themes waiting to be realized. But upright legs rub together regardless of gender.

Phrasing is attraction clamoring for connection organized by jealousy. Emoluments for hands scale up the spine of another's mate. Dust lit on chunk. There were consequences and results never acknowledged by either.

Crashing through the waves with their jaws interlocked, the fighters kill each other then duck under a wreck where the coolest of nights collects their orgasms. Hard insects mingle in soft guts.

A grandstand above is not the place to sit when the psyche below wants revenge. Such arrangements can't control the banality of a wing tickling inside the breast or the ditty that curls down the smooth of a butt or the knee that panics on the outside of a strange creature's toe. It is not safety one seeks in a shadow.

Across sculpted surfaces theories speak to me as poems. Literacy in fields of discourse crumbles amongst freaky sounds. Here are the sirens of not knowing everything. The map of whatever is stilted. More than one bird has pinched an ear, which burns in tenderness and loses a hard-on.

Alternatively, a bird pinches an ear. Alternately, a bird pinched an ear.

Alphabets like insects may triumph over the arrangements made from their parts more than is normally thought. Even as languages disappear the headspace made in the damage converts to tongue.

Between an ecstasy and its other is a factory. Bees nest inside its abandoned parts. In a photo the factory seems old and still. It is never still. The photo is a distraction used to orient brains toward the shell of their prey.

2008

Transparent

Have I ever had a real vision? I wonder about this, even as I can easily describe one associated with something I ate once—several months before I met you. It was during Easter break in the late spring of 1971, and the vision happened on a Laguna Beach mesa overlooking the Pacific Ocean. It was early morning when I went through the ritual of consuming the toxic buttons. After a prolonged bout of nausea from which I could find relief only by lying in my shower with the shower head pointing directly at my body and continuously spraying a soft mist onto my back and stomach, I was at last able to slip on a dress and sometime after midday wander down a short hill to the sandy mesa where a man in a transparent shirt tapped me on the shoulder. I was not exactly startled, but I had been enjoying the feeling of warm sand on my bare feet, so I reacted to this touching with irritation. A personal project in those years was to find fulfillment in being alone—a challenge of sorts for a young person living in zones of rampaging libido. I had to talk myself into turning around to see who was touching me, with the sense that if I didn't something might go wrong. He said something I can no longer recall, but I do remember his shirt, which simultaneously sheathed and revealed his lean high definition body. The shirt was composed of a blend of threads—the sky blue of Pacific air after the fog had burned off and the pale adobe pink of the Spanish style rooftops in the area. When I realized that his shirt *was* the rooftop meeting the sky, he faded in front of my eyes. Until today, however, I hadn't thought that this vision had to do with actual things in the sense that real things were the compositional materials of the hallucination. Instead, I had experienced the things around me as having been constituted by the vision. I believe I relied on that oddly distorted sensation in order to retain the memory, which otherwise might never have been recorded.

2008

Orgasms

tis issue robbing pope sucking spear transit splash oops bore eye fro
eye hire harrow guarded leer trap fire slurry badge adage craze

speak speak speak engineer linger rotund dusty ust ust uh

hoe oat toe below spire rain stamen stick rat earth reeves heavy slob
oh sorrow mow

spot smear spot squashed stadium clinging pillar out hear a-rear
basting let low lyric violet storm

loaned honey nothing doing behind gravy train evil fell to slow
entrance gained a billow in the random rain

never never adumbrate never fever scumbling punchable larynx snot
god sported inside mountain yawn swerve gliding dust to dust hard
shadow phase hammy maverick nut there scratching crevice hording
hot snow ocean bosses suds scribble which ways blacking

chancy chaos gouge loony brighter than tune

may may may may may may max may max may max ayax

razor ruby bird seared near her area reached piper ripping rail

low light lit little tick flea migrant sip pissy wit twill twill low will
piano frill label slain hero palo o opal laughing harrow barracuda
amour our radio crash

not on my time happy not on my time mad not on my time money
not on my time skin not on my time merry not on my time dig not
on my time fanny not on my time sorrow not on my time sand not on
my time sun not on my time moon not on my time hills not on my
time rivers not on my time rinse not on my time cloud not on my
time vapor not on my time film not on my time shame not on my
time hover not on my time blow not on my time sassy not on my time
slow not on my time honey not on my time more

defeat effete defeat effort defeat fort defeat eat eat de teat at art faart
or fete tete ear eat fete tete do to oat to o deaf effort fort ore eee or taa
tort or at eat taa tat or de de ten effete neat tete defeat

lulu lang loop bay bay bay rad hip hole cleave o Decalogue boober
hover mine hammer am

bubble slumber pressure song cover over every wrong abridge my
sigh with over wing oh swim again beyond thy hand

points are reached at every point slimmed mirror prunes mere
mourning rave

Everyone now began to tear at Adorno. An orgasm is an elegy.
I can't explain this rationally. It's site-specific emotion lodged in a

small barking noise—an escape hatch in the negative dialectic.

This is what he might have desired during the student protest in 1969. The emotion that corresponds to the practice of oppression is contempt. If I had been among the students in Frankfurt, would I have opened up my leather jacket and showed him my breasts in a parodic manner, in solidarity with a leaflet that proclaimed "Adorno as an institution is dead?"

Direct socialization is structurally determined by the patriarchal or Oedipal family, so the gender politics of parody is hopeless if you want meaningful social change. In this story however the people live and Adorno dies. Yet I am convinced that I would have refused to think of Adorno or any individual as an institution and instead would have removed myself from the scene and posed as "the small time expert," a sexless menial. In my rejection of revolt, I would have underscored my subject position as a mirror of the fragile component of the social sexual contract. Adorno was attracted to, in fact relied upon, mimesis. Did I desire him even after he forgave me for faking the orgasm? But how do I know that I wouldn't have been instead liberated from this inclination to withdraw, to pose, and to think at a remove? What if I had become activated—I can well imagine this. Even as I write, I can feel some odd source or space that's as much physical sensation as idea located inside—it's probably in everybody's brain—wanting activation.

With a flick of the switch aggression exposes erotic drives to blindness. On the other side of this blindness is an orgasm in the public void.

An orgasm *is* an elegy in which there is no consolation. Machines, like orgasms, are inconsolable things.

Adorno metamorphosed from an instrument to a machine to the unnameable, a figure in the Beckett he had admired. Text is the electricity that moves the body from one thing to the next even as it cannot break out of its instrumental rationality.

With the books in his brain stem shifting their weight hurriedly, he sought comfort in nonhuman Valais in southern Switzerland. The poet Rilke had a few things to say about this spot: I hide my shame below the figure of his agonistic remorse. In respect to mountains like these, Kant refers to "a voluptuousness for the mind in a train of thought that [he] can never fully unravel." Why is it that I wish for the mountain to remain where it is and for the unraveling to continue beyond such words? Adorno has responded thus: "To enter nature," signifies "seeking out unconscious existence at the very place where it is most clearly revealed in the phenomenal world." Adore, whose name became No for an instant, wanted to be elevated by or into the irrational at the site of a gathering of "dissimilar human beings." "The need to protect sexuality has something crazy about it." The need to protect sexuality has something crazy about it.

About has something crazy about "it." About has something crazy about it. About has something crazy about it. About it.

SOURCES: Lorenz Jäge, *Adorno: A Political Biography* (2004), 192–210; Max Hork-heimer and Theodor W. Adorno, *Dialectic of Enlightenment* (1988), 93, 106, 111; Re-becca Comay, "Adorno's Siren Song," and Andrew Hewitt, "A Feminine Dialectic of Enlightenment?" in *Feminist Interpretations of Theodore Adorno,* ed. Renée Heberle (2006), 53, 94.

2008

Laura Moriarty
b. 1952

Laura Moriarty was born in St. Paul, Minnesota, and grew up on Cape Cod. She has lived in the San Francisco area since 1966. From 1986 to 1997 she was the archives director for the Poetry Center and American Poetry Archives at San Francisco State University. She currently serves as deputy director of Small Press Distribution in Berkeley.

Her books of poetry include *Persia* (1983), *Duse* (1987), *like roads* (1990), *Rondeaux* (1990), *L'archiviste* (1991), *Spicer's City* (1998), *Nude Memoir* (2000), *Self-Destruction* (2004), *A Semblance: Selected and New Poems 1975–2007,* and *A Tonalist* (2010). She has also published two novels, *Cunning* (1998) and *Ultravioleta* (2006).

The poet Norma Cole writes: "Moriarty's early chapbook *Duse* . . . is the model for her future works. *Duse* sets up a table of apparent verticals side by side, but reads down and across, and then begins to spiral every which way, a kind of diagramming which threads through *A Semblance,* forming and reforming phonemes, words and phrases, thoughts and tales, rhythm and sound."[1]

In an afterword to her book-length work *A Tonalist,* Moriarty sets out a sprawling poetics that proceeds primarily by *via negativa:*

> A Tonalist is not a style but an attitude or perhaps a context. It is not a set of techniques. The surface(s) of work that might be called A Tonalist are not superficially similar. A Tonalist proposes an anti-lyric whose viability relates to the history of lyrical poetry by resisting as much as enacting it. The table manners are bad. The tranquility being cooked up comes from emptiness. And passing, as everyone knows, means suffering. In *A Tonalist* the lyric "I" is complicated rather than celebrated. There is doubt. There is, as Kafka said, hope, but not for us. Perhaps that is a lot to ask of a poetics—that it write itself out of or up against the canon or the idea of literature, that it shoot itself in the foot. The sense of dissatisfaction or self-destruction, not with the person but with the writing subject, is rife.[2]

The poem "A Tonalist," in fact, reads like a poet's daybook, quoting the works of friends, remembering a detail from an Eisenstein movie, or noting how light glances from aspen leaves, as opposed to the absorbent green of lichen. The encyclopedic form of the work allows for a mosaic of reference and thought: "Out best research is left with its mouth open."

Laura Moriarty lives in Albany, California.

1. Introduction to *A Semblance: New and Selected Poems 1975–2007,* Richmond, CA, 2007, p. 16.   2. "A Tonalist Coda," *A Tonalist,* Callicoon, NY, 2010, p. 119.

FROM Spectrum's Rhetoric

1. Spectrum's Rhetoric

Light changes the sentence. A subject persists in memory sounding. Walks along the edge of the continent. Tea leaves piled like seaweed in a cup in a mind pink on the inside and like the sea dark. Cut orchids and peonies as writing or going out. Green of stems. Green of the sea. A long drive. A longer walk. Movement is aloud.

"It is just this moment of red mind . . ." [Dōgen, *Shobogenzo*]

You as an address various and specific know where you are. Who you are. But what do I know? "What do I know and when did I know it?" you ask later. More on that.

A hill looms like a wave of earth. El Cerrito goes down to the sea, the bay, nearby. The hill intimated by the name is in Albany. Here. In California. Goes to the sea. In green. The sea white.

The city in the distance
Surrounded by

Color drains from it as light recedes but the color remains in this Western version. This version of the West. That being the point (of light visible as) (it is) made complicated by the physicality of thought.

"the circumstances
like a fabric ripping
inside the body"

[Norma Cole, *a little a & a*]

But what is the West? What is light? What is empire? What color? The body as light as perceived from the inside out. The arrangement of color. The arrangement of time. Local time. Thought as action. For time and color's sake. As read. Among the hills golden and yet not empirical or not merely so or empirical and yet not empire, though of it. But what happened?

"I saw the
countryside

for seconds like
a film thru"

[George Albon, *Empire Life*]

What happens to make us believe what we see. To see what we read as being
read we write in color.

"Our best research is left with its mouth open."

Reading a diary backwards. Writing it. Writing the experience before having
it. Thinking of an indistinct town from a distance. Of the city. Thinking
about the war in a store in the midst of the empire. Thinking about Cornell,
not the boxes but the diary. The lack of sentimentality in his Romantic
Museum—or the mad presence of sentiment. Or its ephemerality.

In Eisenstein's *Romance Sentimental* a woman plays a black piano in black
and then a white one in white. She sings an old song of longing. Handwritten
explosions come later after the branches rush by and the sea is included.
There are monsters.

"I may forever lose the light . . ." [Kamau Brathwaite, *Zea Mexican Diary*] "If
she should die . . . I may forever lose the light the light—the open doors."

Aspens like sequins (for example)
Unlike lichen
An arrested splash
Green and light green
Or black with white
The lichen yellow and black

"I don't know where you buy it or whether there is a premium for buying it. I
don't understand how to do it or use it."

The Lotus Sutra

The body in its place
Hybrid of door and face
Present text to be
As you are there then where
Transcribed in its entire

Repetition each day
More patient than anyone
The act of
Who speaking moves
Gives her notes away

"The act of remembering or the vibrations of the sutra
Crash though the real world"

[Philip Whalen, "Four Other Places"]

We see to the bottom of the lake. The stems deep among white rocks. Green
and red leaves flat on the black water. Green to yellow. Yellow lotus buds.
Leaves furled. Magenta inside. Spread out on the lake. Blue now of the sky.
Black and green of trees. Beauty of husband nearby. Lotus and trees in the
background. Husband. Half lake half sky.

Untitled

Mariposa lily

Black and white

Lotus ubiquitous there (East) as here the cross. (West.) It is not about
death, suffering or sacrifice, but about cultivation, recitation, transcription,
translation, genre, gender switching, mud and light. The bright things that
grow there.

Darkly

But silent

Stance

Among the Buddhas in my mother's album is the wooden one in Berkeley
Zen Center pictured with a vase of columbines, a candle and a small statue of
Kwannon. The altar for our wedding. And here we are kissing.

Years missing

Intervene when

Startled from sleep by the wind, I see again the peripheral beings I have lately noticed but who I can't see if I look directly at them. Rows of monks. Known to be Western monks. Rows of pale green robes. Green monks. Eastern but Western. Yellow lotus.

Merely a phenomenon of sight.

The house alight. Water on the floor. The house is empty or needs to be emptied. The room is filled with glasses, keys, keyboards, pillows and cups. It is dark. There are too many bright things. There was a party. A wake. Cabinets are open and broken. What can we do with this place? What are we doing here?

Hereinafter

Things given

Come back

The glass elephant in the painting of the lilacs floating in the photo like a thought over the three of us, my aunt, my mother and I on a couch. My mother's eyes, as if to say "Okay. What the hell. Here I am alive."

"I hold you like a river."
[Esther Tellerman, "Mental Ground," translated by Keith Waldrop]

Like heaven falling, the long line of cloud heads directly for us. It spills over our hill in slow motion. We see the fog in shreds above and descending. Next day we watch as it lightens and dissolving, we pull away.

Wandering at the bottom of the ocean of air, reading two slim volumes. One a translated revelation, the other about the weather.

"And I saw a new sky and a new earth."
[Revelations 21:1;] [Revelations 20:11]

"And books were opened"
Bleeding meaning
Body in time
Just as we said (read)
Red thinking but not

Speaking though speaking
Enough to say

Bleeding meaning in a hospital on Earth sitting—a skinny Buddha with
good hair. I meet your famous friends and say Tonalism with you and you
say "Good." "Title." We agree right there referring to past and future with
sweeping gestures. You point to light with the hand you have making

"The highest heaven in the world of forms form"

The painter in the painting. The gray clouds of paint behind the mailboxes
like her smoke. The black trees. Her signature in the corner. Legible. I did
this.

The name affixed I see

Drains the life

Roars into me from another world

But that painting is unsigned. The autograph is in my mind. This is not my
mother. These are not our mailboxes. They are in the country, in fact, in the
clouds. Ours were on the base, by the house, on a street. I can't remember
them. I can't read this.

People with colors

Arrive and grieve They leave

The receptacles Have left

Petals scattered

Old sunlight. Morning fire. She dreams that she speaks. The lines of the
sea. The distance is complete. The creek swollen. Oaks with moss hung.
The sweep of light from the lighthouse as approaching on Highway 1.
Lens, headlight, windowlight. The trees braided impossibly upward. A gold
rectangle on transparent blue. Thickly pictured. The lens was invented by a
French physicist. This was his room. This, his bed we sleep in. This *we*.

"The landscape
is the portrait of
the sun. Only
skin is skin deep."

[Norma Cole, *Spinoza in Her Youth*]

I can hear as well as see the quiet as you sound it in your mind. Is it my imagination? Is it your speech? A change occurs during the sound. The colors are audible. The sea disappears into the afternoon through a line of gray leafed blue gum. The green is green. The light dark. The artificial log burns down. Books, notebooks, and I reflect like television in the glass doors of the fire. Reading (watching) Alan Halsey's *Memory Screen*. Fire sucked by wind. We take the measure of it. Screen and wind and I. Read him. Read you.

2010

Elaine Equi
b. 1953

Elaine Equi was born and raised in the suburbs of Chicago, and received her B.A. and M.A. in creative writing from Columbia College Chicago.

A minimalist and ironist, Equi's work reflects "deep image" and surrealist influences in its surprising juxtaposition of objects such as "pendants / and bracelets of soot." Her poetry also makes use of the serial organization, or catalogues, common to surrealist poetry. Equi's work draws playfully on traditional forms, as in the pantoum "A Date with Robbe-Grillet," and metaphysical concepts; the unifying conceit of her poem "In a Monotonous Dream" is that the language consists of only one word.

In a review of her work, Tom Clark refers to her "post-punk, Dorothy Parkerish kit of weapons: arched eyebrow barbs, nervy, catchy hooks of pop-conscious metaphor, and double meanings stitched in light-handedly."[1]

Equi's gentle use of irony is evident in the titles of her books, the wryly turned *The Corners of the Mouth* (1986) and *Surface Tension* (1989); other collections include *Accessories* (1988), *Decoy* (1994), *Voice-Over* (1998), *The Cloud of Knowable Things* (2003), *Ripple Effect: New and Selected Poems* (2007), and *Click and Clone* (2011). Her work has appeared on many occasions in the annual anthology *The Best American Poetry*. *Ripple Effect* was on the short list for The Griffin Poetry Prize in 2008.

Equi lives in New York City, where she teaches in the M.F.A. programs at The New School and City College of New York.

1. "Pop Hooks," in *The Poetry Beat,* Ann Arbor, 1990, p. 194.

A Date with Robbe-Grillet

What I remember didn't happen.
Birds stuttering.
Torches huddled together.
The café empty, with no place to sit.

Birds stuttering.
On our ride in the country
the café empty, with no place to sit.
Your hair was like a doll's.

On our ride in the country
it was winter.

Your hair was like a doll's
and when we met it was as children.

It was winter
when it rained
and when we met it was as children.
You, for example, made a lovely girl.

When it rained
the sky turned the color of Pernod.
You, for example, made a lovely girl.
Birds strutted.

The sky turned the color of Pernod.
Within the forest
birds strutted
and we came upon a second forest

within the forest
identical to the first
And we came upon a second forest
where I was alone

identical to the first
only smaller and without music
where I was alone
where I alone could tell the story.

1989

Asking for a Raise

Perhaps there is a color
I can sleep in
like a spare room.

Some uncharted green.

Some state I gladly travel to
in the center of a loud noise
where all is calm.

Snug in my cupcake hut
the difference between
sleeping with pills

and sleeping without them
is the difference between
talking into a telephone
and talking into a jewel.

Depression is an economic state.
Green is also the color of cash.

"All right, but what would you do
with more money if you had it?"

asks the businessman who greets me
with a lei of orchids.

"Shop for clothes," I answer.
"And treat my husband like a whore."

2003

A Quiet Poem

My father screamed whenever the phone rang.

My aunt often screamed when she opened the door.

Out back, the willows caterwauled.

In the kitchen, the faucet screamed
a drop at a time.

At school, they called screaming "recess"
or sometimes "music."

Our neighbors' daughter had a scream
more melodious than my own.

At first, Col. Parker had to pay girls
to get them to scream for Elvis.

I didn't want to scream when I saw The Beatles,
but I did. After that, I screamed for even
mediocre bands.

Late in his career, John Lennon
got into Primal Scream.

Many people find it relaxing to scream.

Just as crawling precedes walking, so screaming
precedes speech.

The roller coaster is just one of many
scream-inducing devices.

The ambulance tries, in its clumsy way, to emulate
the human scream, which in turn tries to emulate nature.

Wind is often said to shriek, but Sylvia Plath
also speaks of "the parched scream of the sun."

Jim Morrison wanted to hear the scream of the butterfly.

With ultra-sensitive equipment, scientists measure
the screams of plants they've tortured.

It's proven that if you scream at a person
for years, then suddenly stop, he will hear even
the tenderest words of love as violent curses.

And to anyone who speaks above a whisper, he will say:
"Don't you dare. Don't you dare raise your voice to me."

2003

Locket without a Face

The name *Equi* means *horses* in Latin.

While growing up, there was a racetrack at the end of our street.

Evening coincided with post time.

Darkness arrived with the flourish and fanfare of trumpets.

During heated races, one could feel even from bed the tremor of the crowd on its feet.

The smell of horses was not the least bit unpleasant.

The jockeys wore bold patterns: diamonds and stripes of warring colors.

Green, white, and black vs. purple, orange, and gold.

There was something medieval about it. There was something abstract and modernist about it too.

Being a child, I rarely went to the racetrack.

I stayed in my room and studied a box.

There was a girl's face in a heart on the box. I think it was bubble bath.

I knew without having to be told that I was supposed to insert my face in place of hers—imagine it was me trapped in someone else's heart.

But by then, I had already developed the habit of trying to see through pictures.

Whenever I looked at photos, drawings, ads, or paintings, I always tried (like Superman) to see the other side— even if it was just blank.

My life at that time seemed bound up in looking through the locket-shaped window like a telescope into a more feudal age.

Inside the box were things I liked: a penknife, a bar of soap in the shape of a flower, a green plastic mermaid, a fuchsia paper umbrella, a blue glass shell. Insignias, emblems.

These things belonged not to me but to the girl whose
face was in the heart.

Or I should say they belonged to me when I imagined
myself to be her.

I served her by collecting them.

She served me by disappearing conveniently whenever I
opened the box.

A face should not be locked inside a heart.

2011

The Collected

for Barbara Guest

I like the feeling of incompleteness,

the icy *un*resolve
(some would say lack of closure)
in your poems.

A good stubborn modernist
refusal to cohere—

chords and wire tendrils left hanging,
semi-seductive exposed brick of midair.

Abrupt exits and entrances.

Modulated chaos.
Easy-listening for fin-de-siecle ghosts.

Like adding zero to wildfire zero,

sharp thoughts etched fine
then abandoned—

the way one sometimes works
with great energy in the morning
going as far as one can.

Are words thought
or afterthought

or something in between
that evaporates yet lingers?

A poem is made of words and spaces—

but can the fiction of words and space
exchange places?   Switch off and on

in fields of bright decoding,

the selvage of blue
remnants worked into unfinished sky.

2011

Harryette Mullen ─────────────────
b. 1953

Born in Florence, Alabama, Harryette Mullen grew up in Fort Worth, Texas, graduated from the University of Texas at Austin, and attended graduate school at the University of California, Santa Cruz.

Her books include *Tree Tall Woman* (1981), *Trimmings* (1991), *S°PeRM°°KT* (1992), *Muse & Drudge* (1995), *Sleeping with the Dictionary* (2002), *Blues Baby: Early Poems* (2002), and *Recyclopedia* (2006).

Mullen is unusual in her poetics, in that she blends the strategies of Oulipo, proceduralism, and conceptual poetry, with themes of African American life. This approach has been consistent throughout her work, with the exception of the more traditionally authored *Tree Tall Woman*. Mullen has written:

> My desires as a poet are contradictory. I aspire to write poetry that would leave no insurmountable obstacle to comprehension and plea-sure other than the ultimate limits of the reader's interest and linguis-tic competence. However, I do not necessarily approach this goal by employing a beautiful, pure, simple, or accessible literary language, or by maintaining a clear, consistent, recognizable, or authentic voice in my work. . . . My inclination is to pursue what is minor, marginal, idio-syncratic, trivial, debased, or aberrant in the language that I speak and write.[1]

Mullen speaks of herself as "one of the last integrationists" because she wants her poems to bring both black and white readers into the same room. Her most effective attempt to do so is the book-length poem *Muse & Drudge*, which she describes as a blending of Sapphire and Sappho. In four terse qua-trains per page that resemble the ballad and the blues, the two cultures are forced to rub against each other: "lifeguard at apartheid park / rough, dirty, a little bit hard / broken blossom poke a possum / park your quark in a hard aardvark." The final line of the quatrain is a homophone for "park your car in Harvard Yard"; likewise, *Muse & Drudge* is a homophonic play on the title of Zora Neale Hurston's novel *Mules and Men*.

Mullen has said in an interview:

> A lot has been said of how American culture is a miscegenated culture, how it is a product of mixing and mingling of diverse races and cultures and languages, and I would agree with that. I would say, yes, my text is deliberately a multi-voiced text, a text that tries to express the actual diversity of my own experience living here, exposed to different cultures. "Mongrel" comes from "among." Among others; we are not alone. We are all mongrels.[2]

In "Dim Lady" and "Variations on a Theme Park," Mullen submits Shake-speare's sonnet 18 to homosyntactic translation, the Oulipo procedure in which the major parts of speech are replaced by other words of the same kind: "My honeybunch's peepers are nothing like neon" and "My Mickey Mouse ears are nothing like sonar." The poem "Denigration" teases the reader with words that sound like racial slurs.

Mullen has received numerous awards including the Academy of American Poets Fellowship in 2009. *Sleeping with the Dictionary* was a finalist for the National Book Award, the National Book Critics Circle Award, and the Los Angeles Times Book Award in poetry. She teaches at UCLA and lives in Los Angeles.

1. "Imagining the Unimagined Reader," *American Women Poets in the 21st Century*, ed. Claudia Rankine and Juliana Spahr, Middletown, CT, 2002, p. 404.   2. Calvin Bedient, "Solo Mysterioso Blues: An Interview with Harryette Mullen," *Callaloo: A Journal of African Diaspora Arts and Letters* 19.3 (1996): 651–669.

FROM *Muse & Drudge*

Sapphire's lyre styles
plucked eyebrows
bow lips and legs
whose lives are lonely too

my last nerve's lucid music
sure chewed up the juicy fruit
you must don't like my peaches
there's some left on the tree

you've had my thrills
a reefer a tub of gin
don't mess with me I'm evil
I'm in your sin

clipped bird eclipsed moon
soon no memory of you
no drive or desire survives
you flutter invisible still

■

another funky Sunday
stone-souled picnic

your heart beats me
as I lie naked on the grass

a name determined by other names
prescribed mediation
unblushingly on display
to one man or all

traveling Jane
no time to settle down
bee in her bonnet
her ants underpants

bittersweet and inescapable
hip signals like later
some handsome man kind on the eyes
a kind man looks good to me

▪

I dream a world
and then what
my soul is resting
but my feet are tired

half the night gone
I'm holding my own
some half forgotten tune
casual funk from a darker back room

handful of gimme
myself when I am real
how would you know
if you've never tasted

a ramble in brambles
the blacker more sweeter juicier
pores sweat into blackberry tangles
going back native natural country wild briers

▪

country clothes hung on her all and sundry
bolt of blue have mercy ink perfume
that snapping turtle pussy
won't let go until thunder comes

call me pessimistic
but I fall for sour pickles
sweets for the heat
awrr reet peteet patootie

shadows crossed her face
distanced by the medium
riffing through it
too poor to pay attention

sepia bronze mahogany
say froggy jump salty
jelly in a vise
buttered up broke ice

▪

sun goes on shining
while the debbil beats his wife
blues played lefthanded
topsy-turvy inside out

under the weather
down by the sea
a broke johnny walker
mister meaner

bigger than a big man
cirrus as a heart attracts
more power than a loco motive
think your shit don't stink

edge against a wall
wearing your colors
soulfully worn out
stylishly distressed

▪

battered like her face
embrazened with ravage
the oxidizing of these
agonizingly worked surfaces

that other scene offstage
where by and for her he descends
a path through tangled sounds
he wants to make a song

blue gum pine barrens
loose booty muddy bosom
my all day contemplation
my midnight dream

something must need fixing
raise your window high
the carpenter's here
with hammer and nail

▪

what you do to me
got to tell it
sing it shout out
all about it

ketchup with reality
built for meat wheels
the diva road kills
comfort shaking on the bones

trouble in mind
naps in the back
if you can't stand
sit in your soul kitsch

pot said kettle's mama must've
burnt them turnip greens

kettle deadpanned not missing a beat
least mine ain't no skillet blonde

1995

Denigration

Did we surprise our teachers who had niggling doubts about the picayune brains of small black children who reminded them of clean pickaninnies on a box of laundry soap? How muddy is the Mississippi compared to the third-longest river of the darkest continent? In the land of the Ibo, the Hausa, and the Yoruba, what is the price per barrel of nigrescence? Though slaves, who were wealth, survived on niggardly provisions, should inheritors of wealth fault the poor enigma for lacking a dictionary? Does the mayor demand a recount of every bullet or does city hall simply neglect the black alderman's district? If I disagree with your beliefs, do you chalk it up to my negligible powers of discrimination, supposing I'm just trifling and not worth considering? Does my niggling concern with trivial matters negate my ability to negotiate in good faith? Though Maroons, who were unruly Africans, not loose horses or lazy sailors, were called renegades in Spanish, will I turn any blacker if I renege on this deal?

2002

Dim Lady

My honeybunch's peepers are nothing like neon. Today's special at Red Lobster is redder than her kisser. If Liquid Paper is white, her racks are institutional beige. If her mop were Slinkys, dishwater Slinkys would grow on her noggin. I have seen tablecloths in Shakey's Pizza Parlors, red and white, but no such picnic colors do I see in her mug. And in some minty-fresh mouthwashes there is more sweetness than in the garlic breeze my main squeeze wheezes. I love to hear her rap, yet I'm aware that Muzak has a hipper beat. I don't know any Marilyn Monroes. My ball and chain is plain from head to toe. And yet, by gosh, my scrumptious Twinkie has as much sex appeal for me as any lanky model or platinum movie idol who's hyped beyond belief.

2002

Elliptical

They just can't seem to . . . They should try harder to . . . They ought to be more . . . We all wish they weren't so . . . They never . . . They always . . . Sometimes they . . . Once in a while they . . . However it is obvious that they . . . Their overall tendency has been . . . The consequences of which have been . . . They don't appear to understand that . . . If only they would make an effort to . . . But we know how difficult it is for them to . . . Many of them remain unaware of . . . Some who should know better simply refuse to . . . Of course, their perspective has been limited by . . . On the other hand, they obviously feel entitled to . . . Certainly we can't forget that they . . . Nor can it be denied that they . . . We know that this has had an enormous impact on their . . . Nevertheless their behavior strikes us as . . . Our interactions unfortunately have been . . .

2002

Variation on a Theme Park

My Mickey Mouse ears are nothing like sonar. Colorado is far less rusty than Walt's lyric riddles. If sorrow is wintergreen, well then Walt's breakdancers are dunderheads. If hoecakes are Wonder Bras, blond Wonder Bras grow on Walt's hornytoad. I have seen roadkill damaged, riddled and wintergreen, but no such roadkill see I in Walt's checkbook. And in some purchases there is more deliberation than in the bargains that my Mickey Mouse redeems. I love to herd Walt's sheep, yet well I know that muskrats have a far more platonic sonogram. I grant I never saw a googolplex groan. My Mickey Mouse, when Walt waddles, trips on garbanzos. And yet, by halogen-light, I think my loneliness as reckless as any souvenir bought with free coupons.

2002

Xenophobic Nightmare in a Foreign Language

waking up with Enrique Chagoya

Whereas, in the opinion of the Government of the United States the coming of bitter labor to this country endangers the good order of certain localities within the territory thereof:

Therefore, be it enacted by the Senate and House of Representatives of the United States of America in Congress assembled,

That from and after the expiration of ninety days next after the passage of this act, and until the expiration of ten years next after the passage of this act, the coming of bitter labor to the United States be, and the same is hereby, suspended; and during such suspension it shall not be lawful for any bitter labor to come, or, having so come after the expiration of said ninety days, to remain within the United States.

That the master of any vessel who shall knowingly bring within the United States on such vessel, and land or permit to be landed, any bitter labor, from any foreign port or place, shall be deemed guilty of a misdemeanor, and on conviction thereof shall be punished by a fine of not more than five hundred dollars for each and every such bitter labor so brought, and may be also imprisoned for a term not exceeding one year.

That any person who shall knowingly bring into or cause to be brought into the United States by land, or who shall knowingly aid or abet the same, or aid or abet the landing in the United States from any vessel of any bitter labor not lawfully entitled to enter the United States, shall be deemed guilty of a misdemeanor, and shall, on conviction thereof, be fined in a sum not exceeding one thousand dollars, and imprisoned for a term not exceeding one year.

That no bitter labor shall be permitted to enter the United States by land without producing to the proper officer of customs the certificate in this act required of bitter labor seeking to land from a vessel. And any bitter labor found unlawfully within the United States shall be caused to be removed therefrom to the country from whence they came, by direction of the United States, after being brought before some justice, judge, or commissioner of a court of the United States and found to be not lawfully entitled to be or remain in the United States.

May 6, 1882

2002

Donald Revell
b. 1954

Born in the Bronx in 1954, Donald Revell is a graduate of SUNY-Binghamton and SUNY-Buffalo, where one of his professors was Robert Creeley. His first collection of poems, *From the Abandoned Cities,* was published in 1983. His other books include *The Gaza of Winter* (1988), *New Dark Ages* (1990), *Erasures* (1992), *Beautiful Shirt* (1994), *There Are Three* (1998), *Arcady* (2002), *My Mojave* (2003), which won the Lenore Marshall Prize for poetry, *Pennyweight Windows: New and Selected Poems* (2005), *A Thief of Strings* (2007), and *The Bitter Withy* (2009). He has also published two essay collections, *The Art of Attention: A Poet's Eye* (2007) and *Invisible Green: Selected Prose* (2005). His translations of Apollinaire's poetry include *Alcools* (1995), and *The Self-Dismembered Man: Selected Later Poems* (2004). He has also translated *A Season in Hell* (2007) and *Illuminations* (2009) by Arthur Rimbaud and *Last Verses* of Jules LaForgue (2011), the poet who so influenced the young T. S. Eliot.

In an age of irony and indeterminacy, Revell's poetry takes up an inspired, even stalwart, defense of poetry as vision and belief: "And now I see that poetry is a form of attention, itself the consequence of attention. And, too, I believe that poems are presences, themselves the consequence of vivid presentations, even as may be called in Dame Julian of Norwich's word, 'showings.'"[1] Showings are emanations (Blake). They are also Pound's "apparitions of these faces in the crowd" (petals on a wet, black bough) and the wooden scent of the paper bag from which Dr. Williams eats his plums. Among Revell's favorite poets are the romantic postmoderns Ronald Johnson and John Ashbery, set against the visionary background of Whitman and Thoreau. Revell writes: "The poem is warm, not with argument, but with attention. I am speaking of intimacy, which is an occasion of attention. It is the intimacy of poetry that makes our art such a beautiful recourse from the disgrace and manipulations of public speech, of empty rhetoric. A poem that begins to see and then continues seeing is not deceived, nor is it deceptive."[2] In Revell's poetics, therefore, the witnessing of a leaf or Hopkins's "stipples upon trout that swim" is an act of great magnitude.

Revell was editor of *Denver Quarterly* from 1988 to 1994 and poetry editor of *Colorado Review* since 1996. He currently lives in Las Vegas, Nevada, and teaches at the University of Nevada.

1. Donald Revell, *The Art of Attention: A Poet's Eye,* Minneapolis, 2007, p. 5.   2. The same, p. 8.

The Secessions on Loan

I and these panels,
not larger than life but only partially
contained, as a landing site or the spindly
oxalis is only partially contained
in a woman's left-hand body,
I and these panels
mount the stair, reaching
the city. We are one size.

The caffeine taken from your eyes
painted the airplane *thus,*
in *that* sky,
daub over daub.
If you must hope, then hope.
If you must die, die.
But don't hope. Do not die.

A lot of corroded images
are just hanging there.
In the blackouts (every
night this week there have been storms
and power-outages, and we have had to travel
to other neighborhoods to read
or to eat or listen to music)
the dead may leave their message flashing.

We are one size.
A lot of corroded images
depict the too many orbits of one day,
a killing tree a cloud at the
center a green zero.

I will say this when she leaves
but to her left hand only:
do not die.
At the landing sites
everywhere on the plateau

we mourn the generals of our city.
They were oceans
in opposite directions.
As I and these panels
mounted the stairs this morning,
wrought-iron uncurved a spindly
oxalis where it became smoke
and rose still higher.
The afterlife gnawed at its small cage
and all the rooftops.

1994

Why and Why Now

There is no through
passage for the rain
between dog and dove.

In defense of Breslau
a pencil-dot an ant
crawled out in sex
onto my tongue. Thus,
I was early to the
construction site.

The schema bites down, as if the spirit were a passing devastation,
as if distance were not a white thing you could hold literally in
hands. I move secessions: lust from hope, hope from acquisition. I
walk on cold flies, no passage to warm their wings or vomiting.

In Europe, six typewriters
clatter without stop or
direction. Did I believe
it was a can of soup to be
warmed so? Idiomatic being

smiles and repaints to the
relief of Breslau. I've tried.
The future unacquired turns out
impossible. Hilt and animal,
it constructs and distances
the actual leafglow. In
the Reichstag, didn't he
smile into the camera of

Some are better than others, repainting, vomiting. The future
condones all that. I am thanking a giant who, wasted yellow
by illness, unconscious in his mother's bed, cannot answer.

1994

Ridiculous Winter Flower

Ridiculous winter flower

    More perfect butter

On the ground the disused

    Ground beloved

Must survive must live to tell

    Another orphan

Something raised us

    Out of the dust

Something gave us color

    A gold also tender

I shall not tell its name

I'm tired

Laughter and piano teacher

Ridiculous winter flower

The gate's wide open now

New Colors

The tree alive with invisible birds in no leaves

Is the soul of winter and says with Yeats

We wither into the truth whose truth is simply

That we die yet behind us the sky deepens

Into the deepest blue I mean to say that I

Could reach my hand forever into it

My hand would be covered with leaves and then

The birds would come in colors new colors

To robe archangels ruined back to life

We wither so to bear the weight of the invisible

Tell me shall I sing another cold day

Or is this merely the ruin before ruin

The shallow breath before no breath at all

Tell me is the sky behind me still

Deluge

I'd like for poetry to die with me:

Not only mine, but all of it. Where's

A good word now for *Louis Quinze?*

Can symmetries survive themselves?

Can the shadows of trees so razor-edged

At the fingertips of untouched women

Possibly survive a single winter,

Much less the oblivion humanity

Justly mistakes for simple change? The nearest heat

Is far. Horses refuse Phaeton.

Awake before anyone, untouched women

Slowly cleanse the body of a day

Never to come. In the east, horizon

Unwrites itself in momentary raiment:

Reddish-gold that blackens into mountains.

Gillian Conoley
b. 1955

Born in Austin, Texas, Gillian Conoley grew up in the nearby farming community of Taylor, where her parents owned a radio station. She holds a B.A. in journalism from Southern Methodist University and an M.F.A. from the Program for Poets and Writers at the University of Massachusetts. After teaching at a number of institutions, she joined the faculty of Sonoma State University, where she is professor of English and Poet in Residence. As a Visiting Poet, she has also taught at the University of Iowa, Denver University, and Tulane University.

A recipient of the Jerome J. Shestack Prize from *The American Poetry Review*, she is founder and editor of the poetry journal *Volt*.

Conoley's poetry books include *Some Gangster Pain* (1987), *Tall Stranger* (1991), *Beckon* (1996), *Lovers in the Used World* (2001), *Profane Halo* (2005), and *The Plot Genie* (2009).

The *American Book Review* comments on Conoley's earlier poetry: "Even above the powerfully inventive language and clear, compressed style is a poetic vision that seems utterly transforming. These are poems born of Flannery O'Connor's short stories, with their oddball grace, their undeniable redemption. Combined with Gillian Conoley's dark humor are an eye for detail and a sensibility that are mysteriously compelling."[1]

A turn in Conoley's work away from narrative and toward abstraction and the fragment occurs with *Profane Halo*, reviewed as follows in *Publishers Weekly:* "Exuberant and challenging, the quick cuts and vibrant, freestanding images in Conoley's fifth volume let her see America from many sides and in all sorts of scales, from the ground level of coastal suburbs to the grand cycles of political history. 'Dear Sunset that was sun of now / Near Greatness, dear tongue my Queen dear rock solid,' the title poem asks, 'how could we know that we are forerunners?' There follows a series of verbally brilliant, sometimes strikingly fragmentary poems, some perhaps inspired by photographs."[2]

The Plot Genie takes its title from a 1930 writer's aid designed for the use of novelists and screenwriters. In the work, "a murky underworld [is] constantly created and re-created, people by hapless characters waiting to be 'dialed up' and sent along multiple and fragmentary narratives."[3]

Gillian Conoley lives in Corte Madera, California.

---

1. *American Book Review*, quoted in *Chicken Bones: A Journal*, http://www.nathanielturner.com/gconoleypoetryreviews.htm/.　　2. *Publishers Weekly*, quoted in the same.　　3. http://www.omnidawn.com/conoley/index.htm.

Native

Let me see
if I can understand you as part of the architecture

though it is the architecture of the place

that keeps killing me, dream of sky that stays
perfect blue foam, dream unfurling

gone and fusing like a hand that has fallen
into place.

You are at the pond

and the beach and over the want ads

and then I have the quieter
impulse to paint
beneath envy's carriage
along eternity's mill.

Earth kicking me up in the form of the human,

and taking the meaning
and giving back the meaning

as the photographs do with the life.

Before rheumy eyes
before young strapping eyes.

A mystery you didn't step over
the white painted hot dog stand

dwarf autumn marigold

a gold chain to look, and look away.

To looky here lies your
empty leg, your empty leg of even gin I would give you

for just the hint of I
I essence
I nuance up the flue.

For the rheumy eyes
For the young strapping eyes.

And begin bicycling a side road in the gaping jaws of

sweet anthem that plays
but follows like murder like entropy like lassitude,

a shade, and then a plain, and then a majesty.

Abandoned on the shore

     a red towel,

      oh my automaton odalisque.

The sun and the wind and the resultant white cloud

then the car gone off in yellow traffic like a "so there"

might we have in conversation,

as in who am I   to write this, who

Who   who is speaking   most whoever-ly,

Who, you are pale

though always

you are social.

As ever,   it is water from a spring

to walk with you

2005

This Land Is My Land

Her bosslady trousseau was crepuscular.

Her remarks half-uttered

the documentary sound of the day.

Traffic salted   the nothing-happening parts,

the whole had been

the whoever-you-are,

frozen, or instamatic,

the rise/fall   orbit,   some kind of

guide figure at the window,

a silence tangled there.

A rim painting over the sun

in which

history would like to do a little unwriting, futurally.

History writing,

spare me.
I am afraid I will die like this,
a human face, of late.

No one understands
the writing.

The words keep saying

     is that

our wordy bride? Cancel and begin,

     oh no,

       she is a dark contemplative.

The Victorian was once a farmhouse.

She was in the task of her biography.

Attention's fan.

In a gorgeous relativity

     a bit like reading the markers

      in a botanical garden,

     California floats its prisons in the sea.

           2005

[My name is the girl with one glass eye said bitterly]

My name is the girl with one glass eye said bitterly.

                      Nightingale

in the birdfeeder hung from the pepper tree opening throat to the body
of light in (was it spring?)

        spring's shipwreck—

high voices. lank hounds
ramping it up over a highway arcing out into empty air—
where we

were resiliencies at the edges of time
dining on upended peach crates—

on lawn chairs dropped into the shaded pool
of the bottomless—where through the murk

Muses and Mediums regenerate the pool's Elysian scum. I am the girl who
   opens the seashell
that stirs the cauldron

that sings us back to the leafy path witch-worn and cobbled thru—
What do you walk upon?
Something already
in the blood.
What line of work you in?
job is Job is Job is job is Job it's all part of an infinite
series foci aperture
⅔ ¾ ⅛ scherzo   pattern I get it,

you look like someone I used to know

drinking out of a garden hose.

Can we summon by the hooks in the water

all the broken—as in the belly of an unsuspecting

mother—can we open the open

the hatchback to hear the Gothic echoes—a virgin forest asway amid the

   Giant's sperm?

Tomb for Tit,

come, wounds—extension cords carried to a midnight execution and left

to dangle there, a beheadedness played over

and over culture soaking it up   I knew a Garden:

meaning of the world is the intaglio of   it's sunny and 75.

What do you walk upon? Something already in the blood drafts an ink,

reconstitutes the flowers. Do you feel a light in the sun

on your back, piercing through the water, it's a light—said the said the I

am the girl with one

glass eye said

bitterly, now let me go, she said, holding the flowers to

long opal tails of moon waving slowly

from time to time

saying No no no no no no no, I am

the girl now that we are on the page of infinite

length,

in the city of uplanded height, on the lawn of rising

green   in the alley tunneled

down to a chambered core,

and I said how many people did you see on the road rolling up their old kit bag

how many people did you see

trying to get where trying to get there

trying to see the many people you have seen on the road

under the star's starkness under the exits entranced

under the mistral of

rain

feeding the lengthening stream we step into—out of—shuttering—

pictured there

2009

Andrew Joron
b. 1955

Born and raised in Stuttgart, Germany, Andrew Joron attended the University of California at Berkeley in order to study with the anarchist philosopher Paul Feyerabend, and graduated with a degree in the philosophy of science. After fifteen years of writing science fiction poetry, culminating in his volume *Science Fiction* (1992), Joron turned to a more speculative form of lyric, influenced by German Romanticism and surrealism, and reflecting his association with poet Philip Lamantia. This later work has been collected in *The Removes* (1999), *Fathom* (2003), *The Sound Mirror* (2008), and *Trance Archive: New and Selected Poems* (2010).

In his volume *The Cry at Zero: Selected Prose* (2010), Joron proposes a theory of the lyric poem based on the Cry:

> American poetry is a marginal genre whose existence is irrelevant to the course of Empire. Yet here, only here, at this very juncture between language and power, can the refused word come back to itself as the word of refusal, as a sign of that which cannot be assimilated to the system—
>
> Word that opens a solar eye in the middle of the Night.
>
> Opens but fails to dispel the dark. Of necessity perhaps, because it fails necessity itself. Opens, if only to make an O, an indwelling of zero, an otherness.
>
> The creative Word comes into its exile here, in the world's most destructive nation.[1]

This Cry opens the "real world" and has "none of the decorative quality of the art of forgetting."[2] Though it does not bring reconciliation or peace, it awakens us and, like the blues, is an "expression of triumph in defeat."[3] The poem is therefore not the shrill cry of the individual. On the contrary, it represents the alienation of all. It brings us back into community.

Joron has translated the *Literary Essays* of the Marxist-Utopian philosopher Ernst Bloch (1988) and *The Perpetual Motion Machine* by German fantasist Paul Scheerbart (2011). He has also written the critical study *Neo-Surrealism: or, The Sun at Night: Transformations of Surrealism in American Poetry 1966–1999* (2010).

Like Nathaniel Mackey and Harryette Mullen, Joron takes delight in homophonic wordplay—for example, the phrases "the *revel* hidden in *reveal*" ("Dolphy at Delphi") and "a knotted Not" ("Skymap under Skin"). Such puns are not casual; they conjure and deepen the Cry.

Joron lives in Berkeley.

1. "The Emergency," in *The Cry at Zero: Selected Prose*, Denver, 2007, p. 4.   2. The same, p. 4.   3. The same, p. 5.

First Drift

If we cannot be anything other than imperfect, a little tired, saddened, or distracted by those things we do not recognize (and familiar because of that)—

If we cannot be anything other than this—disquieted by the slowest possible music, yet listening intently—

Truth is reductive. Therefore, attend to those ideas whose boundaries lack edges, whose tones are just beginning to be infiltrated by disbelief. Allow your body to become a warped effect of that knowledge, a bow drawn backward across the strings—

Toward a blue identity resembling, although not possessing, the roundness of pain.

An excessive chord indwelling, proliferating tendrils, deemed by Lovecraft the *Crawling Chaos*—that which the insomniac writer E. M. Cioran called a "pandemonium of paradoxical symmetries."

To understand the veiled sound of the viol, study the curtains of light that surround extinguished suns.

—In medieval Arabic mathematics, such curvatures reach down to noise; a series of pictures invalidated by the doctrine of the motionless traveler.

We also (wanting elision) recorded the simultaneities' lateness. The round window laid horizontal: a zero. "We," meaning: many other figures of glass, collected at right angles.—Intense repose.

1999

Le Nombre des Ombres

The faster I travel
    the slower the world dies

Inside the head of a flower
The sun's
    a swinging pendulum

—all Radiance is progress
Of a pre-existent stillness

Stone, inspired
To fluency

    curves thought
    toward the drinking of Its shadow

    grail: grille: grid

The lines recursive to impalement

    one point alone
    sings cumulative, crowding negativity

My apparitions
    distorted by star-tides
Fail to approximate zero

Where sensation's tip
Crumbles to ash
Another
Radio-profile turns, edged with dark cries

    objects unfounded
    of medieval prophecy
The heavens too grow cold

1999

Dolphy at Delphi

for Garrett Caples

No lesson but a lessening, a loosening.
The spiral is made to spill its center.

—a name that acts—imperative's axe
Loses its head

As a baritone (the low
   solo's slow slope) sax (imaginary
   gender needs no sleep).

How the wrong notes compose their own song

Parallel to a dream of drowned cities.

After hours, what style of address, what robes
   (robs us
Of daylight) of delight?
Tells, then shows
The *revel* hidden in *reveal*?

   —now's even later than the future. Found
   sound reduced to meaning.

The perpetual emotion of a star-like story.

2003

Skymap under Skin

Ache, a network
Is & is
   a naked
Entirety, a knotted Not.

Bluest semblance of
   myself, the aleph
Unblessed.

Announce
Anything, the name is mine—
   a tear, a ware.

A
   substance
   stood under
The sob at the base of the body.

2010

The Person

But, I have only ever seen The Person—my counterpart—against the grammatical background of interstellar night.

He stands at my door, little realizing the *zero* of predicate is one, while the *prey* of predicate is two. He will say only the errata: *red*, at war with itself; *blue*, always the last instance of blue.

The Person wears a headdress, a dress of thought.

The Person is male with female characteristics, fallen into autumns of stain & substance. His sin is a cinema of seeming, a body-sign of *both & neither* meeting, teeming.

The Person wears what is: a "melancholy cloud." My closed system.

His signs point backward. His eye wants what it cannot have.

Taste waste, the One without mouth, the Eye ever over I.

Icon of the blackness of Blankness, icon of the whiteness of Witness.

Cite I, seer: O deafened hour, defend ear.

My, my, cold, cold, pyre a poor evaluator, & "alive" a lottery of lit particulars.

Because the sun dies in eyes, day is all Idea: a phosphorescent nightscape of skin & bone.

The start of art is always too soon or too late. My statement corrected, as sonically connected, gives only what cannot *not* be given: the empty set, once pieced together; the ware of whereness once aware.

Depart, part: pay per sun; pay per perishing, shadow—

2011

Illocutionary Reels

- Die rolls, rules die.
- Reaper, repairer, here appear.

- Wear sorrow, noiseware.
- Ring, bring news from nowhere.

- Offering fearing, Law of the Father, both neither & nether beard.
- So motion drips down: first & last liquid.

- Voice voice, mark mark, as *voices of ice* is to *vices of eyes*.
- For a chorus is incarcerated in every point of space.

- Every sentence repeats the past.
- "Senseless" alone tunes tense to the height of heat.

- Arc as ark hides hives, swarming in relation to the rest of reason.
- The circle of time is an arc hive.

- Language lies like a block on the tongue.
- So, called, passion, so, cold, position.

- To know no now.
- The animal leaves its senses every moon, every moan. No-man, gnomon.

- *We be,* betrayed: *we* to treat the trait of *alone.*
- *House* has *roof* to refer to *fire.*

- Written rotten: the later the letter, the righter the writer.
- Think, thank, thunk: O god-dawn, gone down.

- Enough of knife, of knife, of of.
- & the wound so wound, the sound so wound.

2011

Cole Swensen
b. 1955

Cole Swensen was born and raised in the San Francisco Bay Area; she received her B.A. and M.A. from San Francisco State University and her Ph.D. in literature from the University of California at Santa Cruz. She taught for a number of years in the University of Iowa Program for Writers, and in 2011 Swensen accepted a position at Brown University.

Her numerous books of poetry include the award-winning *New Math* (1988), *Park* (1991), *Numen* (1995), *Noon* (1997), *Try* (1999), *Oh* (2000), *Such Rich Hour* (2001), *Goest* (Finalist for the National Book Award, 2004), *The Book of a Hundred Hands* (2005), *The Glass Age* (2007), *Ours* (2008), *Greensward* (2010), *Gravesend* (2012), and *Stele* (2012). She is also a prolific translator of French poetry.

Swensen coedited the anthology *American Hybrid* (2009), which proposed the passing of the oppositional "two-camp model" of American poetry: "Hybrid poems often honor the avant-garde mandate to renew the forms and expand the boundaries of poetry—thereby increasing the expressive potential of language itself—while also remaining committed to the emotional spectra of lived experience."[1] Such an analysis was made possible by the wide acceptance of radical modes of writing, especially language poetry, in the late 1990s.

Swensen's books of poetry are unique in being designed as books, around a given theme rather than serving as a collection of disparate poems. In so doing, she recalls the historically researched long poems of Susan Howe. The Bay Area practice of the serial poem, as originally proposed by Jack Spicer, also comes to mind. In the brilliantly structured *Try*, the overall subject is painting. Consisting of three poems, each section plays on the phoneme "try": Triad, Trilogy, Triune, Trio, Triptych, Triarchy, Trinity, Trine, and Triage. Forrest Gander observes, "Swensen often sustains and develops in her poems a major tone, a delicate meditative aura with subtle modulations. The inherent radiance of *Try* lights up not only the paintings which are the poems' ostensible subject material but layers of perception."[2] Her book *Goest*, with its suggestion of Ghost, is researched in the history and future of incandescence. Anne Waldman's comment is therefore especially apt: "Swensen's poetry documents a penetrating 'intellectus'—light of the mind—by turns fragile, incandescent, transcendent."[3]

Swensen is the founding editor of La Presse, a small press that publishes contemporary French poetry translated by English language poets.

1. Introduction to *American Hybrid: A Norton Anthology of New Poetry*, New York, 2009, p. xxi.   2. Jacket comment, *Try*, Iowa City, 1999.   3. Jacket comment, *Goest*, Farmington, ME, 2004.

Trine

Cove

Covey of might

do convey
to my   my most
honor here what not only may
but will
                    that hearts a word

that flight (along the river as well as within the river, migration of dimension;
entire nation as a narrow line that stretches for miles and above, the hovering
dust of what dissolves the city into pieces so small they pass through a salt
shaker, a flour sifter, a human eye by the hundreds moving as a single gesture
down to the smallest finger in which the muscles are nonetheless meticulously
stitched to a longer anger: There is a body in the river. Carried light as
weather. Could not be identified but almost.)
                              my most
distinguished
must
the curving line
          carve
from simple fingers   friend
of a friend to find
within the hand
                    a thousand barely birds
          words for water
and a fire in the harbor. They're flying

(though they is always someone else and in some other country
where the thriving revolt.)

It is with great
and please believe
in my   may this
find you alive.

Dove

Dives, flock after flock

so convened. What lost
to each
        signed,

I beg the pleasure of
and so won this only

measurement of an artery
when and ever shall be
multiple aviary
one less ceiling
one less boat   do send my most

(however lost can only be spoken. It's just a way of speaking. It's not the mouth, but the throat that determines the limits of the vowels. Otherwise the body carries on for years and years later the body in the river becomes thousands, each thinking I should have lowered my eyes, I should have scarred my face, I should have torn out my hair, I should have lied.)

without end and when

the thousandth one turned
and then they will

                all those faces, eyes
and eyes
of my eternal gratitude   I find
(I died in a river but I did not drown, no not I says the body floating says the boat whose leaving came along and then stayed and then kept on staying.)
              one less army
one more throat   to whom it may
it is with great
that I   and will and am
my only   and my always
then.

Woven

Strove the uncommon
           unto custom

Thriving seemed
                     and then arrived
as the thread pulled
and the needle screamed
        friend
                  is searing skin
and then received

one more only
              how oddly
any
        without end
walked all the way to the sea
Entire
                  Please

and that I must

people clustered around fires
(and the harbor still on fire)
may I introduce

(what object with the object of holding was the hand and why does closing
the eyes make the edges more precise. You were born without a face. Stay.
I'm coming to. This which disperses. Names were not entered. Lists were not
made. No one was notified, which is what is meant by why does)

                  took shelter in

invented an

(a lie save only what in any case could not have been altered.)

                                                                    1999

The Girl Who Never Rained

Oddly enough, there was always a city block of clear weather on every side
of her, a space just large enough that the casual passerby simply thought,
"What an odd spot of calm," and often even people who knew her well never
quite put it together, as, after all, it's not that unusual to have a break in a

storm, though they'd develop, after a while, an odd inclination to be with her without really thinking out why. Other than that, her life was neither better nor worse than most, except, of course, for the crowds.

2004

Five Landscapes

One

I'm on a train, watching landscape streaming by, thinking
of the single equation that lets time turn physical,
equivocal, almost equable on a train

where a window is speed, *vertile, vertige.* It will be

one of those beautiful equations, almost visible, almost green. There

in the field, a hundred people, a festival, a lake, a summer, a
hundred thousand fields, a woman
places her hand on the small of a man's back in the middle of the crowd
and leaves it.

Two

A wedding in a field—the old saying: it's good luck to be seen
in white from a train. You must be looking the other way; so many things
work only if you're looking away. A woman in a field is walking away.
Gardens early in the evening. Trees
planted a few hundred years ago to line a road no longer there.
There's a lake, pale teal: its light, field after field. Spire, steeple, sea

of trees that line roads long disappeared along with their houses, which were
great houses in their time.

Three

A vineyard unleashed. The varieties of green. One glances accidently
into entire lives: plumage, habitat, and distance between
the girl raising her head, turning to her friend
lost under the trees—you say it was a ring?
Engraved, the birds rise up from the field like grain
thrown. Into a line of birds planing just above the wheat.

Four

Each scene, as accidental as it is inevitable, so visibly, you look out on, say
a field, say leaves, with a river on the other side, another life, identical
but everyone's this time. Trees in a wallpaper pattern. An horizon
of dusk that barely outruns us. He started with pages and pages

and then erased. This one
will have a thousand pictures.

A field of houses pierced by windows.

Five

There's a wedding in a field I am passing in a train
                                        a field
in the green air, in the white air, an emptier here
                                        the field is everywhere
because it looks like something similar somewhere else.

2004

A Garden as Between

as the articulating tissue between city and ocean, between building and
barren, around a house, a jungle
extends
        a magnet toward a jungle. A match
struck, a tailored knuckle; make it
                        useful. Let it reign
                        between the stilted and the flaming, the crack
in the glaze that lets us flow out again across a plain. A garden marks that plain
with a first principle. It paces off precise and hovers, cartilage between road and
home, a mental stable of dressage roses
                        hovers
                        as a garden is rooted
half in idea, rending the earth unstable, a flying machine with three wings, then
five, then all over the sky, in miniature vistas, a garden
branches from a fist in bridges.

2008

If a Garden of Numbers

If a garden is the world counted
                    and found analogue in nature
One does not become two by ever ending
                              so the stairs must be uneven in number
and not exceed
thirteen without a pause
of two paces' width, which
                    for instance, the golden section
            mitigates between abandon
and an orchestra just behind those trees,
gradations of green that take a stethoscope: we risk:
Length over width
                    to make the horizon run straight
equals
      to make the pond an oval:
                        Width
                        over length minus the width
            in which descending circles curl
into animals exact as a remainder.

            Which means excess. The meaning of the real
always exceeds that of the ideal, said someone.
                        He was speaking of Vaux-le-Vicomte,
but it's equally true of parking, or hunting, or wishing you could take it back. He

            who is Allen Weiss, actually said, "The meaning
of a plastic or pictorial construct always surpasses the ideal meaning of that work."°
Which is something else entirely. Said
the axonometric
divided by
the anamorphic.
            There is nothing that controls our thoughts
more than what we think we see,
which we label "we."

                                                2008

° Allen Weiss, *Mirrors of Infinity: The French Formal Garden and 17th Century Metaphysics,*
Princeton University Press, 1996.

Labyrinths and Mazes

And sometimes you're the door.

Within the stone

is a little maze: Make a list. Make each one different
shades of green and

a certain configuration of bones that ache
is a labyrinth that is,
said Madame de Sévigné, Fouquet's soul

for instance, the man has a garden for a body
and all his organs—the heart topiaried, and the *escalier d'eau*
of the spine.
     One wonders if Fouquet really had either
she said or neither or *history is paltry* he was singing
            one night in the kitchen, as
rummaging about for a midnight snack,
he glanced out the pantry window
into the vegetable patch. Which spiraled, length over width, width over length
minus the width. Planets
are etymologically related to the plants that divide themselves
into carefully proportioned moments when
he turned around to find the kitchen maid staring,
"Monsieur,
    it is dark and entire
orchards are moving
      in the perfect patterns of the quadrille."
Fouquet
followed her gaze, saying, "My
soul is a labyrinth. Madame de Sévigné has said so, and it makes me sad."

                       2008

Susan Wheeler
b. 1955

Susan Wheeler was born in Pittsburgh and grew up in Minnesota and New England. She attended Bennington College and the University of Chicago, and for many years lived in the New York City area, working as a professor, a journalist, and a public affairs director.

Wheeler's first poetry collection, *Bag 'o' Diamonds* (1993), won the Norma Farber First Book Award of the Poetry Society of America. Robert Hass, who selected the book for a publication prize, wrote of her second book, *Smokes* (1998): "The idiom is postmodern: irony, pastiche, non-sequitur, dark wit, wild shifts in diction, a funhouse falling away of narrative continuity from image to image and line to line. . . . What makes *Smokes* such an exhilarating and unexpected performance is not the idiom, which Ms. Wheeler has down and carries off with brio, but her witty ear."[1] In her work *Ledger* (2005), Wheeler creates a thematic book-length work relating to debt, with section headings such as "Short Shrift," "Surfeit," and "Money and God." The critic Marjorie Perloff commented on the book, "Wheeler is that rare thing among poets, a genuine cultural critic." In other of Wheeler's works, the political is sardonically lodged, rather than central.

Her other poetry collections are *Source Codes* (2001); *Assorted Poems* (2009), which collects poems from earlier volumes; and *Meme* (2012). She is the recipient of numerous prizes including a Guggenheim Fellowship (1999), a Yaddo Residency (1999), the Witter Bynner Prize for Poetry (2002), the Boston Review Award for Poetry, and the Iowa Poetry Prize (2004).

In a short essay, "On Form," Wheeler displays her wry common sense:

> Saying a particular poem is "formless" is as nuts as saying it isn't "political": form and politics obtain as soon as there are words. IMHO
>
> You got mascara. Use it.
>
> It's half the score in Olympian judging. Ah, but that other half . . .
>
> Fussiness, cleverness, or adverse polish, results. But sometimes distance is what's called for.[3]

Susan Wheeler teaches at Princeton University.

1. *Smokes,* Marshfield, MA, 1998, p. 55.　　2. *Bag 'o' Diamonds,* Athens, GA, p. 7.　　3. "Poets on Form," contributor, *PSA (Poetry Society of America) Journal,* Summer 1999. Poetry Society of America website: On Poetry Feature: On Form https://www.poetrysociety.org/psa/poetry/crossroads/on_poetry/on_form_susan_wheeler/.

The Belle

Sad, that *porking* verb. I went down
With the fancy dyke to the parts store then
And that Billy crafted up a neurasma
Like as not the bends. *Nice legs.*

Felicity, a mom that's got a skittish grin
For every time the car door slams.
Come again: coquette off, on, and when
That lady turns her eye on you depends.

A girl labels each excretion in a box.
Mom's beat. (I'd like to say the tigers
Then the fear a far cry from complete.)
Come gently, wash those *hi-boys* here.

1993

Bankruptcy & Exile

Along the horizon, the exhausted buildings tilt above
the darkened streets. This silence means
a tarnishing of trade. Before you step into the gaunt
alley, your hand releases a periapt of hope.

Divisions when agreements rent come. This dappled beast
in green finds fault with the quietest prudences, uses the
sword you left behind to hack away at social convocations.
There is no calling for the dream is wavering.

Then the cloud that made the kitchen dark passes.
She is turning the leaves of the magazine and laughing.
She is knowing the silent parting of the skin that soothes the heart.

A crater appears beside the trees, in the dark.
The line that means horizon bends beneath the moon.

1993

The Privilege of Feet

Superb wandering this:
glacier unfed by light,
the object of fidelity,
or the azure wildflower, bending.
It is not so much embellishment,
this reasoning into language.

His first word was *breakfast,* his
second *porridge.* Then he learned
to mate two halves of a
limonite concretion on a shelf.
His Tigers' cap
brushed against his glasses.
He tried peeing
in the sink,
from the top of the toilet seat.
He called geology
jeedocy.

And does this fabric account for
the fiction of family? Too many
highballs. Too much sun.

The starboard tack arrested
the brunt of the luffing, and
several careful swimmers
took a dive, thinking nothing
of the decorative this became:
headfirst, a word
described as *festive.*

1993

He or She That's Got the Limb, That Holds Me Out on It

The girls are drifting in their ponytails
and their pig iron boat. So much for Sunday.
The dodo birds are making a racket
to beat the band. You could have come too.

The girls wave and throw their garters
from their pig iron boat. Why is this charming?
Where they were nailed on their knees
the garters all rip. You were expected.

The youngest sees a Fury in a Sentra
in a cloud. This is her intimation and she balks.
The boat begins rocking from the scourge
of the sunset. The youngest starts the song.

1998

Possessive Case

What are you walking the hamjammies for.
It's always the same argument. The man scrapes
the molt from his forearm and cringes.

The scabs become virulent in their saucer.
The man harnesses their latent energy.
The man continues to prick, pick at the girl.

Seven flight suits are pounding at the door.
Words pound from seven visors. The words
fall in the saucer and make a molten pot hash.

The marquee in the saucer draws waterbugs.
Their inelegant eyebrows make needles for the girl.
He *might* have been capable of love. Worth trying.

The giant engine with its pistons of lamb arms
glides down their street on its skis. The pilots
use their balcony for streamers. Cheers.

Scabrous wasn't such a big deal. Where's the oven?
Under the spreading oak tree a steel filament blew.
He puts his johnson in his pants and begins to stew.

1998

Anthem

after Bill Viola

Five thirty a.m., Gary, Indiana.
The heart under knife, its palpitating fibers,
its onyx strands, its cold lard binders,
chalk, mould, mushroom cavities fibrillating faster,
surgeon in the clank of steel, spears,
flies above the cow's fresh mound—

then, mill at dawn, fires keening at its core,
two men step out. Wet and chill
below the canisters of flames and onyx chutes: two men
bright in a scrub plain's hush.
They light small flames for cigarettes they cup,
needles underfoot.

A Poptart™ hits a plate.
Window smudged, chrome toaster specked,
radio drone on a stirring street,
crabgrass, umbrella grass beyond the glass.
Pursed lines above a woman's lip on a cup
lock, clamp, release, dissolve. Then snow.

2005

Forrest Gander

b. 1956

Born in Barstow, California, a town in the Mojave Desert, Forrest Gander was raised in Virginia, where he attended The College of William and Mary, majoring in geology. Later he received an M.A. in English from San Francisco State University, where he met his wife, the poet C. D. Wright. He then lived in Mexico for four months, where he learned Spanish and began to compile and translate the work published in the bilingual anthology *Mouth to Mouth: Poems by Twelve Contemporary Spanish Women* (1993).

Gander's other poetry translations include *No Shelter: Selected Poems of Pura López-Colomé* (2002); *Firefly Under the Tongue: Selected Poems of Coral Bracho* (2008); two collections by Jaime Saenz, translated in collaboration with Kent Johnson; and *Spectacle & Pigsty* by Kiwao Nomura (2011), translated with Kyoko Yoshida.

Gander's books of poems include *Rush to the Lake* (1988), *Lynchburg* (1993), *Deeds of Utmost Kindness* (1994), *Science & Steepleflower* (1998), *Torn Awake* (2001), *The Blue Rock Collection* (2004), *Eye Against Eye* (2005), *Core Samples from the World* (2011), and *Redstart: a Collaborative Ecopoetics* (with John Kinsella, 2012). He has also published a collection of essays, *A Faithful Existence: Reading, Memory, and Transcendence* (2005), and a novel, *As a Friend* (2008).

Other poets such as Elizabeth Robinson and Donald Revell have taken exception, by the example of their work, to the materialist poetics of language poetry. Gander does so by emphasizing acts of attention. In "The Transparency of a Faithful Existence," he writes, "Neither Jewish, Christian, nor Muslim, when I write I am cloistered, nevertheless, in my own imagination. The basic gesture of my writing is a listening. Perhaps this attitude resembles that of the religious. But my creedal source is worldly. Faith, for me, derives from the most common revelations."[1] These common revelations signal the poetic otherness of being, as found in the work of George Oppen: "We want to be here. // The act of being, the act of being / More than oneself."[2] Gander also cites the poetry of the pre-Romantic visionary Thomas Traherne and the philosophy of Merleau-Ponty, who writes of "the advent of being into consciousness."[3]

In 2010, Forrest Gander was named the Adele Kellenberg Seaver Professor of Literary Arts and Comparative Literature at Brown University, where he began teaching in 2001, after a long tenure at Providence College.

1. *A Faithful Existence: Reading, Memory, and Transcendence*, New York, 2005, p. 43.   2. From Oppen's "World, World," quoted in "Finding the Phenomenal Oppen," the same, p. 135.   3. "The Strange Case of Thomas Traherne," the same, p. 79.

To Eurydice

Like a man who watches from close, like a man
who watches from close the motion of a chorus, the slow
choreography back and forth, hypnotized, like that
man who goes home to drink his black water: I am.
As far as my perceptions refer to what we called
the real world, they are not certain. As far as they are certain
they do not refer to what we called real.

I was there when you began to cheat on the high notes,
gobble lines for extra air. Even at that,
you floored me. The applause, smothering. I shivered
in a cold sweat. Smothering. And when I stepped
from the theater through the cordon of mounted police,
I saw myself upside-down in a horse's eye. Though I
was prepared, a place had yet to be prepared. I rode
the Tenryu ferry under a stand-and-wait moon.
I polished the statue with beeswax.

It's beginning to have a familiar ring, isn't it?
I've instructed myself to speak more slowly. As though
I were in a play.

I stepped from the theater. I kneeled,
kneeled before the statue. *The story has a skip in it.*
What is your distance but my impatience? Lichens live
under crusts of rock for a thousand years. I will never
condescend to be a mere object of turbulent
and decisive verbs. Is leaving whom? Has left whom?

It is not Orpheus speaking. Do you even know
who is speaking? Dear Eurydice. There was a rip in your stocking.
When the cry flashed across the hills (*not your cry,*
but my own), no baffle could muffle it, every hiding place
clenched shut, and a spasm rolled out from me and over the field.
The given is given. How the past waxes fat! Overhead
is now below. There was a rip

in something. Here. No, here on this page.
Whose fingerprints are not smeared across the telling? That
third person beside you. That was my character. Il terzo incomodo.

I have instructed myself to speak more slowly. It is morning.
The fog draws back its thin lavender scent.

When I kicked off my shoes to carry you—*how could I guess*
it was the beginning of my concentration, a test—into
the cramped bedroom, a cross-marked spider crawled my foot.
Upon this intentionality another would impinge. But I
was soaked in pleasure's spittle and you
submitted your willing throat. Wailful. You were. You are.

It was later, later you met Orpheus. His wealth, his fame.
His girlish smile. He went to absurd lengths, he lied
solely to appear mysterious. He played you—
that dreary chorus wending back and forth behind him—
ridiculous *morna* songs for which we hooted him offstage,
but you swallowed it.

When the cry wrung itself from between my teeth. *What*
was the last word? Offstage? There is a sound caught
in my ears, a particular sound like the sound of a breath.
How did it go, the telling? Your face
stayed in the dirt as though you saw into it.

When the cry ricocheted from the hills and screwed
back into me, wasn't it my wakening? It was my castration.
                              Who is that
other one beside her, they asked. It is not Orpheus
speaking. Orpheus, used up in the rashness of his first impulse.

What was torn away is speaking.

Like flakes struck from a stone ax. Like flakes
from a stone ax, the scales have fallen from my eyes
rendering me impervious to panic. Ploughed
and harrowed my soul is. And yet. (*The rip*
is full of voices.) I cannot stop this incessant scheming.
With what word, what gambit,
might a stubborn, remnant hope contract even further
and even further into a summons?

                                                  2001

To Virginia

Every new thing—the sentence began and began
to decay in the dryness of my mouth before I could finish it,
the doctor laying her ear to my chest, listening
for a dead space in the labored
breathing, her fingers probing my ribs for tenderness—
quickens me. Was it something I might insist upon as though
to convince myself?
Sometimes you are more in me than I am
in this room. Sick of myself, I know myself vaguely
as consciousness, image, thing. Here is my dimensional body.
                                        But if there is no frontier
between eloquence and world, in the realm of things
where incoherence is manifest, will we say life presents itself
to that which speaks of itself, as schist
basement rises into the Blue Ridge between valleys? Who would not
read the openness of such long-familiar eyes as a world ready
to be seen, inaugurating itself once more. And
if I received you like that?—
(now that I am vulnerable, but not against my will)
with greediness and delight, entertaining you, exhilarated where
quartz-veins sever beds of black mica in the hills and rains
etch brachiopods from Shenandoah limestone. . . . Begotten
with strange attentiveness, besotted
as I am with you, I feel my response fill in
the routine between us, gathering you into me
in shovelfuls, see myself inverted, a reflection
in a shovel's blade, alone and
desperate and miserable like something unplanted, and then
beatified, wet with intimacy, fine-
tuned to wakefulness. So to hear
tendrils rustle under dead leaves, each thing announcing
its exigence, each tendril, its godly excellence curling out
between ambiguities, to see the beetle in a laurel blossom and
ten pollen-bowed stamens, triggered,
snapping toward the center. If life presents itself. Is—
one horizon ladled into another. Near the window, fragrant
privet. Is nothing—by this means, by this meaning's benevolence,
(the inflammation promising through my lungs)—mended? What then?

2001

FROM Late Summer Entry: The Landscapes of Sally Mann

River and Trees

The passage may be so swollen, limpid, and inviting that it requires considerable effort, a convulsion in seeing's habit, to encounter the drama. In this composition, to wit, the river lavishes-out soft tones, rich detail, and gentle, contrasting textures, but only at first glance. The calm is contradictory. For when we find the river *holding still*—in imitation of itself—it barely impresses a likeness.

The depicted instant: a galvanic pre-storm eclipse. On a bridge, the photographer bends, shrouded behind her tripod. As she guesses the exposure time, lightning hisses and rips so close that the air, for seconds, isn't breathable. At once, the river quicksilvers. Its surface bulks and brightens. The heft of the scene, though, and the dynamic tension flee to the margins. There,

in the rumpled quiet of the trees, we catch the most animate qualities. In the riffle of leafy detail, we sense the respiration of the forest.

And while we absorb this disturbance in a merely apparent repose, our stomach rolls—as when an elevator begins to descend. We detect in the blurred trees a peristaltic contraction. We feel the landscape giving birth to our vision.

Ghost Sonata

The fulcrum of the composition is the sheared off, gnarly trunk. In contradiction of death's irreversibility, it has burst into leaf. It leans forward, toward us, producing an effect similar to the entasis or swelling of a classical pillar. Isolation magnifies its solemnity. Beyond the trunk, the horizon lists. On one side, foliage goes fuzzy, while on the other side, a strange flare burns.

Strain between focal points is sustained by the central figure of the ruptured tree. Mute, but implicative. A leafy explosion crowns the severed totem. So at the border between a tangible and an intangible world, life climbs onto death's shoulders.

Ivy Brick Wall

It never aims to create an illusion of reality. Instead, the warped lens allows for a new set of relationships behind swirling frets. The wall confronts a flotsam of vortical energy and tree limbs transparentize in the blast.

Enmeshed in a field of concentric force, the spectator is drawn toward a wormhole of brightness, not depth but another dimension entire. A light which is life source.

It is this originary force that transforms the ordinary into the exultant. Here, where light authors act and meaning, where whelming ivy overwrites brickwork.

The nucleus of the image is all verb, the seen availing itself to our seeing. When there are no stable terms, there are no faithful things.

Late Summer Entry

Brush-hogged here last week, beckons.

Dog won't sit on the stubble, beckons.

Distant peak, Cambrian quartzite beckons.

Dipping northwest, beckons.

They mine corundum here, beckons.

Grinds her plates with corundum, beckons.

Can you smell collodion, beckons.

Ether and alcohol, cold as an eel, beckons.

Blackening her fingertips, beckons.

Stiffens into membrane, beckons.

Shoot collodion in the full sun, beckons.

So so fragile, beckons.

Pours it onto the plate, beckons.

Three minutes to climb the hill, three minutes to shoot it, beckons.

Under a cape, composing an upside-down image, beckons.

Felt Rider hat in one hand, plate in the other, beckons.

Fingers the lens, beckons.

Pulls out the block, beckons.

The camera quivers, beckons.

Can you photograph a Carolina wren's song, beckons.

The collodion fills with birdsong, beckons.

With the scent of ripening pawpaws, beckons.

From the pawpaw tree behind her, beckons.

Extracts the glass plate, beckons.

Walks back to the truck, beckons.

Over the stiff stubble, the dog following, beckons.

Pulls out the chemical tray, beckons.

The spring-driven trap, thwarting light, beckons.

Click, beckons.

The plate sinks into the tray, beckons.

Gently the dark blows in, beckons.

So figure passes into shadow.

                                                                    2005

Rusty Morrison
b. 1956

Rusty Morrison was born and raised in the Bay Area and worked for several years there as a high school teacher. In her early forties she joined a poetry writing group at the University of California extension, and, inspired by the work of poets Ann Lauterbach and Brenda Hillman, as well as the writings of Bachelard and Blanchot, enrolled in the M.F.A. program at Saint Mary's College. Deciding to devote herself completely to poetry, she resigned her teaching position and worked as a freelance reviewer and part-time teacher. In 2001, she cofounded Omnidawn Publishing, which quickly developed into a leading poetry publisher. With Elizabeth Robinson and others, she also became an editor of the magazine *26*.

In 2003, Morrison won the Colorado Prize, which led to the publication of her first book, *Whethering* (2004). In 2007, she won the Sawtooth Poetry Prize, resulting in the publication of *the true keeps calm biding its story*, which won the James Laughlin Award and the Northern California Book Award, and the DiCatagnola Award from the Poetry Society of America. Written as a cycle of nine numbered sets of six poems each, the work was begun before Morrison's father died suddenly of pneumonia. His death gave urgency to the work's phrasing, each line of which ends with "please," "advise," or "stop." The elegiac repetition of these words has the rhythm of chanted plea, as if the call of "stop" and "please" could in fact change the turn of events.

The poet Claudia Rankine writes of *the true keeps calm biding its story*: "Oddly, what reconstitutes the power of the lyric . . . is the speaker's self-conscious use of metaphor. Because each noun in these poems houses itself as well as its metaphoric possibilities, the speaker eventually follows language beyond the house into a world where nothing looks back at her from the house of the dead father."[1]

Rusty Morrison's third volume, *After Urgency*, won Tupelo Press's Dorset Prize in 2011. She lives in Richmond, California, and teaches at the University of San Francisco.

1. "Please Advise Stop: Claudia Rankine on Rusty Morrison," Poets.org, https://www.poets/printmedia.php/prmMedia11D/21583.

please advise stop

I was dragging a ladder slowly over stones stop
it was only from out of my thoughts that I could climb stop
not from the room please

my father's dying offered an indelicate washing of my perception stop
the way the centers of some syllables scrub away all other sound stop
his corpse merely preparing to speak its new name at the speed of nightfalling
please

each loss grows from a previously unremarkable vestigial organ stop
will I act now as if with a new limb stop
a phantom limb of the familial please advise

please advise stop

only gray rocks with drifting mist but I was so in need of something paired stop
each pairing isolates another world stop
attempted listening in a lower register than I usually speak please

still snapped inside the brackets of my old maneuver but not blindfolded by it stop
teeth grinding down their desperate impulses stop
shine the thought's dark mahogany until it begins to shift like a shoal of mackerel please

soon will I be able to discern the linen texture of right silences stop
there have been emphatic emissaries stop
a pebble cupped in a rose-petal held by a palm resting on the lawn please advise

please advise stop

basin of hills polished with the pour of sunset please
easing down on one knee to touch the oak leaf trapped in a footprint stop
I neglect then compromise the vision I've hidden between eye movements stop

cup my palms together for something new to grow in their microclimate stop
spit as if intending to hit what you aim at stop
a skirtful of fresh pears rolling onto the lawn and into the stealth of narrative please

how to line the pockets of madness with flowerpetals please
the months go but my father's death stays demanding to be reabsorbed stop
sylph-like grass misty rain conceived against claims of other empires please advise

please advise stop

the chainlink fence holds separate the severed air stop
a blond boy sits on a bench his hair dissolving into wind please
etch kohl around each shadow to give it room rather than brightness stop

look up into a starless patch of night and watch it expand stop
stand in its corridor as if in motion stop
as if all four directions had let go of their point of interlocked origin please

indices that at once augment and ridicule the senses stop
a stone floor to step into waist deep stop
too easily I might erect in lieu of sight a stage of sculpted shrines please advise

please advise stop

like water-spiders on a pond the hours pass overhead stop
with each perfected dexterity I thin the surface that carries me stop
traces of an otherwise indiscernible consensus collect under my fingernails please

his face isn't lost to me but traveling now and mostly untended stop
hereafter will I apply rules and avoid content stop
braid wildflower stems peeled of petals stop

scrub gently with a brush to relieve us of the historical present please
listen for the entire circumference of the screen door's arc but hear only its slap stop
even incoherent babbling is usually phonetically accurate please advise

please advise stop

any object inclines away from memory the more energetically I imagine its features stop
featureless is the vault in which I want to hide myself undetected stop
haven't I even a pigeon's sense to fly suddenly the other way please

pecking at seeds and not the shadows of seeds among the gravel stop
we say *materialized out of nothing* to further secure the brackets of that rigid frame stop
a magnet linked tight to other magnets can still pull in new metal stop

impossible to lift the weightless gravity of nightfall please
staring into the dark like digging a grave through an already existing grave stop
tonight Cassiopeia the Pleiades are emitted from the sky like fragrance please advise

2008

Myung Mi Kim
b. 1957

Myung Mi Kim was born in Korea and moved to the United States with her parents at the age of nine. She received an M.F.A. degree in poetry from the University of Iowa and taught for several years at San Francisco State University. She is now a professor of English at the State University of New York Buffalo.

Her books of poetry include *Under Flag* (1991), *The Bounty* (2000), *Dura* (1999), *Commons* (2002), and *Penury* (2009).

Her work is experimental in a line of influence that includes Ezra Pound, language poetry, Kathleen Fraser and the publication *HOW(ever)*, and Theresa Chak Kyung Ha. Its central concern of identity and its shifting borders is made further restless by the open spaces of the page, multiple points of view, and mosaic organization. Her poem "Primer" is prefaced: "To represent 14 single and 5 double consonants, Hangul [Korean] starts with five basic symbols, which are shaped to suggest the articulators pronouncing them. For example, a small square depicts a closed mouth pronouncing /m/."[1] Fragmentary and half-said, much of Kim's work relates to the difficulties of expression. As one critic puts it, "Avant-garde writers like Kim often engage a poetics that seems less concerned with the fabulousness of the production, and more with the struggle to speak itself."[2]

Kim is quoted as saying, "There's something about being nine or so—you have enough access to the language, you feel a connection to the culture fully. And yet again, that culture is and will be embedded in you. In this strange region of knowing and not knowing, I have access to Korea as a language and culture but this access is shaped by rupture (leaving the country, the language). When I engage 'Korea' what resemblance does it have to any 'real' place, culture, or the language spoken there? So in this effort and failure of bridging, reconfiguring, shaping, and being shaped by loss and absence, one enters a difficult negotiation with an Imaginary and a manner of listening which to me is the state of writing."[3] In her essay "Anacrusis," she describes a poetics of "the ellipses": "The meaning of grappling in the interstitial mark between abrasion and adumbration."[4]

Kathleen Fraser writes of *Under Flag*, "One is shaken by this severe and quiet telling—an assemblage of on-going effacements in the life of a child and her family under occupation by American forces in Korea and, later, in her struggle to enter an alien language and culture in the United States. Not since Oppen, has the eroding presence of war on the wholeness of human existence been so vividly located. But the construction of perspective has shifted from male to female, occupier to occupied."[5]

1. Myung Mi Kim, epigraph to "Primer," The Bounty, Minneapolis, 1996, unpaginated. 2. Dawn Lundy Martin, review of *Penury, Critical Quarterly* 53.1, April 27, 2011, p. 98.   3. Woodland Pattern website, http://www.woodlandpattern.org/poems/myung_mi_kim01. shtml.   4. *how2* 1.2, 1999, http://www.asu.edu/pipercwcenter/how2journal/archive/online_ archive/vl_2_1999 current/readings/kim.html.   5. *Under Flag*, Berkeley, 1991, jacket comment.

Into Such Assembly

1.

Can you read and write English? Yes____. No____.
Write down the following sentences in English as I dictate them.
    There is a dog in the road.
    It is raining.
Do you renounce allegiance to any other country but this?
Now tell me, who is the president of the United States?
You will all stand now. Raise your right hands.

Cable car rides over swan flecked ponds
Red lacquer chests in our slateblue house
Chrysanthemums trailing bloom after bloom
Ivory, russet, pale yellow petals crushed
Between fingers, that green smell, if jade would smell
So-Sah's thatched roofs shading miso hung to dry—
Sweet potatoes grow on the rock choked side of the mountain
The other, the pine wet green side of the mountain
Hides a lush clearing where we picnic and sing:
    Sung-Bul-sah, geep eun bahm ae

Neither, neither

Who is mother tongue, who is father country?

2.

Do they have trees in Korea? Do the children eat out of garbage cans?

We had a dalmation

We rode the train on weekends from Seoul to So-Sah where we grew grapes

We ate on the patio surrounded by dahlias

Over there, ass is cheap—those girls live to make you happy

Over there, we had a slateblue house with a flat roof where
I made many snowmen, over there

No, "th", "th", put your tongue against the roof of your mouth,
lean slightly against the back of the top teeth, then bring your
bottom teeth up to barely touch your tongue and breathe out, and
you should feel the tongue vibrating, "th", "th", look in the mirror,
that's better

And with distance traveled, as part of it

How often when it rains here does it rain there?

One gives over to a language and then

What was given, given over?

3.

This rain eats into most anything

> And when we had been scattered over the face of the earth
> We could not speak to one another

The creek rises, the rain-fed current rises

> Color given up, sap given up
> Weeds branches groves what they make as one

This rain gouging already gouged valleys
And they fill, fill, flow over

> What gives way losing gulch, mesa, peak, state, nation

Land, ocean dissolving
The continent and the peninsula, the peninsula and the continent
Of one piece sweeping

One table laden with one crumb
Every mouthful off a spoon whole

Each drop strewn into such assembly

1991

FROM Penury

foundry
mill
warehouse

tannery
refinery
central clearing hall

infirmary
barracks
internment camp

auto plant
containment center
refugee camp

▪

Touching Reception and

Precedence, the Treatment of Audience

Contents of Visiting
Ambassadors

The bird for prosperity we provided you

▪

[conjugate]

she, the weeping work

parade of earnings

|| weight of forelegs and hooves under water

a ripple | birched

alyssum

▪

within a few years it learns to read—if it is a boy—and in this place

the catalogue of books may be inserted

▪

Half a lobe and barricade | as befits a stateroom

Clock-tower and bulwark

: Why don't you take mommy swimming? It'll be fun—

       He is not making rent.
       She is tired of being alone with the child.

▪

plethora of roots || mowed lawns

tendon and refuse, who

cowered | supermarkets, windshield

snap. Does the single tree

list. Disinterred. Would be forced to look.

▪

[conjugate]

A dependent's call

A dependent cries out

A || marvel perceive

■

Through sameness of language is produced

sameness of sentiment and thought

: Got up to cut meat

Stood in that smell all day

beat/th/rone

beat/hrone

bea/t/rone

■

perimeter onset plain crucial corridor

branch full tip time and place

scanned yes sir I do three of those were

fixing it no seeing them elements buffer

in that twitch feel of limbs there's no fixing it

huddle quadrant counting inhabitants

operative swath who is in there who's there blaring

rout will be returned as practicable as possible

▪

mp
lm
ks
nc
lk
lp
nh
gy
td
nc

you speak English so well transcript

2009

Wang Ping

b. 1957

Wang Ping was born in Shanghai and spent her childhood on an island of the People's Republic of China in the East China Sea. When she was eight years old, her mother died and her father was imprisoned in a work camp, leaving her as caretaker of her younger siblings. Despite a limited childhood education, she was admitted to Beijing University, where she earned a B.A. in English literature. The following year she emigrated to the United States and obtained her M.A. in English literature at Long Island University. She obtained her Ph.D. from New York University in 1999.

Wang Ping's first publications were a book of short stories, *American Visa* (1994), and the novel *Foreign Devil* (1996). Two poetry collections followed, *Of Flesh & Spirit* (1998) and *The Magic Whip* (2003). She has published on the Chinese practice of footbinding, *Aching for Beauty* (2000), and edited and translated the anthology *New Generation: Poems from China Today* (2002). In 2006, she published *The Dragon Emperor*, a collection of Chinese folktales. A second collection of stories, *The Last Communist Virgin*, appeared in 2007. With Ron Padgett, she translated *Flash Cards: Poems by Yu Jian* (2010), a leading poet of Yunnan.

Anne Waldman has written of Wang Ping's work: "Riveting, confessional, fierce poetry. In poetic superstitions, Wang Ping makes her singular way with passion and vigor. She explodes the safe boundaries of culture, gender, and female sexuality."[1]

Wang Ping's poems communicate a wealth of cultural knowledge. In "Born in the Year of the Chicken," for instance: "A recipe for mothers who can't produce milk: a hen (the older the better; best if it hasn't laid eggs for three or four years) and five ounces of pangolin scales. Break the scales into small pieces and sew them into the stomach of the hen. Cook until the flesh comes off the bones. Eat the meat and drink the soup."[2]

She has received an NEA Fellowship in Poetry, a Bush Foundation Award for the Arts, and a Lannan Foundation residency in Marfa, Texas.

Wang Ping lives in St. Paul, Minnesota, and teaches at Macalester College.

1. *Of Flesh & Spirit*, St. Paul, MN, 1998, jacket comment.   2. The same, p. 23.

Syntax

She walks to a table
She walk to table

She is walking to a table
She walk to table now

What difference does it make
What difference it make

In Nature, no completeness
No sentence really complete thought

Language, like woman
Look best when free, undressed

1998

Of Flesh & Spirit

I was a virgin till twenty-three, then always had more than one lover at the same time—all secret.

In China, people go to jail for watching porno videos while condoms and pills are given out free.

When I saw the first bra my mom made for me, I screamed and ran out in shame.

For a thousand years, women's bound feet were the most beautiful and erotic objects for Chinese. Tits and asses were nothing compared to a pair of three-inch "golden lotuses." They must have been crazy or had problems with their noses. My grandma's feet, wrapped day and night in layers of bandages, smelled like rotten fish.

The asshole in Chinese: the eye of the fart.

A twenty-five-year-old single woman worries her parents. A twenty-eight-year-old single woman worries her friends and colleagues. A thirty-year-old single woman worries her bosses. A thirty-five-year-old woman is pitied and treated as a sexual pervert.

The most powerful curse: fuck your mother, fuck your grandmother, fuck your great-grandmother of eighteen generations.

One day, my father asked my mother if our young rooster was mature enough to jump, meaning to "mate." I cut in before my mother answered: "Yes, I saw him jump onto the roof of the chicken coop." I was ten years old.

Women call menstruation "the old ghost," science books call it "the moon period," and refined people say "the moonlight is flooding the ditch."

My first lover vowed to marry me in America after he took my virginity. He had two kids and an uneducated wife, and dared not ask the police for a divorce. He took me to see his American Chinese cousin who was staying in the Beijing Hotel and tried to persuade his cousin to sponsor him to come to New York. But his cousin sponsored me instead. That's how I'm here and why he went back to his wife, still cursing me.

Chinese peasants call their wives: that one in my house; old Chinese intellectuals: the doll in a golden house; in socialist China, husbands and wives call each other "my lover."

The story my grandma never tired of telling was about a man who was punished for his greed and had to walk around with a penis hanging from his forehead.

We don't say "fall in love," but "talk love."

When I left home, my father told me: "never talk love before you're twenty-five years old." I waited till twenty-three. Well, my first lover was a married coward. My first marriage lasted a week. My husband slept with me once, and I never saw him again.

1998

Female Marriage

Chinese characters for marriage: *qu* 娶 —a man getting married, and *jia* 嫁 —a woman getting married.

Jia 嫁 is made of two components: the left part is nü 女 —woman, and the right part, *jia* 家 —home.

If a thirty-year-old woman still remains single, every member of her family, every female colleague of hers, gets busy to find her a husband. If she shows no interest, she's suspected of being a hermaphrodite. But if she shows too much interest, or changes boyfriends constantly, she'll be called a "broken shoe," "rotten meat," or *zou ma deng*—lanterns with paper-cut figures made to revolve when it's lit, something like a dizzying merry-go-round.

Every Chinese believes that a husband is a woman's *guisu*—her final home to return to.

Nainai stands for paternal grandma. Its literal translation is "breast breast," or "milk milk."

Waipo stands for maternal grandma. *Wai* means "outside," "stranger." *Po*, "old woman."

My Waipo used to weep when she brushed my hair. "What are you going to do, my baby? Your hair is too tough, so will be your fate. Try not to be so pigheaded, try to learn some obedience. Otherwise you'll never find a husband."

Fu chang fu sui—when man sings, wife follows.

Nuzi wu cai bian shi de—ignorance is woman's virtue.

My father's favorite curse to my mother is *bi yang de*—born out of a cunt, as if he came out of something else.

Other curses for women:
  Cheap stuff
  Losing money commodity
  Disastrous flood
  Stinky whore
  Fox spirit
  Shrew

Even Confucius, the wisest and kindest saint, complained that women and inferior men are hard to raise.

For seventy-five years, my Nainai walked on her heels because all her toes were broken and bent under the soles to make a pair of "golden lotuses." She brought up her two sons alone, by working in the fields and delivering babies for her neighbors. I don't know her name. No one knows her name, not even herself. When she was a girl, she was called a girl, maybe Number 1 or Number 2. When she got married, her neighbors called her "wife of so-and-so," and her husband called her *wei*—equivalent to "hello." After she had her first son, she got the name "mother of so-and-so."

When I was a kid, I was crazy about keeping my hair long. But my father cursed at me every time he saw me brushing it, and my mother chased me around with a pair of scissors.

All our lives, we've never felt attractive enough. But for whom do we struggle to look beautiful?

Chinese proverbs: A married daughter is spilt water. If she marries a chicken, she becomes a chicken; if she marries a dog, she becomes a dog.

Confucius says: "It is not pleasing to have to do with women or people of base condition. If you show them too much affection, they become too excited, and if you keep them at a distance, they are full of resentment."

Never deal with a businesswoman, Chinese men often warn each other. They are too powerful, well-armed with thousands of years of experiences in intrigues and plots to survive in family and society.

With a pair of "golden lotuses," she enters the code of "pure love," a code of tears and suffering.

Thanks to her small feet, my Nainai was able to get married even before her period started. She gave birth to two boys and a girl. When she was 25, her husband died. She was given two choices: marry again and leave her boys, her house and land to the care of her husband's relatives, or stay in her late husband's house as a widow forever and bring up the kids. She chose the second, not only because she couldn't bear separating from her boys, but also because her husband's early death had given her a bad name, and no decent man would go near her.

A woman with high cheek bones brings bad luck to her husband—a sign of "husband killer."

It's also bad luck for men to walk under a clothesline with women's underwear drying on it.

By becoming martyrs, we managed to leave some names for ourselves in the vast army of the anonymous: concubines, courtesans, a few empresses, a few poets and soldiers, the other half of the sky, and the girls of iron.

Yu gui—return home, standing for female marriage, first appeared in the "Book of Songs" about two thousand years ago. Girls are homeless until they get married, until they *chu jia*.

She called in the voice of a human. She called in the voice of a woman. But no one would help her out of the abyss. Only when she pretended to be her own child and report herself as a negligent mother did someone take her away in handcuffs to make her function as a mother again.

Some women cover their faces with veils and some with powder.

Old plus a female noun always makes a good insult: old woman, old girl, old cow, old bitch, old crone, old bat, old hag, old mother-in-law.

I asked my Nainai why she sold her daughter for a morsel of food. "To keep your father and uncle alive," she said. "You'd have done the same. If something happened to my boys, both my daughter and I would be thrown out of the house, and we'd both have died. Everything was under their names, no matter how young."

My sister was divorced for giving birth to a girl. She didn't blame her husband, or her mother-in-law who forced her son to choose another woman. She blamed only her failed womb which couldn't bear an heir for the family.

There are 223 characters with the component of *nü*—woman. Many of them show woman as the source of all misfortunes and evils:

Nü 奴 : slaves, the name women called themselves.

Bi 婢 : woman slave.

Jian 奸 : evil, traitor, and adultery (another way to write this word is to put three women on top of each other).

Ru 如 : follow, obey.

Ji 妓 : prostitute.

Yao 妖 : all the things that are alien, abnormal, monster, evil.

Du 妒 : jealousy. Other words for this meaning (all with woman as the component: *ji, mao, jie*).

Ping 姘 : adultery, a couple living together without a marriage certificate.

Lan 婪 : greedy.

Xian 嫌 : suspicion.

Lan 嬾 : lazy.

Piao 嫖 : go whoring.

Ask a Chinese man why women are associated with disasters, he'll immediately give you a list of those who ruined the greatest emperors and brought down entire kingdoms: Daji, a fox spirit; Yang Guifei, a fat concubine; Chen Yuanyuan, a prostitute.

I think of what happened to my grandmothers, what's happening to my mother and my sister, all those years of not knowing where or who they are. I'm not taking that road. But the only way for help is to think back through my grandmothers and my mother.

The national curse for Chinese is *ta ma de*—his mother's (cunt).

The most vicious curse for men is *jue zi jue sun*—May you have no son!

1998

Tan Lin
b. 1957

Tan Lin was born in Seattle, Washington, in 1957. He grew up in Athens, Ohio, where his mother was a professor of Chinese literature and his father a professor of ceramics and dean of the Fine Arts College at Ohio University. He attended Carleton College and Columbia University, where he received a Ph.D. in English literature with the thesis, "Garbage, Truth and the Recycling of Modern Life." Cultural detritus such as the information that emerges from the World Wide Web and mass media are central to Tan Lin's project as one of the first cybernetic poetics; his first book, *Lotion Bullwhip Giraffe*, published by a press devoted to language poetry, appeared in 1996.

Tan Lin's other published works include *BlipSoak01* (2003); *Heath. Plagiarism/Outsource, Notes Towards the Definition of Culture* (2007); *Seven Controlled Vocabularies and Obituary 2004. The Joy of Cooking* (2010); *Blurb* (2010); *Insomnia and the Aunt* (2011); and *Heath Course Pak* (2011). The awkwardness with which his titles present is indicative of the diversity and interruptiveness of the texts themselves, a good deal of which is cut and pasted directly from the Internet. His 2007 volume *Plagiarism/Outsource* "threads through" text dealing with the death of actor Heath Ledger. Likewise, his texts often retain visual elements that belong to the Web but seem intrusive in the book format.

In a third-person-bio, Tan Lin writes that he "coined the term 'ambient stylistics' and his aim over the past ten years has been to produce an 'ambient' literature, a mode of literature rather than a recognizable genre, that would be permeable and could disable the rigid categorization of work into such categories as poetry, fiction and literary criticism/poetics." Claiming to work "against avant-garde notions of difficulty, Lin's work takes its cue from various popular cultural forms, including yoga, disco, the decorative arts, television, twentieth century sound poetry, and electronica."[1]

In "Do you watch a lot of television?" (Ambient Stylistics 21), Tan Lin writes: "The best poetry is really not what was said but what was almost said without thinking or feeling. It seems everyday conversation revolves precisely around ephemeral things like that. Call it gossip of the mind, or an interambient kind of talking that never actually takes place. Such talking has the same effect for me—especially when I hear it in the cathode-ray tubes and the invisible gasses of color, and the hum and drone of voices on TV—as being in diurnal meadow."[2] He goes on to comment, "Everything that has a subject should be detested; everything that erases its subject should be loved. . . . The greatest poems simply contain what doesn't matter as it happens on the surface of the poem. To have a photograph is not interesting; to have a photograph of a photograph is and this is what a poem does better than any photograph can. . . . A good poem is very boring. A great poem is more boring than the act of reading itself."[3] Moreover, "The best TV and the best poems do not engender memory; they get rid of them. The best cure for memory is a really good poem."[4] This last phrase echoes or overlies T. S. Eliot's statement on the impersonality of poetry in his essay "Tradition and the Individual Talent." Indeed, one of Tan Lin's distinctions is his blending of influences as widespread as T. S. Eliot and Andy Warhol.

He has taught at the University of Virginia, Cal Arts, and Brooklyn College, and teaches currently at New Jersey City University. He resides in New York City with his wife and daughter.

1. Tan Lin, "History," part of a document privately presented to editor of this volume, 2011.   2. In *Telling It Slant: Avant-Garde Poetics of the 1990s*, ed. Mark Wallace and Steven Marks, Tuscaloosa, 2002, p. 341.   3. The same, p. 349.   4. The same, p. 351.

FROM "A Dictionary of Systems Theory"
in: *Seven Controlled Vocabularies and Obituary 2004 The Joy of Cooking*

Preface (1978)

1

[Today]: This is a preface about time not passing and what it means to watch, really not watch a movie. I was in the FedEx office the other day waiting for a package to arrive and I realized that it means being indifferent to the things we are seeing at the moment we are seeing them. And by seeing I mean not [feeling] and not seeing. Only in that way is it possible to see the world repeat itself endlessly. As anyone who has waited for something to arrive can tell you, half an emotion is better than a whole one. The most beautiful emotions are half-hearted. Today I realized that I am [half] in love with my wife. As Herbert Blau noted: "An audience without a history is not an audience."

2

What is that thing known as difference? Like the ocean or a stop sign the film should be the most generic of surfaces imaginable. Because it is true, it should not be about seeing but about the erasure of things that were seen. The retina is boring and absorptive and a film should be no different. The eye scans backwards and forwards when reading. Only in that way can it repeat its own indifference and become all those things it cannot feel. This is known as boredom. In the most accurate movies nothing should be happening. Actors shall stop being actors. All events shall disappear into standardized non-events, like shopping. No emotions shall exist in order to be communicated. It is a well-known fact that shoppers in a supermarket rarely look closely at the things they are buying and this should be true of seeing films. Most of our physical pains, anxieties, and emotions are minor and disorganized like itches. As the authors of *Life and Its Replacement with a Dull Reflection of Itself* [1984] remark, "The observer can see less and less to complain about."

3

Because the retina is [weak], the [universe] tends to resemble nothing but itself. [said]: The world is beautiful because it never stares back at you. Jacques Tati understood this perfectly when in *Playtime* all the interesting things that are not happening are not happening on the periphery of the shot. Most of us see [very little] and that is why the world is such a flat and beautiful place to linger in. Not looking at something is the highest compliment the eyes can pay to a landscape or a face. As anyone [who has been the subject of intense visual adoration] can tell you, staring at someone is the closest most of us will ever get to being a fly or falling in love. Like the bio-anthropology of everyday life [manners, cinema, acting, internet dating, check cashing, vitamin taking, the films of Maurice Pialat, the Discovery Channel, yoga, shopping], the ideal film would not create emotions but arrest them, ever more slowly, like fossils of the retina, and in that way estrange us from the drama of the lives we thought we were living. Vertov said that. An emotion that is waiting to happen is already dead. Not watching a movie is the closest thing to being an animal or reading a book whose pages have turned before we got there. A film should resemble the ambient space created by an airport, ID card photo, hotel, ATM machine, or all those things that happen to be around it. Not watching a movie is generally superior to watching one.

Second Preface (1986)

1

[Yesterday] I was reading a book called *Difference and Repetition* when my wife said: Emotions are the only way we have of making the world repeat itself. This is a preface about time standing still and what it means to not watch, really not watch a movie. I was in the FedEx office yesterday waiting for a package to arrive and I realized that it means to stop seeing the world repeat itself. In very beautiful movies, the film image becomes nothing more than an element in its own sequencing i.e. the sampling of a piece of furniture or a background color or wallpaper or perfume that [   ] occupied a room. Everything in a movie is redundant or everything that we fall in love with is mechanical. The film is as flagrant or lugubrious as a lawn chair. No one has to be an actor to die while speaking her lines.

2

What is that thing known as indifference? Enjoyment, like the face of someone we know, should be a species of dead or missing information. This is a preface about time not repeating like inexactitude and the reasons why so many words mean exactly the same thing. Laura Riding said that. Because the eye is the most relaxing thing we know, it tends to fall in love with only those things it cannot see. In this sense, the tracking number of the package I was waiting for resembles a film [I was not watching] and is meaningless in a distracted kind of way. The most beautiful faces (I have not seen) are the ones that resemble a cell phone or things that are dead. All faces like all films should be as generic, static and empty as possible. Emotions are the only way a human being has of repeating the same thing over and over.

3

What is that thing known as difference? Because the retina is boring and absorptive, I like an actor [who is no longer alive], a [tracking] number, or an obit [of a stranger]. Watching a film should constitute a [pattern] that "produces" highly generic content. The most beautiful emotions are outlines of emotions. I am very inattentive when I fall I love. As I tell my girlfriend who is now my wife, remembrance is a form of neglect. As patterns [of things that are non-existent], emotions are infrequent, dilatory or redundant. Having the same emotion twice is the most beautiful thing that a person can do to herself. Having an emotion once is a species of ugliness. That is why most artworks today are extremely ugly, why most faces are ugly until they become celebrities and we see them all the time, and why TV is the most beautiful medium around. A TV is made for staring at. Today I am half in love with my wife. That is why I love her so much.

4

[Today] [?] Something is [wrong] with this system [Roget]. One [kind] of thing can always be substituted by another [kind] of thing. 62

Third Preface (1998)

1

In Warhol's 3-minute screen tests, everyday people [who want to be stars] become faces and the faces become nothing more than a series of imperceptible twitches or blips on a blank surface. Facial information [input] translates into dull stereotypes. Dull stereotypes transmute occasionally into a system of stars or in Warhol's case, non-stars. The dullest stereotypes that exist today are name brands and generic celebrities. Despite the existence of brands, most shoppers buy w/o thinking or looking at the products they are buying. The same is true of faces. As psychologists have pointed out, staring at a face is one of the most unbearable things a human can do. Whenever I look at Andy Warhol's face I see a room named Delacroix.

2

Warhol understood that a film [every film is the same] is a branding device for the emotions and that the film is a medium wherein the spectator waits to see someone or something arbitrarily repeated. Warhol understood that this process could be systematized and mechanized and that *this,* not any arbitrary conjunction, is how we fall in love or not with people who we have never met. This might be termed a zero mass of events where the rules for genres fall apart. What is the look of an error before it occurs? Before I met my girlfriend, and I have told her this very often, I had fallen in love with her many times. The surface of love is porous and rigorous and illusionistic. The surface of Greta Garbo's face is the most beautiful template for the emotions because the surface is open and dead and arrives too late (for me to see). In much the same way, Warhol's faces are as blank and redundant and mathematical as faces in real life. They are stuck in moments of recurrence. They stare at things that are purely mechanical [the camera] or people who have not yet arrived and so cannot exchange their looks. They wait in celluloid for stardom to arrive. In these cases, it is difficult to tell the difference between a face whose expressiveness seems to trigger hallucinations and the involuntary, meaningless twitches of a face. Likewise it is difficult to distinguish between the drugged, anaphoric look of the smiling celebrity and the static, non-expressive head shot of the common criminal. As Helen Keller remarked: "Since I had no power of thought, I did not compare one mental state with another." What is the relation between an ordinary person and a celebrity? Repetition.

3

Warhol's head shots are quasi-legal documents that seek to regulate the passage of time and in that way the production of artworks, which is just another word for the emotions we probably won't have. In this sense they are like public forms of architecture. That is why people love [to go to] the movies [it is the simplest way of delaying one's emotions] from happening in order to make them appear [as if they are happening] later. Waiting is the greatest aphrodisiac known to humans and animals. Alcohol and drugs buffer the time zone between action and intentionality, and thus elongate the time between events and their interpretation (desired results). A box of chocolates, when ingested, has an amphetamine-like effect that people confuse with love. That is why I love to wait for my wife to show up in restaurants or Laundromats or FedEx counters. She is always who she is even though the ambience of the room she is about to enter has changed in a thousand imperceptible ways before she arrives.

4

Warhol understood that waiting for a loved one was more interesting than actually falling in love and I have to agree. Of course most of the faces we fall in love with in real life never look at us. I have fallen out of love with Parker Posey quite a few times, in *The House of Yes,* in *Party Girl* and in *Basquiat*, and although each movie is different and unbearable to watch in its own way and in its own date/era, each time I fall in love is exactly the same as all the others. My wife looks like Parker Posey. As I was saying, our feelings are mainly repudiations of our feelings. Each of her faces is waiting like a fossil on my retina long before I arrive to interrupt this fact.

Fourth Preface 2000

Poetry, film, novel, architecture and landscape are all management systems for distributing a set of related terms (RT). All generic templates [architecture, landscape, food, poetry, film, painting] possess the same underlying redundancy and exist for the same reason: to lose urgency, erase structural differences and suggest the most generalized of social anxieties as they pass over their surface where they appear to be something other than what they are. Happiness is mildly generic or it is not at all. Tolstoy said that. Waking should be like sleeping. Blandness is the new delivery model for all forms of entertainment. All the paths that our movements take end in repose and then awaken into something they are not.

That is why books we read today tend to resemble reality TV programs or shopping malls why television programs tend to resemble movies airports or parking garages why movies tend to resemble books we don't have time to read why design objects like flyswatters or blenders tend to resemble sculptures or insects or jewelry. Generic forms are much more useless than individual forms and are thus more highly prized. From them can be extracted all necessary i.e. redundant forms of information. Human memory resources are supremely limited and the most beautiful arrangements of reading material would be as immaterial, diffuse and ambient as the memory attached to them. As anyone who has read a book carelessly can tell you, forgetting a book is the most beautiful thing you can do to it. A very short book with lots of pictures can interrupt memory and the various modes of information glut and data blog that go with it.

Fourth Preface Revised 2000

What is the difference when a face is repeated? Like cracks to be repaired, all faces are unnecessarily redundant. Thus, it is possible to fall in love (again) and again and again with the things of the world. As any actor, hypnotized person, or ex-president will tell you, boredom is a form of perfection and everything that happens is ugly or inaccurate.

It would be preferable for a movie, if it were necessary to take place at all, to take place in the ambient corners of a room and in that way become the room in the same way that a novel becomes the place where the eye stops reading the words that are there. Film like reading should be about an unwilling suspension of disbelief. Film like life should not facilitate emotions but prevent them. For this reason, diagrams are useful. It is hard to experience an emotion that is a diagram but of course all our emotions are diagrams. Lars von Trier said that. That is the true nature of the cinema of attractions. Such a cinematic attractor would resemble a decrepit movie house like the Varsity Cinema I used to go to in Athens, Ohio, when I was growing up in the 70s and which was recently converted into a Taco Bell. A fast-food restaurant is the most beautiful kind of wallpaper the world knows how to create. The ideal movie is the most generic form of the thing we are no longer seeing anymore. Nothing could be more decorative than that. In this way, cinema might finally embrace all those inhuman patterns that are a part of our feelings: lifestyle, furniture, clichés, menus, the unread novel, the post office, corporate logos, the backs of books, pop music, soundtracks, bar codes. Seeing like reading should take place in a box or mildly controlled enclosure. The problem with intuitions is that they have too many flaws. The problem with most poems is that they have too many words. Instead of free texts, it would be nice to have extremely controlled vocabularies.

Highly generic, informal surface constraints (objects, organizations, practices, institutions) are the most beautiful ones.

Indexes of significant moments:

Pur

SMASHBOX	TROP-EX	FILTER 14	ETERNITY	VINEFIT LIP
OVERTURE	ADSENSE	STRENESSE	BOOKLAND	SMART TAG
SENSOTRONIC	LOGIXX	RESOLVE	T-57	LCW
PANTYTEC	NIXALITE	DUCO3044	ECLIPSE	MAXI CODE
FLEX DEVELOPMENT	VERY	ISS	PARASITE	ISOO
AGORIC SYSTEMS	NR2B	SANTOPRENE	FRIS	DYSPORT

2010

Laura Mullen
b. 1958

Laura Mullen was born in Los Angeles. She received her undergraduate degree from the University of California at Berkeley and an M.F.A. in poetry from The University of Iowa Writers' Workshop.

She identifies her work as postmodern, hybrid, and postlanguage, but her work is also influenced by Henry James, Edgar Allan Poe, and numerous authors who fall outside of the literary canon. Her books include *The Tales of Horror* (1999), a "postmodern gothic"; *The Surface* (1991), containing poems in traditional form such as "Sestina in Which My Grandmother Is Going Deaf"; and *Murmur* (2007), a postmodern crime novel prose poem sequence. Her other works are *After I Was Dead* (1999), *Subject* (2005), and *Dark Archive* (2011).

Tales of Horror and *Murmur* are, according to Kass Fleisher, "the first and second installments of a trilogy planned by the author. The trilogy aims to unpack three popular genre forms that contribute a great deal, culturally, to defining the construct of woman: horror, mystery, and romance novels (and films). . . . Her books are careful, conceptual wholes—concept albums, if you will."[1]

Mullen's *Dark Archive* opens with a series of poems that relate in one way or another to the Wordsworth poem "I Wandered Lonely as a Cloud," thus her title, "I Wandered Networks like a Cloud." "The concept of a 'dark archive,'" according to poet and UCLA librarian Bruce Whiteman, "comes from the digital world and refers to a copy of a data set to which almost no one has access and that is retained in remote storage against the possibility of disastrous loss. Disasters of several kinds haunt Laura Mullen's book—the loss of love . . . Hurricane Katrina . . . the death by exposure of her stepmother, the artist Ingrid Nickelsen."[2]

Kass Fleisher notes that the occasional opacities of Mullen's work suggest to some that she is a language poet. However, "Mullen does not abandon feeling and evocation, but she does insist that that which is evoked, that which is felt in a poem, is created by *words, words,* unreliable *words.* Mullen rarely lets the reader ignore the materiality of text, the conditions that give rise to her typescript."

Asked if poetry and politics mix, Mullen responded, "Well, you know whenever people start mixing them overtly it turns into propaganda. But poetry is necessarily polysemous—it's necessarily open to criss-crossing meanings, slippages, faults . . . Your ideas are slipping and sliding, coming up against each other in ways you wouldn't have anticipated; you might be denying the same thing you're affirming, if the poem is good enough."[3]

Laura Mullen lives in Baton Rouge and teaches at Louisiana State University.

1. Kass Fleisher, "Laura Mullen: Threatened as Threat: Rethinking Gender and Genre," in *Eleven More American Women Poets in the 21st Century: Poetics Across North America*, ed. Claudia Rankine and Lisa Sewell (Middletown, CT: Wesleyan University Press, 2012), p. 217.   2. Bruce Whiteman, "Dark Archive by Laura Mullen," *Rattle: Poetry for the 21th Century*, Saturday, October 15, 2011, http://rattle.com/blog/2011/10/dark-archive-by-laura-mullen/.   3. Fleisher, p. 216.   4. Cactus May, "An Interview with Laura Mullen," *The Nieve Roja Review* 4 (1998), http:/nieveroja.colostate.edu/issue4/mullen_interview2.htm.

Autumn

Her hair, brown.
Her specialty, damage.
Her specialty, becoming
Something else. Her hair, falling
Leaves, leaf rot, and then soil.
Her specialty, telling us
What we were trying to say
"All along." Her hair,
An introduction—our
Reading—her eyes also
Brown. Conclusion?
The jewelry sold by now.
Her hair, a phone call.
Is anyone home.
Gusts of cold wind
Shifting the leaves a little:
The leaves already married
To the ground. Her hair
The same color, sorrow;
Her sleep, long. I don't need
To tell you. The ground
Keeping her not so far
From the road. Her long
Hair, a transition.
She should have been
Somewhere else.
She should have been
Home. Her shoulders
And belly and throat
Beginning not to be
A secret any longer.
Whatever it was she was

Wearing, gone.
Her specialty, regret.
The skin, the definition
Of the bones. You know.
Her specialty, calculated
Indiscretions. Bothered
By all this activity, the birds
Are still. Was she meant
To be found? The hands
Holding nothing now.
Something has gotten at
Whatever was exposed. Her eyes,
Terror, and her mouth, hope.
We would prefer not to
Feel anything: to watch
As if from far away while
They try to make sense of it.
With one repeated phrase
They are taping the woods off:
"Do not cross." The trees
Are suddenly evidence.
Their specialty, containment.
Hers, regret.
We prefer to think of ourselves
As not restricted. Not like that.
Long arms flung out, holding
The "rocks and stones and trees."
Her hair and her eyes and her mouth
All a part of the ground.
Her specialty, being silent
"As the grave."
Our specialty, looking into it.

1999

After I Was Dead

I had time to think about things,
Time for regrets, like.
The glowing vessel of frozen booze
Lists: *Way a minit: wanna . . . 'scuss shumsing!*

Memory overflowing its salt-rimmed dike?
But your version only, "the" truth . . . —

Sliced. Time folds in on itself: bed to couch.
The sheets (to the wind) come clean:
I gave the keys back.
Comes (in hot water) the stain of love, out.
Comes nobody back from the said, *I mean* . . . ,
To say what lies still under all that black

(Ashes cling): nobody, that is, you'd trust.
I sifted myself, things over between us.

1999

In the Space between Words Begin

In the space between words begin
Attempt
       In the space
At dawn the newly risen dead uncomfortable
      In their restored bodies

Situation: from 'wandering' to rest—
Loneliness to solitude. Believing
Is seeing, experience
An accrual of images

The newly risen dead find their bodies
Uncooperative, awkward, ugly   as in any
Horror flick

I wandered lonely as a van full of hippies
      In Texas

In the space between words   roots
"what shall I talk about"

Situation: a man at his desk pages through
Another's writing closes his eyes seeks rhymes
For the following: daffodils, thought . .

I fear I can no longer think

I fear I am no longer that which thinks
Or that a certain kind of thinking's lost

Light, light, light, light. Let there be a place
From which a way seems clear or clearer

Out of the house into the golden
And never

2011

I Wandered Networks like a Cloud

That floated o'er my couch, remote
In one hand, drink in the other, as a crowd
On the screen (frightened, enraged)
Fled the tanks beneath the leaves
Fluttering and dancing in the breeze.

Continuous as the stars that shine,
These wars, these displaced "refugees,"
Filmed in never-ending lines
Along the margins and at bay.
Ten thousand saw I at a glance,
Hurrying nowhere, like worried ants.

The waves beside them danced; but they
Bent weeping over loved bodies:
A poet could not but be gay,
Far from such desperate company:
I gazed—and gazed—but little thought
What wealth the show to me had brought:

For oft, when on my couch I lie
In vacant or in pensive mood,
They flash upon that satellite dish
Which is the bliss of solitude;
And then my heart with pleasure fills,
To channel surf the world's ills.

2011

Code

S-wings into the light, a swallow in the hall, and out as in over. The context's high flutter: *the roof of the mouth, the mouth of the river.* Roll me over the fluviometer, allowed to doubt the door closed on a loud (and how) cloud cover. Here's a bout with *about* without much of a boat—not to crowd or crow over—but to gloss a glance at the wards (back to for) as key to a would-be warder. Beloved but not a louver. Given our driven and cloven hearts, better hoof it when the storm hovers. Just *go.* Or come to know the shower from the show

glowing lower, after after. Riveting Dada data into yada yada or featherweight father patter, bright assurances slur past disaster. Just a matter of being in clover: light on your feet (on the water), numb to number. Luck's all in a row for the rower still towing the two towers, that fist mover, arriving to rev here his motto motor: heck of a heck of a huckster. Stir that into y'at dat dat dat, back at it: at at. Up to downriver to undo the fluent liar oiling our troubled slaughter. He'd have us dotting the eyes of a storm of forms until ill but we'll not sew to sewer more saltwater waves

we wavers. See underwater and also under *Under.* Rum numbers, numb members. Another bad dad had by hurt, another bird in the band flown like water. A shroud of cloud tears to show how slow clowning around drowns distrusted intelligence out, like, it's all in your head (waters). Blurred word in these submerged streets: bad weather for bed wetters is best for our bettors. They tack back and north, correcting the dots, the daughter. The road her home, the corps her dumb lover: shoveling a brave face on the failure to save her with highway dividers. So go with the flow to

flower or stall in high style, pooled to appeal. Be a pal, be an appalling pallbearer, be there in that blunder. So behave: be a "have"—halve the fictional big picture's *son et lumiere.* Sum for everyone? So know better next crime or be as you were, unsolved and hardly sober, soldier. It's murder getting over now or never. Wet *ever.* It's so long and so latte dough as acoustics accost costumed auditors lost in storm-tossed star-crossed kissed-off echoes: S.O.S. So. So. So solo soul, oh so soluble soma. Dark harbors. Sea? C.O.D. A-lights in the last call a tight swallow—god and gone—a fraud of your own shadow. Cold coda. Cod

2011

The White Box of Mirror Dissolved Is Not Singular

White for diluting dreams
—CY TWOMBLY

Sun or eye or boat or stiff reeds on a small island rising out of their own
reflection

A surface alluded to these ambiguous traces seeming to undulate like a spill
of cloud against cloud or a pale drift net deep in a white ocean

These airs made of what remains of a repeated gesture

To begin with nothing

I won't tell anyone what you say here the water promises and the reeds take
it up as a whisper which reaches at last the very ears gossip discovers

A reiterated *not* makes at once as surface as if removed and as modulated
its horizon too high a landscape the auditor is led always deeper into and
shut out of lead on lead

You'll tell I know you will

A "counter-love . . . the reflection of the love he inspires

Asleep among the stirred swirl of sweet white blossoms asleep or passed out

Felt

The impasto parents

Reading the repeated mark no ear for that

Sun or outstretched hand or boat or empty crown spiky as a battered flower

These airs made of traces of the first repeated gesture "and a cloud came by
and it broke apart on the tower. A small piece of it came in my window and
floated across the room

No ear for that music

Even now I can barely talk about the erasure what should have been
pleasure the sense of something lived through the horizon line over my
head shame a stiff weight parts

Under a thick white sky the impasto parents the edge loss

I sought on surfaces too fragile to breathe on almost the signs of trauma
they endured

2011

Robert Fitterman
b. 1959

Born in St. Louis, Robert Fitterman spent his childhood in Creve Coeur, Missouri. He received his B.A. from the University of Wisconsin–Madison and an M.A. from Temple University.

He is the author of numerous collections of poetry, including *Metropolis 1–15* (2001), *Metropolis 16–29* (2002), *Metropolis 30: The Decline and Fall of the Roman Empire* (2004), *War, the Musical* (2006), *The Sun Also Rises* (2008), *Rob the Plagiarist* (2009), *Sprawl: Metropolis 30A* (2009), and *Now We are Friends* (2011).

With the poet Vanessa Place, he coauthored the theoretical prose work *Notes on Conceptualisms* (2009), which asserts:

> Allegorical writing is necessarily inconsistent, containing elaborations, recursions, sub-metaphors, fictive conceits, projections, and guisings that combine and recombine both to create the allegorical whole, and to discursively threaten this wholeness: In this sense, allegory implicates Gödel's First Incompleteness Theorem: if it is consistent, it is incomplete; if complete, inconsistent.
>
> All conceptual writing is allegorical writing."[1]

Fitterman also edited the anthology *Collective Task* (2009), featuring a large-scale collaboration between poets Mónica de la Torre, Stacy Doris, and Juliana Spahr, among others.

Fitterman currently lives in New York City. He teaches at New York University and Bard College.

1. Vanessa Place & Robert Fitterman, *Notes on Conceptualisms,* Brooklyn, 2009, p. 15.

FROM A Hemingway Reader

The Sun Also Also Rises

Book I

CHAPTER I

I am very much impressed by that. I never met any one of his class who remembered him. I mistrust all frank and simple people. I always had a suspicion. I finally had somebody verify the story. I was his tennis friend. I do not believe that. I first became aware of his lady's attitude toward him one night after the three of us had dined together. I suggested we fly to Strasbourg. I thought it was accidental. I was kicked again under the table. I was not kicked again. I said good-night and went out. I watched him walk back to the café. I rather liked him.

CHAPTER II

I am sure he had never been in love in his life. I did not realize the extent to which it set him off until one day he came into my office. I never wanted to go. I had a boat train to catch. I like this town. I can't stand it to think my life is going so fast and I'm not really living it. I'm not interested. I'm sick of Paris. I walked alone all one night and nothing happened. I was sorry for him but it was not a thing you could do anything about. I sorted out the carbons, stamped on a by-line, put the stuff in a couple of big manila envelopes and rang for a boy to take them to the Gare St. Lazare. I went into the other room. I wanted to lock the office and shove off. I put my hand on his shoulder. I can't do it. I didn't sleep all last night. I could picture it. I have a rotten habit of picturing the bedroom scenes of my friends.

CHAPTER III

I sat at a table on the terrace of the Napolitain. I watched a good-looking girl walk past the table and watched her go up the street and lost sight of her. I caught her eye. I saw why she made a point of not laughing. I paid for the saucers. I hailed a horse-cab. I put my arm around her. I put her hand away. I called to the cocher to stop. I had picked her up because of a vague sentimental idea that it would be nice to eat with some one. I had forgotten how dull it could be. I got hurt in the war. I was bored enough. I went back to the small room. I went over to the bar. I drank a beer. I could see their hands and newly washed, wavy hair in the light from the door. I was very angry. I know they are supposed to be amusing. I walked down the street and had a beer at the bar. I knew then that they would all dance with her. I sat down at a table. I asked him to have a drink. I was a little drunk. I got up and walked over to the dancing-floor. I took my coat off a hanger on the wall and put it on. I stopped at the bar and asked them for an envelope. I took a fifty-franc note from my pocket.

CHAPTER IV

I saw her face in the lights from the open shops. I saw her face clearly. I kissed her. I was pretty well through with the subject. I went out onto the sidewalk. I did not see who it was. I wanted to get home. I stopped and read the inscription. I knocked on the door and she gave me my mail. I wished her good night and went upstairs. I looked at them under the gaslight. I got out my check-book. I felt sure I could remember anybody. I lit the lamp beside the bed. I sat with the windows open and undressed by the bed. I looked at myself in the mirror of the big armoire beside the bed. I put on my pajamas and got into bed. I had the two bull-fight papers, and I took their wrappers off. I read it all the way through. I blew out the lamp. I wonder what became of the others. I was all bandaged up. I never used to realize it. I lay awake thinking and my mind jumping around. I couldn't keep away from it. I started to cry. I woke up. I listened. I thought I recognized a voice. I put on a dressing-gown. I heard my name called down the stairs. I looked at the clock. I was getting brandy and soda and glasses. I went back upstairs. I took them both to the kitchen. I turned off the gas in the dining-room. I had felt like crying. I thought of her walking up the street. I felt like hell again.

CHAPTER V

I walked down the Boulevard. I read the papers with the coffee and then smoked a cigarette. I passed the man with the jumping frogs. I stepped aside. I read the French morning papers. I shared a taxi. I banged on the glass. I went to the office in the elevator. I was looking over my desk. I held him off. I left him to come to the office.

CHAPTER VI

I sat down and wrote some letters. I went down to the bar. I looked for her upstairs on my way out. I saw a string of barges being towed empty down the current. I suppose it is. I walked past the sad tables. I watched him crossing the street through the taxis. I never heard him make one remark. I do not believe he thought about his clothes much. I don't know how people could say such terrible things. I don't even feel an impulse to try to stop it. I stood against the bar looking out. I did not want anything to drink and went out through the side door. I looked back. I went down a side street. I got in and gave the driver the address to my flat.

CHAPTER VII

I went up to the flat. I put the mail on the table. I heard the door-bell pull. I put on a bathrobe and slippers. I filled the big earthenware jug with water. I dressed slowly. I felt tired and pretty rotten. I took up the brandy bottle. I went to the door. I found some ash-trays and spread them around. I looked at the count. I had that feeling of going through something that has already happened before. I had the feeling as in a nightmare of it all being something repeated, something I had been through and that now I must go through again. I took a note out of my pocket. I looked back and there were three girls at his table. I gave him twenty francs and he touched his cap. I went upstairs and went to bed.

2009

LIT

Each section   outlined   below   is   an
independent   treatise   on   a
limited   aspect   of
                      light   and   color :   we hope
         you e**n**joy your   **V**isit   and find

       the answers to your questions. Old light   and
owl light. The light of a spotlight.
    .   **Constable thought that**   "No two days
ar e   a l   ik e,
              nor even two hours; **neither** were there ever
              two l eaves of a tree   **alike since** the cre-
ationof the   w orld"   ,
       then in a   new way   he represented   light
in the open air,
                 the movement of clouds
across the sky.   Picture Lights

by Hogarth. Fine Art are the only   lights   available to
illuminate your   Fine Art exactly.
      Not to sound **overly**   **dramatic,** but
           the LED (light-emitting
diode) is on its way   **d**   to outing
incandescent   an**d**   fluorescent
bulbs.   You need the
           ElectroKraft **Lunar Module,**
which features   multiple photo-sensor light portholes
for   theremin-like
control.   He earned a reputation during
the 1940s and 50s   as one of the...   crisp
shadows   and sculpted   beams

of   light. A majority of th**e Com**mon natural
and artificial light

sources   emit   a broad range of   wavelengths   that
cover   the entire   visible light   spectrum, with some

extending into the ultraviolet and infrared regions
as well.
In this section   we will
investigate   some   of the basic
        theories   about the nature of light.
Understanding   how and where   a rainbow   appears

is

                        tied   to   un   derst
anding   how   light
            travels.
As we know,   life
                would be greatly   hampered
        without light.   We would   bump
into things,   fall off   precipices and   live
our   lives

like albino   cave **salamanders**.

                T h ey m a y n ot   un d e r st a n d
    oth e r   p u l s a   t in g c o d es

            o f s h i n e, b u t   th ey r a p   f o r
e t e r n i t y.
The reference materials listed   in this section are
an excellent   source of   additional   infor-
mation
on   the   diverse   topic of
            anisotropic media.
        I saw shine   forth   a
mighty lite.

We are, in fact, seeing light—
        light that somehow left objects
far or near and reached
    our eyes. Light is all our eyes

can really see. Such human
fabrication must
seem like
Bruises of clustered lights.

Light has   the   quality
to reveal
       it is opposite of dark   or unknown.

The light **of a student lamp**   sapphire   light.

The red panel,
       the third color   of the spectrum, represents   the
       Light   of   Poetry.   Included are refer-
ences   to books, book chapters, and review articles,
which

       discuss the theory and   applications of the refrac-
tion   and   refractive index
and   how they   relate to the

       physics of   light and color.   There   are   many
mil   itar   y   and com me rc ial   ap pli cat i   o
n s   that c an   bene fit fro m fu rth er   innov a tio n s in
the use of lig h t
                     for sen sing   and im
a g ing.

The light   and   shad o w there   de als   wit h
buildings and rooms and objects (whereas in
Caravaggio,   it's people.
To help with   geometric understanding,
we will assume that   light   travels in rays.   We
begin   with
     light rays   moving   through   the   air   at
a constant   speed   and consider
the reflection of light. In 1657
       the mathematician Pierre de Fermat   postulated a simple prin-
ciple: Light bends or refracts
       when   it   moves   from   one transparent
                     material to the   next.

This is what   causes prisms   .   We do lie beneath
the grass

In the moonlight, in the shade   of the yew-tree.
As light passes from one substance
                    into another, it will travel   straight
through   with no change.
            In the center   of   the   panel,
      Poetry is   mounted
      on Pegasus,   holding a   torch in
      one   hand   while reaching
toward   the light of
            the

      ideal.   First of all,   it's not very much
like emerald   light. Sam thought glass
fiber
            and light signals   might work.   If
the angle of the beam   is increased even further,   the light
will   refract with   increasing
      proportion   to the   entry angle.
His use of light still has an influence on modern cinema says director Martin
Scorsese.

To the intelligence   fastened by the senses you are lost   in
                  a   world   of sun light
                        where nothing   is amiss.   As   c it
i e s   flo od   them   selves
with ev er   more

            light,   scientist s wo r ry
                        about   los ing   the nig ht
sky   and   irrevocab ly   dis rupti ng   noc turn al
rhythms.

            Look up   ,   earth child   ,   the
light is   all!

This card just happens to   have been   printed

      a neutral gray color,

but more   importantly it   is a surface

which reflects exactly 18% of the light
                  which   strikes it.
            Ten bright-red LED bulbs flash 120   times

per minute for up to 300 hours
and are   visible for more   than one-half mile.   Light
are the   spinning
            favours, intangible tonight.
                The Molecular Expressions Microscopy
Primer explores   many

of the aspects of visible light starting with   an
introduction to   electromagnetic   radiation
                and con tinuing through to hu man   vision
and

                        the   perception   of c
olor.   Starting with Ole Roemer's **1676**   break-
through endeavors,
    the speed of   light has been
measured at least 163

times by more than **100** investigators   util izing   a
wide variety of different
            techniques.   Many early photographers   were fascinated by
the idea of photographing   at night,   but in
the mid-nineteenth century the slow emulsions   in
use   and the lack of good sources of artificial
light   made this   more or less

impossible.
    The   light of a magnesium   flare. The light of a
magnesium flare.

            Light are the spinning
                    favours, intangible tonight.

The magic of photography   lies   in the
light.   As an example,   a beam **of** light
striking water   vertically will not be refracted, but if
                        the beam enters

            the water   at a   slight angle

it will be refracted   to a very small   degree.   Finally
in 1983,   more   than 300 years after   the first
serious

measurement attempt, the   speed of light was
defined   as   being 299,792.458
       kilometers   per   second   by   the
Seventeenth   General   Congress   on
Weights and   Measures.

     Light is a complex

        phenomenon that is   classically
   explained   with a simple model   **based on** rays
and wavefronts.   But if your means are more
modest,   you can still build a light   tent   that gives you
better results
        when   photographing
small   objects   up close.
     What is   extra light?
         The light in the window
seemed   perpetual

                           2009

Peter Gizzi

b. 1959

Peter Gizzi was born and raised in Pittsfield, Massachusetts, and holds degrees from New York University, Brown University, and the State University of New York at Buffalo. He has taught primarily at the University of California at Santa Cruz and the University of Massachusetts at Amherst, where he is currently a professor of English.

His books include *Periplum* (1992), *Hours of the Book* (1994), *Artificial Heart* (1998), *Some Values of Landscape and Weather* (2003), *The Outernationale* (2007), and *Threshold Songs* (2011).

Gizzi edited the influential periodical *o•blek: a journal of language arts* (with Connell McGrath, 1987–1993), as well as *The House That Jack Built: The Collected Lectures of Jack Spicer* (1998), and *My Vocabulary Did This to Me: The Collected Poetry of Jack Spicer* (with Kevin Killian, 2008). He was poetry editor for *The Nation*, 2007–2011.

Associated early in his career with the New York School influence, Gizzi studied with language poet Charles Bernstein in Buffalo, but he has never fully adopted either the language poetry or New York School manner. He turned instead to an intelligent, distanced, and yet heartfelt expression of lyric. The first section of his serial poem, "History of the Lyric," ends with the lines, "an avant-garde / a backward glance." Gizzi does not mean to suggest that avant-garde is behind us, never to reemerge, but rather that the avant-garde and the traditions of lyric require the navigation of "home" in relation to new conditions of life and language. The same is true of writing a poem, with its collision of inner and outer worlds. "For the record," he says in an interview, "a periplum is a form of reckoning . . . the way Odysseus moves through *The Odyssey*—it's a navigation between the stars and the coast."[1] In writing, "a voice comes to one, and then a poem begins. A world comes to one. And for a moment you are your self and another becoming another thing, a poem."[2] In the same interview, Gizzi remarks, "I am interested though in a poetics of light—a way of reading and seeing its fluid materiality as a phenomenon that comes from far away and in a time frame much larger than our own. It comes to us in a periodicity outside our own. I would say my interest in light is ultimately related to capturing or depicting time."[3] In spreading wide his focus, Gizzi goes to the essentials of space and time rather than rely on the entanglements of theory. His backward and forward glances find home in the world itself, where "what will do" is "that electric tower to the left, one line broken free."[4]

Winner of the Lavan Younger Poet Award from the Academy of American Poets and recipient of a Guggenheim Fellowship, Peter Gizzi lives in Holyoke, Massachusetts.

1. Robert N. Casper, "Interview with Peter Gizzi," *jubilat* 14, 2007, http://poems.com/special_features/prose/essay_gizzi.php.   2. The same.   3. The same.   4. "In Defense of Nothing," *Some Values of Landscape and Weather*, Middletown, CT, 2003, p. 53.

Creeley Madrigal

Where is the stamen she lost
as she has gone solo
as she discarded

or where is the stamen she seeks
as she gave up on
as she thought everything in

then living's flourish to be less
now she's absent without regard
empty space as she was

as open sky is everywhere
of/now the form's recognition
and animal cries animal hunger

. . .

Where is the flourish he missed
as he became faint
as he distilled

or where is the flourish he sought
as he let go of
as he believed deliverance through

then thinking's alembic to be loose
now he's thin without regret
zero place as he is

as close ground is nowhere
of/now the verb's winnow
and foliate list foliate void

. . .

Where is the alembic we ruined
as we have left astray
as we ignored

or where is the alembic we want
as we misplaced
as we sought an approach to

then faith's mystery to be blind
now we've seen without respect
untrodden path as we are

as actual garden is elsewhere
of/now the poem's meaning
and grammar land grammar world

.   .   .

Where is the mystery they glean
as they have pronouns
as they invoke

or where is the mystery they plumb
as they wander
as they make sacrifice for

then healing's balm to be soiled
now their ritual without reflex
open wound as they were

as crisp linen is closeted
of/now the world's stain
and lunar eyes lunar whirr

1998

Revival

for Gregory Corso (1930–2001)

It's good to be dead in America
with the movies, curtains and drift,
the muzak in the theater.
It's good to be in a theater waiting
for The Best Years of Our Lives to begin.

Our first night back, we're here
entertaining a hunch our plane did crash
somewhere over the Rockies, luggage
and manuscripts scattered, charred fragments
attempting to survive the fatal draft.
To be dead in America at the movies
distracted by preview music in dimming lights.
I never once thought of Alfred Deller
or Kathleen Ferrier singing Kindertotenlieder.
It's good to be lost among pillars of grass.
I never once thought of My Last Duchess
or the Pines of Rome. Isn't it great here
just now dying along with azaleas, trilliums,
myrtle, viburnums, daffodils, blue phlox?
It's good to be a ghost in America,
light flooding in at this moment
of never coming back to the same person
who knew certain things, certain people,
shafts of life entering a kitchen
at the end of an age of never coming back now.
To hear reports on the radio,
something about speed, they say, accelerated history.
It's good to share molecular chasm with a friend.
I never once reached for Heisenberg
or The Fall of the Roman Empire.

On this day in history the first antelope was born,
remember The Yearling, like that,
but the footage distressed, handheld.
A hard, closed, linear world at the edge
of caricature, no memory now of the New Science
or The Origin of the Species.
It's good to feel hunted in America.
To be the son of a large man who rose out of depression
and the middle world war, poverty and race
to loom in mid-sixties industrial American air,
survived classic notions of the atom,
to think to be. The official story walks
down the street, enters bars and cafes.
Plays. Airs. Stars. To sing a song of industry,
having forgotten Monte Clift was beaten
for reading Ulysses. It's dark in a theater,
hoping to say never return to the moment

of return, as a hollow ring from Apollo 13
sinks back to burn into the atmosphere
which made it, huh. How come all the best thoughts
are images? How come all the best images
are uncanny? What's the use of The Compleat Angler,
searching for effects at the bottom of a lake
next to a shoe slick with algae, at the base of a cliff
with pine needles and a rotting log?

I was talking about rending, reading, rewriting
what is seen. Put the book down and look into the day.
I want an art that can say how I am feeling
if I am feeling blue sky unrolling a coronation rug
unto the bare toe of a peasant girl
with vague memories of Jeanne d'Arc,
or that transformation in Cinderella.
Where is your mother today?
I think of you, soft skin against soot.
How much has the world turned
since you were a girl in Troy?
In these parts both widow and banker are diminished,
something outside the town defeated them.
In these parts neither possessed their life.
This pageant demands too much,
that we work and not break, that we love
and not lie, and not complain.
It's good to not break in America.
To behave this time
never once looking into Chapman's Homer,
or quoting the Vita Nuova translated
by Dante Rossetti. No, I am thinking
blurry faces, a boy, girl, looking
at New York harbor for a first time,
soil in pockets, missing buttons,
needing glasses, needing shoes.

It was war. A capital experience!
Investing in narratives of working up
from the mail room, basement, kitchen.
It's good to believe in the press kit
sailing away from rear-projection tenements
like a car ride after a good fix,
offset by attractively angled shots,

neo-cartoonish, with massive distorting close-ups,
part lockdown, part interest rate,
part plant, part machine. Part dazzle?
Lulls and high sensations.
I always wished I could be funny ha-ha,
instead of "he's a little funny," if you get my drift,
just courage to accept the facts
that poetry can catch you in the headlights
and it's years refocusing the afterimage,
the depth and passion of its earnest glance.
This part untranslatable, part missing line,
feather in the chest. A description
to account for the lack of detail
the Wealth of Nations conducts on the organs.
We look forward to serving you here
at Managed Health Network.
Thank you for calling, call volume
is still exceptionally heavy. If this is an emergency . . .

All the codes have been compromised.
This is why the boy can't fathom polar lights,
liberty, merry dancer.
Ineluctably the privileged nostalgia of a toy boat.
In the diagram did the vessel survive?
Like an old book, even a beloved book,
its pages give way to a good sneeze.
What have they done, I sit here thinking
of your monuments, trophies, hahahaha.
"Here are my flowers,"
what do they smell like? "Paper."
This is why athenaeum joy, why shiny pathos
intoning the letters, prance and skater,
o say, can you see?
What does it mean to wait for a song
to sit and wait for a story?
For want of a sound to call my own
coming in over the barricades,
to collect rubble at the perimeter
hoping to build a house, part snow, part victory,
ice and sun balancing the untrained shafts,
part sheet music, part dust, sings often—
the parts open, flake, break open, let go.
Why so phantom, searching for a rag

to embellish the holes in my sonnet,
no tracks leading beyond and back,
no more retrograde song cycle tatting air.
These parts wobble, stitching frames
to improvise a document:
all this American life. Strike that.
All our life, all our American lives gathered
into an anthem we thought to rescue us,
over and out. On your way, dust.

2003

In Defense of Nothing

I guess these trailers lined up in the lot off the highway will do.
I guess that crooked eucalyptus tree also.
I guess this highway will have to do and the cars
   and the people in them on their way.
The present is always coming up to us, surrounding us.
It's hard to imagine atoms, hard to imagine
   hydrogen & oxygen binding, it'll have to do.
This sky with its macular clouds also
   and that electric tower to the left, one line broken free.

2003

A Panic That Can Still Come upon Me

If today and today I am calling aloud

If I break into pieces of glitter on asphalt
bits of sun, the din

if tires whine on wet pavement
everything humming

If we find we are still in motion
and have arrived in Zeno's thought, like

if sunshine hits marble and the sea lights up
we might know we were loved, are loved
if flames and harvest, the enchanted plain

If our wishes are met with dirt
and thyme, thistle, oil,
heirloom, and basil

or the end result is worry, chaos
and if "I should know better"

If our loves are anointed with missiles
Apache fire, Tomahawks
did we follow the tablets the pilgrims suggested

If we ask that every song touch its origin
just once and the years engulfed

If problems of identity confound sages,
derelict philosophers, administrators
who can say I am found

if this time you, all of it, this time now

If nothing save Saturdays at the metro and
if rain falls sidelong in the platz
doorways, onto mansard roofs

If enumerations of the fall
and if falling, cities rocked
with gas fires at dawn

Can you rescind the ghost's double nakedness
hungry and waning

if children, soldiers, children
taken down in schools

if burning fuel

Who can't say they have seen this
and can we sing this

if in the auroras' reflecting the sea,
gauze touching the breast

Too bad for you, beautiful singer
unadorned by laurel
child of thunder and scapegoat alike

If the crowd in the mind becoming
crowded in streets and villages, and trains
run next to the freeway

If exit is merely a sign

2007

Hypostasis & New Year

For why am I afraid to sing
the fundamental shape of awe
should I now begin to sing the silvered back of
    the winter willow spear
the sparkling agate blue
would this blade and this sky free me to speak
    intransitive lack—

the vowels themselves free

Of what am I afraid
of what lies in back of me of day
these stars scattered as far as the I
what world and wherefore
will it shake free
why now in the mind of an afternoon is a daisy
    for a while
flagrant and alive

Then what of night
of hours' unpredicated bad luck and the rot
    it clings to
fathomless on the far side in winter dark

Hey shadow world when a thing comes back
comes back unseen but felt and no longer itself
    what then
what silver world mirrors tarnished lenses
what fortune what fate

and the forms not themselves but only itself the sky
by water and wind shaken
I am born in silvered dark

Of what am I to see these things between myself
        and nothing
between the curtain and the stain
between the hypostatic scenes of breathing
and becoming the thing I see
are they not the same

Things don't look good on the street today
beside a tower in a rusting lot
one is a condition the other mystery
even this afternoon light so kind and nourishing
a towering absence vibrating air

Shake and I see pots from old shake
        and I see cities anew
I see robes shake I see desert
I see the farthing in us all the ghost of day

the day inside night as tones decay
        and border air
it is the old songs and the present wind I sing
and say I love the unknown sound in a word

Mother where from did you leave me on the sleeve
        of a dying word
of impish laughter in the midst my joy
I compel and confess open form
my cracked hinged picture doubled

I can't remember now if I made a pact with the devil
        when I was young
when I was high
on a sidewalk I hear "buy a sweatshirt?" and think
buy a shirt from the sweat of children
        hell
I'm just taking a walk in the sun in a poem
        and this sound
caught in the most recent coup

2011

Basement Song

Out of the deep
I dreamt the mother.

How deep the mother
deep the basement

the body, odor of laundry
the soul of a bug.

The grass inside
the song stains me.

The mother stains me.
That was the year

they cut my throat
and toads bloomed

on my voice box.
I have kept my head up.

Have kept myself
out of trouble

but deep is trouble
deep is mother.

Deep the song
inside summer.

Did I tell you it hurt
accepting air in a new body?

And since the change
the air burns.

2011

Claudia Keelan

b. 1959

Claudia Keelan was born in Anaheim, California, and received degrees from Humboldt State University and the Writers' Workshop at the University of Iowa. She has published the poetry collections *Refinery* (1994), *The Secularist* (1997), *Utopic* (2000), *The Devotion Field* (2005), and *Missing Her* (2009).

Writing of Keelan's poem "Everybody's Autobiography," Christina Mengert notes: "Keelan applies the lesson that one should 'distrust / distinctions that separated the simple subject / from the compound subject,' as she weaves the birth of her father into the history of the Southern Pacific railroad, the deaths of eight farmers, and finally the rising power of the oil industry, which culminates in 3,000 dead on September 11th, which occurred just a few months after the death of her father. These poems offer a remarkable vision of the collective and the individual existing within, without, and alongside one another."[1] Politically awakened and not afraid to show the depth of her concern, Keelan is a fierce elegist for a father lost in a lost country. Thereafter, of course, the self goes missing: "So I have / Tried to love my first / Self and so she has / Fled me."[2] She introduces her collection *Missing Her* with a quote from Gerrard Winstanley: "The truth is always experimentall."[3] Now that we have emerged from an age of postmodern theory, the quote may suggest, let's tell the truth directly, rather than obliquely, half turned aside: "Occasion for murder, daily, / The nation's transparent plans / Occasioning the bodies of the new soldier / Sportive in khaki and floppy hat, / Wide-spread Kentucky eyes too blue for horror."[4]

Keelan writes in the essay "A Garden Is a Frame Structure": "A garden tells the story of civilization, our fear of the woods, the need for green within boundaries, order and design. A garden can also be a form of categorization, homage to mimesis, and it is also the place orthodox Christians forever remember in their fallen state. . . . A garden is a paean to Art, and also a plot designed for use. I fool myself, thinking I am cultivating a meadow."[5] What she writes is emblematic of her poetry, which like Charles Olson's defends the polis's garden against the wasteland forces of society.

Claudia Keelan lives in Las Vegas, where she is director of the University of Nevada Las Vegas MFA program.

1. "Missing Her," *The Constant Critic*, January 14, 2010, http://www.constantcritic.com/christina_mengert/missing-her/.   2. Claudia Keelan, "Same Dream," *Missing Her*, Kalamazoo, MI, 2009, p. 76.   3. The same, p. 3.   4. "Sun Going Down," the same, p. 53.   5. "A Garden Is a Frame Structure," Ecstatic Émigré V—An *APR* Column, *The American Poetry Review*, September/October 2010, http://poems.com/special_features/prose/essay_keelan2.php.

Something to Keep

Because this began from love,
a whisper in passing, approval
lighting her hair. Here is where
my name steps in, *Claudia,*
from the Latin meaning
lame, calling come home come home
I will hold us safely together,
we will consider the falling whole.
Cripple with an empire of days
attached to her body.
Do you know enough to say it
the parts ask, do you love
enough to reveal us, paper,
flesh, the face of the rain
on the microscope's slide,
your one good eye?
Nothing ever again free
from the collusion of my entry,
climbing the bus stair promising
to let it all wash over me,
swearing to let it all wash over me
so I may give it back, intact.
All the eddying qualities snarling
in the narrow aisle air,
if I can just be quiet,
not resist them,
let them wash over, not into, me
won't this be ours then?
Won't there be room then,
for my omissions,
his intention to kill,
her three bags of personal sorrow,
the driver's final, unspoken fear of his jo
I need to ask you now, teacher,
why it's destination you defy.
See, I'm on the bus regardless,
some kind of collage of coal and grief,
and sometimes a bird, or the wind,
threading *here* to that other *there*

makes me especially anxious to arrive.
Does the God we believe in want us,
howling and dirty from the listening?
How will I ask forgiveness now,
driving this packed bus
to the only where I know?

1997

Spring

Somewhere in her breath my father's heart, her orphaned mother
lifting buckets. Scatter me in her breath. At this point
I was already (in her breath) far and away grown gone, I was a
    park
the city wrote across a map. Father heart, orphan mother.
I was that which none called back even as I slipped behind.

The depth of that place, the depth and striving disorder of veins
blocking, in her breath I learned this. The depth of that place,
over the phone wires for years, my mother's breath listening,
the struggling veins calling from a back room. Grown far
and gone away, the park assembled its waiting, leaves, snow,
    pages

where flowers stood up each when ordered by name. At this
    point
I am already outside her breath, the sluggish veins pumping
    slowly,
in cold, beyond orphancy. I learned at this point the depth
of that place, far away grown gone, my litter, in her breath
his heart assembling and a park behind gone green, grown away
from a map.

1997

Critical Essay

Anyone writing can come to know
Everything one reading does

Anyone reading might never know
Everyone one writing does

If anyone is really writing
Anyone is really reading

Anyone knows everything writing
Everything anyone reading might never

Anyone for example I I found writing
The experience of the dead gods you

Read in Jane Harrison's *Prolegomena*
The gods dead and gone already in Greece

At the moment Orpheus is born
I for example I found writing the empty

Alpha where the beginning died and I
& Anyone for example Anyone finds writing

Truly writing the end's beginning the empty
Alpha full of the gone God's writing

2004

Sun Going Down

The occasions wouldn't stop occasioning—

Occasion for happiness—
For stupidity with her feathered crown—
Occasion for dreaming—
Jack Spicer the best singer
In a salsa band,
& the evil dwarf in mine,
Looking for our bridal bed
In a room named after a towering plant . . .

Occasion for murder, daily,
The nation's transparent plans

Occasioning the bodies of the new soldier
Sportive in khaki and floppy hat,
Wide-spread Kentucky eyes too blue for horror.

Oh occasionally, occasionally—

Times for murder daily
At "home,"
Both army and Islam
Falling bus driver, shopping ladies,
School boy and all
Waiting at the occasional mall.
The occasion a sequence,
A symptom, a
Spate of minutes held
Momently in place by
Bodies, by action, by architecture
By leaving the scene, not finding the room
Or finishing the song; by dropping your pants

& running freely in green-leaf-sand.

Occasion for nightmares not remembered.
For the radio all through the days,
For the missile shot from the Marshall Islands in the Pacific
To implode freely over our home in Las Vegas.
For my boy's terrible crying then,
And the life we shared together
Ending, I believed,
Until news came of the test—
This is just a test . . .
Is it all a test?
My mother thinks so,
Crooning beside the ashes of my father.

Occasion for hatred
For the men
At the Pistol Range,
For the flags smothering their trucks . . .

Occasion for dreaming
Of burning down the Pistol Range,

Of destroying the bulldozers
And cement trucks paving the Mojave;
Of gathering the flags and sewing them
Each to each into a shroud
For a country going down,
In the aftermath of its occasion.

2004

Pity Boat

I would not blow
      Into the tube
Of the life vest
Not in English
Nyet in Spanish
There were far too many ways to drown
Flying over Texas

      So I'm lying
Next to William Blake
In a big rubber raft
& he's teaching me how to love
Being dead. A slow study,
I fling my arms
After every cactus we pass.
"You're dumb, Claudia," Blake says.
"I am not," I say and poke
Poor William Blake
With a gun.
William Blake is beyond asking why.
And since the many and/or the few
Fuck everyone and/or thing they can
& since to fuck is to hit with a club,
He moved to Paradise.
I drive each day
Down Paradise Road
& one day I saw myself there.
I was 11 and I was crying
Running home through eucalyptus
To the *El Granada* motel.

Those trees knew the future,
Sweet tan bark
Shedding perpetually
In the salty air.
William Blake stretches out,
Happily naked and dead
In the what's next.
He's a singing a song behind my eyelids
Somebody knows where we're going
William Blake is eating stars
& one, very slowly,
Brightens inside my mouth

2009

Joseph Lease
b. 1960

Joseph Lease was born in Chicago and attended Columbia University, Brown University, and Harvard. He is professor of writing and literature at California College of the Arts and a member of the Advisory Board of the *Princeton Encyclopedia of Poetry and Poetics.*

His books of poetry include *Human Rights* (1998), *Broken World* (2007), and *Testify* (2011). Of *Broken World*, poet Dale Smith wrote, "Although his lyric gifts are significant, these poems do not represent the lyric speaker as a vatic medium of personal feeling. . . . Lease's work struggles against social and economic reality to evoke a world beyond the localized subjectivity of the author. . . . He does not represent a world, he relates its basic energies and he argues for an experience of the world held in language."

The poem "Broken World" is written for Lease's friend James Assatly, who died in 1993 of an AIDS-related illness. Lease says that he wrote the poem to honor his friend and his novel *Hejira*, which he completed just before his death. Unfortunately, the manuscript of Assatly's work remains unpublished.

Both a political and lyric poet, Lease maintains a range of subject matters and moods by adopting Whitman's psalmic structure and emotionally open embrace of the reader. The poet Julie Carr writes, "Lease is one of only a few poets writing now who is brave enough and skilled enough to take on the biggest crises of our time while remaining absolutely dedicated to the art of the poem."[1] In his poem "Prayer, Broken Off," included in *Broken World,* he puts Rilke to contemporary use: "If I cried out, / Who among the angelic orders would / Slap my face, who would steal my / Lunch money. . . ."

Joseph Lease lives in Oakland and teaches at California College of the Arts in San Francisco.

1. Jacket comment for *Testify*, St. Paul, MN, 2011.

"Broken World"
(For James Assatly)

1

faith and rain
brightness falls

blank as glass
brightness falls

until he

can't bend
light anymore.

Won't be stronger. Won't be water.
Won't be dancing or floating berries.
Won't be a year. Won't be a song.
Won't be taller. Won't be accounted
a flame. Won't be a boy. Won't be
any relation to the famous rebel.

You are with me
and I shatter

everyone who
hates you.

Arrows on water;
you are with me—

rain on snow—
and I shatter

everyone who
hates you.

2

To be a man, to be, to try. I hate the word *man*. I'm not crazy about the word *husband* or the word *father* either. To try. To heal the night or day. I'm busy selling fighters and bombers. The NASDAQ moves in my face. I'm wired to my greasy self-portrait. Every day in every way. America equals ghost. The wrong side of history. Flat matted yellow weeds. Who could believe "God chose me." Flat matted yellow weeds. God chose? You were dying that spring. Reading at some college I saw ROTC boys in fatigues. The talkiness of winter unwraps me now. In each room someone is fingering her or his soul. The talkiness of winter unwraps me now. The garden made unknowing by the snow. Erased by snow. Erased by snow. Two blocks from campus, a boy, maybe ten or eleven, yelled at a junior-high-school girl: "Ho-bag, incest baby, spread your legs." It's all naked out here. Nothing is here. It's all one big strip mall. We have a Ponderosa.

3

faith and rain
    brightness falls

    blank as glass
      brightness falls

Won't be the magic
lantern or dancer.
won't be despite
the fullness of time,
the other three magic ones.
Won't be a year. Won't be a song.
Won't be a beginning.
Won't be forward.
Won't be on the way.

Won't be a dreary prison.
Won't be the month of May.
Won't be Mary. Won't be the sea road.
Won't be stronger.
Won't be younger.
Won't be pink. Won't be opening from under.

The word.
    The word of God.

The word of God
    in a plastic bag.

I couldn't hear.
    I couldn't hear

your voice.
    You are with me

and I shatter
    everyone who

hates you.
    Arrows on water;

you are with me—
    rain on snow—

and I shatter
    everyone who

hates you.
    faith and rain

brightness falls
    blank as glass

    brightness falls

2007

Send My Roots Rain

presence was broken for a while, stillness was floating in plaid dark like a promise to the living and the dead, and the most horrible heartburn, and the old couple in the kitchen, lights out, lights out, waiting for sound—and the leaves roll just like faces, and the faces blow like thieves, and we all keep our explosions, and you taste joy in the night, and the lost boys answer slowly, and the corpse picks up the phone, and we all claim that we're holy, God won't leave our dreams alone—

▪

       Spin the wind,
Are
You winter—are you summer—here at
The end of the world—at the edge of the
World—every day—gets a little closer—
Moving faster than a rollercoaster—in
The night you kind
Of let go—and let it go—

▪

I wanted to (you know) feel like a giant eyeball—under the trees, where nobody sees—I wanted to cultivate sky-blue emotions like a luminous village in the luminous dream of a luminous painter—sacred is as sacred does. So I watched the spider.

What could I.

What else. I watched it move.

▪

I can't stand my own mind—

You just can't live through this—you're in the rain a million miles from rain, you started and started breaking and thinking and speaking and breaking—might give it back—

might give back—swear you will—if you could only
dream—the saddest dog I dream—then I'd no longer be in
your eyes—

The secret blue lie—

■

　　　　　(eyes shift

like promises, hair wet, apples and linen, just for today)—a
thunderstorm opens—birches in rain, are we breaking,
decorum slits my mouth, he finds a way to lie—lightning
and flat farms confuse me like wine—wine spills—thief,
thief of souls, thief, thief of light—fine, depression it is,
roast beef, Creature Features and Cheetos, Space Food
Sticks, thin birdsong, you your twin—"there was enough—
there was enough *alone* in you" *your eyes like rain eyes like
rain smile like rain* something about green torn silk:

■

"now"—you say take me to Heaven you
say take me to Heaven—

don't you want to say that—don't
you—

"now"

■

When the soul opens, there will be a cheap hotel: tender-
ness at the heart of the sky, the town, and not to hear any
misery in the sound of the wind—you came back to the
world: the green world, the fertile world, the corn world, the
gun world

You came back to the world and there was
nothing there

■

"polity breaks the church greets your faces
every sister against the glass glass wings
glass book glass snow glass secret story"

I believe
       you can do this

         ▪

turn toward night, speak into it: the bright invisible red
blood: you want, you need, which is it—

something tawdry, he writes behind glass, on life, on death,
cast a cold eye—passersby pass by—

the eye, O priests, is on fire, the buried life, the buried life—

       shower door on grass, shower door on grass,
rain beads on jade—"you're it"—

                   2011

Mark McMorris
b. 1960

Mark McMorris was born in Jamaica and attended Excelsior School in Kingston. Since 1979, he has lived and worked in the United States. He has several degrees from Brown University, including an M.A. in creative writing (poetry), an M.A. in Greek and Latin studies, and a Ph.D. in comparative literature.

His collections of poetry include *Palinurus Suite* (1992), *Moth-Wings* (1996), *The Black Reeds* (1997), *The Blaze of the Poui* (2003), *The Café at Light* (2004), and *Entrepôt* (2010).

McMorris is a consummate stylist whose choice of topic varies but whose tone and extension are that of epic. In *Entrepôt*, here selected, war and wounds of soldiers are ever-present. In "Letters to Michael (2)," the reader is provided with a poetics based on bleeding:

> The wound cannot close; language is a formal exit
> is what exists from the wound it documents.
> The wound is deaf to what it makes; is deaf
> to exit and to all, and that is its durable self,
> to be a mayhem that torments a city.

Reviewer Andy Frazee commented on *Entrepôt:* "While the scope of the book's vision is epic—it is in many ways a 'tale of the tribe,' as Ezra Pound described his Cantos—the poems here seem to hold within themselves the very history of epic. They are simultaneously political, erotic, critical, investigatory, prophetic, and linguistically experimental; they are somehow at once Shakespearean, Poundian, Surrealist, Biblical—Yeatsian, perhaps?—and in touch with the avant-garde."[1]

In his essay, "Ah Noh Musik Dat: Speech in the Discourse of Nationalism," McMorris asserts that "no speech is not crooked with other tongues."[2] Because English is necessarily broken by a multiplicity of dialects, its unity is mosaic and provisional. The solution since modernism is therefore the fragment: "Fragments do not pretend to offer the whole and final word; fragments are tentative, they hint rather than prescribe, prefer silence to the consolidation of truth."[3] The language of his native West Indies is therefore "a fugitive echo played on an invisible harmonica, whose location is all around you, and in which you believe you detect the sounds of other things."[4]

McMorris teaches at Georgetown University, where he has served as director of the Lannan Center for Poetics and Social Practice, as well as the university's Lannan Literary Programs. He lives in Washington, D.C.

1. "A Warehouse with an Epic Scope: *Entrepôt* by Mark McMorris," *The Quarterly Conversation,* July 5, 2010, http://quarterlyconversation.com/a-warehouse-with-an-epic-scope-entrept-by-mark-mcmorris.   2. *Diasporic Avant-Gardes: Experimental Poetics and Cultural Displacement*, ed. Carrie Noland and Barrett Watten, Houndmills, Hampshire, England, 2009, p. 171.   3. The same, p. 170.   4. The same.

(a poem)

When the combat finally stops, then I will come to you
like a soldier to his commander, and you will decorate my chest
with fingers too soft and too precious for other uses, asking
my kill rate and praising my accurate eye, the night of lemon
blossoms perfuming your underarms, your heart's land
undressed for my touch and my guilt abolished, the blood
left on the porch. The cicadas will trumpet my coming
and cancel the shriek of Tomahawks and soothe my ears.

When the combat ceases for good, I will put off the clothes
stained with shit and gunpowder, the boots eaten away
and my rusty helmet, and dress up to suit your dignity.
I will have cherry blossoms or the photo of a yellow poui
and they will speak on my behalf of the continuous war
the war that is falling in and out of the signal's compass
the signal I rode on to this gate that creaks behind me.
Combat spells the end of civility but I must begin with you.

When the combat ends, and bulldozers have crushed the shanties
and ploughed a thousand or five corpses under the pasture
the young man has lost his legs, and has questions for someone
and the vehicles head home to Greenwich and the janitors
empty the trash, and the captains hold their fire. At that time
but at no time does the war cease from thunder and the crack
of a rifle, and the book of your labyrinth has no beginning
or foreseeable respite, and I must retreat as I approach.

When the combat closes down, look for me in Tempe
and you should expect some ceremony in my face
because when the war goes bankrupt and is swallowed up
then it will be time to drink a toast, and to get on with it,
one on one, one kiss or word at a time, in good time.

—APRIL 16, 2003   2010

FROM Letters to Michael

Dear Michael (2)

The wound cannot close; language is a formal exit
is what exits from the wound it documents.
The wound is deaf to what it makes; is deaf
to exit and to all, and that is its durable self,
to be a mayhem that torments a city. The sound
comes first and then the word like a wave
lightning and then thunder, a glance then a kiss
follows and destroys the footprint, mark of the source.
It is the source that makes the wound, the wound
that makes a poem. It is defeat that makes
a poem sing of the light and that means to sing
for a while. The soldier leans on his spear.
He sings a song of leaning; he leans on a wound
to sing of other things. Names appear on a page
gentian weeds that talk to gentian words, oral
to local, song talk to sing (Singh), and so
he goes on with the leaning and the talking.
The wound lets him take a breath for a little
because it is a cycle of sorts, a system or a wheel
a circle that becomes a wheel and is not a sound
at all, the idea of a sound and the sound again
of an idea that follows so close; say light
and then is there light or a wound, an idea of being
itself in the thing sound cancels. Is there ever a spear
a soldier that leans in, a song that he sings
waiting for a battle? This soldier is only a doorway.
Say that book is a door. I say the soldier
and the local, the word and the weed, the light
and the kiss make a mayhem and a meeting.
So then that the voice may traverse a field
it transmits the soldier on a causeway to the city
leaning on a spear and talking, just after the wound opens
that never creaks and closes, and has no final page.

Dear Michael (8)

No grammar will console the human
who feeds on utopia, no torque of syntax

will doom the monologue, make it crack
like the spine of a book that hides
a mirror, and my face below glass
pinned to surfaces of type. The outpost
is finally rubble, although some retrieve
fragments as if to store and dissect
and catalogue rumors of other species
anthropophagi who dwell beside canals
to the north, and keep friendly converse
with dwarves who walk on their hands
the pious men with burnt faces, and giants
beneath the mountains of Sicily. No
photograph records them, and yet some
believe they exist, the way islands
humped on the sea-line in morning mist
tell of geological dramas, unseen
because in the trenches, and we are here, today.

So reading your books, I disclose nothing
of what you will become at the noon
of your departure, when the poems falter
and words are only desiccate symbols
given to a mimesis of power. Empty on stage
as perfume that is dreamt of in Créole
islands by a poet, my experiment of echo
bells it is time to concede the limit.
The nouns have gone in. The lexicon wavers.
This was foretold long ago by the seers
and mutes of my country, whom I consulted.

Dear Michael (12)

I could say more about the victory
so much more, so very much more, until
saying the word *sun* is to speak of it
the shining victory in the face of day
that is the nature of semantics, I mean
that is the profit of excess, to see
one throw of dice co-author a page
you learned by heart, in a no-man's-land
the barbed-wire compound called a city
on the eve of combat. The scribe liked

icon dragons and golden leafy capitals.
He was the last scribe, the last page
was his to complete, on the final day
of the last city that was left to him.
You see the logic of his position?
Euclid's theses of imaginary surfaces
point without size, line and area
obedient to pure reason, and perfect cubes
reflecting peerless hyperbolas—
it pleased him to recite such marvels
writing the last law on the last quarto
the last pen moving in the last hand.
The final scribe in the only library
the only river roaring in the forest
are equivalent, and in truth one may say
that the last cricket at the last harvest
describes the same pathos, the last
become the first, the first to be last
the only sun gleaming in the only weather
the only scribe to sit alone in a city
to write the only cursive, primordial
characters of the sole intelligence.
Others agree that it was always thus
—the victor eliminates the victim—
this is the world that thought built.

2010

Inescapable Country

Inside the world, the world is present.
It fills the mind with whistling
of birds, the golden flowers of pouis.

The ravines, along which scouts
pressed their enemies to a standstill,
throw up white blossoms of azaleas.

The paths are steep to the villages
splashed on the blue mountain ridges.
The cows in the pasture barely stir.

Something about pastoral calms
the violent heart, wherein desire
takes form in the visible world.

Bending a corner, you see it green
as it once was and will be then
and always with the mind's deceit.

2010

Sharon Mesmer

b. 1960

Born and raised in Chicago, Sharon Mesmer took her B.A. from Columbia College Chicago. She moved to New York City in 1988 and has lived there ever since, writing music and art reviews for the *Brooklyn Rail* and teaching at The New School.

Associated with the practice of Flarf, her poetry volumes include *Crossing Second Avenue* (1997), *Half Angel, Half Lunch* (1998), *Vertigo Seeks Affinities* (2006), *Annoying Diabetic Bitch* (2008), and *The Virgin Formica* (2008). She has also published the works of fiction *The Empty Quarter* (2000), *In Ordinary Time* (2005), and *Ma Vie a Yonago* (2005, in French translation).

In a postscript to *Annoying Diabetic Bitch*, the most "Flarf" of her works, she writes of being invited by Flarf founder Gary Sullivan to join the group's listserv: "I was delighted with the invitation, and the prospects: I'd been collaging text material in poems almost since I started writing, in 1978, and had always been drawn to running funny, vulgar, non-poetic language—the beef-tongued, stockyards parlance I grew up with on the south side of Chicago—up against 'beautiful' words. . . . It seems like a generous wabi-sabi kind of poetry that could inhabit bodies very different from the poet's own and allow them to speak. Plus a certain amount of control (i.e., ego) would have been surrendered, allowing the word-image to come under the influence of chance. Who knew who would be speaking? People I didn't know, certainly. People I didn't necessarily like."[1] Mesmer also admired the community aspect of Flarf: "The poems seemed to have been written by a meta-mind: in my poems I could see the traces of my friends' poems, and in theirs I could see my own. . . . There's a scene in Werner Herzog's remake of *Nosferatu* where the citizens of a town gripped by the plague dance and sing and carouse among corpses rotting and burning in the town square. In a way, Flarf does pretty much the same thing. But without that awful stench."[2]

Sharon Mesmer lives in Brooklyn.

1. "Postscript," *Annoying Diabetic Bitch*, Cumberland, RI, p. 120.   2. The same.

I Wanna Make Love to You on Mission Accomplished Day

I wanna make love to you on Mission Accomplished Day
On the floor of the main headquarters of the Department of Faith
I wanna make love to you two years ago today
When Bush's carrier offed some old Arab broads who just "got in the way"

When I was a kid we made love in a fun Catholic kind of way
On our bikes, under maypoles, in the Enterprise's cargo bay
I can't wait for Al Qaeda's Call for Papers Day
When I'll make love to you on four million barrels a day

I met FDR once in Vegas, he was a good lay
But not as good as you 'cause you're so ofay
Like an OPEC quote, and bin Laden's protégé
We'll make hot monkey love on Whoopin' Osama's Sorry Ass Day

2007

I Don't Wanna Lose Yer Wholesome Lovefest Forever

I don't wanna lose yer wholesome lovefest forever.
It's like a sparrow singing to my cress in leather,
Or Dennis Rodman changing my kid's diaper,
Or Mike Bloomberg ogling boobs in decent Christian literature.

I wanna ooze yer toothsome goth sex forever
'Cause my onscreen oral scene with Zora just went nowhere.
And human sex trafficking just takes the piss out of daywear.
And a haute-crunchy supermarket chain will just keep identifyin'
with the professor.

I wanna peruse yer mucus in squirrel cress—it's better
Than all the car shows out there AND Great Adventure.
I need you to hold me close 'cause I'm all coarse gorgeous splendor,
And I don't wanna lose that toothsome lovefest forever.

2007

I Never Knew an Orgy Could Be So Much Work

People hosting orgies are always surprised by how much hard work it is.
I think the best way to have an orgy is, in fact, to not prepare for it at all.
An orgy isn't a technological strategy as much as an attitude,
or a chance to provide your kids with a keepsake:
an AT&T orgy with Carrot Top, for example,
contains so much simple wisdom that is immediately applicable
to all areas of life.

I am so happy when an orgy does well because I put so much work into them.
I knew I wanted a funky new conversation thing,
but I also knew I didn't want the usual drumbeats.
Too many times, people make a mad dash for the restrooms—
so much for radical sexual stylin'.
Nevertheless, the Christian symbolism we love so well is constantly present.
In our orgy, the Mole Person took Saddam down to Moleopolis,
which is a gigantic ass vagina in the suburbs.
I got lots of noir work out of that one.
I got to orgy with a little monkey in a Mel Gibson movie.

2007

When the Platypus Kicks Back

I like art movies, books, the duck-billed platypus,
Thai kick-boxing
in the back of a flat-bed,
and the fucking duck-billed platypus,
relaxed and peaceful
from the armpit with a flatulent knee.

I don't like staring at a blurry boob
because I have mud like a nun in her church does,
and when pus comes to shove
I kick back with French cuisine
where peacocks breed,
on a precipitous descent prior to believing
I was a tree.

Oh, shy the platypus, the red rock,
distributed cognition
situations and actions
depending on neighborhood.

Inspect the wine making \ kick back with a spot of sampling
where peacocks breed.

Platypus is semiaquatic
egg-laying
mammal with a broad flat tail—

king monotreme—
propelling itself through the water
with alternate kicks of its webbed front limbs.
His spurs administer a cocktail of at least six different toxins.
That's getting physical.
And every time that happens
the platypus dies inside.
He's used to it.

Not everyone can do the platypus,
you need strength and
great glutes moving
against the stress
of Howie Mandel: he makes me laugh,
platypus enthusiast, 20 years old,
watching platypus on a kangaroo
like a duck-billed cowboy
in Princess Leia.

                                                              2007

Kenneth Goldsmith

b. 1961

Kenneth Goldsmith was born in Freeport, New York, and received his B.F.A. degree in sculpture at the Rhode Island School of Design. He worked for many years within the art world as a successful text-based artist and sculptor before becoming a writer. He is also a DJ for the alternative radio station WFMU (91.1 New York) and the original editor and compiler of the online archive of avant-garde poetries UbuWeb (www.ubuweb.com).

Working in the avant-garde traditions of Dada, Futurism, Concretism, and Fluxus, Kenneth Goldsmith is one of the leading figures of conceptual poetry, taking his influences from a range of artists including John Cage and Andy Warhol. His early conceptual poetry volumes include *No. 105* (1992), in which he collects words and phrases ending with the "e" sound, listing them in alphabetical order by syllable count, and *73 Poems* (1993), a visual poetry sequence based on textual overlays of e. e. cummings's 1963 book of the same title.[1] In *Fidget* (2000), Goldsmith turns to an exhaustive minimalism of the everyday by listing every physical movement of his body in a thirteen-hour period. Moreover, he chose Joyce's Bloomsday (June 16th) to do so. Many of his projects are similarly based on exhaustive examination of the quotidian. In *Soliloquy* (2001), he tape-recorded and made an unedited transcript of everything he said during one week in 1996. In his best-known project, *Day* (2003), he types every word of the Friday, September 1, 2000, issue of *The New York Times*. In *Head Citations* (2002), however, he brings his creative wit to bear by presenting misheard lines or titles of pop songs; the book's title is a mishearing of the Beach Boys song "Good Vibrations." "Seven American Deaths and Disasters," here represented, consists of transcripts of media broadcasts and police tapes.

In short, Goldsmith is the hardest-working conceptual poet in the business. He is also, proudly, the most unoriginal. His essay collection *Uncreative Writing* (2011) calls for the "repurposing of preexisting texts." But in order to work with such text, "words must first be rendered opaque and material."[2] With respect to the resituating of a found text, Goldsmith follows Dada and Situationism; in his call for opacity, he is consistent with language poetry. The text is, in a sense, unbaptized; it loses its sanctity, ill-gotten aura, and lyric purpose. But an infallible realism is gained, which Goldsmith calls "hyperrealism." He believes for instance that global capitalism is best revealed by replicating and reframing its own words: "Let the text speak for itself: in the case of the G8, they'll hang themselves through their own stupidity. I call this poetry."[3] Goldsmith argues further that "uncreative writing is a postidentity literature."[4] Anyone with a tape recorder or photocopier can stand in as the author. Liberating and communal, this development may take poetry beyond "the shipwreck of the singular" (George Oppen). Communion of a profound kind comes through reading, but it is greatly intensified when the reading and writing acts are instantaneous on the Internet.

Goldsmith's other works include the trilogy *The Weather* (2005), *Traffic* (2007), and *Sports* (2008). With Craig Dworkin, he edited the anthology *Against Expression: An Anthology of Conceptual Writing* (2011). A professor of poetics and poetic practice at the University of Pennsylvania, he lives in New York City.

1. Kenneth Goldsmith entry in *The Greenwood Encyclopedia of American Poetry*, http://epc/ buffalo.edu/authors/goldsmith/greenwood.html.   2. "Language as Material," *Uncreative Writing*, New York, 2011, pp. 35–36.   3. "Towards a Poetics of Hyperrealism," the same, p. 85.   4. The same.

FROM *Day*

"All the News That's Fit to Print"
The New York Times
Late Edition
New York: Today, mostly cloudy, high 83. Tonight, warm and muggy, low 73. Tomorrow, cloudy with a few showers, high 80. Yesterday, high 83, low 72. Weather map is on Page A20.
VOL. CXLIX . . . No. 51, 498
Copyright © 2000 The New York Times
NEW YORK, FRIDAY, SEPTEMBER 1, 2000
$1 beyond the greater New York metropolitan area.
75 CENTS
PENTAGON LIKELY TO DELAY NEW TEST FOR MISSILE SHIELD
JANUARY DATE EXPECTED
Deployment Decision Would Fall to Next President—Treaty Issue Remains
By ERIC SCHMITT
WASHINGTON, Aug. 31—The Pentagon will probably postpone the next test of a national missile defense system until January, administration officials said yesterday. Any decision to deploy the antimissile shield now seems certain to pass out of President Clinton's hands to his successor's.

Administration officials had previously said Mr. Clinton would decide this summer on deploying a $60 billion antimissile system that would be ready by 2005. To meet that schedule, the Pentagon has been under heavy pressure for two years to conduct enough flights to show Mr. Clinton and his advisors whether the system was technologically feasible.

But now officials are signaling that Mr. Clinton merely plans to decide whether to go ahead with the program's initial development. The change follows events that include test failure, opposition from Russia as well as European allies and a legal dispute over how far the system could proceed before violating an important arms control treaty.

To keep that option of initial development open for Mr. Clinton, the Pentagon has requested bids for initial construction of a radar site in Alaska, setting Sept. 7 as the deadline for technical and cost proposals from contractors. The first contracts would have to be awarded by December to permit building to begin next spring and to have a working system in place by 2005. Under the schedule the Pentagon has set in light of conditions in Alaska, it has to start the process soon, subject to later presidential approval.

The more politically volatile decision of whether to field the system—and break the Antiballistic Missile treaty of 1972—would be left to the administration, whether that of Al Gore or George W. Bush.

In a sign of this political evolution, senior military officers, including the program's executive officer, Maj. Gen. Willie Nance of the Army, have argued that there is no more reason to rush more tests. Critics of the program have consistently complained that the military operation was on an artificially fast schedule.

"General Nance is not going to conduct a test unless he's fully confident that everything is fully ready for the test," said Lt. Col. Rick Lehner, a spokesman for the Ballistic Missile Defense Organization.

Mr. Clinton is awaiting a recommendation from Defense Secretary William S. Cohen on the project and

Continued on Page A9

Ozier Muhammad / The New York Times

Exit Agassi

The top-seeded Andre Agassi, right, congratulating Arnaud Clément of France yesterday after Clément defeated him, 6-3, 6-2, 6-4, in the second round of the United States Open in Queens. SportsFriday, Page D1.

Lazio Closes In On Mrs. Clinton In Money Race

By CLIFFORD J. LEVY

Representative Rick A. Lazio may be less well known than his opponent in the New York Senate contest (not to mention the Republican who dropped out), but in terms of fundraising, he has already entered her league. Mr. Lazio collected $10.7 million in just seven weeks this summer, his aides said yesterday, leaving little doubt that he will have the means to battle for the seat despite his late start.

Mr. Lazio has taken in a total of $19.2 million since jumping into the Senate race in May, nearly as much as Hillary Rodham Clinton, who has been raising money for more than a year and has collected $21.9 million. She raised $3.3 million in the seven-week period this summer: July 1 to Aug. 23.

Mr. Lazio's success with donors suggest that no matter who is on the Republican line—mayor, congressman, school board member—the checks will pour in because of hostility among some people across the country to the Democrat, Mrs. Clinton. And Mr. Lazio, a once-obscure congressman from Suffolk County, has readily harnessed that sentiment.

"I'm Rick Lazio," he wrote in an unusually short, one-page fund-raising letter this summer. "It won't take me six pages to convince you to send me an urgently needed contribution for my United States Senate campaign in New York. It will take

Continued on Page B7

Religion on the Hastings

Signs of Shift in Attitudes Suggest Blurring Of the Line Between Faith and Politics

By GUSTAV NIEBUHR

When Senator Joseph I. Lieberman urged a greater role for religion in public life in campaign speeches this week, he touched off a new round in the sharp but unsettled debate over the role that personal beliefs should play

News Analysis

in American politics.

Some critics of Mr. Lieberman's remarks, including the Anti-Defamation League, cast the issue in terms of separation of church and state, suggesting that the senator had infringed on that principle.

But another way to look at what Mr. Lieberman, a Connecticut Democrat, said is to ask whether American culture has changed enough of late so that his remarks are more acceptable, socially and politically, than before.

Those who say such a change has taken place can cite various reasons— public unease over the political scandals of the late 1990's, for example, or the longer-term emergence of religious conservatives as a political force or a less tangible but pervasive interest in the personal over the political.

"I think the Christian Coalition has added to our dialogue on politics and religion," said Paul Simon, the former Democratic senator from Illinois, referring both to the conservative organization of that name and also to the broader political movement of religious conservatives. "Now, some of that is not good, but some of that is good, too."

Mr. Simon, who now directs the Public Policy Institute at Southern Illinois University, said he thought Mr. Lieberman had made his remarks "with great care." But he also said that some of the religious language used in the presidential campaign had left him uncomfortable.

"My overall impression," Mr. Simon said, "is the deeply religious people don't talk about it as much."

Mr. Lieberman, the first Jew on a major American presidential ticket, said in a speech last Sunday that Americans needed to "renew that dedication of our nation and ourselves to God and God's purpose." And while he said the Constitution "wisely separates church from state," he added that there must be a place for faith in the nation's public

Continued on Page A23
Bush Approves New Attack Ad Mocking Gore
Democrats Say G.O.P. Has Turned Negative
By JAMES DAO

LOUISVILLE, Ky., Aug. 31—After struggling for a week to seize the offensive from Vice President Al Gore, aides to Gov. George W. Bush said today that they had approved a new and sharp attack commercial that strikes directly at Mr. Gore's character and mocks his appearance at a Buddhist temple four years ago.

The 30-second spot, paid for by the Republican National Committee, will go on the air Friday in 16 states, and comes just a week after Mr. Bush personally blocked another commercial sponsored by the party that also questioned Mr. Gore's truthfulness. The move exposed rifts within the Republican camp over how to attack Mr. Gore without violating Mr. Bush's vow to keep his campaign positive.

Mr. Bush's aides said they had wholeheartedly approved the contents and tone of the new spot, which they described as "tongue-in-cheek." They said it was a response to critical advertisements run by the Democrats against Mr. Bush.

The commercial shows a television set on a kitchen counter with Mr. Gore on the screen and an unseen woman complaining that the vice president is "reinventing himself on television again." At one point the commercial shows a picture of Mr. Gore at the Buddhist temple event in 1996 and another segment shows him saying, "I took the initiative in creating the Internet." At that point, the narrator says, "Yeah, and I invented the remote control."

Predictably, the commercial sparked accusations and counteraccusations between the two campaigns over which one had "gone negative" first. Mr. Gore's camp wasted no time responding to the commercial, which was widely shown on television news programs and on the Internet during the day.

Mr. Gore also scaled back plans to focus on a patient's bill of rights in the belief that the Republican advertisement would backfire and that the Democrats should not create news that would distract public attention from it.

The new commercial is part of a broader, coordinated effort by the Republicans to raise doubts about Mr. Gore's ethics and integrity, which the Bush campaign clearly views as the vice president's greatest vulnerability.

All this week, Mr. Bush has criti-
Continued on Page A22
PRESIDENT VETOES EFFORT TO REPEAL TAXES ON ESTATES
REPUBLICANS VOW A FIGHT
Clinton, Echoing Gore, Calls Bill Too Costly and Says It Mainly Helps the Rich

2003

FROM Seven American Deaths and Disasters

4.

. . . John Smith is on the line and I don't care what's on the line, Howard Cosell, you have got to say that we know in the booth.

Yes we have to say it. Remember this is just a football game no matter who wins or loses. An unspeakable tragedy confirmed to us by ABC news in New York City. John Lennon, outside of his apartment building on the West Side of New York City, the most famous perhaps of all of The Beatles, shot twice in the back, rushed Roosevelt Hospital, dead on arrival. Hard to go back to the game after that newsflash. Frank Gifford?

Indeed, Howard, it is.

We interrupt this program to bring you a special bulletin from NBC news. Former Beatle John Lennon is dead. Lennon died in a hospital shortly after being shot outside his New York apartment tonight. A suspect is in custody but has not been identified. Again, John Lennon is dead tonight of gunshot wounds at the age of forty. We now return to *The Tonight Show.*

In the, uh, latest, um, report that we've got from the Associated Press, a police spokesman says a suspect in the killing of Lennon is in custody but he would give no further details. The, uh, spokesman did say it was not a robbery and that Lennon was killed most likely by a deranged person. It's eleven fifteen right now and, uh, were gonna be doing a full hour of The Beatles in lieu of, uh, Boston on Moon Rocks tonight.

It's eighteen minutes after eleven on this, a rather gloomy Monday now for, uh, I was going to say for fans of music but certainly anyone. John Lennon, former Beatle, shot to death in New York City this evening. It happened outside his apartment building on the city's Upper West Side. Lennon, who just had his fortieth birthday in October, was rushed by police to Roosevelt Hospital and pronounced dead upon arrival. According to police, the shooting took place outside The Dakota, that is the century-old luxury apartment building where Lennon and wife Yoko Ono lived. Police have a suspect in custody. They describe him as, quote, a local screwball. And they say there doesn't seem to have been any motive for the shooting. It was just two months ago that, uh, John released his first single in more than five years and, uh, ironically titled "(Just Like) Starting Over." John Lennon, dead tonight in New York at the age of forty.

None of us will probably ever forget where we were and what we were doing when we first got word. When we heard the first reports that John Lennon, the man who gave birth to The Beatles was dead, felled by a lone gunman in front of his New York City home.

. . . every other song for the remainder of his hour will be, uh, a track of music by The Beatles, as we, uh, kind of, uh, shall we say, think or exist in memorial for the death of John Lennon.

. . . his wife Yoko Ono was with him when he died. They do have a suspect in custody but the police have, ah, released no other details at this time. We will keep you posted on that situation of course.

John Lennon was shot tonight in New York and, uh, he is dead. And I think if you're looking for a radio station tonight, that's not playing Beatle music, you will have a long hunt.

Stereo 101, uh, doing a complete hour of, uh, Beatles songs, some written by Lennon some written by, uh, Lennon and McCartney, but all, uh, John Lennon was a part of. It's eleven forty-nine right now in case, uh, you haven't had your radio on, uh, former Beatle John Lennon was shot and killed in front of his home on Manhattan's Upper West Side tonight. Uh, he was forty. Police said Lennon was shot three times about eleven o'clock tonight and died in the Emergency Room at Roosevelt Hospital. His wife Yoko was with him when he died. One witness, Sean Strub, says the man who shot Lennon had what was described as almost a smirk as he pulled the trigger and he describes the suspect.

We'll be doing a Devo / Hall and Oates concert coming right up at midnight and, uh, any news about the Lennon situation that we have, um, we'll be, uh, interrupting the concert, uh, as soon as we get the news. Okay? Let's try some material from the former Beatle, John Lennon at Q92.

It's midnight. Good evening. I'm Michelle Diamond. John Lennon dead, shot down about ten PM tonight outside of his Manhattan apartment. And tonight on KCLD-FM, instead of Full Trackin', we have an hour of John Lennon and Beatles music, in honor and memory of the great man, a great musician. Here's a track from the album *Yesterday and Today,* "I'm Only Sleeping."

. . . 1971. Uh, good question for everybody to ask themselves, uh, when they are going over this event in their minds, I would say, particularly those that are hovering around thirty, between twenty-five and thirty-five maybe, ask yourself where you would be, what you would be thinking, how you would look, possibly, even today, if it wasn't for John Lennon? Good night.

2011

Elizabeth Robinson
b. 1961

Born in Denver, Colorado, Elizabeth Robinson grew up in Southern California. After taking degrees from Bard College and Brown University, she moved to the Bay Area of San Francisco, where she earned an M.A. in divinity and also in ethics from Pacific School of Religion. During that time, she ran the notable Deakin Street reading series in the backyard of her house in Berkeley.

Her poetry volumes include *In the Sequence of Falling Things* (1990), *Bed of Lists* (1990), *House Made of Silver* (2000), *Harrow* (2001), *Pure Descent* (2003), *Apprehend* (2002), *Apostrophe* (2006), *Under That Silky Roof* (2006), *The Orphan & Its Relations* (2008), *Also Known As* (2009), *Three Novels* (2011), and *Counterpart* (2012).

"I understand the writing of poetry as processual and exploratory, not as a means of landing upon ultimate discovery," Robinson writes in a note on her poetics. "In a sense, I find that writing poetry, like the practice of any art, maximizes a sense of suspension during which my/our usual conclusions are held at bay and I/we can enter a different mode of attentiveness. Lately I have been experimenting with writing as less an act of utterance than of listening. My sustaining preoccupations have been with spirituality, ethics, and the formation and operation of community."[1]

Robinson responded to a question about her writing process: "Poems tend to come from what I call 'soaking.' I will have a preoccupation, or a little ghost lingering at the edge of my consciousness, and I carry that around, sometimes, for a long time. Then it will be ready to articulate itself, and even what I may have thought I would say is interrupted by what actually gets said. I love the balance of discipline and volitionlessness in that process. It feels both mystical and erotic. And humorous. I think I write multidirectionally, and so at any given time, I am making some random poems and also some poems that seem to deliberately converse with each other."[2]

In an essay on *Apprehend* (2004), Patrick Pritchett writes: "The kind of daring found in Robinson's poetry evinces a spiritual courage and moral acuity that recalls Simone Weil and Abraham Joshua Heschel. Her deeply informed suspicion of language has not robbed her of an underlying assurance in the hermeneutical circle of meaning. There's a willingness in her poems to grapple with the aporia of faith and doubt that places her in a line extending from Hadewijch of Brabant and Julian of Norwich to H.D., Robert Duncan and Fanny Howe."[3]

Coeditor of EtherDome Chapbooks, Elizabeth Robinson lives in Boulder, Colorado.

1. Unpublished statement for Paul Hoover, 2011.   2. Rob McLennan's Blog, "12 or 20 Questions: with Elizabeth Robinson," Sunday, August 22, 2010, http://robmclennan.blogspot .com/2010/08/12-or-20-questions-with-elizabeth.html.   3. *Jacket 23*, http://jacketmagazine .com/23/prit-robin.html.

Apollo

I know the way the funnel works. The part of the fact seen
between columns. Gibberish unearthed from dirt. Mother
and husband.

I know you were proximate. Assign me the Ion. The flaw
of grace is proof. Stones become restless too, tired of being
encoded, a trinity. But a temple should carry the memory
of narrative.

The mothering hand falls to the shoulder, architecture.
Her act is secured, the garment discarded, the gown obdurate.
Profligate. She has not committed the reading to its proper
time. The rape buried in the hill and its lateness.

We always hear her voice from the other room, overburdening
our married life. I have my hand to your jaw, finger over
tongue. A boy would grow up. So you should succumb, that
I talk jerkily, my foreign way. That he has been reassigned to
me; wreathing.

For this, the lady takes her shovel in hand and buries the
instruments of the cloth. There is irony to legitimacy,
tiredness.

I ask as if I were the one to be recognized. A pressure of
utterance, he then came forward in drapery pieced together
from their unearthings. A god's body formed in the
translation, viscous aftereffect of speaking.

2001

Experience

I try to defend the orthodoxy of the icon, of uranos and gaia:
Any sane person can compare. But, heretic,
you move among the forms of illogic while the form speaks
    to you.
Where vision precedes hearing. Can't the form
of the evangel be reborn alike in eclipse?

Or hypostasis:
What is created, like a word, is circumscribed, a man in the
form of the moon
with all his singular deformities—
simultaneous in time, God and God, the word in its state
     of experience
is never spoken.
But we do act, visually, to remember its timelessness.

Then the question: You find a space,
heretic, whose width conveys meaninglessness.
The prod of that glow in memory.
The womb,
like groping the moon, opens to creatures and the son of man
has no size.
A desire created by seeing and impiety,
in this case, becomes the object of its own lunar orbit, perhaps,
worthy of veneration.

2001

Doorway

This is the house of conviction
you come into.

Characters play here,
blurred, coming into

movement
made inside frame.

Passive hardware. The address
is resistless at its new site.

The characters crave their old positions. Once,

they stood, so,

on their parts. The frame of address

first laid upon.

And then implanted.

Where one finds oneself. The roof-peak,
the angle of wall to floor.

Where one finds oneself, one imagines,
is as one fell.

The characters that comprise a house
exist in this:

like weather falling down, you did
enter, the shape of the house bent aside.

The atmosphere is nailed together.
Limb marking threshold.

Each element struggles to
make threat subservient

to shelter.

2006

Stained Syllogism

I find myself floating face-down in the sea, and am grateful that my
hands have been bound behind my back so as not to obstruct my
view. Appalled by my nakedness, the sea batters itself with itself,
such belaboring a form of embarrassment.

You should feel no humiliation, though, to see my naked back, that
on itself frets only its gagged hands, and no other mouth. 'Soldier' is
the action that arranges flesh on a moving horizon.

I am afraid only that I might not be permitted to drown, that a
well-intentioned hand will peel my body from the liquid skin to
which it adheres. The forms of kindness flay us. Kindness, too,
being tidal; it leaves behind.

See the posture of the sea, its salt made to dissolve me. Tentacular, the water insinuates, is my familiar, a consummation. It turns me before your gaze, mauls my face with my face.

2008

Mary and No Savior

Here you see me, all gold, but rubbed serenely raw so that the maroon below palpitates. At my feet there is nothing. I am absolved of history. But behind me, my ancestry grows, luxurious, a full head of hair lifted on wind.

I had wanted to give birth to an orphan, but his problems superceded mine, and history turns again. Now to work out the terms for an intimacy that can disassemble and re-create itself. Naming colors had seemed so important to establishing relation, but this comes over me vaguely. Painted over, milky, a tone and not a color. If there is not an object to love, there is still the impulse, a devotion to time itself.

Light comes from behind me, not attaching to my line of sight, but offering friction. A perverse and transparent kindness.

What lies behind me when I wake, a sort of history, the braid of bodies that engendered this self, the discord of the body's waking stretch. Even flesh is speculative. What was once skin can no longer be rubbed away, but inserts itself in one's surface like a blemish. All color revealed is a funnel pouring away what would come next, and then revolving onto the antecedents that would shape it. Doing away with sequence as well, and unfailingly.

Blue: the color unhindered space would be. History's refining abrasion.

2008

Having Words

You, perhaps, only wanted to know how many words
fit on a page,

but the variables are contingent on season.
And in this heat the words slide right off

the surface of the paper. Meaning to touch you,
I found my hand full instead of oily letters.

I could feel by the curl of the page that
your discouragement infused the writing

entirely. Holding this sample, damp and
tattered with the grease of summer rain, I was at an impasse

myself. Do you realize that you talk incessantly
about breathing, about what it's like

to pull something into your lungs? But suddenly, what had
always been as tiresome as hearing a family member

recite his dreams became
real for me: the thickness of the air, the muggy downpour,
all played cinematically before the both of us. That is,

the idea of the page seemed laughable while
the pure liquid viscosity of what we sucked in as
"breath" ran full with syllables. The number of words,

the exact delight of them, was exactly what I did know.
Sultry, unglued,

I threw your document away. I no longer needed
to count on your behalf. Nor ask how to persist

through the day's scorch. My one sigh was that precise.

2009

A Stitch in the Side

Accuracy aches, going uphill. The sun peers down
on my belly, constricting it.

I am in the sun.

That the sun shines down on me is my motto.

Motto: "one's guiding principle." Guiding:

the sun leading me uphill, the specific hill
where the blind lead the blind

and a stitch is eventually a suture.

2009

Elizabeth Willis
b. 1961

Born in Bahrain and raised in the Midwestern United States, Elizabeth Willis received her undergraduate degree from the University of Wisconsin Eau Claire. She received her Ph.D. from the Poetics Program at SUNY Buffalo and has won several awards for her poetry including the National Poetry Series, resulting in the publication of her collection *The Human Abstract* in 1995.

Willis has taught at several institutions including Brown University, Mills College, and the University of Denver. Since 2002 she has taught at Wesleyan University, where she currently serves as the Shapiro-Silverberg Professor of Creative Writing.

In her essay "The Arena in the Garden: Some Thoughts on the Late Lyric," Willis doubts the validity of such terms as "post" and "new" with regard to literary categories: "The language of progress tyrannizes poetry. . . . What's new is obsolete within seconds."[1] She prefers therefore the term *late lyric*. Seeking to avoid the reductionist rhetoric that poses language poetry on the one end and lyric as necessarily confessional and epiphanic on the other, Willis believes that contemporary lyric "overlaps with, rather than opposes, the aesthetics of 'language' or 'post-language' writing."[2] Moreover, "A number of poets who have been swept into the 'language' category for lack of a more precise grouping are primarily lyrically driven—Susan and Fanny Howe, for instance, or the recent work of Barbara Guest."[3] Willis makes no totalizing claim for the lyric qualities of language poetry or the advantages of lyric's "divergence in time signature; its divergence from mimesis." The suggestion is, rather, that an experimental lyric is not only possible, but has been with us all along. Many of those associated with such a lyric—for instance, Ann Lauterbach, Barbara Guest, and Marjorie Welish—wrote what has been called the "abstract lyric," an aspect of New York School practice. Their stylistic negotiation of that mode with language poetics made for a more dispersed, oblique form of expression and often the use of the white space of the page.

Willis's other poetry collections are *Second Law* (1992), *Turneresque* (2003), *Meteoric Flowers* (2007), and *Address* (2011). She is also editor of *Radical Vernacular: Lorine Niedecker and the Poetics of Place* (2008).

Elizabeth Willis lives in central Massachusetts.

1. *Telling It Slant: Avant-Garde Poetics of the 1990s*, ed. Mark Wallace and Steven Marks, Tuscaloosa, 2002, p. 225.   2. The same, p. 228.   3. The same.

Autographeme

A thought on the lip
of little sand island

An easy messenger
who forgot where to go

I came to laugh
in a dirty garden

A thwarted pauselessness
considering pearls

I was fluent in salamander

Everything wrote itself onto skin
with a tangled blowing

An opal eye looking down
on an errant package

A sky wrung of tint

What is the meaning
of this minor error?

The reflecting pool
no one could read

A beach fire snagged me
with its bright emergent eye

My colony sought revolt
in every yard

The present was a relic
of a past I was older than

Taking its language, I became an abridgement
of whatever I contained

A social imperative of silky fears

I wanted air
I wanted the balloon

Darkness flaked down like bottle glass
invented by a poor oily sea

A house made of soup

Others formed an invisible order
felt in every part

The male of the species was
louder than the female

Females made the mush
a sound of offstage sweeping

Boys played a game of torment
and sleepy forgiveness

while girls read their books on the rocks
containers of a solar plot

Little bird, fox on a string

A caravan of foreign number
staging death

So?

A smudge against the smallest dress
buried creature, of sly erasures

in the storied night, long *e*
cricketing awake, asleep

2003

A Woman's Face

Doctors sculpt a monster to disprove everything. Scaling mountains, she forgives herself the climbs of youth. Nothing can stop her dark mouth. She governs boys carelessly. You can't forge her dazzle. She stars all the time. Acts accrue against her inner caning. She lifts and shoots in furs, criming her way to newness, men.

She carries herself like a parcel over waterfalls bejeweled in salt. Her breath is honeysuckle in winter. Mourning doves carry her by the shoulders. Shaking curls against her neck, caught in a lie, she mines inwardly for change. Her forehead glows like cream above the Austrian ego. She can read.

2003

Clash by Night

A good man's up to his waist in mackerel. Sometimes there are no other fish in the sea. A stormcloud roils over his primitive kitchen. Her eyes are starlight headed for a crash. She wants the part, but not for long. Dancing shows everyone where she comes from. The projectionist is a dark horse, but he's at home there. The pin-up's a bunny in jeans, drinking milk, thinking up babies, a lesson in endurance. The martyr trades her wings for a day at the beach, but who can blame her? You can't reform a lighthouse. The worker knows he's been gulled. His catch is no match for *noir*.

2003

A Species Is an Idea (2)

The vine is just a vine
a substitute for nothing:
little mitten
bellwether friend

Or you, my landscape
a sensory derangement
next to Ireland's forgeries
the dream of her gigantic ear

on the poem's longest coastline
The poem that is America
America a prophecy
like reason in atomic winter

We think its magic wheel
is but a dress
that calls this city home
Unpeopled, architectural

2011

The Witch

A witch can charm milk from an ax handle.

A witch bewitches a man's shoe.

A witch sleeps naked.

"Witch ointment" on the back will allow you to fly
through the air.

A witch carries the four of clubs in her sleeve.

A witch may be sickened at the scent of roasting meat.

A witch will neither sink nor swim.

When crushed, a witch's bones will make a fine glue.

A witch will pretend not to be looking at her own
image in a window.

A witch will gaze wistfully at the glitter of a clear night.

A witch may take the form of a cat in order to sneak
into a good man's chamber.

A witch's breasts will be pointed rather than round, as
discovered in the trials of the 1950s.

A powerful witch may cause a storm at sea.

With a glance, she will make rancid the fresh butter of
her righteous neighbor.

Even our fastest dogs cannot catch a witch-hare.

A witch has been known to cry out while her husband
places inside her the image of a child.

A witch may be burned for tying knots in a marriage
bed.

A witch may produce no child for years at a time.

A witch may speak a foreign language to no one in particular.

She may appear to frown when she believes she is smiling.

If her husband dies unexpectedly, she may refuse to marry his brother.

A witch has been known to weep at the sight of her own child.

She may appear to be acting in a silent film whose placards are missing.

In Hollywood the sky is made of tin.

A witch makes her world of air, then fire, then the planets. Of cardboard, then ink, then a compass.

A witch desires to walk rather than be carried or pushed in a cart.

When walking a witch will turn suddenly and pretend to look at something very small.

The happiness of an entire house may be ruined by witch hair touching a metal cross.

The devil does not speak to a witch. He only moves his tongue.

An executioner may find the body of a witch insensitive to an iron spike.

An unrepentant witch may be converted with a little lead in the eye.

Enchanting witchpowder may be hidden in a girl's hair.

When a witch is hungry, she can make a soup by stirring water with her hand.

I have heard of a poor woman changing herself into a pigeon.

At times a witch will seem to struggle against an unknown force stronger than herself.

She will know things she has not seen with her eyes. She will have opinions about distant cities.

A witch may cry out sharply at the sight of a known criminal dying of thirst.

She finds it difficult to overcome the sadness of the last war.

A nightmare is witchwork.

The witch elm is sometimes referred to as "all heart." As in, "she was thrown into a common chest of witch elm."

When a witch desires something that is not hers, she will slip it into her glove.

An overwhelming power compels her to take something from a rich man's shelf.

I have personally known a nervous young woman who often walked in her sleep.

Isn't there something witchlike about a sleepwalker who wanders through the house with matches?

The skin of a real witch makes a delicate binding for a book of common prayer.

When all the witches in your town have been set on fire, their smoke will fill your mouth. It will teach you new words. It will tell you what you've done.

2011

Stacy Doris
1962–2012

Stacy Doris was born in Bridgeport, Connecticut. She received her A.B. in literature and society from Brown University and an M.F.A. from the Program for Writers at the University of Iowa.

Doris's books include *Kildare* (1994), *La vie de Chester Steven Wiener ecrite par sa femme* (1998), *Paramour* (2000), *Une année à New York avec Chester* (2000), *Conference* (2001), *Cheerleader's Guide to the World: Council Book* (2006), *Knot* (2006), and *Fledge: A Phenomenology of Spirit* (2012). She also published two books written in collaboration with visual artists, *Mop Factory Incident* (with Melissa Smedley, 1996) and, with Anne Slacik, *Implements (for Use)* (1995).

A translator from French and Spanish, she coedited anthologies of French writing, including *Twenty One New (to North America) French Writers* (1997) and *Violence of the White Page* (1991).

A tireless and exuberant experimenter, Doris changed her approaches with each project. In a preface to *Cheerleader's Guide,* Doris writes: "The text in general is a sort of sandwich-translation read-through of four books: *Popul Vuh, Paterson, Tibetan Book of the Dead,* and *The Secret Autobiographies of Jigne Lingpa.*"[1] Many poems in the text are accompanied by diagrams of American football plays, such as coaches would draw on the sideline. In a preface to *Knot,* which is vastly different in form and thrust, Doris explains, "Form means we keep changing our minds, at every velocity, due to life; poetry is that fact's lucidity. This book's actual shape is a meander that articulates its construct by showing all of its vantages at once, including the movement which creates them."[2] In *Paramour,* virtually each page is of a different form and design, variations that are unified by the book's sensuality.

The poet and critic Alan Sondheim writes of *Paramour*: "By virtue of virtue, of the embodiment of the Latinate, of the swerve. As if the body were virtual, and the writing a performance or dance around it. . . . Everyone is linked, including the sentence reading sometimes shuddering like branches, back and forth, the palindromic of the word, not the letter. Or the palindromic of the book itself."[3]

Stacy Doris lived in San Francisco and taught at San Francisco State University. She died in 2012 after a prolonged battle with cancer.

1. *Cheerleader's Guide to the World: Council Book,* New York, 2006, p. 7.   2. "Entrance," *Knot,* Athens, GA, 2006, unpaginated.   3. Alan Sondheim, http://home.jps.net/~nada/paramour.htm.

Synopsis of KILDARE

(Motley sketch of everything that has never been believed):

Sheila is a talk show hostess whose luster can't make up for her crummy sense of timing. Nonetheless worshipped, full of karma, ambitions, and cash, she sallies forth in quest of past lives during the course of minor surgery (a mere routine procedure), while under the influence of a local (anesthetic).

From an Arcadian operating scenario Sheila's consciousness spins back through a series of past lives (mostly her own) in the guise (not in chronological order) of a petty thief, Benedictine (captured by pirates), "All Gums" Evelyn, Tinkerbell (down home), Homecoming Queen, a contortionist, Herself – but zapped to Mars, and other girl champion archetypes.

After a brief interview, soul search, reminiscences, and Time Trip (a stroll down involuntary memory lane), Sheila stumbles at length upon the real New Age (future and post-nuclear) where, incarnated as Carmen, she takes a central part (that of Good) in a struggle against the crazy Doctor Kildare, right in the midst of his gamble for universal (what remains of it) leadership. Due to shape-shifting, an equivocating slave, and other set-backs, the duel ends in a draw (though Sheila maintains an upper hand). Kildare is dissolved (or is he?).

Finally, in any case, in a triumphal cross of bliss with unemployment, in the spirit(s) of beating and joining both, Sheila merges with the (putrid, stinking) half-life of the still moldering Kildare, giving rise (before it's too late) to a prodigious chorus of somewhat interchangeable (36 - 24 - 36) nurses who, along with their ever-faithful servant-breeder Klink, make off to the pastoral eternity of laughing gas.

(*Trumpets.*)

1994

Love Letter (Lament)

Dear Embers,

I warble then melt, rousing. This me infinitely, Thus. Your dark breaths course kisses, hand swooning between. I cut open, unravel, shower.

The honeysuckles marking, a long way down, we sink. First endless drifts, the path leading only deep, only nowhere, dark firs, This thick smell on the wind, windowless, a jumble. Thrust me.

Convulsing, This never awake or asleep, eye on eye.

Burrow softer then, then bind me blind. Under the wall of thorns, clip violets. When your hand Thus I swoon. Loosening tangles in me—oh, where? In a cave, sunless, opened quick to plunder This. Now pebbles could swallow me. I'm Thus wrenched and bundled.

If honey, This suckles. If hammered, This spins me. I clip deep juices, thin white body's hidden stems.

Thus down, in a burn of sun, Thus wastes, thin but stronger, wind-sheltered so seared, hidden stems with moss-skirts darting in the quiet of an afternoon, only eternal.

What hammers This shred, so I'm adrift yet fastened? What crawled in streams to this moister nesting, what crouches on This?

This coos, Oh, adore, oh more. Trust it to. Trickle and wait Thus:

Are you my now?

Geliebter

2000

As SEQUEL:
Second Slogan Poem:
A Song for Twins

My mother take me on the under side,
      Where I am black, but wow, my stuff is white!
White as ice cream is the little flood,
      Under my neck, all whipped up nice.

My mother lead me underneath a bush,
      And, sitting down on top the heaving part,
She lift me in her lap and kissed my mush,
      And, reaching to the place, she puff a lot:

"Look at the sort of sun: there rise and shine,
      And give your fist, and give the arm way high,
And flower pots with weeds and men to hang
      First in the morning; if you're good at night.

There's put in back a little hole,
      So she or he can fist the red fish tide;
And these black bottoms and their rosy cheeks
      Are just a fog made for a shady pole.

One day your arms will like to hold the weight,
      The fog lift, but don't forget that face,
Call, 'Come out in the woods, my ache and hate,
      And from my shiny waist the chains release.'"

That's what my mother show, with kissing rash,
      And next I try it out on little English boy.
When I from back and he from front place pry,
      And round and round the rosy spot we push.

I'll shake him in a heat 'til he can beg
      To press in joy upon each other's lap;
And then I'll stand and stroke his other leg,
      And go with him, and we will drink good sap.

2000

FROM *Knot*

Are collisions entrances? Even if inhuman, can't they merit collapse,
Without ingress, seeding, or proper nourishment? Detonations, no order,
Range increasingly discrete with the tear of—was it a garment? If we aren't
Propelling ourself, was somebody? With magnets? A kiss? Whatever's
Small and round, a purchase.

"Tick, tick," says the cat. "Tick." Here's a present. Here's a collection,
The real Halloween. Here's a gift, an igloo, so incubate, now. Something
With its eyes sealed inspects obscurity. If the lids burst: luminousness.
Here's a flowering, top-secret, then. In imagination it's hard, to invade,
And elsewhere easy or soft. A disappointment. Is this electric? With a

Switch? You shows up where somebody makes you's. Otherwise curtaining,
Present of red. Anyone comes and colors in another, filled, replaced. Unless
A burning, slight, an itch, all along the knuckles, expand, unconcerned.
Pinching continues until my's cover—was it a dress, milk?—becomes scrim.
A screen's demise, where sifting files texture's collapse, through noticing.
To see is not credulity, just dissolution.

2006

▪

Into some distance, everything empties. Explosions riddle nightfalls now,
And bombs partly originate sound; thus echo unending. In radiance, cells
Determine clashes and covering. Convert. Somebody, numb, sheathes in
Incomprehension. But touch medicates. In each caress, we takes shape as
Dwelling's axis. So another's hand insulates us, cocoons meaning cordons.

"Harmony" and "form," each song, these constructs serve law. So in a
Realm independent of time, there's disequilibrium's chance. In accepting
Erosion, embracing drowning, anyone could indefinitely swim. In giving up
You's a permanence, soaked rather than encircled, confusion of saturate
With restore, in lost recourse to fixing. Reparation's repartition, a sharing
For those who won't recognize others, so invent them as subservience.
Then living forever predicates eruption. Repatriation. The bullets stand
For blessings, so freedom's enduring.

Exposure's a safety. Stripped to the invisible. Security heats what it protects
Into bursting. Attracts to the lasting cover of ash. Any benison targets
Believers. Marks or wounds them thus, as winding too cuts off.

2006

▪

Is there a dalliance that stops putting all its eggs in one basket? Somebody's
Prerogative and potential—just sight—roots or roosts, which may construct
Reflecting, the finest indifference. Otherwise apprehension mostly hatches
Designs, virulent; a flagrant conflagration which authenticates, even invents,
Time in its casting. Ritual thus, counting's cupped, a poured vacancy.

Why do cognition, reservation and discomfort; fear, grasp, arrest share this
Term? Why all imply an end? If there's culture, thus tools of expressing
Some figure, each, slid into a gravity, will orbit. Where action counts
With respect to others, foreign, anyone's course designs their isolation,
A path that sinks in more than expands; a gravity, wearing. So attraction's
A projection of collapse.

Contact acts in declining; marks a trail, burn that wearies, the shaping
Of age, where sharpness comes at an instrument's expense. Any structure
Hungers, digesting all contents. What's held stews, makes celebrations,
Builds hospitably, hosting thus ghosted as revelry echoes. It echoes
Creation to a fault of uniformity. There, every couple twists potential,
Contemplative, so are objects and beyond opposition. Divinity's thingly,
And rule, plain immortal.

2006

■

Detail, a sip of tea, warps anyone's day to desperation because only
Ceaseless adjustment, only fidgeting, realigns time into expanse where
Vacancy's the price and they pay. Glazed, anyone takes refuge in
Expecting, follows a fly or an eyelash. Repetition's to blame. Once disgusts.
Somebody adds on a minute by relinquishing. Lives as a suspension,
Corrosive, any thread lost. Sequence names diminishment. Occurrence lifts
Away to respite: gull or gulf. Origin everywhere boils, a recession. That
Seethes and leaks. Makes dates; crosses them out.

Anyone's interest's to make each hour memory, whether or not this
Builds a collection at last. Work is then entombment. Fertile, meaning
Dirt; what sloughs off. As sun on moisture, which eradicate won't chart,
Some death may store absorption. Or, idea equals air.

A ladder takes ownership. To settle on it swaying, in an edifice of fissures,
To dwell that way not as honesty's last resort, not to favor even spring
Or the primeval, just dragged by negligence, by instability's drift,
Claustrophobic and a-dangle, thus febrile, thus food chain, suffices.

2006

K. Silem Mohammad
b. 1962

K. Silem Mohammad received his B.A. from the University of California, Santa Cruz, and a Ph.D. from Stanford University. An original member of the Flarf Collective, he published the first full-length collection of Flarf writing, *Deer Head Nation*, in 2003. His other works include *A Thousand Devils* (2004), *Breathalyzer* (2008), *The Front* (2009), and *Sonnagrams* (2011). He edits two magazines, *Abraham Lincoln: A Magazine of Poetry* and *West Wind Review*. He also maintains the weblog Lime Tree.

Mohammad's early works involve the "sculpting" of material derived from the use of an online search engine. In *Sonnagrams,* however, he uses a different but related procedure influenced by his study of the Renaissance lyric in graduate school:

> I feed Shakespeare's sonnets one line at a time into an anagram engine, thus generating a new group of words from each line, which I then paste into a Microsoft Word document. This initial textual output gives me a bank of raw material that is quantitatively equivalent to Shakespeare's poem at the most basic linguistic level: the letter. At the same time, it sufficiently alters the lexical structure of the original poem so that I am not overtly influenced by Shakespeare's semantic content. I click and drag the text generated by the anagram engine letter by letter until I am able to rework it into a new sonnet in iambic pentameter, with the English rhyme scheme ABAB CDCD EFEF GG. The letters that are inevitably left over are used to make a title."[1]

Mohammad changed his procedure after sensing the limitations of Google sculpting over the long term.

Both Flarf and the refitting of Shakespeare are proceduralist in their exhaustive use of a poetry machine. Mohammad comments: "Process is sleazy in this sense because it represents ulterior motives, i.e., desires, for which any justification is de facto sleazy. I think sleaze is an interesting part of poetry. And life. I associate sleaziness with wanting/needing something so badly that you 'readjust' reality to support that desire. That people are sleazy is also what makes them poetic, creative."[2]

Mohammad's essay "Excessivism" (see p. 929), which parodies Frank O'Hara's "Personism: A Manifesto," may seem to offer little in the way of poetics. However, in its obsession with popular culture, it offers a prime example of Flarf's uses of the burlesque and excessive, which by challenging political correctness and good taste serve the daily texture of our lives back to us. The essay's ethics are more transparent in its final paragraph, which begins with

"What can we expect from a country where the candidate that gets more votes loses?"

K. Silem Mohammad lives in Ashland, Oregon, and teaches at South Oregon University.

1. Slack Buddha Press website, *Sonnagrams* 1–20, 2011, http://slackbuddha.com/chapbooks/ la_perruque/sonnagrams.html.   2. Tom Beckett, "Interview with K. Silem Mohammad," Tuesday, July 28, 2005, E-X-C-H-A-N-G-E-V-A-L-U-E-S poetry blog, http://willtoexhange .blogspot.com/2005/06/interview-with-k-silem-mohammad.html.

Spooked

for David Larsen

first we get a spooky guitar echo intro
to help you gear up for this spooky time
the voices have no source
(pretty, spooky, quiet)
spooky

downtown area was a ghost town
massive buildings along the edge of a ghost lake
where she handed the package to the unseen ghost
spooky, half seen world of night
ski masks conceal terracotta faces
"drink, Madame?" the manager had appeared
NAFTA, 6 pesos to the dollar
this is downright spooky

a mother dies while being exorcised of a ghost
people view these experiences
as too weird, far out, spooky

a vampiric tree spirit who controls a lovely ghost
turning the recently deceased into
broadly mesmeric collages
of highly politicized anti-imperialist dogma
sung to the tune of "Ghost Riders in the Sky"
(you know, *spooky*)

spooky Arab hero who confronted the West
painted over in favor of the new ghost

"he was an imperialist"
"he was a good imperialist"
like waiting for the spaceship or something is spooky

SECRETARY [*Galadriel-spooky*]: you know of whom I speak
no, I think you've told me too many ghost stories
too spooky!

here some feed for the goose: SPOOKY
ooooohhh, spooky
spooky

2003

Cosmic Deer Head Freakout

1.

a disembodied head and leg poke out of a cart set in imaginary states
conjuring up haunting beings that are half-animal, half-human
deer man in deep-space / deer-antlers / deer discussion-panel / disembodied-hand

watersnake swimming disembodied head stitches seams in the warm pond
no moon: everywhere in the orchard, deer eyes   butterfly
 droplets and froth
sensing too late the occult phenomenon manifested as a talking, thinking
disembodied head
               you can see his hair waving in the wind
a disembodied head bobbed furtively into his field of view, drifting in from above
images: a warrior with a spear holding a circular object above his head
    his disembodied head floats
the noble man acquiring the feet of a deer
the camera is pulled back and he is seen as a disembodied head

2.

a black prostitute is decapitated by her drug dealer
her disembodied head is continually sensitive to diverse ways of "seeing"
there are aspects of deer: *pregnancy / bizarre throat-slitting*
decapitation / disembodied-head / Jeri-curl-hairstyle

the disembodied head spoke to her in a deep, authoritative voice
it's a disembodied head called the Silly Slammer, it's ugly as sin
also, its eyebrows are purple: when punched it yells "get a life" or "get real"
"lie back and fast asleep"   "if you could see what I could see"
"drip drop a lovely dream"
she yelps and wipes the blood out of her eyes and pushes ahead
she makes her way to the disembodied head of Hag C-SNO-62
Hag flees thru stormy woods   C-SNO-63 Grumpy, astride deer
the strange and disturbing skinned deer floating and singing
replaced by the image of her

3.

Billy Corgan's disembodied head:
"so do you want me to speak to you, or not?"
"there's a baby deer" I repeated
I could see his disembodied head talking to me
    could see the blood still spurting
"did you have to kill a deer right next to me?"
answer me! I kill you!   it was the little deer over by frozen treats

"I've lost various appendages in my struggles with The Specter
and have been reduced to a disembodied head"
        the disembodied head goes spinning through the air
before hitting the ground with a thud simultaneously with the body
    in the distance, we see a deer run away
then the camera is pulled back and he is seen as a disembodied head

2003

FROM *Sonnagrams*

H.D., H.D., Tetchy H.D.! Why Punch "Punchy," BBW Spy?

Medieval fishsticks on my lonesome mind;
Lonesome medieval fishsticks, yessiree.
"Medieval fishsticks," lonesomely I whined,
"Oh lonesome, lonesome, lonesome, lonesome me."

I want a golden walrus for the pool;
I want one for the hot tub and the sauna;

I want this golden walrus, it would rule;
I wanna wanna wanna wanna wanna.

My hot Virginia farm nurse does me right:
Shes tighter than the Cylon alphabet.
Yes! hot Virginia farm nurse, hold me tight—
Oh, tighter, tighter, tighter, tighter yet!

Medieval fishsticks, golden walrus: sure.
Virginia farm nurse: too cute to endure.

[Sonnet 33 ("Full many a glorious morning have I seen")]

Vac-U-Cash Devo Vogue

On melancholy airlines of abstraction,
The doomsday cheetahs hotly do pursue
Geometries that lose the name of action,
Together with the album *Kind of Blue*.

Through subway tunnels hardly worth a token,
Nightmarish offshore lurkers make their way
Toward a Gypsy shelter in Hoboken,
Where everything authentic is outré.

From Sarasota Springs to Mohawk Valley,
Socratic horses bear their creepy lords;
They stumble not, and neither do they dally,
But speed with all the haste their form affords.

They cross the dunes, the dust, the muck, the sand,
And soon fantastic cavemen tame the land.

[Sonnet 34 ("Why didst thou promise such a beauteous day")]

The the the the the the the the the the Death (Hey Hey)

Hell yeah, this is an English sonnet, bitch:
Three quatrains and a couplet, motherfucker.

I write that yummy shit to get me rich:
My iambs got more drive than Preston Tucker.

I also got that English rhyme shit straight,
That alternating shit the verses do.
Word: every foxy mama that I date
Feels how my goddam prosody is true.

And I don't mess with no Italian shit;
I only blow your mind the one way, ho.
I line it up four-four-four-two, that's it:
That's how I do my sonnet bidness, yo.

My mad Shakespearean moves are "phat," or "def":
They weave my pet eel Lenny—what the eff?

[Sonnet 47 ("Betwixt mine eye and heart a league is took")]

Ohhhhhhhhhhhhhhhh, J.M.L.: Flit Flit Flit, Fold Fold Fold, My Violent DDT Doll™

I celebrate the lordly Fluxus bard
Whose duly ordered rhetoric of chance
Procured advantage for the avant-garde
In crafting forty curious ways to dance.

The Pronouns, Words nd Ends, the poems of light,
The happy hundred Twenties without peer:
His hearty hair at last shone snowy white,
But those do stay like ivy never sere.

The bloodless bones of lofty randomness,
The sinews of intention rendered plain:
His art to fold them both in beauty's dress,
So to admit no odds betwixt the twain.

If mourners seek their oratorio,
Oh bid them merely say the name Mac Low.

[Sonnet 99 ("The forward violet thus did I chide")]

2008–2011

Linh Dinh

b. 1963

Linh Dinh was born in Saigon, Vietnam, and came to the United States in 1975. Before becoming established as a poet, Dinh studied painting at the University of the Arts in Philadelphia (he left before getting a degree), painted houses for more than a decade, and worked as a file clerk. Awards for his writing include a Pew Fellowship, a David T. K. Wong Fellowship, and residencies from the Lannan Foundation and the International Parliament of Writers. He is currently working on a book of photos and political essays, *Postcards from the End of America*. He has also edited an anthology of contemporary Vietnamese poetry.

His poetry collections include *All Around What Empties Out* (2003), *American Tatts* (2005), *Borderless Bodies* (2006), *Jam Alerts* (2007), and *Some Kind of Cheese Orgy* (2009). He has also written the short story collections *Fake House* (2000) and *Blood and Soap* (2004) and the novel *Love Like Hate* (2010).

The poet John Yau writes of Linh Dinh's work, "The ever-precise and brilliant James Schuyler characterized Vladimir Mayakovsky's poetry as brimming with the 'intimate yell.' Frank O'Hara got that energy pulsing in his work, but was tenderer, while Linh Dinh is more preposterous and full of outrage than either. Imagine a concoction that mixes Shakespeare's Falstaff and Celine's Bardum, frank, rollicking humor and hair-raising disgust. After adding fish sauce, a smelly cheese and sexual sweat, shake vigorously. Out of the bottle rises Linh Dinh."[1]

Asked by an interviewer about the violence in his poetry, Linh Dinh responded: "I see violence as a common misfortune and, by extension, fate. It's what awaits each one of us just around the corner. One cannot think seriously about life without contemplating the destruction of the body. Born in Vietnam, I was baptized early into this awareness. As an adult in Philadelphia, I had many opportunities to gather my evidence."[2]

The poet and critic Sianne Ngai has written, "In contrast to the striking number of critical abstractions produced around the category of 'desire' that have strategically informed theoretical writing for the past twenty years (for example jouissance, polysemia, and libidinal economy), disgust has no well-known paradigms associated with it and has largely remained outside the range of any theoretical zone. This is surprising given that this affect often plays a prominent role in structuring our responses to capitalism and patriarchy."[3] Perhaps this is one way to approach Linh Dinh's often profane writing, reminiscent of Artaud. To unveil the real violence, it must first pierce the shield of decorum and stand in excess of the case. Linh Dinh's poem "The Death of English" ends with the lines, "It's all japlish or ebonics, or perhaps

Harold Bloom's / Boneless hand fondling a feminist's thigh." He challenges every politically correct instinct with a knowing wink, as if to say, "Discuss *that* with your Introduction to Poetry class."

Linh Dinh lives in Philadelphia.

1. Jacket comment, *Some Kind of Cheese Orgy*, Tucson, 2009.   2. *Philly Sound Feature* 2, December 31, 2003, in Susan M. Schultz, "Most Beautiful Words: Linh Dinh's Poetics of Disgust," *Jacket* 27, April 2005, http://jacketmagazine.com/27/schu-linh.html.   3. "Raw Matter: A Poetics of Disgust," in *Telling It Slant: Avant-Garde Poetics of the 1990s*, ed. Mark Wallace and Steven Marks, Tuscaloosa, 2002, pp. 162–163.

Continuous Bullets Over Flattened Earth

Like horizontal couriers of a vertical fate,
Like troop rotations at a service station,
Like English lessons in Guantánamo,
Like draping towels onto a bronze head,
Like spraying love onto the sand.
I went as one and came back as two.
I went as one and came back as zero.

2005

Fifteen Rounds with a Nobody

I can only show my happy self
To A, and my angry self to B;
Thus, when I'm with both A and B,
I do not know how to behave.

Jolted by an unpleasant memory,
I punch myself—hard!—in the face.

In my defense I can only say:
"The point is universality and solidarity.
Unity, transparency, efficiency,
Collectivity and objectivity.
These are the key words."

2005

The Death of English

It stang me to sang of such thang:
This language, like all others, will be deep fried,
Will die, then be reborn as another tongue
Sloshed in too many mouths. What of
"That kiff joint has conked me on a dime"?
"Them cedars, like quills, writing the ground"?
It's all japlish or ebonics, or perhaps Harold Bloom's
Boneless hand fondling a feminist's thigh.

2005

Vocab Lab

This word means yes,
however, maybe, or no,
depending on the situation.

This word means desire,
love, friendship, rape, or a sudden urge
to engage someone in a philosophical
conversation.

This word is unlearnable,
its meaning hermetic to all outsiders.
It can neither be pronounced
nor memorized.

This word is protean and can be spelled
an *infinite* number of ways.
Its meaning, however, is exact.

This word is also protean,
and may be used in place of any other word,
without loss of meaning.

This word can only be hinted at, implied,
and thus appears in no books,
not even in a dictionary.

This word can neither be spoken nor seen.
It can be freely written, however,
but only in complete darkness.

This word means one thing when spoken by a man,
and another thing, altogether different, when said by a woman.

This word means now, soon, or never,
depending on the age of the speaker.

This word means here, there, or nowhere,
depending on the speaker's nationality.

It has often been said that the natives
will only teach foreigners a fake, degraded language,
a mock system of signs
parodying the real language.

It has also been said that the natives
don't know their own language,
and must mimic the phony languages of foreigners,
to make sense out of their lives.

2005

Body Eats

The word *mình*, body, has wide application in Vietnamese. It is sometimes used as a first person pronoun, as in "body has lived here for a long time," or "body does not know him." Body as I. It is also we or us. As in: "Body eat rice; they eat bread." Body is also used to address one's spouse. As in: "Body, what would you like to eat today?"

A spouse can also be referred to as "my house." As in: "My house is not home at the moment. Please call back later." To be married is to live in a new house, to be engulfed in another body.

The core of the Vietnamese body is not the heart but the stomach. Instead of saying "I don't know what's in his heart," a Vietnamese would say, "I don't know what's in his stomach." To be content is to have a happy stomach, *vui lòng*. To be in grief is to have a rotting stomach, *thúi ruột*. To be in extreme anguish is to have one's stomach chopped into pieces, *đứt ruột*.

Eating is the body's primary function. Whatever else the body does, it must *ăn,* must eat. To dress is to *ăn mặc,* eat and dress. To talk is to *ăn nói,* eat and talk. To have sex is to *ăn nằm,* eat and lie down with somebody. To be married is to *ăn ở,* eat and live with somebody.

To win at anything, a bet, a soccer match, is simply to *ăn,* to eat, an echo back to the days when to win is to swallow one's opponent whole, perhaps. To dominate or decisively defeat someone is to *ăn sống,* eat raw.

To indulge in pleasures is to eat and play, *ăn chơi.* To celebrate is to eat with happiness, *ăn mừng.* To go to a party is to eat at a party, *ăn tiệc.* One doesn't celebrate the New Year, one eats during the New Year, *ăn Tết.*

To look for work is to look for something to eat, *kiếm ăn.* To work is to make and eat, *làm ăn.* A good business prospect is described as having something easy to eat, *dễ ăn.* To do well in business is to eat customers, *ăn khách.*

To spend money is to eat and digest, *ăn tiêu.* To take a bribe is to eat money, *ăn tiền.* To work an illicit job, thievery, prostitution, is to eat dew, *ăn sương.* To steal is to eat in secret, *ăn trộm.*

Eating, and how one eats, becomes a metaphor for nearly everything, as these proverbs testify:

> *A magpie, starved, eats banyan fruit. A phoenix, starved, eats chicken shit.*
> *Fish eat ants, ants eat fish.*
> *Have vegetable, eat vegetable. Have rice gruel, eat rice gruel.*
> *The smart eat men, the stupid are eaten.*
> *Tailors eat rags, artists eat paints.*
> *Father eats salty food, son's thirsty.*
> *Eating new rice, telling old stories.*
> *Eat in front, swim behind.*
> *Eat for real, fake work.*
> *Arrive late, gnaw on a bone.*
> *Ate rice gruel, pissed in the bowl.*
> *A bowl of sweat for a bowl of rice.*
> *A piece of meat is a piece of shame.*
> *Selling ass to feed mouth.*
> *Two hands, two eyes are just enough to feed one stomach.*
> *Better to die sated than to live hungry.*

To be homeless is to eat the wind and lie with the dew, *ăn gió nằm sương.* This phrase used to refer to the hardships of a long journey, a concept similar to the English "travel," a variation on travail, from the French *travailler*, to work.

To inherit property is to eat fragrance and fire, *ăn hương hỏa,* which refer to the incense and oil lamp on the ancestral altar present in most Vietnamese homes.

A remote place is described as where "dogs eat rocks, chickens eat pebbles," *chó ăn đá gà ăn sôi.*

To be primitive is to eat fur while living in a hole, *ăn lông ở lỗ.*

To die is to eat dirt, *ăn đất.*

A common Vietnamese greeting is "Have you eaten yet?"

One should always answer, "After eating dew all night, I'm more than ready to eat and to lie down."

2009

Claudia Rankine ──────────────
b. 1963

Claudia Rankine was born in Kingston, Jamaica, and was raised there and in the South Bronx, New York City. Educated at Williams College and Columbia University, she is currently the Henry G. Lee Professor of Poetry at Pomona College.

Her books of poetry include *Nothing in Nature Is Private* (1994), *The End of the Alphabet* (1998), *PLOT* (2001), and the much-praised multigenre work *Don't Let Me Be Lonely: An American Lyric* (2004), which uniquely blends poetry, essay, lyric, and television imagery.

In an interview, Rankine says: "*PLOT* started with the idea that there are certain subjects you can't write about without being sentimental—the issue of sentimentality in poetry and the sacredness of certain objects intrigues me. I hadn't yet had a child, but I was thinking about motherhood in the abstract—thinking about it intellectually—and I was able to build a world before I sat down to write. Also, at the time I was watching all of Ingmar Bergman's films. The characters' names in *PLOT* came from the names of the actors in *Scenes from a Marriage*, Liv Ullmann and Erland Josephson. I loved that Erland sounded like 'her land' and that Liv dovetailed into *life, live, livelihood*. But Bergman's film *Wild Strawberries* probably influenced the plot of *PLOT* most."[1] Rankine further states, "The idea with *PLOT* was pregnancy, so the thought was quite literally: how many things engender another? How can the subject inform the form? Since *PLOT* was an investigation of shape within shape, and language was my tool—the words became lives themselves, and I began to see words within words."[2] The nonexistent child of *PLOT* goes by the name of Ersatz.

Rankine admires poets like Muriel Rukeyser and Susan Howe who bring literature and the reality of the world into close relation. Among her other influences she includes Samuel Beckett's plays, Ben Marcus's fiction, Lyn Hejinian's poetry, and Cornell West's essays.[3]

Rankine has coedited the anthologies *American Women Poets in the 21st Century: Where Lyric Meets Language* (2002) and *American Poets in the 21st Century: The New Poetics* (2007). Her plays include *Provenance of Beauty: A South Bronx Travelogue* and *Existing Conditions*, coauthored with Casey Llewellyn. She has also produced a number of videos in collaboration with John Lucas.

1. Jennifer Flescher and Robert N. Caspar, "Interview with Claudia Rankine," *jubilat* 12, 2006, reprinted in *Poetry Daily*, http://poems.com/special_features/prose/essarank.htm.   2. The same.   3. The same.

from *PLOT*

Coherence in Consequence

Imagine them in black, the morning heat losing within this day that floats. And always there is the being, and the not-seeing on their way to—

The days they approach and their sharpest aches will wrap experience until knowledge is translucent, the frost on which they find themselves slipping. Never mind the loose mindless grip of their forms reflected in the eye-watering hues of the surface, these two will survive in their capacity to meet, to hold the other beneath the plummeting, in the depths below each step full of avoidance. What they create will be held up, will resume: the appetite is bigger than joy. indestructible. for never was it independent from who they are. who will be.

Were we ever to arrive at knowing the other as the same pulsing compassion would break the most orthodox heart.

2001

Proximity of Inner to In Her

More flesh of their flesh? What was it that they wanted?
In the days they were not careful. too much fluttering to not
respond, not reenter, not laugh and not swallow the laugh.
what was it they wanted?

He does not call out. except with his eyes.

He passes each moment and knows it is never that. never the
moment calling. it is he who calls out. awakening each moment.

Blink and the link is gone.

Blinded, she wonders away, increasingly encased by the
projected angled scar of a perhaps C-section. Surely it too will
cost: a newer fear in the cut or did she cut a fear. a thought
spill. involving the womb's pace. its face.

Then the anterior view:

She's turning back to look you in the eye. wry-neck bird, Ersatz.

A groove in her palm says a boy will be born. says they will not
be blind forever though the marriage would cry "no,"

though the marriage would cry "please,"

and always their sighs would be the sighs that mattered.

When a breath comes would they let go in relief?

This figured equation takes Liv awry down the broad hallway
(we live in each other, hold each other up like able tables). she
asks the bathroom to be her escape. below being. in the still.
moment the house chokes. in the gnashing of low. oh blue
violence of true. in tolerable decision. decide a child beneath
the eye. unborn infant in the still-illumined mind.

The moment wakened. awakening soul of. cape to warm herself.
in she steps from the swarming arms of her own insides where
a ticking sticks to the mind like a drip a room away. urethral
resistance lowers. a stream sprays the bowl.

She lets the tissue fall, wondering, Is the new always a form
of a truce? a bruising?

2001

Intermission in Four Acts

The thing in play (Act I)

A world outside this plot prevents our intermission from being
uninvolved—a present, its past in the queue outside the toilet,
in each drink dulling the room. Hence our overwhelming desire
to forgive some, forget others. Even so, we are here and, as yet,
I cannot release us to here, cannot know and still go on as if all
the world were staged. Who believes, "Not a big mess but rather
an unfortunate accident arrived us here." Our plot assumes
presence. It stays awkward, clumping in the mouth: I shall so
want. And this is necessary time. Only now do we respect
(or is it forget) the depths of our mistakes. There often rises
from the fatigue of the surface a great affection for order. Plot,
its grammar, is the linen no one disgorges into. Excuse me.
From that which is systemic we try to detach ourselves; we cling
to, cellophane ourselves into man-made regulations, so neatly
educated, so nearly laid: *He maketh me to die down.* But some

of us have drowned and coughed ourselves up. The deep
morning lifts its swollen legs high upon the stage. Some wanting
amnesia float personified abstractions. Some wash ashore, but
not into the audience, not able to look on. Help me if who you
are now helps you to know the world differently, if who you are
wants not to live life so.

Still in play (Act II)

On the street where children now reside, the speed limit is 25.
Green owns the season and will be God. A rain, that was, put
a chill in every leaf, every blade of grass. The red brick, the
asphalt, cold, cold. The front step, the doorknob, the banister,
the knife, the fork. A faucet opens and the woman, Liv, arrives
as debris formed in the sea's intestine, floating in to be washed
ashore and perfumed. In time she opens her mouth and out
rushes, "Why is the feeling this? Am I offal? Has an unfortunate
accident arrived me here? Does anyone whisper *Stay awhile,* or
the blasphemous *Resemble me, resemble me?*" Those watching
say with their silence, That is Liv, she has styes on her eyes,
or she needs to forget the why of some moment. She doesn't
look right. She is pulling the red plastic handle toward her,
checking around her. She's washing, then watching hands, feet
and shouting *Assemble me. Assemble me.* She is wearing shoes
and avoiding electrical wires, others, steep drops, forgotten
luggage. Those are her dangers. She cannot regret. A hook out of
its eye, she's the underside of a turtle shell. Riveted, and riven,
the others stare, contemplating the proximity of prison to person
before realizing the quickest route *away from* is to wave her on.
They are waving her on. Liv is waved on. Everything remains
but the shouting. A cake is cooling on a rack. Someone is
squeezing out excess water. Another is seasoning with salt. The
blacker cat is in heat. A man sucks the mint in his mouth. The
minutes are letting go. A hose is invisible on the darkened lawn.

Musical interlude (Act III)

A certain type of life is plot-driven. A certain slant in life. A man
sucking his mint lozenge. He is waiting for the other foot to
drop: his own, mind you. In a wide second he will be center
stage.

His song will be the congregation of hope. He will drain his voice to let Liv know she cannot move toward birth without trespassing on here: To succumb to life is to be gummed to the reverberating scum seemingly arrested.

Erland knows Liv is as if in a sling, broken in the disappeared essence, the spirit perhaps: catfoot in a moist soil, at the lowest altitude or simply streamside, though seeming fine.

He knows he too, sometimes, is as if below, pained, non-circulatory, in an interval, the spirit perhaps in an interval. But then frictionized, rubbed hard—

sweet-life-everlasting, he is singing softly beneath his meaning in the sediment of connotation where everyone's nervously missing, so missed. His melody is vertical, surrendering suddenly to outcome, affording a heart,

recalling, after all, another sort of knowing because some remainder, some ladder leftover, is biddy-bop, biddy-bop, and again. His voice catches. It feels like tenderness beckoning and it is into her voice, rejoicing.

In mortal theater (Act IV)

blessedly the absolute miscarries

and in its release this birth pulls me toward that which is without comparison. in the still water. of green pasture. Lord and Lamb and Shepherd in all circumstances. daylight in increase. always the floating clouds. ceaseless the bustling leaves. we exist as if conceived by our whole lives—the upsurge. its insides. in all our yesterdays. moreover

asking and borne into residence. the life that fills fills in a world without synonym. I labor. this is the applause. This—mercy grown within complexity. and in truth these lies cannot be separated out: I see as deep as the deep flows. I am as willing as is recognized.

I am.

am almost to be touching

2001

Nada Gordon
b. 1964
and Gary Sullivan
b. 1962

Nada Gordon was born in Oakland, California, and spent a colorful, seminomadic childhood in the Bay Area and Chicago. She graduated from San Francisco State University's creative writing program in 1984, and received her M.A. in literature from the University of California at Berkeley in 1986. She is the author of *More Hungry* (1985), *Rodomontade* (1985), *Lip* (1988), *Koi Maneuver* (1990), *Anime* (2000), *Are Not Are Lowing Heifers Sleeker than Night-Swollen Mushrooms* (2001), *Foriegnn Bodie* (2001), *Folly* (2007), and *Scented Rushes* (2010). Rick Snyder, who wrote a history of Flarf, comments that her work is propelled by "a liberatory, ludic excess."[1] A founding member of the Flarf Collective, she lives in Brooklyn and blogs at http://ululate.blogspot.com.

Born in California, Gary Sullivan is a poet, cartoonist, and blogger. Sullivan coined the term Flarf, wrote the first Flarf poem, "Mm-hmm," designed to be the worst poem he could produce, and founded the Flarflist, an email list for sharing poems, in May, 2001. In 2005, he started drawing and writing his online comic book, *Elsewhere*, an exploration in biography as an artistic construct. His exchange of email messages with Nada Gordon is the substance of the book *Swoon* (2001); the same correspondence caused them to fall in love and brought Nada to Brooklyn from Japan, where she had been living for twelve years. Sullivan's other books include *How to Proceed in the Arts* (2001) and *Ppl in a Depot* (2008), which consists of ten plays. His blog, also called *Elsewhere*, is located at http://garysullivan.blogspot.com/. Gary Sullivan lives in Astoria, New York.

Nada Gordon has said of their collaborative project *Swoon*:

> Gary and I had a crisis, and one of the ways we dealt with it was to write a blog to each other. The material of the blog was therefore "natural" "expressive" language. I used a random poem generator program to generate thirty pages of stuff from the language on that blog. Then I edited it down to thirteen pages. . . .
> Gary and I both craved, well before ever having written each other, a total removal of the cardboard boundary between "art" and "life." In *Swoon* we were able to give that to each other. *Swoon* is absolutely about wishes and, more importantly, wishes coming true. This, not surprisingly, is not a terribly common theme in the jaded contemporary environment. If I do say so myself, it's a kind of lotus in the marsh. . . .

I call it an e-pistolary non-fiction novel. It certainly is something that was willfully constructed, as a novel is, though without any blueprint (except for love's urgency and all its cultural trappings), and of course, it is the product of our dual artificing. "Construction of self" is a pomo cliché, but you really get to see it in action in *Swoon* as we each build our personality for the other, aiming to charm and fascinate. . . .

Suffice it to say that I cannot endure the trendy (and possibly deeply sexist) villainization of "the interior" any longer. . . .

Without lyric voicings and personalities, even mutable ones, the risk a writer takes is only formal, is only art-historical. That's a valid and important kind of risk, but for me, it doesn't satisfy. . . .[2]

1. Rick Snyder, "The New Pandemonium: A Brief Overview of Flarf," *Jacket* 31, October 2006, http://jackmagazine.com/31/snyder-flarf.html.   2. "Nada Gordon in Conversation with Tom Beckett," *Jacket* 23, August 2003, http://jacketmagazine.com/23/beck-gord-iv.html.

FROM *Swoon*

Among the Living

From: Gary
Date: November 2
Subject: First answer ("explained" in later e-mail)

Among the Living

1

The aim of constructive uncertainty
lies in the corner between two windows. Such that
we, welcoming the indistinct, unlocks the door
because it likes the sound.
We abstracts the whistled body
of the word. The hazards of this opposition
become clear: the ear listens to what
becomes it, to the blood flowing through it.
Your hand on the paper doesn't belong to me;
the mysterious invisible placed on the tongue,
I, has a thing in its throat.
The air is colder than the room.
To have no place in it flattens perception
to the usual table; your hand on it can't stop talking,

is grammatically correct. Is this the way writing looks
looking back? The dignity of the road,
the hazards of water. I, aspiring to the dignity
of one who may not be brilliant
but upon whom you can rely,
rolls the thick word, the mouthful of light.

2

So great is the influence of language,
we can speak only for itself. If we is a manifesto,
I wields a deliberate response
to the aesthetic problem of simple communication.
This idea unfolds into two equal parts:
a spaciousness filled by the vernacular
that feels it, I, passing unnoticed
in the wake watching is.
We lay awake watching television
while we and our children slept.
So great is the hatred of others that they
placed itself there so that we couldn't sit down.
If the menace of numbers is only so many stones,
so many teeth, we sounds a ledge to lean from,
is grammatically correct. Sound is never enough.
I looks for what she really is, if there is such a thing.
We share nothing but space: the space you occupies
long after you is gone. Thus, you is renamed
for what I am, whom I love: what's left
unfolds, that we placed itself there.

3

Rubbed raw by the world's noise
we buries itself into focus. This picture
is porous; not only water conceals
what it shows. Where we lives becomes insolvent.
What you likes is there, in that sound, flattened
against the world. Not one another, not you
sits down, buries the first stone.
"Unseen I sees it all," walks
because it is its nature
to be coming towards. What speaks

breaks. With this rope, we cannot tell
if we are going to pull ourselves to safety
or simply hang there.
Is this a case of unconscious
distortion? "Hope is resurrected upon loss,"
so as to look more like you
than your reflection. Only this room,
a cloak to wrap around you,
warms itself. Is what we warms, a vow?
Enough to hold what focused, veers.

4

Because words mention each other
they are literally true: "I stole words and lines
from magazines," that line, that's just me,
for instance: "to make me seem more
calm." Because I reads your absence
in the space you haven't yet filled.
"So calm it could be a photograph of you."
I measures the house in this room, places
itself on its shelf. Love, beloved,
is what makes me, takes you; your tongue
is my heart in what speaking subsides.
If it's boring, that's just me. The dead
should have known better. Each line returns
to its quiet exterior, our origin.
Once spoken, we enters, is grammatically correct.
How it is that you can see this
is a mystery to me. The lights go out,
brushing against the bruised blue books.
Whatever is a possibility is therefore a necessity,
save these few minutes.

5

I, any want, wants to take your place,
lies in wait, awake for you everywhere.
Tall grass waving you on, the tug of this system
must be willing to subside into it, too.
The music comes straight through the forehead.
To the extent this is poetry,

it occludes translation;
to the extent this must be read
I lies down in your mouth;
puts his hands upon her head and disappears.
Disappears into those spare moments of inspiration,
we: "need something lovely" or: "kill our selves
to propagate our kind." A picture always leads you
to someone else, and we eat everything. Certain chewed up words
wiped from the face, face down in the river
drawing you forward. "Murder me, too." Language
claps its lid on the "when" of seeing you in bed.
Looking again at the photograph, the river
slides under our hands; the closer we look
the greater the distance from where we look back.

6

We arms itself against our invasion;
not by the noise, but by the illustration.
The telephone rings, the mailbox
is empty. It rests, it calms,
it placed a chair in the room and then went far away.
Everything in this room is covered with white dust,
as close or as thin as you. How long have you been down
where my speech is? We bear its shame,
its disfigurement; those days are in a thousand pieces.
"We haven't a prayer" is merely silence,
though perfectly white.
As recognition of reluctance begins to lapse,
sense of self begins to show: a single tear,
a silver airplane. "You are" and its audience,
strewn; the many, a form of order.
The vernacular that sheds it,
sheds itself. We curves beyond reach,
careless of index and anticipation.
This sentence driven deep into the grooves
of its shoulders, bent, as though they were true.

2001

Moonscape with Earthlings

From: nada
Date: December 18
Subject: Moonscape with Earthlings

> i really tried to sleep
> but woke up excitedly at four
> needing to finish this poem
> well it isn't finished
> but i'm sending it anyway
> to you
> my inspiration . . .

Moonscape with Earthlings

"You don't have to LIKE me if you don't want to. Just LOVE me, that's all."
>   —today's train neighbor's stationery

up against a word wall, pushed
by voluble groin

your (o)men's ferocity
eats at me.

my sentences feel simple.
they make sense.
this is how I touch you.

                    *

no anvils anytime, no
nor no bricks suddenly dropping
no no no no no—gentle.

>   our communication
>   a fabulous peony
>   bending its stem
>   in early morning
>   insomniac mist

communication
a silly straw breath
goes through—wilting
for love
of that breath

*

yearning for a dilatory cat
every sound's a melody
silence more suggestive

yesterday a secret
everyone could hear:
sibilance

you took notice
endings force beginnings
so why worry

yammering
effervescent doll-boy leaps in
sweet-tasting sea water

younger than ever
enlightenment reveals
shine on leaves' surface

*

the brassiere
makes an oath
of containment
things with wings
look on: flies
in oils

a small black eggplant
appears before the eyes
as a mirage

I quit!

and put the plum
in the exact mouth

on the mound of love

you in a folder
beside me

my head
like a sumo
on Quaaludes
filled
with the voicings
of a sister mind

and this brotherly
l o v e

*

From Satoko Nishimura's sweatshirt:

EVEN when you're not in YOUR room

imagine there is AN invisible HEART above you
all the time
that WAY, you'll feel SAFE and

comfortable wherever you are.

it's not just a DECORATION

it also gives you

HAPPINESS and courage

(insert image: kissing dogs wagging tails)

HANABANA DAYS

°advertisement° °advertisement° °advertisement° °advertisement°

I really enjoyed this lesson in my life. There is no lesson but this how many times we can laugh. The first time I talked to you, you answered my question about the difference of MAN and WOMAN. NADA said I don't like distinguish MEN and WOMEN. I was surprised because you said clearly NO, for the first time. But I understand what you said, now. I like your way of thinking as one personal. You have a good eye that everything and everyone is equal.

And this lesson is just like Nada.

—Akiko Yamada

Through Nada's class the members of the class became more friendly. Because we are needed to cooperate. I also found what Nada was like. For example, she is cheerful, charming and likes skirts better than pants. Nada's skirts were always pretty, I think. I rarely wear a skirt but I felt skirt is also pretty thing. I want to wear skirt more often.

—Yumi Shintani

*

I think I should get a C in this class. . . . I was not energetic in the class but in that small room that was the best I can do. It was really hard. This is one reason. The other main reason is that I like the shape of a C. It's very artistic sophisticated and even intelligent. When I think about a C, I feel the history of a C being so deep, and I like the word it's initial stars from C, for example coca-cola, cheeseburger, camisole, cheerleader, cabaret, celibacy, cynical and so on. That's why I'm glad if I could get a C.

—Takashi Yamada

*

This man has had an oppression on his astonish.
You can see the long star.
He is also having trouble with his choice.
The doctor is examining one of his air bows, and he has a bandage around his need.

This girl is a trip girl.
She is holding an envy in her hand.
There is an erection near the typewriter.
Behind her there is a glow on the desk, and an eternal is open at a

map of Japan behind it.
There is a picture of freedom on the wall.

*

adventure.

tumult.

the poets come out of the crevices to look at each other

jitsu wa ne
        atta koto wa nai n desu ga
    zutto zutto
        anata no soba ni itai
kore ga   *honto ni*
        sono mae ni oshieta
   inochi

   kurenai
        sugoku sugoku

    fushigi da ne

       love,
       nada

2001

Jennifer Moxley
b. 1964

Jennifer Moxley was born in San Diego and studied for three years at the University of California at San Diego. In 1989, she moved with scholar and critic Steve Evans to Providence, Rhode Island, where she completed her B.A. at the University of Rhode Island. She received an M.F.A. degree from Brown University in 1994. From 1992 to 1995, she edited *The Impercipient*, a literary magazine, and founded, with Steve Evans, The Impercipient Lecture Series, a monthly poetics pamphlet. Moxley also served as poetry editor of *The Baffler* from 1997 to 2010.

Moxley's poetry volumes include *Imagination Verses* (1996/2003), *The Sense Record and Other Poems* (2002/2003), *Often Capital* (2004), *The Line* (2007), and *Clampdown* (2009). She has also published a memoir, *The Middle Room* (2007), and *There Are Things We Live Among: Essays on the Object World* (2012).

Ron Silliman has commented that each of Moxley's works is a distinct departure from those that preceded it: "I can't think of another writer who manages this sort of effect from book to book beyond, say, the later publications of Jack Spicer."[1]

In "Fragments of a Broken Poetics," which may be viewed as a statement of her own poetics of divergence, Moxley writes:

I

The poet's psychology, visible only to the poet's friends, floats lightly over the surface of the poem. It discolors some words temporarily, but never quite settles into them—provided those words belong together. If so, they will eventually cast off this shadow; if not, it will eventually smother them. Thus, it is the poem, not the poet, that we love. Through it the singular becomes shared, the transitory eternal.

II

The eternal, typically a conceit standing in for the hope of civilizations, acts differently in poetry. The words of the poem, once happily configured, may wait a very long time for a reader to read them as they were meant to be read. This is the eternity of the poem.[2]

Moxley lives in Orono, Maine, and teaches poetry and poetics at the University of Maine.

1. Silliman's Blog, Monday, July 2, 2007, http://ronsilliman.blogspot.com/2007/07/no-two-books-of-jennifer-moxleys-really.html.   2. *Chicago Review*, Spring 2010.

Wreath of a Similar Year

A circlet ring of light
        beneath our feet
a door, a possible path
        of very best will,
placed before us
        in infinite intervals.
Such facets of mind
        might sustain us
if luck runs over, or love
        provide the lost,
more bodily
        forms of warmth.

The inconsolable mind
        has created
abundant distress—
        the scarcity required
to bury a world
        of living evidence.
Abandoned so, in an idea
        of innermost anguish,
we have become accustomed
        to the unheard music,
the quiet accompaniment
        of water,
being disturbed within.

Thought intent
        upon contentment
may temper the guests of our greater being,
        unearth
the hourly questions
        burned down from youth
with energy and light. As in the wake
        of awakening
wrong attempts
        and wrongful death
will fall adjacent
        careful Hope.

Hope,
how strangely of untold direction
it sounds, blind as
the first letter on the first stone
written down
as if a wreath to circle
the last sound spoken
on some distant, though similar
Earth.

2003

The Price of Silence

It's very early in the century.
We are awake, like a futureless youth
tired from a night of dreary drinking.
The sun warms the synthetic bedspread
hoary with sprouts of nylon thread.
Its topography of occasional craters
formed by errant burning cherries
bespeaks the vintage of its dying surface.

Who will benefit from the use of such things?
Is there coffee being made in the kitchen,
wafting up the stairway, now carpeted
in plush rose fibers, once a well-worn
maple with a squeak around step three?
Are there eggs sizzling on the stove?
A smooth blueprint of linen across
an old wooden breakfast table?
Clean utensils slightly tarnished,
fresh cream in a cream-colored creamer,
a little mottled with attractive cracks?
Austere dreams of outdated poetry.

The century has just begun.
Shall we roll over and go back to sleep?
Such an impossibility: the time it takes
to maintain these things we've worked

so hard to gain. As to grow a tree.
Who has it? Let us sleep a while longer.

We shall dream of the sober aesthetics
of an old stone farmhouse, the quiet
as it sounds in religious contrast
to a lovingly crafted grandfather clock.
Wake up! Supper has been prepared.
But by whom? It's mysteriously delicious
and wholesome besides.

But let's not forget the naughty bit.
A milkmaid astride the knees of an undertaker.
Toothless disowned relations
vulgarly hocking our beloved trousseau.
Just punishment for our haughty treatment
of the downstairs workers all these years.

A ghostly cloud of beige pressed powder
drifts from the maw of a silver compact
which sits on a doily atop an armoire
in the master's bedroom. The master
whose servants all ran away.

Is the new century a failure?
A failure locked in an image,
to which we don't have access.
Things are happening out of spite.
The exhaustion is one of heat, sticky skin
against the texture of aggressively pilled
flannel sheets. Shall we meet again?
I'm off to where the job takes me, and you?
To a downtown revival in a stucco mall.

Beautiful austerity. Europe, after the fact.
It still works nicely in poetry, like
worshipping outdated gods.
We wish light flooded into this century
as light once used to do. A warm aura
of color against a cold interior,
a Hammershøi painting from which
we are barred, trapped here as we are

with the waste of an outdated system
in a landscape bereaved by unusual weather.

It is suffocating beneath this vinyl window,
in whose fake glued-on mullions we see a cross.
But it doesn't mean anything. No word
can be uttered or kept in store to chant us
out of losing. The whir of the washing machine
as it pours detergent down the sewer pipes,
chlorine rising up from the drains. The compact
fluorescent bulb in the gooseneck lamp
with a broken spring neither mutters
nor sputters playfully. Things don't speak
our distance. The phone, though loud, tinny,
and insistent, cannot, it seems, be found.
We oppress in a way we cannot pay for
in any direct or meaningful way. All is fake.

Why should we awake?

2009

Eleni Sikelianos

b. 1965

Born and raised in Santa Barbara, California, Eleni Sikelianos left the United States at age twenty to travel in Europe, Turkey, Israel, and Africa for nearly two years. She then lived in Paris, attended the Jack Kerouac School of Disembodied Poetics at Naropa Institute in Colorado and lived in New York for six years, where she cocurated the Wednesday night reading series at St. Mark's Church. She now lives in Boulder and teaches at the University of Denver.

Sikelianos's poetry books include *To Speak While Dreaming* (1993), *The Book of Tendons* (1997), *Earliest Worlds* (2001), which won the James P. Phelan Award, the book-length work *The Monster Lives of Boys and Girls* (2003), *The California Poem* (2004), and *Body Clock* (2008). She has also published a memoir, *The Book of Jon* (2004).

The poet Karla Kelsey writes: "In scope and mode *The California Poem* directly descends from the epic tradition carried so stunningly through the twentieth century in America, and the project could not have been written without Pound's *Cantos,* Eliot's *Wasteland,* H.D.'s *Trilogy,* Williams's *Paterson,* Olson's *Maximus Poems,* Johnson's *Ark,* and Zukofsky's 'A.'" Sikelianos continues the twentieth-century epic's exploration of the material, constructed nature of history by 'sampling' various historical and cultural texts and stitching them into the body of her work."[1] These samplings include *The Log from the Sea of Cortez* by John Steinbeck and Edward F. Ricketts and *December's Child: A Book of Chumash Oral Narratives.*

Sikelianos has been a Princeton University Seeger Fellow, a Yaddo Fellow, and a Fulbright Scholar to Greece. She has also received a National Endowment for the Arts fellowship in poetry.

Sikelianos's great-grandfather was the distinguished Greek poet Angelos Sikelianos.

1. Karla Kelsey, "The California Poem and The Book of John," *Double Room* 5, Winter/Spring 2005, http://www.webdelsol.com/Double_Room/issue_five/Eline_Sikelianos.html.

Campo santo

—Non ai, voir, mere, non ai, non!

I learned to say no in the old language
studying at the Night-school

of Electricity on Rocket Street
Before I got my eye put out

on a teeth of forests—No

to the angels, no to electricity

No to pretending to read when the ear is open

the Pearl

of venery, this vertical blanking
about ten lines outside the TV's frame

No, no, for what is not No
hid by umber & alcove

1999

Of the True Human Fold

& I am of the skull & corpus vertebrata hiding inside
the microscopic structure of a bone

& my osteoclasts will tear it down & my osteoblasts will build it back

& I am of chordata & endoskeleton hiding inside
a star the buildings of dust that stuff

& I am of hominidae & anthropoidea Look my 2000 cc brain capacity

& this is my heart's atrium & the a. of my tympanic cavity
& here is my hepatic vein
& here my oral hood
my vestibular canal   organ of Corti
my homo sapiens' larynx   mons pubis
& here, my axillae armpits milk-lines along each side & I am hiding between
the dawn ape & nuclear fission

If you can't find me at the Lake of Aegyptopithecus
Look for me at Child of the Hook, my black-bone burning

my blank
spine

1999

Essay: Delicately

The father pollutes his body and
this is illegal and yet he does not
knowingly or purposefully pollute rivers
except by the small necessities
of daily living. Chevron pollutes rivers
and dirt and children are born
into brain cells in wrong places. If my father
smokes in a public place, this could
get him into trouble. If he shoots
heroin at home and someone
official finds him he
will be fined or arrested, maybe jailed.
This is the classic story in which a hero
sets out on a voyage, like Homer's or Dante's, and
along the way finds out something about
her / himself, only this time there's nothing
left to find out. For the world like Sappho was either

small, dark, and ugly
or small, dark, and beautiful.

2001

Essay: Seven Aspects of Milking Time

I had it in my mind to move
my left knee toward kathenotheism or Calgary, worshiping
one god at a time

In it, the alphabet was an abolitionist

Fire was a messenger
the smoke sent up & ash. The message

: Do you want scientific replacements or creative additions : was :
: A celestial mechanics problem : How long have you been involved
   in Earth's politics

(this message is : blank) the answer is

ever since I'm in my strong suit, my weak

spackling the walls with bandages of light. I (may I
say we) was

trying to fix the place up, (we) was
to finish the procedure, it was
an architectural question, a spirit / spit one

    (could not)
change cavalry to Calgary to calligram

Is each generation a further fragmentation? Was it
    Omegaville?   . . .   I think the thing is
a conquistador built of prunes & glue. The Grand Combustion

Carnival, Columbus the Cat Dancing in Flames; there are
white boys on the corner and cherry

bombs. There was only enough water to support a

an A, or B; a boy or a   grill

There was not enough water to put out a fire
They had to import a river & kill a bunch of Black Feet. Who / I declare
a season is an agreement that hangs between heaven and here

My heroes start out in the meadowdust
& end up in the gutter

    2001

Be Honeyed Bush

    Draw the poison
    from the Lake with sweet
    bait: dip in
    sugar sachets & watch
    the sirens quake: like
    Robot Angels they rise
    with eyes of industrial imagination

Sky rolls back to its black
bones & hooks;   We hang.

Could I hear this air tear   to see it
all again—life
with its private   history
moving   particle by particle

Create in us a clean
shirt, clean lake, & of my tongue shall sting

for I have always said
by my true human monster
you too shall be honeyed
in palindromes of gold
when the train divides
your wrong from right

2008

A Radiant Countess of What's It

I love it
when women eat sweet ribbon, sweet
rabbit, sweet meat, when women

are the scene
of several utopias

when the body melts back into shadow
beginning with the feet

2008

Edwin Torres
b. 1965

Edwin Torres was born in the Bronx to Puerto Rican parents. After the death of his father, Torres received comfort and support during his teenage years from his Uncle Martin, whom he describes as a "Puerto Rican Benny Hill." This humor served as a motivating force for Torres, and led him to discover poetry in the pages of *Mad* magazine. In 1989, Torres discovered the Nuyorican Poets Café, founded by poet Miguel Algarín and playwright Miguel Piñero. Inspired by the poetry performance scene, he created the movements Interactive Eclecticism, which combines movement, music, and audience participation, and Poets Neurotica, in which dancers and musicians performed in the company of poets. He was also a member of the Real Live Poetry performance group, 1993–1999.

After years of emphasizing the performance of poetry, Torres began to publish books of his poetry. They include *Fractured Humorous* (1999), *The All-Union Day of the Shock Worker* (2001), *The Popedology of an Ambient Language* (2007), *In the Function of External Circumstances* (2010), and *Yes Thing No Thing* (2010).

Torres claims among his influences the Soviet Cubo-Futurist poet Velimir Khlebnikov and his notion of *zaum,* a transrational language that employs sound-oriented neologisms; the aleatory and cybernetic poetics of Jackson Mac Low and John Cage; the collage methods of German Dadaist Kurt Schwitters; and the "sprung rhythm" poetics of nineteenth-century British poet Gerard Manley Hopkins.

In a panel discussion, Torres commented: "In a time of crisis, if you have something to say and choose to say it, you are claiming your right to freedom-slash-interference. Which would then bring up a point about freedom itself being interference. If we used what empowers to free us, when is freedom needed? Are we captives of interference? Performance poetry is an ultimate freedom-slash-interference since it combines poetry, an already daring motion to undertake in this society, with performance . . . the body's vulnerability and by turns its strength . . . the voice's command of breath *as* stage."[1]

Edwin Torres lives in Hopewell Junction, New York, and works as a graphic designer.

1. Edwin Torres, "The Limit Is Limitless: Freedom in Crisis, Breathing Life into Words," http://poetry.about.com/cs/reviewsessays/a/perfpoetorres_2.htm.

Slipped Curve

danger is the birth of angles
shazz'd; lettroin; marved; eld
enticing; the shape beckons
rip in sky; throat opens

when ungorged; a curve
features formless, out of reshaped voweletter
yellow vegas bundesbähn
welcome to the four-eyed boys

zizz'd; mreckt; taon; vevved
shell-shocked leather-clad; mad punkt
takes over soundpakt; easier to listen
if you take away; fear; peligrøtz

lover street; luuversträsse
jammed mother's vilk-kummen; mira
the minister's house; shadowblakt
by nicht-shak; danger is the birth of angles

geo-momo; retric-meutschland
the birth of danger is *ingles*
curve un-complished; comfort word
anglish saxo; birth of dango

finding the approaching; storm approached
patriarch-tactic; tac-toe tolerant
skinned by scarlet; stripes and stars
o ruby riff; o long ago

alexanderplatz; loco
boricua; das chicaletz
sank pakt; acht-man
sleeper leaps; a million sans omen

glowning echo; what is free; is not the feather
that is feathered but; the feather
torqued horizon; foontakt remora
crossed crag; gleamed; by curve just missed

what is danger pinched; nasal-ostroso
look; more graffiti by esl punks
graphis on danger; wall to wall
"look more" it sez; call attention

to calling; nasal punkt?
no; esl; oh; messers
lander ünd platz; einer poesie
existen der rim of der; planetun

tight birth; nicht night
enticing; no?
the shape
that beckons

2007

Sorry, I Don't Talk Poetry

*don't want fixing
to happen just yet
dont wanna lose such fragile heat*

mere is mirror's ass scent
sorry I have a crib to assemble in the morning
just one wish, close eyes and breathe
altogether
no war is the chant
dear man
I would help you
and all your awakefulness at hypocrisy
and how the yang has been shifting without provocation
and how the ice cap is melting the wireless
and how language cuts chase by half
and how mirror spells faith inside out
I would arrange to stand by your side
during this most desperate time of your roar—
but I have a crib to assemble in the morning
and my screws need to soak in sweat

2007

The Intermission Clown

The man, the woman, the dog, the ball.
The black man, the white woman, the black dog, the red ball.
Not once did I mention
the relationship between the man and the dog.

Never the lover, the ball. Nor the woman kiss
the man before the ball returned by dog.
Nor did I bother with waves, or ocean
or beach. The sun hitting the hair of the woman.

As the man came close to her cheek. The dog
caught in the sun, by the ball's
returning gaze. Never do we learn
how intimate the man has been

with the woman or the dog. How long
have they been in each other's lives, arms. What is the ball's
relationship to the dog, to the color. New or favorite.
The same could be said as red.

And not once have I mentioned if the dog belongs
to the woman or the man or the black or the beach.
And the woman, trying to escape the man's
grasp. And this, a prelude to a breakup

in a matter of minutes. The ball in the red mouth
a transition in orbit. The shoreline baked
in golden sandstorms. Blue waves
on a fading shift of ardent erosion.

Nor do we smell the way they both
ignore the dog. Joyously retrieving the ball
from the ocean. And what about
the manner in which this viewer came upon them.

How I used walk to cross
that part of the telling. That obvious alert
into when we enter, and when we go.
The porous weight that follows echo.

Trailing talk behind each tiny summit of rock,

strewn with reminders of what belongs together.
Catching the size of sirens before they drift apart.
The travel to never-be in the giant size of things.

Never did I mention, how they all tried to become
the other. The man, the woman, the woman, the man.
The dog, the ball, the ball, the dog. The secret
of each other's knowing. The red, the black, the white, the gold,

unearthed in my viewing. Nor did I allow my witness
a true flight. A risen consequence from the pit
of what I brought with me. My history attached to theirs,
in alignment with my telling.

And when did I leave out how I left. Where,
in this story, is the time or position of the shoreline's
pass. Every change affecting its greeting.
Each wave, another frame, another stone.

And in what I've just told you
did I ever mention thought
or gift or carnival. The horizon's volume
relived as a tremor, doing its vertical remember in you.

Its impulse for legs, to stand apart
from perspective and light.
To walk
in the telling of things.

                                                              2010

Lunar Shift

The breath implied from where it
bends, calls you and me to song again.
Maybe the animals know more than
we do about change and what happens
in flight. If I've given you too many
choices it's only because your
bravery is an illusion, a whisper
from where I stand. If I had
all the answers, I'd be done now

and ease would suffocate night
with routine. What does that
sound like to you? Here in my spot
far from yours, your smell spins
a circle. A night borrows a dog,
lands him on the other side.
A star finds me, burns its point
through my skull. An hour floats
a bird, glass pretends to be sky.
If I knew where to go, would we
be there now?

2010

Of Natural Disasters and Love

I haven't the right to record what I haven't lived through
I can only write what I know — and how empty is that
and who cares
                    I am capturing the essence
of what I live through — everyday
the wonder of another breath seems like a new beginning
                    and here at the gathering
of reader, writer and page — I am made aware
that there is no matter
                    when what's outside your grasp
can slip away so easily if you don't let go first
and my love — has just asked me what I want to eat
                    because dinner is ready
and I write that down — to remind myself
and who cares besides me
                    and that's the point

2010

Christian Bök

b. 1966

Christian Bök was born in Toronto, Ontario, and began writing while study-
ing at Carleton University in Ottawa. He completed his Ph.D. degree at York
University, where he became part of the poetry community that included
Steve McCaffery. Like McCaffery, he is known for his performance of sound
poetry, including a condensed version of Kurt Schwitters's *Ursonate*. He was
also hired to provide the languages of nonhuman creatures for Gene Rodden-
berry's *Earth: Final Conflict* and Peter Benchley's *Amazon*.

Bök is the author of two works of poetry, *Eunoia* (2001), for which he won
the Griffin Poetry Prize, and *Crystallography* (2003). He has also written
a brilliant critical study, *'Pataphysics: The Poetics of an Imaginary Science*
(2001). The word *eunoia* means "beautiful thinking" in Greek; it is also the
shortest word in English to contain all five vowels (in French that word is
oiseau).[1] Like Harryette Mullen's, Bök's work displays the Oulipo aspect of
proceduralism. In *Eunoia*, the Oulipo device employed is primarily the lipo-
gram, which rules certain letters of the alphabet out of the work. Thus, the
poems that comprise "Chapter A" employ only the vowel "A." Bök's lyrical
poem "Vowels" is anagrammatic; the only letters allowed in the poem are
those in its title.

Unique among contemporary poets for his ability to blend poetry and sci-
ence, Bök is currently working on the Xenotext Experiment, which involves
the implanting of language into the cell structure of a bacterium. Bök writes:

> The Xenotext is my nine-year long attempt to create an example of "living
> poetry." I have been striving to write a short verse about language and
> genetics, whereupon I use a "chemical alphabet" to translate this poem
> into a sequence of DNA for subsequent implantation into the genome of
> a bacterium (in this case, a microbe called Deinococcus radiodurans—
> an extremophile, capable of surviving, without mutation, in even the
> most hostile milieus, including the vacuum of outer space).[2]

As part of a vital Canadian avant-garde, Bök, Steve McCaffery, and Lisa
Robertson publish and perform many of their works in the United States and
are associated with such camps as the language poets, performance poetry,
and the Dada and Oulipian influences felt within New York School poetics.
Bök currently lives in Calgary, Canada, where he teaches at the University of
Calgary.

1. Darren Werschler-Henry, "The New Ennui," afterword to *Eunoia*, Toronto, 2001,
p. 104.   2. Christian Bök, "The Xenotext Works," Harriet the Blog, April 2011, http://www
.poetryfoundation.org/harriet/2011/04/the-xenotext-works/.

Vowels

loveless vessels

we vow
solo love

we see
love solve loss

else we see
love sow woe

selves we woo
we lose

losses we levee
we owe

we sell
loose vows

so we love
less well

so low
so level

wolves evolve

2001

FROM Chapter A

for Hans Arp

Awkward grammar appals a craftsman. A Dada bard
as daft as Tzara damns stagnant art and scrawls an
alpha (a slapdash arc and a backward zag) that mars
all stanzas and jams all ballads (what a scandal). A
madcap vandal crafts a small black ankh — a hand-
stamp that can stamp a wax pad and at last plant a

mark that sparks an *ars magna* (an abstract art that charts a phrasal anagram). A pagan skald chants a dark saga (a Mahabharata), as a papal cabal blackballs all annals and tracts, all dramas and psalms: Kant and Kafka, Marx and Marat. A law as harsh as a *fatwa* bans all paragraphs that lack an A as a standard hallmark.

*

Hassan Abd al-Hassad, an Agha Khan, basks at an ashram — a Taj Mahal that has grand parks and grass lawns, all as vast as parklands at Alhambra and Valhalla. Hassan can, at a handclap, call a vassal at hand and ask that all staff plan a bacchanal — a gala ball that has what pagan charm small galas lack. Hassan claps, and (*tah-dah*) an Arab lass at a swank spa can draw a man's bath and wash a man's back, as Arab lads fawn and hang, athwart an altar, amaranth garlands as fragrant as attar — a balm that calms all angst. A dwarf can flap a palm branch that fans a fat maharajah. A naphtha lamp can cast a calm warmth.

FROM Chapter E

for René Crevel

Enfettered, these sentences repress free speech. The text deletes selected letters. We see the revered exegete reject metred verse: the sestet, the tercet — even les *scènes élevées en grec*. He rebels. He sets new precedents. He lets cleverness exceed decent levels. He eschews the esteemed genres, the expected themes — even *les belles lettres en vers*. He prefers the perverse French esthetes: Verne, Péret, Genet, Perec — hence, he pens fervent screeds, then enters the street, where he sells these letterpress newsletters, three cents per sheet. He engenders perfect newness wherever we need fresh terms.

*

Relentless, the rebel peddles these theses, even when vexed peers deem the new precepts 'mere dreck'. The plebes resent newer verse; nevertheless, the rebel perseveres, never deterred, never dejected, heedless, even when hecklers heckle the vehement speeches. We feel perplexed whenever we see these excerpted sentences. We sneer when we detect the clever scheme — the emergent repetend: the letter E. We jeer; we jest. We express resentment. We detest these depthless pretenses — these present-tense verbs, expressed pell-mell. We prefer genteel speech, where sense redeems senselessness.

FROM Chapter U

for Zhu Yu

Kultur spurns Ubu — thus Ubu pulls stunts. Ubu shuns *Skulptur:* Uruk urns (plus busts), Zulu jugs (plus tusks). Ubu sculpts junk *für Kunst und Glück.* Ubu busks. Ubu drums drums, plus Ubu strums cruths (such hubbub, such ruckus): *thump, thump; thrum, thrum.* Ubu puns puns. Ubu blurts untruth: much bunkum (plus bull), much humbug (plus bunk) — but trustful schmucks trust such untruthful stuff; thus Ubu (cult guru) must bluff dumbstruck numbskulls (such chumps). Ubu mulcts surplus funds (trust funds plus slush funds). Ubu usurps much usufruct. Ubu sums up lump sums. Ubu trumps dumb luck.

*

Ubu gulps up brunch: duck, hummus, nuts, fugu, bulgur, buns (crusts plus crumbs), blutwurst, brühwurst, spuds, curds, plums: *munch, munch.* Ubu sups. Ubu slurps rum punch. Ubu chugs full cups (plus mugs), full tubs (plus tuns): *glug, glug.* Ubu gluts up grup; thus Ubu's plump gut hurts. Ubu grunts: *ugh, ugh.* Ubu burps up mucus sputum. Ubu upchucks lunch: Ubu slumps. Ubu sulks. Ubu shrugs.

Ubu slurs drunk chums. Ubu snubs such drunks;
thus curt churls cuss: 'shut up, Ubu, shut up'. Gruff
punks club Ubu. Butch thugs drub Ubu. Ku-klux cults
kung-fu punch Ubu. Rumdum bums bust up pubs.

2001

Kalokagathia

stars are bubbles of air
rising through an infinite
depth: we rise with them
through this dark, slow
motion snowfall in reverse

sleep through our ascent
bound at wrist and ankle
by the chains from silver
watches, anchors without
weight: even as we dream

we hold our breath against
the moment when we crash
up through the surface
tension, as though through
a sheet of glass, into still

another depth with other
stars, the fragments of our
last collision in our wake
eyes shut tight, and every
mouth a photo of a scream

2003

Laynie Browne

b. 1966

Born and raised in Los Angeles, Laynie Browne received her undergraduate degree from the University of California at Berkeley and her M.F.A. in poetry from Brown University.

Her poetry collections include *Pollen Memory* (2003), *Mermaid's Purse* (2005), *Drawing of a Swan Before Memory* (2005), *Daily Sonnets* (2007), *The Scented Fox* (2007), *The Desires of Letters* (2010), and *Roseate, Points of Gold* (2011). She has also published a novel, *Acts of Levitation* (2002). She has curated the Subtext Reading Series in Seattle and The Ear Inn in New York City. She teaches creative writing at the University of Arizona. With Caroline Bergvall, Teresa Carmody, and Vanessa Place, she has edited the anthology *I'll Drown My Book: Conceptual Writing by Women* (2011).

Browne is both a lyric poet of person and place and a proceduralist committed to alternative structures. *Daily Sonnets* consists of 151 sonnets written in one-minute writing intervals while she was caring for her two sons to whom the book is dedicated. Reviewer Cecily Parks writes of the book, "As she transmits multiple frequencies of discourse—becoming, as she outlines in the book's closing essay, the 'permeable I'—the poet becomes difficult to locate: 'You might have written this / I certainly did not / but don't let that stop you.'"[1]

Kathleen Fraser writes of *Drawing of a Swan Before Memory*: "With Bachelard's 'surveyor's map of (his) lost fields' as her memory ground, Browne seeks—through the figures of child, swan, and lover—to recover a wholeness from the holographic splittings of recovered film, minute interference patterns in which the hood of childhood is poised as mythic antidote to the lover's body."[2]

Browne lives in Tucson and teaches at the University of Arizona.

1. *Boston Review*, May/June 2008, http://www.bostonreview.net/BR33.3/microreviews .php.   2. Jacket comment, *Drawing of a Swan Before Memory*, Athens, GA, 2005.

FROM Possession

1

Even at this hour you are mine.
When you are not here you are elsewhere—traces of an ancient
gallery whose object permanence, a scoundrel.

His sorrow was polyvalent, those otherwise knowing glances of trees.

Does he see darkness, a picture mind which taunts?

And so he steamed off to that book of fallen yellow
where all engines return when they are not busy.

Detachment is that cloud he carries until the drenched face of an
angel collides with unlovely sentiments.

We've otherwise perplexed the landscape.

Longer since carved a dream above light.

2

The hours he names 'mine' and 'now' as the interior of a hive reflects
the concept of person elongated.

How his mind seeds within hers from great distances.

If they have reached the park her sense of distance is muted by the
possibility of light falling onto his face.

If once solutions could be culled from sight to furnish resolutions
of endeavor, now inner sight marks an image like a frontlet between
eyes. The iris is lined with white. Dimensions of pulling have the
opposite effect of blindness.

The hood heightens the face of her vehicle with sight.

3

He builds with red towers which comely circumstances provide. She
cannot abandon even that which he has entirely forgotten. Ruins of
dual bodies. His memory of being carried. Hers of walking redly
towards birth.

Pictures broken at odd angles which he carries close to his chest,
running.

From where is the red stone ferreted, she asks? How is it concealed
ships now appear within his mineral eyes?

4

To lose one must first possess

To possess one must bind matter to matter

With loss as guide, one desires to be matterless

The matterless guide resides in a borrowed form, contains no loss.

Residing within a body, this bodilessness is not confined to the invisible strictures of any given form.

Rapid soiling of hands, linens, hangings of rooms, hollows of lungs.

The self possessed form—abandoned

upon departure from the matterful hemisphere.

5

If you will cull, I will not insist

Where you kiss, you have undone the premise of insisting

He walks towards a red stone which contains absence.
He covets the berry, the sand, the rock and the water. The pharaoh's emeralds.

If you curl yourself about me so that your feet refuse to reach the floor you will only be held.

2005

Crown of Larks

She saw in the middle of the room face of white, hair of flax, a crown of larks. A person seemed transparent.

She held the red stem of the white rose. The green bud with crème petal edged with spot of crimson. Stem cut, inside the flesh crème sinewy, exuding scent of apple.

To posture the rose is such. As marble marks itself, as a hillside gathers onlookers.

Thus, the rose, more apparent than person.

Only when flushed would she have contained color. Thus, the difficulty of the girl watching was that of an appetite for lifting an illustration of berries from a page. The blood of water is blind in concentration against a hillside transparency.

2007

Sentencing

There is more waiting than one thought possible, began the female sentence. But how then must one proceed?

Simply, replied the pear. One proceeds. One need not wait.

Not wait, asked the sentence?

All will befall, replied the pear, and none will be forsaken. One may lose regardless of gazing lookingly. This episode of yours is hardly less meek. It will befall everyone.

But when the sentence gazed into the pear and saw herself reflected in its golden skin, she knew otherwise. How then can my befallen state be the same as any other?

When one has just heard brave news, replied the pear, that one has been granted a wish, the sentence must contrive to complete itself.

Confound the one who first distinguished the hours, continued the sentence. Thus, my body becomes a question.

Who assembled the first sundial whose shadows plague these letters to no end?

2007

The Girl of Wax

The girl of wax is plausible. An unfixed entity. She frequents the rose coast to pluck plasticity. What is real fastens pretend. What is pretend—the furthermore real. She is liquid, solid, necessity.

She has spilled her premonition upon volumes. Perhaps the counter desired to be bathed in tea. There is a formless experience. Where she spilled tea on whoever was king. In that history, if the tea hadn't spilled he wouldn't have been king.

Then she goes outside to tell that storm to be quiet.

Hair flew in rivers and rivulets of coal
in pale fronds her fingers flock to the child's laughter

She believes she has lost the pretend coast where once she had gathered an estuary, though one cannot misplace a pretend landscape, though the description might be awake elsewhere, borrowed. This is not seen, only a flutter and the dark rivulet fallen across one's eyes. Wax flowers alongside, these have been riveted to a cloth. Burrs as well and brambles held in place by fasteners. The view, more or less, is the painted imagined. One edge of color is enough to lead eyes astray. True light is the only member which must ring false and fall upon the palm of an ashen hand.

But also she wanted to speak of the unspeakable. He has torn one of the owl's wings. That which gathers and falls along the pretend coast. It is not as shocking as the wet smear of madrona bark, smartingly red. One may gather there only news which has no surrounding. The owl with one wing continues to wait. Surrounding itself with unspeakable vistas. She wanted to speak of what she dare not speak of. The body in part a gesture, surrounding a jet black night. A superstition, that the days followed the nights and so forth. The night, a gladdening gesture. One's own thoughts—if we cease to see them passing—approach non-seeing acres and rejoice. Thus to say one has lost the pretend coast might be to presume that one is finished with artificiality. One is finished taping the torn wing. Therefore complete. But, she may say, she is intrigued by the beauty of falseness, here where all tasks have completed themselves.

2007

Julie Carr
b. 1966

Julie Carr was born in Cambridge, Massachusetts, and attended Barnard College. Even though she was interested in becoming a writer, she danced for ten years in New York with local companies and choreographers. In 1995, she enrolled in the M.F.A. program in creative writing at New York University. With the birth of her first child, poetry became her chief pursuit. She received her Ph.D. from the University of California, Berkeley in 2006.

Her first collection of poetry, *Mead: An Epithalamion* (2004), was selected by Cole Swensen as winner of the Contemporary Poetry Prize. Her other collections include *Equivocal* (2007), *Sarah—of Fragments and Lines* (National Poetry Series, 2010, selected by Eileen Myles), and *100 Notes on Violence* (2010), selected by Rae Armantrout as winner of the 2009 Sawtooth Poetry Prize.

In her books, Carr explores marriage, the birth of children, and family life as they relate to history and identity. In one section of *Equivocal,* "Illiadic Familias," she inserts quotes from Homer's *Iliad* into a prose poem sequence, joining war with a recollection of her mother crying while driving. Carr's poetry is personal, often searingly so. But it is so various in strategy, mood, and detail that it never falls into the confessional. Gillian Conoley captures this balance regarding *Equivocal*:

> It is nothing less than thrilling to see the delight, the pain, the opposition, the contradiction, the logic and the illogic of the mysterious, unlanguaged correspondences between mother and child, child and mother, and then adult and mother meet with such a fierce intelligence. And there is brilliant formal invention.[1]

The reviewer Andy Frazee credits Carr's lyric objectivity to the influence of George Oppen, but Carr's momentum and mood are more far-flung. Her work is precise but also thrillingly unpredictable, as a knife thrown is precise. Frazee puts it this way, "Lyric and constructivist, investigative and synthetic, *Equivocal* works to express the paradoxes of being in the world, of contending with the multiplicity of roles one performs in becoming—or un-becoming—whatever 'oneself' may be."[2]

In an "Author's Statement" that accompanies the press materials for *100 Notes on Violence,* Carr writes: "This is not, for me, not a book about other people's violence. Rather, it is an investigation into the violent experiences and tendencies that we all harbor. As the wars have carried on, I wanted to turn the focus domestic: toward our country, our streets, and homes—'Everyone's life is riddled.'

Carr lives in Denver and teaches creative writing in the English Department at the University of Colorado Boulder. With Tim Roberts, she is copublisher of Counterpath Press.

1. Jacket comment, *Equivocal*, Farmington, ME, 2007.   2. *Jacket* 36, 2008, http://jacketmagazine.com/36/r-carr-rb-frazee.shtml. p. 5.

Equivocal

If that bird in my hand and that bear in the trees
were to read what I store in the crease of my eye,

if the green infant shoots and the blond bomb blooms
in the garden we measured with the width of our arms,

in the gate-guarded seed-spill we plotted and pooled

might nativity carry our cure?

2007

House / Boat

Broad, the river belled in a thud of sun.

I climbed aboard, I rowed. A border flew open like a cough.
I leaned back to balance

my oars as they dipped
to green and red furrows of light.

My boat rocked, steady, un-steady.
Was I welcomed? It seemed I was as I gripped

and privately beheld.

The night soon lost its head.
Pulling up now, parking,

looking for something to eat,
to redeem.

The wind shook the seedpod but the seedpod
wasn't moved.

And though I thought I'd done the damage I was born for,

there was still so much to step through,
so much to mar.

2007

Of Sarah

Years having passed, the foliage is wet: the final morning on which you, in freedom, lie awake. I see your entrapment as a fault of my own, my failure to house you in my own face.

A girl we know has memorized the witches' song. Her serious mouth, unbrushed hair hiding black eyes: Fillet-of-a-fenny-snake-in-the-cauldron-boil-and-bake-eye-of-newt-and-toe-of-frog-wool-of-bat-and-tongue-of-dog. No pause, no breath, as if forced as if always as if gripped.

And you, ungripped, have been trained to know less. The training arduous, lasting for ages—your entire lifetime. First you had to give up the meaning of words. And then water.

2010

Of Sarah

Decay to the lemon. To the crust of bread. But not to the dog that leaps against the door, not to its owner in camouflage, his lank hair and heavy glasses. Decay, Sarah, also far from you, your place in the trees—the way their fullness makes the landscape three-dimensional now, almost June. That green before green before green, that roundness we perceive as the air—this is your roundness, your green.

As a child on the boardwalk you seemed patient, contemplative. In fact, you were angry and for good cause. Then, your anger turned quiet. Now it peels from the throats of birds: rage in song.

But when I sleep your face remains placid: the face of all women who were not my mother but who I imagined as my mother. Wander through.

2010

FROM *100 Notes on Violence*

83.
NOTE ON VENGEANCE

If I agree to the terms, if I agree to my cast. If I attempt to see into the ordinary to make it break, to see how it is already broken:

One woman comes daily to drink her coffee, her cup shaped like the head of a pig. Gazes out the window with her pen in her hand: streetlights, headlights, dawn. She'd not seen me in a dozen weeks and came over to say hello: "Joe was talking to a girl. We were fighting a little bit. But the girl was his cousin! I made him so angry he swore at me and grabbed my arm, he threw me down. That's what jealousy does: helps you play games in the worst possible way."

A family had a special anger room, a room to sit in and count. Another had a bell to ring that meant, I cannot speak to you now or I will say something hateful.

In a third family the parents will, at moments of crisis, leave the house, walk the neighborhood, staring at the concrete until something lifts. I'm not thinking logically when day turns to night. Couples dance ankle-deep in a fountain—dance the tango, kick up lit sprays. I'm not looking into mirrors now for fear of another's face. Not recording my dreams. Don't want that radio to speak to me: "My daughter's death must not go unavenged!" Let the car idle; will the mother say more?

You cannot put a fire out

. . .

Pretty is the light now
Prettier than trees

Can go itself without a fan
Upon the slowest night
(Dickinson)

2010

84.

But what was I up to?

There was a bush growing skyward really needed pruning, sun getting stymied and stumped by cloud-stock, like cardstock, so stiff.

There was something to know and no way to know it. What's a normal living, a protected? Said,

Kids at the pool, at every moment you're going under: blurred and unidentifiable, said, watch it I told you stay near me stay shallow,

no way to.

Some shit on the men's room floor and my son dropped his pants on it. Un-

protected.

Is fear what we want? To keep us? Women stand watching—the curves of their backs, their gently sloping waists.

Then, just as I feared, violence began to seem banal. One student of it, in a 20-year-search, traveled to Korea, Iraq, Beirut, in search of it, carried a gun in his hometown as if to court it, interviewed the murdered by peering at their corpses: anything to keep

the smell of it alive.

2010

Lisa Jarnot

b. 1967

Lisa Jarnot was born in Buffalo, New York, and received degrees from the State University of New York at Buffalo and Brown University. Since the mid-1990s, she has resided in New York City, where she has been actively involved in The Poetry Project at Saint Mark's Church.

Jarnot's full-length books of poetry include *Some Other Kind of Mission* (1996), *Ring of Fire* (2003), *Black Dog Songs* (2003), and *Night Scenes* (2008). She has also published numerous chapbooks. Her biography, *Robert Duncan: The Ambassador from Venus*, was published in 2012.

Jarnot has edited two magazines, *No Trees* and *Troubled Surfer*, as well as *An Anthology of New (American) Poetry* (1998). As a fervent antiwar activist, she maintains the One Hundred Hat Memorial Site, which documents the hats she knits in memory of soldiers and civilians who have died in the conflicts in Iraq and Afghanistan.

Influenced by Robert Duncan, Jack Spicer, and Gertrude Stein, Jarnot has stated in an interview that her practice is to collect scraps of paper that she finds on the street, as if to bring the world itself directly into her poetry. In addition to the practice of collage, she also enjoys the masonry and music of line relations:

> and in the inside there is sleeping sleep
> and in the outside there is reddening red
> and in the morning there is meeting meat
> and in the evening there is feeling fed[1]

The publisher of *Ring of Fire* states: "Jarnot's work represents a synthesis of traditional modes of verse alongside more fragmented avant-garde writing practices. The poems in this collection resonate with homages to the metaphysical masters of the 17th Century while commenting on popular culture in the Western world."[2]

In her essay "On Identity," Jarnot writes: "It would be difficult for me to talk about my identity as a writer without acknowledging first my identity as a reader. What I learned to do early in life, as a survival mechanism of sorts, was to invent a self, or a composite of selves, as if my own life was formed out of a distant memory of who all the other versions of me had been throughout the history of my kind."[3]

Lisa Jarnot has taught at Long Island University, Bard, and Naropa. Currently she works as a horticulturalist and lives in Sunnyside, Queens.

1. "Stein Meat Work," *Night Scenes*, Chicago, 2008, p. 6.   2. Salt Publishing website, http://www.saltpublishing.com/books/smp/1844710076.htm.   3. Lisa Jarnot, "On Identity," Symposium at St. Mark's Church in the Bowery, 1998, http:/www.poetspath.com/Scholarship_Project/jarnot.html.

They Loved the Sea

They loved those things, him, her, the ocean, and the sea. They loved the lighthouse and the moon. They loved to sing about the sea. They loved the birds that were at sea, and sang the sea songs even far from shore. The sea sang and they sang its sea songs too. The sea sang songs and near the sea they sang. And they were not the sea, the sea was what it was, the sea, a lighthouse near the moon. It was a big sea. It was the sea and it was loved, near the light of the sea, being what it was.

2002

Gang Angles

for Greg

as an age
an agéd glade

as a green deer
seed and eden

as a ragged
deer gear slang

and as grange gangs
lease seed edens

lanes and gardens
lanes and grange

angles, angels,
grease rags, sage

agéd glades
an eagle grange,

a green deer land lease
seed sage lane.

2002

Manx Kippers

for Jeremy

the song of all the bushes green
the first class bushes with a theme
the theme of all the escalope
the red-winged bushes, posted home
the cups of tea of bushes winged,
the home team bushes red-winged trees,
the trucks of loaf bread, fine and wide,
the train song shoe horns, porcupine,
the escalope of downy quills,
for lamb and Webster, shiny pills,

for all the otters as they gleam,
a pine bed splendor with no seam,
that am the something that is real,
the sun that may be stars and wheels,
the palace of the clothesline stars
run over clotheslines, doves and cars,
iberian exploding night
the dark wood wingspan cattle light
the palace of the small bird fens,
the music, cattle, deers and hens,
the dark wood angles of the doves,
the doves on clotheslines, shift and hum,
the lighted wingspans of the cows,
the traffic happy run down thou
the dark wood of one hundred skies,
exploding stars of twilight by

the letters of repeating space
the peating of the garden place,
the chicked limbs of hence repeat,
behind the place in focus green,
the place that tries to be itself,
repeating, spaces, empty shelf,
the lakefront, I, the cattle, sing
the signs of doves, run over bring
the shifts of stars in otter light,

the twilight chicked limbs delight
the shifts of stars exploding how,
the place that goes there goes there now.

2002

Husband Sonnet One

o calm sheep in the fields asleep
be quiet while my husband sleeps
ride bicycles or drive your jeeps
in pastures where the snow is deep
the roads that bend o pay no heed
nor wonder where the neighbor speeds
nor ponder at the road's sad fork
just plow on forward brave and dark
like Dante in his mid-life's wood,
a sheep's mid-life is stout and good
like beer that ambers from a tap
or maple running wine tree sap
you sheep of silence play along
in dreams my husband sleeps among

2008

Right Poem

This is the best way to do things. This is the very best way to do things. This is
the very best way to do things exactly right right now and these are the right
people doing the right things and these are the right people doing the right
things at the right time and these are the right people doing the right things at
the right time in the right places and these are the right people doing the right
things to the right things at the right places and these are the people that are
exactly right and these exactly right people are doing their thing which is right
and this is the right thing to do at the right time which is right now and right
now everything is exactly right right now where it is.

2008

Drew Gardner
b. 1968

Editor of *Snare* Magazine and a jazz drummer, Drew Gardner is one of the original Flarf founders and the author of *Sugar Pill* (2002), *Petroleum Hat* (2005), and *Chomp Away* (2011). With some other members of the Flarf Collective, his work also appears on the audio CD *Flarf Orchestra* (2012). His poem "Chicks Dig War," which appears in *Petroleum Hat*, is a prime example of Flarf's ability to hold the mirror of language up to the U.S. culture since September 11, 2001. The poet Ange Mlinko writes of the work: "*Petroleum Hat* is natural language for a country at war. Unlike the old model of protest poetry, Drew Gardner isn't interested in earnest appeals to reason and compassion. He'll match the political spectacle absurdity for absurdity—and in the case of the funny and chilling 'Chicks Dig War,' I'm struck by how thoroughly he understands the logic of our times."[1]

Of the history of Flarf, Gardner writes: "In the early 2000s Nada Gordon, Gary Sullivan and I were friends, and Gary wrote his now well known 'Mmhmm' poem—an intentionally bad satire written to make fun of a fake poetry anthology. This was typical of Gary's practice—he had been writing poetry satire for years. The poem didn't involve Google or collage. Around this time I was working on my first book *Sugar Pill* and had developed the technique of collaging language from Google searches. Several of the poems in that book use Google collage. Gary and Nada and I had been emailing poems in the 'intentionally bad' mode a little and I had the idea to combine the Google search technique with it. Gary and Nada, and soon after, Katie Degentesh, picked up on this approach and it grew from there into Flarf as the list grew into a listserv. So there was a satire + google collage you got your peanut butter in my chocolate thing. The third element that made things happen was that later K. Silem Mohammad was the first to collect and print a full book of material from the Flarflist."[2] That book was of course *Deer Head Nation* (2003).

In his essay "Why Flarf Is Better Than Conceptualism," Gardner strikes at Flarf's essential difference with conceptualism and, by extension, with poetry's many worlds: "Conceptualism is composed. / Flarf is compost." Most poets including the conceptual are dedicated to shaping the work, which includes its concision, music, and formal boundaries. This is true even of language poetry's New Sentence. But Flarf misbehaves by leaving "the mess" (Beckett) in messy condition. Compost is trash; its awfulness is undeniable. But it is also rich in earth. We are reminded of O'Hara's demand that the poem retain "love's lifegiving vulgarity."[3] And indeed Flarf resembles Dada in its proceduralism; the New York School, in its love of the everyday.

Drew Gardner lives in the Harlem neighborhood of New York City.

1. Jacket comment, *Petroleum Hat*, New York, 2005.   2. Email to Paul Hoover, 9/23/2011.   3. "Personism: A Manifesto," *The Collected Poems of Frank O'Hara*, Berkeley, 1995, p. 499.

Chicks Dig War

Story time: Trojan Oil War (part 2)
The Trojan War, chicks dig it
and such hits as "Chicks Dig War,"
"Wizards Have Landed on my Face,"
"God Made Girls Who Like War,"
and "Colin Powell's the Lay of the Land."

More women than men are enjoying the war
with two-fisted truth
before changing clothes
by portraying war as
chicks digging the phones of war.

Phallocentric chicks:
they dig guys with big wars.
I just cannot, you know, believe in a war
against chicks when they've got the anti-chick war
thing goin' on.
The women will be like "Ooh, what a cute war!"

Your mission, captain, is complete:
enjoy the spoils of war.
It's so romantic.
chicks dig war (especially chicks on the pill).
The experience is just magical.
Oh, and you can get a really awesome war on.
Chicks like a nice war.

Women are excellent teachers
of the bitter lesson that being
anti-war does not get a man laid.
An "anti-war" guy (who is often the one most capable
of love and trust) is routinely brushed off
as a "pacifist," and passed over
for an abusive jerk who starts a war.
The pacifist wanders through life in a state
of psychic castration,
his heart scarred by the talons of female avarice
and flawed psychology. He is a poor fool who has
listened too literally
to the women who lie and say that what they want

from men is adoration and understanding.
What they want is war.

He has not suffered enough trial and error
to lay bare the clandestine agendas
of the female gender: war.
War makes you a woman.
Chicks dig war. Military
service is the only true expression of war.
Also, chicks dig it.
Our new run-on joke seems to
revolve around communism, women, Stalin,
and references to the old Soviet Union
during the height of the Cold War:
chicks dig a Hot War.

But what of the "war boy" phenomenon?
Every man knows, or has seen in action,
that the more wars he starts,
the more successful he will be in attracting women,
and the more peaceful he is,
the more likely he will wind up as a "pacifist."
But most men are socialized to cultivate harmony,
not discord, and so they refuse to participate
in such pathology.
Most men are pacifists, who have no interest in war.

What a woman really wants is a war-mongering Republican
who turns out in the end to be a pacifist (to her).
He is the storybook hero of her novels and evening news.
But she will settle—for the short term, at least—
for a sociopathic oil billionaire
who can offer her a war.
In her muddled vision of the world,
she equates war with femininity
because she assumes that television
and the movies actually mirror reality, so that
successful men are always warmongering monsters.

Bad boys are dull, tamed, safe
and charged with sexuality.
They are a challenge (meaning that
they don't instantly fall prey to her Pussy Power).

Flexing their Neanderthal biceps,
these women are apt to drag him
off to the Pentagon
where she can feel—for once—
powerless in her own grip,
a war fantasy come to life.
A woman's hormone-driven "logic"
will equate power with war.
She glories in the sensation of raw war.
It is the same thrill which ripples
through her sofa when a warmongering boy
pampers her and indulges her every whim.
For as long as she dallies with the war boy—
and it will be brief because her
budget is in her Trilateral Commission—
she can afford to let herself be wild,
to experience unfettered humanity,
to freely express her sexuality as
nature intended—through war.
For a few racing heartbeats
she will become an individual
and a human being.

Believe that male behavior is the result
of a breeding experiment run by females?
In case you missed it,
the basic implication is that by following
their natural proclivity to breed with
John Ashcroft
women are an anti-civilizing force,
actively creating more male aggressiveness.
It would seem that a wise society would have an
interest in creating a counter-force to oppose this.

2005

The Mayim Bialik-Kruschev Fig Rearrangement

if the father of us all
was a father-turd,
was it wrong to leave him
for an intelligently designed corn-oud-on-a-stick

that could be used
for the igneous livestock to linger with
like pissed-off mouse hazard lights in the rain?

this guy isn't so much of a
horrible barrier to the future
as he is the flat-screen
minimum-possible-effort
sharpest-cheese-slicer-in-the-world project
we've been looking for.

you can't use a secrecy to make a mullet,
only to prevent one from being detected.
but you have to stand for something.

2010

Superstar

Gotta love the boring crazy people switching places with my eyes.
This trading spouses with The Price Is Right is wrong, but you cannot
deny the look on a puppy's face when the silence is broken by Tori Spelling.
Don't dream about things.

Never dream about forests.
Titanium forests—
Presidential arcade radio system shit log titanium forests:
Don't dream about them.

I hate it when people spend money on astronauts, or jugglers.
You have to dream to invert life.
I think I'm in Amherst, MA, and I'm getting cocky about it.
Material: It is surely not charm-free.

Boring crazy people fill the future, the feeling almost fascistic.
I fear being part of some larger cause.

Why don't you do so without putting it in realms?
How they charge your inclinations to the lands on their hands.
Your dreams are within your dreams.
And yes, you can come over later.

2010

Why Do I Hate Flarf So Much?

She came from the mountains, killing zombies at will. Some people cried "but that was cool!" and I could only whisper "we should NOT be killing zombies!" What have you gotten yourself to do? Did it ever occur to you that you may in fact hate yourself? I know I do. . . . I'm not nearly high enough yet—and you're not helping. My group got invited to join the Flarfist Collective, set up some hibachis and do what we do best, if you know what I mean. I wouldn't have so much of a problem with this writing if it were a library and I checked out the entire world as if it were a single book. Strike "helpful" off your list. The 4th quarter gets pretty intense and the announcers are usually trying to figure out who is going to become overwhelmed by their own arrogant nightmares. It would upset the stomach of the balance of nature. I always go red over the stupidest things and I have no clue why. Whether it's speaking in front of the class or someone asking me why I think I have the right to say anything. Why do I need an enemy to feel okay about what I'm doing? Observe yourself as you browse with sophistication through the topic of Authorship & Credibility. Why do I hate the surface of the world so much that I want to poison it? Why do I hate this so much? Well. . . you Hate Your Fucking Dad! Why is the screen so damn small? And why does the car turn so sharply? And why is the only sound I hear the sound of a raft of marmosets? BECAUSE I'm fucking ANXIOUS AS HELL about EVERYTHING. AAAAAAAAARGH. It's even worse: "I'll tell you later." The medium is literally made of thousands of beautiful, living, breathing wolves. Why do I hate the moon so much? Unpublish your ideas in reverse. People hate any new way of writing. My girlfriend really hates it. There is not so much daytime left. Life is like spring snow tossing off mercurial Creeley-like escapes from life-threatening health problems. In summer we love winter in winter we love summer—all poetry is written in social mercurochrome. Since I hate the abridgement of life, a function of needing to please unpleaseable parents is more what this is about. Hate and love—if those are the options I just want to love and hate *lobsters*. The oddity is not so much that Blake held these eccentric views for most of his life, but that in modern civilization they not only extend the hand, so that it could not complain about complaining about something it hadn't even bothered to read, and instead formed a halfway decent indie rock band. I'm actually starting to get much more interested in white people than I used to be. Why do I hate Flarf so much? Because it is against everything good this country once espoused. Why do I hate Flarf so much? Because of the awful conflict it places the law-abiding or police-fearing poets under.

2010

Vanessa Place
b. 1968

Vanessa Place is a leading conceptual poet living in Los Angeles. She received a B.A. from the University of Massachusetts in Amherst, an M.F.A. from Antioch University, and a J.D. from Boston University. In addition to founding and codirecting Les Figues Press, which publishes conceptual and procedural writing, she works as an appellate criminal defense attorney.

Place is the author of *Dies: A Sentence* (2006), a 50,000-word, one-sentence novel in verse; *La Medusa* (2008); *Statement of Facts* (2010), which focuses on the statements of victims and perpetrators in violent sex crime cases; *Notes on Conceptualisms* (with Robert Fitterman, 2009), an exploration of contemporary conceptual theory, and *The Guilt Project: Rape, Morality, and the Law* (2010), an analysis of the prosecution of sexual offenders. A trilogy of her conceptual work, *Tragodia*, containing *Statement of Facts, Statement of the Case,* and *Argument,* was published 2010–2011. A regular contributor to *X-tra Contemporary Art Quarterly*, she lectures and performs internationally.

Place and Fitterman write in *Notes on Conceptualisms:*

> Consider the retyping of a random issue of *The New York Times* as an act of radical mimesis, an act of monastic fidelity to the word as flesh. Consider the retyping of the September 11, 2001 edition (a day that would not be) as an act of radical mimicry, an act of monastic fidelity to Word as Flesh. If these gestures are both critiques of the leveling and loading medium of media, their combined critique is inseparable from the replication of the error under critique. Replication is a sign of desire.
>
> Radical mimesis is original sin.[1]

About her texts, Place says: "Authorship doesn't matter. Content doesn't matter. Form doesn't matter. Meter doesn't matter. All that matters is the trace of poetry. Put another way, I am a mouthpiece." Susan McCabe describes her poetry as "both humbling and beyond paraphrase, both mythic and contemporary."[2]

Vanessa Place lives in Los Angeles, California.

1. *Notes on Conceptualisms*, Brooklyn, 2009, p. 20.   2. Vanessa Place author profile, Academy of American Poets website, https://www.poets.org/poet.php/prmPID/2117.

FROM *Dies: A Sentence*

The maw that rends without tearing, the maggoty claw that serves you, what, my baby buttercup, prunes stewed softly in their own juices or a good slap in the face, there's no accounting for history in any event, even such a one as this one, O, we're knee-deep in this one, you and me, we're practically puppets, making all sorts of fingers dance above us, what do you say, shall we give it another whirl, we can go naked, I suppose, there's nothing to stop us and everything points in that direction, do you think there will be much music later and of what variety, we've that, at least, now that there's nothing left, though there's plenty of pieces to be gathered by the wool-coated orphans and their musty mums, they'll put us in warm wicker baskets, cover us with a cozy blanket of snow, and carry us home, walking carefully through the rubble and around the landmines, or visa versa, poor little laddy's lost his daddy, *pauvre* unminted lamb, you'd give him a chuck on the chin if you still had arms, sure as I'd pitch myself into a highland fling for the sake of the neighbors, but they say or at least said once and if we're very quiet we might hear them again, that all of us will reune with all of us when the time comes, our bits and pieces will cling-a-ling to our cores like fillings rag a magnet, think how big we'll be then, we'll spread from sea to see, sky's the limit for philomel and firmament, and there will be Indians and buffalo and a hero's welcome, I've always wanted a hero's welcome, it's due, said the capitulate archduke, doubtless they'll put us in long black cars and someone's sure to have a picnic, that's the beauty of it, someone's always sure to have a picnic, and we'll laugh when they salt and pepper their hard eggs and be glad to lend our long bones for rude goalposts, what's that, that sound, nothing, you say, right again, nothing walks heavily, nothing stomps about, the big turd, carding its beard with a baleen comb, and lovingly licking the mirror in the eggcup, it fixes red-hot ingots to its ears and pirouettes in a pineneedle shawl, showing itself off to one and all, it's a braggart and a pimp, this nothing, ups the short hairs nonetheless, doesn't it, but that's all right, continue making your stew, sun's swallowed and we've plenty of hours to morn, assuming there's to be another dawn, I'm keeping the faith on that one, my friend, my comrade, my comparison, why I'd light a candle and pray, if I weren't afraid of snipers, still, a campfire seems safe enough, at least for cooking, no one'd be so mean as to shoot a man before his supper, what's the sport in that, better to let a body leisure and sup, knowing there's no time to digest, for it's utter contempt you're after, that and the absolute beauty of wasted sweet butter, it was important that the last bite taste better, though saltless, we've St. Maladroit to clap for that, the silvertongued one, he who proved birds traitors for singing what must be sung, thoughtless, *dolce* thoughtless, still, perhaps the next one will use a beer batter, make a nice soda bread, slather it with the whitest spread, that's good shooting, my darling, right between hiccoughs, speaking of which, how's your arm, you complained earlier, though quietly, you didn't want to disturb my concentration, I was squeezing oranges into cans and setting up camp, there's so much to do before a battle, don't you agree, put shoes into trees and try our hair in different styles, I thoughtfully chalked some names and addresses on our backs to facilitate false identification of our remains, unfortunately it makes us better targets, but this sort of thing can't be helped, still, I heard you, for a cold moment I thought you were saying your morning prayers, till I remembered our night had fallen and tomorrow was a holiday, or will be, certainly they'll take time off to commemorate our exhausted sacrifice and someone else's dry valor with a parade and a picnic, someone will cook a chicken before or after as they always do, the cowards, but I'm looking forward to the little boy eating watermelon and the girl who sucks a spoonful of Nutella while twisting her hair in rings around her forefinger, no, of course you don't, you lost your arms, I remember, wasn't I just asking you about that as well, you think I don't pay attention, but I do, you've no idea how much I care, why I cried when you lost your right arm, though I confess I was a bit annoyed about the left, it seemed careless at that point, and what was the point of that, surely you were signaling something, everyone's known for some time now there's meaning to be evacuated from everything, lined up and airlifted, not unlike Saigon, years from now, it was, we'll be so proud then, we'll see the world with the eyes of dead men, don't get technical, the thing is then we'll understand the raw fruit of our labors as if we'd set up a stand and sold them by the side of the road, and maybe we will, hang a white sign saying something and display them in green plastic baskets, like summer strawberries, or stack them in Euclidean pyramids, like melons or mangos or even apples, something with its seeds safely inside, that's the problem with history, you once said, spitting into the fire, it treats itself vegetable, or oak, you altered and opined, awkward it is, too, boasting of its spread and shade when you and I both know it's got nothing to go on about, and they'd see it too, in the next millennium, this time slouching to Brigadoon, but not in Jerusalem, watch it, now, laugh like that and you're sure to attract shooters, I'm telling you, next to picking off a man with a snootful of *cerises aux chocolat,* or a brandy Alexander, they like nothing better than to go gunning for the grinning, the sorry bastard busting a gut, there it goes, you can wave bye-bye to your intestine, if you still had arms, that is, again, but why are you complaining, you've got your legs, more than I can say, I've come permanently seated, lost them both at the knee in one fell bloody swoop, must have been a cannonball or missile or maybe a villanelle, I wasn't paying attention, leaving me my itemless list, unpinned as an unfoundling, with the same untoward prospects, and I loved those legs as well, especially the left, he followed the right so unthinkingly, he was a good soldier, if I can be so bold, he swung in a rhythm not his own, quite contented, he was enormously attuned to the beat of the street and the sound of the violin, though he didn't care much for opera or what passes these days as poetry, he was a simpler sort, purer of heart, his mind unarticulated and most refined, why most evenings you'd find him propped on an Ottoman, one of the real ones, Oriental, with a pointed red hat and a furious mustache, most ornamental, though still and all a good Christian, couched in fickle malice, but the leg didn't mind, he was a good egg, name was Bob, he laughed at that one, said it suited him consonant, being nothing fancy, not like that other leg, Warrington, Warrington E. Wanderlick, or Augenblich, no, that's not it, he had no agnomination, didn't think he needed it, he was egg-proud, independent, struck out on his own each morning and never looked forward or back, I suppose in his own way he was decent enough, though somewhat stand-offish to good old Bob, now they're both gone and I'm not sure why, losing one leg is stuffed with significance, but to have both devested like a couple of breadcrumbs, what's the point of that, I'm not certain, I'm stumped, that's the truth of it, sure as I'm squatting poolside, though there's still the fire, and that's nice, given the dark, do you think the wolves're out yet, they ought be, the air's suffuse with the stench of brave young muscle, which by tomorrow'll be jugged meat, but no matter, the great beasts will slather the pale unwed flanks with spittle and savory barbeque, lick their lips, thickly purpled and caked at the corners with wet white foam, their eyes're Maundy Thursday moons and the heat from their beating tongues'd melt any man's mold and when's the last time you got eaten by a bit player in a fairy tale, sure it's an honor, it's an honor to be such a goner, if I had a hat, I'd doff it, lend me yours for a moment, that's a good man, there, there's a tip of the lid to what'll make a meal out of me and you, to the time-honored tradition of finding the creature inside whose potted stomach we might nestle safe and round, though you and I are hardly twins and Rome wasn't built in a day, not like today, but you have to start somewhere, especially to finish, and a dog's gut is as good as it gets for a sonovabitch such as myself, I'm being modest, mostly, but you have to admit there's a striking resemblance between the halves of us, and if I still had my legs, you'd allow how we're about equal height in our stocking feet, I miss my legs, did I mention that, and my boots, beautiful in their very addition, beautiful as a lady's bare bottom, those skins stitched together with the care of a surgeon, one of the good ones, a set of silver pens in his breast pocket, and a cat's unsleeved touch, why those boots were alive, they breathed easy as kittens and stayed dog-faithful at the feet, they had the soles of a saint, ignorant of stones, slings and arrows, though not, I would qualify, impervious to the odd nail, they were long-suffering and lucky, lucky as a pair of sevens or a single eleven, lucky as four-leaf clovers and four-eyed Irishmen, not for me, naturally, but certainly for the one who got me, a tall blond man, I imagine, strapping, if that can still be said without blinking, big, in any event, a man with hands like hams and thighs the size of roast pigs, a happy man, content in his apple-scented way, a man who wipes his mouth with the back of a broad palm and keeps a dark pint running through the veins, a stouthearted man in the days when there were such fellows, and ever shall be, if I'm any judge of the Almighty, the Lord God has seen fit in His Infinite to keep a steady supply of bricks and bracks on Hand, to create, one can copiously presume, aqueducts and arcades, bridges and barricades, cook's chambers and campanile, Darby & Joan, egesta and elevators, family trees and fantasies, geoducks and geographies, hibachis and high persuaded reliefs, incandescent lamps, the impresa of great gentlemen, jets, jerkins and joss houses, all ajumble, Kremlins and Kulturkamfs, languid lance corporals, major league Mahdi, the vertical spread of Mrs. Murphy's bed, nabobs, netherworlds, Oregon and onanistic ontology, pater's noster and the queen's quadrangle, riverrun with steelhead rocketships, sarcophagi and sarsaparilla, sugar-free soda water, suitable for silksoaks, tin tabernacles and throbbing temples, the salted substitution of you for me and visa versa, wonder and winsome exultation, the reptilian wisdom of Yankeedom and the ever-fêted zymosis, though let us not omit His marketplaces, department stores, all floors, and their pomped coteries, barbarous butchers, decant bankers, evangels who strap feathers to fish, commanding flies, blind beggars beggaring all written prescription, a slack-bellied dancer, canvassing for sonnet crowns, and genuine cowboys with mirrored eyes, there's brass bistoury and scarlet barrooms, there's where they make wigs from plaits of brunet hair and minds from yellow paper, there's a peripatetic baker but no candlestick maker, He's finished fashioning light, been there, done that, as the newer testaments will affix, His huts to and for, His homemade ironworks, steelworks, plasticworks, rubber and siliconworks, sites of pomp deconstruction and the blackberry patch . . .

2005

G. C. Waldrep

b. 1968

G. C. Waldrep was born in South Boston, Virginia. He earned a B.A. from Harvard University and a Ph.D. from Duke, both in U.S. history, before leaving academia to join an Amish community, where he started his own bakery and later worked in a vinyl window shop. Later he enrolled in the University of Iowa Writers' Workshop, receiving his M.F.A. in 2005. His engagement with poetry is directly related to his commitment to Anabaptism and pacifism, which began with his interest in shape note singing. Consistent with Anabaptism, he is not programmatic about his poetics and seems reluctant to make statements about it. Moreover, his idiom seems to shift from book to book. His stated influences are not what one would expect of a postmodern; they include Robert Penn Warren, Thomas McGrath, Flannery O'Connor (whose religious devotion he admires), the British poet Geoffrey Hill, Thomas Merton, and the nineteenth-century Scottish writer George MacDonald. He does however admire the Mexican poet Raul Zurita and C. D. Wright's *Deepstep Come Shining*.[1] Wright comments on his most neo-baroque work, *Archicembalo*: "It is almost over the top—cultishly formal, closely set with visual features, hyper-referential—but it is lavishly invented, detailed, particular in its language, and so fully realized."[2]

Waldrep's books include *Goldbeater's Skin* (2003), *Disclamor* (2007), *Archicembalo* (2009), and, with John Gallaher, the collaborative volume *Your Father on the Train of Ghosts* (2011).

He has won the Alice Fay Di Castagnola Award, the Cecil Hemley Memorial Award, and the George Bogin Memorial Award from the Poetry Society of America. He has also received the Dorset and Colorado publication prizes.

Waldrep teaches at Bucknell University, where he is Margaret Ley Professor of Poetry and Creative Writing, edits the journal *West Branch*, and directs the Bucknell Seminar for Younger Poets.

Since 2005 Waldrep has been affiliated with the Old Order River Brethren, a conservative Anabaptist group related to the Amish. He lives in Lewisburg, Pennsylvania.

1. "Messages to Strangers," unpublished author's statement, 2011.   2. Jacket comment, *Archicembalo*, Dorset, VT, 2008.

Pharisee's Lament

I am haphazard in my ministrations
but take some comfort in order.
The burden rests on others: the gas man,
the postman, those other faithful

in their convocations, all flesh
moving foursquare across this lively grid.
Even the horses—creatures of habit—
profess their devotion to gods
of oat-box and grass-pasture, twice daily
east and west before the crude stations
of their desire. A ritual, this sacrament of appetite
renewed each morning as the mind
works its soft way from darkness
to the satisfactions of eye, of lip,
a pleasure. The light frays, the horses rise
from the lower field; they know
they will be compensated yet in this dispensation
though their faith is rooted
in the doubtful sinews of an angry man.
I stand in the shadow of the mow
and listen as their bodies touch
and touch again, proximate, expectant.
The stars spin from their dark autoclave.
I draw a long breath, hold it. The mare nickers.
This is one way of loving the world.

2003

Goldbeater's Skin

Ask for an axe, a syringe, a length of rope
plein air, coiled or loose. Working from nature dilates focus,
draws form from its pale circuit—point beyond which
each sphere reckons its ovation.

Ask for a clip, a pin, a charge, a powder.
Denounce the offset: heaven knows the personal
expands to fill a visual field, colonnade or any aural space
incurred as penalty. Ask for self, ask

whether the white you see is application
or absence, content or context, eight ducks rubbed

into glacial moraine, pinfeathers scarlet against slate-grey scree:
one landscape out of many, call it "Off-Season,"

call it "'58 Chevy," ask for a blade, a vial,
a flashcube, a spool of fresh film. It's important
that the work have a handmade quality, not the disconnect
of digitized tablets scaled just short of empathy

or market value. Request a hearing,
query the epic. Notice how images rise to within
a finger's breadth but come no further, pain excised from touch.
This is the refuge between notation and balance.

It shreds in transposition. So ask for a permit,
a thrombus, a roadside stand; hot wax, at least a thimbleful.
Somewhere in these battlements an egg lies hidden.
I promise, when we find it, Naples falls.

2003

Wunderkammern

I have lived in several worlds, all of them fine.
There was never any question of punishment, rather
representation of a like crystalline faith,
that the blower holds within herself
the unriddling ligature,
that the winter, pierce of ice, the snow
in its intricate fingering can be arrested, and hailed as beauty.
In this fashion the world remains with us.
I buy and I buy; with each receipt
something shredding and translucent breaks upward
from darkness. This is unavoidable.
With a light step and minimal violence I make
myself a tintype. As if invisible.
And thus escape that union.
I would rather, as some do, have left the road for the forest.
I would rather, as some do, bind the alternatives
and set them ablaze on a low hill.
Instead I raise a stone and leave my own

token in that cold place.
Each weight bears the memory of its slow burn,
its origin. What I am describing is what comes after.
I wanted to prolong the wishes, the wishing.
My patron turns in his slow flame.

2007

On the Seventh Anniversary
of the U.S. Invasion of Afghanistan

Your body is a white palette
covering a sacrifice of gills, some moon's clement
misanthropy: I do not mean
it does not love us, only
                    that inside the ash-gold
camber physics makes, your breath exerts a gravity
trapped in winter's porcelain teeth
through which hunger like some history

keeps peering. The dogs run round & round
the salt well of your hair
barking—I almost wrote "banking"—

in the language of fur coats,
                    something already dead &
ornamental, a bamboo grove in January
offering its own guided tour

of the war, its broad cranium,
its massive hips. Sometimes I think
we are all figures in a portrait
                    war is painting,
other times the canvas on which war paints.
If I say devotion is a candle
in the shape of a bell, you are already
six thousand miles away from the neighboring

        place setting, a French forest
through which soldiers sight

my sister

bent low over thrust's smoking flare.
I like to imagine it—in this penultimate moment—

as a breathing thing, that turns in current,
            with eyes that magnify;
that feels pain after all, scientists now maintain.
What we call darkness, it calls desert.
Before language there was an *idea*
of language: to record
            the empathy, the mirage, the attractions

of both chance and surgery,
of *body* to *bomb*. The chapped hand of the one
who stoops now to trouble this water.

2010

discrete series:
Selinsgrove

one town hides another:

we live there, & like it
most of the time, we say:

to the artifacts of
evening: processional:

the mercy seat, or
just a bit of architecture:

tinder / consequence:

is a matter of faith,
not of style so much

as that word's
usually meant: field-

stubble, as opportunity
for photography,

something the figure
can do that plants can't:

cf. duplicity: to vuln:

no I am not done
bearing upward: this

body, its glands &
constituent organ stops:

porous: sympathetic,
i.e. receptive of vibrations

at certain frequencies:

incoming: as ordnance:

duck & cover, shallow
gibbet of astringent sun:

2011

Craig Dworkin
b. 1969

Craig Dworkin was born and raised in southern Indiana. He received his B.A. from Stanford University and his Ph.D. from the University of California at Berkeley.

An important conceptual poet and one of conceptualism's leading theorists, his works of poetry include *Dure* (2004), *Strand* (2005), *Parse* (2008), *The Perverse Library* (2010), and *Motes* (2011). He has written the critical studies *Reading the Illegible* (2003) and *There Is No Medium* (2012) and edited *Architectures of Poetry* (2004), *Language to Cover a Page: The Early Writing of Vito Acconci* (2006), *The Consequence of Innovation: 21st Century Poetics* (2008), *The Sound of Poetry* (with Marjorie Perloff, 2009), *Against Expression: An Anthology of Conceptual Writing* (with Kenneth Goldsmith, 2011), and the online archive The Eclipse Archive (http://english.utah.edu/eclipse).

Brian Reed writes of *Parse*: "Although poets nowadays are designated 'creative writers'—presumably to differentiate their labor from 'technical,' 'commercial,' and 'critical' writing—Dworkin presents his work as manifestly uncreative, that is generated in a rote manner. He hints that poetry is at base just another commodity mechanically reproduced by the infotainment industry to satisfy a niche market."[1] Works like *Parse* involve the exhaustive "working" of a preexisting text; in the present case, the parsing of Edwin A. Abbott's *How to Parse: An Attempt to Apply the Principles of Scholarship to English Grammar,* which was first published in 1874. The work's exhaustiveness is part of its conceptual humor. Dworkin's tongue-in-cheek note further explains, "When I first came across the book I was reminded of a confession by Gertrude Stein (another product of 1874): 'I really do not know that anything has even been more exciting than diagramming sentences.' And so, of course, I parsed Abbott's book into its own idiosyncratic system of analysis."[2]

According to Dworkin, "The text of 'Legion' comes from the true/false questions of the first edition of The Minnesota Multiphasic Personality Inventory (1942)."[3] The constant shifting of the neurotic "I" speaker brings to mind the multivocality of Ashbery's poetry. But Dworkin's work and conceptualist writing in general prefers the flat rhetoric of the machine to that of expression. Likewise, the dialogic aspect of such works can be more convincing as détournement. Dworkin explains that his work "Shift" is the result "of replacing a handful of vocabulary words in the introductory chapter of a geology textbook from the introductory chapter of a linguistic textbook. No further editing took place."[4]

Dworkin teaches at the University of Utah, across the lake from sculptor Robert Smithson's *Spiral Jetty.*

1. "Grammar Trouble," *boundary* 2 36:3 (2009), p. 150.   2. *Parse,* Berkeley, CA, 2008, p. 289.   3. "Notes and Acknowledgments," *Strand,* New York, 2005, p. 109.   4. The same.

Chapter One: Tectonic Grammar

INTRODUCTION

Tectonic grammar, which has so profoundly influenced linguistic thinking since the early 1970's, provides a valuable insight into the mechanisms by which language's semantic floor and surface crust have evolved [Figure 1]. **Tectonic grammar** is a unifying model that attempts to explain the origin of patterns of deformation in the crust, asemantic distribution, semantic drift, and mid-morphemic ridges, as well as providing a mechanism for language to cool (in simple terms, language is just an immense spheroid of magmatic inscription which has crystallized into solid words where it has been exposed to the coldness of space). Two major premises of tectonic grammar are:

> 1. the outermost layer of language, known as the **text**, behaves as a strong, rigid substance and reacts to many stresses as a tensile solid, resting on a weaker region in the semantics known as the sign [Figure 1.1]. The hotter this textual crust becomes, the more it behaves like a ductile solid deforming by plastic flow, whereas if it cools, it behaves as an elastic solid deforming by both brittle fracture and frictional gliding.

> 2. the text is broken into numerous segments or **lexical plates** which have been set in motion with respect to one another; continually changing in shape and size (from partial minims and incomplete bows to areas the size of dialects), these plates are constantly subjected to stresses that impactively compress, laterally sheer, extrude, deform and fragment them in all directions.

The origin and evolution of language's **crust** is a topic of considerable controversy even today. Results from film and other media indicate that language's crust may be a unique feature in semiotic systems. Evidence favors a source for the materials composing the crust from within language itself, and although its interior is inaccessible even to the most sophisticated measuring and modeling techniques, it seems certain that the absolute temperature of language rapidly increases in a geometrical progression pitched in direct proportion to the depth of the crust, and that it soon reaches a temperature where even the words will melt.

Originally, the partial melting of language's semantics may have produced inscriptive magmas that moved to the surface and formed the crust. That textual crust, being less dense than the underlying semantics, has subsequently risen isostatically above the level of the page and hence is subjected to weathering and erosion. Eroded materials are then partially deposited on narrative margins (paratactic collisions in which the strain sequences are variable along great strike lengths of forepage flexures and oblique indentures which need not parallel the regional plate movement), and partially returned to the semantic by subduction to be recycled and perhaps become part of the crust at a later time.

Within the magma's vast suspension of undifferentiated inscription, alphabetic droplets accumulate, coalesce, and percolate through the surface tensile boundaries with an oscillatory sink and segregatory float. Although the data do not exclude alphabetic layering, the non-random occurrence of submorphemic components in passive plume source fanning would seem to require communication between the denotative and connotative semantic strata. This suggests that a substantial portion of semantics keels beneath the narratives formed at the same time as the overlying textual crust, and that they have remained firmly attached to that crust ever since.

In a crustal **melt**, the process of fluid vowel transport affects both the rheology and lettristic evolution of the crust. The melt-producing capacity of a source word is determined chiefly by its alphabetic characteristics and their affinities with deep crustal granulities. Although it may not itself remain after slow melt extraction, a fertile connotative crust can generate a range of compositions in which the melt partitions preferentially form source-words, zoning itself according to density. Experiments indicate that melt segregation is enhanced by increased vowel pressures and consonantal fracturing within surrounding words.

Many scientists consider the widespread acceptance of the tectonic grammar model as a 'revolution' in Literary Theory. As pointed out by J. Tuzo Wilson in 1968, scientific disciplines tend to evolve from a stage primarily of data gathering, characterized by transient hypotheses, to a stage where a new unifying theory or theories are proposed that explain a great deal of the accumulated data. Physics and chemistry underwent such revolutions around the beginning of the twentieth century, whereas Literary Theory entered such a revolution in the late 1960s. As with scientific revolutions in other fields, new ideas and interpretations do not invalidate earlier observations. On the contrary, the theories of graphemic spreading and tectonic grammar offer for the first time unified explanation of what, before, had seemed unrelated observations in the fields of linguistics, paleography, etymology, and poetics [Figure 1.2].

2005

FROM Legion

Once in a while I think of things too bad to talk about. Bad words, often terrible words, come into my mind and I cannot get rid of them. I am bothered by acid stomach several times a week. I am likely not to speak to people until they speak to me. Often I cross the street in order not to meet someone else. I am often sorry because I am so cross and grouchy. I can't understand why I have been so cross and grouchy. I frequently ask people for advice. I am liked by most people who know me. I commonly wonder what hidden reason another person may have for doing something nice for me. I believe in the second coming of Christ. I find it hard to keep my mind on a task or a job. I am not afraid of mice. I am not usually self-conscious. I used to keep a diary. I cannot understand what I read as well as I used to. My daily life is full of things that keep me interested. At times it has been impossible for me to keep from stealing or shoplifting something. I don't blame anyone for trying to grab everything he can get in this world. I would rather win than lose in a game. Sometimes I'm strongly attracted by other's personal effects, shoes, gloves, etc., so that I want to handle or steal them though I have no use for them. I have been disappointed in love. I have no dread of going into a room by myself where other people have already gathered and are talking. My family does not like the work I have chosen (or the work I intend to choose for my life work). I am more sensitive than most other people. At times I hear so well it bothers me. I have no fear of water. I have periods in which I feel unusually cheerful without any special reason. At times I feel that I can make up my mind with unusually great ease. I am afraid of using a knife or anything very sharp or pointed. My feelings are not easily hurt. I have not lived the right kind of life. Dirt frightens or disgusts me. It is safer to trust nobody. At parties I am more likely to sit by myself or with just one other person than to join in with the crowd. I must admit that I have at times been worried beyond reason over something that really did not matter. I worry over money and business. When someone does me a wrong I feel I should pay him back if I can, just for the principle of the thing. People say insulting and vulgar things about me. I am against giving money to beggars. I readily become one hundred percent sold on a good idea. I am very careful about my manner of dress. I would like to be a soldier. At times I feel like picking a fist fight with someone. I would like to be a journalist. My memory seems to be all right. I frequently have to fight against showing that I am bashful. My hardest battles are with myself. At times I feel like smashing things. I have very few headaches. It is all right to get around the law if you don't actually break it. When I leave home I do not worry about whether the door is locked and the windows closed. I like repairing a door latch. At times I have a strong urge to do something harmful or shocking. I would like to wear expensive clothes. Someone has been trying to rob me. There are persons who are trying to steal my thoughts and ideas. I often feel as though things were not real. No one cares much what happens to you. Most of the time I feel blue. I am not afraid of picking up a disease or germs from door knobs. I do not dread seeing a doctor about a sickness or injury. I sometimes keep on at a thing until others lose their patience with me. When I get bored I like to stir up some excitement. I am sure I am being talked about. I have never had any breaking out on my skin that has worried me. It makes me angry to have people hurry me. I wish I were not so shy. When I was a child, I didn't care to be a member of a crowd or gang. Except by a doctor's orders I never take drugs or sleeping powders. I usually work things out for myself rather than get someone to show me how. I seldom worry about my health. During the past few years I have been well most of the time. I have never had a fit or convulsion. Several times I have been the last to give up trying to do a thing. Most people make friends because friends are likely to be useful to them. I have reason for feeling jealous of one or more members of my family. There is something wrong with my sex organs. I do many things which I regret afterwards (I regret things more or more often than others seem to). I have often felt guilty because I have pretended to feel more sorry about something than I really was. There is very little love and companionship in my family as compared to other homes. At one or more times in my life I felt that someone was making me do things by hypnotizing me. I think most people would lie in order to get ahead. Much of the time my head seems to hurt all over. I am certainly lacking in self confidence. If given the chance I could do some things that would be of great benefit to the world. I have difficulty in starting to do things. If I were an artist I would like to draw flowers. I have never been in trouble with the law. I believe I am being plotted against. I like collecting flowers or growing house plants. I would like to be a florist. At times I have very much wanted to leave home. My plans have frequently seemed so full of difficulties that I have had to give them up. I feel like giving up quickly when things go wrong. Horses that don't pull should be beaten or kicked. The sight of blood neither frightens me nor makes me sick. Peculiar odors come to me at times. I feel uneasy indoors. I do not try to cover up my poor opinion or pity of a person so that he won't know how I feel. I am troubled by discomfort in the pit of my stomach every few days or oftener. Some of my family have habits that bother and annoy me very much. I never attend a sexy show if I can avoid it. I like poetry. I have several times given up doing a thing because I thought too little of my ability. Most people inwardly dislike putting themselves out to help people. I resent having anyone take me in so cleverly that I have to admit that it was one on me. I believe that my home life is as pleasant as that of most people I know. My people treat me more like a child than a grown up. In school I was sometimes sent to the principal for cutting up. As a youngster I was suspended from school one or more times for cutting up. I don't seem to care what happens to me. I am a good mixer. I have never been in trouble because of my sex behavior. Sometimes I am sure that other people can tell what I am thinking. I believe that a person should never taste an alcoholic drink. I wish I could get over worrying about things I have said that may have injured other people's feelings. It makes me feel like a failure when I hear of the success of someone I know well. I am worried about sex matters. I have had blank spells in which my activities were interrupted and I did not know what was going on around me. It is always a good thing to be frank. I used to like drop-the-handkerchief. I have often felt badly over being misunderstood when trying to keep someone from making a mistake. I feel weak all over much of the time. I pray several times a week. I am about as able to work as I ever was. I cannot do anything well. Sometimes when I am not feeling well I am cross. Criticism or scolding hurts me terribly. Sometimes my voice leaves me or changes even though I have no cold. My hands and feet are usually warm enough. These days I find it hard not to give up hope of amounting to something. Once a week or oftener I feel suddenly hot all over, without apparent cause. I sweat very easily even on cool days. Sometimes, when embarrassed, I break out in a sweat which annoys me greatly. At times I feel like swearing. I am embarrassed by dirty stories. My way of doing things is apt to be misunderstood by others. My parents and family find more fault with me than they should. Parts of my body often have feelings like burning, tingling, crawling, or like "going to sleep." I have nightmares every few nights. My sleep is fitful and disturbed. I can sleep during the day but not at night. I am often afraid of the dark. I am very strongly attracted by members of my own sex. I am afraid of finding myself in a closet or small closed space. I am afraid to be alone in the dark. I have been told that I walk during sleep. I have no difficulty in keeping my balance in walking. I like to let people know where I stand on things. I would rather sit and daydream than to do anything else. I can stand as much pain as others can. I have one or more faults which are so big that it seems better to accept them and try to control them rather than to try to get rid of them. I am often said to be hotheaded. I dread the thought of an earthquake. I have had periods when I felt so full of pep that sleep did not seem necessary for days at a time. When a man is with a woman he is usually thinking about things related to sex. Usually I would prefer to work with women. Once a week or oftener I become very excited. I have a habit of counting things that are not important such as bulbs on electric signs and so forth. At times I am full of energy. Lightening is one of my fears. If I were a reporter I would very much like to report sporting news. I am not bothered by a great deal of belching of gas from my stomach. A windstorm terrifies me . . .

2005

FROM *Parse*

Noun Cardinal Arabic Numerical Period

Noun Copulative Conjunction Noun Period

Definite Article Noun Implied Subject locative preposition indefinite article Active Participle Used As An Adjective Prepositional Object period

Adjective Of Number Plural Noun relative pronoun active present tense verb indefinite article object modal verbal auxiliary appositional verb participle used subjectively as an appositional adjective preposition adjective prepositional object comma alternative disjunctive coordinate conjunction implied definite article preposition indefinite article prepositional object comma preposition relative pronoun definite article object present tense singular appositional intransitive verb and intransitive verb as part of a passive form verbal compound colon dash

parenthesis cardinal arabic numeral parenthesis marks of quotation *Proper Name Used As The Subject* past tense verb period marks of quotation parenthesis cardinal arabic numeral parenthesis marks of quotation *Third Person Singular Masculine Pronoun Used As The Subject* past tense verb period marks of quotation

parenthesis cardinal arabic numeral parenthesis marks of quotation *Definite Article subject preposition of the infinitive active present tense transitive verb infinitive mood definite article direct object* past tense verb period marks of quotation

parenthesis cardinal arabic numeral parenthesis marks of quotation *Relative Pronoun indicative masculine pronoun used as the subject present indicative in the third person singular present tense appositional intransitive verb supplemental appositional adjective subjectively used* period marks of quotation

Locative Preposition adjective of number genitive preposition definite article adjective plural noun locative preposition comma conditional conjunction second person singular pronoun active present tense transitive verb conditional subjunctive implied definite article direct object marks of quotation Interrogative Subject Pronoun alternative disjunctive coordinate conjunction relative interrogative pronoun past tense verb question mark marks of quotation definite article subject comma verbal appositive definite article *appositional noun objectively used* genitive preposition third person genitive pronoun noun comma present tense singular appositional intransitive verb supplemental appositional adjective subjectively used definite article *Appositional Onomastic* genitive preposition definite article Noun period

  Singular Deictic Pronoun active transitive present tense verb third person plural pronoun used as a direct object preposition indicative of movement indefinite article object of the preposition colon
  Definite Article noun genitive preposition indefinite article Noun locative preposition indefinite article active participle used as an adjective prepositional object present tense singular appositional intransitive verb definite article appositional noun alternative disjunctive coordinate conjunction appositional plural noun declined in the singular compositional preposition plural noun taken as the object of the preposition relative construction implied adjectival gerund preposition definite article noun adjectival past participle preposition of agency gerundive infinitive marks of quotation Interrogative Subject Pronoun question mark marks of quotation alternative disjunctive coordinate conjunction relative interrogative pronoun question mark marks of quotation adverbial preposition indefinite article Noun period ^{superscript cardinal arabic numeral}

Direct Object transitive verb imperative mood and second person singular personal pronoun implied Ordinal Roman Numeral period conditional conjunction definite article Noun present tense singular appositional intransitive verb and past participle used as part of a passive form verbal compound preposition indefinite article singular Noun used as an object comma adverb dash

parenthesis cardinal arabic numeral parenthesis marks of quotation Third Person Singular Masculine Pronoun Used As The Subject *adverb* active intransitive incomplete present tense verb period marks of quotation

parenthesis cardinal arabic numeral parenthesis marks of quotation Third Person Singular Feminine Pronoun Used As The Subject active transitive present tense

---

^{superscript cardinal arabic numeral} Third Person Neuter Accusative Pronoun present tense singular appositional intransitive verb adverb of negation adjective used as an appositional noun preposition of the infinitive active transitive present tense verb relative pronoun definite article Noun present tense singular appositional intransitive verb marks of quotation relative pronoun adjective relative pronoun definite article noun present tense singular appositional intransitive verb as part of a passive form verbal compound period marks of quotation Conjunction comma locative preposition marks of quotation Indefinite Article noun transitive past tense verb third person plural genitive pronoun direct object marks of quotation semicolon conjunction of exception marks of quotation Noun marks of quotation present tense singular appositional intransitive verb adverb of negation definite article marks of quotation Noun period marks of quotation

third person singular verb *adverb of negation* verbal direct object period marks of quotation

dash definite article Noun modal verbal auxiliary of obligation present tense appositional intransitive verb infinitive mood and past participle as part of a passive form verbal compound locative preposition definite article noun colon

parenthesis cardinal arabic numeral parenthesis marks of quotation Interrogative Subject Pronoun *adverb* active intransitive incomplete present tense verb question mark marks of quotation Indicative Noun colon marks of quotation Third Person Singular Masculine Pronoun comma marks of quotation Noun period

parenthesis cardinal arabic numeral parenthesis marks of quotation Interrogative Subject Pronoun active transitive present tense third person singular verb *adverb of negation* verbal direct object question mark marks of quotation Indicative Noun colon marks of quotation Third Person Singular Feminine Pronoun comma marks of quotation Noun period

Direct Object transitive verb imperative mood and second person singular personal pronoun implied Ordinal Roman Numeral period conditional conjunction definite article Noun present tense singular appositional intransitive verb and past participle used as part of a passive form verbal compound preposition indefinite article plural noun used as an object adjective preposition of the infinitive active indefinite present tense transitive verb infinitive mood definite article direct object comma adverb dash

2008

Brian Kim Stefans
b. 1969

Brian Kim Stefans was born and raised in Rutherford, New Jersey, and received his B.A. in literature from Bard College and M.F.A. in electronic literature from Brown University.

Stefans's poetry publications include *Free Space Comix* (1998), *Gulf* (1998), *Angry Penguins* (2000), *What Is Said to the Poet Concerning Flowers* (2006), and *Kluge: A Meditation, and Other Works* (2007). He has also published a collection of essays and poetry, *Fashionable Noise: On Digital Poetics* (2003) and *Before Starting Over: Selected Essays and Interviews 1994–2005* (2006).

Stefans is one of the most effective theorists and practitioners of digital poetics. Noah Eli Gordon writes in a review of *Kluge: A Meditation*: "With an erudite wit, a swerving, campy, sonic thickness, and an adherence to recombinatory exercises in the subversion of style, *Kluge* . . . reads like a handbook for the future avant-garde. The book merges the erstwhile artistic breakthroughs of the Black Mountain School and Oulipo-inspired procedural methods with a forward-looking faith in digital aesthetics to concoct a poetry as flat-out funny as it is furiously intelligent."[1]

Stefans follows Veronica Forrest-Thomson, author of *Poetic Artifice,* in her use of the terms "good naturalization" and "bad naturalization." In the case of cyberpoetry, bad naturalization occurs when radical artifice such as software is used to traditional ends such as lyric poetry.[2] Cyberpoetry should seek noise rather than silence, interference and discontinuity rather than a smooth, unimpeded progress. "The terms of engagement are changed when power shifts hands to the machine, and one's identity as digital pilgrim, as a 'data cowboy,' becomes banalized if the promise of the link does not produce a significant sense of self-creativity, or (in Situationist terms) 'spontaneous creation.' "[3] In an interview with Gary Sullivan, Stefans refers to a divide in the musician Brian Eno's work between "idiot energy," meaning the focused excitement of pop songs, and his comparatively "ambient" work. "Idiot energy," he says, "could be that energy that comes from alienation, in which one cannot acknowledge any sort of social contracts with others . . . whereas ambient energy seems to create this contract, even if it's ephemeral, essentially private, soothing, I would also say 'pragmatic.' "[4] The performative aspect of "idiot energy" would seem to be that of the solitary singer, while "ambient energy" is a more dialogical process of being in digital community with others.

Brian Kim Stefans teaches at UCLA.

1. *Boston Review,* March/April 2008, http://bostonreview.net/BR33.2/microreviews.php.
2. "Stops and Rebels or, The Battle of Brunaburh," *Fashionable Noise: On Digital Poetics,* Berkeley, 2003, p. 139.   3. The same, p. 132.   4. Gary Sullivan, "Brian Stefans Interview," undated, http://home.jps.net/~nada/bks.htm.

Elementary Buddhism

Strike a match, a pun in the wind, the window pain. The stitch elegant against splitting, a suture, a way of sitting, a winning. Boy, they say, play play until the tremors go away: I don't know, don't care to know, now. This is the wind speaking—echoing, state to state. This is the crime oblivious, the fright elastic, and signs curve me ever inward, puck's balance, talentless. These chords of connective tissue that I ordered in the mail, wrapped in preserving plastic, starved in their institution, pronouncing its final syllables of revolution—with a doctorate or a general acceptance, within doctrine, these chords are not vibrating, they've stopped, placating. And all the truths are relevant dragging a desperate mile through bogs of shit and temperaments that argue for, or against, style. These truths we've come to believe are hardly material, but only gaseous, or like some lump sum that never approaches, from its third realm, the physical. In its condom: striking a match, a pun. The raw, the unrefined find again in the cooked mind, a way to sleep, slip happy domestic in a challenging way, a map against all becoming. Calm, he wipes it down, clean again.

2007

Searchbot

Phrase here, and then
    "Funny how that
works out!"

Silly narcissists,
    heads of goldilocks,
better spit out your gum, better walk tall
    in the city
of the projective maw.

The proleptic mall
    sits on a barren hill
(this for you, inveterate Brasilia!)
    —I pop the pock
and prepare for dinner
    with the family.

A sentence elides meaning.

A DNA strand recovers it,
twisting in fanciful curves
    of the sperm cell
running to the elk.

This book is boring,
    put it down.

As the weight deludes its content,
    denudes its irreverent content,
we palm each others'
    heads, then dribble them
to Brooklyn.

Say, the shores of Brighton
    Beach, where that restaurant
was.

Don't try it.

There's a hair in the soup.

Video emanations
    arbitrary as a tie die,
a visual corsair:
    "I like the poems
in which the letters do all sorts of
    things."

A nude
entropy stares
    at the hermaphrodite's face,
vandal of Kunduns,
    dribble, babble, stubble-faced
Hermes.

They walk
    in their calisthenics,
phi beta therapied,
    frisson as an aperitif
in the goyim onions of the State.

So that:
"The proliferation of frames,
    publications that are permitted
fixation bears a family resemblance
    to Charles Bernstein:
formalist, a
    social formalist." (Bernstein).

I have eaten the dumdums
    that were in coalition,
forbid me,
    they were free, and old, sold
to me.

Sort of resemble me.

    Lapidary LAPD,
you stoned the coroners
    of a poet named Guillaume
X, from Berkeley, mistaking
    him for your own,
sliding down the panty leg with a
    zip, a static cling,
sing!

All the
    sentences got flushed out,
then, attention
    faltered, a wiffle-
ball placed back where the
    heart should be.

It goes:
tick, tick, tick, now,
    smooth and sincere.

There is a koala in the daydream,
    smooth and sincere.

There is a pageant in the daydream,
    smooth and sincere.

Now,
for a joke:
   as a blue _____ over the water
stinks of _____, I
   disown you, parent
of my sickle and starfire.

2007

Bishop Bedlam's Entreaties

a poem for Brown's "Cave"

Please reject me after plagiarizing this.
Please turn me over if you think you can.
Please rewrite me if you know a bad joke.
Please seduce me if you want to touch me.
Please advise me how to invest my income.
Please navigate me if that's your fetish.
Please rotate me if you believe in magic.
Please sanitize what you read for school.
Please translate me into classical Greek.
Please take shoes off before entering me.
Please ridicule me if you feel I'm bland.
Please eulogize me after I kick the pail.
Please flub the pronunciation of my name.
Please advertise that you think I'm sexy.
Please revert to earlier stages of being.
Please flabbergast me with impious slang.
Please retort that I stroke you unkindly.
Please refrain from smoking the tomatoes.
Please undulate me like a jellyfish robe.
Please shoot me if you can aim the thing.
Please reboot me if my framerate's jerky.
Please undercut me like the Wizard of Oz.
Please exacerbate me with your lamer wit.
Please reward me if I am moving prettily.
Please please me if you want me to smile.
Please don't be afraid of me this moment.

Please don't be shy if you want to strip.
Please excuse me while I check my emails.
Please perform better next time you come.
Please resort to speaking rather bluntly.
Please grease me if you hear any screech.
Please archive me if I'm getting too old.
Please praise me like a software Madonna.
Please resist me if you've good strength.
Please animate me with BASIC programming.
Please recommend me to rich text editors.
Please modify me if you've got the balls.
Please don't reply I am a suckass friend.
Please forage for some scrap meat for me.
Please promise me some day I'll be human.
Please regret that you never have met me.
Please do not turn off the Cave just yet.
Please restart me at a later Brown event.
Please regurgitate me in your MFA thesis.
Please hoax me into making myself expire.
Please don't tell her I've spoken to you.
Please understand it is too late to quit.
Please imitate me with your recombinance.
Please illustrate me with childlike glee.
Please excommunicate me for being adless.
Please thrash me until I spill the beans.

2007

Catherine Wagner ────────────────────────
b. 1969

Catherine Wagner was born in Rangoon, Burma. She grew up in Asia, the Middle East, and Baltimore, Maryland, and was educated at the University of Tennessee and the University of Iowa Writers' Workshop.

Her poetry collections include *Miss America* (2001), *Macular Hole* (2004), *My New Job* (2009), and *Nervous Device* (2012).

Of *My New Job,* Eileen Myles wrote, "Catherine Wagner's 'new job' might be the last great book of the oughts. Part of its delight is that it is not constant. Its eyelid adjusts and flutters throughout. It's three books at least: fuzzy portraiture of energy and thought like early moderns: Arthur Dove and Georgia O'Keeffe—and even like Pound, in Wagner's familial way of tugging at language. It's also a bit Don Juan (as in Castaneda). It's a new age book: searching, awkward and useful too—a momentary sex manual for girls—then a dirty adult notebook."[1]

Associated with the Gurlesque, a burlesque "girly" poetics, Wagner's poetry is among the most vividly personal and self-disclosing of the contemporary period. Sometimes the poems are notational and diaristic ("Haven't clean the house since Martin left, and living out of the freezer, the old food, / and no fresh") and sometimes heroic in their cry ("an extreme change, so it's obvious what to do / (dig my way out of the rubble, toward the cries) / and make my now golden?"). One reviewer notes, "The reader senses her attachment to the craft, even if this rare feeling originates from self-love. Someone else's narcissism often brings bees to the honey, if they aren't already drowning in their own emissions. Wagner has a specific way of speaking; she breaks down and ultimately responds to her desires and demands—like an eager child arguing to get what she wants without caring about established social dictations. . . . Wagner's speech is free, uninhibited yet aware."[2]

A review of *Macular Hole* notes: "Wagner's musical poems rely often on nursery-rhyme rhythms and refrains. With their gutter humor and comic images they become part dare, part self-satisfied smirk and part despair."[3]

Catherine Wagner lives in Oxford, Ohio, and teaches at Miami University.

1. http://www.units.muohio.edu/creativewriting/faculty/wagnerc.html.   2. Jacquelyn Davis, review of *My New Job, Coldfront,* August 1, 2010, http://coldfrontmag.com/reviews/my-new -job.   3. Molly Bendall, *Slope,* 2006, http://www.slope.org/bendall.html.

Fraction Anthem[8]

Still asleep in its bunny
the world arrives. Lyre,
pinch, a gale.
                    A pigeon
leaps the furry straits

paint mucked all round the window edges,
pbus gone by
no Martin. 2 tiny red bugs
cross the white swoosh. Martin!
Fuzzy round the edges and kinder
than Lance even, or Jeff Clark
Ruddy, and kind   shall I compare you.
first-rate, with a freckle on your temple.

Still asleep in it, honey,
asleep in the bunny.
I will get cold. Demur, with fur.
Get cellulite, and pubes. Morose,
in there, the veinfugue, limited.
Pasted-on formica, winestain bellybutton
rabid nipple, ha.
Why stain. Why

wriggle free of haunches.
Curl up toes, demesne.

                    Then Martin sit in the car with Chris,
agossip, needing a shave.
Rise bun! Slant home,
good Chris, fogged up,
please send him gesturing in.
Knee clamp, wrist clamp, mine.
Big ol chest, mine, sit by refrigerator,
sleep mouth open, funny. Here minus.
Here he mine come smile.

                                                        2001

Fraction Anthem[15]

A little bell in the tree, ha ha
It shed on me
A ting and a ting and I saw it not
I sat around in my linen shirt
Beneath the tree on a mat, ha ha
Displeased, and displeased
For I had not worked and I had just sat
And I had not exercised
But to blow a fly off the mat

I remembered Marvell's Garden
Where the drunk falls down on grass
Drunk on grapes or on thinking
And he thinks a peacock thought
He thinks he can think
A bigger than a this
That's to think with a peacock's eyes
The eye is a coin and it sees the realm
The realm it is coin of the realm in
The realm real money
Reflective and exchange
I will have caught the sun sitting here
Drunk on fir.

2001

Exercise 34 (1/3/02 PM)

Snow
  starred when I looked straight up
  sky dark gray, geese rose
in alarmed soft shh and hasping
long-necked geese
agossip all upset

Home I immed. dial
        does anyone love me, and Karen does.
Muscle under collarbone hurt today
from fooling with computer.

Look left and up   pulls like a bitch
Haven't cleaned the house since Martin left, and living out of the freezer,
  the old food,
and no fresh, and living high alone and secret way up high a cloud ranch
twisted threw me on the bank spurred my own cheek
Cloud at the level of my eye
I was high up in my head with cheek-hollows like the Red Sea
To reward me my email is up
Chelsey, Rebecca with news of a plug from Powell's, and Janet; not bad
  yellowredpearl and interrupting twigs
                Somebody liked my booooook
    Do I want something scary
an extreme change, so it's obvious what to do
  (dig my way out the rubble, toward the cries)
and make my now golden?
                    fadeproof/waterproof
  I knew I was a sign to myself
      I couldn't see myself except in the mirror
which 1) wasn't me 2) was me backwards was 3) flat was 4) making me
vain or 5) making me embarrassed to go out, that was all a sign to me
  not a sign of me
all along I was alone to that
though everyone saw me
  checking myself out by talking to them
when they checked themselves out in me
I tried to say Oh here have it all
       warm woolen flood   welcomer
      some spider-netting held it back,
kept growing over my warm and my intention to befriend
      I could use it to disinfect
a wound and it abstracted me, which was salvation.

                                          2009

Exercise 38 (1/7/02 PM)

Monster planet buzzing around
    the bursting-forth gold flash arrival
        Martin Corless-Smith
I will have to cover my eyes
        Shy Martin Corless-Smith
Seventy angels with ruthless eyes

maxxing the jets of the plane
massaging the red lights green
   as he sways in the back of the cab
    I subducted the clouds
from the path of the plane
   & they roil & burl up in Kansas
King of the silent Tetons
 in white phosphorescence below
enjoy your journey Sir

                2009

For the Boys

Can you imagine dear men
what it is to be a woman being fucked.
The men installing a new gate
—ran past them prickling, face
prickling, back of neck
sensitive and tight, and they *do*
say something to/about me

      Now there was
in a transparent skybox
someone watching my body and giving it
a score. I berated myself for letting it
hover; then the man in the orange construction helmet
 crashed through the skybox glass
with his head,
and the transparent box
filled with color and a stone support
under it. I did not make it up.

Will you just fuck me or
will I just fuck without the skybox.
There is no fucking without the skybox.

This part is for girls, college highschool girls

The guy fucks you five eight minutes
you think you are supposed to come
you do not. What's wrong with you?
Frigidaire girl.
"—But prior girl came all the time!"
To have to learn to be pleasing
throws his image
as successful lover

—image he needs, to continue sexing—

   in doubt.

The problem lies
with you.

This situation   lie on both sides

is the rule. There are exceptions.

Now let us have ceremonial
sex.

Who is the pauper?

I will be.   I will be.

2009

Song

Penis regis, penis immediate, penis
        tremendous, penis offend us; penis
ferule us, penis protrude from us,
        wrinkly rule us; penis intrudes us.
Penis surrender. Penis precede us,
        penis resented, penis emended:

penis between us,
      penis regis.

Vagina regina, vagina align us,
      vagina astride us, vagina assault
us. Vagina inside her.
      Vagina for punches,
vagina for lunches, vagina dentata,
      vagina regatta;
vagina behind us, vagina refined us,
      vagina before us,
vagina regina.

2009

Graham Foust
b. 1970

Graham Foust was born in Knoxville, Tennessee, and raised in Eau Claire, Wisconsin. He has degrees from Beloit College, George Mason University, and the State University of New York at Buffalo. He teaches at St. Mary's College of California.

Foust's publisher offers the following description of his style: "*A Mouth in California* [2009], Graham Foust's fourth book of poetry, uses the ironies and anxieties of contemporary life as a foil for mordant and sometimes violent humor. Through mangled aphorisms, misheard song lyrics, and off-key phrasing, Foust creates a unique idiom of tragicomic pratfalls, a ballet of falling down. Yet the elasticity of Foust's language repels the stiff-necked adversaries of thought: "what's the wrong way to break / that brick of truth back into music?"[1]

His other works include *As in Every Deafness* (2003), *Leave the Room to Itself* (Sawtooth Poetry Prize, 2003), *Necessary Stranger* (2007) and *To Anacreon in Heaven and Other Poems* (2013). With Samuel Frederick, he has translated two volumes of Ernst Meister, *Wallless Space* (*Wandloser Raum*) and *In Time's Rift* (*Im Zeitspalt*).

In a review of *Necessary Stranger*, Chris McCreary notes: "Foust works in a compact form that features often enjambed lines holding close to the left-hand margin, and he employs a terse but carefully chosen vocabulary. Within those basic parameters, though, he explores a number of modes. The title of "Shift Change, the Old Pink. Buffalo, New York" suggest that it is an occasional poem, and in a sense it surely is, but Foust doesn't exactly rely on conventional narrative strategies: "I'll have / whatever shadows // you say / I've been having // for the last / blank elixir // of your unborn afternoon."[2]

In his commentary on *A Mouth in California*, Ray McDaniel strikes upon an important aspect of Foust's considerable appeal: "As many of us have noted, the pendulum has begun to swing away from poetry operative wholly at the level of the book, a move that itself marked a certain generational disenchantment with poems as bite-sized universes resplendent with guaranteed but perhaps cheap and certainly suspect pleasures and meanings."[3] In other words, it's this generation's task to move beyond breathlessness and forced silence of the serial poem, at least as currently practiced. Foust offers instead the bitten-off realism and exactitude of the slur, the flaw, and the stumble.

1. Flood Editions website, http://www.floodeditions.com/foust-a-mouth-in-california. 2. *Rain Taxi* Online Edition, Spring 2007, http://www.raintaxi.com/online/2007spring/foust .shtml. 3. The Constant Critic, 10/24/2011, http://www.constantcritic.com/ray_mcdaniel/a -mouth-in-california.

1984

Look at the sky, go
back inside. Cocaine
makes its way to Wisconsin.

The TV's thick with burial, hilarious
with seed, and while the moon,
my mind, and the real world stay home,

I will walk walk
walk unkilled around
a new year's clumsy gallows.

Anything's impossible. I'm not
you. Here's to music
to be in the movies to.

2007

Of What Seems Like My Father

I met him in the candy store.
He turned around and smiled at me—
you get the picture.
Yes, we see.

You get the picture.
If it would all please stop for what seems like forever,
I could walk through spanking dark across
America on car tops.

I could walk through spanking dark among
these pharmacies, canyons, and flags.
It's not unusual to be loved by anyone.
The moon's got a fake side tonight, but still—

it's not unusual to be loved by anyone.
Wanting to hear what I don't want to hear
is hardly possible. *And then?* I'll come
to where what's said here disappears.

is hardly possible. *And then?* I'll come
and from an airplane jump
to open his piss-stained chute.
I am leaping like the pieces of a bomb, do you hear me?

Just to open his piss-stained chute?
I'm precisely the quiet of his blind spot's eye:
part heartache, part affect; part heartache, part arsenal.
Embroidered with cold—

part heartache, part affect; part heartache, part arsenal—
and to this sudden edge of city not a bird.
A border's bruised clarity, an ocean an ocean.
Try closing your eyes with your eyes closed.

2007

Interstate Eighty

This world is conclusion. On a clear day, you can go
blind. The unknown is almost
interesting, with its infinite *I'm-not-
kidding.* Who are you.

Why is it we can't
touch when I so want to. That is,
to kiss and be kissed
slick, be gripped as ash.

Would you look at those trucks
of trucks—they're only facts. We've years
of brightest cold and fewer roads.
Don't yet be amazing. There's such a thing

as sentimental peril, you'll see. One needs only
a few songs, really. There's no beginning to decay.

2007

Panama

Fruit thumps in the pointless
grass, has no hand in itself.
Complaint's a sort of orchard.
A summer flower plucked black's
another tool.

If only I couldn't
understand, I'd imagine
some sarcastic new Christ and say
something someone would say.

*

Pain is okay—
it's the practical
that murders.
Birdsongs now

in the trash-
thicketed blackout.
I want something to not
do with my hands.

2007

FROM *To Anacreon in Heaven*

Like the docent who would suck all hint of interest from his subject, I'll warn
you now that I've been known to cheat at reverie.

I wake apart to dark, suggest a presence, some lone imagination gummed
with time.

And still the city hides a sentence, its parade of strokes and serifs only weeds
and clumps of broken bricks derive.

Come daybreak, one more heat wave, an all-day hate crime in the sky.

And the kiss?

I got behind on it.

Do I know the drill?

I *am* the drill.

Or rather, I am until an hour of clumsy silences renders me otherwise.

I should pretend myself to sleep again.

A few more injuries are scheduled to arrive.

2013

I could break into slavery, certain songs hung on my bones.

The poem: Think to listen at me fix that.

I've come straight into the room as if the poem was to be for me.

Vague scraping at the shingles, vaguer flashing in the air—I get it.

S'all evil.

The poem is briars and bells of poison.

The torn half of a book is in the wine that's crawling toward me on the floor.

Has a hard, bright eye, today does, and with one fist and a finger in the world I've come to hell.

The poem peels its speech from me.

The revolution will probably be pantomimed.

The poem keeps away when I can't see or there's nothing to see.

2013

Noelle Kocot

b. 1970

Noelle Kocot was born and raised in Brooklyn, New York. She holds a B.A. from Oberlin College and an M.F.A. from the University of Florida, and was awarded a fellowship from the National Endowment for the Arts for 2001.

Kocot's first collection of poems, *4* (2001), won the Levis Poetry Prize. Her other works include *The Raving Fortune* (2004), *Poem for the End of Time and Other Poems* (2006), *Sunny Wednesday* (2009), and *The Bigger World* (2011). She has also published *Poet by Default,* her translation of the poetry of Tristan Corbière (2011).

"Imagine Rilke with a sense of humor," Jordan Davis writes of Kocot's *The Raving Fortune.* "She can be simultaneously brutal and self-glorifying, too, as when she begins 'The Maddest Kind of Love' with 'Two retarded men are kicking off their shoes' and ends it 'I want to save the world.' Her contemporaneity is more deliciously off when she uses *Snuffelufagus* as the end word in a sestina, announces that 'Long Black Veil' was her shower song, or writes an ode to the person who, during a subway bomb threat, pickpocketed her Tao Teh Ching."[1] Craig Morgan Teicher notes the significance to Kocot's poetry of her husband's death on a sunny Wednesday in 2004: "Many of the poems about [Damon] Tomblin's death do more than mourn his death; they also describe and carry out an ongoing relationship with his spirit and influence, a slow, subtle transformation of the beloved into an energy that inhabits every aspect of life: 'I want to be intimate with everyone // And most of all with you, my only. / I want to taste the flavor of a leaf / . . ./ Wear the collar of a pregnant deli cat.' There is also a pervasive, and surprising, silliness throughout the poems, and Kocot's penchant for wordplay is on full display."[2]

Noelle Kocot lives in New Jersey and teaches at various colleges in the New York City area.

1. Jordan Davis, "Power-Word Wiz Kocot: Traces of Plath—Or Snuffelufagus?" *The Village Voice Books,* 9/21/2004.   2. "Beginning with an Elegy: Interview with Poet Noelle Kocot," *Publishers Weekly,* April 20, 2009, http://www.publishersweekly.com/pw/by-topic/authors/interviews/article/7562-beginning-with-an-elegy-interview-with-poet-noelle-kocot-.html.

Love Poem on the Anniversary of Nowhere

The ground is failing in my memory.
This shade is deafening. A false story
Welds me to a space where I neither
Wash my hair, nor fold my clothes,

Nor speak, nor even breathe, and I ask myself,
What favor can you do for me
That you have not already done? For instance,
When I wrote my name in the datebooks of angels

And I did not care whether they were fallen,
You didn't say a word.
But I heard your crystal clanging
From afar and I knew you'd finally come

To doubt the bodiless fire of marvelous dark
Fading softly into nearest stars above us. You wept.
The leaves fell one, two, three, infinity,
And you, my stalled train bound for eternity,

Remain sunk into the burning snow that caps the evil
River pumping my heart across the empty edge of space,
Where an intermezzo sleep of shadows writhes
Lightly on the throbbing, failing ground.

2001

Abortion Elegy

And there you were, emerging alone into the light,
A sort of halo, scattering despite
My fierce and silent request, too late
To defer to my bird's-eye hindsight

Sinking to eye-level now before the portrait
Of you I'll never see, ever. Yet you are concrete
Somehow; I know, I've heard your bee-like buzzing
In all the tiny leaves bursting from their sacs to greet

A magical universe, where everything grows, and sings
In harmony for we know not what. Everything
Grows, even you, my little one, and your sanctity
Is that of a dim and stormy summer evening

With its regard for all things temporary.
So go now, dear, and go with dignity
Into the stark, mid-winter air, which is your birthright.
May your sleep keep you as warm as a September tree.

2001

For My Father the Poet

I look and look for you in the eyes of other men,
Go on singing under the spires of the city
And its symphony of iron like a knife through wax
While the evening raises its scarred wrists
Over the stained awning of the sky
And again I find myself without you.
I want to say, I have fed the young, changed the seasons,
Banged into the silken necks of giraffes
Craning over the deep night of the truly dead.
I want to tell you that I carry your gifts
To where the outlines of waves remain,
Where everything in the wild universe
Can be traced to its ontic source,
So that you in your error and I in mine
May someday be able to join each other
Far from the call of illusion and metal
And the light feet of my dreams can sprout wings
And fly off to greet you on the axis of the one true language.

2001

Passing Over Water

The sunset is blinding today.
The bridge seems to have shed its cables,
And everything tapers to a methodical hissing, a calm.
I cannot hear above the wheels that softly sing

What seems a lullaby to soothe all of creation,
Meant to reach even into the rich marrow of stars.
I dreamed this once,
The bridge, the sea, the song of the train,

And in the dream there were fluorescent trees,
Fuchsia, bright yellow, electric teal,
Brushing against the sky in the breeze like fiber-optic lamps.
In the dream there was a feeling of utter silence,

Palpable as sketches for buildings,
And I wondered when it would leave, if it would leave at all,
Or if it would exist only in the prism of that instant
Where earlier I'd heard a voice urging me

Through an anguished mesh of faces and rain:
Forget everything you know, it is of no use to anyone,
And your ominous conjectures will shrivel away
In the salt of your own affliction.

I remember I sat in my seat just as I am now sitting,
Whispering over and over *dark is right, dark is right,*
And when I turned my face to the clear, dark window
I saw lions struggling to climb out of the sea.

2004

Over, Under, Through, With

for Rainer Maria Rilke

It is a particle lodged between you and everything,
This fragile pet I hold up to the light.
To watch with soft eyes.
To grant grace to the innocent.

You whistle like a royal bird in morning.
I am nursing a sincere desire,
A maze of species in the green humming of trees.
I see that I am truly my own progeny.

The Apollonian clover-wife sings, *behold in wonder,*
And I applaud the purity of sound.
It is everything I always thought.
But then some kind of revision overtakes me,

Overtakes the ones still out at sea,
And I realize I have cried in rhyme.
I only wanted it to stop and stop,
Not to slide full-force into the heavy grist of things.

I have instead watched my star unravel,
Watched the wisp of an invisibility
Live like a blonde object I have long since put to bed.
And the tree that grows in the ear

Is the apple of my eye,
Over, under, through, with.
I dress the wounds of my unsatisfactory life,
A fallacy that translates all too well.

2004

Lithium

I have my finger on the pulse of something.
My mind is a sea that eats me,
The fidgety harmony of two trains passing.
A car bathes in its own blueness,
The moon is a yolk that beyolks us,
While I am daring to fault the ergonomics of destiny.
And the helpless word propels itself through the inkjets,
The word that dashes itself against the rocks like an actor.

And affliction cannot speak to non-affliction,
Counting its wounds on the abacus of time.
I know what it is to mourn,
And to breathe bliss into the wormhole of the senses,
And that I must disabuse myself of the lion's share of who-knows-where
And the whirring of new grasses on the rainy side of spring.

2006

Katie Degentesh

b. 1974

Born in Fairfax, Virginia, Katie Degentesh was raised in Maryland and Virginia. She attended Washington College in Chestertown, Maryland, and the University of California at Davis. Since 2000, she has lived in New York City, where she works in marketing as a creative director and brand consultant. An early member of the Flarfist Collective, she uses Google sculpting as part of her writing process.

Degentesh's one volume, *The Anger Scale* (2006), holds a special position because, unlike the free play of many Flarfist works, its project is so well planned and executed. In an afterword to the book, she explains that "Every poem in this book is titled with a question from the MMPI, or Minnesota Multiphasic Personality Inventory, a psychological test consisting of 556 true/false questions that has been the benchmark for determining people's mental pathologies as well as their fitness for court trials and military service." Degentesh fed phrases from the test questions into Internet search engines. "This process was a little different for each poem. For instances for 'I LOVED MY FATHER' some results might come from a search for 'LOVED MY FATHER' + turtleneck, some from 'HATED MY FATHER,' some from 'HATED MY FATHER' + pussy; etc. I might also then replace words or phrases with the results." She further explains that the title of her book is taken from the "psychopathic deviate" scale, or Scale 4, sometimes referred to as "the anger scale."

Critic Stephen Burt comments: "All the Flarf I've seen, including Degentesh's debut collection, reflects annoyance, tetchiness, a prankster mind-set, and a frank sense of exhaustion, even boredom, with older, subtler techniques. . . . Unlike most Flarf—and like, say, most Stooges tracks—Degentesh's poems hold together despite their raggedness, roar with resentment against the world as is, and resonate with joy."[1]

Katie Degentesh is currently working on *Reasons to Have Sex*, a book of poems with titles taken from a scientific study listing reasons why people have sex, as well as poems constructed from children's writing found by searching for these reasons on the Internet.

Degentesh lives in the Harlem neighborhood of New York City.

1. *Review of The Anger Scale*, "Central Question: How many Google searches make a good poem?" *The Believer*, April 2007, http://www.believermag.com/issues/200704/?read=review_degentesh.

I Sometimes Tease Animals

because my husband and I have given one another
the freedom to stay alive and growing, we

have never engaged in serious investigation
of the nature of Being in any of the more august

forms of child abuse or verbal harassment
(plus telepathy from the sitter or other living persons)

My son takes showers for the longest time and
he has the cutest bounce to his little step

the backs of his legs look like the little lines on a road map
I'll snip them off and make pillowcases out of them

I know what he's doing, masturbating,
being such a tightwad just makes plain sense

in a world where everyone's someone's private dancer, boy-toy
and we will not worry where our water came from

The houses in this town are very neat
The scats are the products of the forest
And are covered with people of both sexes

Whenever we gently stroke a little pet, or give a surprise gift
the wicked boys do sometimes tease the old
by shouting "police, police" on these occasions

and shock the politeness of the inhabitants of the town
—Oh My PetPet! This is Pork, my Zebbra!

When I first start to get to know people
especially some sad seedy tosser

I tell them about my son having this lust
for someone else's small perky breast

and that although I found nursing while walking to be easy
he now buys nothing but wargame manuals

She looked at me and asked if "Dickson" is my son's name
And do we wrestle as a way of showing our fondness for each other

Then my son gave a pint of gin for a squaw
and lived with her as such until his death

2006

I Feel Uneasy Indoors

When I'm near someone missing an arm or a leg
I feel weighed down by clothes,
the faithful and celebrities

Already I have been spanked twice by my new stepdad
sometimes gay guys look at me for more than a moment
right outside the door to the boy's department

I cannot understand science.
It just got done raining like hell outside
and now it's darker than hell inside.

A fire flickered always, regardless
White paper. White wool. In the dark . . .
. . . That was almost too much for me

The balloon is obviously greater than
whatever is around me that seems to want to scare me
And my long curly hair is all tangled

At this point, it seems to affect only driving,
but what can be done besides driving?

the two military guys, who sleep outside in the snow as usual
seem creepy and messed-up
as if they talk too loud in restaurants
and think all my days have been misspent
I wish they would tell me who she is

To my delight, even outside the Matrix, she is nonsmoking
and takes her anger out on a rock

The wind swollen by ill-temper
without a single bomb falling
the rubbish that people put in their bodies
pierced her eyes like shards of glass

Faced with the heroicity of this girl
I see not only Mars, but its moons

I told her, "I stand outside the gates of the world
which your sex can make a paradise."
"That is well," she replied, "but I feel uneasy."

2006

At Times I Have Fits of Laughing and Crying That I Cannot Control

Susan picked up a 19-year-old at the reception
and encouraged everyone she knew to do the same

laid on his shoulder and bore him twenty or thirty children
with a wild, staring expression and strabismus of the right eye

The doctor said that was usual.
We were daily overtaken back then
With the mass of hair she had

We had to wait until she left the room
to speak to God about the vibrator,
masturbation and women's sexuality
and the vulgarity of walking

Part of a Sunday my brother and I then used to spend
in walking in the meadows and singing psalms
alternating with intervals of stupidity

But one day, just as we were beginning to sing,
I noticed on the other side of the bath
a rather large circle, set below the hallway proper

she of the hair took the fiery torch
and knelt down with the circle ever growing smaller,
until she was at the center of a group hug
in which she was heartily joined by all the merry party!

then she falls and rolls off the roof onto the ground
into a circle drawn on the floor of the garage
which doubled as a brothel containing two whores
swaying their bodies until by and by their heads were rotating in a large circle

many nasty falls I've taken into the future
are to be ascribed to Susan

2006

Noah Eli Gordon
b. 1975

Noah Eli Gordon was born in Cleveland, and studied at the University of Massachusetts at Amherst. Copublisher of Letter Machine Editions, he currently teaches in the M.F.A. program at the University of Colorado Boulder, where he also directs Subito Press.

His books include: *The Frequencies* (2003); *The Area of Sound Called the Subtone* (2004), winner of the Sawtooth Poetry Prize; a conceptual memoir, *Inbox* (2006); *A Fiddle Pulled from the Throat of a Sparrow* (2007); *Figures for a Darkroom Voice* (2007), a collaboration with Joshua Marie Wilkinson; *Novel Pictorial Noise* (2007), a National Poetry Series selection and subsequently chosen for the San Francisco State Poetry Center Book Award; and *The Source* (2011).

Influenced early on by Wallace Stevens and Edmond Jabès, and later by Clark Coolidge and Michael Palmer, Gordon's poetry represents a fusion of many strains of experimental practice. "A lot of my work . . . deals with stretching expected rhetorical tropes," notes Gordon. "I like to twist and expand the arc of the sentence. Ideally, there's an affinity here to the Surrealist impulse to expand the possible."[2] Often syntactically complex, while still driven by an underlying musicality, his prose poetry has been described as playing "freely in the realm between theory and lyric."[2]

Gordon includes a "process note" as an afterword to *The Source*: "From January of 2008 to September of 2009, I read only page 26 of nearly ten thousand books at the Denver Public Library, culling from them bits of language, which I then fused together, altering some nouns to read 'the Source.'" Such a process associates Gordon with proceduralism, even though, on the whole, his work is lyric rather than machinic. "The choice of page 26," he continues, "is also important in Kabbalist terms; it represents the numerical value of the Tetragrammaton, the four Hebrew letters that form the name of God."[3] His volume *Inbox* is also based in a procedure: "to take the body-text of every email that was addressed specifically to me . . . currently in my inbox (over 200) and let all of the voices collide into one continuous text."[4]

Noah Eli Gordon lives in Denver.

1. Joshua Marie Wilkinson, "Reconsidering the World: an interview with Noah Eli Gordon," *Rain Taxi*, Online Edition (Spring 2007).   2. http://www.publishersweekly.com/978-0 -06125-703-2.   3. *The Source*, New York, 2011, p. 125.   4. Thomas Fink, "Interview with Noah Eli Gordon," E-X-C-H-A-N-G-E-V-A-L-U-E-S, October 3, 2007, http://willtoexchange .blogspot.com/2007/10/interview-with-noah-eli-gordon-by.html.

The book of forgetting

Sun-bleached into memory,
ribbon scars—
    a notch for the bloodletting table,
& each knot, loosened:
    ropes gone slack

    Payment in a pound of flesh;
how a breath links its fingers
    —the canary quieted,
called: history gone down
    —buried to the hilt

    Extraction without a drop,
hooks & curves for tearing,
    learned retrieval,
an empty suitcase or pile of shoes,
    soot-nails & tongue-salt

    The veins, a sea;
open-valved & splayed,
    two wings of red velvet
called a cool heart,
    though culled,
both blood-deep & drifting

2007

The book of signs

Icons were no longer icons
& their eye-sacks unlaced
In the field, testing the full range of motion
All wicks removed, each stump sanded down
Stripped of rank & arms at their sides,
counted each ring, regardless
their equivalent for the word winter

Collected shoes called acceptable losses,
so without hitting the bottom
the next sign read: lasso, lash, lesson
Still, one went on playing her violin
Slits cut in hems & bricks left unstacked
Icons were icons & the book remained open

2007

An approximation of the actual letter

I died in a book

& couldn't touch the ink around me

it was autumn

I died in a book asking

the word for leaf for leave

I died in a book on the eve of music

in the distance, another distance

2007

Dove song

A dove makes a sentence in the window
unendurably the lack of dove

This plausible form thinks itself a garden
predicate to the shape of dove ideas

Now the air is thick, internal
A dove makes a sentence in the window

& a dove-made, noun-less conjecture
makes of the thinker a vacant dove sound

This plausible form thinks itself a garden
unpunctuated by reckless duration

reiterated from margin to margin, where
a dove makes a sentence in the window

unrestrained, a concerted dimmer silence
The weight of dove & the waiting dove

2007

FROM *The Source*

The Source sits atop an alp as if it were a throne. I record it here. Others memorize a pattern and work with it, whereas the Source understands a pattern and works against it. Like a nutritive substance surrounding a growing embryo, the Source feeds upon its enclosure. My point is its incompleteness.

Various sources force us to assume that the so-called earliest Source leaves no trace but an elaboration. It was simple for it to give unpleasant orders, yet one can no longer simply speculate or reason about the Source, for the very framework within which traditional speculation and reasoning proceeds has been shaken to its foundation.

Clearly one does the Source the greatest service by quoting as much as space allows. So much so that from one day to the next, while outside the weather remains consistent in its uncertainties, we might begin to build within it a storm.

2011

▪

On what account are we not condemned to servitude? The Source was never a system of imperial exploitation, nor was it full of sentiments of unity, brotherhood, and common interests. If it were your choreographer, then it would devise dances to make you appear a virtuoso dodging dead horses lining the road, though still bound by the rules of deportment. Is it really a matter of indifference to the people in the marketplace? Each account confirms every other account. As we all exhibit the kind of behavior predicted by the Source, the next step is to ask whether this behavior has its origins elsewhere. Can we respond to silence in the presence of speech by saying: the Source has no beginning?

Do we not have terms in the English tongue to define and shade pastel painted rows of block-and-plaster houses scattered haphazardly across forlorn landscapes? Do our decision-making mechanisms, as a whole, not resemble a herd of deer or a covey of quail after the hunting season?

There are days when I find myself longing to be near a river or lake, to let the familiar argument of analogy break down. This is not an ethical view of life. I've told at least one person everything I am aware of that I've done or that's been done to me. Thus, one emerges from the blind alleys and pitfalls of the Source, tasting an orange or touching a velvet cloth or listening to Mozart.

2011

Joshua Marie Wilkinson

b. 1977

Joshua Marie Wilkinson was born and grew up in Seattle's Haller Lake neighborhood and attended Western Washington University's Woodring College of Education and the M.F.A. program at the University of Arizona. He has an M.A. in film studies from University College Dublin and a Ph.D. in English from the University of Denver.

Wilkinson's books include *Suspension of Secret in Abandoned Rooms* (2005); *Lug Your Careless Body out of the Careful Dusk: A Poem in Fragments* (Iowa Poetry Prize, 2006); *Figures for a Darkroom Voice* (2008), a collaborative work with Noah Eli Gordon and the visual artist Noah Saterstrom; *The Book of Whispering in the Projection Booth* (Tupelo Prize, 2009); and *Selenography* (2010), with Polaroids by Tim Rutili. *Selenography* is the first book of a pentalogy, *No Volta*, the second book of which, *Swamp Isthmus*, will appear in 2013.

Wilkinson favors the long poem, which he organizes serially and in sequences. He also likes to establish a dialogue between his book-length writing project and the work of an artist. His second book, *Lug Your Careless Body*, is for instance an "ekphrastic conversation" with the paintings of Susan Rothenberg. On his work in general, Wilkinson comments: "I'm a huge Basil Bunting fan. And Hart Crane's lyricism is entrancing to me. I love, too, the bluntness of somebody like Oppen, where the fluidity is always thwarted. . . . I love friction and interruption and collage more than an overarching fluidity, I suppose."[1]

"I like befuddlement," Wilkinson declared in another interview, "I like a quagmire, but I like a seduction, too. It's easy as hell to be vague—and thus adopt a pseudo-philosophical stance—in a poem."[2] Like many of his generation, he is wary of the well-made poem: "There's so much clunk and awkward (lovely, arresting) phrasing in Dickinson that it's just stupefying. . . . I think this is why Spicer is so startling, and Guest too."[3]

Wilkinson is coeditor of *12 × 12: Conversations in 21st-Century Poetry and Poetics* (2009) and editor of *Poets on Teaching: A Sourcebook*, featuring ninety-nine short essays on the art of teaching (2010). He founded a "poem-film" journal, *Rabbit Light Movies*; the publishing enterprise Letter Machine Editions (with Noah Eli Gordon); and a monthly online journal of poetics, *Evening Will Come*.

Wilkinson teaches at the University of Arizona.

1. "Mike Young Interviews Joshua Marie Wilkinson," Studio One Reading Series blog, Monday February 22, 2010, http://studioonereadingseries.blogspot.com/2010/02/mike-young-interviews-joshua-marie.html.   2. Peter Moyseanko, "Literature: Joshua Marie Wilkinson: Part I," BOMBLOG, August 30, 2010, http://bombsite.com/issues/1000/articles/4470.   3. The same.

Wolf Dust

the woods pulled on your
sleeve

& the bathtub water went
black your

little brother's
curtain wrapped
around your other little
brother's quiet

what light comes
between
your nightgown & you?

*

an owl breaks the
fold a cut tree spills

a soft crutch
hits

this dust
a freezer stocked
with I

happened
to myself in these very woods

*

carry your
own dancing shoes

your tin suitcase filled
with bricks & wolf dust

you are coming
through the phone wires
& ice at once

little
hunter in the chimney of

your throat

birds caught in
blocks of ice

*

blind colt
new bees a spun
snaky light

& laughter I know
the way
you

hold pencils to
a settling this
is the

hidden warning this
is

opened dusk
thwarting your
swallows

*

a fresh field
underfoot held
together between the cold radio

killer wasps
easing into the
doorjamb

a proving swamp circle of
blue flies & the reeds
chafe

toads bolster us it
is
again
nightfall

*

a bit
of speech scored

into the bathroom
door revolved stars dropped
us in

& we are forever here a child
spoke through

the dressmaker's dummy's cupped hand
to tell

us
again which way not
to go

a storm like
thousands of locusts
listening

*

not cigarettes
enough to trade us
through the

dead men
put their mouths on
the backs of

our hands little

airport slowly sank
into the

swamp with the rest
of the zoo

& its
city

a thin envelope
quicklime
goofer dust a

red telephone box
& coarse powder
for taking
the meanest layer of
skin off our backs

*

cuttings
shoveled

up into a fortress
hiding behind where
the dead
woman bakes lemon
& mincemeat pies
we live inside the

seam of the wind the
breaker's froth the
swarm's
sleepy landing

a pond divided

by an upside-down moon more
animals learn to hollow
grow wary

& withhold their math from us

*

yields memory's
search for a dancehall
with huge
aluminum ceilings
& an old water closet

a convex mirror in
the great entry
ghosts in the red
liquor

we are
reared
in the

sheepish sounds
of christmas foot-traffic
our breathing split like
a peach

*

we are falling sparrow-aligned
useless against

even the slenderest breeze or apologies
we are built without tools or

recording devices without the
fat whoosh of the
woodchopper

without legends
of the legendary child thieves

there was

almost nothing before us or at
our feet yet

this spinning black set negates us
names us revokes

our calls
made
in the yard the light is a foil &

it stomps
us out like a wick until our
eavesdropping is what
stuns us
awake

2010

Ben Lerner
b. 1979

Ben Lerner was born and raised in Topeka, Kansas. At Brown University, he earned a B.A. in political theory and an M.F.A. in poetry.

His first book, *The Lichtenberg Figures* (2004), a cycle of fifty-two sonnets, was awarded the Hayden Carruth Prize and named by *Library Journal* as one of the year's best books of poetry. When the book was published in a German translation, it received the Preis der Stadt Münster für internationale Poesie for 2011.

Lerner's second book, *Angle of Yaw* (2006), was written in Spain on a Fulbright Scholarship and was later named a finalist for the National Book Award. His third poetry volume, *Mean Free Path*, was published in 2010. His novel, *Leaving the Atocha Station* (2011), was named one of the best books of the year by *The Guardian* and *The New Statesman.*

In *The Lichtenberg Figures,* Lerner's quick intelligence and humor overlie a cutting critique of contemporary culture: "We must retract our offerings burnt as they are. / We must recall our lines of verse like faulty tires. / We must flay the curatoriat, invest our sackcloth, // And enter the academy single file."[1] Like Michael Palmer, he has a fondness for parallel structure as a way of both steadying and unsteadying the discourse. A mysterious character named Orlando Duran comes and goes throughout the sequence, as if drawn from a novel: "I beat Orlando Duran with a ratchet until he bled from his eye."

Asked about the relationship of the text to the body in his writing, Lerner responded, "It's a violent relationship. Violence is, after all, our global condition. I have a tendency to write in and about the violence of language, the language of violence. I don't just mean that when bodies appear in my poems they tend to come to blows. I mean that I consider the poem a space in which rhetorical forms can be opposed or juxtaposed in a manner that makes their violence manifest."[2]

The publisher's description of *Mean Free Path* is apt: "In physics, the 'mean free path' of a particle is the average distance it travels before colliding with another particle. The poems in Ben Lerner's third collection are full of discrete collisions—stutters, repetitions, fragments, recombinations—that track how language breaks up or changes course under the emotional pressures of the utterance." In "The Doppler Elegies" sequence especially, broken and discontinued sentences suggest use of the cut-up method.

Poetry editor for the British publication *Critical Quarterly,* Lerner has taught at California College for the Arts and the University of Pittsburgh. In 2010, he joined the faculty of the M.F.A. program at Brooklyn College.

1. *The Lichtenberg Figures,* Port Townsend, WA, 2004, p. 5.   2. Ben Lerner interviewed by Lance Phillips, Here Comes Everybody website, http://herecomeseverybody.blogspot.com/2005/03/ben-lerner-is-from-topeka-kansas.html.

FROM *The Lichtenberg Figures*

■

The dark collects our empties, empties our ashtrays.
Did you mean "this could go on forever" in a good way?
Up in the fragrant rafters, moths seek out a finer dust.
Please feel free to cue or cut

the lights. Along the order of magnitudes, a glyph,
portable, narrow—Damn. I've lost it. But its shadow. Cast
in the long run. As the dark touches us up.
Earlier you asked if I would enter the data like a room, well,

either the sun has begun to burn
its manuscripts or I'm an idiot, an idiot
with my eleven semiprecious rings. Real snow
on the stage. Fake blood on the snow. Could this go

on forever in a good way? A brain left lace from age or lightning.
The chicken is a little dry and/or you've ruined my life.

2004

■

I had meant to apologize in advance.
I had meant to jettison all dogmatism in theory and all sclerosis in organization.
I had meant to place my hand in a position to receive the sun.
I imagined such a gesture would amount to batter, battery. A cookie

is not the only substance that receives the shape
of the instrument with which it's cut. The man-child tucks
a flare gun into his sweatpants and sets out
for a bench of great beauty and peacefulness.

Like the girl my neighbors sent to Catholic school, tonight
the moon lies down with any boy who talks of leaving town.
My cowardice may or may not have a concrete economic foundation.
I beat Orlando Duran with a ratchet till he bled from his eye.

I like it when you cut the crust off my sandwiches.
The name of our state flower changes as it dries.

2004

▪

In my day, we knew how to drown plausibly,
to renounce the body's seven claims to buoyancy. In my day,
our fragrances had agency, our exhausted clocks complained so beautifully
that cause began to shed its calories

like sparks. With great ostentation, I began to bald. With great ostentation,
I built a small door in my door for dogs. In my day,
we were reasonable men. Even you women and children
were reasonable men. And there was the promise of pleasure in every question
we postponed. Like a blouse, the most elegant crimes were left undone.

Now I am the only one who knows
the story of the baleful forms
our valences assumed in winter light. My people, are you not

horrified of how these verbs decline—
their great ostentation, their doors of different sizes?

2004

FROM The Doppler Elegies

▪

I want to finish the book in time
        period. Confused bees
In a perfect world
a willow-effect. Rain on the recording
Fine with this particular form
of late everything, a spherical
        break of colored stars
a voice described as torn in places
        Why am I always

asleep in your poems
      Soft static falling through
The life we've chosen
from a drop-down menu
of available drives. Look at me
Ben, when am I
      This isn't my voice
At such-and-such smooth rate, the lines
      Stream at night

and love. Why not speak of it
      as all work now
is late work. Leafage, fountain, cloud
into whose sunlit depths
I'm quoting. Is there a place for this
she cut her hair
      She held it toward me
In your long dream
      money changes hands

▪

I'm worried about a friend
      among panicles of spent
flowers. I'm on the phone
There's an argument here regarding
Cathedral windows thicker at the base
It does not concern you
      flowing glass. Can we talk
about the drinking
      They call them smoke trees

I'm pretty much dead
      by any measure
already. When we were kids, the leaves
but that's a story, fallen or reflected
obscured the well. I cut this
In the dream, they are always
      younger. Ari woke me
You were screaming
      Everything is so

easy for you
>You mean was
so easy, like walking slowly
Out of the photo, even those
They are blooming early. I mean that
literally. You can see it from space
>he took. Can we talk
about the drinking
>Sometime in May

▪

The passengers are asked to clap
>It was always the same
window in his poems
for the two soldiers. We were delayed
In every seat, a tiny screen
A tiny bottle. The same traffic
>High up in the trees, small
rain. He held the subject
>constant. Now I

get it. I looked out
>over Denver, but could see
only our reflection. Dim
the cabin lights. Robert is dead
Articles may have shifted
I didn't know him. Why am I
>clapping. We are beginning
our final descent into
>A voice described as torn

On the recording, I could hear
>the hesitation
A certain courage. I can't explain
as music. We could watch
our own plane crash. We would be
Our men and women
>permitted to call down
in uniform. When I heard him live
>it was lost on me

▪

A flowering no one attends
         The enterprise known
variously as waking, April, or
Bats are disappearing like
color into function. I wanted to open
In a new window
         the eyes of a friend
by force if necessary. Amber light
         is a useless phrase

but will have to do
         what painting did
Dense smoke from the burning wells
for our parents. Ben
there is a man at the door who says
I've made small changes
         he found your notebook
throughout in red. The recurring dream
         contrived in places

Of waning significance
         it resembles the hand
after a difficult passage
opening, a key word in the early
Blue of rippled glass
atonal circles. The phased us out
         across the backward capitals
like paper money
         Or is that two words

▪

They are passing quickly, those
         houses I wanted to
speak in. Empty sets
Among my friends, there is a fight about
The important questions

cannot arise, so those must be hills
        where the famous
winter. I am familiar with the dream
        Windmills enlarge

experience, killing birds
        but I have already used
dream too often in my book
of relevance. Nothing can be predicated
Along the vanishing coast
tonight. You'll have to wait until
        remnants of small fires
the eye can pull new features from
        The stars

eat here. There is a private room
        Are you concerned
about foreign energy
In your work, I sense a certain
distance, like a radio left on
Across the water, you can see
        the new construction going up
in glass. The electric cars
        unmanned

▪

Somewhere in this book I broke
        There is a passage
with a friend. I regret it now
lifted verbatim from
Then began again, my focus on
moving the lips, failures in
        The fuselage glows red against
rinsed skies. Rehearsing sleep
        I think of him from time

in a competitive field,
        facedown, a familiar scene
composed entirely of stills

to time. It's hard to believe
When he calls, I pretend
he's gone. He was letting himself go
     I'm on the other line
in a cluster of eight poems
     all winter. The tenses disagreed

for Ari. Sorry if I've seemed
     distant, it's been a difficult
period, striking as many keys
with the flat of the hand
as possible, then leaning the head
against the window, unable to recall
     April, like overheard speech
at the time of writing
     soaked into its length

2010

POETICS

Charles Olson ──────────────────────

Projective   Verse

(projectile   (percussive   (prospective

vs.

The NON-Projective

(or what a French critic calls "closed" verse, that verse which print bred and which is pretty much what we have had, in English & American, and have still got, despite the work of Pound & Williams:

it led Keats, already a hundred years ago, to see it (Wordsworth's, Milton's) in the light of "the Egotistical Sublime"; and it persists, at this latter day, as what you might call the private-soul-at-any-public-wall)

Verse now, 1950, if it is to go ahead, if it is to be of *essential* use, must, I take it, catch up and put into itself certain laws and possibilities of the breath, of the breathing of the man who writes as well as of his listenings. (The revolution of the ear, 1910, the trochee's heave, asks it of the younger poets.)

I want to do two things: first, try to show what projective or OPEN verse is, what it involves, in its act of composition, how, in distinction from the nonprojective, it is accomplished; and II, suggest a few ideas about what stance toward reality brings such verse into being, what that stance does, both to the poet and to his reader. (The stance involves, for example, a change beyond, and larger than, the technical, and may, the way things look, lead to new poetics and to new concepts from which some sort of drama, say, or of epic, perhaps, may emerge.)

FROM *Charles Olson: Selected Writings*, 1966. First published in *Poetry New York*, No. 3, 1950.

I

First, some simplicities that a man learns, if he works in OPEN, or what can also be called COMPOSITION BY FIELD, as opposed to inherited line, stanza, over-all form, what is the "old" base of the non-projective.

(1) the *kinetics* of the thing. A poem is energy transferred from where the poet got it (he will have some several causations), by way of the poem itself to, all the way over to, the reader. Okay. Then the poem itself must, at all points, be a high energy-construct and, at all points, an energy-discharge. So: how is the poet to accomplish same energy, how is he, what is the process by which a poet gets in, at all points energy at least the equivalent of the energy which propelled him in the first place, yet an energy which is peculiar to verse alone and which will be, obviously, also different from the energy which the reader, because he is a third term, will take away?

This is the problem which any poet who departs from closed form is specially confronted by. And it involves a whole series of new recognitions. From the moment he ventures into FIELD COMPOSITION—put himself in the open—he can go by no track other than the one the poem under hand declares, for itself. Thus he has to behave, and be, instant by instant, aware of some several forces just now beginning to be examined. (It is much more, for example, this push, than simply such a one as Pound put, so wisely, to get us started: "the musical phrase," go by it, boys, rather than by, the metronome.)

(2) is the *principle,* the law which presides conspicuously over such composition, and, when obeyed, is the reason why a projective poem can come into being. It is this: FORM IS NEVER MORE THAN AN EXTENSION OF CONTENT. (Or so it got phrased by one, R. Creeley, and it makes absolute sense to me, with this possible corollary, that right form, in any given poem, is the only and exclusively possible extension of content under hand.) There it is, brothers, sitting there, for USE.

Now (3) the *process* of the thing, how the principle can be made so to shape the energies that the form is accomplished. And I think it can be boiled down to one statement (first pounded into my head by Edward Dahlberg). ONE PERCEPTION MUST IMMEDIATELY AND DIRECTLY LEAD TO A FURTHER PERCEPTION. It means exactly what it says, is a matter of, at *all* points (even, I should say, of our management of daily reality as of the daily work) get on with it, keep moving, keep in, speed, the nerves, their speed, the perceptions, theirs, the acts, the split second acts, the whole business, keep it moving as fast as you can, citizen. And if you also set up as a poet, USE USE USE the process at all points in any given poem always, always one perception must must must MOVE, INSTANTER, ON ANOTHER!

So there we are, fast, there's the dogma. And its excuse, its usableness, in practice. Which gets us, it ought to get us, inside the machinery now, 1950, of how projective verse is made.

If I hammer, if I recall in, and keep calling in, the breath, the breathing as distinguished from the hearing, it is for cause, it is to insist upon a part that breath plays in verse which has not (due, I think, to the smothering of the power of the line by too set a concept of foot) has not been sufficiently observed or practiced, but which has to be if verse is to advance to its proper force and place in the day, now, and ahead. I take it that PROJECTIVE VERSE teaches, is, this lesson, that that verse will only do in which a poet manages to register both the acquisitions of his ear *and* the pressures of his breath.

Let's start from the smallest particle of all, the syllable. It is the king and pin of versification, what rules and holds together the lines, the larger forms, of a poem. I would suggest that verse here and in England dropped this secret from the late Elizabethans to Ezra Pound, lost it, in the sweetness of meter and rime, in a honey-head. (The syllable is one way to distinguish the original success of blank verse, and its falling off, with Milton.)

It is by their syllables that words juxtapose in beauty, by these particles of sound as clearly as by the sense of the words which they compose. In any given instance, because there is a choice of words, the choice, if a man is in there, will be, spontaneously, the obedience of his ear to the syllables. The fineness, and the practice, lie here, at the minimum and source of speech.

> O western wynd, when wilt thou blow
> And the small rain down shall rain
> O Christ that my love were in my arms
> And I in my bed again

It would do no harm, as an act of correction to both prose and verse as now written, if both rime and meter, and, in the quantity words, both sense and sound, were less in the forefront of the mind than the syllable, if the syllable, that fine creature, were more allowed to lead the harmony on. With this warning, to those who would try: to step back here to this place of the elements and minims of language, is to engage speech where it is least careless—and least logical. Listening for the syllables must be so constant and so scrupulous, the exaction must be so complete, that the assurance of the ear is purchased at the highest—40 hours a day—price. For from the root out, from all over the place, the syllable comes, the figures of, the dance:

> "Is" comes from the Aryan root, *as*, to breathe. The English "not" equals
> the Sanscrit *na*, which may come from the root *na,* to be lost, to perish.
> "Be" is from *bhu*, to grow.

I say the syllable, king, and that it is spontaneous, this way: the ear, the ear which has collected, which has listened, the ear, which is so close to the mind that it is the mind's, that it has the mind's speed . . .

it is close, another way: the mind is brother to this sister and is, because it is so close, is the drying force, the incest, the sharpener . . .

it is from the union of the mind and the ear that the syllable is born.

But the syllable is only the first child of the incest of verse (always, that Egyptian thing, it produces twins!). The other child is the LINE. And together, these two, the syllable *and* the line, they make a poem, they make that thing, the—what shall we call it, the Boss of all, the "Single Intelligence." And the line comes (I swear it) from the breath, from the breathing of the man who writes, at the moment that he writes, and thus is, it is here that, the daily work, the WORK, gets in, for only he, the man who writes, can declare, at every moment, the line its metric and its ending—where its breathing, shall come to, termination.

The trouble with most work, to my taking, since the breaking away from traditional lines and stanzas, and from such wholes as, say, Chaucer's *Troilus* or S's *Lear,* is: contemporary workers go lazy RIGHT HERE WHERE THE LINE IS BORN.

Let me put it baldly: The two halves are:

the HEAD, by way of the EAR, to the SYLLABLE

the HEART, by way of the BREATH, to the LINE

And the joker? that it is in the 1st half of the proposition that, in composing, one lets-it-rip; and that it is in the 2nd half, surprise, it is the LINE that's the baby that gets, as the poem is getting made, the attention, the control, that it is right here, in the line, that the shaping takes place, each moment of the going.

I am dogmatic, that the head shows in the syllable. The dance of the intellect is there, among them, prose or verse. Consider the best minds you know in this here business: where does the head show, is it not, precise, here, in the swift currents of the syllable? can't you tell a brain when you see what it does, just there? It is true, what the master says he picked up from Confusion: all the thots men are capable of can be entered on the back of a postage stamp. So, is it not the PLAY of a mind we are after, is not that that shows whether a mind is there at all?

And the threshing floor for the dance? Is it anything but the LINE? And when the line has, is, a deadness, is it not a heart which has gone lazy, is it not, suddenly, slow things, similes, say, adjectives, or such, that we are bored by?

For there is a whole flock of rhetorical devices which have now to be brought under a new bead, now that we sight with the line. Simile is only one bird who comes down, too easily. The descriptive functions generally have to be watched, every second, in projective verse, because of their easiness, and thus their drain on the energy which composition by field allows into a poem. *Any* slackness takes off attention, that crucial thing, from the job in hand, from the *push* of the line under hand at the moment, under the reader's eye, in his moment. Observation of any kind is, like argument in prose, properly previous to the act of the poem, and, if allowed in, must be so juxtaposed, apposed, set in, that it does not, for an instant, sap the going energy of the content toward its form.

It comes to this, this whole aspect of the newer problems. (We now enter, actually, the large area of the whole poem, into the FIELD, if you like, where all the syllables and all the lines must be managed in their relations to each other.) It is a matter, finally, of OBJECTS, what they are, what they are inside a poem, how they got there, and, once there, how they are to be used. This is something I want to get to in another way in Part II, but, for the moment, let me indicate this, that every element in an open poem (the syllable, the line, as well as the image, the sound, the sense) must be taken up as participants in the kinetic of the poem just as solidly as we are accustomed to take what we call the objects of reality; and that these elements are to be seen as creating the tensions of a poem just as totally as do those other objects create what we know as the world.

The objects which occur at every given moment of composition (of recognition, we can call it) are, can be, must be treated exactly as they do occur therein and not by any ideas or preconceptions from outside the poem, must be handled as a series of objects in field in such a way that a series of tensions (which they also are) are made to *hold,* and to hold exactly inside the content and the context of the poem which has forced itself, through the poet and them, into being.

Because breath allows *all* the speech-force of language back in (speech is the "solid" of verse, is the secret of a poem's energy), because, now, a poem has, by speech, solidity, everything in it can now be treated as solids, objects, things: and, though insisting upon the absolute difference of the reality of verse from that other dispersed and distributed thing, yet each of these elements of a poem can be allowed to have the play of their separate energies and can be allowed, once the poem is well composed, to keep, as those other objects do, their proper confusions.

Which brings us up, immediately, bang, against tenses, in fact against syntax, in fact against grammar generally, that is, as we have inherited it. Do not tenses, must they not also be kicked around anew, in order that time, that other governing absolute, may be kept, as must the space-tensions of a poem, immediate, contemporary to the acting-on-you of the poem? I would argue that here, too, the LAW OF THE LINE, which projective verse creates, must be hewn to, obeyed, and that the conventions which logic has forced on syntax must be broken open as quietly as must the too set feet of the old line. But an analysis of how far a new poet can stretch the very conventions on which communication by language rests, is too big for these notes, which are meant, I hope it is obvious, merely to get things started.

Let me just throw in this. It is my impression that *all* parts of speech suddenly, in composition by field, are fresh for both sound and percussive use, spring up like unknown, unnamed vegetables in the patch, when you work it, come spring. Now take Hart Crane. What strikes me in him is the singleness of the push to the nominative, his push along that one arc of freshness, the attempt to get back to word as handle. (If logos is word as thought, what is word as noun, as, pass me that, as Newman Shea used to ask, at the galley table, put a jib on the blood, will ya.) But there is a loss in Crane of what Fenollosa is so right about, in syntax, the sentence as first act of nature, as lightning, as passage of force from subject to object, quick, in this case, from Hart to me, in every case, from me to you, the VERB, between two nouns. Does not Hart miss the advantages, by such an isolated push, miss the point of the whole front of syllable, line, field, and what happened to all language, and to the poem, as a result?

I return you now to London, to beginnings, to the syllable, for the pleasures of it, to intermit:

> If music be the food of love, play on,
> give me excess of it, that, surfeiting,
> the appetite may sicken, and so die.
> That strain again. It had a dying fall,
> o, it came over my ear like the sweet sound
> that breathes upon a bank of violets,
> stealing and giving odour.

What we have suffered from, is manuscript, press, the removal of verse from its producer and its reproducer, the voice, a removal by one, by two removes from its place of origin *and* its destination. For the breath has a double meaning which latin had not yet lost.

The irony is, from the machine has come one gain not yet sufficiently observed or used, but which leads directly on toward projective verse and its consequences. It is the advantage of the typewriter that, due to its rigidity and its space precisions, it can, for a poet, indicate exactly the breath, the pauses, the suspensions even of syllables, the juxtapositions even of parts of phrases, which he intends. For the first time the poet has the stave and the bar a musician has had. For the first time he can, without the convention of rime and meter, record the listening he has done to his own speech and by that one act indicate how he would want any reader, silently or otherwise, to voice his work.

It is time we picked the fruits of the experiments of Cummings, Pound, Williams, each of whom has, after his way already used the machine as a scoring to his composing, as a script to its vocalization. It is now only a matter of the recognition of the conventions of composition by field for us to bring into being an open verse as formal as the closed with all its traditional advantages.

If a contemporary poet leaves a space as long as the phrase before it, he means that space to be held, by the breath, an equal length of time. If he suspends a word or syllable at the end of a line (this was most Cummings' addition) he means that time to pass that it takes the eye—that hair of time suspended—to pick up the next line. If he wishes a pause so light it hardly separates the words, yet does not want a comma—which is an interruption of the meaning rather than the sounding of the line—follow him when he uses a symbol the typewriter has ready to hand.

> "What does not change / is the will to change"

Observe him, when he takes advantage of the machine's multiple margins, to juxtapose:

> "Sd he:
>   to dream takes no effort
>   to think is easy
>   to act is more difficult
>
>   but for a man to act after he has taken thought, this!
> is the most difficult thing of all"

Each of these lines is a progressing of both the meaning and the breathing forward, and then a backing up, without a progress or any kind of movement outside the unit of time local to the idea.

There is more to be said in order that this convention be recognized, especially in order that the revolution out of which it came may be so forwarded that work will get published to offset the reaction now afoot to return verse to inherited forms of cadence and rime. But what I want to emphasize here, by this emphasis on the typewriter as the personal and instantaneous recorder of the poet's work, is the already projective nature of verse as the sons of Pound and Williams are practicing it. Already they are composing as though verse was to have the reading its writing involved, as though not the eye but the ear was to be its measurer, as though the intervals of its composition could be so carefully put down as to be precisely the intervals of its registration. For the ear, which once had the burden of memory to quicken it (rime & regular cadence were its aids and have merely lived on in print after the oral necessities were ended) can now again, that the poet has his means, be the threshold of projective verse.

II

Which gets us to what I promised, the degree to which the projective involves a stance toward reality outside a poem as well as a new stance towards the reality of a poem itself. It is a matter of content, the content of Homer or of Euripides or of Seami as distinct from that which I might call the more "literary" masters. From the moment the projective purpose of the act of verse is recognized, the content does—it will—change. If the beginning and the end is breath, voice in its largest sense, then the material of verse shifts. It has to. It starts with the composer. The dimension of his line itself changes, not to speak of the change in his conceiving, of the matter he will turn to, of the scale in which he imagines that matter's use. I myself would pose the difference by a physical image. It is no accident that Pound and Williams both were involved variously in a movement which got called "objectivism." But that word was then used in some sort of a necessary quarrel, I take it, with "subjectivism." It is now too late to be bothered with the latter. It has excellently done itself to death, even though we are all caught in its dying. What seems to me a more valid formulation for present use is "objectism," a word to be taken to stand for the kind of relation of man to experience which a poet might state as the necessity of a line or a work to be as wood is, to be as clean as wood is as it issues from the hand of nature, to be shaped as wood can be when a man has had his hand to it. Objectism is the getting rid of the lyrical interference of the individual as ego, of the "subject" and his soul, that peculiar presumption by which western man has interposed himself between what he is as a creature of nature (with certain instructions to carry out) and those other creations of nature which we may, with no derogation, call objects. For a man is himself an object, whatever he may take to be his advantages, the more likely to recognize himself as such the greater his advantages, particularly at that moment that he achieves an humilitas sufficient to make him of use.

It comes to this: the use of a man, by himself and thus by others, lies in how he conceives his relation to nature, that force to which he owes his somewhat small existence. If he sprawl, he shall find little to sing but himself, and shall sing, nature has such paradoxical ways, by way of artificial forms outside himself. But if he stays inside himself, if he is contained within his nature as he is participant in the larger force, he will be able to listen, and his hearing through himself will give him secrets objects share. And by an inverse law his shapes will make their own way. It is in this sense that the projective act, which is the artist's act in the larger field of objects, leads to dimensions larger than the man. For a man's problem, the moment he takes speech up in all its fullness, is to give his work his seriousness, a seriousness sufficient to cause the thing he makes to try to take its place alongside the things of nature. This is not easy. Nature works from reverence, even in her destructions (species go down with a crash). But breath is man's special qualification as animal. Sound is a dimension he has extended. Language is one of his proudest acts. And when a poet rests in these as they are in himself (in his physiology, if you like, but the life in him, for all that) then he, if he chooses to speak from these roots, works in that area where nature has given him size, projective size.

It is projective size that the play, *The Trojan Women*, possesses, for it is able to stand, is it not, as its people do, beside the Aegean—and neither Andromache or the sea suffer diminution. In a less "heroic" but equally "natural" dimension Seami causes the Fisherman and the Angel to stand clear in *Hagoromo*. And Homer, who is such an unexamined cliche that I do not think I need to press home in what scale Nausicaa's girls wash their clothes.

Such works, I should argue—and I use them simply because their equivalents are yet to be done—could not issue from men who conceived verse without the full relevance of human voice, without reference to where lines come from, in the individual who writes. Nor do I think it accident that, at this end point of the argument, I should use, for examples, two dramatists and an epic poet. For I would hazard the guess that, if projective verse is practiced long enough, is driven ahead hard enough along the course I think it dictates, verse again can carry much larger material than it has carried in our language since the Elizabethans. But it can't be jumped. We are only at its beginnings, and if I think that the *Cantos* make more "dramatic" sense than do the plays of Mr. Eliot, it is not because I think they have solved the problem but because the methodology of the verse in them points a way by which, one day, the problem of larger content and of larger forms may be solved. Eliot is, in fact, a proof of a present danger, of "too easy" a going on the practice of verse as it has been, rather than as it must be, practiced. There is no question, for example, that Eliot's line, from "Prufrock" on down, has speech-force, is "dramatic," is, in fact, one of the most notable lines since Dryden. I suppose it stemmed immediately to him from Browning, as did so many of Pound's early things. In any case Eliot's line has obvious relations backward to the Elizabethans, especially to the soliloquy. Yet O. M. Eliot is *not* projective. It could even be argued (and I say this carefully, as I have said all things about the non-projective, having considered how each of us must save himself after his own fashion and how much, for that matter, each of us owes to the non-projective, and will continue to owe, as both go alongside each other) but it could be argued that it is because Eliot has stayed inside the non-projective that he fails as a dramatist—that his root is the mind alone, and a scholastic mind at that (no high *intelletto* despite his apparent clarities)—and that, in his listenings he has stayed there where the ear and the mind are, has only gone from his fine ear outward rather than, as I say a projective poet will, down through the workings of his own throat to that place where breath comes from, where breath has its beginnings, where drama has to come from, where, the coincidence is, all act springs.

Barbara Guest

A Reason for Poetics

For all his purple, the purple bird must have
Notes for his comfort that he may repeat
Through the gross tedium of being rare.
—Wallace Stevens

The Infancy of Poetics

The poem begins in silence.

Poetic Codes

A pull in both directions between the physical reality of place and the metaphysics of space. This pull will build up a tension within the poem giving a view of the poem from both the interior and the exterior.

Ideally a poem will be both mysterious (incunabula, driftwood of the unconscious), and organic (secular) at the same time. If the tension becomes irregular, like a heartbeat, then a series of questions enters the poem. What is now happening? What does the poem, itself, consider to be its probabilities? The poem needs to take care not to flounder, or become rigid, or to come to such a halt the reader hangs over a sudden cliff. It is noticeable that a poem has a secret grip of its own, separate from its creator.

The poem is quite willing to forget its begetter and take off in its own direction. It likes to be known as spontaneous. Some poets then become firm and send out admonitory hints. Others become anxious. A few become pleased with the trickster and want to adopt it. There are moments when mistaken imageries can lead in interesting directions. Poets even try to charm the poem. We have all taken these positions.

The conflict between a poet and the poem creates an atmosphere of mystery. When this mystery is penetrated, when the dark reaches of the poem succumb and shine with a clarity projected by the mental lamp of the reader, then an experience called *illumination* takes place. This is the most beautiful experience literature can present us with, and more precious for being extremely rare, arrived at through concentration, through meditation of the

Appeared in *Ironwood*, No. 24, 1984; Michael Cuddihy, editor.

poem, through those faculties we often associate with a religious experience, as indeed it is. The reader is converted to the poem. (Invisible magic also passes between poet and reader.)

Mystery, with its element of surprise and, better word, audacity. At once unexpected dramas have entered the poem. The search for its originating mystery now becomes an adventure. Poet and reader perform together on a highwire strung on a platform between their separated selves. Now an applause for the shared vigilance.

The usefulness of the tension set up in a poem is to arrange its dimensions. The poem stretches, looking outwardly and inwardly, thus obtaining a plasticity that the flat, the basic words—what we call the language of a poem—demands and, further, depends upon. This cannot be achieved through language alone, but arrives from tensions placed on the poem's structure: variability of meter, fleeting moods of expression, trebled sound.

Each poet owns a private language. The poet relies on the pitch within the ear. The ear is also a private affair, and so is pitch. Much poetry betrays a tin ear. There is also trouble in possessing perfect pitch, which can lead to an obsessive need to listen to it. Like ravens quothing. But this is not a common trouble. Pitch and ear are the servants of language and cannot make their living anywhere else, even by escapades. Language can lead to trouble when words are selected solely for their sound, and meaning is then forced to hurry along after, trying to catch up. Sometimes it is necessary to dispense with a word, or rather to be cautious, when it intrudes upon form.

The structure of the poem should create an embrasure inside of which language is seated in watchful docility, like the unicorn. Poems develop a terrible possessiveness toward their language because they admire the decoration of their structure.

The Poetics of Survival

Poetry sometimes develops a grayness; the light can never get in. The surface is smudgy. Cézanne was irritated by this murkiness in painting and complained "the contour eludes me."

How splendid when a poem is both prospective and introspective, obeying tensions within itself until a classic plasticity is reached.

I have little regard for poems of mine which have become votives of obsolete reactions. These poems appear to have no conscience, and worse, are passionless.

There is nothing fearsome about the chrome attic. There are more mad poets out on the lawn. And very few wear cloud trousers.

I wish the Emperor's new clothes were less a visual phenomenon and more poetry's plaintive sigh.

And then there is saving laughter. I don't mean by "laughter" what is known as "comic relief." That seems to me to be part of a philosophical argument surrounding questions such as "why did Shakespeare, or Meredith bring in such and such a character?" My laughter is bittersweet and brings us closer to irony, the mole of poetry. Irony is a coagulant of pain when the subject of the poem (the interior meaning) begins to draw blood. Robust poets, it seems to me, too seldom acknowledge this weapon against poetry's sores, the most suppurating of which is sentimentality.

Mandelstam once wrote of "sound spilling into fingers." That could be the noise of a poem when it experiences an ecstasy of recognition.

To keep the poem alive after its many varnishings.

                                                                    2003

Frank O'Hara ———————————————

Personism: A Manifesto

Everything is in the poems, but at the risk of sounding like the poor wealthy man's Allen Ginsberg I will write to you because I just heard that one of my fellow poets thinks that a poem of mine that can't be got at one reading is because I was confused too. Now, come on. I don't believe in god, so I don't have to make elaborately sounded structures. I hate Vachel Lindsay, always have, I don't even like rhythm, assonance, all that stuff. You just go on your nerve. If someone's chasing you down the street with a knife you just run, you don't turn around and shout, "Give it up! I was a track star for Mineola Prep."

That's for the writing poems part. As for their reception, suppose you're in love and someone's mistreating *(mal aimé)* you, you don't say, "Hey, you can't hurt me this way, I *care!*" you just let all the different bodies fall where they may, and they always do may after a few months. But that's not why you fell in love in the first place, just to hang onto life, so you have to take your chances and try to avoid being logical. Pain always produces logic, which is very bad for you.

I'm not saying that I don't have practically the most lofty ideas of anyone writing today, but what difference does that make? they're just ideas. The only good thing about it is that when I get lofty enough I've stopped thinking and that's when refreshment arrives.

But how can you really care if anybody gets it, or gets what it means, or if it improves them. Improves them for what? for death? Why hurry them along? Too many poets act like a middle-aged mother trying to get her kids to eat too much cooked meat, and potatoes with drippings (tears). I don't give a damn whether they eat or not. Forced feeding leads to excessive thinness (effete). Nobody should experience anything they don't need to, if they don't need poetry bully for them, I like the movies too. And after all, only Whitman and Crane and Williams, of the American poets, are better than the movies. As for measure and other technical apparatus, that's just common sense: if you're going to buy a pair of pants you want them to be tight enough so everyone will want to go to bed with you. There's nothing metaphysical about it. Unless, of course, you flatter yourself into thinking that what you're experiencing is "yearning."

FROM *The Collected Poems of Frank O'Hara*, 1972. First published in *Yugen*, No. 7, 1961, where its date of composition was given as September 3, 1959. According to critic Marjorie Perloff in *Frank O'Hara: Poet Among Painters* (1977), this essay was written in response to an essay by Allen Ginsberg, "Abstraction in Poetry," which appeared in the journal *It Is*, No. 3, Winter/Spring, 1959. O'Hara's essay also parodies Charles Olson's "Projective Verse."

Abstraction in poetry, which Allen recently commented on in *It is,* is intriguing. I think it appears mostly in the minute particulars where decision is necessary. Abstraction (in poetry, not in painting) involves personal removal by the poet. For instance, the decision involved in the choice between "the nostalgia of the infinite" and "the nostalgia *for* the infinite" defines an attitude towards degree of abstraction. The nostalgia *of* the infinite representing the greater degree of abstraction, removal, and negative capability (as in Keats and Mallarmé). Personism, a movement which I recently founded and which nobody yet knows about, interests me a great deal, being so totally opposed to this kind of abstract removal that it is verging on a true abstraction for the first time, really, in the history of poetry. Personism is to Wallace Stevens what *la poésie pure* was to Béranger. Personism has nothing to do with philosophy, it's all art. It does not have to do with personality or intimacy, far from it! But to give you a vague idea, one of its minimal aspects is to address itself to one person (other than the poet himself), thus evoking overtones of love without destroying love's life-giving vulgarity, and sustaining the poet's feelings towards the poem while preventing love from distracting him into feeling about the person. That's part of personism. It was founded by me after lunch with LeRoi Jones on August 27, 1959, a day in which I was in love with someone (not Roi, by the way, a blond). I went back to work and wrote a poem for this person. While I was writing it I was realizing that if I wanted to I could use the telephone instead of writing the poem, and so Personism was born. It's a very exciting movement which will undoubtedly have lots of adherents. It puts the poem squarely between the poet and the person, Lucky Pierre style, and the poem is correspondingly gratified. The poem is at last between two persons instead of two pages. In all modesty, I confess that it may be the death of literature as we know it. While I have certain regrets, I am still glad I got there before Alain Robbe-Grillet did. Poetry being quicker and surer than prose, it is only just that poetry finish literature off. For a time people thought that Artaud was going to accomplish this, but actually, for all their magnificence, his polemical writings are not more outside literature than Bear Mountain is outside New York State. His relation is no more astounding than Dubuffet's to painting.

What can we expect of Personism? (This is getting good, isn't it?) Everything, but we won't get it. It is too new, too vital a movement to promise anything. But it, like Africa, is on the way. The recent propagandists for technique on the one hand, and for content on the other, had better watch out.

Allen Ginsberg

Notes for *Howl and Other Poems*

By 1955 I wrote poetry adapted from prose seeds, journals, scratchings, arranged by phrasing or breath groups into little short-line patterns according to ideas of measure of American speech I'd picked up from W. C. Williams' imagist preoccupations. I suddenly turned aside in San Francisco, unemployment compensation leisure, to follow my romantic inspiration—Hebraic-Melvillian bardic breath. I thought I wouldn't write a *poem*, but just write what I wanted to without fear, let my imagination go, open secrecy, and scribble magic lines from my real mind—sum up my life—something I wouldn't be able to show anybody, write for my own soul's ear and a few other golden ears. So the first line of *Howl*, "I saw the best minds," etc. the whole first section typed out madly in one afternoon, a huge sad comedy of wild phrasing, meaningless images for the beauty of abstract poetry of mind running along making awkward combinations like Charlie Chaplin's walk, long saxophone-like chorus lines I knew Kerouac would hear the *sound* of—taking off from his own inspired prose line really a new poetry.

I depended on the word "who" to keep the beat, a base to keep measure, return to and take off from again onto another streak of invention: "who lit cigarettes in boxcars boxcars boxcars," continuing to prophesy what I really knew despite the drear consciousness of the world: "who were visionary indian angels." Have I really been attacked for this sort of joy? So the poem got serious, I went on to what my imagination believed true to Eternity (for I'd had a beatific illumination years before during which I'd heard Blake's ancient voice & saw the universe unfold in my brain), & what my memory could reconstitute of the data of celestial experience.

But how sustain a long line of poetry (lest it lapse into prosaic)? It's natural inspiration of the moment that keeps it moving, disparate thinks put down together, shorthand notations of visual imagery, juxtapositions of hydrogen juke-box—abstract haikus sustain the mystery & put iron poetry back into the line: the last line of "Sunflower Sutra" is the extreme, one stream of single word associations, summing up. Mind is shapely, Art is shapely. Meaning Mind practiced in spontaneity invents forms in its own image & gets to Last Thoughts. Loose ghosts wailing for body try to invade the bodies of living men. I hear ghostly Academics in Limbo screeching about form.

Ideally each line of *Howl* is a single breath unit. Tho in this recording it's

FROM *The New American Poetry: 1945–1960*, 1960. First published as the liner note to the recording of *Howl and Other Poems* issued in 1959 by the Fantasy record label (Fantasy 7006), where its date of composition was given as Independence Day 1959.

not pronounced so, I was exhausted at climax of 3 hour Chicago reading with Corso & Orlovsky. My breath is long—that's the Measure, one physical-mental inspiration of thought contained in the elastic of a breath. It probably bugs Williams now, but it's a natural consequence, my own heightened conversation, not cooler average-dailytalk short breath. I got to mouth more madly this way.

So these poems are a series of experiments with the formal organization of the long line. Explanations follow. I realized at the time that Whitman's form had rarely been further explored (improved on even) in the U.S. Whitman always a mountain too vast to be seen. Everybody assumes (with Pound?) (except Jeffers) that his line is a big freakish uncontrollable necessary prosaic goof. No attempt's been made to use it in the light of early XX Century organization of new speech-rhythm prosody to *build up* large organic structures.

I had an apt on Nob Hill, got high on Peyote, & saw an image of the robot skullface of Moloch in the upper stories of a big hotel glaring into my window; got high weeks later again, the Visage was still there in red smokey downtown Metropolis, I wandered down Powell Street muttering, "Moloch Moloch" all night & wrote *Howl* II nearly intact in cafeteria at foot of Drake Hotel, deep in the hellish vale. Here the long line is used as a stanza form broken within into exclamatory units punctuated by a base repetition, Moloch.

The rhythmic paradigm for Part III was conceived & half-written same day as the beginning of *Howl*, I went back later & filled it out. Part I, a lament for the Lamb in America with instances of remarkable lamblike youths; Part II names the monster of mental consciousness that preys on the Lamb; Part III a litany of affirmation of the Lamb in its glory: "O starry spangled shock of Mercy." The structure of Part III, pyramidal, with a graduated longer response to the fixed base.

A lot of these forms developed out of an extreme rhapsodic wail I once heard in a madhouse. Later I wondered if short quiet lyrical poems could be written using the long line. "Cottage in Berkeley" & "Supermarket in California" (written same day) fell in place later that year. Not purposely, I simply followed my Angel in the course of compositions.

What if I just simply wrote, in long units & broken short lines, spontaneously noting prosaic realities mixed with emotional upsurges, solitaries? "Transcription of Organ Music" (sensual data), strange writing which passes from prose to poetry & back, like the mind.

What about poem with rhythmic buildup power equal to *Howl* without use of repeated base to sustain it? "The Sunflower Sutra" (composition time 20 minutes, me at desk scribbling, Kerouac at cottage door waiting for me to finish so we could go off somewhere party) did that, it surprised me, one long Who . . .

Last, the Proem to *Kaddish* (NY 1959 work)—finally, completely free composition, the long line breaking up within itself into short staccato breath units—notations of one spontaneous phrase after another linked within the line by dashes mostly: the long line now perhaps a variable stanzaic unit, measuring groups of related ideas, marking them—a method of notation. Ending with a hymn in rhythm similar to the synagogue death lament. Passing into dactylic? says Williams? Perhaps not: at least the ear hears itself in Promethian natural measure, not in mechanical count of accent.

I used Chicago Big Table readings (Jan. 1959) of *Howl,* "Sunflower" and *Kaddish* on this record because they're the best I can find. Though the tapes were coarse. And hope the reproduction of that reading will permanently give lie to much philistine slander by the capitalist press and various brain-washed academies. And convince the Lamb. I tried recording *Howl* under better mechanical conditions in studio but the spirit wasn't in me by then. I'm not in control. The rest of the poems were recorded in June '59 Fantasy Studios in SF. "Footnote to *Howl*" may seem sick and strange, I've included it because I trust it will be heard in Heaven, though some cruel ear in U.S. may mock. Let it be raw, there is beauty. These are recorded as best I can now, though with scared love, imperfect to an angelic trumpet in mind, I quit reading in front of live audiences for while. I began in obscurity to communicate a live poetry, it's become more a trap and duty than the spontaneous ball it was first.

A word on Academies; poetry has been attacked by an ignorant & frightened bunch of bores who don't understand how it's made, & the trouble with these creeps is they wouldn't know Poetry if it came up and buggered them in broad daylight.

A word on the Politicians: my poetry is Angelical Ravings, & has nothing to do with dull materialistic vagaries about who should shoot who. The secrets of individual imagination—which are transconceptual & non-verbal—I mean unconditioned Spirit—are not for sale to this consciousness, are of no use to this world, except perhaps to make it shut its trap & listen to the music of the Spheres. Who denies the music of the spheres denies poetry, denies man, & spits on Blake, Shelley, Christ & Buddha. Meanwhile have a ball. The universe is a new flower. America will be discovered. Who wants a war against roses will have it. Fate tells big lies, & the gay Creator dances on his own body in Eternity.

Robert Creeley ─────────────────────────────

To Define

The process of definition is the intent of the poem, or is to that sense—"Peace comes of communication." Poetry stands in no need of any sympathy, or even goodwill. One acts from bottom, the root is the purpose quite beyond any kindness.

A poetry can act on this: "A poem is energy transferred from where the poet got it (he will have some several causations), by way of the poem itself to, all the way over to, the reader." One breaks the line of aesthetics, or that outcrop of a general division of knowledge. A sense of the KINETIC impels recognition of force. Force is, and therefore stays.

The means of a poetry are, perhaps, related to Pound's sense of the *increment of association;* usage coheres value. Tradition is an aspect of what anyone is now thinking—not what someone once thought. We make with what we have, and in this way anything is worth looking at. A tradition becomes inept when it blocks the necessary conclusion; it says we have felt nothing, it implies others have felt more.

A poetry denies its end in any *descriptive* act, I mean any act which leaves the attention outside the poem. Our anger cannot exist usefully without its objects, but a description of them is also a perpetuation. There is that confusion—one wants the thing to act on, and yet hates it. *Description* does nothing, it includes the objects—it neither hates nor loves.

If one can junk these things, of the content which relates only to denial, the negative, the impact of dissolution—act otherwise, on other things. There is no country. Speech is an assertion of one man, by one man. "Therefore each speech having its own character the poetry it engenders will be peculiar to that speech also in its own intrinsic form."

FROM *The Collected Essays of Robert Creeley*, 1989. First published in *Nine American Poets*, Liverpool, 1953.

Form

The Whip

I spent a night turning in bed,
my love was a feather, a flat

sleeping thing. She was
very white

and quiet, and above us on
the roof, there was another woman I

also loved, had
addressed myself to in

a fit she
returned. That

encompasses it. But now I was
lonely, I yelled,

but what is that? Ugh,
she said, beside me, she put

her hand on
my back, for which act

I think to say this
wrongly.

Form has such a diversity of associations and it seems obvious enough that it would have—like *like*. Like a girl of my generation used to get a formal for the big dance, or else it could be someone's formalizing the situation, which was a little more serious. Form a circle, etc.

It was something one intended, clearly, that came of defined terms. But in what respect, of course, made a great difference. As advice for editing a magazine, Pound wrote, "Verse consists of a constant and a variant . . ." His

FROM *The Collected Essays of Robert Creeley*, 1989. First published in *Ecstatic Occasions, Expedient Forms*, 1987, in which poets were asked to comment on the formal decisions that went into the making of one of their poems. "The Whip," the poem Creeley chose for comment, was first published in *For Love: Poems, 1950–1960*, 1962.

point was that any element might be made the stable, recurrent event, and that any other might be let to go "hog wild," as he put it, and such a form could prove "a center around which, not a box within which, every item . . ."

Pound was of great use to me as a young writer, as were also Williams and Stevens. I recall the latter's saying there were those who thought of form as a variant of plastic shape. Pound's point was that poetry is a form cut in time as sculpture is a form cut in space. Williams' introduction to *The Wedge* (1944) I took as absolute credo.

"The Whip" was written in the middle fifties, and now reading it I can vividly remember the bleak confusion from which it moves emotionally. There is a parallel, a story called "The Musicians," and if one wants to know more of the implied narrative of the poem, it's in this sad story. The title is to the point, because it is music, specifically jazz, that informs the poem's manner in large part. Not that it's jazzy, or about jazz—rather, it's trying to use a rhythmic base much as jazz of this time would—or what was especially characteristic of Charlie Parker's playing, or Miles Davis', Thelonious Monk's, or Milt Jackson's. That is, the beat is used to delay, detail, prompt, define the content of the statement or, more aptly, the emotional field of the statement. It's trying to do this while moving in time to a set periodicity—durational units, call them. It will say as much as it can, or as little, in the "time" given. So each line is figured as taking the same time, like they say, and each line ending works as a distinct pause. I used to listen to Parker's endless variations on "I Got Rhythm" and all the various times in which he'd play it, all the tempi, up, down, you name it. What fascinated me was that he'd write silences as actively as sounds, which of course they were. Just so in poetry.

So it isn't writing like jazz, trying to be some curious social edge of that imagined permission. It's a time one's keeping, which could be the variations of hopscotch, or clapping, or just traffic's blurred racket. It was what you could do with what you got, or words to that effect.

Being shy as a young man, I was very formal, and still am. I make my moves fast but very self-consciously. I would say that from "Ugh . . ." on the poem moves as cannily and as solidly as whatever. "Listen to the sound that it makes," said Pound. Fair enough.

Susan Howe

There Are Not Leaves Enough to Crown
to Cover to Crown to Cover

For me there was no silence before armies. I was born in Boston Massachusetts on June 10th, 1937, to an Irish mother and an American father. My mother had come to Boston on a short visit two years earlier. My father had never been to Europe. She is a wit and he was a scholar. They met at a dinner party when her earring dropped into his soup.

By 1937 the Nazi dictatorship was well-established in Germany. All dissenting political parties had been liquidated and Concentration camps had already been set up to hold political prisoners. The Berlin-Rome axis was a year old. So was the Spanish Civil War. On April 25th Franco's Luftwaffe pilots bombed the village of Guernica. That November Hitler and the leaders of his armed forces made secret plans to invade Austria, Czechoslovakia, Poland, and Russia.

In the summer of 1938 my mother and I were staying with my grandmother, uncle, aunt, great-aunts, cousins, and friends in Ireland, and I had just learned to walk, when Czechoslovakia was dismembered by Hitler, Ribbentrop, Mussolini, Chamberlain, and Daladier, during the Conference and Agreement at Munich. That October we sailed home on a ship crowded with refugees fleeing various countries in Europe.

When I was two the German army invaded Poland and World War II began in the West.

The fledgling Republic of Ireland distrusted England with good reason, and remained neutral during the struggle. But there was the Battle of the Atlantic to be won, so we couldn't cross the sea again until after 1945. That half of the family was temporarily cut off.

In Buffalo New York, where we lived at first, we seemed to be safe. We were there when my sister was born and the Japanese bombed Pearl Harbor.

Now there were armies in the west called East.

American fathers marched off into the hot Chronicle of global struggle but mothers were left. Our law-professor father, a man of pure principles, quickly included violence in his principles, put on a soldier suit and disappeared with the others into the thick of the threat to the east called West.

FROM *The Europe of Trusts,* 1990.

Buffalo
12. 7. 41
(Late afternoon light.)
(Going to meet him in snow.)
HE
(Comes through the hall door.)
The research of scholars, lawyers, investigators, judges
Demands!

SHE

(With her arms around his neck
whispers.)

Herod had all the little children murdered!

It is dark
The floor is ice

they stand on the edge of a hole singing—

In Rama
Rachel weeping for her children

refuses
to be comforted

because they *are* not.

Malice dominates the history of Power and Progress. History is the record of winners. Documents were written by the Masters. But fright is formed by what we see not by what they say.

From 1939 until 1946 in news photographs, day after day I saw signs of culture exploding into murder. Shots of children being herded into trucks by hideous helmeted conquerors—shots of children who were orphaned and lost—shots of the emaciated bodies of Jews dumped into mass graves on top of more emaciated bodies—nameless numberless men women and children, uprooted in a world almost demented. God had abandoned them to history's sovereign Necessity.

If to see is to *have* at a distance, I had so many dead Innocents distance was abolished. Substance broke loose from the domain of time and obedient intention. I became part of the ruin. In the blank skies over Europe I was Strife represented.

Things overlap in space and are hidden. Those black and white picture shots—moving or fixed—were a subversive generation. "The hawk, with his long claws / Pulled down the stones. / The dove, with her rough bill / Brought me them home."

> Buffalo roam in herds
> up the broad streets connected by boulevards
> and fences
>
> their eyes are ancient and a thousand years
> too old
>
> hear murder throng their muting
>
> Old as time in the center of a room
> doubt is spun
>
> and measured
>
> Throned wrath
> I know your worth
>
> a chain of parks encircles the city

Pain is nailed to the landscape in time. Bombs are seeds of Science and the sun.

2,000 years ago the dictator Creon said to Antigone who was the daughter of Oedipus and Jocasta: "Go to the dead and love them."

Life opens into conceptless perspectives. Language surrounds Chaos.

During World War II my father's letters were a sign he was safe. A miniature photographic negative of his handwritten message was reproduced by the army and a microfilm copy forwarded to us. In the top left-hand corner someone always stamped PASSED BY EXAMINER.

This is my historical consciousness. I have no choice in it. In my poetry, time and again, questions of assigning *the cause* of history dictate the sound of what is thought.

> Summary of fleeting summary
> Pseudonym cast across empty
>
> Peak proud heart

Majestic caparisoned cloud cumuli
East sweeps hewn flank

Scion on a ledge of Constitution
Wedged sequences of system

Causeway of faint famed city
Human ferocity

Dim mirror Naught formula

archaic hallucinatory laughter
Kneel to intellect in our work
Chaos cast cold intellect back

Poetry brings similitude and representation to configurations waiting from forever to be spoken. North Americans have tended to confuse human fate with their own salvation. In this I am North American. "We are coming Father Abraham, three hundred thousand more," sang the Union troops at Gettysburg.

I write to break out into perfect primeval Consent. I wish I could tenderly lift from the dark side of history, voices that are anonymous, slighted—inarticulate.

Fanny Howe

FROM Bewilderment

What I have been thinking about, lately, is bewilderment as a way of entering the day as much as the work.

Bewilderment as a poetics and a politics.

I have developed this idea from living in the world and also through testing it out in my poems and through the characters in my fiction—women and children, and even the occasional man, who rushed backwards and forwards within an irreconcilable set of imperatives.

What sent them running was a double bind established in childhood, or a sudden confrontation with evil in the world—that is, in themselves—when they were older, yet unprepared.

These characters remained as uncertain in the end as they were in the beginning, though both author and reader could place them within a pattern of causalities.

In their story they were unable to handle the complexities of the world or the shock of making a difference. In fact, to make a difference was to be inherently compromised. From their author's point of view the shape and form of their stories were responses to events long past, maybe even forgotten.

Increasingly my stories joined my poems in their methods of sequencing and counting. Effects can never change what made them, but they can't stop trying to.

Like a scroll or a comic book that shows the same exact character in multiple points and situations, the look of the daily world was governed only by which point you happened to be focused on at a particular time. Everything was occurring at once. So what if the globe is round? The manifest reality is flat.

There is a Muslim prayer that says, "Lord, increase my bewilderment," and this prayer belongs both to me and to the strange Whoever who goes under the name of "I" in my poems—and under multiple names in my fiction—where error, errancy, and bewilderment are the main forces that signal a story.

A signal does not necessarily mean that you want to be located or described. It can mean that you want to be known as Unlocatable and Hidden. This

FROM *The Wedding Dress*, 2003.

contradiction can drive the "I" in the lyrical poem into a series of techniques that are the reverse of the usual narrative movements around courage, discipline, conquest, and fame.

Instead, weakness, fluidity, concealment, and solitude assume their place in a kind of dream world, where the sleeping witness finally feels safe enough to lie down in mystery. These qualities are not the usual stuff of stories of initiation and success, but they may survive more than they are given credit for. They have the endurance of tramps who travel light, discarding acquisitions like water drops off a dog.

It is to the dream model that I return as a writer involved in the problem of sequencing events and thoughts—because in the weirdness of dreaming there is a dimension of plot, but a greater consciousness of randomness and uncertainty as the basic stock in which it is brewed.

Too clever a reading of a dream, too serious a closure given to its subject, the more disappointing the dream becomes in retrospect. If the dream's curious activities are subjected to an excess of interpretation, they are better forgotten. The same demystification can happen with the close reading of a text; sometimes a surface reading seems to bring you closer to the intention of the poem.

Sustaining a balance between the necessity associated with plot and the blindness associated with experience—in both poetry and fiction—is the trick for me. Dreams are constantly reassuring happenings that illuminate methods for pulling this off.

▪

As we all know, a dream hesitates, it doesn't grasp, it stands back, it jokes, it makes itself scared, it circles, and it fizzles.

A dream often undermines the narratives of power and winning.

It is instead dazzled and horrified.

The dreamer is aware that only everything else but this tiny dream exists and in this way the dream itself is free to act without restraint.

A dream breaks into parts and contradicts its own will, even as it travels around and around.

For me, bewilderment is like a dream: one continually returning pause on a gyre and in both my stories and my poems it could be the shape of the spiral that imprints itself in my interior before anything emerges on paper.

For to the spiral-walker there is no plain path, no up and down, no inside or outside. But there are strange returns and recognitions and never a conclusion.

What goes in, goes out. Just as a well-known street or house forms a living and expressive face that looks back at you, so do all the weirdly familiar bends in the spiral.

▪

However I can't really talk about bewilderment as a poetics and an ethics without first recollecting the two fundamental and oppositional life-views that coexist in many of us. That is, the materialist-skeptical view and the invisible-faithful view.

Many of us know only too well the first one—we live it.

According to some Sufis, it was God's loneliness and desire to be known that set creation going. Unmanifest things, lacking names, remained unmanifest until the violence of God's sense of isolation sent the heavens into a spasm of procreating words that then became matter.

God was nowhere until it was present to itself as the embodied names of animals, minerals, and vegetables.

On the day of creation Divine transcendence was such an emotional force, energy coalesced into these forms and words.

Now the One who wanted to be known dwells in the hearts of humans who carry the pulse of the One's own wanting to be known by the ones who want in return to be known by it.

Lacking is in this case expressed by the presence of something—the longing to be loved—and so humanity, composed of this longing, misses the very quality that inhabits itself.

Ordinary problems of logic like: Where were you before you got here? How did you arrive before my eyes?—foment in the background of this creation story.

Just as language evolves with increasing specificity, breaking further and further into qualifying parts, so words, as weak as birds, survive because they move collectively and restlessly, as if under siege.

This is at the root of the incarnational experience of being—that one is inhabited by the witness who is oneself and by that witness's creator simultaneously.

The question is, what is it to be familiar? (Why am I familiar to myself at all? Or is it my self that is familiar to some inhabitant behind my existence?)

The mystery of thought can only be solved by thought itself—which is what?

Martin Buber has written, "Every name is a step toward the consummate Name, as everything broken points to the unbroken." The awareness of both continuum and rupture occurring together may form the very rhythm of consciousness.

To the Sufis, words precede existence, perhaps because a cry brings people running.

Using a small grammatical ploy, the poet and philosopher Ibn Arabi reveals the overlap between the caller and the called when he writes that the Spirit wanted "to reveal, to it, through it, its mystery."
   One "it" is not distinguished from another "it" by a capital I, or by quotes, or by calling "it" "itself"—as in "the Spirit wanted to reveal itself through its mystery."
   Instead the sentence is deliberately constructed so that the Divine It and its "it" are indistinguishable and confusing.

▪

When someone is incapable of telling you the truth, when there is no certain way to go, when you are caught in a double bind, bewilderment—which, because of its root meaning—will never lead you back to common sense, but will offer you a walk into a further wild place on "the threshold of love's sanctuary which lies above that of reason."

> The summer's flower is to the summer sweet
> Though to itself it only live and die.

This walk into the wilderness is full of falls and stumbles and pains. Strangely one tries to get in deeper and to get home at the same time. There is a sense of repetition and unfamiliarity being in collusion.
   Each bruise on you is like the difference between a signature semiconsciously scrawled across a page and a forgery deliberately and systematically copied by a person who stops and watches her own hand producing shapes.
   The forgery has more contour, more weight. In its effort to seem real, it cuts deeper into the paper and the fingers.

A liar can reproduce the feeling that a wilderness does.
   In Sufism "the pupil of the eye" is the owner of each member of the body, even the heart, and each part becomes a tool under its lens. It is in and through and with the pupil of the eye that the catch locks between just-being and

always-being. The less focused the gesture, the more true to the eye of the heart it is.

You are progressing at one level and becoming more lost at another.

■

The owner of the eye is the Divine Non-Existent about whom one can only speculate.

At certain points, wandering around lost produces the (perhaps false) impression that events approach you from ahead, that time is moving backwards onto you, and that the whole scenario is operating in reverse from the way it is ordinarily perceived.

You may have the impression that time is repeating with only slight variations, because here you are again!

Each movement forwards is actually a catching of what is coming at you, as if someone you are facing across a field has thrown a ball and stands watching you catch it.

Watching and catching combine as a forward action that has come from ahead.

All intention then is reversed into attention.

Mentally, an effect precedes its cause because the whole event needs to unravel in order for it all to be interpreted.

The serial poem attempts to demonstrate this attention to what is cyclical, returning, but empty at its axis. To me, the serial poem is a spiral poem.

In this poetry circling can take form as sublimations, inversions, echolalia, digressions, glossolalia, and rhymes.

An aesthetic that organizes its subject around a set of interlocking symbols and metaphors describes a world that is fixed and fatally subject to itself alone.

Decorating and perfecting any subject can be a way of removing all stench of the real until it becomes an astral corpse.

■

In an itinerant and disposable work each event is greeted as an alternative, either the equivalent of respite or a way out.

Space may only indicate something else going on, somewhere else, all that lies beyond perceptions.

There is a new relationship to time and narrative, when the approach through events and observations is not sequential but dizzying and repetitive. The dance of the dervish is all about this experience.

> Since the upright man is kin to the stumbling drunk
> to whose sultry glance should we give our heart? What is choice?
> —*Hafiz*

The whirling that is central to bewilderment is the natural way for the lyric poet. A dissolving of particularities into one solid braid of sound is her inspiration.

Each poem is a different take on an idea, an experience, each poem is another day, another mood, another revelation, another conversion.

> A void was made in Nature; all her bonds
> Cracked; and I saw the flaring atom-streams
> And torrents of her myriad universe
> Running along the illimitable inane.
> —*Tennyson*

What Shelley called "the One Spirit's plastic stress" and Hopkins called "instress" is this matching up of the outwardly observed with the internally heard.

A call and response to and from a stranger is implied.

Or a polishing of a looking glass where someone is looking in and out at the same time.

Particularities are crushed and compacted and redesigned to produce a new sound.

The new sound has muted the specific meanings of each word and a perplexing music follows.

Themes of pilgrimage of an unrequited love, of wounding and seeking come up a lot in this tradition.

Every experience that is personal is simultaneously an experience that is supernatural.

How you love another person might be a reflection of your relationship to God or the world itself, not to the other person, not to any other person, mother, father, sister, brother. Untrusting? Suspicious? Jealous? Indifferent? Abject? These feelings may be an indication of your larger existential position, hardly personal.

And the heart is an organ of the soul, in such a case, not the reverse.

In your cyclical movements you often have to separate from situations and people you love, and the more you love them the more difficult it is to allow anyone new to replace them.

This action can produce guilt, withdrawal, and rumination that some might read as depression. But to preserve, and return to a past you have voluntarily left—to suffer remorse—has always signaled a station in spiritual progress.

The human heart, transforming on a seventy-two-hour basis (the Muslim measurement of a day in relation to conversion of faith and conduct) in a state of bewilderment, doesn't want to answer questions so much as to lengthen the resonance of those questions.

Bewilderment circumnavigates, believing that at the center of errant or circular movement is the empty but ultimate referent.

> Shall I compare thee to a summer's day?
> Thou art more lovely and more temperate.
> Rough winds do shake the darling buds of May
> and summer's lease hath all too short a date.
> —*Shakespeare*

For poets, the obliquity of a bewildered poetry is its own theme.

Q—the Quidam, Whoever, the unknown one—or I, is turning in a circle and keeps passing herself on her way around, her former self, her later self, and the trace of this passage is marked by a rhyme, a coded message for "I have been here before, I will return."

The same sound splays the sound waves into a polyvalence, a rose. A bloom is not a parade.

A big error comes when you believe that a form, name, or position in which the subject is viewed is the only way that the subject can be viewed. This is called "binding" and it leads directly to painful contradiction and clashes. It leads to war in the larger world.

No monolithic answers that are not soon disproved are allowed into a bewildered poetry or life.

According to a Kabbalistic rabbi, in the Messianic age people will no longer quarrel with others but only with themselves.

This is what poets are doing already.

Lyn Hejinian

FROM The Rejection of Closure

.

My title, "The Rejection of Closure," sounds judgmental, which is a little misleading—though only a little—since I am a happy reader of detective novels and an admiring, a very admiring, reader of Charles Dickens' novels.

Nevertheless, whatever the pleasures, in a fundamental way closure is a fiction—one of the amenities that fantasy or falsehood provides.

What then is the fundamental necessity for openness? Or, rather, what is there in language itself that compels and implements the rejection of closure?

I perceive the world as vast and overwhelming; each moment stands under an enormous vertical and horizontal pressure of information, potent with ambiguity, meaning-full, unfixed, and certainly incomplete. What saves this from becoming a vast undifferentiated mass of data and situation is one's ability to make distinctions. Each written text may act as a distinction, may be a distinction. The experience of feeling overwhelmed by undifferentiated material is like claustrophobia. One feels panicky, closed in. The open text is one which both acknowledges the vastness of the world and is formally differentiating. It is the form that opens it, in that case.

.

Two dangers never cease threatening in the world: order and disorder.

Language discovers what one might know. Therefore, the limits of language are the limits of what we might know. We discover the limits of language early, as children. Anything with limits can be imagined (correctly or incorrectly) as an object, by analogy with other objects—balls and rivers. Children objectify language when they render it their plaything, in jokes, puns, and riddles, or in glossolaliac chants and rhymes. They discover that words are not equal to the world, that a shift, analogous to parallax in photography, occurs between things (events, ideas, objects) and the words for them—a displacement that leaves a gap. Among the most prevalent and persistent category of joke is that which identifies and makes use of the fallacious comparison of words to the world and delights in the ambiguity resulting from the discrepancy:

FROM *Writing/Talks*, ed. Bob Perelman, Carbondale, Ill., 1985. First given as a talk at 544 Natoma Street, San Francisco, on April 17, 1983. The essay was also published, in a different form, in *Poetics Journal*, No. 4, May 1984.

Why did the moron eat hay?
To feed his hoarse voice.

Because we have language we find ourselves in a peculiar relationship to the objects, events, and situations which constitute what we imagine of the world. Language generates its own characteristics in the human psychological and spiritual condition. This psychology is generated by the struggle between language and that which it claims to depict or express, by our overwhelming experience of the vastness and uncertainty of the world and by what often seems to be the inadequacy of the imagination that longs to know it, and, for the poet, the even greater inadequacy of the language that appears to describe, discuss, or disclose it.

This inadequacy, however, is merely a disguise for other virtues.

"What mind worthy of the name," said Flaubert, "ever reached a conclusion?"

Language is one of the principal forms our curiosity takes. It makes us restless. As Francis Ponge puts it, "Man is a curious body whose center of gravity is not in himself." Instead it seems to be located in language, by virtue of which we negotiate our mentalities and the world; off-balance, heavy at the mouth, we are pulled forward.

> She is lying on her stomach with one eye closed, driving a toy truck along the road she has cleared with her fingers. Then the tantrum broke out, blue, without a breath of air. . . . You could increase the height by making lateral additions and building over them a sequence of steps, leaving tunnels, or windows, between the blocks, and I did. I made signs to them to be as quiet as possible. But a word is a bottomless pit. It became magically pregnant and one day split open, giving birth to a stone egg, about as big as a football.
>
> —*My Life*

Language itself is never in a state of rest. And the experience of using it, which includes the experience of understanding it, either as speech or as writing, is inevitably active. I mean both intellectually and emotionally active.

The progress of a line or sentence, or a series of lines or sentences, has spatial properties as well as temporal properties. The spatial density is both vertical and horizontal. The meaning of a word in its place derives both from the word's lateral reach, its contacts with its neighbors in a statement, and from its reach through and out of the text into the other world, the matrix of its contemporary and historical reference. The very idea of reference is spatial: over here is word, over there is thing at which word is shooting amiable love-arrows.

■

Writing develops subjects that mean the words we have for them.

Even words in storage, in the dictionary, seem frenetic with activity, as each individual entry attracts to itself other words as definition, example, and amplification. Thus, to open the dictionary at random, mastoid attracts nipplelike, temporal, bone, ear, and behind. Then turning to temporal we find that the definition includes time, space, life, world, transitory, and near the temples, but, significantly, not mastoid. There is no entry for nipplelike, but the definition for nipple brings protuberance, breast, udder, the female, milk, discharge, mouthpiece, and nursing bottle, and not mastoid, nor temporal, nor time, bone, ear, space, or world, etc. It is relevant that the exchanges are incompletely reciprocal.

> and how did this happen like an excerpt
>   beginning in a square white boat abob on a gray sea
>   tootling of another message by the hacking lark
>   as a child to the rescue and its spring
>   many comedies emerge and in particular a group of girls
>   in a great lock of letters
>   like knock look
>   a restless storage of a thousand boastings
>   but cow dull bulge clump
>   slippage thinks random patterns through wishes
>   I intend greed as I intend pride
>   patterns of roll extend over the wish
>   —*Writing is an Aid to Memory*

The "rage to know" is one expression of restlessness produced by language.

> As long as man keeps hearing words
> He's sure that there's a meaning somewhere

says Mephistopheles in Goethe's *Faust*.

It's in the nature of language to encourage, and in part to justify, such Faustian longings. The notion that language is the means and medium for attaining knowledge, and, concomitantly, power, is old, of course. The knowledge towards which we seem to be driven by language, or which language seems to promise, is inherently sacred as well as secular, redemptive as well as satisfying. The *nomina sunt numina* position (i.e., that there is an essential identity between name and thing, that the real nature of a thing is immanent and present in its name, that nouns are numinous) suggests that it is possible to find a language which will meet its object with perfect identity. If this were the case, we could, in speaking or in writing, achieve the at-oneness with the universe, at least in its particulars, that is the condition of paradise, or complete and perfect knowing—or of perfect mental health.

But if in the Edenic scenarios we acquired knowledge of the animals by naming them, it was not by virtue of any numinous immanence in the name but because Adam was a taxonomist. He distinguished the individual animals, discovered the concept of categories, and then organized the species according to their functions and relationships in a system.

What the naming provides is structure, not individual words.

As Benjamin Lee Whorf points out, ". . . every language is a vast pattern-system, different from others, in which are culturally ordained the forms and categories by which the personality not only communicates, but also analyzes nature, notices or neglects types of relationships and phenomena, channels his reasoning, and builds the house of his consciousness."

In this same essay, which appears to be the last he ever wrote (1941), entitled "Language, Mind, Reality," Whorf goes on to express what seems to be stirrings of a religious motivation: ". . . what I have called patterns are basic in a really cosmic sense." There is a "PREMONITION IN LANGUAGE of the unknown vaster world." The idea

> is too drastic to be penned up in a catch phrase. I would rather leave it unnamed. It is the view that a noumenal world—a world of hyperspace, of higher dimension—awaits discovery by all the sciences [linguistics being one of them], which it will unite and unify, awaits discovery under its first aspect of a realm of PATTERNED RELATIONS, inconceivably manifold and yet bearing a recognizable affinity to the rich and systematic organization of LANGUAGE.

It is as if what I've been calling, from *Faust,* the "rage to know," which is in some respects a libidinous drive, seeks also a redemptive value from language. Both are appropriate to the Faustian legend.

Both also seem in many respects appropriate to psychoanalytic theory, if one can say that in the psychoanalytic vision the "cure" is social and cultural as well as personal.

Coming in part out of Freudian psychoanalytic theory, especially in France, is a body of feminist thought that is even more explicit in its identification of language with power and knowledge—a power and knowledge that is political, psychological, and aesthetic—and that is identified specifically with desire.

The project for these French feminist writers is to direct their attention to "language and the unconscious, not as separate entities, but language as a passageway, and the only one, to the unconscious, to that which has been repressed and which would, if allowed to rise, disrupt the established symbolic order, which Jacques Lacan has dubbed the Law of the Father" (Elaine Marks, *Signs,* Summer 1978).

If the established symbolic order is the "Law of the Father," and it is discovered to be repressive and incomplete, then the new symbolic order is to be a "woman's language," corresponding to a woman's desire.

Luce Irigaray:

> But woman has sex organs just about everywhere. She experiences pleasure almost everywhere. Even without speaking of the hysterization of her entire body, one can say that the geography of her pleasure is much more diversified, more multiple in its differences, more complex, more subtle, than is imagined. . . . "She" is indefinitely other in herself. That is undoubtedly the reason she is called temperamental, perturbed, capricious—not to mention her language in which "she" goes off in all directions. . . .
>
> —*New French Feminisms*

I find myself in disagreement with the too narrow definition of desire, with the identification of desire solely with sexuality, and with the literalness of the genital model of women's language that some of these writers insist on.

But what was striking to me in reading the collection of essays from which the above quote was taken was that the kinds of language that many of these writers advocate seem very close to, if not identical with, what I think of as characteristic of many contemporary avant-garde texts—including an interest in syntactic disjunctures and realignments, in montage and pastiche as structural devices, in the fragmentation and explosion of subject, etc., as well as an antagonism to closed structures of meaning. Yet of the writers from this area whom I have read to date, only Julia Kristeva is exploring this connection.

For me, too, the desire that is stirred by language seems to be located more interestingly within language, and hence it is androgynous. It is a desire to say, a desire to create the subject by saying, and even a feeling of doubt very like jealousy that springs from the impossibility of satisfying this desire.

This desire is like Wordsworth's "underthirst / Of vigor seldom utterly allayed."

Carla Harryman:

> When I'm eating I want food. . . . The I expands. The individual is caught in a devouring machine, but she shines like the lone star on the horizon when we enter her thoughts, when she expounds on the immensity of her condition, the subject of the problem which interests nature.
>
> —"Realisms"

If language induces a yearning for comprehension, for perfect and complete expression, it also guards against it. Hence the title of my poem "The Guard."

Windows closed on wind in rows
Night lights, unrumorlike, the reserve for events
All day our postures were the same
Next day the gentleman was very depressed and had a
    headache; so much laughing had upset him he thought
The urge to tell the truth is strong
Delightful, being somewhere else so much the moment of
    equivalence
To be lucky a mediation
To look like life in the face
The definition quotes happiness
The egg is peafowl
The kitchen: everyone eats in different cycles—yeh,
the dishes are all over the counter. . . . yeh, food's
    left out, things are on the stove. . . . yeh, the floor's
filthy—that's amazing! have you been there?
Like the wind that by its bulk inspires confidence
Red and yellow surefire reflect on the breakdown
The forest is a vehicle of tremors
When mad, aged nine, and dressed in calico
Confusion is good for signs of generosity
Each sentence replaces an hallucination
But these distractions can't safeguard my privacy
During its absence, my presence
Every hour demonstrates time's porosity
The ghosts that blend with daylight come out like stars
    in the dark longing to have their feet fit in boots
And finish in Eden.

Faust complains:

> It is written: "In the beginning was the Word!"
> Already I have to stop! Who'll help me on?
> It is impossible to put such trust in the
> Word!

Such is a recurrent element in the argument of the lyric:

> Alack, what poverty my Muse brings forth. . . .

> Those lines that I before have writ do lie. . . .

> For we / Have eyes to wonder but lack tongues to praise. . . .

In the gap between what one wants to say (or what one perceives there is to say) and what one can say (what is sayable), words provide for a collaboration and a desertion. We delight in our sensuous involvement with the materials of language, we long to join words to the world—to close the gap between ourselves and things, and we suffer from doubt and anxiety as to our capacity to do so because of the limits of language itself.

Yet the very incapacity of language to match the world allows it to do service as a medium of differentiation. The undifferentiated is one mass, the differentiated is multiple. The (unimaginable) complete text, the text that contains everything, would be in fact a closed text. It would be insufferable.

For me, a central activity of poetic language is formal. In being formal, in making form distinct, it opens—makes variousness and multiplicity and possibility articulate and clear. While failing in the attempt to match the world, we discover structure, distinction, the integrity and separateness of things.

Will Alexander ————————————————

My Interior Vita

I was born under Leo, under its signpost of heat, and what has evolved from such coloration is a verbal momentum always magnetized to the uranic. A verbal rhythm prone to the upper hamlets of starlight, my predilection being instinctively honed to the fluidic motion of the sidereal. This is not to say that the protean aspects of Earth cease to amaze me, or cease to enthrall me with its natural magic. The winds, the bays, the deserts, ceaseless in my mind like a teeming field of Flamingo flowers, or a sun-charged clepsydra. Yet above all, the earth being for me the specificity of Africa, as revealed by Diop, and Jackson, and Van Sertima, and its electrical scent in the writings of Damas.

Because of this purview I have never been drawn to provincial description, or to the quiescent chemistry of a condensed domestic horizon. I've always been prone to exploring the larger scope of predominant mental criteria as exhibited by the influential civilizations over the span of time which we name as history. For instance, within the Roman or American criteria I see the active involvement of what is called the left brain and its natural gravitation towards separating life by means of active fragmentation. Yet at a more ancient remove there exists the example of Nubia and Kemet unconcerned with life as secular confiscation, but with the unification of disciplines, such as astronomy, mathematics, philosophy, law, as paths to the revelation of the self. Knowledge then, as alchemical operation, rather than an isolated expertise. So when various knowledges fuse in my writings, insights occur, revealing an inward light whose source is simultaneous with the riveting connection between flashes of lightning.

For me, language, by its very operation, is alchemical, mesmeric, totalic in the way that it condenses and at the same time proves capable of leaping the boundaries of genre. Be it the drama, the poem, the essay, the novel, language operates at a level of concentration modulated by the necessity of the character or the circumstance which is speaking. My feeling is that language is capable of creating shifts in the human neural field, capable of transmuting behaviours and judgments. Humans conduct themselves through language, and, when the latter transmutes, the human transmutes. The advertisers know this linkage, but to a superficial degree, so when language is mined at a more seminal depth of poetic strata, chance can take on a more lasting significance. And I do not

FROM *Compression & Purity*, 2011, and *Callaloo*, Vol. 22, No. 2 (Spring 1999), pp. 371–73.

mean in a didactic manner, but in the way that osmosis transpires, allowing one to see areas of reality that heretofore had remained elided or obscured. I'm speaking here of an organic imaginal level which rises far beyond the narrow perspective of up and down, or left side and right side, which is the mind working in the service of mechanical reaction. Rather, I am thinking of magnetic savor, allowing the mind to live at a pitch far beyond the garish modes of the quotidian. One's life then begins to expand into the quality of nuance naturally superseding a bleak statistical diorama.

I was always drawn to realms outside the normal reaches of comment even at an early age. I would sustain imaginary dialogues with myself by continuously creating imaginal characters very specific in their cryptic ability to spur continuous inward rotation. Imaginal kings, warriors, athletes, angels, always igniting my mind with their ability to overcome limits, to sustain themselves beyond the confines of normal fatigue. And it was during this period that I had my first confrontation with a spectre. It spoke to me in the dead of night, commanding me to rise from my bed and follow its presence into I know not where. I remained frozen as it spoke to me, and as I vividly recall I could utter no sound. I knew I was not dreaming, because as I stared into the darkness its strange niveous image formed in my vision, and took on for those unbelievable moments a staggering animation. Of course I was not believed the next day when I reported my contact to my mother. And years later she could never recall me recording the incident or my reaction to the incident, something totally out of character for her. Nevertheless it confirmed for me the activity of the supra-physical world which has remained with me in all my subsequent moments. Thus the rational world has never been able to annul my alacrity for what the mechanically-sighted call the invisible.

This reality was further strengthened when first hearing the recordings of Eric Dolphy and John Coltrane. It was during my early teens and listening to the music was absolutely electric. It made me feel that I had allies, that there were others who knew that the material world was completely permeable, and that none of the rationally stated boundaries could contain the imaginal. Of course all of this happened before I knew anything of poetry. Yet I was already in the poetic, the music already opening me up to creativity linked as it is to the inner and outer plane. The inner burst of creative power and its circulation in the world on an international scale. Eric Dolphy in Berlin, John Coltrane in Antibes, Cecil Taylor at Moosham Castle in Austria, Duke Ellington in Dakar. So by the time I read a book on Rimbaud some seven years later I felt a definite relation between his inner experience and my own. Close to finishing the book I found myself writing my first poem, and I immediately felt a great liberty transpire within me, a liberty which suddenly flashed to creative fruition.

And I've found over time that this liberty continuously burns, and is capable of transmuting all that it touches. I've found no discipline which is foreign to it. Architecture, politics, mathematics, mysticism, all prone to a higher verbal kindling, to a different archery of usage. This is not to say that poetry serves as a didactic device, no, but as a magical instrument with the prowess to overcome the mortality of the temporal. It is fiesta outside the limits of the measured diurnal regime where the constraints of the conscious mind vanish without trace. So by the time I discovered Surrealism and the writings of Artaud, Césaire, Breton, Lamantia, and Bob Kaufman, I felt ripe for exploring the subconscious levels of the mind. Then connecting the power of such writing with Sri Aurobindo's supra-conscious mind, the Tibetan Book of the Dead, and the Egyptian connective between visible and invisible domains, I was able to develop within an instinctive motif of linguistic arousal. And as was for Césaire earlier, the Surrealism opened me up to animate use of language not unlike the ancient African atmosphere of consciousness. Life being an unbroken motion of consciousness, poetry is for me the celebration of that unbrokenness.

Creativity being an ongoing praxis, is a continuous trance, in which one deals with the unification of worlds, rather than fostering inclement fragments. Insights, worlds within worlds, which include not only scintillations of the conscious mind, but more importantly, its ability to both elevate and descend, thereby traversing the triple levels of the mind, the conscious, the supra-conscious, and the subconscious minds, creating in the process a concert of worlds.

2011

Leslie Scalapino

Note on My Writing, 1985

On that they were at the beach — aeolotropic series.

The ship (so it's in the foreground) — with the man who's the beggar in back of it, the soil is in back of him — is active. So it's mechanical — there aren't other people's actions — I don't know how old the man in back is. Who's older than I, desire'd been had by him for something else. I'm not old.

And with him being inactive back then.

––––––––

Playing ball — so it's like paradise, not because it's in the past, we're on a field; we are creamed by the girls who get together on the other team. They're nubile, but in age they're thirteen or so — so they're strong.

(No one knows each other, aligning according to race as it happens, the color of the girls, and our being creamed in the foreground — as part of it's being that — the net is behind us).

––––––––

I intended this work to be the repetition of historically real events the writing of which punches a hole in reality. (As if to void them, but actively).

Also, to know what an event is. An event isn't anything, it isn't a person.

No events occur. Because these are in the past. They don't exist.

Conversely as there is no commentary external to the events, the children on the playing field can commune with each other. It is entirely from the inside out.

There was when writing the work something else occurring besides what's going on in the segments. But the events do not represent that.

A segment in the poem is the actual act or event itself — occurring long after it occurred; or acts put into it which occurred more recently. They somehow come up as the same sound pattern.

The self is unraveled as an example in investigating particular historical events, which are potentially infinite.

The self is a guinea pig.

The piece in *that they were at the beach* titled "A Sequence" is erotica, a

FROM *It's Go in Horizontal: Selected Poems, 1974–2006* (Berkeley: University of California Press, 2008).

genre being artificial which can 'comment on itself' as a surface because it is without external commentary.

External commentary does not exist as it's being entirely erotica genre, which is what?

By its nature as erotica genre, it is convention. Though it may not have people's character or appear to be social convention. Nor does there appear to be domination.

In a Godard film such as *Hail Mary,* one doesn't know whether it is just its surface or it is from the inside out.

Similarly, in "A Sequence" the surface(s) is (are) the same.

The camera lens of writing is the split between oneself and reality. Which one sees first — view of dying and life — is inside, looking out into untroubled 'experience.'

Which is the beggar who's lying back from the dock (in the above example).

So that repression would not be a way of giving depth.

"Chameleon series" in *that they were at the beach* are (multiple) cartoons, distortions of the (inner) self, which have a slight quality of refined Medieval songs.

Interpreting phenomena is deciphering one's view. This is related to poems which are cartoons or writing which uses the genre of comic books, as commentary being the surface.

The form has the 'objective' quality of life — i.e., the comic book, from which life is excluded, has freedom in the actions of the 'characters.'

A recent work of mine in such a chameleon cartoon mode is a short 'novel' titled THE PEARL. It is the form of the comic book as writing. Each line or paragraph is a frame, so that each action occurs in the moment.

The writing does not have actual pictures. It 'functions' as does a comic book — in being read.

And read aloud to someone the picture has to be described or seen and

then what the figure in it says read.

So it's private.

Cartoons are a self-revealing surface as the comic strip is continuous, multiple, and within it have simultaneous future and past dimensions.

Being inside each frame, is the present moment. But at the same time the writing (the frame) is really behind, in the rear of 'what is really occurring.' The things are happening out ahead of the writing.

The following is five or more frames:

And there's this pink sky that's in front but as if — beforehand. To the

events (of that night) that entire day goes, and then there's this incredible

vast corrugated rungs of rose colored yet extreme sunset as if it had covered

the sky and is behind it, pushing.

She's driving up the street of small flat porched houses and it's behind

her, and stretching in front as well.

And as if the events are pushed — from it.

What's happened — ? — she'd slept during the day. Checking the
man's

apartment, he's not there.

What is in the frame is occurring — but what's going on (which is 'free') is
ahead of, being pushed by, the writing.

The title is a reference to the Medieval poem *The Pearl.* But the work is
made up, from experience.

There are similar possibilities in using the form of plays composed of
poems. These are 'experience' in that the surface is the same: each poem is an
act, done by the actor. It takes place exactly in and as that moment.

The actors, as for example in the play *fin de siècle,* can be made to be
something other than what they are. Which causes that thing to be gently
internalized by them. People don't usually speak in poems. They aren't that.
Nobody's any thing.

The setting and tone of these plays are both realistic and artificial.

Nathaniel Mackey ────────────────────────────

FROM Sound and Sentiment, Sound and Symbol

I

Senses of music in a number of texts is what I'd like to address—ways of regarding and responding to music in a few instances of writings which bear on the subject. This essay owes its title to two such texts, Steven Feld's *Sound and Sentiment: Birds, Weeping, Poetics and Song in Kaluli Expression* and Victor Zuckerkandl's *Sound and Symbol: Music and the External World.* These two contribute to the paradigm I bring to my reading of the reading of music in the literary works I wish to address.

Steven Feld is a musician as well as an anthropologist and he dedicates *Sound and Sentiment* to the memory of Charlie Parker, John Coltrane, and Charles Mingus. His book, as the subtitle tells us, discusses the way in which the Kaluli of Papua New Guinea conceptualize music and poetic language. These the Kaluli associate with birds and weeping. They arise from a breach in human solidarity, a violation of kinship, community, connection. *Gisalo,* the quintessential Kaluli song from (the only one of the five varieties they sing that they claim to have invented rather than borrowed from a neighboring people), provokes and crosses over into weeping—weeping which has to do with some such breach, usually death. *Gisalo* songs are sung at funerals and during spirit-medium seances and have the melodic contour of the cry of a kind of fruitdove, the *muni* bird.[1] This reflects and is founded on the myth regarding the origin of music, the myth of the boy who became a *muni* bird. The myth tells of a boy who goes to catch crayfish with his older sister. He catches none and repeatedly begs for those caught by his sister, who again and again refuses his request. Finally he catches a shrimp and puts it over his nose, causing it to turn a bright purple red, the color of a *muni* bird's beak. His hands turn into wings and when he opens his mouth to speak the falsetto cry of a *muni* bird comes out. As he flies away his sister begs him to come back and have some of the crayfish but his cries continue and become a song, semiwept, semisung: "Your crayfish you didn't give me. I have no sister. I'm hungry. . . ." For the

---

1. Examples of *gisalo* and other varieties of Kaluli song can be heard on the album *The Kaluli of Papua Niugini: Weeping and Song* (Musicaphon BM 30 SL 2702). [Mackey's note.]   2. *Slavery and Social Death: A Comparative Study* (Cambridge, 1982). [Mackey's note.]

FROM *The Politics of Poetic Form: Poetry and Public Policy*, 1990. Originally presented on April 26, 1983, as part of the St. Mark's Talks series and first published in *Callaloo*, Vol. 10., No. 1., 1987. This excerpt is Part 1 of a five-part essay.

Kaluli, then, the quintessential source of music is the orphan's ordeal—an orphan being anyone denied kinship, social sustenance, anyone who suffers, to use Orlando Patterson's phrase, "social death,"[2] the prototype for which is the boy who becomes a *muni* bird. Song is both a complaint and a consolation dialectically tied to that ordeal, where in back of "orphan" one hears echoes of "orphic," a music which turns on abandonment, absence, loss. Think of the black spiritual "Motherless Child." Music is wounded kinship's last resort.

In *Sound and Symbol*, whose title Feld alludes to and echoes, Victor Zuckerkandl offers "a musical concept of the external world," something he also calls "a critique of our concept of reality from the point of view of music." He goes to great lengths to assert that music bears witness to what's left out of that concept of reality, or, if not exactly what, to the fact that something *is* left out. The world, music reminds us, inhabits while extending beyond what meets the eye, resides in but rises above what's apprehensible to the senses. This coinherence of immanence and transcendence the Kaluli attribute to and symbolize through birds, which for them are both the spirits of the dead and the major source of the everyday sounds they listen to as indicators of time, location and distance in their physical environment. In Zuckerkandl's analysis, immanence and transcendence meet in what the terms "the dynamic quality of tones," the relational valence or vectorial give and take bestowed on tones by their musical context. He takes great pains to show that "no material process can be co-ordinated with it," which allows him to conclude:

> Certainly, music transcends the physical; but it does not therefore transcend tones. Music rather helps the thing "tone" to transcend its own physical constituent, to break through into a nonphysical mode of being, and there to develop in a life of unexpected fullness. Nothing but tones! As if tone were not the point where the world that our senses encounter becomes transparent to the action of nonphysical forces, where we as perceivers find ourselves eye to eye, as it were, with a purely dynamic reality—the point where the external world gives up its secret and manifests itself, immediately, *as symbol*. To be sure, tones say, signify, point to—what? Not to something lying "beyond tones." Nor would it suffice to say that tones point to other tones—as if we had first tones, and then pointing as their attribute. No—in musical tones, being, existence, is indistinguishable from, *is*, pointing-beyond-itself, meaning, saying.[3]

One easily sees the compatibility of this musical concept of the world, this assertion of the intrinsic symbolicity of the world, with poetry. Yeats' view that

3. *Sound and Symbol: Music and the External World* (Princeton, 1956), 371. Subsequent citations are incorporated into the text. [Mackey's note.]   4. Stephanie A. Judy, "The Grand Concord of What: Preliminary Thoughts on Musical Composition and Poetry," *Boundary 2*, VI, 1 (Fall 1977): 267–85. [Mackey's note.]   5. *Prepositions* (Berkeley, 1981), 19. [Mackey's note.]

the artist "belongs to the invisible life" or Rilke's notion of poets as "bees of the invisible" sits agreeably beside Zuckerkandl's assertion that "because music exists, the tangible and visible cannot be the whole of the given world. The intangible and invisible is itself a part of this world, something we encounter, something to which we respond." His analysis lends itself to more recent formulations as well. His explanation of dynamic tonal events in terms of a "field concept," to give an example, isn't far from Charles Olson's "composition by field." And one commentator, to give another, has brought *Sound and Symbol* to bear on Jack Spicer's work.[4]

The analogy between tone-pointing and word-pointing isn't lost on Zuckerkandl, who, having observed that "in musical tones, being, existence, is indistinguishable from, *is,* pointing-beyond-itself, meaning, saying," immediately adds: "Certainly, the being of words could be characterized the same way." He goes on to distinguish tone-pointing from word-pointing on the basis of the conventionally agreed-upon referentiality of the latter, a referentiality writers have repeatedly called into question, frequently doing so by way of "aspiring to the condition of music." "Thus poetry," Louis Zukofsky notes, "may be defined as an order of words that as movement and tone (rhythm and pitch) approaches in varying degrees the wordless art of music as a kind of mathematical limit."[5] Music encourages us to see that the symbolic is the orphic, that the symbolic realm is the realm of the orphan. Music is prod and precedent for a recognition that the linguistic realm is also the realm of the orphan, as in Octavio Paz's characterization of language as an orphan severed from the presence to which it refers and which presumably gave it birth. This recognition troubles, complicates, and contends with the unequivocal referentiality taken for granted in ordinary language:

> Each time we are served by words, we mutilate them. But the poet is not served by words. He is their servant. In serving them, he returns them to the plenitude of their nature, makes them recover their being. Thanks to poetry, language reconquers its original state. First, its plastic and sonorous values, generally disdained by thought; next, the affective values; and, finally, the expressive ones. To purify language, the poet's task, means to give it back its original nature. And here we come to one of the central themes of this reflection. The word, in itself, is a plurality of meanings.[6]

Paz is only one of many who have noted the ascendancy of musicality and multivocal meaning in poetic language. (Julia Kristeva: "The poet . . . wants to turn rhythm into a dominant element . . . wants to make language perceive

6. *The Bow and the Lure* (New York, 1973), 37. [Mackey's note.]

what it doesn't want to say, provide it with its matter independently of the sign, and free it from denotation."[7])

Poetic language is language owning up to being an orphan, to its tenuous kinship with the things it ostensibly refers to. This is why in the Kaluli myth the origin of music is also the origin of poetic language. The words of the song the boy who becomes a *muni* bird resorts to are different from those of ordinary speech. Song language "amplifies, multiplies, or intensifies the relationship of the word to its referent," as Feld explains:

> In song, text is not primarily a proxy for a denoted subject but self-consciously multiplies the intent of the word.
>
> . . . Song poetry goes beyond pragmatic referential communication because it is explicitly organized by canons of reflexiveness and self-consciousness that are not found in ordinary talk.
>
> The uniqueness of poetic language is unveiled in the story of "the boy who became a *muni* bird." Once the boy has exhausted the speech codes for begging, he must resort to another communication frame. Conversational talk, what the Kaluli call *to halaido*, "hard words," is useless once the boy has become a bird; now he resorts to talk from a bird's point of view . . . Poetic language is bird language.[8]

It bears emphasizing that this break with conventional language is brought about by a breach of expected behavior. In saying no to her brother's request for food the older sister violates kinship etiquette.

What I wish to do is work *Sound and Sentiment* together with *Sound and Symbol* in such a way that the latter's metaphysical accent aids and is in turn abetted by the former's emphasis on the social meaning of sound. What I'm after is a range of implication which will stretch, to quote Stanley Crouch, "from the cottonfields to the cosmos." You notice again that it's black music I'm talking about, a music whose "critique of our concept of reality" is notoriously a critique of social reality, a critique of social arrangements in which, because of racism, one finds oneself deprived of community and kinship, cut off. The two modes of this critique which I'll be emphasizing Robert Farris Thompson notes among the "ancient African organizing principles of song and dance":

> *suspended accentuation patterning* (offbeat phrasing of melodic and choreographic accents); and, at a slightly different but equally recurrent level of exposition, *songs and dances of social allusion* (music which, however danceable and "swinging," remorselessly contrasts social imperfections against implied criteria for perfect living).[9]

7. *Desire in Language: A Semiotic Approach to Literature and Art* (New York, 1980), 31. [Mackey's note.]   8. *Sound and Sentiment: Birds, Weeping, Poetics and Song in Kaluli Expression* (Philadelphia, 1982), 34. [Mackey's note.]   9. *Flash of the Spirit: African and Afro-American Art and Philosophy* (New York, 1984), xiii. [Mackey's note.]

Still, the social isn't all of it. One needs to hear alongside Amiri Baraka listening to Jay McNeeley, that "the horn spat enraged sociologies,"[10] but not without noting a simultaneous mystic thrust. Immanence and transcendence meet, making the music social as well as cosmic, political and metaphysical as well. The composer of "Fables of Faubus" asks Fats Navarro, "What's *outside* the universe?"[11]

This meeting of transcendence and immanence I evoke, in my own work, through the figure of the phantom limb. In the letter which opens *From a Broken Bottle Traces of Perfume Still Emanate* N. begins:

> You should've heard me in the dream last night. I found myself walking down a sidewalk and came upon an open manhole off to the right out of which came (or strewn around which lay) the disassembled parts of a bass clarinet. Only the funny thing was that, except for the bell of the horn, all the parts looked more like plumbing fixtures than like parts of a bass clarinet. Anyway, I picked up a particularly long piece of "pipe" and proceeded to play. I don't recall seeing anyone around but somehow I knew the "crowd" wanted to hear "Naima." I decided I'd give it a try. In any event, I blew into heaven knows what but instead of "Naima" what came out was Shepp's solo on his version of "Cousin Mary" on the *Four for Trane* album—only infinitely more gruffly resonant and varied and warm. (I even threw in a few licks of my own.) The last thing I remember is coming to the realization that what I was playing already existed on a record. I could hear scratches coming from somewhere in back and to the left of me. This realization turned out, of course, to be what woke me up.
>
> Perhaps Wilson Harris is right. There are musics which haunt us like a phantom limb. Thus the abrupt breaking off. Therefore the "of course." No more than the ache of some such would-be extension.[12]

I'll say more about Wilson Harris later. For now, let me simply say that the phantom limb is a felt recovery, a felt advance beyond severance and limitation which contends with and questions conventional reality, that it's a feeling for what's not there which reaches beyond as it calls into question what is. Music as phantom limb arises from a capacity for feeling which holds itself apart from numb contingency. The phantom limb haunts or critiques a condition in which feeling, consciousness itself, would seem to have been cut off. It's this condition, the non-objective character of reality, to which Michael Taussig applies the expression "phantom objectivity," by which he means the veil by way of which a social order renders its role in the construction of reality

10. *Tales* (New York, 1967), 77. [Mackey's note.]   11. Charles Mingus, *Beneath the Underdog* (New York, 1980), 262. [Mackey's note.]   12. *Bedouin Hornbook* (Charlottesville, 1986), 1. [Mackey's note.]

invisible: "a commodity-based society produces such phantom objectivity, and in so doing it obscures its roots—the relations between people. This amounts to a socially instituted paradox with bewildering manifestations, the chief of which is the denial by the society's members of the social construction of reality."[13] "Phantom," then, is a relative, relativizing term which cuts both ways, occasioning a shift in perspective between real and unreal, an exchange of attributes between the two. So the narrator in Josef Skvorecky's *The Bass Saxophone* says of the band he's inducted into: "They were no longer a vision, a fantasy, it was rather the sticky-sweet panorama of the town square that was unreal."[14] The phantom limb reveals the illusory rule of the world it haunts.

13. *The Devil and Commodity Fetishism in South America* (Chapel Hill, 1980), 4. [Mackey's note.]   14. *The Bass Saxophone* (London, 1980), 109. [Mackey's note.]

Steve McCaffery ━━━━━━━━━━━━━━━━━━━━━

Language Writing: from Productive to Libidinal Economy

Barthes, in his masterly reading of Balzac's *Sarrasine,* distinguishes two fundamental types of texts: the readerly (*lisible*) and the writerly (*scriptable*). The readerly is the classic text, grounded in a transmission theory of communication and in an ideology of exchange, the human condition of whose reader Barthes sums up in the following way:

> Our literature is characterized by the pitiless divorce which the liter-
> ary institution maintains between the producer of the text and its user,
> between its owner and its customer, between its author and its reader. This
> reader is thereby plunged into a kind of idleness—he is intransitive; he is, in
> short, *serious*: instead of gaining access to the magic of the signifier, to the
> pleasure of writing, he is left with no more than the poor freedom either to
> accept or reject the text: reading is nothing more than a referendum.[1]

The writerly text by contrast is resistant to habitual reading; it is "the novelistic without the novel, poetry without the poem . . . production without product"[2] making the reader no longer a consumer but a producer of the text. The writerly proposes the *unreadable* as the ideological site of a departure from consumption to production, presenting the domain of its own interior, interacting elements (Barthes' "magic of the signifiers") as the networks and circuits of an ultimately intractible and untotalized meaning.

What I would like to question in this approach to the unreadable is Barthes' and subsequent writers' tacit identification of *production, creativity* and *value* that attains the status of an ideological occlusion. Or to phrase it differently: what alternative approaches are open to the opaque text other than semantic production?

I

Semantic Production and the Issue of the Unreadable Text

I refer to Language Writing as an heterogenous body of writerly texts that made its appearance throughout the seventies and early eighties in the

1. Roland Barthes, *S/Z*, tr. Richard Miller (New York: Hill and Wang, 1974), p. 4.   2. Ibid. p. 5.

This paper was first presented as part of The Festival of Canadian Poetry, organized by Robert Bertholf and Robert Creeley, State University of New York at Buffalo in October 1980. Reprinted from *North of Invention: Critical Writings 1973–1986*, 3rd ed. New York, 2000.

magazines *Hills, Roof, This, Tottel's*; the small presses of *Tuumba, Burning Deck, Sun & Moon,* and whose major theoretical articulations have appeared in *Open Letter, Alcheringa* and *L=A=N=G=UA=G=E*. This list is not exhaustive and neither is the following one of significant practitioners: Bruce Andrews, Charles Bernstein, Clark Coolidge, Robert Grenier, Lyn Hejinian, Jackson Mac Low, Bob Perelman, Stephen Rodefer, Peter Seaton, Ron Silliman, Barrett Watten and Diane Ward. A certain definitional miasma has arisen that has argued for a consistent *school* or *movement* in this body of work, but such imputed consistency is contradicted by the facts themselves. My own attempt here is to release a few flies into the ointment by outlining three major notions that relate significantly to the historical and epistemological situation of Language Writing and to take account of the major critical implications that issue from the "theoretical wound" of any appeal to defetishization by way of a return to semantic productivity. In the paper's second part, two alternative economies to the utilitarian value of semantic production are proposed: libidinal and general economies. There will be no argument along the lines of an excluded middle and the three economies are presented in mutually non-privileged situations.

Writing emerges as a profound dialectic of its occasion, one which is both personal and historical. I will take as a premise that writing must emerge inside the problematics of the concept of writing itself (which today in the light of Deleuze, Kristeva, Lacan and Derrida are enormous), that the purpose of a certain writing should be to raise these problems, that writing's contemporaneity is always an historical problem and that the problem of history itself is, to a large extent, the problem of ideological inscription.

There are at least three major structural-epistemological shifts of great significance that we should measure against their historical ideological antecedents; they are not intended to project a set theory of Language Writing but are nevertheless important to an understanding of the complex context that forms the ground for any new scriptural practice.

1. FROM WORD TO SIGN

In Language Writing it is the sign rather than the word that is the critical unit of inscription. This shift of writing *from a verbal to a semiological context* was certainly anticipated as early as the *Course* of Saussure where he describes the linguistic sign as a binary, oppositive relation that involves two functional elements: a discharging signifier and a discharged signified.[3] The signifying act

3. The roots of western semiotics can be traced back through Saussure to the Stoics. There are no complete texts on the subject, however, and any notion of Stoic language theory must be gleaned from the scattered fragments and quotations surviving in such anti-Stoic works as the Pyrrhonistic tracts of Sextus Empiricus. From Sextus, we learn of frequent references to a *signifier* and a *signified*, but reference to the *sign* itself is lacking. Early Greek writing on language theory (in both the Stoics and in Aristotle) illustrate the symptoms of confused

(from which all linguistic meaning arises) comprises a passage from the sounds and formal graphic shapes that make up the signifier over to what those shapes represent (or discharge) in the form of a mental or acoustic image. Implicit in Saussure's theory of the sign is the notion of meaning presenting itself as a *diacritical dependency* on the oppositions of one signifier to another, which marks a fundamental break with the earlier atomistic theory of meaning that the classic notion of the word as a container supports. Saussure breaks with the belief that linguistic identity is substantial; he shows that language comprises only differences without positive terms and linguistic identity takes the form of such formal relational differences within the total system.[4]

A writing grounded on this notion of the sign takes the form of a negative articulation along an axis of absence and betweeness and upon which meanings are effected through differential relations and more by what words *don't* say than by what they do.

2. FROM WRITING AS META-SIGN TO WRITING AS WRITING

From the dawning of a consciousness about their opposition, writing and speech have been hierarchized with writing condemned to a secondary position as a debased system of silent markers. Lying behind phonetic ideology's devaluation of writing is the dream of a union of form and meaning in some kind of suppressed, but recuperable, plenitude. Plato in the *Phaedrus* and Aristotle in the *Peri Hermeneton* both treat writing as the sign of a sign.[5]

---

argumentation through an inadequate separation of the logic of the sign from theories of both rhetoric and logic. For a concise summary of the development of semiotics from the Stoics, through Aristotle to St. Augustine, see Tzvetan Todorov, *Theories of the Symbol,* tr. Catherine Porter (Ithaca: Cornell University Press, 1982).

4. Whilst Saussure's *Course in General Linguistics* stands as probably the key document in the turning point of Sign Theory it should be pointed out that Saussure himself did not write the book. The *Course,* as we have it, was compiled in 1916—three years after his death—from his students' notes taken down during his lectures at the *Ecole practique des hautes études* in Paris. Saussure's "actual" beliefs, like many of Wittgenstein's and the entirety of Socrates', are quite literally hearsay. There is a revealing, interrupted passage (Ms. fr. 3957/2) in the collection of Saussure's papers at the Public and University Library of Geneva which reads:

> absolutely incomprehensible if I were not forced to confess that I suffer from a morbid horror of the pen, and that this work is for me an experience of sheer torture.

5. For a full discussion of the Platonic attack on writing see Jacques Derrida, "Plato's Pharmacy" in *Dissemination,* tr. Barbara Johnson (University of Chicago Press, 1981). Derrida argues that Plato's condemnation of writing involves a covert appeal to a double sense of writing: the one physical, the other metaphorical. The well-known passage in the *Phaedrus* where King Thamus responds to Theuth's proffered gift writing is appended here for convenience:

> The fact is that this invention [writing] will produce forgetfulness in the souls of those who have learned it because they will not need to exercise their memories, being able to rely on what is written, using the stimulus of external marks that are alien to themselves rather than, from within, their own unaided powers to call things to mind. So it's not a remedy for memory, but for reminding that you have discovered.

Speech, being closer to the breath and body of the subject is thereby seen as closer to an authentic presence and is granted a fundamental anteriority to the written mark. Writing, at best, is an untrustworthy representation of a representation. Speech is the living and the living is the originary of all value. This phonetic-pneumatic myth of a breath governed, anterior authenticity has been protected at the expense of the written through western thought from Plato to Nietzsche; it is significantly virulent in Charles Olson and the aesthetics of presence that grew up around his notions of projective verse. In his *Letter to Elaine Feinstein*, Olson comes remarkably close to the anti-representational, anti-referential position that Language Writing grounds itself within: the attack on the completed thought, the dead-spot of description and the centripetal, self-annihilating push of language chained by reference to reality all promise a sense of writing based on textual immanence. But in many places come the appeals to primaries, origins, returns and anti-miasmic backtrackings that betray this link to phonetic ideology:

> Verse now, 1950, if it is to go ahead, if it is to be of *essential* use, must, I take it, catch up and put into itself certain laws and possibilities of the breath, of the breathing of the man who writes as well as of his listenings.[6]
>
> Because breath allows *all* the speech-force of language back in (speech is the "solid" of verse, is the secret of a poem's energy), because now, a poem has, by speech, solidity, everything in it can now be treated as solids, objects, things . . . [7]

This is reminiscent of Plato's attack on writing in the *Phaedrus* as a dead and rigid knowledge learned by heart, promoting of a repetition without knowing. The link is clear and can be easily verified in parallel readings of the *Cratylus, Phaedrus* and Olson's *Human Universe.* In his essay on Projective Verse (which arose out of the contemporary issues of prosody circa 1950) we can detect this underlying ideological seam that permits Olson to argue for a specific value in verse without questioning the problematics of a value *per se.* His criticism of closed poetics actually reduces to a criticism of a closed interior and moves by a line of argument that derives its ammunition from a long tradition of western metaphysics. And the ideological operation is not too covert: breath, by providing "solidity", "thing-ness" is closer to a presence and must therefore be fixed anterior to writing, whilst writing has the status of a repressive exterior that constrains the authentic structure of breath. In the double appeal of breath and syllable, Olson attempts to externalize a closed interior. The typewriter (as Olson defends it) ironically rescues writing from

---

6. Charles Olson, "Projective Verse" in *The Human Universe and Other Essays*, ed. Donald Allen (New York: Grove Press, 1967) p. 51.   7. Ibid, p. 56.

its historical villain's role by pushing writing further away from its traditionally tight, symplegmatic involvement with speech, giving it the formal (and ideological) distance of a *notation* as distinct from a supplement.

Writing, however, is neither a fixed, repressive exterior nor a meta-sign; it is, as Derrida and others have convincingly argued, a fundamental trace structure and as such is *always* present in speech *as speech's necessary condition.* (Derrida announces this structure by various terms—the supplement, the hinge, the *differance,* the *pharmakon*—as the most general structure of semantic economy). Sign production (the discharge-discharged dynamic of the signifier-signified) operates as a delay that also differentiates. It is the nature of the linguistic sign to be neither itself nor any other thing (Saussure fails to point out this violently contradictory logic of signification which is, nevertheless, implicit within his own diacritical formulation of the sign). The signifier—because it is always standing for a signified—can never be itself; whilst the signified—in always being stood for—is constantly withheld and likewise never present. This is what Derrida terms *differance* (difference *and* deferral) which cannot be fixed in space and time but constitutes the pre-logical basis of all sign production:

> We provisionally give the name *differance* to this *sameness* which is not *identical:* by the silent writing of its *a,* it has the desired advantage of referring to differing, *both* as spacing/temporalizing and as the movement that structures every dissociation . . . *Differance* is neither a *word* nor a *concept.*[8]

Implicit in *differance* is the fact that sound can certainly be heard in language but likewise *can never be present inside it.*[9]

3. FROM POEM TO TEXT

Text here is not simply a lexical preference but marks a shift in the conception of scriptive work from a fixed object of analysis or conception, to an open, methodological field for semantic production. Language today no longer poses problems of meaning but practical issues of use; the relevant question being not "what does this piece of writing mean"? (as if meaning was somehow a represented essence in a sign the activity of reading substantially extracts) but "how does this writing work"? There is a radical shift in Language Writing from the poem as object, to the text as a methodological field that implies also the issue of a sociological detachment of the writer from his historical

8. Jacques Derrida, "Differance" in *Speech and Phenomena,* tr. David B. Allison (Evanston: Northwestern University Press, 1973) p. 129–30.   9. What is at issue is not a triumphant return to writing of its appropriated rights, nor a reversal of the valuational poles in the binary opposition of speech/writing. Rather it is the issue of re-situating writing *within an expanded notion of itself.*

role and ideological identity of author. Language Writing resists reduction to a monological message, offering instead an organized surface of signifiers whose signifieds are undetermined. There is a primacy lent to readership as a productive engagement with a text in order to generate local pockets of meaning as semantic eruptions or events that do not accumulate into aggregated masses. The texts, whilst written, demand writers to produce *from* them, for what the texts deliberately lack are *authors*: the traditional literary fiction of a central, detached but recoverable source of origin. Vicki Mistacco has suggested the term "ludism" for this type of writing:

> 'Ludism' may be simply defined as the open play of signification, as the free and productive interaction of forms, of signifiers and signifieds, without regard for an original or ultimate meaning. In literature, ludism signifies textual play; the text is viewed as a game affording both author and reader the possibility of producing endless meanings and relationships.[10]

Language, in the following text, reveals itself as a primary, nonintentional scriptive play, incapable of being foreclosed or exceeded and offering itself as a highly volatile circulation of signifiers.

my high
mallorca
tailored
sitten (s)ought sunk
ogled a blond
(pilaf)
()unched
th... b...rb...n th...mb...l...n...
mAgiC
"moon" and "stars" and lentil
agaze[11]

There are obvious iconic constraints: why the justified left-hand margin? why the symmetrical elisions? And equally there are resonating alter-texts: do the parentheses suggest a reading of Husserlian bracketing? are the words hung in quotations textual complications or textural echoes? does the eighth line suggest a move towards completion (plenitude) or decomposition (absence)? What is the semiotic suggestion in the eruptive capitalizations in line nine? Do these suggest an intentional presence or semantic freeplay? What is important to grasp here is the characteristic *excess* of this text. In a way it cannot be spoken about but only participated within and a criticism would comprise the documentation of

10. Precise source not located.   11. Charles Bernstein, *Disfrutes* (Peter Ganick, 1980).

its reading as an extended writing. It might be argued that texts like the above have no concern with communication (or at least with the dominant theory of communication that sees it as a transmission from producer to receiver along a semiotic axis of production-consumption, giver-recipient) but rather with establishing a politicized effervescence within the code in which signs can never settle into messages from "authors" and intentional language can hold no power. At this point semantics would seem to get returned to the order of production and use value as part of the historical step towards the re-politicization of language as an open field of truly human engagements.

What Language Writing is proposing is a shift for writing away from literature and the readable, towards the dialectical domain of its own interiorities as primarily an interacting surface of signifiers in the course of which a sociological shift in the nature of readership must be proposed. For the texts of Andrews, Bernstein, Coolidge, Watten cannot be consumed but only produced. There is an operation in excess of Barthes' unreadability, however, for beyond the appeal to semantic production is a certain revelation and critique of the ideological contamination operative upon the very order of sign production. The issue, of course, is political, but it is not an issue of extra-linguistic concerns to be discussed by means of language, but one of detecting the hidden operation of those repressive mechanisms that language and the socio-economic base actually share. In Language Writing this critique has so far taken the form of exposing through their political analogies two major fetishisms operating in language: grammar and the referent.

GRAMMAR, STATE AND CAPITAL

Grammatical effects obtain not only in language but in state operation also. Deleuze and Guattari describe the State as "the transcendent law that governs fragments"—a description that applies equally to grammatical as to political control. As a transcendent law, grammar acts as a mechanism that regulates the free circulation of meaning, organizing the fragmentary and local into compound, totalized wholes. Through grammatical constraint then, meanings coalesce into meaning. Denied independent and undetermined discharge through a surface play, the controlled parts are thrust into an aggregated phrase that projects meaning as a destination or culmination to a gaze. Like capital (its economic counterpart) grammar extends a law of value to new objects by a process of totalization, reducing the free play of the fragments to the status of delimited, organizing parts within an intended larger whole. Signifiers appear and are then subordinately organized into these larger units whose culmination is a meaning which is then invested in a further aggregation. Grammar's law is a combinatory, totalizing logic that excludes at all costs any fragmentary life. It is clear that grammar effects a meaning whose form is that of *a surplus value generated by an aggregated group of working parts for immediate investment into an extending chain of meaning.* The concern of grammar homologizes the capitalistic concern for accumulation, profit and investment in a future goal. Language Writing, in contrast, emerges more as an expenditure of meanings in the forms of isolated active parts and for the sake of the present moment which the aggregative, accumulative disposition of the grammatical text seeks to shun. (We must return shortly to this point and see how Language Writing conceived as semantic production is not entirely free of this "grammatical" concern).

REFERENCE, REPRESENTATION AND COMMODITY FETISHISM

Fetishism is a mechanism of occlusion that displaces and eclipses the true nature of commodities as the products of human labour and interaction, detaching them magically from their productive bases and presenting them as self-perpetuating "things" that take their place within social circulation as an exchange value. The referential fetish in language is inseparable from the representational theory of the sign. Proposed as intentional, as always "about" some extra-linguistic thing, language must always refer beyond itself to a corresponding reality. The linguistic task is not to draw in and centre a productive activity within itself, but to fulfill a deictic function that points beyond itself to an exterior goal. The referential fetish thrives on the myth of *transparent signification,* on words as innocent, unproblematic sign-posts to a monological message or intention; it wants a message as a product to be consumed with as little attention as possible drawn to the words' dialectical engagements. Reference reaches its most fetishized form in the readable bestseller, the world of rapid and simple linguistic movement in which language reduces to the status of perfect fenestration: a clear window of words to carry a reader effectively along a story line.

I have argued that Language Writing involves a shift away from literary concerns and back to the ground of semantic production; it chooses a context of productive play for a repoliticization of the word as a scene for common human engagement; it similarly exposes the fetishization of the linguistic sign by ideological constraint that brings the linguistic order disturbingly close to that of the political order. Central to both this shift and exposé is the felt need to extend writing beyond a simple relation to consciousness towards a dialectical relation with production. This is seen as a primordial political act that detaches the reader from language as a communicative subject in order to re-attach her as an agent of production. Behind this is an implicit operation of judgement: a commitment to the primacy of utilarian values and a commitment that will be examined in this paper's second part.

II

From Semantic Productivity to Libidinal Intensity and General Economy

Work corresponds to the care of tomorrow, pleasure to that of the present moment. Work is useful and satisfactory, pleasure useless, leaving a feeling of unsatisfaction. These considerations put economy at the basis of morality and at the basis of poetry.[12]

If Language Writing successfully detaches Language from the historical purpose of summarizing global meaning replacing the goal of totality with the free polydynamic drive of parts, it nevertheless falls short in addressing the full implications of this break and seems especially to fail in taking full account of the impact of the human subject with the thresholds of linguistic meaning. It is at the critical locus of productive desire that this writing opens itself up to an alternative "libidinal" economy which operates across the precarious boundaries of the symbolic and the biological and has its basis in intensities. François Fourquet describes the libidinal complex as a complex not of representations "but of intensive forces, active only in the realm of power in the most material, the most 'political' sense of the word . . . The libido is force, pure power . . . the libido does not have an image. It is not representable".[13] Libidinal intensities are oppositionally related to the fixity of the written; they are decoding drives that seep through and among texts, jamming codes and pulverizing language chains; they are liberative of the energy trapped inside linguistic structures. Libidinal circuits, however, are intractable, intensely permeative and impossible to locate as specific, operational factors; they derive from the pre-linguistic (infantile) drives of both the writing and reading subjects. It is at that pivotal point, where language is simultaneously composed and dissolved, made and unmade, consumed and regurgitated, that language connects with the unconscious and its drives.

Barthes:
THERE EXISTS FUNDAMENTALLY IN WRITING A "CIRCUMSTANCE" FOREIGN TO LANGUAGE.

Kristeva:
COMMUNICATION DOES NOT EQUAL WRITING.

Bataille:
IN A SENSE POETRY IS ALWAYS THE OPPOSITE OF POETRY.

12. Georges Bataille, *Literature and Evil*, tr. Alastair Hamilton (London: Calder & Boyars, 1973) p. 36.   13. François Fourquet, "Libidinal Nietzsche" in *Semiotext(e)*, III, 1, 1978, p. 71–74.

Charles Bernstein

FROM Artifice of Absorption

By *absorption* I mean engrossing, engulfing
completely, engaging, arresting attention, reverie,
attention intensification, rhapsodic, spellbinding,
mesmerizing, hypnotic, total, riveting,
enthralling: belief, conviction, silence.

Impermeability suggests artifice, boredom,
exaggeration, attention scattering, distraction,
digression, interruptive, transgressive,
undecorous, anticonventional, unintegrated, fractured,
fragmented, fanciful, ornately stylized, rococo,
baroque, structural, mannered, fanciful, ironic,
iconic, schtick, camp, diffuse, decorative,
repellent, inchoate, programmatic, didactic,
theatrical, background muzak, amusing: skepticism,
doubt, noise, resistance.

Absorptive & antiabsorptive
works both require artifice, but the former may hide
this while the latter may *flaunt*
it. & absorption may dissolve
into theater as these distinctions chimerically
shift & slide. Especially since,
as in much of my own work, antiabsorptive
techniques are used toward
absorptive ends; or, in satiric writing (it's a put
on, get it?), absorptive means are used
toward antiabsorptive ends. It remains
an open question, & an unresolvable
one, what
will produce an absorptive poem & what will
produce a nonabsorptive one.

These
textual
dynamics

FROM *A Poetics*, 1992.

can
be
thought
about
in
relation
to
the
reader
&
to
the
structure
of
the
poem.

On Fordian absorptive terms, the reader
(a.k.a. beholder) must be ignored, as in
the "fourth wall" convention in theater, where what
takes place on the stage is assumed to be sealed
off from the audience. Nothing
in the text should cause self-consciousness
about the reading process: it should be as if
the writer & the reader are not present.
As Diderot puts it, also (if unwittingly) articulating
the dilemma of the role assigned to women in
sexist society, *"It is the difference between a
woman who is seen and a woman who exhibits
herself."*[1] This distinction is
a fiction; texts are written to be read or heard,
that is, exhibited; but the degree the "teller"

1. Quoted by Fried, p. 97; italics added. Diderot's remark epitomizes the double bind of women being defined by a male gaze: to be seen as a woman one must be passive, while to stare back (as in Manet's *Olympia*) is to exhibit oneself, to become a whore. This implicitly valorizes the woman as subject, absorbed in the world as opposed to acting on it. As Nicole Brossard made clear at the New Poetics Colloquium in Vancouver, discussing her *Journal intime* (Montreal: Editions Herbes Rouges, 1984), the subjective space is treacherous for a woman since it risks accepting the subjectification of women in the model described by Diderot. Brossard's response is to write something called an "intimate journal", a diary (the traditionally accepted form of women's writing) that refuses the primary terms of that form, refuses, that is, to absorb the gaze of the reader but rather deflects this gaze onto the artificial/actual process of self-construction: "ma vie qui n'est qu'un tissue de mots" [my life which is only a tissue of words] (p. 15). This transformed, you might also say evacuated, journal requires the name *poetry*.

or "way it's told" are allowed to come
into focus affects the experience of "what"
is being told or "what" is
unfolding. Nor is poetry,
by nature emphasizing its artifice,
immune from this dynamic. For poems
do not necessarily make the beholder conscious
of his or her role as a reader, nor can such
self-consciousness be obliterated only by
presenting highly visualizable scenes of sea
voyages or Homeric adventure.

Many nineteenth-century lyric poems involve a self-
absorbed address to a beloved, the gods, or
the poet her/himself: an address that, because
it is *not* to the reader but to some presence
anterior or
interior to
the poem, induces readerly absorption
by creating an effect of overhearing in contrast to
confronting.

Absorption can be broken
by any direct address
to the reader, whether as in
a how-to book ("now go get that leaky poem"), an
instruction manual ("stop here and complete the
test questions"), a sermon ("I'm calling
on you, not your neighbor, not the Jew Boy
next door, not them playdough inverts"), the Ten
Commandments ("I/thou"), or just by asking
you to look at the period at the end of this
sentence & pointing
out that it's about the size of your macula.—"Who
are you calling a macula!" Don't get huffy. Don't
get "huffy". Why just yesterday (but when was
today, dear reader?) Bob Perelman was saying "I'm
also using more repetition, deictics [words that
point, like 'this' word but which word is *this*
word 'this' or this], speechlike elements which posit
a co-presence of 'speaker & listener', i.e., writer

and reader." Perelman quotes from "Cliff Notes":
"It can't be the knobs' fault because this is back
before knobs" & from "Let's Say":

> A page is being beaten
> back across the face of 'things'.
> . . . . .
> and the you and I spends its life
> trying to read the bill
> alone in the dark
> big wide streets lined with language glue

Perelman comments:

> The reader and the writer, "the you and the I," are such languages
> transforming into pulp language, non-languages and back, degraded,
> exploded, overburdened systems of public & private address. There's no
> inner escape from our environment, where such powerful emblems of
> coercion as USA TODAY constantly conflate the initials U.S. with their
> editorial staff and with "us," so that "we" read that "we" are buoyed by
> the progress of the Salvadoran army or that "we" are attending more
> ballgames than ever this summer.[2]

Or, as he writes in "Binary": "Finally the I
writing / and the you reading (breath still misting
the glass) / examples of the body partitioned by the
word" [*The First World*, p. 47].

---

2. Bob Perelman, "Notes on *The First World*", *Line* 6 (1985), 101, 108–109; this talk was originally presented at the New Poetics Colloquium in Vancouver. The poems quoted by Perelman in his talk, as well as the citations that follow, are from *The First World* (Great Barrington, Mass.: The Figures, 1986).—"If only the plot would leave people alone", Perelman writes in "Anti-Oedipus" (p. 20). His passionate refusal to be housed by the poem, his insistence on breaking loose from the social hypnosis that deadens response, nonetheless cannot readily be understood as preventing absorption, despite its striking awareness of itself as a poetry & its forthright address to the reader. For Perelman has created poetry that is funny, political, engaging—and does not distance itself from the reader in ways we have grown accustomed to. In a recent interview Perelman was careful to put off the suggestion that because his poems do not employ causal unity (are not "little short stories"), they are therefore not coherent. "China", a work in *The First World*, "coheres grammatically, thematically, politically in terms of tone. It's certainly not something that throws you off the track, like playing trains as a kid, whipping from side to side until someone falls off—it's not that." This last image of a train flipping the tracks is precisely a description of the effect of the antiabsorptive on reading. Interview by George Hartley, conducted in Berkeley in 1986, quoted in "Jameson's Perelman: Reification and the Material Signifier", a draft chapter of Hartley's dissertation (University of New Mexico); not included in the chapter of the same name in Hartley's *Textual Politics of the Language Poets* (Bloomington: Indiana University Press, 1989).

Absorption is blocked by misting
this glass, or by breaking it, or
by painting on its surface. Any
typographic irregularity,
any glitch in expected
syntax, any
digression . . .

Introjective Verse

)introversive   )implosive   )introspeculative

incorporating

The Rejected

Verse, what? if it is to trip and flail and fall, if it is to be *inessential,* useless, maybe could consider, losing it, forgetting laws and breadth: the breathlessness of the person who refuses to be a man when she listens.

I won't do two things: first, I won't show what introjective or CENTRIPETAL verse is, how it recoils, in its fate as decomposition, how, in distinction to the projective, it is dismayed, and 2, I'll hold back from suggesting a few contradictions about how the ebullient denial of reality takes such a verse out of believing, what that aversion does, both to the poet and her nonreaders. (Such aversion involves, for example, a return to the technical, and may, the way things hokey-poke around, lead away from drama and epic and toward the materials of poems, their sounds and shapes.)

I

First, some complexities that a person learns, if she works INTROJECTIVELY, or what can be called MISCOMPOSITION BY EAR.

(1) the *pataphysics* of the thing. A poem is energy absconded by the poet from where she got it (she will have several stashes), by way of the nonreaders themselves, all the way over to, the poem. Oy!

This is the problem which any poet who departs from adenoidal forms is specially coddled by. And it involves a whole series of blunders. From the moment she jumps back into CENTRIPETAL MISCOMPOSITION—puts herself in the bin—she can aver by no tack other than the one the poem refuses.

FROM *My Way: Speeches and Poems,* 1999.

(It is much more, for example, this backward somersaulting, than simply such a one as Wilde put, so giddily, to get us startled: life imitates art, not the other way round. Come on, girls & boys, think complex, act to redistribute the wealth!)

(2) is the *abandonment of principle*, the ludicrousness that presides so conspicuously over such dysraphisms, and, when averred, is the reason why an introjective poem refuses belief. It is this: FORM IS NEVER MORE THAN AN EXTENSION OF MALCONTENT. There it went, flapping, more USELESSNESS.

Now (2) the clumsiness of the thing, how the awkwardness of the thing can be made to dishevel the energies that the form thought it accomplished. It can never be boiled down to a statement: ONE PERCEPTION MUST NEVER LEAD DIRECTLY TO ANOTHER PERCEPTION. It means something very different than what it says, is never a matter of, at *no* points, (even—I shouldn't say—of our injuring reality as our weekly bliss) get off it, invoke arrestation, keep out of it, slow down, the perceptions, ours, the evasions, the long-term evasions, none of it, stop it as much as you can, citizen. And if you also slouch as a poet, REFUSE REFUSE REFUSE the process at some points, in some poems, once in a blue while: one perception STOPPED, SLOWED, BY ANOTHER!

So there we were, looping, where there's no dogma. And its inexcusable-ness, its uselessness, in theory. Which doesn't get us, ought not to get us, outside the cyberfactory, then, or 1995, where centripetal verse is made.

If I sing tunelessly—if I forget, and keep crying wolf, out of breath—of the sound as distinguished from the voice, it is for no cause except to loosen the part that breath plays in verse, which has been observed and practiced too well, so that verse may retreat to its proper immobility and placelessness in the mouths that are already lost. I take it that INTROJECTIVE VERSE teaches nothing, that that verse will never do what the poet intends either by the tones of her voice or theater of her breath . . .

Because the centripetal questions the speech-force of language (speech is the "red herring" of verse, the secret of the poem's delusions), because, then, a poem has, by language, evanescence, nothing that can be mistreated as solid, objectified, thinged.

II

Which makes no promises, no realities outside the poem: no stances only dances. It is the matter of content, this discontent. The content of Cleave, of Bruce, of Ball, as distinct from what I might call more "literary" ministers. There is no moment in which the introjective evasion of verse is finished, the form fuels blame. If the beginning and end is the breathlessness of words, sound in that material sense, then the domain of poetry blurs and blurts.

It's hardly this: the uselessness of a baby, by itself and thus by others, crying in its misconception of its relation to culture, that semiotic fluidlessness to which it owes its gigantic existence. If it squall, it shall find much to squall about, and shall squirm too, culture has such flummoxing ways of terrorizing all that is outside. But if it stays inside itself, if it is contained in its infancy as if it is a participant in the life immediately surrounding, it will be able to babble and in its babbling hear what is shared. It is in this sense that the introjective ache, which is the artist's artlessness in the intimate streets of enfoldment, leads to scales more intimate than the child's. It's all so easy. Culture works from irreverence, even in its constructions. Irreverence is the human's special qualification as vegetable, as mineral, as *animalady*. Language is our profanest act. And when a poet squalls about what is outside herself (in "the material world", if you object, but also the materiality in her, for that matter), then she, if she chooses to reflect on this restlessness, pays in the street where culture has given her scale, centripetal scale.

Such works, though it's no argument, could not issue from persons who conceive verse without the full resonance of human voicelessness. The introjective poet staggers from the failings of her own boasts to that syntaxophony where language digs in, where sound echoes, where utterances concatenate, where, inevitably, all acts stall.

K. Silem Mohammad

Excessivism

Everything is in the European fund blinko (whatever that means), but
at the risk of sounding like the Powerline Boys on a corndog-and-Super-
Squishee bender, I will write to you because I just heard that The Police
are reuniting for the Grammies. Now, come on. I don't believe in God,
so I don't have a problem. I hate Southwest Airlines, I always have. I may
be spoiled, but I like airlines that offer advance seat assignments and
first-class cabins for upgrades. I don't even like whales. Please, feel free
to observe the irony of my current situation: I love to sleep. You just go on
your merry way and try and explain to the bio majors that dinosaur fossils
were put in the earth to fool sinners. It's quite simple really. If someone's
chasing you, you're advised to call 911. If someone's chasing you, try
running backwards. If someone's chasing you around the house, it's super
creepy, because where do you have to run? Seriously, it freaks me out. If
someone's chasing you, kill them. You don't turn around and say "Mac users
rarely expand their computers, so the Firewire ports don't matter." Many of
you will be screaming, if I may use your expression, like *whores* when your
deeds are read before you. That's for the writing part, but one can make
the same with music (that's how David Bowie recorded "Outside"). As for
their reception, after the friendly stabs of their welcoming committee,
things got better, Sgt. Kevin Smette, of Fargo, ND, said. Suppose you're
in love with a skilled piano player who loves the look and feel of her old
acoustic piano. Suppose you're in love with Mrs. Forrest, and Mrs. Forrest
is in love with you, and you run away together in the big limousine.
Suppose you're in love with that rustler, Bern Venters. Suppose you're in
love with Ikea Corp, and watch Captain Planet cartoons to be reminded
that the main goal of corporations is rape. You don't say, "hey you wanna
go get some parfait" and they be like, "no I don't like no parfait." You just
let all the judgment and shittiness of high school go and you're free to be
yourself and stop caring. But that's not why you own a train. A train is a toy,
and a toy is to have fun with or look at and play with. You don't buy a toy
for investment, so you have to take your chances with eBay and the like. It's
like forbidden Halloween. Pain always comes during the menstrual cycle,
which is very Chibi, and animelike, and approximately four feet tall.

I'm not saying that I don't have an ego problem at times also, but when
you treat your readers like that, it's just freakin' wrong. I'm not saying that
I don't have anything to say to a fifteen-year-old. I'm not saying that I don't

FROM *Action Yes Online Quarterly* 1.5 (Spring 2007).

have moments when it's "Because Mommy Says So!" I'm not saying that I
don't have problems with *The Vagina Monologues*. But I wouldn't argue
that this is a reason to discard the Vag-Mos altogether. I'm not saying that I
don't have a EVAP solenoid, just that my scanner tells me that it's not in the
list of PIDs that I can look at. I'm not saying that I don't have nerdy dream
women lurking in my imagination. I'm not saying that I don't have days when
I look in the mirror and I'm like "silly frizzy-haired girl with no discernible
eyelashes." I'm not saying that I don't have opinions about nappy hair (clearly
my signature says I do), I'm just not comfortable making my opinion apply
to everyone. I'm not saying that I don't have a touch of carb-face myself, but
remember how hot Vince Vaughn used to be? Vaughncute. Now he's a potato.
I'm not saying that I don't have a butt or anything but I am curious. I'm
not saying that I don't have a few CDs in my iTunes library that I no longer
own. I'm not saying that I don't have an iPod, because I do. I just haven't put
anything on it yet. I finally broke down and bought one a couple weeks ago.
I'm not saying that I don't have the urge to lick it or anything. I mean . . .
uh . . . I'm offended? I'm not saying that I don't have dope-ass friends I can
already talk to. I love you guys. I'm just saying that I have deep shit inside
me, but what difference does that make? They're just ideas. The only good
thing about it is that when stop, head eventually stops hurting! The midget
arrives, and the rancher asks if he would like a male or female horse. And
that's when I shot the son of a bitch.

But how can you really care when you've got a top ten album and just did
a big successful tour? C'mon. Improves them for use in fruit leather? For
death? Why even ask? We're already a nation of living dead zombies working
day in and out like walking flesh. Too many poets and poetry clubs have
risen across the country. All of their members are now calling themselves
cowboy poets. They all have porcelain hands & arms (from the elbow), legs
from the knee down, head and necks, red painted lips, sad painted faces
(with dripping tears). I don't give a damn whether they're lifelong season-
ticket holders, fair weather fans or members of some neofascist organization.
I don't give a damn whether they're a government or not. I don't give a
damn whether they like me, President Bush or the United States or not.
I don't give a damn whether they're killed by the patriots, slaughtered
by the rebels or bombed to hell by us. I don't give a damn whether they
have an intercontinental missile or not. I don't give a damn whether they
have the Pope come over and bless the damn thing. I don't give a damn
whether they get nominated for the Grammy at all. Forced feeding leads to
gross inefficiency and low absorption coefficients (effete). Nobody should
experience anything. Don't hand-feed kittens if they don't need it. I like
the movies too and television if I can lie on the floor when I watch it. I like
the movies too, but dressing up like Frodo Baggins and poking my girl's

ass with a toy sword isn't my idea of an exciting Saturday night. I like the movies too, I am left-handed and I just had a cheeseburger and I should be asleep right now. And after all, only humans have a point of view, plants don't. As for measure and attack quality, it is necessary to avoid them as much as possible: If you're going to buy a pair of LCD monitors, why not buy them from the same manufacturer? That's the logic behind the GVLM1928 and GVLM1728. There's nothing metaphysical about your "message" that would prevent it from being destroyed if I could get my hands on all the manifestations. There's nothing metaphysical about shadows and how they come to be. Unless of course you are working for the Seattle Chamber of Commerce.

Abstraction in poetry is a phrase or word that pulls away from reality, or is one filtered step above the true meaning. I think it appears in a Ford commercial running now. Abstraction involves creating a simplified problem description in which the amount of small isolated forbidden zones and their removal becomes the determinant of water balance. For instance, the decision of whether or not to go indoors during a lightning storm is obvious. *The Nostalgia of the Infinite* is a painting by the Italian artist Giorgio de Chirico. This is all part of a movement, which I have seen through the multitudes of books I receive from publishers, to capture a picture of Jesus that is so totally opposed to computers in chess that it is verging on technofeudalism—one of my pet hates. Georgetown is to Catholic as Pepsi is to Wallace Stevens. It has nothing to do with philosophy. It's just a style of music like zydeco. The long streams of uninterrupted music have nothing to do with philosophy. There's just no money for more announcers. The Brooklyn Bridge is a nice bridge, but it has nothing to do with philosophy no matter how you slice it. Not all these young people want to be farmers, far from it! But to give you a vague idea, it's in the Midlands on the outskirts of Warwickshire. Great to know you're reading my diary, thus evoking pragmatic protests against that play with abstractions which "fiddles to a logical tune while the throbbing city burns," and sustaining the illusion that it MIGHT really be possible for one person to "Mommy" while preventing "the great American public" from spilling coffee on books. That's part of the beauty of the Web, as we see it. The beauty is, Slam was invented by a blue collar white guy in Chicago on August 27, 1959, a day in which I was tied to a cactus and assaulted by snakes (like I was a child). I went back to work and wrote my resignation letter. That leads me to where I am now. Unemployed and as happy as I've felt in years. While I was writing it I got to thinking about all of the Nintendo merchandise I had. I am guilty of spending money in Beijing (duh), but I am increasingly annoyed with blatant excessivism (is that a word?). It puts the poem in the sound hole. About. Every morning I take something I wrote on paper the day before and I put it in my guitar. It puts the poem in another language. It puts the poem in perspective and it's different. It puts the poem between the reader, or the listener, the reader and the subject, or the world, rather than delivering the reader into the world. It puts the poem and the poet under terrible pressure. The poem is at last fifteen words long. The poem is at last 2500 years old. The poem is at last a symbol for all church doors. Excessivism to the max. In all modesty I must tell you that I am a remarkable fellow, even among the talented cat family of which I am a part. In all modesty, I type faster than a court reporter, baby. While I have certain areas that usually burn easily, like the tops of my feet and my chest area, using this product has prevented the need for me to worry. While I have certain tastes that drift toward the indie/emo side of the spectrum, I can really groove with Alain Robbe-Grillet. Poetry being one of the global fields of human endeavor, it is only a matter of time and talented graduate students. For a time, people thought that electrical brainwaves indicated very clearly whether a person was alive or dead. For a time, people thought I went to high school with them or something. For a time people thought they could drug millions of baby-boom women. For a time people thought the author was a man. Excessivism is when it starts to become a problem—when it causes you to drop out of high school, become a bum and die of alcoholism at the age of 26.

What can we expect from a country where the candidate that gets more votes loses? (This is getting good, isn't it?) Everything, but we won't go into that now. Everything, but we won't have to waste our time trying to do anything. Everything, but we won't be able to afford such a fantasy. Everything, but we won't give it back if something's not right. Everything, but we won't be sure till the cooking is over. Everything, but we won't use magic to undo everything. Everything, but we won't all get to see it. It is too new, too uncertain, too strange to vote Green. It is too new, too aggressive, or too disturbing to the ego structure. It is too new, too hard, and smells like department store. But it, like our cultural tourism industry, is a kind of weird story from Africa about some nuns. You could call it nicotinism or excessivism or whatever you want. The recent propagandists still do not read F. H. Bradley. The result is that they are content.

Kenneth Goldsmith

Conceptual Poetics

. . . i had always had mixed feelings

about being considered a poet   "if robert lowell is a
poet i dont want to be a poet   if robert frost was a
poet i dont want to be a poet   if socrates was a poet
ill consider it"

—David Antin

A poet finds a grammar book from the late nineteenth century and, inspired by Gertrude Stein's confession, "I really do not know that anything has ever been more exciting than diagramming sentences," proceeds to parse the entire 185-page book—every word and letter, from the table of contents to the index—by its own system of analysis.

Another poet teams up with a scientist to create an example of living poetry by infusing a chemical alphabet into a sequence of DNA, which is then implanted into a bacterium. Thousands of research dollars later, they are in the process of creating an organism embedded with this poem, strong enough to survive a nuclear holocaust, thereby creating a poem which will outlast humanity and perhaps even the lifespan of the planet earth.

Yet another poet decides to retype an entire edition of a day's copy of *The New York Times*. Everywhere there is a letter or numeral, it is transcribed onto a page. Like a medieval scribe, the poet sequesters himself for over a year until he is finished. The resulting text is published as a 900-page book.

Sounds like something out of a Borgesian fantasy? No. These works are key examples of conceptual poetry, a broad movement that has been receiving a fair amount of attention lately. Conceptual writing or uncreative writing is a poetics of the moment, fusing the avant-garde impulses of the last century with the technologies of the present, one that proposes an expanded field for twenty-first century poetry. Not satisfied to exclusively be bound between the pages of a book, this new writing continually morphs from the printed page to the webpage, from the gallery space to the science lab, from the social space of the poetry reading to social space of the blog. It's a poetics of flux, one that celebrates instability and uncertainty. And although its practitioners often come from disciplines outside of literature, the work is framed through the discourse and economy of poetry: these works are

FROM http://www.sibila.com.br/index.php/sibila-english/410-conceptual-poetics.

received by, written about, and studied by readers of poetry. Freed from the market constraints of the art world or the commercial constraints of the computing & science worlds, the non-economics of poetry create a perfectly valueless space in which these valueless works can flourish.

Conceptual writing's concerns are generally two pronged, as manifested in the tensions between materiality and concept. On the materiality side, traditional notions of a poem's meaning, emotion, metaphor, image, and song are subservient to the raw physicality of language. On the conceptual side, it's the machine that drives the poem's construction that matters. The conceptual writer assumes that the mere trace of any language in a work—be it morphemes, words, or sentences—will carry enough semantic and emotional weight on its own without any further subjective meddling from the poet, known as non-interventionalist tactic. To work with a machine that is preset is one way of avoiding subjectivity. It obviates the necessity of designing each work in turn; thus, it is the plan that designs the work.

In his introduction to the UbuWeb Anthology of Conceptual Writing, Craig Dworkin posits, "What would a non-expressive poetry look like? A poetry of intellect rather than emotion? One in which the substitutions at the heart of metaphor and image were replaced by the direct presentation of language itself, with 'spontaneous overflow' supplanted by meticulous procedure and exhaustively logical process? In which the self-regard of the poet's ego were turned back onto the self-reflexive language of the poem itself? So that the test of poetry were no longer whether it could have been done better (the question of the workshop), but whether it could conceivably have been done otherwise."

If it all sounds familiar, it is. Conceptual writing obstinately makes no claims on originality. On the contrary, it employs intentionally self and ego effacing tactics using uncreativity, unoriginality, illegibility, appropriation, plagiarism, fraud, theft, and falsification as its precepts; information management, word processing, databasing, and extreme process as its methodologies; and boredom, valuelessness, and nutritionlessness as its ethos.

Language as material, language as process, language as something to be shoveled into a machine and spread across pages, only to be discarded and recycled once again. Language as junk, language as detritus. Nutritionless language, meaningless language, unloved language, entartete sprache, everyday speech, illegibility, unreadability, machinistic repetition. Obsessive archiving & cataloging, the debased language of media & advertising; language more concerned with quantity than quality. How much did you say that paragraph weighed?

Conceptual writing's primary influences are Gertrude Stein's densely unreadable texts, John Cage & Jackson Mac Low's procedural compositions, and Andy Warhol's epically unwatchable films. Conceptual writing adds a twenty-first-century-prong to a constellation of certain twentieth-century avant-garde movements that were concerned with the materiality of language and sound: Mallarmé's spatialist concerns, the Futurist page, Zaum's invented languages, concrete & sound poetry, Musique concrete, plunderphonics, sampling, and rap. On the conceptual side, it claims allegiance to the works of "pataphysics," Marcel Duchamp, James Joyce, process & conceptual art, as well as aspects of 1980s consumerist-based appropriation in the fine arts.

In its self-reflexive use of appropriated language, the conceptual writer embraces the inherent and inherited politics of the borrowed words: far be it for the conceptual writer to morally or politically dictate words that aren't theirs. The choice or machine that makes the poem sets the political agenda in motion, which is often times morally or politically reprehensible to the author (in retyping the every word of a day's copy of *The New York Times*, am I to exclude an unsavory editorial?). While John Cage claimed that any sound could be music, his moral filter was on too high to accept certain sounds of pop music, agitation, politics, or violence. To Cage, not all sounds were music. Andy Warhol, on the other hand, was a model of permeability, transparency, and silver reflectivity; everything was fodder for Warhol's art, regardless of its often unsavory content. Our world turned out to be Andy's world. Conceptual writing celebrates this circumstance.

With the rise of appropriation-based literary practices, the familiar or quotidian is made unfamiliar or strange when left semantically intact. No need to blast apart syntax. The New Sentence? The Old Sentence, reframed, is enough. How to proceed after the deconstruction and pulverization of language that is the twentieth-century's legacy. Should we continue to pound language into ever smaller bits or should we take some other approach? The need to view language again as a whole—syntactically and grammatically intact—but to acknowledge the cracks in the surface of the reconstructed linguistic vessel. Therefore, in order to proceed, we need to employ a strategy of opposites—unboring boring, uncreative writing, valueless speech (these will all be explored this week in depth)—all methods of disorientation used in order to re-imagine our normative relationship to language.

David Antin's sentiments in the epigraph are correct: conceptual writing is more interested in a thinkership rather than a readership. Readability is the last thing on this poetry's mind. Conceptual writing is good only when the idea is good; often, the idea is much more interesting than the resultant texts.

And yet . . . there are moments of unanticipated beauty, sometimes grammatical, some structural, many philosophical: the wonderful rhythms of repetition, the spectacle of the mundane reframed as literature, a reorientation to the poetics of time, and fresh perspectives on readerliness, but to name a few. For an ethos claiming so much valuelessness, there's a shocking amount of beauty and experience to be siphoned from these texts.

Uncreative Writing

I teach a class at the University of Pennsylvania called "Uncreative Writing," which is a pedagogical extension of my own poetics. In it, students are penalized for showing any shred of originality and creativity. Instead, they are rewarded for plagiarism, identity theft, repurposing papers, patchwriting, sampling, plundering, and stealing. Not surprisingly, they thrive. Suddenly, what they've surreptitiously become expert at is brought out into the open and explored in a safe environment, reframed in terms of responsibility instead of recklessness.

Well, you might ask, what's wrong with creativity? "I mean, we can always use more creativity." (1) "The world needs to become a more creative place." (2) "If only individuals could express themselves creatively, they'd be freer, happier." (3) "I'm a strong believer in the therapeutic value of creative pursuits." (4) "To be creative, relax and let your mind go to work, otherwise the result is either a copy of something you did before or reads like an army manual." (5) "I don't follow any system. All the laws you can lay down are only so many props to be cast aside when the hour of creation arrives." (6) "An original writer is not one who imitates nobody, but one whom nobody can imitate." (7)

When our notions of what is considered creative became this hackneyed, this scripted, this sentimental, this debased, this romanticized . . . this uncreative, it's time to run in the opposite direction. Do we really need another "creative" poem about the way the sunlight is hitting your writing table? No. Or another "creative" work of fiction that tracks the magnificent rise and the even more spectacular fall? Absolutely not.

One exercise I do with my students is to give them the simple instructions to retype five pages of their choice. Their responses are varied and full of revelations: some find it enlightening to become a machine (without ever having known Warhol's famous dictum "I want to be a machine"). Others say that it was the most intense reading experience they ever had, with many actually embodying the characters they were retyping. Several students become aware that the act of typing or writing is actually an act of performance, involving their whole body in a physically durational act (even down to noticing the cramps in their hands). Some of the students become intensely aware of the text's formal properties and for the first time in their lives began to think of texts not only as transparent, but as opaque objects to be moved around a white space. Others find the task zen-like and amnesia-inducing (without ever having known Satie's "Memoirs of an Amnesiac" or Duchamp's desire to live without memory), alternately having the text lose then regain meaning.

In the act of retyping, what differentiates each student is their choice of what to retype. One student once retyped a story about a man's inability to complete the sexual act, finding the perfect metaphor for this assignment. Another student retyped her favorite high school short story, only to discover during the act of retyping it, just how poorly written it was. Yet another was a waitress who took it upon herself to retype her restaurant's menu in order to learn it better for work. She ended up hating the task and even hating her job more. The spell was broken when purposefulness and goal-orientation entered into the process.

The trick in uncreative writing is airtight accountability. If you can defend your choices from every angle, then the writing is a success. On the other hand, if your methodology and justification is sloppy, the work is doomed to fail. You can no longer have a workshop where people worry about adjusting a comma here or a word there. You must insist that the procedure was well articulated and accurately executed.

We proceed through a rigorous examination of the circumstances that are normally considered outside of the scope of writing but, in fact, have everything to do with writing. Question arise, among them:

What kind of paper did you use? Why is it on generic white computer paper when the original edition was on thick, yellowed, pulpy stock? What does it say about you: your aesthetic, economic, social, and political circumstances?

Do you reproduce exactly the original text's layout page by page or do you simply flow the words from one page to another, the way your word processing program does? Will the texts be received differently if it is in Times Roman or Verdana?

For a task so seemingly simple, the questions never end.

A few years ago I was lecturing to a class at Princeton. After the class, a small group of students came up to me to tell me about a workshop that they were taking with one of the most well-known fiction writers in America. They were complaining about her lack of imagination. For example, she had them pick their favorite writer and come in next week with an "original" work in the style of that author. I asked one of the students which author they chose. She answered Jack Kerouac. She then added that the assignment felt meaningless to her because the night before she tried to "get into Kerouac's head" and scribbled a piece in "his style" to fulfill the assignment. It occurred to me that for this student to actually write in the style of Kerouac, she would have been better off taking a road trip across the country in a '48 Buick with the convertible roof down, gulping Benzedrine by the fistful, washing 'em down with bourbon, all the while typing furiously away on a manual typewriter, going eighty-five miles per hour down a ribbon of desert highway. And even then, it would've been a completely different experience, not to mention a very different piece of writing, than Kerouac's.

Instead, my mind drifted to those aspiring painters who fill up the Metropolitan Museum of Art every day, spending hours learning by copying the Old Masters. If it's good enough for them, why isn't it good enough for us? I would think that should this student have retyped a chunk—or if she was ambitious the whole thing—of *On the Road*. Wouldn't she have really understood Kerouac's style in a profound way that was bound to stick with her? I think she really would've learned something had she retyped Kerouac. But no—she had to bring in an "original" piece of writing.

At the start of each semester, I ask my students to simply suspend their disbelief for the duration of the class and to fully buy into uncreative writing. I tell them that one good thing that can come out of the class is that they completely reject this way of working. At least their own conservative positions become fortified and accountable; they are able to claim that they have spent time with these attitudes for a prolonged period of time and quite frankly, they've found them to be a load of crap. Another fine result is that the uncreative writing exercises become yet another tool in their writing toolbox, upon which they will draw from for the rest of their careers. Of course, the very best result—and the unlikeliest one—is that they dedicate their life to uncreative writing. Later in the week, we will actually look at works of uncreative and conceptual writing by mature writers who, in fact, have dedicated their oeuvre to this type of practice.

1. Marc Chagall
2. Philip Yeo
3. Richard Florida
4. Dr. Wayne Dwyer
5. Kimon Nicoliades
6. Raoul Dufy
7. Gail Sheehy

Information Management

I am a word processor. I sympathize with the protagonist of a cartoon claiming to have transferred x amount of megabytes, physically exhausted after a day of downloading. The simple act of moving information from one place to another today constitutes a significant cultural act in and of itself. I think it's fair to say that most of us spend hours each day shifting content into different containers. Some of us call this writing.

In 1969, the conceptual artist Douglas Huebler wrote, "The world is full of objects, more or less interesting; I do not wish to add any more." I've come to embrace Huebler's ideas, though it might be retooled as, "The world is full of texts, more or less interesting; I do not wish to add any more." It seems an appropriate response to a new condition in writing today: faced with an unprecedented amount of available text, the problem is not needing to write more of it; instead, we must learn to negotiate the vast quantity that exists.

Contemporary writing requires the expertise of a secretary crossed with the attitude of a pirate: replicating, organizing, mirroring, archiving, and reprinting, along with a more clandestine proclivity for bootlegging, plundering, hoarding, and file-sharing. We've needed to acquire a whole new skill set: we've become master typists, exacting cut-and-pasters, and OCR demons. There's nothing we love more than transcription; we find few things more satisfying than collation.

There is no museum or bookstore in the world better than our local Staples.

The writer's solitary lair is transformed into a networked alchemical laboratory, dedicated to the brute physicality of textual transference. The sensuality of copying gigabytes from one drive to another: the whirr of the drive, intellectual matter manifested as sound. The carnal excitement from supercomputing heat generated in the service of poetry.

The weight of holding a book's worth of language in the clipboard waiting to be dumped: the magic is in the suspension.

The grind of the scanner as it peels language off the page, thawing it, liberating it. The endless cycle of textual fluidity: from imprisonment to emancipation, back to imprisonment, then freed once more. The balance between dormant text warehoused locally and active text in play on the Web. Language in play. Language out of play. Language frozen. Language melted.

The text of a newspaper is released from its paper prison of fonts and columns, its thousands of designs, corporate, political decisions, now flattened into a nonhierarchical expanse of sheer potentiality as a generic text document begging to be repurposed, dumped into a reconditioning machine and cast into a new form.

A radio broadcast is captured and materialized, rendered into text. The ephemeral made permanent; every utterance made by the broadcaster—every um and uh—goes onto the ever-increasing textual record. The gradual accumulation of words; a blizzard of the evanescent.

Cruising the Web for new language. The sexiness of the cursor as it sucks up words from anonymous Web pages, like a stealth encounter. The dumping of those words, sticky with residual junk, back into the local environment; scrubbed with text soap, returned to their virginal state, filed away, ready to be reemployed.

Sculpting with text.
Data mining.
Sucking on words.
Our task is to simply mind the machines.

> ANDY WARHOL: I think everybody should be a machine. I think everybody should like everybody.
>
> INTERVIEWER: Is that what Pop Art is all about?
>
> WARHOL: Yes. It's liking things.
>
> INTERVIEWER: And liking things is like being a machine?
>
> WARHOL: Yes, because you do the same thing every time. You do it over and over again.
>
> INTERVIEWER: And you approve of that?
>
> WARHOL: Yes, because it's all fantasy.[1]

Writing is finally catching up to Warhol. And it's just the beginning. Soon we will not have to be bothered minding the machines for they will mind themselves. As poet Christian Bök[2] states:

> We are probably the first generation of poets who can reasonably expect to write literature for a machinic audience of artificially intellectual peers. Is it not already evident by our presence at conferences on digital poetics that the poets of tomorrow are likely to resemble programmers, exalted, not because they can write great poems, but because they can build a small drone out of words to write great poems for us? If poetry already lacks any meaningful readership among our own anthropoid population, what have we to lose by writing poetry for a robotic culture that must inevitably succeed our own? If we want to commit an act of poetic innovation in an era of formal exhaustion, we may have to consider this heretofore unimagined, but nevertheless prohibited, option: writing poetry for inhuman readers, who do not yet exist, because such aliens, clones, or robots have not yet evolved to read it.

Boredom

I am the most boring writer that has ever lived. If there were an Olympic sport for extreme boredom, I would get a gold medal. My books are

---

1. G. R. Swenson, "What Is Pop Art? Answers from 8 Painters, Part I," *ARTnews*, November 1963.   2. Christian Bök, "The Piecemeal Bard Is Deconstructed: Notes Toward a Potential Robopoetics," *Object 10: Cyber Poetics*, Kenneth Goldsmith, ed. (2001), http://www.ubu.com/papers/object/03_bok.pdf.

impossible to read straight through. In fact, every time I have to proofread them before sending them off to the publisher, I fall asleep repeatedly. You really don't need to read my books to get the idea of what they're like; you just need to know the general concept.

Over the past ten years, my practice has boiled down to simply retyping existing texts. I've thought about my practice in relation to Borges's Pierre Menard, but even Menard was more original than I am: he, independent of any knowledge of *Don Quixote*, reinvented Cervantes' masterpiece word for word. By contrast, I don't invent anything. I just keep rewriting the same book.

John Cage said, "If something is boring after two minutes, try it for four. If still boring, then eight. Then sixteen. Then thirty-two. Eventually one discovers that it is not boring at all." He's right: there's a certain kind of unboring boredom that's fascinating, engrossing, transcendent, and downright sexy. And then there's the other kind of boring: let's call it boring boring. Boring boring is a client meeting; boring boring is having to endure someone's self-indulgent poetry reading; boring boring is watching a toddler for an afternoon; boring boring is the seder at Aunt Fanny's. Boring boring is being somewhere we don't want to be; boring boring is doing something we don't want to do.

Unboring boring is a voluntary state; boring boring is a forced one. Unboring boring is the sort of boredom that we surrender ourselves to when, say, we go to see a piece of minimalist music. I recall once having seen a restaging of an early Robert Wilson piece from the 1970s. It took four hours for two people to cross the stage; when they met in the middle, one of them raised their arm and stabbed the other. The actual stabbing itself took a good hour to complete. Because I volunteered to be bored, it was the most exciting thing I've ever seen.

The twentieth-century avant-garde liked to embrace boredom as a way of getting around what it considered to be the vapid "excitement" of popular culture. A powerful way to combat such crap was to do the opposite of it, to be purposely boring.

By the '60s and '70s in art circles this type of boredom—boring boring—was often the norm. I'm glad I wasn't around to have to sit through all of that stuff. Boredom, it seems, became a forced condition, be it in theater, music, art, or literature. It's no wonder people bailed out of boredom in the late '70s and early '80s to go into punk rock or expressionistic painting. After a while, boredom got boring.

And then, a few decades later, things changed again: excitement became dull and boring started to look good again. So here we are, ready to be bored once more. But this time, boredom has changed. We've embraced unboring boring, modified boredom, boredom with all the boring parts cut out of it. Reality TV, for example, is a new kind of boredom. *An American Family,* broadcast in the early '70s—strutting its ennui—was the old boredom; *The Osbournes*—action-packed boredom—is the new. There's no one more tedious than Ozzy Osbourne, but his television presence is the most engagingly constructed tedium that has ever existed. We can't take our eyes off the guy, stumbling through the dullness of his own life.

Our taste for the unboring boring won't last forever. I assume that someday soon it'll go back to boring boring once again, though for reasons and conditions I can't predict at this time.

I don't expect you to even read my books cover to cover. It's for that reason I like the idea that you can know each of my books in one sentence. For instance, there's the book of every word I spoke for a week unedited. Or the book of every move my body made over the course of a day, a process so dry and tedious that I had to get drunk halfway through the day in order to make it to the end. Or a book in which I retyped a day's copy of *The New York Times* and published it as a 900-page book. I've transcribed a year's worth of weather reports and a twenty-four-hour cycle of one-minute traffic reports every ten minutes, resulting in textual gridlock.

Now you know what I do without ever having to have read a word of it.

I think that there were a handful of artists in the twentieth century who intentionally made boring work, but didn't expect their audiences to fully engage with it in a durational sense. It's these artists, I feel, who predicted the sort of unboring boredom that we're so fond of today.

Andy Warhol, for instance, said of his films that the real action wasn't on the screen. He's right. Nothing happened in the early Warhol films: a static image of the Empire State Building for eight hours, a man sleeping for six. It is nearly impossible to watch them straight through. Warhol often claimed that his films were better thought about than seen. He also said that the films were catalysts for other types of actions: conversation that took place in the theater during the screening, the audience walking in and out, and thoughts that happened in the heads of the moviegoers. Warhol conceived of his films as a staging for a performance, in which the audience members were the Superstars, not the actors or objects on the screen.

Gertrude Stein, too, often set up a situation of skimming, knowing that few were going to be reading her epic works straight through. (How many people have linearly read every word of *The Making of Americans*? Not too many, I suppose.) The scholar Ulla Dydo, in her magnificent compilation of the writings of Gertrude Stein, remarked that much of Stein's work was never meant to be read closely at all, rather she was deploying visual means of reading. What appeared to be densely unreadable and repetitive was, in fact, designed to be skimmed, and to delight the eye (in a visual sense) while holding the book. Stein, as usual, was prescient in predicting our reading habits.

John Cage proved to be the avant-garde's Evelyn Wood, boiling down dense modernist works into deconstructed, remixed Cliff Notes; in his Writing for the Second Time Through "Finnegans Wake" he reduced a 628-page tome to a slim 39 pages, and Ezra Pound's 824-page Cantos to a mere handful of words.

At a reading I gave recently, the other reader came up to me after my reading and said incredulously, "You didn't write a word of what you read." I thought for a moment and, sure, in one sense—the traditional sense—he was right; but in the expanded field of appropriation, uncreativity, sampling, and language management in which we all habit today, he couldn't have been more wrong. Each and every word was "written" by me: sometimes mediated by a machine, sometimes transcribed, and sometimes copied; but without my intervention, slight as it may be, these works would never have found their way into the world. When retyping a book, I often stop and ask myself if what I am doing is really writing. As I sit there, in front of the computer screen, punching keys, the answer is invariably yes.

Why Flarf Is Better Than Conceptualism

Conceptualism asks what is Conceptualism?

Flarf turns poetry up to 11.

Conceptualism is never about anything other than Conceptualism itself.

Flarf is poetry. It is about everything that is not poetry.

Flarf is the court's most feared group of space pirates. As such, it is still a member of Moby Grape.

Conceptualism courts jest, but is not Elvis' dong.

Conceptualism is composed.

Flarf is compost.

Conceptualism employs a variety of techniques that compromise and complicate the question of blah blah blah blah. . . .

Flarf is a tricked-out unicorn that rides another tricked-out unicorn into eternity.

Conceptualism says I want you to show me love but I don't want to show you love.

Flarf gives you more love than you can deal with.

Flarf is a smutty, expressive swan-bear hybrid at a clam bake.

Conceptualism is a kink. The penis is Bilbo Baggins.

Flarf wants you.

Conceptualism wants to put you in a state where you want to be put out of your misery.

Flarf wants to be even fluffier.

Flarf maintains a super collider attitude towards the world-at-large.

Conceptualism wants you to know it has read Lacan.

Flarf has an anaphylactic shock for every situation. It involves the Spin Doctors or the schmear of interpretation on the bagel of social context, such as is favored by Ken Russell filming spontaneous human combustion as orc lactation. Thus, its sororal underpinnings lie primarily in the conical promise of a radioactively milk fed ethanol-fueled dinosaur, in the sense that the dinosaur as represented must contain a more or less stable relationship to Adderall, with a larger sense of relief at not having to write torturous prose in an attempt to ascribe institutionally reinforced intellectual authority to one's self, equally stable, preferably central, in order to frame Conceptualism as a function both relevant to the fiduciary realities of the art world and the stock market of other Conceptualism readers who increase the value of the holdings by reading more at a higher price. Conceptualism repeats gestures that were vetted and digested forty years ago in the art world and displays them in the poetry world virtually unchanged: it is a remake. Poetry is too out of it to notice. And thus Conceptualism hits an intellectual pitch. The intellectual pitch, it could be noted, of the art history professor.

Conceptualism has one answer, and that is: being boring without being alienating. Through the deployment of multiple strategies that serve to present writers as destabilizing texts (extant or made) via reframed reiterations and multiple sites of rhetorical deployment, conceptualism is neo-Canadian, though it doesn't seem to read enough Dan Farrell, epistemologically concerned with the ongoing subject and the instantiation of Sandy Duncan, in other words, the affirmative will to Sandy Duncan that manifests the fact of Sandy Duncan herself. In other words, the instantiation of that which is consciously contra-textual in the sense of all that has made text make contextual sense to Sandy Duncan, the rendering immaterial of every materiality of poetry. The contra-text being the new con-text, con-, as I have pointed out elsewhere, in the sense of Sandy Duncan.

Flarf is Fortran roid rage: leggo my ego.

Conceptualism is a can-can in the bathroom mirror, the discourse of the shave.

Flarf is gangster in the sense of the drive-by shooting during a virtual dérive. As such, it must be sans repression: Marie Osmond.

Conceptualism is Lacanian in the sense of desire by way of Jude Law by way of the petit dejeuner. As such: Donny Osmond.

Conceptualism, by emphasizing the notes on the gallery wall which spell out exactly how art is to be taken and how it was made, deactivates thought.

Flarf, by not providing a motherfucking note to tell you what it's supposed to be, activates thought.

Flarf plays kissing cousin while playing a little too rough. It uses the language of the people when poets are supposed to seem smarter than the people. Flarf is always the first to see other poetry groups as opportunities for Mrs. Buttersworth Jell-O shot orgies, and it will stay up late and party party party. It might bleed out from the head injury later, but it'll probably survive. Yes, it sells out — it sells out Madison Square Garden. It's smurfs watching Point Break while reading Finnegans Wake. You can't help but like it, can you? It wants to play even dirtier.

Flarf is the new style, center stage on the mic, And they're puttin' it on wax. Those who write flarf write poetry, or, to use their terminology: "You're from Secaucus — we're from Manhattan, you're jealous of us because your girlfriend is cattin'. Poets with movements are the kind I like. I'll steal your poets like I stole your bike." Eventually all Conceptual poets will be Flarfists.

Flarf is nature. Conceptualism is denature. In this sense, Flarf is making Chuck Woolery watch them get it on. Conceptualism is a starve.

Marjorie Perloff likes Conceptualism.

Perloff does not like Flarf.

The best conceptualism is readable and successful.

Flarf fails in doing what it sets its mind to, to be bad. Flarf is Goooooooooooood.

Poetry is Conceptualism.

Flarf is life.

April 19, 2010

Permissions Acknowledgments

Katie Degentesh: "I Sometimes Tease Animals," "I Feel Uneasy Indoors," and "At Times I Have Fits of Laughing and Crying That I Cannot Control" from *The Anger Scale* (Combo Books, 2006). Copyright 2006 by Katie Degentesh. Reprinted by permission of the author.

Linh Dinh: "Continuous Bullets Over Flattened Earth," "Fifteen Rounds with a Nobody," "The Death of English," and "Vocab Lab" from *American Tatts* (Chax Press, 2005). "Body Eats" from *Some Kind of Cheese Orgy* (Chax Press, 2009). Both reprinted by permission of the author.

Diane di Prima: "The Practice of Magical Evocation," "On Sitting Down to Write, I Decide Instead to Go to Fred Herko's Concert," "For H.D.," "Backyard," and "The Loba Addresses the Goddess / or The Poet as Priestess Addresses the Loba-Goddess" from *Pieces of a Song* (City Lights Books, 1990), copyright by Diane di Prima. Reprinted by her permission.

Stacy Doris: "Synopsis of KILDARE" from *Kildare* (Roof Books, 1994). "Love Letter (Lament)" and "As SEQUEL: Second Slogan Poem: A Song for Twins" from *Paramour* (Krupskaya Press, 2000). All reprinted by permission of the author. "[Are collisions entrances?]," "[Into some distance, everything empties]," "[Is there a dalliance that stops]," and "[Detail, a sip of tea]" from *Knot* (The University of Georgia Press, 2006). © 2006. Reprinted by permission of the University of Georgia Press.

Ed Dorn: "The Rick of Green Wood," "Geranium," "From Gloucester Out," and "On the Debt My Mother Owed to Sears Roebuck" from *Edward Dorn: The Collected Poems*, Enlarged Edition (Four Seasons Foundation, 1975). Reprinted by permission of the Edward Dorn Literary Estate.

Robert Duncan: "Bending the Bow" and "The Torso: Passages 18" from *Bending the Bow*. Copyright © 1960 by New Directions Publishing Corp. "Often I Am Permitted to Return to a Meadow" and "Poetry, a Natural Thing" from *The Opening of the Field*. Copyright © 1960 by Robert Duncan. "Songs of an Other" from *Ground Work: Before the War*. Copyright © 1984 by Robert Duncan. "Close" from *Ground Work II: In the Dark*. Copyright © 1987 by Robert Duncan. All reprinted by permission of New Directions Publishing Corp.

Craig Dworkin: "Chapter One: Tectonic Grammar" and excerpts from "Legion" from *Strands* (Roof Books, 2005). Reprinted by permission of the author. Excerpts from "Definite Article Noun Implied Subject locative preposition indefinite article Active Participle Used As An Adjective Prepositional Object period" from *Parse* (Atelos Books, 2008). Reprinted by permission of Atelos Books.

Kenward Elmslie: "Shirley Temple Surrounded by Lions," "Japanese City," and "Feathered Dancers" from *Routine Disruptions: Selected Poems & Lyrics 1960–1998*. Copyright © 1998 by Kenward Elmslie. Reprinted by permission of Coffee House Press.

Elaine Equi: "A Date with Robbe-Grillet" is reprinted by permission from *Surface Tension* (Coffee House Press, 1989). Copyright © 1989 Elaine Equi. "Asking for a Raise" and "A Quiet Poem" are reprinted by permission from *The Cloud of Knowable Things* (Coffee House Press, 2003). Copyright © 2003 Elaine Equi. "Locket without a Face" and "The Collected" are reprinted by permission from *Click and Clone* (Coffee House Press, 2011). Copyright © 2011 Elaine Equi.

Clayton Eshleman: "The Lich Gate" from *Hades in Manganese* (Black Sparrow Press, 1981). "Iraqi Morgue" from *An Alchemist with One Eye on Fire* (Black Widow Press, 2006). "In Memory of George Butterick," "Combarelles," and "Eternity at Domme" from Anticline (Black Widow Press, 2010). All reprinted by permission of Clayton Eshleman.

Lawrence Ferlinghetti: "[In Goya's greatest scenes we seem to see]," "[In Golden Gate Park that day]," and "[Constantly risking absurdity]" from *A Coney Island of the Mind*. Copyright © 1958 by Lawrence Ferlinghetti. "A Dark Portrait" from *European Poems and Transitions*. Copyright © 1984 by Lawrence Ferlinghetti. Reprinted by permission of New Directions Publishing Corp.

Robert Fitterman: "From A Hemingway Reader: The Sun Also Also Rises, Book I" and "LIT" from *Rob the Plagiarist* (Roof Books, 2009). Reprinted by permission of the author.

Graham Foust: "1984," "Of What Seems Like My Father," "Interstate Eighty," and "Panama" from *Necessary Stranger*. Copyright © 2007. Reprinted with permission of Flood Editions. Excerpts from *To Anacreon in Heaven and Other Poems* [Forthcoming 2013]. Reprinted with permission of Flood Editions.

Kathleen Fraser: "re : searches (fragments, after Anakreon, for Emily Dickinson)" from *Notes preceding trust* (Lapis Press, 1987). Reprinted by permission of Kathleen Fraser. "your back to me inside the black suit" and "notebook

5: 'in spite of gradual deficits' " from *Discrete Categories Forced into Coupling* (Apogee Press, 2004). Reprinted by permission of Apogee Press.

Forrest Gander: "Ghost Sonata," "Ivy Brick Wall," "Late Summer Entry," and "River and Trees" from *Eye Against Eye*. Copyright © 2001, 2002, 2004, 2005 by Forrest Gander. "To Eurydice" and "To Virginia" from *Torn Awake*. Copyright © 1996, 1998, 1999, 2000, 2001 by Forrest Gander. All reprinted by permission of New Directions Publishing Corp.

Drew Gardner: "Chicks Dig War" from *Petroleum Hat* (Roof Books, 2005). "The Mayim Bialik-Kruschev Fig Rearrangement," "Superstar," and "Why Do I Hate Flarf So Much?" from *Chomp Away* (Combo Books, 2010). "Why Flarf Is Better Than Conceptualism" from *Harriet blog of Poetry magazine*: http://www.poetryfoundation.org/harriet/2010/04/ill-steal-your-poets-like-i-stole-your-bike/. All reprinted by permission of the author.

Allen Ginsberg: "*Howl*," "A Supermarket in California," "To Aunt Rose," "First Party at Ken Kesey's with Hell's Angels," and "On Neal's Ashes" from *Collected Poems 1947–1980*. Copyright © 1984 by Allen Ginsberg. Reprinted by permission of HarperCollins Publishers. Used outside of North America by permission of The Wylie Agency, LLC. "Notes for *Howl and Other Poems*" from *The Poetics of the New American Poetry* (Grove Press, 1973). Copyright © The Allen Ginsberg Estate. Reprinted by permission of the Allen Ginsberg Estate.

Cecil S. Giscombe: "All (Facts, Stories, Chance): 1–3," from *Here* (Dalkey Archive, 1994). "Far," "Day Song," and "Prairie Style" from *Prairie Style* (Dalkey Archive, 2008). All reprinted with the permission of Dalkey Archive Press.

Peter Gizzi: "Creeley Madrigal" from *Artificial Heart* (Burning Deck Press, 1998). Reprinted by permission of Burning Deck Press. "In Defense of Nothing" and "Revival" from *Some Values of Landscape and Weather*. Copyright © 2003 by Peter Gizzi. "A Panic That Can Still Come upon Me" from *The Outernationale*. Copyright © 2007 by Peter Gizzi. "Hypostasis & New Year" and "Basement Song" from *Threshold Songs*. Copyright 2011 by Peter Gizzi. Reprinted by permission of Wesleyan University Press.

Kenneth Goldsmith: Excerpts from *Day* and "Seven American Deaths and Disasters" reprinted courtesy of powerHouse Books.

Nada Gordon and **Gary Sullivan**: "Among the Living (Date: November 2)" and "Moonscape with Earthlings (Date: December 18)" from *Swoon* (Granary Books, 2001). Reprinted by permission of Gary Sullivan and Nada Gordon.

Susan Howe: Excerpts from "Girl with Forest Shoulder" from *Singularities* (Wesleyan University Press, 1990). Copyright © 1990 by Susan Howe. Reprinted with permission of Wesleyan University Press. "Bedhangings I: To the Compiler of Memories" from *The Midnight*. Copyright © 2003 Susan Howe. Reprinted by permission of New Directions Publishing Corp. "There Are Not Leaves Enough to Crown to Cover to Crown to Cover" from *The Europe of Trusts* (Sun and Moon Press, 1990). Reprinted by permission of the author.

Lisa Jarnot: "They Loved the Sea," "Gang Angles," and "Manx Kippers" from *Black Dog Songs*. Copyright © 2010 by Lisa Jarnot. Reprinted with the permission of Flood Editions. "Husband Sonnet One" and "Right Poem" from *Night Scenes*. Copyright © 2006 by Lisa Jarnot. Reprinted with the permission of Flood Editions.

Ronald Johnson: "O I" from *RADI OS*. Copyright © 2005 by the Estate of Ronald Johnson. "Beam 6, The Musics," "Beam 8," and "Beam 33" excerpts from *Ark*. Copyright © 1980 by the Estate of Ronald Johnson. Reprinted with the permission of Flood Editions.

Andrew Joron: "First Drift" and "Le Nombres des Ombres" from *The Removes* (Hard Press, 1999). "Dolphy at Delphi" from *Fathom* (Black Square Editions, 2003). "The Person" and "Illocutionary Reels" from *New American Writing 29* (2011). All reprinted by permission of the author. "Skymap under Skin" from *Trance Archive* (City Lights Books, 2010). Copyright © 2010 by Andrew Joron. Reprinted by permission of City Lights Books.

Claudia Keelan: "Pity Boat" from *Missing Her* (New Issues Press, 2009). Reprinted by permission of New Issues Poetry and Prose. "Critical Essay" and "Sun Going Down" from *The Devotion Field*. Copyright © 2004 by Claudia Keelan. Reprinted with the permission of The Permissions Company, Inc., on behalf of Alice James Books, www.alicejamesbooks.com. "Something to Keep" and "Spring" from *The Secularist* (The University of Georgia Press, 1997). Reprinted with the permission of The University of Georgia Press.

Myung Mi Kim: "Into Such Assembly" from *Under Flag* (Kelsey Street Press, 1991). Reprinted by permission of Kelsey Street Press. A podcast of the author reading from *Under Flag* is available on the press website, www.kelseyst.com. Excerpt from *Penury* (Omnidawn, 2009). Reprinted with the permission of Omnidawn Publishing.

Caroline Knox: "Sleepers Wake" and "Famous Bigshots" from *Sleepers Wake* (Timken Publishers, 2004). Reprinted by permission of the author. "Quaker

Guns" and "Dreyken / Bathrobes" from *Quaker Guns*. Copyright 2008. Reprinted with permission of Wave Books and the author. "Freudian Shoes" and "Movement Along the Frieze" from *To Newfoundland* (University of Georgia Press, 1989). Reprinted by permission of the University of Georgia Press.

Kenneth Koch: "To You," "Variations on a Theme by William Carlos Williams," "Alive for an Instant," and excerpts from "On Aesthetics" from *The Collected Poems of Kenneth Koch*. Copyright © 2005 by The Kenneth Koch Literary Estate. Used by permission of Alfred A. Knopf, a division of Random House, Inc. Any third party use of this material, outside of this publication, is prohibited. Interested parties must apply directly to Random House, Inc., for permission.

Noelle Kocot: "Lithium" from *Poem for the End of Time and Other Poems*. Copyright 2006. Reprinted with permission of Wave Books and the author. "Love Poem on the Anniversary of Nowhere," "Abortion Elegy," and "For My Father the Poet" from *4*. Copyright © 2001 by Noelle Kocot. "Passing Over Water" and "Over, Under, Through, With" from *The Raving Fortune*. Copyright © 2004 by Noelle Kocot. All reprinted with the permission of The Permissions Company, Inc., on behalf of Four Way Books, www.fourwaybooks.com.

Ann Lauterbach: "Clamor" from *Clamor*. Copyright © 1991 by Ann Lauterbach. "New Brooms" from *If in Time: Selected Poems 1975–2000*. Copyright © 2001 by Ann Lauterbach. "Instruction" from *Hum*. Copyright © 2005 by Ann Lauterbach. All used by permission of Viking Penguin, a division of Penguin Group (USA) Inc. "Platonic Subject" from *Before Reflection* (Princeton University Press, 1987). Reprinted with permission of the author. "Constellation in Chalk" from *Or to Begin Again* (Penguin Poets, 2009). Reprinted by permission of the author.

Joseph Lease: "Broken World" is reprinted with permission from *Broken World* (Coffee House Press, 2007). Copyright © 2007 Joseph Lease. "Send My Roots Rain" is reprinted with permission from *Testify* (Coffee House Press, 2011). Copyright © 2011 Joseph Lease.

Ben Lerner: "[The dark collects our empties, empties our ashtrays]," "[I had meant to apologize in advance]," and "[In my day, we knew how to drown plausibly]" from *The Lichtenberg Figures*. Copyright © 2004 by Ben Lerner. "[I want to finish the book in time]," "[I'm worried about a friend]," "[The passengers are asked to clap]," "[A flowering no one attends]," "[They are passing quickly, those]," and "[Somewhere in this book I broke]" from "The Doppler Elegies" from *Mean Free Path*. Copyright © 2010 by Ben Lerner. All reprinted

Steve McCaffery: "Apologia Pro Vita Sua," "Suggestion but No Insult," "The Dangers of Poetry," "The Poem as a Thing to See," "Correlata for a Cryptogram," and "Digital Poetics" from *Verse and Worse: Selected and New Poems by Steve McCaffery 1989–2009* (Wilfred Laurier University Press, 2010). "Language Writing: from Productive to Libidinal Economy," Part I, pp. 143–52, from *North of Intention: Critical Writings 1973–1986* (Roof Books, 2000). Reprinted with the permission of the author.

Michael McClure: "Mexico Seen from the Moving Car," "The Butterfly," and "The Cheetah" from *Simple Eyes & Other Poems*. Copyright © 1994 by Michael McClure. Reprinted by permission of New Directions Publishing Corp. "Gray Fox at Solstice" from *Of Indigo and Saffron* (University of California Press, 2011). Copyright © 2011 by the Regents of the University of California and reprinted by permission of the University of California Press. "Thoreau's Eyes" from *Plum Stones: Cartoons of No Heaven* (O Books, 2002). Reprinted by permission of the author.

Mark McMorris: "(a poem) [When the combat finally stops, then I will come to you]," "Inescapable Country," and excerpts from "Letters to Michael" (Dear Michael 2, 8, and 12) are reprinted by permission from *Entrepôt* (Coffee House Press, 2010). Copyright © 2010 Mark McMorris.

Sharon Mesmer: "I Wanna Make Love to You on Mission Accomplished Day," "I Don't Wanna Lose Yer Wholesome Lovefest Forever," "I Never Knew an Orgy Could Be So Much Work," and "When the Platypus Kicks Back" from *Annoying Diabetic Bitch* (Combo Books, 2007). Reprinted by permission of the author.

K. Silem Mohammad: "Spooked" and "Cosmic Deer Head Freakout" from *Deer Head Nation* (Tougher Disguises, 2003). Reprinted by permission of the author. "H.D., H.D., Tetchy H.D.! Why Punch 'Punchy,' BBW Spy? (Sonnet 33)," "Vac-U-Cash Devo Vogue (Sonnet 34)," "The the the the the the the the the the the Death (Hey Hey) (Sonnet 47)," and "Ohhhhhhhhhhhhhhhhh, J.M.L.: Flit Flit Flit, Fold Fold Fold, My Violent DDT Doll™ (Sonnet 99)" from *Sonnograms* (Unpublished). "Excessivism" from *Action Yes Online Quarterly* 1.5 (Spring 2007). Reprinted by permission of the author.

Laura Moriarty: Excerpt from "Spectrum's Rhetoric" pp. 3–10 from *A Tonalist* (Nightboat Books, 2010). Reprinted by permission of Nightboat Books.

Rusty Morrison: "Part 2" from *the true keeps calming biding its story*. Copyright © 2008 by Rusty Morrison. Reprinted with the permission of The Permissions Company, Inc., on behalf of Ahsahta Press, http://ahsahtapress.boisestate.edu.

Jennifer Moxley: "Wreath of a Similar Year" from *Imagination Verses* (Salt Publications, 2003). Reprinted by permission of the author. "The Price of Silence" from *Clampdown*. Copyright © 2009 by Jennifer Moxley. Reprinted by permission of Flood Editions.

Harryette Mullen: "Denigration," "Dim Lady," "Elliptical," "Variations on a Theme Park," and "Xenophobic Nightmare in a Foreign Language" from *Sleeping with the Dictionary* (University of California Press, 2002). Copyright © 2002 by the Regents of the University of California. Reprinted by permission of the University of California Press. Excerpt from "Muse & Drudge" from *Recyclopedia: Trimmings, S*PeRM**K*T, and Muse & Drudge*. Copyright © 1995 by Harryette Mullen. Reprinted with the permission of The Permissions Company, Inc., on behalf of Graywolf Press, Minneapolis, Minnesota, www .graywolfpress.org.

Laura Mullen: "In the Space between Words Begin," "I Wandered Networks like a Cloud," "Code," and "The White Box of Mirror Dissolved Is Not Singular" from *Dark Archive* (University of California Press, 2011). Copyright © 2011 by the Regents of the University of California. Reprinted with permission of the University of California Press. "Autumn" and "After I Was Dead" from *After I Was Dead* (University of Georgia Press, 1999). Reprinted by permission of the University of Georgia Press.

Eileen Myles: "Bleeding Hearts" and "Immanence" from *Maxfield Parrish: Early & New Poems* (Black Sparrow Press, 1985). Reprinted by permission of Black Sparrow Press. "Each Defeat" and "The Frames" from *Sorry, Tree*. Copyright © 2007. Reprinted with permission of Wave Books and the author. "December 9th" and "The Sadness of Leaving" from *Not Me* (Semiotext(e) Native Agent Series, MIT Press, 1991). © 1991, Eileen Myles. Reprinted by permission of the author.

Alice Notley: "I Must Have Called and So He Comes" and "April Not an Inventory but a Blizzard" from *Mysteries of Small Houses*. Copyright © 1998 by Alice Notley. Used by permission of Viking Penguin, a division of Penguin Group (USA) Inc. "From *Beginning with a Stain*" from *The Scarlet Cabinet* (Scarlet Editions, 1992). Reprinted with permission of Alice Notley. "Poem (You hear that heroic big land music?)," "Jack Would Speak through the Imperfect Medium of Alice," and "A California Girlhood" from *How Spring Comes* (Coffee House Press, 1981). Copyright © 1981 by Alice Notley. Reprinted by permission of Coffee House Press.

Frank O'Hara: "Poem (The eager note on my door . . .)" and "Meditations in an Emergency" from *Meditations in an Emergency*. Copyright © 1957 by Frank

Wang Ping: "Syntax," "Of Flesh & Spirit," and "Female Marriage" are reprinted by permission from *Of Flesh & Spirit* (Coffee House Press, 1998). Copyright © 1998 Wang Ping.

Vanessa Place: Excerpt from *Dies: A Sentence* (Les Figues Press, 2005). Reprinted by permission of Les Figues Press.

Bin Ramke: "The Ruined World" from *Theory of Mind: New & Selected Poems* (Omnidawn Publishing, 2009). Reprinted by permission of Omnidawn Publishing.

Claudia Rankine: "Coherence in Consequence," "Proximity of Inner to In Her," "Intermission in Four Acts" from *Plot*. Copyright © 2001 by Claudia Rankine. Used by permission of Grove/Atlantic, Inc.

Stephen Ratcliffe: "10/31 to 11/5," excerpts from *Real* (Avenue B Press, 2007). Reprinted by permission of Avenue B Press.

Joan Retallack: "Curiosity and the Claim to Happiness," "Present Tense," "Present Tense: Choice," and "Present Tense: Still" from *Memnoir* (The Post-Apollo Press, 2004). Reprinted by permission of the author.

Donald Revell: "The Secessions on Loan" and "Why and Why Now" from *Beautiful Shirt* (Wesleyan University Press, 1994). Copyright © 1994 by Donald Revell. Reprinted by permission of Wesleyan University Press. "Ridiculous Winter Flower," "New Colors," and "Deluge" (Unpublished, 2011) reprinted with the permission of the author.

Ed Roberson: "Sit in What City We're In," "Urban Nature," "Open / Back Up (breadth of field)," "Monk's Bird Book," "A Sampler," "Psalm," and "The Counsel of Birds" from *City Eclogue* (Atelos Press, 2006). Reprinted with permission of the author and Atelos Press.

Elizabeth Robinson: "Apollo" and "Experience" from *Harrow* (Omnidawn Publishing, 2001). Reprinted by permission of Omnidawn Publishing. "Doorway" from *Apostrophe* (Apogee Press, 2006). "Having Words" and "A Stitch in the Side" from *Also Known As* (Apogee Press, 2009). Both reprinted by permission of Apogee Press. "Stained Syllogism" and "Mary and No Savior" from *The Orphan and Its Relations* (Fence Books, 2008). Reprinted by permission of Fence Books.

Leslie Scalapino: Excerpt from *Zither & Autobiography* (Wesleyan University Press, 2003). Copyright © 2003 by Leslie Scalapino. "Note on My Writing" from *It's go in horizontal: Selected Poems, 1974–2006* (Wesleyan University Press, 2008). Copyright © 2008 by Leslie Scalapino. Reprinted by permission of Wesleyan University Press.

James Schuyler: "The Crystal Lithium," "Korean Mums," "Letter to a Friend: Who Is Nancy Daum?" and "A Man in Blue" from *Collected Poems* by James Schuyler. Copyright © 1993 by the Estate of James Schuyler. Reprinted by permission of Farrar, Straus, and Giroux, LLC.

Aaron Shurin: "VIII (I come to café, I sit, I bear)," "XVIII (Those guys with Christmas tree untrimmed)," "XXXVII (It's a country road forty years ago)," "LXVI (Disabled / by seeing them touch)," "CII (if you would come for days)," "CXLI (Claudio, Steffano, Salo, Jésus)," and "CXLII (friends walk; bones begin to creak)" from *Involuntary Lyrics* (Omnidawn Publishing, 2005). Reprinted with the permission of Omnidawn Publishing.

Eleni Sikelianos: "Campo santo" and "Of the True Human Fold" are reprinted by permission from *Blue Guide* in *Earliest Worlds* (Coffee House Press, 2001). Copyright © 2001 Eleni Sikelianos. "Essay: Delicately" and "Essay: Seven Aspects of Milking Time" are reprinted by permission from *Of Sun, of History, of Seeing* in *Earliest Worlds* (Coffee House Press, 2001). Copyright © 2001 Eleni Sikelianos. "Be Honeyed Bush" and "A Radiant Countess of What's It" are reprinted by permission from *Body Clock* (Coffee House Press, 2008). Copyright © 2008 Eleni Sikelianos.

Ron Silliman: "A SENTENCE in the evening" from *Paradise* (Burning Deck Press, 1985). Reprinted by permission of Burning Deck Press. Excerpt from *Tjanting*. Copyright © Ron Silliman, 1981, 2002. Used with permission of the author. "(G)hosts final passage" from *The Alphabet* (University of Alabama Press, 2008). Reprinted by permission of the University of Alabama Press. *The Chinese Notebook* from *The Age of Huts (compleat)* (University of California Press, 2007). Copyright © 2007 by the Regents for the University of California. Reprinted by permission of the University of California Press.

Gary Snyder: "As for Poets," "Avocado," and "The Bath" from *Turtle Island*. Copyright © 1974 by Gary Snyder. Reprinted by permission of New Directions Publishing Corp. "Hay for the Horses," "Riprap," "Axe Handles," and "Right in the Trail" from *The Gary Snyder Reader*. Copyright © 1999 by Gary Snyder. "No Shadow" from *Danger on Peaks*. Copyright © 2004 by Gary Snyder. Reprinted by permission of Counterpoint.

Gustaf Sobin: "Genesis" and "Under the Bright Orchards" from *Towards the Blanched Alphabets* (Talisman House, 1998). Reprinted by permission of

on behalf of BOA Editions Ltd., www.boaeditions.org. "Pharisee's Lament" and "Goldbeater's Skin" from *Goldbeater's Skin*. Copyright © 2003 by G. C. Waldrep. Reprinted by permission of the Center for Literary Publishing and the author. "On the Seventh Anniversary of the U.S. Invasion of Afghanistan" first appeared in *New American Writing* and "Selinsgrove" in *Conjunctions*. Reprinted by permission of the author.

Keith Waldrop: *A Shipwreck in Haven*, "Plurality of Worlds," and "Competing Depth" from *Transcendental Studies: A Trilogy* (University of California Press, 2009). Copyright © 2009 by the Regents of the University of California. Reprinted by permission of the University of California Press.

Rosmarie Waldrop: "Object Relations" and "We Will Always Ask, What Happened?" from *Love, Like Pronouns* (Omnidawn Publishing, 2003). Reprinted by permission of Omnidawn Publishing. "Pre & Con or Positions and Junctions 1–5" from *Split Infinites* (Singing Horse Press, 1998). Reprinted by permission of Singing Horse Press. "Conversation I: On the Horizontal" and "Conversation 2: On the Vertical" from *Curves to the Apple*. Copyright © 1984, 1985, 1986, 1987, 1993, 1999, 2006 by Rosemarie Waldrop. "Conversation 3: On Vertigo" from *Reluctant Gravities*. Copyright © 1999 by Rosemarie Waldrop. Both reprinted by permission of New Directions Publishing Corp.

Marjorie Welish: "Respected, Feared, and Somehow Loved," "Within This Book, Called Marguerite," "Twenty-three Modern Stories," and "The World Map" are reprinted by permission from *The Annotated "Here" and Selected Poems* (Coffee House Press, 2000). Copyright © 2000 Marjorie Welish. "Possible Fires" is reprinted by permission from *Word Group* (Coffee House Press, 2004). Copyright © 2004 Marjorie Welish.

Philip Whalen: "Sourdough Mountain Lookout" and "The Chariot" from *The Collected Poems of Philip Whalen* (Wesleyan University Press, 2007). Copyright © 2007 by Phillip Whalen and reprinted by permission of Wesleyan University Press.

Susan Wheeler: "The Belle," "Bankruptcy & Exile," and "The Privilege of Feet" from *Bag 'o' Diamonds* (University of Georgia Press, 1993). Reprinted by permission of the author. "Anthem" from *Ledger* (University of Iowa Press, 2005). Reprinted by permission of the University of Iowa Press. "He or She That's Got the Limb, That Holds Me Out on It" and "Possessive Case" from *Smokes*. Copyright © 1998 by Susan Wheeler. Reprinted with the permission of The Permissions Company, Inc., on behalf of Four Way Books, www.fourwaybooks.com.

Joshua Marie Wilkinson: "Wolf Dust" was first published in *Selenography* by Sidebrow Books in 2010. Reprinted by permission of Sidebrow Books.

Elizabeth Willis: "Autographeme," "A Woman's Face," and "Clash by Night" from *Turneresque* (Burning Deck Press, 2003). Reprinted by permission of Burning Deck Press. "A Species Is an Idea" and "The Witch" from *Address* (Wesleyan University Press, 2011). Copyright © 2011 by Donald Revell. Reprinted by permission of Wesleyan University Press.

C. D. Wright: Excerpt from *One Big Self: An Investigation*. Copyright © 2003, 2007 by C. D. Wright. Reprinted with permission of The Permissions Company, Inc., on behalf of Copper Canyon Press, www.coppercanyonpress.org.

John Yau: "Unpromising Poem," "Screen Name," and "Ing Grish" from *Ing Grish* (Saturnalia, 2005). Reprinted with permission of Saturnalia Books, Inc.

Index